A History of American Poetry

1900-1940

A History of
AMERICAN
POETRY
1900 - 1940

HORACE GREGORY *and*
MARYA ZATURENSKA

GORDIAN PRESS
NEW YORK
1969

Originally Published 1946
Reprinted 1969, With a New Foreword

PS
324
.G7

Published by Gordian Press, Inc.,
By Arrangement with
Horace Gregory and Marya Zaturenska

Library of Congress Catalog Card Number: 70-84695

TO

LOUIS UNTERMEYER

ACKNOWLEDGMENT is made to the editors of *The Sewanee Review, Accent* and *The American Bookman* in whose magazines certain early drafts of some chapters in our history have appeared. We also thank the many poets who have made a history of twentieth-century American poetry possible and whose poems enliven and illuminate so many of our pages. We wish to thank those who through correspondence, conversation, the lending of rare books, editorial advice, or a reading of the manuscript have sustained and encouraged us, and for these services we owe particular debts of gratitude to the following: Ermine Stone, Librarian of Sarah Lawrence College; Adele Brebner and Helen McMaster of the English faculty at Sarah Lawrence College; Norman Holmes Pearson of Yale University; A. J. Putnam, Morton Dauwen Zabel, Charles Madison and James T. Farrell; H. D. Aldington, Allen Tate, Christopher Lazare, Dunstan Thompson, T. C. Wilson and Lewis Nichols; Elizabeth Shepley Sergeant; Frank V. Morley, Sylvia Dudley and Jacqueline Embree. And all whom we have mentioned are not, of course, responsible for any errors or opinions in the text.

CONTENTS

FOREWORD   xiii

Prologue   3

PART I: THE "TWILIGHT INTERVAL"

WILLIAM VAUGHN MOODY AND HIS CIRCLE   25

THREE POETS OF THE SIERRAS:
JOAQUIN MILLER, EDWIN MARKHAM, GEORGE STERLING   44

THE BAREFOOT BOY OF INDIANA:
JAMES WHITCOMB RILEY   59

A NOTE ON THE POETRY OF GEORGE SANTAYANA   67

FOUR WOMEN OF THE "TWILIGHT INTERVAL":
REESE, GUINEY, CRAPSEY, AND TEASDALE   79

"LA COMÉDIE HUMAINE" OF E. A. ROBINSON   107

A NOTE ON STEPHEN CRANE   133

PART II: THE "POETIC RENAISSANCE"

HARRIET MONROE AND THE "POETIC RENAISSANCE"   141

THE HORATIAN SERENITY OF ROBERT FROST   150

EZRA POUND AND THE SPIRIT OF ROMANCE   163

AMY LOWELL, LITERARY STATESMAN   182

THE ISLANDS OF H.D.   192

THE POSTIMPRESSIONISM OF JOHN GOULD FLETCHER   201

A FORMAL "OBJECTIVIST":
WILLIAM CARLOS WILLIAMS   207

THE HERITAGE OF "THE YELLOW BOOK"
AND CONRAD AIKEN   217

THREE MIDDLE WESTERN POETS:
MASTERS, LINDSAY, AND SANDBURG   226

PART III: THE 1920's

DONALD EVANS:
PREFACE TO THE 1920'S   255

EDNA ST. VINCENT MILLAY AND THE POETRY
OF FEMININE REVOLT AND SELF-EXPRESSION   265

ELINOR WYLIE AND LÉONIE ADAMS:
THE POETRY OF FEMININE SENSIBILITY   282

"THE ROMANTIC TRADITIONISTS":
WILLIAM ELLERY LEONARD, LOUIS UNTERMEYER,
ROBERT HILLYER, AND MARK VAN DOREN   300

MARIANNE MOORE: THE GENIUS OF "THE DIAL"   317

THE HARMONIUM OF WALLACE STEVENS   326

THREE POETS OF BRATTLE STREET:
E. E. CUMMINGS, JOHN WHEELWRIGHT, DUDLEY FITTS   336

JOHN CROWE RANSOM, ALLEN TATE,
    ROBERT PENN WARREN, AND A NOTE ON LAURA RIDING   360

THE NEGRO POET IN AMERICA   387

ROBINSON JEFFERS AND THE BIRTH OF TRAGEDY   398

T. S. ELIOT, THE TWENTIETH-CENTURY
    "MAN OF FEELING" IN AMERICAN POETRY   413

PART IV: THE 1930's

THE NATIONAL SPIRIT OF STEPHEN VINCENT
    AND WILLIAM ROSE BENÉT, WITH NOTES
      ON LOLA RIDGE AND MURIEL RUKEYSER   431

ARCHIBALD MAC LEISH AND THE
    "INVOCATION TO THE SOCIAL MUSE"   448

THE LOST GENERATION OF JOHN PEALE BISHOP   458

THE CRITICAL REALISM OF KENNETH FEARING   462

HART CRANE: DEATH AND THE SEA   468

EPILOGUE

RECENT AMERICAN POETRY   483

A Descriptive Bibliography   497

Index   505

FOREWORD

Since we have given permission for a reprinting of *A History of American Poetry 1900-1940*, there is a question that might well be answered: "Why didn't we extend our Epilogue and bring the book up to date?" Had the book been an anthology of verse, that would have been an easy thing to do. But the book was a history with a life and character of its own. Truly, some histories can be revised, but we felt that this book should stand as it is, a sturdy, not unsympathetic record of the period which it represents. To attempt to add to it at length, would throw it out of perspective.

The making of the book was singular enough. We entered an era where only a few had ventured. Historical criticism had dropped out of fashion. We were forced to start afresh, and we began our research by blowing the dust off the tops of half-forgotten books to make sure whether or not they were worth the trouble of mentioning at all. Not much of this could be described as pleasure, but it was invaluable in providing a setting of the stage—as well as a preview for the central action of our narrative, the arrival of the new poetry of the 20th century. For five years we were deep in our readings, and another year was spent in the composition and rewriting of the *History,* and this was followed by a year of checking and rechecking its many details.

Beyond our belief in the significance of historical criticism, we had other convictions. We believed that poems cannot be paraphrased, that poetry exists only in the very words that make the poem. Therefore, our book contained a great number of quotations, so as to illustrate the course of its narrative. We believed that a formal history had a beginning, a middle, and a close. Whatever its faults may have been, or continue to be, it would be more comprehensive than a mere series of comments on modern poetry.

Looking back at the period covered by our history, one can see it as "a coming of age" in American poetry. At the very least, it found room for highly individual, variously inspired poets, a range that reached from the writings of Edwin Arlington Robinson and Robert Frost to Pound and Eliot and Cummings, and from Cummings to Robinson Jeffers, and from Jeffers to Wallace Stevens. Each had a language he had made his own; each had his own projection of a world that was not entirely of earth. Their very presence set a standard of high accomplishment in poetry.

In their writings, and at one time or another, each of the seven voiced unpopular sentiments and ideas. As poets, each outgrew the temporary shelters of literary movements: each stood his ground; however intractable he was, each sought a truth that was larger than himself. Under their hands, poetry had reassumed something of its ancient and traditional power to move its audiences, and to evoke a spell. And from their example, one may draw a moral, a moral too obvious to demand lengthy explanation.

But, of course, since the first publication of this book, there have been a few changes in perspective. These were natural enough, and it is, perhaps, appropriate for us to make a few critical appraisals. In our book, some stress had been placed on the English heritage in American verse. That heritage, we assume, is a vital one: it contains our culture as well as our language. For several centuries, poetry in English has had the deceptive appearance of being extremely frail, yet it has had a way of surviving through "twilight intervals" and nights of darkness. And the survival is closely related to the English tradition of "speaking one's own mind," of the right to express one's own temperament and feelings. It has become a truism that totalitarian states, from ancient Sparta to modern Russia, have destroyed the very right of the artist to speak aloud—and it is also well known to all of us that where politicians command the arts, poetry flies out of the window.

During the late 1940s and the decade following them, several poets mentioned in our history increased in influence and favor. The first of these was W. H. Auden, the young Englishman who had become a citizen of the United States. In England, where, so he wrote,

Encased in talent like a uniform,
The rank of every poet was well known.

He had been readily accepted as head of his own generation
of poets. During the 30s, no one freshly stepping down from
Oxford or Cambridge could match the quickness of his perception, his wit, or his sudden plunges into straight-faced
dialogues with the world. In a so-called "political decade," his
was a new and singular voice, and whether it was heard in prose
or verse, it was didactic, often stimulating; it was a renewed
"call to order" in modern poetry. Everything he writes, trans-
lates, or edits bears the impress of his personality, which is that
of an inquiring, restless spirit whose autobiography he brilliantly
recited in his *Letters from Iceland* (with Louis MacNiece).

Another poet was Wallace Stevens who, as the trans-Atlantic
influences of Pound and Eliot began to recede from American
shores, came into general favor. In an historical view of American
poetry, Stevens' writings take their place with Emily Dickinson's
on the same side of a line that separates them from Whitman's
Leaves of Grass. Like Emily Dickinson's, his verse is aphoristic
and sharp in contour. And behind his elegance, his excellent
display of wit, one discerns his shifting scenes of transcendental
order.

Since Robinson Jeffers' death in 1962, his lonely figure on the
Pacific coast seems to have grown in stature. Certainly his masterpieces, including "The Tower Beyond Tragedy," have lost none
of their power. In "The Cretan Woman" there was further
evidence that he was a poet of the first order. His brushing aside
of ephemeral themes in favor of Nietzschean truths gave his later
writings a strength of conviction that few of his contemporaries
had attained. To this may be added his posthumous volume of
poems, *The Beginning and the End,* with its "Ode to Hengist
and Horsa," lines occasioned by the disinterment of a Saxon
warrior in the south of England, his bones broken, "Lest he
come back . . ." His buriers speak the lines that close the poem:

He was our loyal captain and friend,
But now he is changed, he belongs to another nation,
The grim tribes underground. We break their bones

To hold them down. We must not be destroyed
By the dead or the living. We have all history ahead of us.

Another poet whose writings have gained in appreciation and prestige since his death in 1963 is E. E. Cummings. Unlike Jeffers, he had seldom suffered lack of recognition—though during the 1930s, his attacks on left-wing literary liberal attitudes meant that no publisher would accept the manuscript of his book of poems, _No Thanks_ (1935) —which was privately printed. Cummings as satirist and creator of glorious light verse had delighted his readers for almost fifty years, yet after his death, young people, and those who scarcely read poetry at all, rediscovered him as the poet of imperishable love lyrics. It would seem Cummings had proved (as 17th century poets had done before him) that lyric verse, given the touch of genius he possessed, has a hardiness that outlives changes in critical fashions and public taste.

In this brief survey something should be said of recent revivals of the Whitman tradition in American verse. Although the revivals have not produced poets of the first order, it has been a persistent force—a "know-nothing," anti-intellectual attitude, with the voice of Jean-Jacques Rousseau in the confession-box subconsciously echoed and overheard. Carl Sandburg was one result of the tradition; in the 1930s, Kenneth Fearing was another. Less often noted, but no less pertinent, was Ezra Pound's remark, early in the century, "I make a pact with you, Walt Whitman," a forecast of the weary, anti-intellectual aspect of Pound himself, the Pound of the more disorderly, disjointed Cantos, the Pound who so significantly encouraged and influenced William Carlos Williams. Through Williams, and not unlike an an apostolic succession, the Whitman tradition has been passed on as "a defense of ignorance," making its appeal to anyone willing to call himself a poet. Williams led his followers in the same fashion that Amy Lowell with her prosaic unrhymed "Amygism" inspired school children to write verse that has its counter-part in "finger-painting." In this friendly guidance the poet is neither a responsible artist nor human being, for indiscriminate praise is a sign of indifference to both moral and aesthetic values, rather than the benevolence it appears to be.

The best of Williams' own verse remained, of course, far superior to that of his imitators: it had and still retains the craft, the charm of a full-rigged model ship fitted into a glass-bottle; it also has the transient purity and brilliance of a snap-shot taken at noon on a cloudless day. It has never equalled the depth, the color and richness of Pound's poetry—whenever it drew on the resources of his European inspirations.

Dominating the fashions of current verse during the 1950s, the poetry of Robert Lowell took the center of the scene. At its right hand was the verse of Elizabeth Bishop, at its left, the less well-poised, often shrill confessions of Theodore Roethke. Of these three, Lowell's public image acquired almost instant notoriety, for he had behind him the legend of the Lowell family, with rumours of its wealth, its eccentricities, its literary heritage. In this picture, supported by his writings in two of his books of poems, *Life Studies,* and *For the Union Dead,* his position in opposing war—the Vietnam war in particular—is consistent with that of an ancestor, James Russell Lowell, who wrote against the Mexican-American war of the 1840s. In a group, Lowell's ability to take the center of attention also resembles the forwardness of another relative, Amy Lowell—and with these figures as part of his heritage and identity, it would be strange to find his gifts neglected.

The inner tensions of Lowell's verse, with their tightly woven lines, give it character and resonance, and one sees the action of triple drama within the poems, a family feud between madness and death, death and life. Since the greater number of his poems are frankly autobiographical, it is only natural that the Latin classical references within them come by way of Boston and New England: his image of the old man falling asleep after reading Vergil's *Aeneid* is a case in point, and the feud goes on. This is certainly brilliant writing!

> Now the scythe-wheeled chariot rolls
> Before their lances long as vaulting poles,
> And I stand up and heil the thousand men,
> Who carry Pallas to the bird-priest. Then
> The bird-priest groans, and, as his birds foretold,
> I greet the body, lip to lip. I hold

The sword that Dido used. It tries to speak,
A bird with Dido's sworded breast. Its beak
Clangs and ejaculates the Punic word
I hear the bird-priest chirping like a bird.
I groan a little. "Who am I, and why?"
It asks, a boy's face, though its arrow-eye
Is working from its socket. "Brother, try
O Child of Aphrodite, try to die:
To die is life."

The triple conflict of dream-madness, life and death is clear enough—the point is that within it, Lowell created his own world, his own poetic diction which draws its strength from New England soil: its creatures, its grotesques, its intimate heroes and heroines: all at their best, however, in clipped, nervous verse. As his lines relax, the tensions sag, and the poetry in them dissipates and wanders; that is why Lowell's books beyond 1959 are less impressive than his earlier writings. His many imitations of other poets may be viewed as another aspect of his heritage, this time, from Longfellow, who delighted in making new versions of his favorite European poets. But in Lowell's case, the practice seems to have diffused too broadly the language and skill of his interpretations.

The rise of Robert Lowell's reputation brings us up to 1960—but if we attempted to mention all the new poets worthy of attention, and some of them younger than he, we would have to write another book. *A History of American Poetry 1900-1940* makes no pretense of telling what may happen in the future, yet readers of poetry—and this is part of the pleasure of reading it—should always be ready to face the unexpected. For a further understanding of how—and not so very long ago—the unexpected came into being, the following pages may offer a tentative explanation.

March 8th 1969
Palisades, Rockland County,
New York.

Horace Gregory

Marya Zaturenska

A History of American Poetry

1900-1940

PROLOGUE

In justice to the readers of this book, we have decided that a prologue is required. First of all, it is our obligation to say a word or two concerning the general nature of the book, to present a vantage point as briefly as we can from which the present survey of recent American poetry arrives in view. A history of anything, whether it is of politics or poetry, of religion or economics, or of the familiar and sometimes highly deceptive recording of military events, has its own scopes and limitations. The limitations are clearly those of time and of environment, and because of them certain phenomena of whatever subject we choose to talk about must be included. In the present instance, the subject is twentieth-century American poetry, and poetry, as all of us know well, has always maintained its own discriminations against history. At the risk of making what may seem to be an obvious understatement, let us say that historic truth and poetic truth do not always coincide. Poetry claims its own right to being an immortal, and like other creations of the human imagination, not excluding history and social science, it also claims a jealous disregard of trivial, literal, and often faulty statements of external fact. It is at this point that the historian of poetry becomes a critic; he must reject everything that stands in the way of his presenting a clear picture of chronological progression. He cannot indulge himself in a prolonged discussion of esthetic or social theory for its own sake. (And parenthetically it should be said that during the past fifteen years discussions of poetry have been clouded rather than illuminated by the sustained effort to unveil the secrets of the closet and the bedchamber and the writing table. Certain of these discussions were both worthy and serious in their intentions, but the public, justly enough, began to regard them as curiously incestuous forms of literary criticism: and as the num-

3

ber of footnotes enlarged upon the page, the value of reading a particular poem or the work of a particular poet seemed to diminish.) The historical critic has responsibilities of a different order: he cannot exclude biographical information, and his notable precedent for quoting facts of this nature may be found in Samuel Johnson's *Lives of the Poets;* and he must pay his respects to the legends, the *fabulae* of poetic history, for however dubious the surface qualities of these phenomena may appear to the naked eye they are among the generative forces of poetry itself, and are commonly referred to under the large and all too often meaningless names of "culture," "folklore," and "tradition."

Since we have brought up the subject of the poetic phenomenon, a further word of explanation should be devoted to its North American peculiarities. The American genius has long delighted in its own gifts of exaggeration, and within the confusions of youthful self-criticism and local shrewdness, a love of bigness for its own sake, and the rapid spending of countless lives and dollars, there is a tendency to regard art as one might look at a waterfall caused by the bursting of a dam, or a prairie fire, or an earthquake, or a mountain. To say the least, such a phenomenon is scarcely human, and yet its production is assumed to be the work of the average man. Once seen, the contradiction is plain enough, and Matthew Arnold in his lecture on Milton was among the first to remark upon its existence:

A lady in the State of Ohio sent to me only the other day a volume on American authors; the praise given throughout was of such high pitch that in thanking her I could not forbear saying that for only one or two of the authors named was such a strain of praise admissible, and that we lost all real standard of excellence by praising so uniformly and immoderately. She answered me with charming good temper, that very likely I was quite right, but it was pleasant to her to think that excellence was common and abundant. But excellence is not common and abundant; on the contrary, as the Greek poet long ago said, excellence dwells among rocks hardly accessible, and a man must almost wear his heart out before he can reach her. Whoever talks of excellence as common and abundant, is on the way to lose all right standard of excellence. And when the right standard of excellence is lost, it is not likely that much which is excellent will be produced.[1]

[1] *Essays in Criticism,* Second Series, used by permission of The Macmillan Company.

Let us say further that it is our intention to present a history of American poetry since 1900 that is humane in its interest rather than humanitarian, and that the chronological order which we have preserved with few exceptions throughout the book allows us to speak with more attention to the work of individual writers than to the various literary "movements" which have introduced them or modified their talents. Since the end of the nineteenth century there has been a tendency to over-rate the importance of literary movements in poetry; Arthur Symons' valuable little book, *The Symbolist Movement in Literature,* which was dedicated so pertinently to W. B. Yeats in the spring of 1899, marks the date, and from that time onward, and in this country since the "poetic renaissance" of about 1912, there has been an abundance, there has been (to remark politely) a confusion of talk about what "modern" poetry is, where it is going, and what it hopes to do. Now, one is always grateful to overhear conversations that seem to transcend the amenities and impertinent familiarities of personal gossip in respect to poets and poetry, yet to speak of literary movements in terms that ignore individual values as well as that degree of excellence which "dwells among rocks hardly accessible" is often "shop talk" that is considerably less charming and good tempered than Matthew Arnold's lady from Ohio and is quite as pernicious as that lady's desire to find excellence as common as the grass on her front lawn. Our saying this does not mean that we have ignored the existence of literary movements in America—far from it—but we have placed them (since this book is a history) in the strictly historical setting where they belong.

Within the span of time that our book covers there is scarcely a poem mentioned that has not been called (at one time or another) "modern poetry." Let us grant that the term has been somewhat overused and cheerfully admit that American poetry, painting, and architecture is of the "modern" world and that all of us are living for good or ill—and some of us indifferently—within the twentieth century itself. In poetry (since poetry is an art) whatever truly refreshes and delights the eye and ear is likely to have an innocent air of modernity for many centuries to come. We hope we need not remind many readers that this phenomenon has often happened in the past; and even as recently as 1922, when *The Waste Land* made its spectacular appearance in *The Dial,* among its more shocking innovations were those passages that had been inspired by T. S. Eliot's readings in Ovid's *Metamorphoses.* Barring the facts that Ovid wrote in Latin and died in the year 17 A.D., an excellent case could be presented for the "modernity" of some few of his love elegies.

Throughout our book we have assumed that American poetry has inherited the responsibilities of the familiarly called "great tradition" of poetic literature in English. But to say this also requires a paragraph of explanation, for an unspoken claim of this character can be readily misunderstood. It can be made to seem that American poetry in acknowledging its heritage still tends to ignore its native climate and its speech in favor of an elder language, an island geography, and west European psychology and culture. All this is, of course, historically false: we happen to agree with Bernard Shaw and H. L. Mencken when they insist that the British and the Americans "speak a different language," and we believe that a particular "difference" in temperament and spirit made its arrival as early as the year of 1776, which was a "difference" that led to a famous misunderstanding, and was, undoubtedly, a strong "difference" of opinion. But the heritage of which we speak is of a character that it is not always easy to define; it lies within the province of what some people would call "an unconscious will or knowledge," and that belongs, so we believe, to that rich substratum of poetic consciousness, the myths or *fabulae* of a national literature. The heritage may seem to be in violent contradiction to other "unconscious wills" that stir so restlessly in its near company; and its existence can be simply and calmly recognized by admitting that American poetry as a vehicle of human expression and as a major form of art has never been unaware of the great example set before it.

Since we have touched upon the difference in language, an extremely subtle difference, yet a clear one, that distinguishes the English of New York from that of London, it is appropriate to observe how profoundly that difference has affected poetic diction. During the past four decades, it would seem that American poetry has gained in the virility and brilliance of its speech, and by contrasting it with British poetry written in the same period, it would also seem that the creative forces of the language itself are to be found on this side of the Atlantic. The historian is in a position to record this phenomenon in proper detail—and so we shall, from the vantage point that we have chosen. But in this particular place, the Prologue of the book, the reader deserves a broader view, so as to prepare him for the progression of events which are to follow.

2

We are, of course, too close to the period in which the gains and losses of poetic speech occurred to give final answers to all the questions that may be raised. Briefly the series of circumstances are these: the last great master of English verse, Thomas Hardy, died in 1928; Robert Bridges died in 1930, and Rudyard Kipling in 1936. Meanwhile, two American poets, Ezra Pound and T. S. Eliot, exerted a subterranean and slowly increasing influence upon a younger generation of British poets. Between the death of Hardy and the declaration of a second world war the celebrity of William Butler Yeats grew into eminence on both sides of the Atlantic, but Yeats's speech was of Anglo-Irish Dublin, and during his last years, the maturity of his poetic gifts had met no rival from an indigenous British source. These circumstances and events are offered for what they are worth; in another fifty years—and in poetry the unpredictable is always to be anticipated—another generation may bring to maturity a British poet whose stature and influence will revive what now seems to be a dying inflection of a once vigorous and resourceful language. "Poetry is made with words" and the imaginative life of the individual poet is always closely related to the strength and resources of the language that he has at his command; if inventiveness in the very use of language seems to decline, if a general public attitude toward a memorable poetic tradition tends to become academic and remote, the individual poet faces a prospect of mediocre accomplishment that is more deadly to the spirit than the lack of money or public recognition. "History seems to have struck a bad patch," wrote W. H. Auden, but such disasters are of lesser consequence than the absence of mature and gifted masters of poetic speech combined with the loss of an indigenous vitality which exists in the spoken word and its inflections.

In expressing the foregoing convictions—and it would seem that there is sufficient and visible evidence to support them—we hope that we do not convey the impression of being blindly partisan in favor of our subject. What we do believe is that American poetry of the past four decades has grown beyond the needs of the somewhat maternal concern which had been voiced by Matthew Arnold's charming correspondent from Ohio. Since Arnold's lecture was delivered in 1888, it is not unreasonable to suppose that his lady was a third cousin (unhappily her name is unknown) of Henry James's equally charming and unfortunate Daisy Miller. If Daisy Miller's death in Rome did not impede the journeyings of American heiresses eastward across the Atlantic, their less adventurous cousins probably felt the necessity of protecting all—everything—that could be gathered under the imposing name of "culture" at home. That necessity is, of course, no longer urgent; and if American poetry has survived the misadventures of excessive praise, it will certainly find salutary relief in whatever critical discriminations we have to offer.

3

Our history has its own prologue in Edmund Clarence Stedman's *An American Anthology* and the dinner given to celebrate the occasion of its publication at Carnegie Hall in the City of New York on December 6, 1900. The invited guests were an impressive company and, among those who wrote telegrams and letters because they could not come, were John Hay, William Dean Howells, Edward Eggleston, Henry Van Dyke, S. Weir Mitchell, and James Whitcomb Riley, who honored his host with rhymed regrets that were read to spirited applause. To speed the welcome of a new era in American poetry William Winter, the dramatic critic (who is remembered chiefly for his instructions to Mrs. Patrick Campbell's *Second Mrs. Tanqueray* to "go away and sin no more"), had prepared a speech to be read at the

dinner table. "The deadliest foe of the creative impulse is criticism," he remarked. "Genius is something that comes without
effort and impels its possessor to heroic labor." If William Winter
seems to have indulged himself in an overstatement that in its
very exuberance denied his own usefulness in writing criticism
of the stage, there is little doubt that his intentions were sincere.
Proof of their heat was all too evident in the lines of his verses
to Stedman which brought his recitation to a close:

> So rest thy regal throne, thou hast ascended,
> The standards blaze, the golden trumpets ring,
> And in one voice, our loyal hearts are blended:
> God bless the poet and God save the King!

It has not been recorded what Stedman thought at being
called a "King"; but he probably knew that Winter meant no
harm by it, and that his friend at this high moment of excitement was visibly overwrought. The plain facts of the matter
were that Stedman was a prosperous Connecticut Yankee, had
been briefly educated at Yale, had been a newspaper editor, had
been an assistant in the office of the Attorney General of the
United States, had entered Wall Street in 1863, and like his
contemporaries, Richard Watson Gilder and R. H. Stoddard,
had earned the distinction of being among "the squires of
poetry." The leisure that he had acquired from his wealth had
been devoted to a wide reading of both British and American
verse, and with equal verve he composed Civil War ballads.
These were written with a quick-marching beat of rhythms that
recalled the political satires of James Russell Lowell's *The Biglow Papers,* and the most frequently quoted of them all was
Stedman's "How Old Brown Took Harper's Ferry" which might
well have been inspired by Hosea Biglow's notorious lines:

> God sends country lawyers, an' other wise fellers,
> To start the world's team wen it gits in a slough;
> Fer John P.
> Robinson he
> Sez the world'll go right, ef he hollers out Gee! [2]

---

[2] *The Biglow Papers* by James Russell Lowell, First Series, III, Cam. ed.,
used by permission of Houghton Mifflin Company.

The refrain of Stedman's ballad is equally swift and emphatic:

> And each drop from Old Brown's life-veins, like the red gore
>   of the dragon,
>   May spring up a vengeful Fury, hissing through your slave-
>   worn lands!
>   And Old Brown,
>   Osawatomie Brown,
> May trouble you more than ever, when you've nailed his coffin
>   down! [3]

This was, of course, thoroughly acceptable journalistic verse, but Stedman's *An American Anthology,* like Lowell's *The Vision of Sir Launfal,* aimed at higher things. Compared with Rufus W. Griswold's *The Poets and Poetry of America,* which had been its weightiest predecessor, Stedman's compilation was a model of scholarship and critical discrimination. It was not without some show of courage that Stedman approached his editorial labors; his book of British verse, *A Victorian Anthology,* had been well received in 1895, and when a friend heard that he was about to publish a compendium of American verse which was to be its equal in size and format, the editor was warned: "We have nothing to compare with what is being done in England." The task was, no doubt, a formidable one, for aside from the general optimism that was felt and shared by many Americans who were eager to greet "the dawn of a new century," editorial confidence in the quality of American verse was extremely rare. During the twenty years before 1900, Emerson, Longfellow, Holmes, Lowell, and even the lesser known Whitman had completed the course of their careers on earth; and a skeptical group of American critics who were by no means certain that "when half-gods go, the gods arrive," had scarcely recovered from the deaths of Browning and Tennyson. Stedman himself spoke of the hour in which his *An American Anthology* appeared as "a twilight interval"; and the excitements of both popular and semiesoteric "literary discovery" were reserved for those who had read Kipling's *Barrack Room Ballads,* Stevenson's *A Child's Garden of Verses,* W. E. Henley's *Hospital Sketches,* and A. E. Housman's

---

[3] "How Old Brown Took Harper's Ferry" from *Poems,* used by permission of Houghton Mifflin Company.

A Shropshire Lad, none of which could claim an American origin.

Although a present rereading of *An American Anthology* would scarcely reawaken the enthusiasms and diligent responses of its editor's labors, it can still be read with historical interest and renewed understanding of the necessities which prompted its arrival. Across the span of the nineteenth century, one sees the beginnings of a national poetry: in a few of Philip Freneau's lyrics, despite their clear indebtedness to studious rereadings of Gray's "Elegy Written in a Country Church-Yard," a change of poetic climate may be discerned, a forecast (since we read them in retrospect) of what we now define as an "American brilliance" and sharpness of visual imagery. *An American Anthology* was a work that gave historical perspective to its choices, and however generously Stedman represented the tastes and prejudices of his day which were schooled in an uncritical appreciation of Victorian verse, including the false vigor, mediocre diction, and belated Byronism of Bayard Taylor, his anthology brought to light submerged contrasts and vitalities in American poetry. At a time when Emily Dickinson's name was hardly known, he represented her work with fullness and enthusiasm, nor did he ignore the unique quality of Jones Very's devotional verse, nor the poetry of Herman Melville when only the very few remembered the existence of Melville's *Battle-Pieces* and *Clarel*. If the majority of Stedman's selections from the work of younger poets did little more than reflect the minor graces of a period in which Richard Hovey and Bliss Carman seemed to invite their readers to the joys of Vagabondia, he also took pains to extend the fame of George Santayana beyond the elms of Harvard Yard and to introduce the early poems of E. A. Robinson. To Stedman's home in the village of Bronxville, Westchester County, New York, young Robinson came to hear the elder man's reminiscences of Whitman. For Stedman had a genuine admiration for Whitman, and he once admitted (as though the fact were a dangerously open secret) that Emerson, Poe, and Whitman were the three American poets from whom Europe had much to learn. The handsomely bearded, delicately profiled, urbane Edmund C. Stedman was an excellent host to young men and women who "showed promise." If he possessed the art of putting shy E. A. Robinson at ease, he also had the gift of extending nicely tempered encouragement to poets who had not quite arrived, and his conduct probably (since she was often among his younger guests) offered an example to Harriet Monroe. Certainly the heritage of courteous and yet inspiring hospitality (that made a visit to *Poetry's* office in Chicago an event in the lives of many younger poets) remained unbroken.

Meanwhile a large measure of Stedman's enthusiasm had been reserved for the young authors of three books of *Songs from Vagabondia*—Richard Hovey, the Dartmouth poet; the Canadian, Bliss Carman, and the forgotten Tom Buford Meteyard, who designed the covers and end papers of the little volumes with a touch of Pre-Raphaelite craftsmanship. Before the publication of the first book in 1894, the three friends had spent a holiday together, including a winter in New York, a journey to Nova Scotia, the Acadie of Longfellow's *Evangeline,* and an autumn tour of Washington, D. C. Hovey's education at Dartmouth College where he enjoyed the honors of being "class poet" as well as the author of "Men of Dartmouth"—a song still sung at Hanover—and subsequent trips across the Atlantic to Paris and Avignon (a passion for travel which rivaled the earlier European wanderings of Bayard Taylor whose peregrinations resulted in a fustian and now unreadable translation of Goethe's *Faust*), furnished the background for the kind of lyricism that the American public welcomed as the poetry of Vagabondia. However far he traveled he never lost the spirit of:

> The campus is reborn in us today;
> The old grip stirs our hearts with new-old joy;
> Again bursts bonds for madcap holiday
> The eternal boy.[4]

Hovey attempted to combine and succeeded in confusing the Transcendentalism of Emerson and Whitman with his admiration for whatever ecstatic utterances he could find in the poetry

---

[4] "Spring—Read at the 63d Annual Convention of the ψ Upsilon Fraternity at the University of Michigan, Ann Arbor, Michigan, May 7, 1896" from *Along the Trail* by Richard Hovey and Bliss Carman. Reprinted by permission of Dodd, Mead & Company, Inc.

of the French Symbolists and the Parnassians. He delighted in his attempts to translate Maurice Maeterlinck, and Bliss Carman shared with him the exuberance of "the wine that maketh glad the heart, of the bully-boy, gay, jolly," an innocence which overrode whatever contradictions may have been felt in an equal love for Paul Verlaine, the "Prince of Vagabonds," and Walt Whitman, the "King of Free-Versists." While Bliss Carman wrote

> The world is Vagabondia
> To him who is a vagabond [5]

Hovey composed lines to "Isabel" [6] which read

> In her body's perfect sweet
> Suppleness and languor meet,—
> Arms that move like lapsing billows,
> Breasts that Love would make his pillows,

as well as "A Stein Song" that had the merits of diverting his enthusiasm into more appropriate channels than are to be discovered in the phrasing of his stanzas to "Isabel"; certainly he recaptured the joys of an American undergraduate drinking beer in

> it's always fair weather
> When good fellows get together,
> With a stein on the table and a good song ringing clear. [7]

At the time of his death in 1900, and perhaps anticipating E. A. Robinson's interest in the Arthurian legends (for which Tennyson's *Idylls of the King* had provided a Victorian precedent), Hovey was engaged in writing a long poem on Launcelot and Guenevere, "in Five Dramas."

It may well be difficult for the reader of the mid-twentieth century to appreciate fully the underlying seriousness with which Hovey and Carman wrote their *Songs from Vagabondia;* in 1900 their intentions were readily understood and widely applauded. Muriel Miller in her *Bliss Carman: A Portrait* (1935, Toronto)

[5] "The Vagabonds" from *Ballads and Lyrics* by Richard Hovey and Bliss Carman. Reprinted by permission of Dodd, Mead & Company, Inc.

[6] From *Songs from Vagabondia* by Richard Hovey and Bliss Carman. Reprinted by permission of Dodd, Mead & Company, Inc.

[7] "A Stein Song" from *Songs from Vagabondia* by Richard Hovey and Bliss Carman. Reprinted by permission of Dodd, Mead & Company, Inc.

has the best explanation of the purpose which briefly animated—
one almost says "galvanized"—Hovey and Carman into the activity of writing verses:

> However, the two poets did not mean their Vagabondian scheme to
> be a mere idle pastime of a summer's day; it represented far more to
> them: It was their joint protest against the warped convention-bound
> lives of the material, money-making American citizen of their day.

As a "message of protest" against the materialism of the day,
the verses now seem harmless enough, and if it were not for the
loud and certainly aggressive note that Carman and Hovey
sounded in their praise of a globe-circling Bohemia, one might
feel more regret at the decline of their "promise" into the gray
expanses of mediocre and inept poetic phrasing. Bliss Carman
outlived Hovey by more than a quarter of a century; in his
latter years he edited *The Oxford Book of American Verse,* a
task for which he was obviously unfit, and to the end of his days
he continued a habit he had acquired of writing rhymed descriptions of the Connecticut countryside—with all the inoffensive
and polished banality of another Richard Watson Gilder. Padraic
Colum who knew him in these years writes of his courtesy, his
distinction of manner, and then concludes, "though the tweeds
that he wore had given him long service, they were always carefully pressed and spotless." And in Carman's last book, *Wild
Garden* (1929), the landscape is always seen from the distance
of a pleasant country house; from the earliest hours of its inception his Vagabondia had been an overtly conscious and "literary"
invention. The youthful voices that announced its discovery were
highly pitched, and in their lack of art were often strained. The
historical value of its existence lies neither in its criticism of
social evils, nor in its effort to import the latest styles in Parisian
verse to the American continent. Both Hovey and Carman lacked
the depths of feeling, understanding, and serious application to
their art which were necessary to endow their readings in Mallarmé, Verlaine, and Verhaeren with the strength of a memorable
influence upon American poetry. But what they did convey (and
this was probably something that concerned them least) was the
recurrent theme of youth for its own sake and glory, and that

theme with the image of Bohemia at its side was sustained for twenty years after Hovey's death. It soon found expression in the verse of George Sterling on the Pacific Coast, and it re-emerged, less innocently perhaps, in Witter Bynner's *Young Harvard* (1917) and his "Grenstone" verses (1917), and the notes of Vagabondia were heard in the "kinds of love" that John Reed, Max Eastman, Edna St. Vincent Millay, and Floyd Dell pursued through the streets of New York's Greenwich Village. By this time it had presumably left college and was slightly soiled by early sorrows and disillusionments, but touches of its gaiety remained—and no one can rightly say that Stedman had been far wrong in his conviction that *Songs from Vagabondia* looked forward to a future.

Perhaps something should be said of the immediate effect that W. E. Henley's "Invictus" had on Hovey's verse. The Romantic didacticism of Henley's

> It matters not how strait the gate,
>   How charged with punishments the scroll,
> I am the master of my fate:
>   I am the captain of my soul . . .[8]

has a persistent heritage in American newspaper verse; its voice literally thunders through the lines of Edwin Markham's "The Man with the Hoe" (1899), but it has never found a more exact imitation of a particular model than in Hovey's patriotic stanzas to an "Unmanifest Destiny": [9]

> I do not know beneath what sky
>   Nor on what seas shall be thy fate;
> I only know it shall be high,
>   I only know it shall be great.

This literal devotion to contemporary British models was widely practiced among lesser American poets of Stedman's day, but there has been some confusion in referring to them as though they were slaves of "traditional form," or "members of a genteel

[8] "Invictus" from *Poems*, 1926, used by permission of Charles Scribner's Sons.

[9] From *Along the Trail* by Richard Hovey and Bliss Carman. Reprinted by permission of Dodd, Mead & Company, Inc.

tradition." Briefly, they followed too closely the fashions of the day, placing a standard for their own skill no higher than the demands of being published in a magazine. Of these Thomas Bailey Aldrich (1836-1907) was the most gifted, and since he was a popular and able editor of *The Atlantic Monthly,* he practiced the art of writing verses that were acceptable to the *Atlantic's* temperament and needs. The index to his charm may be found in his prose narrative, a semiautobiographical account of a New England childhood, *The Story of a Bad Boy,* which places the quality of his imagination at a measurable distance from the genius that inspired Whittier's *Snow-bound;* his observations in verse were slight, exact, and as he grew older, markedly feminine. The concluding stanzas of his "Heredity" [10] may be read for their lack of pretension and for their quiet utterance of a true sensibility:

> In Grantham church they lie asleep;
> Just where, the verger may not know.
> Strange that two hundred years should keep
> The old ancestral fires aglow!
>
> In me these two have met again;
> To each my nature owes a part:
> To one, the cool and reasoning brain;
> To one, the quick, unreasoning heart.

As Van Wyck Brooks implies in his *New England: Indian Summer,* Aldrich seems to fill a space that would have been otherwise left vacant between the death of James Russell Lowell and the arrival, in a descending order, of George Edward Woodberry.

4

In Aldrich whatever may be called a New England tradition in American poetry had come to a halting place; it had not died, but in 1900 it is perhaps significant that Stedman's dinner to announce the publication of *An American Anthology* was held in New York and not in Boston. The perfect example of the well-established poet was Madison Cawein (1865-1914) of Ken-

---

[10] From *Poems,* used by permission of Houghton Mifflin Company.

tucky whose verse had been praised by Edmund Gosse, the British critic, and by William Dean Howells. Cawein's verse had the same relationship to poetry as the once-popular canvases sketched so fluently by Maxfield Parrish have to painting, which means that it was by no means as artful as it seemed. A quotation of one stanza from "The Rain-Crow" is quite enough to show him at his best, and if it does small credit to his memory, it helps to define the kind of verse that was accepted and enjoyed by reputable editors and critics:

> The butterfly, safe under leaf and flower,
>   Has found a roof, knowing how true thou art;
> The bumble-bee, within the last half-hour,
>   Has ceased to hug the honey to its heart;
> While in the barnyard, under shed and cart,
> Brood-hens have housed.—But I, who scorned thy power,
>   Barometer of birds,—like August there,—
>   Beneath a beech, dripping from foot to hair,
>   Like some drenched truant, cower.[11]

Another figure of the period was John Bannister Tabb (familiarly known as "Father Tabb") (1845-1909), and the merit that his verse acquired rests in its brevity. His air was modest and his self-knowledge led him to disclaim the enthusiasm of a friend who had likened the quality of his verse to that of Robert Herrick's. Tabb wrote in reply: "Of this poet, the *Golden Treasury* has all I know . . . Nothing, I am glad to observe, is detected of my worship of Keats, whom I know best of the gods."

Actually his verse has the quality of remarks that might well have been made by a less gifted, less intense, but not less charming Emily Dickinson. And there is little likelihood that the Baltimore priest who was born in Virginia had ever heard of his New England contemporary. His verses written for children are less memorable than those composed by Robert Louis Stevenson; and the "minute particulars" of his wisdom were too facile, too neatly trained in glib generalities, to express the depth of religious emotion that they imply:

[11] From "The Rain-Crow," *Poems of Madison Cawein,* used by permission of Bobbs-Merrill Company.

The least to man, the most to God—
A fragrant mystery
Where love, with beauty glorified,
Forgets utility.[12]

Often enough his verse ran dangerously near to the lyrics that
Carrie Jacobs Bond wrote and set to music of the same quality,
but Tabb's restraint (and perhaps his readings in Keats) preserved his dignity:

Out of the dusk a shadow,
Then a spark;
Out of the cloud a silence,
Then a lark . . .[13]

Tabb's verse was praised extravagantly in the British press and
in particular by Alice Meynell, whose critical influence was felt
in the pages of W. E. Henley's *National Observer,* and the *Pall
Mall Gazette.* After Tabb's death in 1909, Mrs. Meynell in a
flush of praise dramatized the affliction of blindness which over-
took him in his latter years:

Such is one, and not the least, assuredly not to be the last, of the
poets of America. That great nation has looked ardently for her poets.
She has found them in places unransacked. She must have been much
amazed to find one of them here, in the less literary South, in the
person of a Catholic priest, in the seclusion of an ecclesiastical college,
and finally, in one of the deprived and afflicted of this troublous life,
a man blind for his few last years but alight within, who has now gone
down quietly to an illustrious grave.[14]

With considerably fewer overtones of rhetoric and with the
same modest courage that many of his little verses had expressed
Tabb wrote more fittingly his own epitaph in "Going Blind": [15]

12 "Blossom" from *The Poetry of Father Tabb.* Reprinted by permission of
Dodd, Mead & Company, Inc.
13 "Evolution" from *The Poetry of Father Tabb.* Reprinted by permission
of Dodd, Mead & Company, Inc.
14 From *Alice Meynell: A Memoir* by Viola Meynell, used by permission
of Charles Scribner's Sons.
15 From *The Poetry of Father Tabb.* Reprinted by permission of Dodd,
Mead & Company, Inc.

> Back to the primal gloom
> Where life began,
> As to my mother's womb
> Must I a man
> Return:
> Not to be born again,
> But to remain;
> And in the School of Darkness learn
> What mean
> "The things unseen."

Years later, Edgar Lee Masters (then an unknown young poet who wrote verses that were as ineffectual as any) was to personify the versifier of Stedman's day in his *Spoon River Anthology*. "Petit, the poet," [16] he called him, and the type is too obvious to be mistaken:

> Seeds in a dry pod, tick, tick, tick,
> Tick, tick, tick, like mites in a quarrel—
> Faint iambics that the full breeze wakens—
>
> . . . .
>
> Tick, tick, tick, what little iambics,
> While Homer and Whitman roared in the pines?

It was that consciousness that Stedman felt when he spoke of Whitman to E. A. Robinson. Whitman's loose and not altogether convincingly expressed desire to "hear America singing" was communicated to such hearty souls as Stedman, who beneath his urbane and carefully sustained disguise of a Wall Street broker, cherished an apparently inexhaustible feeling of warmth for poets.

In the year following the publication of Stedman's anthology, no signs of a portentous revival of American poetry made their appearance; and E. A. Robinson, who was to become the significant exception to the mediocrity which surrounded him, was still unacknowledged. He, unlike William Vaughn Moody, George Cabot Lodge, and Trumbull Stickney, was to fulfill his early promise with work of an impressive maturity which was to make

[16] From *Spoon River Anthology*, Macmillan, used by permission of the Author.

the legend of his neglect no less notorious than the sudden blaze
of celebrity that was a warning (as he might well have read it)
of his future fame. Before 1902, he had published two small books
of poems, and through a series of fortuitous accidents, they had
been brought to the attention of Theodore Roosevelt, who with
energetic promptness offered Robinson his patronage. This was
the kind of celebrity which was of a piece with everything in
American life that Robinson distrusted. He had learned to be
skeptical of the fame that had attended the careers of many
poets in Stedman's *Anthology* in which there were only two, or
perhaps three, of his contemporaries, Moody, Torrence, and
Stickney (and the latter had been excluded from its pages) who
like him perceived "the valley of the shadow" through which
they moved. To be acknowledged as a poet by the same critical
estimate that had welcomed Hovey, Carman, and Cawein was
dubious praise, and to be subjected to the well-intentioned enthusiasm of the President of the United States was an irony as
profound and as dramatic as the reversal from good fortune to
bad which fell upon the characters in his own poems. He who
seemed the least likely to fulfill Whitman's prophecies of poets
to come after him, and he who in temperament and accomplishment was least like Whitman, began to assume the responsibilities of the position thrust upon him. A friend described his reception of the eulogy written of his work by Roosevelt in a weekly
periodical; Robinson stood up and began to pace the floor, saying half-humorously to himself over and over again, "I shall
never live it down, I shall never live it down."

5

With this brief summary of events which immediately surrounded the publication of *An American Anthology,* our history
begins. From here onward we write of our far and near contemporaries, and as the historical perspective grows shorter, we
shall be faced with those hazards that Edward Gibbon saw when,
as in a nightmare, he viewed the prospect of writing a history of
his own times and his own country:

I should shrink with terror [Gibbon wrote] from the modern history of England, where every character is a problem, and every reader a friend or an enemy; where a writer is supposed to hoist a flag of party, and is devoted to damnation by the adverse faction. . . . I must embrace a safer and more extensive theme.[17]

We have no wish to quarrel with Gibbon's wisdom, but we can take comfort in the fact that no theme is safe, and that no history, however close at hand or far removed, is entirely free from error, or impervious to the "adverse factions" that Gibbon had in mind. Even though the historical critic carry Achilles' shield before him, it will be discovered by those who follow him that he also possesses an Achilles' heel. As yet there is no sign that Gibbon's flags of party have been taken down, but we, speaking frankly for ourselves, are not concerned with them: political rewards have little relevance to our subject, and for the poet, the historian, and the critic, such rewards are often unrealistic in prospect, and as many a writer from Ben Jonson's day to this will testify, they are frequently shabby once they come to hand.

Like the face of Janus, poetry, ancient or modern, has its ambiguities, and we have spoken before of that reserved and sometimes properly snobbish air with which its "timeless" face looks down at history. But at that moment and in that place one of the wisest of contemporary poets has a word to say; Robert Frost (who has substituted a Vermont hillside for a Sabine farm) once wrote in a glow of optimism, ". . . permanence in poetry is perceived instantly. It hasn't to await the test of time." That is one view that modifies by several degrees the fixities of an historical perspective; and there are occasions at which even the historical critic must regard his subject with a "timeless", and let us hope, an equally steady eye.

It is possible that some readers of our book will discover the omission of a poet's name or the title of a poem that they had long held in high regard. Here we must (though for the moment it may seem discourteous to do so) take our position with that guest of princes and their historian, Voltaire:

17 From *Edward Gibbon's Autobiography*, Everyman's Library, used by permission of E. P. Dutton & Company, Inc., publisher in the United States.

My great difficulty [he wrote] has not been to find memoirs, but to sift out the good ones. There is another inconvenience inseparable from writing contemporary history. Every captain of infantry who has served in the armies of Charles XII and lost his knapsack on the march thinks I ought to mention it. If the subalterns complain of my silence, the generals and ministers complain of my outspokenness. Whoso writes the history of his own time must expect to be blamed for everything he has said and everything he has not said; but these little drawbacks should not discourage a man who loves truth and liberty, expects nothing, fears nothing, asks nothing, and who limits his ambition to the cultivation of letters.[18]

For the rest we have only to say that we have tried to cultivate that uncommon merit, common sense, of which Samuel Johnson's *Lives of the Poets* furnishes so brilliantly and humanely an example. In respect to literary history the twentieth century is less fortunate than the eighteenth, and in the hope of making some contribution toward righting an unequal balance we offer the following pages to our readers.

[18] From *Life of Voltaire* by S. G. Tallentyre, used by permission of G. P. Putnam's Sons.

PART I

THE "TWILIGHT INTERVAL"

WILLIAM VAUGHN MOODY AND HIS CIRCLE

The best introduction to William Vaughn Moody and his circle is found in the pages of Henry Adams' little-known biography, *The Life of George Cabot Lodge* (1911). The inner circle consisted of three friends, Moody, Lodge, and Trumbull Stickney, who had met at Harvard and were undergraduates there in the early and mid-years of the 1890's; at that moment all three were "poetic personalities" rather than poets: they discussed literature and literary movements fervently, they exchanged the latest ideas imported from the British Isles and continental Europe, and Moody, a Middle Westerner, who had been born in Indiana in 1869, seemed to possess more energy, more awareness of a poetic "mission" in life, and more initiative than his two friends who came from well-established New England families. What Henry Adams had to say of the cultural climate that produced a George Cabot Lodge has been repeated many times since the publication of his biography in 1911, but no one has written of that climate with a more quickening perception of its lights and shadows:

Poetry was a suppressed instinct: and except where, as in Longfellow, it kept the old character of ornament, it became a reaction against society, as in Emerson and the Concord school, or, further away and more roughly, in Walt Whitman. Less and less it appeared, as in earlier ages, the natural, favorite expression of society itself. In the last half of the nineteenth century, the poet became everywhere a rebel against his surroundings. What had been begun by Wordsworth, Byron, and Shelley, was carried on by Algernon Swinburne in London or Paul Verlaine in Paris or Walt Whitman in Washington, by a common instinct of revolt. Even the atmosphere of Beacon Street [in Boston] was at times faintly redolent of Schopenhauer.

. . . but young Lodge's nature was itself as elementary and simple as the salt water. . . . Robust in figure, healthy in appetite, careless of consequences, he could feel complex and introspective only as his ideal, the Norse faun, might feel astonished and angry at finding nature perverse and unintelligible in a tropical jungle. Since nature could not be immoral or futile, the immorality and futility must be in the mind that conceived it. Man became an outrage;—society an artificial device for the distortion of truth;—civilization a wrong. Many millions of simple natures have thought, and still think, the same thing, and the more complex have never quite made up their minds whether to agree with them or not; but the thought that was simple and sufficient for the Norseman exploring the tropics, or for an exuberant young savage sailing his boat off the rude shores of Gloucester and Cape Ann, could not long survive in the atmosphere of State Street. Commonly, the poet dies young.[1]

Literally the three friends did die young, Moody at the age of forty-one in 1910, Lodge at thirty-six in 1909, and Stickney, the youngest and most highly gifted of the three, at the age of thirty in 1904. The mortality rate was so high and the extinction so complete that one almost thinks of them in the same terms in which W. B. Yeats referred to his own "tragic generation," which was their contemporary and which was marked by the early deaths of Lionel Johnson, Ernest Dowson, and John Synge.

2

The present reader of William Vaughn Moody's verse is almost certain to be faced with embarrassment. At the time he wrote it, Moody seemed to possess all the right answers that were demanded of poetry, he seemed to embrace large themes with remarkable ease, and while he taught English literature at the University of Chicago,[2] which followed his promising career at Harvard, he sought to revive poetic drama in an heroic and Miltonic strain; it would seem that he feared no subject and could write of relationships between Man and God, between Man and Woman, of social injustice, of Right and Wrong, of Good and Evil with equal facility and resonance. His ambitions were so great that they seemed to blunt his sensibilities, and apparently such mock-heroic lines as

I am the Woman, ark of the law and its breaker,

[1] From *The Life of George Cabot Lodge* by Henry Adams, Houghton Mifflin, by permission of Elizabeth Lodge.

[2] Moody had also taught at Radcliffe and Harvard before going to Chicago.

were to him an appropriate expression of moral grandeur, and
with the same lack of feeling for the true strength of language
he wrote of America, "the eagle nation Milton saw Mewing its
mighty youth." Nor were his verses on intimate themes less unfortunate. "The Daguerreotype" written in memory of his mother
seems to echo persistently the lack of sensibility and taste that
subjected Coventry Patmore's *The Angel in the House* to Gerard
Manley Hopkins' severest criticism. In "The Daguerreotype" [3]
Moody wrote:

> Nine moons I fed
> Deep of divine unrest,
> While over and over in the dark she said,
> "Blessèd but not as happier children blessed"—
> That this should be
> Even she . . .
> God, how with time and change
> Thou makest thy footsteps strange!
> Ah, now I know
> They play upon me, and it is not so.
> Why, 't is a girl I never saw before,
> A little thing to flatter and make weep,
> To tease until her heart is sore,
> Then kiss and clear the score;
> A gypsy run-the-fields,
> A little liberal daughter of the earth,
> Good for what hour of truancy and mirth
> The careless season yields.

The faulty diction betrayed a curious lack of respect for his
subject and equal lack of feeling in the line,

> A little thing to flatter and make weep.

Our concern with Moody's verse is almost solely a matter of
historical interest: in 1931 a volume of his *Selected Poems* was
edited by Robert Morss Lovett, an admiring friend and a colleague at the University of Chicago; and Moody's memory was
also kept green through the good offices of his wife, whose hospitality to young poets (including Hart Crane) at her Chicago
home created a center of literary activity in the Middle West

[3] From *Poems of William Vaughn Moody*, used by permission of Houghton
Mifflin Company.

until the closing years of the 1920's. Several of Moody's occasional pieces, "Gloucester Moors," a record of economic disaster in New England, caused by the industrial revolution's maladjustments in New England's fishing towns, the famous "Ode in Time of Hesitation," and "On a Soldier Fallen in the Philippines," the last two written in the first wave of disillusionment following the patriotic enthusiasm of the Spanish-American War, still occupy a place in larger anthologies of American verse. Their spirit and diction are less noisy, less suspiciously robust, and a shade more thoughtful than Edwin Markham's "The Man with the Hoe." A few lines from "On a Soldier Fallen in the Philippines" [4] illustrate the resemblance to Markham's histrionic mannerisms as well as the note of irony which distinguished Moody from his more clearly extraverted contemporary:

> A flag for a soldier's bier
> Who dies that his land may live;
> O, banners, banners here,
> That he doubt not nor misgive!
> That he heed not from the tomb
> The evil days draw near
> When the nation, robed in gloom,
> With its faithless past shall strive.

Let him never dream that his bullet's scream went wide of its island mark,
Home to the heart of his darling land where she stumbled and sinned in the dark.

3

The excellence of Henry Adams' mordant and penetrating *Life of George Cabot Lodge* almost convinces one that its subject was at least a "promising young poet." But however hard we may try to discover actual poems in the memorial edition of his poems and dramas issued in 1911, the effort fails. Young Lodge was more deeply concerned with the ideas that entered the writing of a poem than with the poem's accomplishment. He had been disturbed and genuinely moved by the rich flow of talk which surrounded him at Harvard, and his travels on the

[4] From *The Poems and Plays of William Vaughn Moody*, Vol. I, used by permission of Houghton Mifflin Company.

European continent stirred inner wells of literary appreciation that could easily be mistaken by his friends for the existence of poetic talent. If a reading of his work yields no greater rewards than the rhetoric of such lines as these:

> The Thought of Buddha in our mortal brain,
> The human heart of Jesus in our breast,
> And in our will the strength of Herakles! [5]

his career as an archetypical Bostonian of his day endows him with an interest that we usually reserve for one of Henry James's heroes. And truly enough, since George Cabot was the son of Senator Henry Cabot Lodge, his career follows the course of James's charming young Englishman, Nicholas Dormer, son of Lady Agnes in *The Tragic Muse,* who inherited the prospects of a seat in Parliament and relinquished them in favor of the more difficult and less assured rewards of pursuing the dim lights of art in a portrait painter's unswept, ill-cared-for, London studio.

The very latest modes in Continental literature held great and luminous attractions for the eager mind of young George Cabot Lodge; in 1895 his self-imposed and accelerated course in reading embraced the names of Balzac, Flaubert, de Vigny, Leconte de Lisle, Alfred de Musset, Victor Hugo, Renan, Sully-Prudhomme, and Schopenhauer. In 1897, after encountering the delights and disillusionments of German arts and philosophic letters in Berlin, he returned to America, and in the following year he permitted the publication of a first book, *The Song of the Wave,* of which Henry Adams dryly remarked, "Lodge felt himself unpleasantly placed between . . . two needs,—that of justifying his existence, on the one hand, and that of challenging premature recognition, on the other."

In Europe, "Bay" Lodge had sought out intellectual stimulation and salvation, but his mind and talents were both too restless and unformed to grasp meanings clearly or to put them into words:

[5] "The Soul's Inheritance" from *The Poems and Dramas of George Cabot Lodge,* Houghton Mifflin, used by permission of Elizabeth Lodge.

> And I shall answer thee as one who calls
> Through the dumb places of the haunted past,
> Drinking its fulness ere the moment dies [6]

he wrote, and the true expression of what he had seen and read and felt was left for Adams to record in his *Education of Henry Adams:* [7]

> Bay Lodge and Joe Stickney had given birth to the wholly new and original party of Conservative Christian Anarchists, to restore true poetry under the inspiration of the "Götterdämmerung." . . . The conservative Christian anarchist could have no associate, no object, no faith except the nature of nature itself; and his "larger synthesis" had only the fault of being so supremely true that even the highest obligation of duty could scarcely oblige Bay Lodge to deny it in order to prove it. Only the self-evident truth that no philosophy of order—except the Church—had ever satisfied the philosopher reconciled the conservative Christian anarchist to prove his own. . . . Naturally these ideas were so far in advance of the age that hardly more people could understand them than understood Wagner or Hegel.

Obviously young Lodge's speculations in philosophy were too ambitious for his undeveloped skills in writing verse, and indeed the heavily weighted periods of his "conservative anarchy," as Adams phrased it, were scarcely conducive to writing poetry. Throughout his commentaries on Lodge's esthetic aspirations, there is rather more than a hint that Henry Adams himself was a "spoiled poet"; his admiration for Swinburne had the air of being a vicarious adventure into a forbidden world, a world that was ill suited to his temperamental austerities and his melancholy wit—and if Swinburne's poetry was "poetry" in the sense of creating a standard for excellence in its day, Adams was all too willing to admit himself no poet. As he looked at "poetry" and observed its flaws as it fell from the lips of his American contemporaries, he peered more closely in his *Mont-Saint-Michel and Chartres* (1905), and then withdrew from "poetry" entirely, and turned at last, with more finality than ever, to the writing of his prose.

But his withdrawal did not blunt the keener edges of his sensi-

[6] "XXXIII" from *The Poems and Dramas of George Cabot Lodge,* Houghton Mifflin, Vol. I, used by permission of Elizabeth Lodge.
[7] Used by permission of Houghton Mifflin Company.

bility; in 1911 he saw the phenomenal aspects of poetry in America; "In America," he wrote, "the male is not only a bad listener, but also, for poetry, a distinctly hostile audience." It will be observed that this remark was made one year before the arrival of a so-called "poetic renaissance" in the United States, in *Poetry* (Chicago), yet its essential truth remained unchanged, nor is it modified greatly by those who listen to poetry read today. When Harriet Monroe founded her magazine, *Poetry,* she quoted boldly, and with insistence on its back cover, Whitman's "To have great poets there must be great audiences too." Adams was objectively correct, and his discontent, his gloom were salutary.

Meanwhile Adams' "exuberant young savage," George Cabot Lodge, continued his career of transatlantic speculations in philosophy and writing verses. An elegiac note, which was perhaps derived from his friend Stickney, entered his lines, and to Giacomo Leopardi he inscribed:

> Despair is musical, the wings of pain
>> Are stirred in rhythms of large winds that bear
>> A mute divinity of human prayer
>> And human sorrow that is prayer in vain.[8]

Of course he had been rereading Tennyson and was under the spell of *In Memoriam;* and characteristically enough, he could not invent a way of breaking it. On the occasion of Stickney's death in 1904, the spell returned:

> We bore the chill, persistent dread
>> Here in the long, tree-shaded way;
>> And here the things we could not say
>> Were more, I know, than man has said.[9]

"The things we could not say" were all too evident because Lodge lacked the wit and the power to discover his own language; it was not that Tennyson's influence was "bad" for him, any more than Milton's influence was "bad" for Moody or for Markham; the difficulty was that all three poets were trapped in

[8] "To Giacomo Leopardi" from *The Poems and Dramas of George Cabot Lodge,* Houghton Mifflin, Vol. I, used by permission of Elizabeth Lodge.

[9] "XXIII" from *The Poems and Dramas of George Cabot Lodge,* Houghton Mifflin, Vol. II, used by permission of Elizabeth Lodge.

a fatal circle of literary reminiscence in the same way that lesser poets of the mid-twentieth century imitate with literal serious-ness the language of W. H. Auden; and it is obvious that masters are not to be blamed for the lack of inventiveness shown by their ardent, if not too brilliant, pupils.

Lodge had married happily, and as his sudden and unforeseen death approached in 1909, he turned from the effort to write long poetic dramas (which has remained a persistent tendency in American poetry since his day) to the writing of dramatic narra-tives in verse. None was successful, and it seemed as though his energy had been expended in the hope of becoming a "conserva-tive Christian anarchist" as well as a poet. One concludes that his devotion to the writing of poetry was less pure, less concen-trated than Nicholas Dormer's devotion to portrait painting in *The Tragic Muse*. But Dormer, despite the active opposition of his family and his friends, had finally secured a hard-won peace with his surroundings; Lodge lacked that valuable experience; his verse was imitative, restless, "sad, bewildered," and he seemed to look forward with the gaze of an adolescent into a hazy, "larger, lovelier unknown heaven beyond the known!"

4

At the time of his death in 1904, the rewards of Joseph Trum-bull Stickney's life (1874-1904) seemed smaller than those earned by Moody and too easily secured by George Cabot Lodge. Time has restored a balance in his favor; the existence of his poetry has not been forgotten, and what has been written of his person-ality seems to hint that his wit and learning ignited the imagi-nation of his fellows. As recently as 1940 Edmund Wilson, as he paid his respects to Van Wyck Brooks's *New England: Indian Summer* in the pages of *The New Republic*,[10] rediscovered Stick-ney in one of the finest of his shorter essays:

Trumbull Stickney [Edmund Wilson wrote] was one of those New Englanders of the last half of the last century who oscillated between

[10] October 14, 1940, used by permission of *The New Republic*.

Europe and Boston. He was born in Geneva in Switzerland, was graduated with classical honors at Harvard, and went back, as soon as he left college, to Europe, where he spent seven years studying in Paris and afterwards traveled in Greece. He returned to teach Greek at Harvard in the fall of 1903 and died suddenly a year later in Boston of tumor of the brain. His brilliance as a scholar had been a prodigy. He had taken at the University of Paris the only *Doctorat ès Lettres* that had ever been given an Anglo-Saxon. There is an interesting footnote in Brooks, in which he quotes a description by Shane Leslie of Stickney's doctor's examination at the Sorbonne: "With what learning and subtlety he defended himself against their sleight of tongue! How they pricked and tore and tossed his thesis! With his beautiful gray eyes and sad bewildered face, he met them on his own ground and in their own tongue. How carelessly the Greek flowed from his lips, and with what unperturbed French he met all their objections for hour after hour. When the strife was over, they were all polite congratulations." His thesis on "Les Sentences dans la Poésie Grecque" was greatly praised in France. I have heard one of his friends at Harvard, whose experience of American writers and scholars was as wide as that of anyone of his time, declare that Trumbull Stickney was the most cultivated man he had ever known.

As one turns the pages of Stickney's posthumous *Poems,* which was a memorial volume, edited by George Cabot Lodge, John Ellerton Lodge, and William Vaughn Moody, published in Boston, 1905, one seems to stand in the unshaded presence of poetic genius. But one is still turning pages, and as one stops to read, shadows begin to fall. Individual lines and phrases hold the eye and sound within the ear:

It rains across the country I remember . . .[11]

then an entire stanza from some verses to Lucretius:

> To him this verse, to him this crown of leaves,
> My supreme piety shall I commend:
> This is my last,
> Wreathed of what Youth endows and Age bereaves,
> Bound by the fingers of a lover and friend,
> Green with the vital past . . .[12]

[11] "Mnemosyne" from *Poems of Trumbull Stickney,* ed. by Lodge and Moody, Houghton Mifflin. Used by permission of Henry A. Stickney.

[12] "Lucretius" from *Poems of Trumbull Stickney,* ed. by Lodge and Moody, Houghton Mifflin. Used by permission of Henry A. Stickney.

then a fragment entitled by the Roman numeral, *IV:* [13]

> Be patient, very patient; for the skies
> Within my human soul now sunset-flushed
> Break desperate magic on the world I knew,
> And in the crimson evening flying down
> Bell-sounds and birds of ancient ecstasy
> Most wonderfully carol one time more

which promises so much and even as a fragment is not quite good enough. One turns to a poem called "Age in Youth," [14] and from it a single stanza, the last, comes into view:

> In vain the flower-lifting morn
> With golden fingers to uprear;
> The weak Spring here shall pause awhile:
> This is a scar upon the year.

And after this the last two lines of a sonnet:

> Apollo springing naked to the light,
> And all his island shivered into flowers. [15]

There is a great distance between the quality of these lines and anything that may be found in Moody's verse and Lodge's. The haze of literary reminiscence, of grandiose sentiment, of witless, uninventive rhetoric begins to lift, and the first impression conveyed to the reader—and especially to a reader who has been wearied by the coy and adolescent charms of *Songs from Vagabondia*—is one of brilliance and the promise of poetic maturity. Read individually the lines are better than those written in moments of unfelicity by the early E. A. Robinson who permitted these lines to close his sonnet on "The Garden": [16]

> Whose every leaf, miraculously signed,
> Outrolled itself from Thought's eternal seed.
> Love-rooted in God's garden of the mind.

[13] From *Poems of Trumbull Stickney*, ed. by Lodge and Moody, Houghton Mifflin. Used by permission of Henry A. Stickney.

[14] *Ibid.*

[15] "Live Blindly and Upon the Hour, The Lord" from *Poems of Trumbull Stickney*, Houghton Mifflin. Used by permission of Henry A. Stickney.

[16] From *Children of the Night*, used by permission of Charles Scribner's Sons.

If one looks for literary influence in its best sense, it would seem that Stickney read Keats and John Webster with more understanding and intelligence than his contemporaries. There is a touch of Webster's violence in Stickney's brief:

> Sir, say no more,
> Within me 'tis as if
> The green and climbing eyesight of a cat
> Crawled near my mind's poor birds.[17]

And it is as if from Keats he had learned a youthful respect for exact phrasing by placing familiar nouns and adjectives in fresh associations:

> Sorapis and the rocks of Mezzodì
> Crumble by foamy miles into the azure
> Mediterranean sea . . .[18]

Nor was this kind of brilliance reserved for the choice of visual imagery alone; Stickney possessed an "ear"; and however light or fragmentary the impulse for writing it may have been, a stanza from his "Song"[19] is ample proof of his delight in hearing verbal music:

> Good-bye, for the pretty leaves are down
> (The linnet sang in my heart to-day);
> The last gold bit of upland's mown,
> And most of the summer has blown away
> Thro' the garden gate
> (A cuckoo said in my brain: "Too late").

In his "In Ampezzo"[20] there are flashes of his enjoyment in writing descriptive passages for themselves alone, and through the twenty stanzas of the poem, the Mediterranean sea and its

17 "Fragment V" from *Poems of Trumbull Stickney*, ed. by Lodge and Moody, Houghton Mifflin. Used by permission of Henry A. Stickney. These lines become more interesting when it is known that they were written shortly before his death of a brain tumor.

18 "In Ampezzo" from *Poems of Trumbull Stickney*, ed. by Lodge and Moody, Houghton Mifflin. Used by permission of Henry A. Stickney.

19 From *Poems of Trumbull Stickney*, ed. by Lodge and Moody, Houghton Mifflin. Used by permission of Henry A. Stickney.

20 *Ibid.*

shore lines wheel and glitter, reflecting light across the yellowed pages of his book:

> Only once more and not again—the larches
> Shake to the wind their echo, "Not again,"—
> We see, below the sky that over-arches
> Heavy and blue, the plain
>
> Between Tofana lying and Cristallo
> In meadowy earths above the ringing stream:
> Whence interchangeably desire may follow,
> Hesitant as in a dream,
>
> At sunset, south, by lilac promontories
> Under green skies to Italy, or forth
> By calms of morning beyond Lavinores
> Tyrolward and to north . . .

Images remembered from Greek and Latin pastorals begin to rise and one is convinced that the honor bestowed on Stickney at the University of Paris was not merely academic in its tribute; it had been, one concludes, an early recognition of his gifts which are scattered so negligently through the pages of his book.

But if individual lines and stanzas revive a personality precociously gifted in its sensibility to an elegiac note in poetry (which is a classical heritage that British and American literature has carried from the past into our own day) what of the entire poems in Stickney's posthumously published volume? It is there that the shadow falls and it is there that the enthusiastic reader meets with disappointment. His poems, viewed as completed poems within themselves, show flaws of heady rhetoric and histrionic gestures that without the "beautiful gray eyes and sad, bewildered face" of their author distract the reader and leave him with the feeling that the sight of Stickney's inspiration vanished almost as soon as his pen struck paper. Or if the strained, theatrical gesture does not intervene:

> To this hot clay
> Must sing my shells, where yet the primal day,
> Its roar and rhythm and splendour will not sleep . . .[21]

[21] "On Some Shells Found Inland' from *Poems of Trumbull Stickney,* ed. by Lodge and Moody, Houghton Mifflin. Used by permission of Henry A. Stickney.

the diction suddenly falls out of tone and becomes flaccid and inappropriately colloquial:

> The babble of our children fills my ears,
> And on our hearth I stare the perished ember
> To flames that show all starry thro' my tears.

It's dark about the country I remember.[22]

One is certain that Stickney, like Lodge, diffused his energies; and in Stickney's book there is no poem that sustains its own atmosphere as completely as Lionel Johnson's stanzas to the statue of King Charles at Charing Cross or, more significantly, Robinson's memorable "Luke Havergal." His gifts were so lavish and his personal attractions so evident that there was apparently no need to sacrifice their immediate rewards to the demands of "a single talent, well employed"; it was the latter course that Robinson pursued, and with Stickney's death that difficult, narrow, and empty road opened its way to welcome him.

5

Before Robinson's road had made itself clear to the sight of his contemporaries, there were many attractive bypaths on which Moody and his friends traveled lightly and easily. One was the direction sketched out on the chart by Bliss Carman and Richard Hovey—with the broad hint that Vagabondia offered both the joy of wandering and the privilege of rejecting (as long as poets remained young) those evils inherent in modern civilization. This was the cult of the tramp, the clown, the fool, or of the shrewd, yet feeble-minded provincial, who could claim an ancestor in Wordsworth's Peter Bell, the idiot boy. And his path was admittedly a well-traveled and many-peopled highway. The other road was writing verse to be spoken on the stage, that had been crowded with failures since the seventeenth century, but the road still held its fascinations because it was so populous, because of its rare chance of presenting poetry to large audiences,

---

[22] "It's Autumn in the Country I Remember" from *Poems of Trumbull Stickney,* ed. by Lodge and Moody, Houghton Mifflin. Used by permission of Henry A. Stickney.

and because of the hope of "making poetry pay." But before we speak of the latter road, the first demands attention, for its tradition (if it may be called such) runs backward to the songs of Tom o' Bedlam, and beyond him to those who were the wandering, singing Latinists of the Middle Ages. If the conduct of several heroes and masters (for Villon's name cannot be excluded) in this company was, at times, unfortunate or resolutely wayward, the antiquity of the line was unassailable.

With this we arrive at the work of a man who was six years younger than Moody and had been born in Xenia, Ohio. Ridgely Torrence's first book, published under the title, *The House of a Hundred Lights,* appeared in 1900; a second volume, *Hesperides,* was published in 1925, and his last book, *Poems,* in 1941. Through the years, his verses were written carefully and sparely. The verses of social relevance in his scrupulously edited, *Poems* (which contained many titles that had previously been gathered into *Hesperides*), owed a debt to the spirit and language of *Songs from Vagabondia* as well as the touch of humanitarian protest that had been voiced by Tom Hood in mid-nineteenth-century England and was later revived in America by Moody. In "Eye-Witness," one of the best known of Torrence's longer pieces, whose theme recalls, without the narrative excitement, John Masefield's *The Everlasting Mercy* (1911), echoes of Vagabondia are heard through the lips of a tramp who sings:

> I will sing, I will go, and never ask me why.
> I was born a rover and a passer-by.
>
> I seem to myself like water and sky,
> A river and a rover and a passer-by.[23]

For some half-dozen years, the years 1897 through the turn of the old century into the twentieth, Torrence was a librarian at the Astor Library in New York, and for several years he was poetry editor of *The New Republic.* He had been educated at Miami and Princeton universities, and a reading of his verse seems to indicate that his interests revolved around two centers—

[23] "Eye-Witness" from *Poems,* used by permission of The Macmillan Company.

the Negro problem in the United States, eloquently stated in a lynching sermon, "The Bird and the Tree," and the standards achieved by acceptable verse published in current British and American periodicals. In the latter, his position was not unlike that of Thomas Bailey Aldrich. He had also listened attentively to the strains of A. E. Housman nor could he summon the strength to endow them with a speech that was his own: in his "Prothalamion (To a bride in wartime)" written as late as the Second World War the first and last stanzas reveal the power of Housman's influence:

> Now the doom on land and sea
>   Lengthens toward the wedding day,
> Let the bridal bravely be
>   Though the world should burn away.
>
> .   .   .   .
>
> Speed the mating, crown the vow
>   While the brand of havoc gleams.
> Now's the time to mate and now
>   Breed the men with better dreams.[24]

Torrence's gifts were far too frail to support the weight of dominating influences and social themes, and if one looks for something that defines his own sensibility, the answer is an insubstantial one:

> When grass rises again (I thought) the sorrow
> Will lie hidden forever under beauty;
> So I longed for the time of apple blossoms,
> All my dreams were upon the blowing lilacs.
>
> But some whirlwind that held the winter's secret
> Rose and lifting the frozen days as curtains
> Showed me Time as an upper sky of crystal
> Flushed with images yet to be reflected.[25]

And from these lines the same vague, wandering images unfold:

> With beacons, with dawns that unveil it, the hidden and strange,
> As it lifts from the steadfast tides of the ocean of change,

[24] "Prothalamion" from *Poems,* used by permission of The Macmillan Company.

[25] "Winter Crystal" from *Poems,* used by permisison of The Macmillan Company.

With rays on footholds gaining to summits more proud
And won more surely than under a sky without cloud.[26]

The atmosphere, the aspirations of the *fin de siècle,* "the dying fall," are the clearest impressions that one gains from reading the later verses in Ridgely Torrence's book. In 1941 the hour that welcomed Moody was definitely passed, yet it is interesting to observe how persistently its mannerisms and its overtones lingered on in the verse of Ridgely Torrence; it may be an impertinence to say that the sensibility that Torrence possesses belongs to any school, but if schools are to be named, the most appropriate title for the frailties and refinements that he and his verses represent would be "The School of Gossamer and Old Gauze."

6

The other road, on which hope is always expressed for the revival of poetic drama in America, had one traveler whose round eyes, curved lips, and pretty, bare shoulders still gleam from faded photographs. The lady was one of Moody's friends and her name was Josephine Preston Peabody. She was born in New York in 1874, and was brought up in Boston, educated at Radcliffe, and in 1906 married Lionel Marks, who was then an instructor at Wellesley—and one might say that she seemed to bloom and to flourish in an academic atmosphere. As a young girl Josephine Peabody drew attention through her good looks, her enthusiasm for "culture," and her avid reading—and among her friends were many survivors of the elder Boston literary tradition, of whom Van Wyck Brooks has remarked, "they reacted against the world they lived in by falling back on mediaeval themes." Josephine Peabody herself defined poetry as "the richest expression of noblest ideals," which was commendable enough, but decidedly vague. One is certain, however, that she numbered among her "ideals" the success of Tennyson's play in verse, *Becket,* which had had a long run in London, aided by the mimetic talents of Ellen Terry; and one is also certain that they embraced the "ideals" of Browning's lighter narratives in verse

[26] "Light" from *Poems,* used by permission of The Macmillan Company.

and those of the Pre-Raphaelite Brotherhood. Her charming, graceful, and unmistakably rhapsodic journals reflect the stream of her literary activity; and it is highly doubtful if she ever thought of its adventures as an "escape" from the life of her own day. She was carried lightly on a fashionable road toward Stratford-on-Avon in England where her play, *The Piper,* received an award and was produced before admiring audiences. The play was a thoroughly emasculated version of Browning's "The Pied Piper of Hamelin," and the piper was a poet who led the children away from the sordid aspects of a naughty world. The royalties from the play mounted to a small fortune, and *The Piper* is still revived with undergraduates as its performers in women's colleges. In America the literary attraction of the Middle Ages has always rested on unsure foundations, and of American poets Poe alone seems to have penetrated the darker recesses of the Gothic imagination. It remained for Henry Adams in his *Mont-Saint-Michel and Chartres* to approach anything like a clear understanding of what the Middle Ages meant through western and Anglo-American eyes. For the rest, and particularly among lesser poets, the reach toward medieval themes went no further than transitory imitations of Stephen Phillips and the more spectacular figures in the Pre-Raphaelite Brotherhood.

Not unlike Lodge and Stickney, Josephine Peabody continued to exert her true gifts of personal charm upon those who met her; her fanciful verses which appeared so frequently in magazines, lines to the "Cedars" that called to her from Lebanon, to the little house that said, "Stay," and the little road that said, "Go," and the domestic pieces which included a "Cradle Song" to her son, were among the least important contributions of her literary talent. Her actual value was that of a popular woman writer who possessed both grace and some learning, and she stood in a position far removed from the women poets of a later generation who voiced loud commands to the east and to the west, and who affected the false vigor of would-be masculine and public speech. Though she wrote a letter of protest to Bernard Shaw for daring to publish *Man and Superman* (a play which offended her sensibilities), she secured a publisher for E. A. Robinson's *Captain Craig,* and in biographies and histories of her day her name is still remembered as the author of *Marlowe*, which was among the more valiant attempts to revive Elizabethan blank verse for production on the modern stage.

The height of excitement in writing for the stage was reached when in 1906 William Vaughn Moody's play in prose, *The Great Divide*, had won applause and commercial success on Broadway. Seen through the colder eyes of a later generation, the merits of *The Great Divide* are slight and their brilliance has considerably paled. The story of the play was of a New England girl who had eloped to the West with an Arizona outlaw, and the conflict or "problem" of the play was the contrast between the "Puritanism" of the girl and the "Paganism" of the man who had seduced her. The reception of the play was fortunate and its theme was well-suited to Moody's imagination.

E. A. Robinson had once written to Josephine Peabody that much as he admired Moody, he felt that Moody had much to unlearn. It was this process of unlearning that made possible the "new poetry" of the following decade in America, and the success of *The Great Divide* did no harm whatsoever to the development of Robinson's poetry. As Hermann Hagedorn, Robinson's biographer, remarked, he went home from the first night of the play, "walking on air." And it is said that the play inspired what we now recognize as one of the best and most characteristic of his early poems:

THE WHITE LIGHTS (BROADWAY, 1906) [27]

When in from Delos came the gold
That held the dream of Pericles,
When first Athenian ears were told
The tumult of Euripides,
When men met Aristophanes,
Who fledged them with immortal quills—
Here, where the time knew none of these,
There were some islands and some hills.

When Rome went ravening to see
The sons of mothers end their days,

[27] From *The Town Down by the River,* used by permission of Charles Scribner's Sons.

When Flaccus bade Leuconoë
To banish her Chaldean ways,
When first the pearled, alembic phrase
Of Maro into music ran—
Here there was neither blame nor praise
For Rome, or for the Mantuan.

When Avon, like a faëry floor,
Lay freighted, for the eyes of One,
With galleons laden long before
By moonlit wharves in Avalon—
Here, where the white lights have begun
To seethe a way for something fair,
No prophet knew, from what was done,
That there was triumph in the air.

The poem does not, of course, refer to anything that Moody placed before his audiences, but it expressed, rather, the hopes of a generation who had "begun to seethe a way for something fair."

A year later, Robinson, urged by Moody and Josephine Peabody (whose *Marlowe* had been produced at Radcliffe with George Pierce Baker in the title role) attempted to experiment with the writing of two plays; they were failures and he seemed to know that they were. Moody, as Hagedorn has described him, "stocky, bearded, with his blue eyes and his ruddy face, a plodding figure outwardly, but a volcano inside . . . had become a factor on Broadway." But Robinson's weakness of will in the writing of plays set him back on the singular road that was his to follow and, disassociated as it was from the far more facile rewards of William Vaughn Moody and his circle, it opened the way a few steps further toward true self-knowledge and maturity.

THREE POETS OF THE SIERRAS

Nothing is more difficult or sadder for the literary historian than to examine the works of Joaquin Miller (1841-1913), of Edwin Markham (1852-1940), of George Sterling (1869-1926). For they were serious poets, and two of them had a large share of the public's affection, if not the critical esteem of the literary journals. Yet their work in its attempts and attitudes holds so much that is revealing of the American attitude toward poetry and the writing of poetry in the early years of the twentieth century that a study of their verse may be more valuable than the ultimate value of their work may seem to justify. In their personalities, in their grandiose attempts at large themes and whole philosophic concepts, these men were at one, and when we study their individual failures, it is easy to agree with Stuart P. Sherman that they reward our study most sympathetically, "when one regards and studies them as a register of the power excited upon the individual by the American environment, even at the thinnest and crudest."

Nor is revaluation of what they were a task which can be accomplished by the use of facile speculation and dismissal. George Sterling's and Edwin Markham's deaths are of comparatively recent date, and their personalities are still alive within the memory of friends who loved them and who would naturally resent a rigidly critical attitude. When Charles Hanson Towne writing in *Poetry, A Magazine of Verse* of April, 1940, says of Markham, "He stood for nobility of character, for everything that is great in the American spirit," one agrees that Edwin Markham actually stood for all this to many Americans of Towne's generation, and one becomes eager to analyze the reasons for such a positive statement and its implications.

JOAQUIN MILLER

Of the three poets, Joaquin Miller is the most available for judgment, since his death occurred in 1913 and his collected works have had sufficient exposure to the critical partiality of time. They have not prospered under the severe gaze of this greatest critic of us all, and Miller's name has been mentioned (if spoken at all in recent years) with half-contemptuous brevity or put aside with humorous disdain. But to generations of public-school children in the United States, his name has other and more lively connotations; he has been and is still known as the author of a well-liked recitation piece which was often recited, and with gestures, in school auditoriums before admiring parents, friends, fellow students, and members of the board of education. The recitation was, of course, Miller's poem on Columbus: [1]

> Behind him lay the gray Azores,
> Behind the Gates of Hercules;
> Before him not the ghost of shores;
> Before him only shoreless seas.
> The good mate said: "Now must we pray,
> For lo! the very stars are gone,
> Brave Adm'r'l, speak; what shall I say?"
> "Why, say: 'Sail on! sail on! and on!'"

Those who recall this poem from classroom memories—and it was especially popular with Americanization committees in their instruction of the "foreign born"—often confuse it with a similar poem equally popular with those who taught the arts of becoming an American and which was recited as frequently as Joaquin Miller's "Columbus." It was an equally vocal and demonstrative poem by a better poet on the death of Lincoln which was called "O Captain! My Captain!" In their bombastic imagery and hollow rhetoric, and in their "false vigor," these two poets seemed to travel common ground. The great difference between them was that Whitman soon recovered from his brief "O Captain! My Captain!" period and went onward in his more char-

[1] From *Poetical Works of Joaquin Miller*, The Whitaker, Ray and Wiggin Co. By permission of Juanita Miller.

acteristic vein, while Miller never traveled far beyond the verbal gestures and mannerisms of his "Columbus." The two poems were in the admired convention of their time, and if recited from a platform, they were certain to receive immediate acclaim from thoroughly respectable audiences: they sounded vigorous, they uttered noble and uplifting sentiments, they seemed to stir the blood or wring the heart, they were based on references to heroic American figures, and it was easy to suppose that anyone could understand them. Here were no subtleties and no refinements, and their booming stanzas seemed to echo from the very classroom walls on which hung a portrait series of forbidding elderly gentlemen, each face half covered by an impressive beard, and all answering to the title of "Our Poets." It is not wholly unjust to say that "O Captain! My Captain!" and "Columbus" had contributed their share in spreading an active dislike and a false conception of poetry to many young Americans who outgrew and fled from the elocution classes of the public schools. For it is well to remember that whenever Whitman's portrait appeared in the "Our Poets" series, it was the Whitman of "O Captain! My Captain!" who was commemorated, and not the poet who wrote "When Lilacs Last in the Dooryard Bloom'd" and "Passage to India." And Joaquin Miller, by rarely deviating from the qualities that made his poem on Columbus famous, was among those who fixed an attitude toward poetry in the opening years of the twentieth century in America.

Though Miller had a healthy respect for what was being said about poetry in England and in New York and Boston, the extraliterary sources of his verse were made respectable by those who hailed the Frederic Remington conventions of the Western frontier as opposed to the so-called "genteel" aspirations of poetry written ·in the East. Joaquin Miller was not unlike Bret Harte (1836-1902) in his ability to create a nostalgia for the life of a frontier that was already dwindling into a romantic past. In this respect his work also resembles the color and activity of Mark Twain's Western sketches and the backward glancing pages of Hamlin Garland's autobiographies.

Another analogy to Whitman's reputation appears in the fact that Miller, like Whitman, received an early recognition of his work in England and from exactly the same people. These were the members of the Pre-Raphaelite Brotherhood and their friends, who had continued to exert more influence on literary and esthetic judgment in England than almost any other group. In the opening years of the present century Pre-Raphaelite taste was something that corresponds to our definition of "esoteric": they "discovered" Victor Hugo, Baudelaire, and Verlaine as key figures in French poetry, and with notable discrimination, revived for a brief period Walter Savage Landor's waning reputation; they popularized the poetry of William Blake; they first praised, and then when shocking revelations seemed to appear, quickly dropped and ultimately lost the manuscripts of Thomas Lovell Beddoes. With American poets they seemed to allow their love of the esoteric to take full rein: they showed equal enthusiasm for Joaquin Miller and for Walt Whitman, and one is not sure that they did not like the two poets for the same reason— a novelty of subject matter. In reviewing Miller's *Songs of the Sierras* in 1871, *The Westminster Review* said, and this opinion seemed to express an attitude that was held for many years, that "Joaquin Miller . . . is another Whitman without coarseness." Other magazines compared him to Byron and to Victor Hugo, and this was the praise that Miller appreciated most of all, for it was as the American Byron that he wished to shine, and indeed, one aspect of his poetry was an actual, though curious manifestation of the Byronic temper, a little more noisy than the original, and, of course, diluted, and to English friends the remote Sierras held the same attractions as the memory of Byron's *Tales, Chiefly Oriental.* Nor would such praise have seemed extraordinary to Americans in the generation preceding Miller's English fame, and though Miller was not the author of "Marco Bozzaris," since Fitz-Greene Halleck (1790-1867) had published it sixteen years before Miller's birth, one feels that he would have liked to have written it, and, in fact, wrote many poems that resembled it in every characteristic feature.

It was Miller's fate to live far into the American period of the *fin de siècle,* to be influenced by Browning and Tennyson as well as the Pre-Raphaelites, and he had undoubtedly read the early Kipling and found him attractive. But as time went on, he became known in the United States as a Californian, and something of the giganticism that creeps into the boasting, the very idiom of so many who live under Californian skies, entered Miller's poetry. His flowers seem always to be greater than life size, his women amazons, his valleys always "gorgeous and glorious," his snow-topped mountains always covering half the globe, and his hard-fighting heroes always seem more cleanly amorous, hardier, and hard-riding than nature itself dared to demand. There is the charm of the Hollywood Wild West in some of his poems, a pace of narrative action that disarms serious criticism and yet awakens general disbelief in what he had to say. Such poems as "Kit Carson's Ride" (which was properly filled with rent clouds, thunderbolts, and lightning flashes), "Isles of the Amazons," "The Gold that Grew by Shasta Town," and "Comanche," [2] with all its blood and fury, are still guaranteed to thrill and charm those who remember Buffalo Bill's Wild West Show and even today listen with children at their side to the Lone Ranger series on the radio.

> A blazing home, a blood-soaked hearth;
> Fair women's hair with blood upon!
> The Ishmaelite of all the earth
> Has like a cyclone, come and gone—
>
> .   .   .   .
>
> "To horse! to horse!" the rangers shout,
> And red revenge is on his track. . . .[3]

[2] From *Poetical Works of Joaquin Miller*, The Whitaker, Ray and Wiggin Co. By permission of Juanita Miller.

[3] "In 1912 my father told me that his so-called 'Comanche' was really a Modoc Massacre and written about the battle of Castle Crags, also Castle Rocks, that the Indians were not Comanches but Shasta Modocs. It was at that time he received the arrows through his face and neck, shooting out two teeth. The lines should have been:

> A blazing home, a blood-soaked hearth,
> White women's hair with blood upon;
> The Indian of Modoc birth has, like a cyclone, come and gone.
>
> His feet are as the flying earth,
> His hands are arrows drawn, . . .

"He said he had titled it 'Skirmish' but because of writing with a split quill the Reader read differently and he let it go. He seldom corrected anything." (Juanita Miller in a letter to the authors.)

Meanwhile Joaquin Miller himself became a colorful and typical American figure of this extended period that leaned over and into the first ten years of the new century, and his appearances, however spectacular, contained their own measure of Byronic contradiction, for as Stuart P. Sherman wrote, "he was never quite sure of what costume to assume to adorn our national gallery." But whether in high-heeled and spurred boots, with sombrero, revolver on hip, and complete cowboy costume so as to dazzle English duchesses in their drawing rooms, or during his declining years in his home overlooking San Francisco Bay, in a house built to resemble a Greek temple, containing statues of Frémont, Robert Browning, and Moses, Miller himself, the full-bearded American bard and student of East Indian philosophy, was a national phenomenon, and, one might say, hearteningly Californian.

His work gained in prophetic fervor, and like George Sterling and Edwin Markham, his fellow Californians, he also took an interest in socialism. He protested in favor of the Boers in South Africa during the Boer War, of the Jews in Russia during the Kishinev massacres and the later pogroms as, with a like impulse during our Civil War, he had been driven from a small town in Ohio because he edited a newspaper that strongly favored the cause of the Confederacy. "I am always getting on the wrong side with the weak," he had said later, which perhaps indicates more of an effort to display a kindly disposition than any strict adherence to a principle.

To Dante Gabriel Rossetti, who had asked him what he thought poetry should be, he had answered, "To me, a poem must be a picture," and this reply must have delighted Rossetti, of whom it has been so often said that he painted his poems and wrote his canvases. Miller always retained his frontiersman's love for the culture and refinements of life that had been denied him in his youth, for as a boy he had traveled in covered wagons from Mississippi to Oregon, and then had run away from his new home to a Californian mining camp. His four years of travel on the European continent during the 1870's had whetted rather than cultivated his eager tastes. "All life, all action that is grand and good is poetry waiting for expression," he wrote; and with this easy and too optimistic attitude toward life and poetry, it is not surprising that the same poet who wrote Wild West adventure stories in verse, even in his best work wrote poems that tended to become feeble, secondhand impressions of Pre-Raphaelite illustrations.

> . . . lovers, would you love with zest,
> Win love and hold her fast and well,
> Believe, believe the best, the best
> Though she had singed her skirts in hell! [4]

But most of all, in his later years, he was again strongly compelled to portray the Californian landscape, its immensity, its large and all-pervading sunlight, and here he failed, as many Californians have done, leaving behind him only the sound of echoes whirling through an empty cave.

Perhaps his finest poem was his commemoration of Walker's ill-fated expedition into Nicaragua, his tribute to the memory of Walker's bravery.

> He lies low in the level'd sand,
> Unshelter'd from the tropic sun,
> And now, of all he knew, not one
> Will speak him fair in that far land.[5]
>
> .   .   .   .
>
> I said some things with folded hands,
> Soft-whisper'd in the dim sea-sound,
> And eyes held humbly on the ground,
> And frail knees sunken in the sands.
> He had done more than this for me,
> And yet I could not well do more;
> I turned me down the olive shore,
> And set a sad face to the sea.[6]

Behind a rhetorical gesture that has now become quaint and was never as brilliant as it once seemed, one may detect the genuine notes of pathos, with a suggestion of a dignity that had never been fully expressed.

[4] "Walker in Nicaragua" from *Poetical Works of Joaquin Miller,* The Whitaker, Ray and Wiggin Co. By permission of Juanita Miller.
[5] *Ibid.*
[6] "LXXIII" from *Poetical Works of Joaquin Miller,* The Whitaker, Ray and Wiggin Co. By permission of Juanita Miller.

EDWIN MARKHAM

When Edwin Markham died at the age of eighty-eight, filled with his many years and uncounted honors, a few critics wondered if he remembered Ambrose Bierce's warning that "The Man with the Hoe" would eventually kill him. This was perhaps unfair to Markham's fame in the small town on Staten Island where he had made his home for forty years and where he died. Since the publication of "The Man with the Hoe" in the *San Francisco Examiner* of January 15, 1899, he had written five books of poems, was an editor of one of the most voluminous anthologies of "world poetry" ever published on the North American continent, had written several books of prose and many articles on social problems. These tended to solidify his reputation among members of The Poetry Society of America as well as with the president of Richmond Borough who in 1930 declared his birthday a holiday on Staten Island, at which hundreds of schoolchildren took part in a parade to Markham's home in Westerleigh and a pageant was held in his honor.

But to the majority of the American reading public, he was inevitably known as "the author of 'The Man with the Hoe'" and even his poem on Lincoln, which contained similar faults and virtues, never superseded the popularity of the earlier poem. To the younger generations of poets growing up during the first forty years of the present century, Markham was a picturesque, Whitman-bearded figure of the past, and if any of them read his books of verse, *The Man with the Hoe and Other Poems* (1899), *Lincoln, and Other Poems* (1901), *The Shoes of Happiness* (1914), *The Gates of Paradise* (1920), and *New Poems: Eighty Songs at 80* (1932), no influence of that reading can be discerned. Even when the poetry of social protest had gained momentum during the late 1920's and the mid-thirties, Markham never became more than an elderly figure in what is sometimes thought to be a simple and innocently flamboyant era, which included Christian Socialism, the fading memory of Joaquin Miller, pioneer activity and its enthusiasms, and Edward Bellamy's *Looking Backward*. Almost all of Markham's first forty-eight years were spent in California; and his work seemed to exist solely in an atmosphere that had made possible a faith in the natural goodness of man and the evolutionary triumph of democracy. If his work contained some few of the Byronic and naïve attitudes of Joaquin Miller, it was also distinguished by a greater restraint and modesty than anything that Miller wrote, and as Louis Untermeyer has remarked, it contained the rhetoric without the resonance of the elder poet's more exuberant moments.

Like Miller's, Markham's early childhood bore the marks of pioneer restlessness, hardiness, excitement, and privation; his family had moved westward from Michigan to Oregon, and at the age of five, Markham's boyhood career took a fresh start in California. The Markham legend includes a wide range of early activities; he was said to have been a sheep herder, farmer, blacksmith, and cowboy—but the most important influence upon his future life seems to have been the encouragement he received from a country schoolteacher, who recognized in Markham, then a boy of seventeen, the abilities that were to make him famous. It is significant that Markham himself became a teacher, and before he earned his fame as "the author of 'The Man with the Hoe,'" he was engaged as superintendent and principal of schools in California.

Though his childhood privations have been said to have provided a background for his interest in social problems, his general optimism readily cleared him of all tendencies toward bitterness. Violent methods for changing social conditions shocked him, and thinking of such possibilities, he wrote:

I am neither an economist, nor a politician. In my writings I have only attempted to depict life as it appears to me. If they disclose there is something wrong, that is as much as can be expected from them. I am no back-seat driver. I leave the guidance of our political State to the men who have learned to direct it.

There can be no doubt of the essential goodwill contained in these remarks, nor of their honesty; and they explain why his personal qualities endeared his memory to many friends. The same atmosphere of goodwill and hopefulness enters his famous quatrain, with its triumphant title, "Outwitted": [7]

> He drew a circle that shut me out—
> Heretic, rebel, a thing to flout.
> But Love and I had the wit to win:
> We drew a circle that took him in!

The voice of the nineteenth-century Californian schoolteacher, who had read textbook anthologies of verse, may be found in his test for greatness in poetry: "Sublimity is the test. Very few poets have it—Homer, Aeschylus, Dante, Shakespeare, Victor Hugo— that's about all." But unfortunately, even the greatest names, particularly if they remain no more than and solely "great names" to the reader, are not always the best influences. It is sometimes to be feared that Markham read the best poets for the worst reasons. He took from them all the sublimity and rhetoric and ornamentation he could find, and to these elements he added a fondness for Miltonic blank verse, and in his latter years, an unguarded admiration for Edgar Allan Poe. When he forgot his own grim resolution that

> Life is a mission stern as fate,
> And Song a dread apostolate.[8]

he turned to such attempted graces as

> Ah, once of old in some forgotten tongue
> Forgotten land, I was a shepherd boy,
> And you a Nereid, a wingèd joy.[9]

Here, as in his "Song of the Followers of Pan," he seemed to express, more than all else, a confused and boyish delight in finding scraps of knowledge floating through his mind. '

His incorrigible optimism led the way through many varieties of verse and public affirmations. He seemed always willing to lend his name to anything that had the appearance of being a

[7] From *Eighty Songs at 80,* Doubleday, Doran. Reprinted by permission of Virgil Markham.

[8] "The Poet" from *The Man with the Hoe,* Doubleday, Doran. Reprinted by permission of Virgil Markham.

[9] "Shepherd Boy and Nereid" from *The Man with the Hoe,* Doubleday, Doran. Reprinted by permission of Virgil Markham.

worthy cause. He celebrated the Russian Revolution in his best
Miltonic manner (in a poem which was translated into Russian
and greatly admired), and he appeared before a convention of
pharmacists with the avowed purpose of creating sympathy for
the drug addict. His poem, "Slaves of the Drug," was enthusiastically applauded and was reputed to have done much good. He
also wrote an ode of welcome to Ramsay MacDonald and the
British Labour Party when MacDonald visited the United States
in 1929.

But throughout his campaigns for outmoded political figures
and dimly realized social ideals, he kept his soul, as he once said,
"as simple as a flower."

His remark concerning the welfare of his soul was by no means
inappropriate; of the many featured contributors to the Hearst
newspapers, Markham, like Art Young, the cartoonist, was among
the few who retained a personal integrity. And it is in this setting
and environment that the Populist sentiment of his poem, "The
Man with the Hoe," still retains its brightest colors. Its language
has the same character that earned for the young Arthur Brisbane the reputation for being the best editorial writer on
Hearst's large staff. Although the sources of its inspiration have
been credited by Markham himself to Jean François Millet's
painting of the same title, its diction and imagery as well as its
expert touches of journalistic craftsmanship bear a stronger relationship to whatever virtues might be found on the Hearst editorial page during the period when Hearst had found it profit-
able to champion the cause of the poor against the rich.

It was reputed that before Markham died his famous poem
had earned for him the round sum of two hundred and fifty
thousand dollars. Few Californians of the old mining days had
struck so rich a mine, and Markham had an honest and almost
humble faith in his good fortune. He once said to those who
asked him for the secret of his success: "A chance stroke: I caught
the eye and ear of the world."

GEORGE STERLING

Like Edwin Markham whose birthplace was Oregon City, or like Joaquin Miller, or Robinson Jeffers and Yvor Winters, in fact, like many others who seemed rooted in California, George Sterling (1869-1926) was not born there. Sterling's actual birthplace was Sag Harbor, New York, and he received his education in local schools and at St. Charles' College, Ellicott City, Maryland. At the age of twenty-five, he migrated westward to the Pacific Coast, and under the literary patronage of Ambrose Bierce, which was supported and sustained by the friendships of Joaquin Miller and Jack London, Sterling stepped into the charmed circle of San Francisco's Latin Quarter—and the Bohemian Club.

This entry into the literary life of the Pacific Coast in the early 1890's may be said to have been young Sterling's substitute for a trip to Paris. He had arrived at a moment when the smoky atmosphere of San Francisco's Bohemian resorts was stirred and lighted by Gelett Burgess' little magazine, *The Lark*. His adjustment to the Californian environment seems to have been spontaneous and all embracing; and to it he brought his own sensitivity, which, by the way, had a finer grain of literary intelligence than can be found in the work of either Joaquin Miller or Edwin Markham. If Joaquin Miller's later work can be said to bear traces of Pre-Raphaelite influences, it could be said with equal justice that Sterling's verse seems to have been inspired by a thorough, and perhaps overserious, devotion to the poetry that found its way into the pages of *The Savoy* and *The Yellow Book*. The influences of Oscar Wilde and Ernest Dowson can be quickly noted in almost everything that Sterling wrote and, with them, the characteristic literary vices of their time and school. In fact, all the flaws of the lesser romantic poets may be found in Sterling's poetry, each marked by a vague striving for exalted subject matter and the frequent use of an unconvincing archaic diction. "He never thinks, he *deems,* he is *fain* for this and that, he deals in emperies and auguries, in *casual throes* and *lethal voids,*" wrote Harriet Monroe. And he himself went halfway toward explaining his literary weaknesses in his attempts to find a definition for poetry. "Poetry," he said, "must abjure every literal and familiar element, accumulate as many images of strange loveliness, and cherish all the past embodiments of visionary beauty, such as the beings of classical mythology." This theory as he practiced it did him irrevocable harm—and though it may be properly elucidated in the works of a highly sensitized composer, such as Debussy, or a poet like Walter de la Mare with comparatively small damage to music and to verse, the very confusion of the wording in this confused belief seems to prove the ultimate vagueness of Sterling's intentions.

At its best, Sterling's poetry displays the sensitivity to line and image that his friends admired; flashes of the true poet he might have become can be discerned through the rapid courses of many poems. Excerpts from his "Ode on the Centenary of Robert Browning" [10] may be taken to illustrate his worst mannerisms and his occasional felicity:

> Clear truth with her cold agate of the well
> . . . with thee trace
> Her footprints passing upwards to the snows,
> But sought a phantom rose,
> And islands where the ghastly siren sings,
> Nor would I dwell
> Where star-forsaking wings
> On mortal thresholds hide their mystery
> The light of heaven cast on common things!

If the "ghastly siren" seems strained and, to say the least, unfortunately phrased, the rest of the poem is well sustained and shows him in his better moments. His first volume, *The Testimony of the Suns*, published in 1903, won the immediate applause of Ambrose Bierce and made his reputation. Though it appeared as the first of his many books, it still remains his most ambitious work: its astronomical vastitudes seem limitless, large visions of the universe and whole constellations seem to be employed in the effort to repeat the names that Sterling loved, names which were to be recited over and over again from this

[10] From *The Lyric Year*. Reprinted by permission of the publisher, Mitchell Kennerley.

first volume to his last, "Betelgeuse," "Antares," Procyon," and "Altair."

George Sterling had many friends, among whom were Bierce, Dreiser, Upton Sinclair, and Jack London. But the feeling of partisanship that he aroused seems to have been related to the great physical charm and beauty he possessed in his youth, which can be noted even in Jack London's half ironical, half affection-ate remark: "He looks like a Greek coin run over by a Roman chariot." But this was a portrait of the later Sterling.

His personal life was in the best neoromantic tradition, and if one were looking (as some critics have of late been doing) for the penalties and dangers attendant upon those who fail to exercise complete decorum and the action of the "inner check," Sterling's life could point a moral and adorn a tale as vividly as any legend of Hart Crane. Though his suicide in 1926 brought him to the unfortunate end which is frequently predicted of romantic poets, the brighter moments of his career were filled with the applause of many loyal readers. A brief glimpse of the kind of worship he inspired among those who knew him is reflected in the pages of Harriet Monroe's autobiography, *A Poet's Life:* [11]

In San Francisco I met George Sterling for the first time, a poet whose somewhat battered physical beauty was a reminder of the Apollo-like perfection of his youth. . . . But charming, always witty and charming, and always unconquerably modest about his work. I knew that the Pacific states were loyal to their own, but I was hardly prepared to hear Sterling's publisher—that amiable enthusiast, A. M. Robertson—pro-nounce him "the greatest poet since Dante," or to find him quoted (the only living poet) along with Confucius and Firdousi, Shakespeare and Goethe, on the high triumphal arches of the Panama-Pacific Exposition. . . . Sterling himself laughed at this futile exaltation of his fame . . . he knew that he had never done his best.

In reply to an unfavorable review Harriet Monroe had written of his work, Sterling wrote:

It gave me much satisfaction to bring that keen review of yours to dear old Robertson, as further evidence of my perennial claim to him that he was only making me ridiculous by quoting Joaquin Miller's "Dante" remark—and other comments just as absurd by Ambrose Bierce

[11] By permission of The Macmillan Company.

and others. Joaquin had a way of making his rivals (?) ridiculous by overheaping praise on them—I've wondered more than once whether there wasn't a pinch of malice in the habit.[12]

Sterling took Miss Monroe's objections to his excesses and facilities with gentlemanly grace, and an unexpected meekness; he reminded her that he had been reading Ezra Pound's "A Few Don'ts by an Imagiste" published in *Poetry*, March, 1913, and while he confessed that Pound was not one of his "enthusiasms," he agreed that most members of his generation were a "mass of dolts." In this instance, his sensitivities seemed to take the form of self-criticism. If he had failed to convey in his wild and sometimes effective imagery the physical phenomena of Californian landscape, which had made so powerful an appeal to his nervous fancies, he was quick to realize their successful creation in the work of a younger and more gifted poet. He was among the first to acknowledge the potential abilities of Robinson Jeffers and he seemed to realize that though he had also been greatly attracted by the massive grandeur of Point Lobos and the scenery surrounding Carmel, Jeffers had actually caught the very quality and soul of that country, making it as real as Thomas Hardy's re-creation of his Wessex countryside.

Underlying Sterling's reaches toward floating planets and wild constellations, there was a persistent note of pathos as well as a fitfully expressed sense of evil. Unlike Markham and unlike Miller, he seemed to feel the presence of a darkness, a Spenglerian melodrama that Jeffers was to enter and explore. And as his years rounded to a close, one is reminded by the circumstances of his death that he had been for many years a close friend of "Bitter" Bierce. The characteristic touch of pathos, unmarred by the least suggestion of self-pity, may be found in these few lines written in his middle years. Sterling writes of himself as

> Scanning the shadows with a sense of haste
> Where fade the tracks of all who went before,
> A dim and solitary traveller
> On ways that end in evening and the waste.[13]

[12] From *A Poet's Life* by Harriet Monroe. By permission of The Macmillan Company.
[13] Sonnet from *Omnia Exeunt Mysterium*.

THE BAREFOOT BOY OF INDIANA

Although contemporary historians of American poetry tend to grow uneasy or shy at the mention of James Whitcomb Riley (1849-1916), it would be an error of self-conscious embarrassment to underrate the phenomenon of his popularity and its significance. Of recent years, his reputation has been linked with the notoriety achieved by Ella Wheeler Wilcox (1855-1919), whom he admired, and it is all too easy to see why the mechanical optimism which flows so freely through the verse of both poets has brought to light an acceptable if not profound association. It is also true that both were born in the Middle West during a period when literary reputations owed their existence to the encouragement received from editors and readers of small-town newspapers and when the yearning for culture spread like a low prairie wind over the land; yet Riley's verse sustained and has continued to sustain its hold upon the popular imagination with greater tenacity than the work of any newspaper poet in his generation.

Another association that Riley's popularity brings to mind is the name of Eugene Field (1850-95) whose verse held similar appeal to like audiences and whose legend flourished in the daily columns of a local newspaper. Again the resemblance is one of surface qualities that fail to account for the kind of fame that made Riley a national spokesman for the State of Indiana. Clues to the secret lie in his early graduation from newspaper offices to lecture platforms; and successful tours with Bill Nye at small-town one-night stands as well as a facility in the craftsmanship of writing dialect verse enabled him to fill a position that had been left vacant since the day James Russell Lowell published the last installment of *The Biglow Papers*. After many years of applause from audiences in one-night lecture halls, Riley lived long enough to receive an honorary degree from Yale among the cheers of its student body, and during these later triumphs he also gained recognition from editors of New York and Boston magazines—the magazines of national circulation, toward which his youthful eyes had once wistfully turned—*Harper's, Scribner's, The Atlantic Monthly, The Century*. His birthday became a state of Indiana holiday: no poet since Longfellow had been so loved by school-children, and as Riley neared his death in 1916 Woodrow Wilson, then President of the United States, sent anxious messages of inquiry concerning his last illness. To this day, he remains a poet whose lines are frequently quoted by schoolchildren and the sale of his books in popular reprint editions shows few signs of falling off.

Though it would be unwise to overestimate the quality of Riley's verse on the mere evidence of its popularity, it is also clear that his gifts aroused a public response that is seldom if ever earned by grace of empty rhyming and familiar music. Those who read through the bulky volume of his letters, edited by William Lyon Phelps in 1930, will be impressed by a native shrewdness, by a mature as well as boyish energy and sly humor, by a touch of gentleness that, however worldly, remains un-spoiled, and by a kind of literary cultivation that was self-taught and yet well disciplined. He had taken as his motto "The heart is all," and he kept his ear tuned to the music that stirred the heart of his native state and, later, the whole nation. Perhaps because he, like "O. Henry," was a true provincial, and because the large cities of the nation were filled with men and women from small towns and villages, he found a national audience. To them his verse contained accurate and beloved pictures of In-diana pastures and farmyards, of side roads that led to hidden streams and ponds, and these were re-created in the speech of provincial characters, who were recognized not only on Middle Western small-town streets, but in all small towns—they were the people who stayed at home, who loved the familiar sight of things at home, who were tenacious of old ways and were moved by simple sentiment. When someone questioned Riley concern-ing the accuracy of his Hoosier dialect, he admitted that its sources were in the memory of his own childhood, a childhood which had been spent during the same years that welcomed the publication of the second series of *The Biglow Papers*. Perhaps it was not surprising that Riley's own rules for writing dialect verse were of but the slightest variation from the Yankee idiom of Birdofredum Sawin and Ezekiel Biglow; Lowell had fixed the literary pattern for the speech and attitudes of small-town characters in America, and the sentiment of "The Courtin'" [1] with its lines,

> All kin' o' smily roun' the lips
> An' teary roun' the lashes . . .

set the standard in which provincial America saw itself reflected as in a mirror.

Riley was obsessed by childhood, as some greater poets have been, and it is easy to see why someone once said of him that all his verses read as if they had been written by the very old and the very young against the middle-aged. In his obituary address on Riley before The Academy of Arts and Letters, Hamlin Garland said: "He expressed something of the wistful sadness of the middle-aged man who is looking back on the sunlit streams of his boyhood."

In the same address, Garland also recalled a trip that he had made to Greenfield, Indiana, to visit Riley. To him, after the beauty of his own Wisconsin lake country, Indiana landscape seemed dull, flat, and unlovely, an unpromising place for the birth of poets and poetry. Nor did Riley himself look particularly poetic. Garland described Riley as "short, square-shouldered, very blond, and with the face of an actor." He spoke of Riley's clear, precise diction, which only momentarily dropped into a familiar Hoosier drawl. "Wise, rather than learned," Garland remarked, and then went on to say that Riley's way of expressing his ideas and prejudices contained the sententiousness of a farmer and the charm of those who are not brought up in cities, which was "a native fragrance," Garland said, "as of basswood and buckwheat bloom" rising from his poetry.

"*The face of an actor* . . ."—though it is doubtful if Garland intended his brief memoir of Riley to be taken as a clew toward defining the nature of his verse and its popularity, the remark sheds light upon those qualities that made his appearance on

[1] *The Biglow Papers,* second series, Houghton Mifflin Company.

lecture platforms and what he said remembered. It goes far toward explaining the eager welcome he received at schools, church socials, and women's clubs. What was more, Riley tested the value of his verses by the response from his audiences and learned through their physical reactions how to gauge the taste of a larger, national public. Riley himself told how on one of his first lecture tours, he read his lines to "A Happy Little Cripple," a composition artfully contrived to bring an immediate response from those who heard it. He saw two people in the audience suddenly get up and walk out. In making inquiries he discovered that the verses had affected his two listeners too deeply, and that they had a crippled child waiting for them at home. This incident distressed Riley profoundly, who took great care to recite lines that would not depress his audiences, nor strike too deeply into the darkness of their fears and doubts. He had a great dread of the darker places in the soul, and of the sinister or complicated recesses of the mind. Coupled with his dread of darkness was his deep and genuine dislike of Whitman; and William Lyon Phelps remarked that on this subject in private conversation he often gave way to unprintable language. "A cult-reputation," Riley once wrote of Whitman, "he began by writing bad verses for magazines. These attracted no attention, so he decided to write something startling and eccentric." He also insisted, and not without justice, that Whitman lacked a sense of humor. Though Riley admired Poe, he also thought him much too "morbid." Ambrose Bierce was another writer who offended every instinct by which he lived, who was miles away from Riley's world of circus parades, of village bands, of small white clapboard houses set off by wide lawns and shaded by heavy trees, his world of a remembered childhood in which the emotions of pathos could be felt, if not fully understood, and which by its childlike character held no room for tragedy.

It might be said that to those who read and heard him, Riley never failed to hearten and console. It was not for nothing that his Indianapolis neighbors seeing him leave the yellow and white frame house on Lockerbie Street, faultlessly attired, gold-headed cane in hand, stopping to call children by name and sometimes giving them copper one-cent pieces, called him "Sunny Jim."

And it was not for nothing that he had dedicated one of his books to "all Americans who were ever boys, to all at least who had the good luck to be country boys, and to go barefoot."

Nor had he always lived in a house on Lockerbie Street with its terraced stone steps and its flower urns and its shade trees darkening the lawn, a house that looked as though its existence had been forgotten as the little town grew into the city of Indianapolis. Before coming here, he had lived in Greenfield, Indiana, a very small town, some twenty miles outside the city limits. His father, contrary to popular legend, had not been a farmer, but a prosperous lawyer, and Riley had been offered the opportunities of a conventional education and a chance to train for the law. At eighteen, he ran away from home and joined a one-night-stand theatrical troupe, who embellished their scant earnings by selling patent medicines to their audiences during intermissions. During the summers when such jobs grew scarce, he would spend his time loafing or reading, "knee-deep in June" through the torpid, mellow, Midwestern summer weather that he was never tired of celebrating. Many years later, when he was old and famous and had been the recipient of many letters asking him to reveal the reasons for his success, he replied to inquiries made by a young poetess, and in his answer there is perhaps a broad hint of how he conducted his summer courses in a self-instructed, private education:

"Study—study—study—Read! Read! Read! Study to discover the real secret of success in writing, and read only successful books—to discover and hunt out the deep down secret of the successful poet's song. Avoid reading the older poets . . . read only the successful modern poets." [2]

Of the "modern" poets, he placed Longfellow first, and next to him Tennyson, whose craftsmanship he heartily admired.

As his own admirers were never tired of repeating, Riley had kept intact the heart, the emotions of a boy; and it was his unquestioning faith in the essential goodness of boyish work and play that continued to win the hearts of his many readers. If he sang of the old swimming hole, the old trundle bed, the old

[2] From *The Letters of James Whitcomb Riley*, ed. by Wm. Lyon Phelps, Copyright 1931. Used by special permission of the Publishers, The Bobbs-Merrill Company.

haymow, the old glee club, and going out again to visit old Aunt Mary—and recited each stanza as though it had been written for the millions of children who also recited verse on Thursday afternoons in public schools—every note he struck found an answering response in the breasts of those who stopped to listen to the song. What he had found and brought to light in a re-membered childhood may not have been what childhood was, but to those who heard him, it was what childhood should have been in a world that was slowly drifting toward the instabilities which preceded and came after the First World War. The drift was noted in certain undercurrents of unrest that were to lead toward disillusionments and to an embittered analysis of the same milieu in the *Winesburg, Ohio* of Sherwood Anderson and the *Spoon River Anthology* of Edgar Lee Masters.

Meanwhile and throughout the first decade of a self-con-sciously American twentieth century, Riley continued to supply his publishers with scores of poems written in two languages, the first in what came to be known as a "Hoosier dialect," and the second in the readily acceptable idiom of conventional magazine verse. There were times when Riley himself preferred the latter idiom and was fond of recalling an anecdote in which a Brown-ing Club member asked him whether or not he enjoyed reading dialect verse. "Some of it," Riley replied. "Eugene Field's is all right. But the other day I read some verse by a fellow named Chaucer, and I think he went altogether too far." This touch of wit, carefully phrased so as to offend no one, was characteristic of the particular craftsmanship he employed, as well as the not unworldly elegance in dress and manner that was so brilliantly reflected in the Sargent canvas which became his official portrait.

More than all else, he was the versifier of the long, bright summer holiday:

> With all your harvest stores of olden joys,
> Vast overhanging meadow-lands of grain . . .[3]

> The yearning cry of some bewildered bird
> Above an empty nest, and truant boys

[3] "An Old Friend" from *Home Folks*, Copyright 1902, 1930. Used by special permission of the Publishers, The Bobbs-Merrill Company.

Along the river's shady margin heard,
A harmony of noise.[4]

And down the woods to the swimmin' hole
Where the big white hollow old sycamore grows . . .[5]

And through the image of a summer's day, again and again,
Riley's insistent longing for the past appears; and this emotion
has never been more fortunately expressed than in his "Where-
Away": [6]

> Children at the pasture-bars,
> Through the dusk, like glimmering stars,
> Waved their hands that we should bide
> With them over eventide:
> Down the dark their voices failed
> Falteringly, as they hailed,
> And died into yesterday—
> Night ahead and—Where-Away?

It is for the clear statement of this emotion, accompanied by
his thumbnail sketches of small-town characters, that Riley's
verse has been remembered and among the *fabulae* of American
literature it may endure. For twenty years he was the poet of
American family life in the same sense that Booth Tarkington
became the novelist of the humorously perceived and yet idealized American home. And from the oblique position of his
bachelorhood, for Riley never married, it is perhaps significant
that his frequent spokesman was the man of all work and odd
jobs, "the Raggedy Man," who was the traditional figure of the
American "Uncle," as well as the romantic "Tramp" of Ridgely
Torrence's "Eyewitness."

Riley, in a letter of advice to the young Booth Tarkington,
told him that his stories should be "Godlike, Manlike, Childlike," and this instruction was, of course, a rule that he had tried
to follow in the writing of his own verse.

[4] "August" from *Green Fields and Running Brooks,* Copyright 1892, 1920.
Used by special permission of the Publishers, The Bobbs-Merrill Company.

[5] "A Backward Look" from *Pipes O'Pan at Zekesbury.* Used by special permission of the Publishers, The Bobbs-Merrill Company.

[6] From *Green Fields and Running Brooks,* Copyright 1892, 1920. Used by
special permission of the Publishers, The Bobbs-Merrill Company.

On Riley's brief visit to London, the great object of his admiration was Sir Henry Irving and there is no doubt that Sir Henry returned the compliment. After this exchange of warm approval, Riley was all too glad to return to Lockerbie Street and to resume at intervals his recital tours on which he had once met Matthew Arnold. He had been happy to note that Arnold was by no means snobbish and yet he felt uneasy in his presence. Riley wrote of him: "I think he has no sense of humor whatever. A joke that tackled him would hide its head in shame and skulk away and weep." It is sometimes well to remember that Riley once made the same criticism of Whitman.

His fame had continued to grow until one day Samuel L. Clemens sent him a letter addressed from Vienna inscribed:

> James Whitcomb Riley,
> Practicing Poet,
>   and a dern capable one, too,
>   Indianapolis,
>   Indiana.[7]

The letter reached him without the slightest difficulty, and when he died in 1916, his native state founded a children's hospital in his name.

Before Riley's death, two books of poems, *Spoon River Anthology* (1915) and *General William Booth Enters into Heaven* (1913) appeared and one tends to associate Lindsay's name as well as Masters' with the memory of Riley's Middle Western countryside. Lindsay would have loved to have gained the local recognition that Riley received. But Lindsay's verse touched deeper springs of emotion than the people of his native Illinois would have cared to see revealed, and Masters' *Spoon River Anthology* opened the tombs of a thousand Lockerbie Streets in as many Middle Western towns.

[7] From *Letters of James Whitcomb Riley*, ed. by Wm. Lyon Phelps. Copyright 1931. Used by special permission of the Publishers, The Bobbs-Merrill Company.

A NOTE

ON THE POETRY OF GEORGE SANTAYANA

In the years when Riley's *Rhymes of Childhood* were increasing their popularity and Sterling had made his first discoveries of the Bohemian life in California, George Santayana, a young instructor of philosophy at Harvard, who had been born in 1863, returned to Europe for a year of graduate work at King's College, Cambridge, England. This was his sabbatical year, 1896-1897, and in 1897 President Eliot of Harvard wrote a confidential report concerning the inadvisability of promoting him to an assistant professorship:

The withdrawn, contemplative man who takes no part in the everyday work of the institution, or of the world, seems to me a person of very uncertain value. He does not dig ditches, or lay bricks, or write school-books, his product is not of the ordinary, useful, though humble kind. What will it be? It may be something of the highest utility; but, on the other hand, it may be something futile, or even harmful because unnatural and untimely.[1]

In respect to Santayana's particular virtues, President Eliot later modified his worst fears, yet his retreat carried with it this gloomy reservation: he could not see his young instructor as a professor at the age of fifty. His later prophecy came so near to literal truth that it justified its somber warning. At the age of forty-nine, Santayana, upon receiving an inheritance which enabled him to be free of colleges and teaching, left Harvard and he also left behind him the legend that he had walked out of his classroom one fine afternoon and never showed up again in Cambridge.

To the reader who appreciates the best of Santayana's poetry as it appears in *Poems,* selected and revised by its author in 1922,

[1] From *Life of George Santayana* by George Howgate, used by permission of Charles Scribner's Sons.

his poetic contribution to American literature seems extraordinarily slender. But between 1894 and 1901, his writing of verse was extraordinarily prolific. These years included the publication of a first book, *Sonnets and Poems, Lucifer,* a theological drama in blank verse, and *A Hermit of Carmel,* and these volumes, if reprinted in their original format, would make a collection of some four hundred pages of published verse that would more than equal the life work of most twentieth-century poets.

To his admirers, it may also seem ironic that Santayana's poetic reputation since 1901 has been obscured by his other activities, by his distinction as the author of valuable studies in philosophy and esthetics, and by his notoriety in this country as the author of a best-selling novel, *The Last Puritan.* In his prose, as in his poetry, the same qualities appear, an absence of concrete imagery, a pure, limpid diction, great intellectual charm, graceful cadences and the implied desire to contemplate man and his destinies wisely—but at a distance. In his carefully guarded and thoroughly witty preface to the 1922 edition of his selected *Poems,* he wrote, "My own moral philosophy . . . may not seem very robust or joyous. Its fortitude and happiness are those of but one type of soul." And in that same preface he said, sustaining always the note of individual irony which so clearly distinguishes his early sonnets from those of his contemporaries:

In one sense I think that my verses, mental and thin as their texture may be, represent a true inspiration, a true docility. A Muse—not exactly an English Muse—actually visited me in my isolation; the same, or a ghost of the same, that visited Boethius or Alfred de Musset or Leopardi. It was literally impossible for me then not to re-echo her eloquence. When that compulsion ceased, I ceased to write verses.[2]

His "Muse," rightly enough, was of un-English origin. Born in Madrid, Santayana had spent the first nine years of his life in Spain. Both of his parents were Spanish, but his mother had had three children by a previous marriage to an American, and had pledged herself to bring them (as well as her younger son)

[2] From preface to *Poems,* 1923, used by permission of Charles Scribner's Sons.

to Boston where they had relatives and property. Santayana's father remained in Spain, a man of wide cultural interests, who had at one time studied under a painter of the Goya school, and who had translated Seneca into Spanish.

Though Santayana was educated at the Brimmer School, the Boston Latin School, and then at Harvard, he never overcame a sense of not being native to the English language, which may well have entered and set up limitations for his poetry, but in speaking of his family, he was quick to add, "We were not immigrants, we never changed our country, class, or religion."

Though it would be difficult to seek out the mere evidence of a Roman Catholic heritage in his poetry, it seems clear that his imagination recoiled from or was ill at ease whenever it faced the disorderly aspects of the Anglo-American liberal tradition. His very facility in the use of English (quite as though the language were without an Anglo-Saxon backbone) resembled the ease and "foreign" inflection of poetry written by the Rossettis. His position was that of a stranger in a world he had not made, which may be said to have created a habit of detachment from those around him, even in his family circle, where as a child he had often been lonely and had pleaded, to his elders, "Entertain me."

One can almost discern an answer to President Eliot's attitude and general philosophy of education in a paragraph of Santayana's *Interpretations of Poetry and Religion,* which was published four years after his return to Harvard to resume his instruction of courses in Scholasticism and European philosophies:

> The liberal school that attempts to fortify religion by minimizing its expression, both theoretic and devotional, seems, . . . to be merely impoverishing religious symbols and vulgarizing religious aims; it subtracts from faith that imagination by which faith becomes an interpretation and idealization of human life, and retains only a stark and superfluous principle of superstition.

This is of the same conviction that led him to say of poetry, ". . . the innate freedom of poets to hazard new forms does not abolish the freedom of all men to adopt the old ones." And again he wrote, thinking of poetry as one might think of a religious faith that transcends humanity, and not without some display of philosophic wit, "Poetry was made for man, not man for poetry."

All these remarks indicate and may be offered as an explanation of the far distance between him and President Eliot, and indeed, he seemed to stand at an oblique angle to a Boston Back Bay Protestant environment, and in this respect, his position was not unlike André Gide's Protestantism in Roman Catholic France. It is not surprising that his distinction brought to its support men such as Josiah Royce, William James, and Hugo Münsterberg, who, however strongly they may have differed from him in their philosophic views, recognized his essential qualities and their importance. In the years when he lectured and taught at Harvard he also attracted such undergraduates as Felix Frankfurter, Walter Lippmann, Conrad Aiken, and T. S. Eliot.

Meanwhile, the ironies of Santayana's position as a poet, however individual their origins may have been, were not as singular as it might be supposed. At the close of the nineteenth century Henry James, George Cabot Lodge, Joseph Trumbull Stickney, and Henry Adams would have understood, each with a difference, Santayana's remark in *The Life of Reason:* "All prophets are homeless, and all inspired artists, all philosophers think out some communism or other, and monks put it into practice." Each could say with Santayana:

> My heart rebels against my generation,
> That talks of freedom and is slave to riches,
> And, toiling 'neath each day's ignoble burden,
> Boasts of the morrow.[3]

Nor can we say, remembering the later figures of Matthew Josephson's *Portrait of the Artist as American* (1930), that Santayana was "less American" than other sensitive and intelligent American writers of that day, particularly when we recall the passionate spirit contained in the stanzas of his Sapphic "Odes":

> Gathering the echoes of forgotten wisdom,
> And mastered by a proud, adventurous purpose,
> Columbus sought the golden shores of India
> Opposite Europe.

[3] "Sapphic Odes" from *Poems*, 1927, used by permission of Charles Scribner's Sons.

He gave the world another world, and ruin
Brought upon blameless, river-loving nations,
Cursed Spain with barren gold, and made the Andes
    Fiefs of Saint Peter;

While in the cheerless North the thrifty Saxon
Planted his corn, and, narrowing his bosom,
Made covenant with God, and by keen virtue
    Trebled his riches.

What venture hast thou left us, bold Columbus?
What honour left thy brothers, brave Magellan?
Daily the children of the rich for pastime
    Circle the planet.

And what good comes to us of all your dangers?
A smaller earth and smaller hope of heaven.
Ye have but cheapened gold, and, measuring ocean,
    Counted the islands.

No Ponce de Leon shall drink in fountains,
On any flowering Easter, youth eternal;
No Cortes look upon another ocean;
    No Alexander . . .[4]

George W. Howgate in his *George Santayana,* an extended
study of Santayana's life and work, offers a number of speculations concerning the nature of his temperament. He suggests
that Santayana's family, since they were from Madrid, were
Spaniards of the austere Castilian tablelands which are described
in one of Santayana's poems:

> Realm proudly desolate and nobly poor,
> Scorched by the sky's inexorable zeal . . .[5]

It was of this Castilian tableland that Salvador de Madariaga
spoke: ". . . a country with grandeur and majesty which make
it the worthy companion of the great scenes of nature, seas and
skies—and of the great moods of the spirit, the poetry of contemplation."

However much or little this distant background may have
influenced the character of Santayana's poetry, it is clear that its

[4] "Odes, III" from *Poems,* 1923, used by permission of Charles Scribner's
Sons.
[5] "Avila" from *Poems,* 1923, used by permission of Charles Scribner's Sons.

existence in his memory contributed to his sense of exile, both from Spain itself and from the America of Boston's State Street and President Eliot's Harvard. Even his view of the "sacred Mediterranean" was shadowed with the thought of his own exile:

> The more should I, O fatal sea, before thee
> Of alien words make echoes to thy music;
> For I was born where first the rills of Tagus
> Turn to the westward.[6]

If, as Archibald MacLeish observes, "for all their decorum, the work strikes fire," the best of Santayana's poems disclose the conflict of emotion that lies within a sense of loss and homelessness:

> Exile not only from the wind-swept moor
> Where Guadarrama lifts his purple crest,
> But from the spirit's realm, celestial, sure
> Goal of all hope.[7]

And in "Avila," one of his few poems in which a Spanish landscape is consciously recalled, one rediscovers the persistent undertone of his poetic themes:

> Nor world nor desert hath a home for thee.

It is little wonder that President Eliot felt uneasy particularly if, as Howgate says, the younger Santayana was best known at Cambridge as a teacher who attracted only certain types of students, was distinctly a poet, a Spanish "exotic," and a social favorite with the cultivated ladies of Boston.

Though his restrained emotions and his philosophic idealism, wedded as it was to the scholastic humanism of the early Renaissance, may have confused and bewildered those around him, his poetic wit seems to have resolved its problems in this excellent sonnet which is quoted from his earliest collection:

> Dreamt I to-day the dream of yesternight,
> Sleep ever feigning one evolving theme,—
> Of my two lives which should I call the dream?

[6] "Odes, V" from *Poems*, 1923, used by permission of Charles Scribner's Sons.

[7] "Sapphic Odes" from *Poems*, 1923, used by permission of Charles Scribner's Sons.

Which action vanity? which vision sight?
Some greater waking must pronounce aright,
If aught abideth of the things that seem,
And with both currents swell the flooded stream
Into an ocean infinite of light.
Even such a dream I dream, and know full well
My waking passeth like a midnight spell,
But know not if my dreaming breaketh through
Into the deeps of heaven and of hell.
I know but this of all I would I knew:
Truth is a dream, unless my dream is true.[8]

The same felicity, touched briefly with the "sensuous and ideal" for which he seemed always to be seeking, enters these lines:

And heaven shines as if the Gods were there.
Had Dian passed there could no deeper peace
Embalm the purple stretches of the air.[9]

Howgate hints that a true "dark lady" is the subject of Santayana's love sonnets, but the actuality of the event should not concern us as much as the true felicity of phrasing that gives the 1894 sonnet sequence an air of personal reality:

O too late love, O flight on wounded wing,
Infinite hope my lips should not suspire,
Why, when the world is thine, my grief require,
Or mock my dear-bought patience with thy sting?
Though I be mute, the birds will in the boughs
Sing as in every April they have sung,
And, though I die, the incense of heart-vows
Will float to heaven, as when I was young.
But, O ye beauties I must never see,
How great a lover have you lost in me! [10]

In rereading the 1923 edition of Santayana's *Poems* there can be little doubt that his work deserves greater prominence in current anthologies or studies of American verse. Of the many

8 Sonnet "V" from *Poems*, 1923, used by permission of Charles Scribner's Sons.

9 Sonnet "XVI" from *Poems*, 1923, used by permission of Charles Scribner's Sons.

10 Sonnet "XXI" from *Poems*, 1923, used by permission of Charles Scribner's Sons.

lesser poets grouped together under the general heading of a
so-called "genteel tradition" his work alone possesses the distinction that earns respect from future generations. Even Bruce
Weirick in his survey of American poetry from Whitman to
Sandburg reluctantly confesses, "A society able to produce so
fine a flower of culture . . . has in some sense grown up." The
very least that one can say regarding Santayana's selected *Poems*
is that no American poet of the twentieth century has so skillfully edited and revised his own contribution to modern literature, and the last lines of his preface are an irresistible invitation
to readers who have yet to recognize the enduring eloquence of
his un-English "Muse." His book is "addressed only to those
whose ear it might strike sympathetically and who, crossing the
same dark wood on their own errands, may pause for a moment
to listen gladly."

Since 1914 Santayana has lived in London and in Rome, a
welcome exile that the late Sir Edmund Gosse described with
awe and half-bewildered reverence in *The Times Literary Supplement.* Something of the same bewilderment fell upon the
critics of Santayana's autobiography in prose, *Persons and Places,*
at the time of its distribution by the Book of the Month Club
in 1944, while its author continued to live under the protection
of the Roman Catholic Church in Fascist Rome. Beneath the
general tones of reverence that each assumed came the com-
plaints that Santayana was "devious," "uncandid," "cold," and
"possibly in sympathy with Fascism." The simple—and complex—
truth of the matter is that Santayana has identified himself with
Spain; and the only sense of unity that the stricken, tortured,
passionate, and austere country has ever found springs from the
intensity of its religious life. This is a truth that has always been
flagrantly misunderstood on this side of the Atlantic by the
critics of Santayana's poetry and prose who have resented his
restraint, his perception of a private world (which by the way
has kept his poetry alive), and his right to accept the terms of
individual existence. For him those terms have always been the
position of an exile, a condition that had been fully realized by
both Henry Adams and Henry James—with the singular differ-

ence that Santayana's emotional responses lie within the contradictions of the Spanish psyche. Perhaps a quotation from Miguel de Unamuno will throw further light on what has been viewed as the unsolved mystery of Santayana's position:

> If we take away from the mind of each man that which is his own, that way of looking at things that is peculiar to him, everything that he takes care to hide for fear people should think him mad, we are left with that which he has in common with everyone else, and this common element gives us that wretched thing that is called common sense and which is nothing more than the abstract of the practical intelligence. But if we fuse into one the differing judgments of people, with all that they jealously preserve, and bring their caprices, their oddities, their singularities into agreement, we shall have human sense, which, in those who are rich in it, is not common but private sense.
>
> The best that occurs to men is that which occurs to them when they are alone, that which they dare not confess, not only not to their neighbor but very often not even to themselves, that which they fly from, that which they imprison within themselves while it is in a state of pure thought and before it can flower into words. . . . The solitary . . . surprises others by saying that which they think beneath their breath. . . . All this will help you to deduce for yourself in what way and to what extent solitude is the great school of sociability, and how right it is that we should sometimes withdraw ourselves from men in order that we may the better serve them.[11]

All this is said, of course, in a manner that is less sensitively balanced than anything that Santayana has written in verse, yet in it one finds a reason why Santayana's *Poems* have sold through several editions, and why his work "surprises others" in that slightly foreign use of English which has become the mark of his individual style. In Santayana's poetry those rough distinctions which are usually applied in defining a national literature tend to break down, and with them those equally coarse definitions which separate major and minor verse also tend to disappear. The foregoing remarks on his identity with Spain were given to explain his temperamental affinities which have been so often and so generally misunderstood, but such an explanation does not exclude Santayana's name from whatever we mean when we

[11] From *Essays and Soliloquies*, by permission of Alfred A. Knopf, Inc. Copyright 1924 by Alfred A. Knopf, Inc.

speak of American poetry. On the contrary, his early statement, "My heart rebels against my generation," now seems to have anticipated, though slightly in reverse, the feeling expressed by young Americans of a later generation, who were "lost" in Paris in the years immediately following the First World War, and it now seems certain that Santayana expressed that feeling with deeper penetration and with more enduring art than some few of the "exiles" who came after him.

But Santayana's sensibilities were not without flaws of their kind, and the curse of dullness descended on his long novel, *The Last Puritan;* in *A Letter to Robert Frost,*[12] Robert Hillyer, speaking of Santayana and *The Last Puritan,* wrote:

> Who after years of rightful fame defrauded,
> Wrote one bad book at last,—and all applauded.

And in criticism of Santayana's work when it is less firm than his best, one is tempted to quote his own lines "On an unfinished statue by Michael Angelo in the Bargello, called an Apollo, or a David":[13]

> . . . the torpid and unwilling mass
> Misknew the sweetness of the mind's control,
> And the quick shifting of the winds, alas!
> Denied a body to that flickering soul.

Unlike Trumbull Stickney, Santayana possessed the art of sustaining his gifts throughout the length of a poem, so that the poem itself fulfills its own intentions, its own laws, its own identity. That is why certain of Santayana's poems have the quality of "timelessness" which is so difficult to describe, and whenever it appears it implies that the author has reached his maturity. The elegiac note which Lodge and Stickney sounded at the turn of the century has its fulfillment in Santayana's "A Minuet on Reaching the Age of Fifty":[14]

[12] By permission of Alfred A. Knopf, Inc. Copyright 1936, 1937 by Robert Hillyer.

[13] From *Poems,* used by permission of Charles Scribner's Sons.

[14] *Ibid.*

I

Old Age, on tiptoe, lays her jewelled hand
Lightly in mine.—Come, tread a stately measure,
Most gracious partner, nobly poised and bland.
　　Ours be no boisterous pleasure,
But smiling conversation, with quick glance
And memories dancing lightlier than we dance,
　　Friends who a thousand joys
Divide and double, save one joy supreme
　　Which many a pang alloys.
　　Let wanton girls and boys
Cry over lovers' woes and broken toys.
Our waking life is sweeter than their dream.

II

Dame Nature, with unwitting hand,
Has sparsely strewn the black abyss with lights
Minute, remote, and numberless. We stand
　　Measuring far depths and heights,
　　Arched over by a laughing heaven,
Intangible and never to be scaled.
If we confess our sins, they are forgiven.
　　We triumph, if we know we failed.

III

　　Tears that in youth you shed,
Congealed to pearls, now deck your silvery hair;
　　Sighs breathed for loves long dead
Frosted the glittering atoms of the air
　　Into the veils you wear
Round your soft bosom and most queenly head;
　　The shimmer of your gown
Catches all tints of autumn, and the dew
Of gardens where the damask roses blew;
The myriad tapers from these arches hung
　　Play on your diamonded crown;
And stars, whose light angelical caressed
　　Your virgin days,
Give back in your calm eyes their holier rays.
　　The deep past living in your breast
　　Heaves these half-merry sighs;
　　And the soft accents of your tongue
　　Breathe unrecorded charities.

IV

Hasten not; the feast will wait.
This is a master-night without a morrow.
No chill and haggard dawn, with after-sorrow,
    Will snuff the spluttering candle out,
Or blanch the revelers homeward straggling late.
    Before the rout
Wearies or wanes, will come a calmer trance.
Lulled by the poppied fragrance of this bower,
    We'll cheat the lapsing hour,
And close our eyes, still smiling, on the dance.

Serenity, grace, and lightness are in these lines; in twentieth-century verse these qualities are rare and, as if in spite of the slightly archaic overtone that is always present in Santayana's diction, the poem has an air of distinction that transcends the moment.

FOUR WOMEN
OF THE "TWILIGHT INTERVAL":
REESE, GUINEY, CRAPSEY, AND TEASDALE

LIZETTE REESE

There is a kind of poetry before which criticism seems almost helpless and painstaking analysis becomes irrelevant and un-gracious. Such is the poetry of Lizette Reese (1856-1935) with its lightly poised simplicity and its delicately tuned music. If her songs seem to resemble, more than all else, the smaller seventeenth-century masters of lyric verse, to be accompanied always by the spinet and the lute, her accents also sound a muted yet clear note of authority, a musical rather than verbal precision that is her own.

Lizette Reese was born in Waverly, Baltimore County, Maryland, of English and German stock, the daughter of a Confederate veteran of the Civil War. In her reminiscences, *A Victorian Village*, published in 1929, she speaks of the soft, rolling landscape which had traced its color and line upon her visual imagination, a Maryland landscape, with its innocent resemblances to Devonshire, Kent, and Buckinghamshire of southern England. It was a country peopled by those whose ancestors had come in early Colonial days from these very shires, a heritage whose sympathies had been Cavalier rather than Puritan. She was a poet whose work has a true if slender kinship with Herrick's poetry in its quick sensory impressions, its immediacy, its light touch, its sense of atmosphere and of transient moods, however gay, or grave, or swift, set down with sudden clarity. One thinks of her verses as one recalls Herrick's lines "To Dianeme": [1]

> When as that *Rubie,* which you weare,
> Sunk from the tip of your soft eare,

[1] From *Herrick's Poetical Works,* Oxford University Press.

Will last to be a precious Stone,
When all your world of Beautie's gone.

Hers was a world, indeed, that was not dependent upon the changing poetic fashions of her long lifetime; it was of things within her reach, of Maryland orchards, flowers, houses, weather, trees, gardens, all seemingly renewed as though looked at for the first time, and always with the slight shock of that first glance as if it were an actual discovery of new beauty in an old world:

> Carved out against a tender sky,
> The convent gables lift,
> Half-way below the old boughs lie,
> Heaped in a great white drift.
>
> .   .   .   .   .   .
>
> They tremble in the passionate air,
> They part, and clean and sweet,
> The cherry flakes fall here, fall there,
> A handful stirs the street.
>
> The workmen look up as they go,
> And one remembering plain
> How white the Irish orchards blow,
> Turns back and looks again.[2]

And again one reads:

> Dark, thinned, beside the wall of stone,
> The box dripped in the air;
> Its odor through my house was blown
> Into the chamber there.
>
> Remote and yet distinct the scent,
> The sole thing of the kind,
> As though one spoke a word half-meant
> That left a sting behind.[3]

Lizette Reese's first book, *A Branch of May,* was published in 1887, and even then she had already struck the note her verse

[2] "A Street Scene" from *The Selected Poems of Lizette Woodworth Reese,* copyright, 1926, by Lizette Woodworth Reese, and reprinted by permission of Farrar & Rinehart, Inc.

[3] "In Time of Grief" from *The Selected Poems of Lizette Woodworth Reese,* copyright, 1926, by Lizette Woodworth Reese, and reprinted by permission of Farrar & Rinehart, Inc.

sustained from its first volume to its last. "A Girl's Mood" [4]
expresses this quality in her verse with the same unaffected ease
that distinguishes so many of her poems; the girl who speaks
seems to be discovered at the very moment when she is artless
and unposed:

> I love a prayer-book;
> I love a thorn-tree
> That blows in the grass
> As white as can be.
>
> I love an old house
> Set down in the sun,
> And the windy old roads
> That thereabout run.
>
> I love blue, thin frocks;
> Green stones one and all;
> A sky full of stars,
> A rose at the fall.
>
> A lover I love;
> O, had I but one,
> I would give him all these,
> Myself, and the sun!

One might say, reading her *Selected Poems,* published in 1926,
that her entire work seems miraculously unchanging and intact,
as though the book that covers a span of nearly forty years had
been the work of a young girl of undoubted talent.

John Farrar had shrewdly caught an essential part of her
poetic character when he wrote the introduction to her novel,
Worleys, in 1936:

She never seemed to me to be a southerner in the accepted sense of
the word, though she was deeply rooted in the country and towns of
Maryland. She was rather typical of the fine type of schoolmistress and
librarian of virginal heart and active mind, cultured, broad-minded,
and yet almost fierce in a defense of tradition.

If we are consistently made aware of the young girl of great
talent in her work, we also find glimpses of the little school-

[4] From *Wild Cherry,* copyright, by Lizette Woodworth Reese, and reprinted
by permission of Farrar & Rinehart, Inc.

mistress whose favorite reading list always included the names of Herrick, George Herbert, Thomas à Kempis, Trollope, Charles Lamb, Bunyan, Dickens of *Pickwick Papers* (though on the whole, she preferred Thackeray), Jane Austen, and Charlotte and Emily Brontë. Of *Wuthering Heights* she wrote: "a book so great that it is startling; she [Emily Brontë] more than her sisters felt the pricking of the modern spirit." At a later moment she grew to love the prose of Robert Louis Stevenson and the novels but not the poems of Thomas Hardy. Thackeray, though she admired him, shocked her by his cynicism. "It made me feel," she wrote, "as though I were in a room filled with smoke from a long-disused chimney, mentally I smarted and choked." An "equally cruel experience" was her shock at reading Hawthorne's *Scarlet Letter,* and yet she felt close to Hawthorne, for the sharp, tart quality of his prose was also present in her poetry, and the very keenness of its clarity, however deceptively English its exterior may seem, identifies it as peculiarly American.

As time went on, her later preferences in reading poetry included such diverse poets as Henry Vaughan, the seventeenth-century Welsh mystic, and Dante Gabriel and Christina Rossetti. John Farrar and Louis Untermeyer made a point of remarking her indifference to the experiments of the 1920's in poetry, an indifference which was mildly stressed by her enjoyment of the delicate faintly mystical poetry of Marguerite Wilkinson (1883-1928), a poet whose slight but rare qualities (which may be discerned in a few of her devotional poems) do not deserve the complete oblivion into which they have fallen.

The very titles of Lizette Reese's thin volumes, *A Branch of May, A Handful of Lavender, A Quiet Road, Spicewood, Wild Cherry, Pastures,* bear witness to the limitations of her subject matter and its attractions. Her sensitivity was of a kind that was always quickened by the imagery of flowers. She wrote of "streaked cowslips half of honey and of fire," of "poppies tingling scarlet" or of "the glare of bitter marigold." There were times, however, when her flowers tended to become a shade too neatly patterned and one is reminded of the completely inanimate charms of early nineteenth-century wallpaper in a country house as well as of the fragrance of a Baltimore suburban garden.

Her moods of sadness were never quite so fortunate in their expression, yet her poem "Tears" brought fame to her well-established reputation and the alumnae of the high school where she taught had the poem engraved upon a bronze tablet to be placed on a wall of the building.

It is always well to remember that Stedman was among Lizette Reese's first admirers, and that he once wrote:

> The novelist has outstripped the poet in absorbing the new ideality conditioned by the advance of science [a statement, by the way, that has been repeated many times since 1900 with countless variations]. But [continued Stedman whose optimism never long deserted him] there continues an exercise of the art by many whose trick of song persists under all conditions. We have a twilight interval with minor voices and their tentative modes and notes.[5]

It is extremely doubtful if any interval, however twilight, could have kept Lizette Reese from writing the poetry she chose to write for, as it has been said before, she was one of those rare writers whose seemingly effortless grace and freshness sustained the illusion of her being a "born poet" and her undidactic lyricism gathered its rewards throughout three decades, when in the full tide of poetic upheaval and experimentation, all sides paused to do her honor.

LOUISE IMOGEN GUINEY

"Damn the age," Charles Lamb is reputed to have said as someone warned him that his work was out of tone with his own time; "if the age cannot take me, I shall write for antiquity." And today it seems as if Louise Imogen Guiney (1861-1920) wrote for antiquity thirty-six years of her life, or rather, for the England of Lord Clarendon's *Rebellion* in which she had found her deepest inspiration. She was one who had turned to the poetry of Herbert and of Vaughan long before the generation that matured in 1920 had heard of the "metaphysicals." Born in Boston, Massachusetts, in 1861, her first book, *Songs at the Start,* was published in 1884. Within the fastnesses of the seventeenth

---

[5] From *An American Anthology* ed. by E. C. Stedman, used by permission of Houghton Mifflin Company.

century Louise Guiney had discovered a congenial and secure vantage ground; she had an "original" temperament, and a feeling for excellence in poetry in the work of others that was by no means neglible. Near the end of her life (she died in 1920) she was one of the first to praise Gerard Manley Hopkins, and she was one of the few Americans, Ezra Pound among them, to respect the fine gifts of the often neglected British poet, Lionel Johnson. But her soul was with the minor Caroline poets, "my men," she called them—Cartwright, Quarles, Habington, Stanley, Fanshawe, Rochester, and lesser figures, "those golden lyricists who have not come . . . into their inheritance." Something of their grace, wit, delicate precision, and elegant wildness—and for her, there is no other word but "wildness" for it—entered her verse; and with the "wildness" she took their virtues to her heart:

> Take temperance to thy breast,
> While yet is the hour of choosing,
> An arbitress exquisite
> Of all that shall thee betide.
> For better than fortune's best
> Is mastery in the using,
> And sweeter than any thing sweet
> The art to lay it aside.[6]

In prose as well as in verse her models were of the various styles of her favorite century: Sir Thomas Browne, Jeremy Taylor, and Lord Clarendon; and it is said that she once absentmindedly dated a letter to a friend, "March 12th, 1667." Among her more "modern" masters were Lamb, Hazlitt, and, since she, too, was a devout Roman Catholic, Cardinal Newman; and when she turned to the century that followed the seventeenth, it was to the prose of Burke and to the poetry of Christopher Smart, whose phrase, "the quick, peculiar quince," had caught her eye and became the touchstone of her appreciation in reading poetry. The search for things that were "peculiar," romantic, and quaint both spurred and lightened her literary enthusiasms and her learning. She wrote of her passion for an age, a century other

[6] "A Talisman" from *Happy Ending*, used by permission of Houghton Mifflin Company.

than her own, with all the eloquence of her Irish ancestry, and never did she betray that ancestry more clearly than when she wrote of an England whose supernatural beauty could have existed only in her imagination:

> . . . the soul hath sight
> Of passionate yesterdays, all gold and large,
> Arisen to enrich our narrow night.[7]

Nor did she forget in writing of a time other than her own the figure of Robert Emmet and his love for Sarah Curran; and some of the most moving and eloquent passages of her prose are to be found in her study of James Clarence Mangan, the temperamentally unhappy and unfortunate Irish poet. The sublime failure and the gallant and royal martyr held her interest equally; and her extraordinary enthusiasm, which offered the contradictions of well-controlled hysteria, was also reserved for such figures as the Earl of Surrey, poet and soldier, who died on the block during the reign of King Henry VIII and the learned and saintly Edmund Campion, the Jesuit priest who suffered martyrdom for his faith in England under the rule of Queen Elizabeth.

In 1901 Louise Guiney left Boston for the British Isles where she spent the rest of her life, and there, as she walked London's streets, she saw the shade of William Hazlitt who also aroused her romantic sensibilities.

> Between the wet trees and the sorry steeple,
> Keep, Time, in dark Soho, what once was Hazlitt,
> Seeker of Truth, and finder oft of Beauty.[8]

After a visit to the neighborhood of a seventeenth-century battlefield Louise Guiney wrote:

I didn't see the battlefield as it happened. . . . Nothing more personal ever got hold of me than that war. . . . I can bear any grief of my own better than I can King Charles's.

[7] "On Leaving Winchester" from *Happy Ending,* used by permission of Houghton Mifflin Company.
[8] "Beside Hazlitt's Grave" from *Happy Ending,* used by permission of Houghton Mifflin Company.

It was to celebrate this veritable King Charles's head that she wrote in her copy of Lord Clarendon's *History of the Rebellion* one of her most characteristic poems:

> How life hath cheapen'd, and how blank
> The Worlde is! like a fen
> Where long ago unstainèd sank
> The starrie gentlemen:
> Since Marston Moor and Newbury drank
> King Charles his gentlemen.
>
> If Fate in any aire accords
> What Fate deny'd, Oh, then
> I ask to be among your Swordes,
> My joyous gentlemen;
> Towards Honours heaven to goe, and towards
> King Charles his gentlemen! [9]

When this poem first appeared in a magazine, young H. G. Wells (who even in his youth had been properly insulated from poetic flights and fancies) clipped it for quotation in one of his lesser-known "scientific" novels; the poem in its new setting reappeared as evidence of the queer modes of thinking and writing that Wells's Utopians of the Millennium looked back upon with horror. But kindly H. G. Wells could have spared himself that trouble: the poem was as uncommon to the day that he discovered it as it was to the seventeenth century; its spirit and its spelling were Louise Guiney's contributions to her own enthusiasms, and it is probable that the poem would have puzzled her favorite, Lord Falkland, and certainly John Wilmot, Earl of Rochester, as much as it charmed and bewildered her contemporaries. For many years, it had been her ambition to compile the wealth of her singular "discoveries" among the poets of the sixteenth and seventeenth century, and when the anthology at last appeared under the title of *Recusant Poets* (1919) it was more a tribute to her Celtic imagination, her lively and perceptive wit, and her deceptively artless charm than an example of anything that remotely resembled scholarship. Not since Chatterton's day

[9] "Writ in my Lord Clarendon, His History of the Rebellion" from *Happy Ending*, used by permission of Houghton Mifflin Company.

had anyone attempted a resurrection of the past with so marked a gift of poetic discernment and fervor. If one of Louise Guiney's friends, Sir Edmund Gosse, brushed the book aside and could not read it (he was no great scholar himself), another friend, Alice Meynell, who had more seriousness than he, was delighted by it.

Louise Guiney's versions of seventeenth-century spelling often produced mildly exciting and not unpleasant effects; if they were artless, which is to be doubted, they were remarkably consistent in their waywardness, and if they were not, they created an atmosphere, which she undoubtedly desired, of writing poems from a world that had escaped the limitations of time and space:

> The Ox he openeth wide the Doore,
> And from the Snowe he calls her inne,
> And he hath seen her Smile therefor,
> Our Ladye without Sinne.
> Now soone from Sleep
> A Starre shall leap,
> And soone arrive both King and Hinde:
>   *Amen, Amen:*
> But O, the Place co'd I but finde!
>
> .   .   .   .
>
> The Ox is host in Judah stall
> And Host of more than onelie one,
> For close she gathereth withal
> Our Lorde her littel Sonne.
> Glad Hinde and King
> Their Gyfte may bring,
> But wo'd to-night my Teares were there,
>   *Amen, Amen:*
> Between her Bosom and His hayre! [10]

Louise Guiney wrote a number of "cavalier rhymes," but the true image of what she saw was neither Prince Rupert nor his men, but the image of her father, the Irish-born General Patrick Guiney of whom Van Wyck Brooks wrote:

[He was] an Irish lawyer who had commanded a regiment in the American Civil War. Brevetted a brigadier-general . . . he had been hopelessly wounded; and one day in Boston, twelve years later, he sud-

[10] "Five Cards for Christmastide" from *Happy Ending*, used by permission of Houghton Mifflin Company.

denly stopped in the street, removed his hat, knelt, crossed himself and died. Miss Guiney's spirit rode forward in her father's stirrups.[11]

His portrait shows an attractive and intelligent face, one that seems well suited to the son and grandson of men who had been out in "the '98," and "the '45." "My preux chevalier of a father," Louise Guiney called him, and perhaps it was—and that likeliness seems very clear—in loyal deference to his memory that her verses were filled with gallant soldiers who rode forth to battle during which, of course, they always fell:

> A dipping of plumes, a tear, a shake of the bridle,
> A passing salute to this world and her pitiful beauty:
> We hurry with never a word in the track of our fathers.
>
> .   .   .   .
>
> We spur to a land of no name, out-racing the storm-wind;
> We leap to the infinite dark like sparks from the anvil.
> Thou leadest, O God! All's well with Thy troopers that follow.[12]

It was in England that Louise Guiney, possessed by the very daemon of antiquarian research, did her most characteristic work, and became "a Bodleian mole." Many years of her life were spent in searching for and at last discovering the grave of her beloved Vaughan. As a friend once wrote of her, "a half-effaced inscription was more dear to her than whole broadsides of modern paeans to success." In 1903 and of America Miss Guiney herself had written:

> I can't go home. It gives me the most genuine and involuntary fit of trembling. . . . The pace at which everything goes there, the noise, the publicity, the icicles, the mosquitoes, the extreme climatic conditions, I am not equal to them any more.[13]

Her remarks were not unlike those in another letter, written by Mrs. Church, in New York, to Madame Galopin, at Geneva, dated October 17, 1880, in Henry James's "The Point of View": [14]

---

[11] From *New England: Indian Summer*, E. P. Dutton & Company, Inc.

[12] "The Wild Ride" from *Happy Ending*, used by permission of Houghton Mifflin Company.

[13] From *Letters of Louise Imogen Guiney*, ed. by Grace Guiney, by permission of Harper & Brothers.

[14] From *The Siege of London*, used by permission of Houghton Mifflin Company.

We have found a refuge in a boarding-house which has been highly recommended to me, and where the arrangements partake of that barbarous magnificence which in this country is the only alternative from primitive rudeness. . . . There is no wine given at dinner, and I have vainly requested the person who conducts the establishment to garnish her table more liberally. She says I may have all the wine I want if I will order it at the merchant's, and settle the matter with him. But I have never, as you know, consented to regard our modest allowance of *eau rougie* as an extra. . . . In this country the people have rights, but the person has none.

It was her "person" that Louise Guiney wished to retain, and with it the right to live in her own world, "that green and growing England" where "the gracious parks, the clean-cut hedges, the old abbeys" were "the evidences everywhere of nature controlled and enjoyed to the full." And unlike Mrs. Church, Louise Guiney had of course no daughter to marry off, and she had none of Mrs. Church's concern for the material advantages of those who on a small income found sufficient means to live away from home; living in England was her means of preserving an individuality, of fulfilling the particular nature of her gifts. Her antiquarian researches and her devotions to her faith kept her mind employed and her talents fresh and young; in her chosen environment, she held the motto of her saint, St. Francis de Sales, before her eyes: "In the royal galley of Divine Love there are no galley slaves; all the rowers are volunteers."

> In loneliness, in quaint
> Perpetual constraint [15]

she wrote her essays and her verses, and within them she preserved the quality of seeming to live in pastures above the earth which is the secret of their charm:

> Hither felicity
> Doth climb to me,
> And bank me in with turf and marjoram
> Such as bees lip, or the new-weanèd lamb . . .[16]

[15] "Planting the Poplar" from *Happy Ending*, used by permission of Houghton Mifflin Company.

[16] "Sanctuary" from *Happy Ending*, used by permission of Houghton Mifflin Company.

Through the eyes of her early friends in Boston, she was re-membered as "a slight, blue-eyed girl, delicate as a wild rose, elusive as thistledown," which was perhaps another way of say-ing that she was both reserved and shy. A few of her verses will always speak to the initiate who share an interest in her favorite themes; however willful and extravagant her fancies became, she rarely wrote a shoddy line of verse—and she was the author of one extraordinary poem, "A Friend's Song for Simoisius": [17]

> The breath of dew and twilight's grace
> Be on the lonely battle-place,
> And to so young, so kind a face,
> The long protecting grasses cling!
> (Alas, alas,
> That one inexorable thing!)
>
> In rocky hollows cool and deep,
> The honey-bees unrifled sleep;
> The early moon from Ida steep
> Comes to the empty wrestling-ring;
>
> Upon the widowed wind recede
> No echoes of the shepherd's reed;
> And children without laughter lead
> The war-horse to the watering;
>
> With footstep separate and slow
> The father and the mother go,
> Not now upon an urn they know
> To mingle tears for comforting.
>
> Thou stranger Ajax Telamon!
> What to the lovely hast thou done,
> That nevermore a maid may run
> With him across the flowery Spring?
>
> The world to me has nothing dear
> Beyond the namesake river here:
> Oh, Simois is wild and clear!
> And to his brink my heart I bring;
>
> My heart, if only this might be,
> Would stay his waters from the sea,
> To cover Troy, to cover me,

[17] From *Happy Ending*, used by permission of Houghton Mifflin Company.

To haste the hour of perishing.
(Alas, alas,
That one inexorable thing!)

The expression of classical imagery in Louise Guiney's fresh, clean diction reminds one of what an early critic of her work had written—that it was often felt in reading it as if one had suddenly encountered a Greek temple, standing alone, in an American woodland. In her "Song for Simoisius" Miss Guiney as early as 1893 seems to have anticipated the spirit of a finer poet, who followed her exactly a decade later to London and who wrote memorable poems out of her private vision of another age, H.D.

ADELAIDE CRAPSEY

If there is a pantheon where the memory and the verse of all true poets endure, then Adelaide Crapsey (1878-1914) would indeed be possessed of a distinguished reputation. Unlike Lizette Reese's, her verse had an intellectual quality, a studied, if not strained, simplicity; yet in its way, it was equally delicate and quite as fine as the more freely spontaneous lyricism of the elder poet. Most of her creative years were troubled by ill health, and this circumstance, along with her desire for perfection, seems to have hindered as fine a minor talent as has ever appeared in American poetry. The slim volume of her *Verse,* which was first published in 1915, the year after her death (and was reissued in a final edition in 1922), and *A Study in English Metrics,* also posthumously published in 1918, in which she made an application of theories in phonetics to metrical problems in writing verse, are all we have of her literary remains. But that little, especially in the verse itself, gives evidence of a personality that united sensibility with passion, and fine perceptions with intellectual strength.

She was best known for her "Cinquains," which she had written as an experiment in verse form, an attempt to find the shortest and simplest form for writing English verse, and which were, as her biographer, Mary Elizabeth Osborn, described them, "a working up to and falling away from a climax; with the syllables always two, four, six, eight, two." As her biographer also relates, Milton's use of vowels in "Lycidas" had given her her first interest in prosody. Not unlike Sidney Lanier (1842-81), but with considerably less technical knowledge and sophistication than he possessed, Adelaide Crapsey "felt that certain combinations of sound were particularly effective." Her "Cinquains" bore the characteristic marks of her studies in prosody and if their contribution to the technics of modern poetry is negligible and quite unlikely to be revived, it is all the more certain that they reflected one aspect of her personality and may be said to have lived and died with her. A study, therefore, of her longer poems in other forms gives us a far better impression of her promise and achievements and is far more rewarding than a prolonged review of her frequently quoted "Cinquains."

Adelaide Crapsey was the third of the nine children of the Reverend Algernon Crapsey, "a personality of fire and enthusiasm," who had had a stormy career within the Episcopal Church by leading a revolt against certain of its rituals and who was at last formally deposed from its ministry. Adelaide Crapsey had shared her father's love for the church itself, but she had also received from him an attitude of dissent toward dogma and ritual which became an essential part of her character. "Being brought up in the Crapsey family," wrote Miss Osborn, "meant being brought up in the midst of intellectual experiment." Adelaide Crapsey's mother did not take part in theological disputes, but devoted her energies to church charities and the care of her many children. "To her a family was a collection of personalities, to each of whom courtesy was a duty and reserve was a right." This attitude of aloofness was carried so far that, as Miss Osborn wrote, "Not until after the daughter who was named for her was dead did Mrs. Crapsey know that she had been a poet."

Though Adelaide Crapsey was born in Brooklyn Heights, Brooklyn, her early childhood was spent in Rochester, New York, where her father had accepted a call as rector of St. Andrew's Church. She was sent off to Kemper Hall at Kenosha, Wisconsin, and there was described as being "very tall, delicate, and so vivid and active that no one thought of her as fragile." Up to her graduation from Kemper Hall, she wore her brown hair in two braids, and with characteristic independence, she dressed in a quaint fashion that best suited her—in "Kate Greenaway dresses which set off admirably her delicate features, her vivid eyes and . . . her quick, reticent smile." At Kemper Hall she had begun to write, but almost all of her literary efforts were in prose, and she had received an award for her school work in French.

In 1897 she went to Vassar College where her roommate was Jean Webster, a niece of Mark Twain, who afterwards enjoyed brief fame as the author of a popular novel called *Daddy Long-Legs.* Jean Webster had a lively admiration for poetry and her companionship seems to have been a source of inspiration for Adelaide Crapsey. Miss Florence V. Keys, who was among Adelaide Crapsey's instructors at Vassar, observed in a long letter:

> Her work . . . was of a sound kind; it was "literary" in its quality, by which I mean that while it showed a mind trained in its perceptions it did not have the warmth, concreteness, and individuality that awakened the interest one gives to "originality." Her treatment of things was rather diffuse, and mediated by a mass of critical reading, than concentrated and immediate; literature supporting literature for comparison, not life. . . . At the same time, Adelaide was very popular with quite unliterary girls. . . . Her nature was very wholesome, open, and genial, in an easy, quiet, humorous way that made her thoroughly liked by all kinds. . . . What I have been driving at in the foregoing is this: that she herself was much larger and more vitally interesting than her work as such. . . . Adelaide was deliberate in the use to which she put her thinking and her literary enjoyment.[18]

In 1902, she went back to Kemper Hall as an instructor. She liked to teach, and the opening lines of Milton's "Lycidas" she considered the purest poetry in the language. She delighted in reminding people of:

> Yet once more, O ye Laurels, and once more,
> Ye Myrtles brown, with ivy never-sear,
> I come to pluck your Berries harsh and crude,
> And with forc'd fingers rude,
> Shatter your leaves before the mellowing year.

At Kemper Hall she began her first inquiries into *A Study in English Metrics,* on which she worked until her death and yet left unfinished.

[18] From *Adelaide Crapsey,* by Mary Elizabeth Osborn. Copyright 1933; used by permission of Bruce Humphries, Inc.

After returning from a long stay in Europe in 1911, she accepted a post as instructor at Smith College where a number of her students were to remember her with deep affection. Even her appearance filled them with "love and foreboding. . . . She wore gray now all the time, shades of gray in dresses, coats and hats." They noted her delight in accuracy for the sake of accuracy, and the beauty that she always found in the forms and technics of literature. It was at this time that she began to write her "Cinquains," which had followed the writing of one of her loveliest poems, which had begun as a metrical exercise, an "experiment . . . to show the sequence of rising and falling tone":

> I make my shroud but no one knows,
> So shimmering fine it is and fair,
> With stitches set in even rows.
> I make my shroud but no one knows.
>
> In door-way where the lilac blows,
> Humming a little wandering air,
> I make my shroud and no one knows,
> So shimmering fine it is and fair.[19]

The "experiment," of course, was the most delicate of variations in the form of the French triolet, a form, by the way, which during the 1890's had become the vehicle in English of supposedly light and usually banal verse. Her craftsmanship was so fine that it never seems obtrusive, and whatever personality shines through it, even the "personal" touches, never (as in the case of Edna St. Vincent Millay's poetry which in some early, shorter pieces resembles hers) dominate the poem. Her "Cinquains" are possessed of the same tenuous charm:

THE GUARDED WOUND [20]

> If it
> Were lighter touch
> Than petal of flower resting
> On grass, oh still too heavy it were,
> Too heavy!

[19] "Song" from *Verse*, by permission of Alfred A. Knopf, Inc. Copyright 1934 by Adelaide T. Crapsey. Copyright 1915, 1922 by Algernon S. Crapsey.

[20] From *Verse*, by permission of Alfred A. Knopf, Inc. Copyright 1934 by Adelaide T. Crapsey. Copyright 1915, 1922 by Algernon S. Crapsey.

ARBUTUS [21]

Not Spring's
Thou art, but her's,
Most cool, most virginal,
Winter's, with thy faint breath, thy snows
Rose-tinged.

In 1912, her health, never too robust and of great concern during her stay in Europe, began to fail rapidly. She was forced to give up her teaching and to relax her studies in English prosody. Already her poems had begun to reflect images of an increasing awareness of death, not the heroic image of death, which is so often the common coinage of romantic poetry, but a sense of death that took on a painful and almost physical manifestation of reality in her poetry. In her poem to John Keats she wrote:

> . . . for thou art come
> Upon the remote, cold place
> Of ultimate dissolution and
> With dumb, wide look
> Thou impotent, dost feel
> Impotence creeping on
> Thy potent soul . . .[22]

And in her lyric "Angélique," the image of death became an all-abiding presence, as brilliantly and as sharply realized as the sophisticated simplicity, the "insouciance" of her frequently quoted, "Vendor's Song":

> Have you seen Angélique,
> What way she went?
> A white robe she wore,
> A flickering light near spent
> Her pale hand bore.
>
> Have you seen Angélique?
> Will she know the place
> Dead feet must find,

[21] From *Verse*, by permission of Alfred A. Knopf, Inc. Copyright 1934 by Adelaide T. Crapsey. Copyright 1915, 1922 by Algernon S. Crapsey.

[22] "Poem to John Keats" from *Verse*, by permission of Alfred A. Knopf, Inc. Copyright 1934 by Adelaide T. Crapsey. Copyright 1915, 1922 by Algernon S. Crapsey.

> The grave-cloth on her face
> To make her blind?
>
> Have you seen Angélique . . .
> At night I hear her moan,
> And I shiver in my bed;
> She wanders all alone,
> She cannot find the dead.[23]

She had a room with a balcony in a sanatorium at Saranac, New York, "a room with a view" of what she called "Trudeau's Garden," an old graveyard that had been abandoned many years before by a village population. It was the sight of the graveyard that moved her to restlessness, even to the quick edge of anger, and finally to the writing of one of the longest poems in her collection, "To the Dead in the Graveyard Underneath My Window." This poem, though by no means one of her best, holds its position in her small volume by its value as a personal document. The emotion she attempted to convey is clear enough, but as she wrote it down an unassimilated, all too Miltonic passion seemed to possess her lines, and that full expression of all she had to say seems thwarted of its final purpose and desires. Yet, with all its faults, the poem never fails to attract the reader; the strength as well as the pathos of her intellectual courage seem to flash between its lines, and fragments of her speech to an unanswering audience of the dead might well be quoted as further evidence of the promise she extended toward the poetry of a generation which followed hers:

> Oh, have you no rebellion in your bones?
> The very worms must scorn you where you lie,
> A pallid, mouldering, acquiescent folk,
> Meek habitants of unresented graves.
>
> .   .   .   .   .
>
> And in ironic quietude who is
> The despot of our days and lord of dust
> Needs but, scarce heeding, wait to drop
> Grim casual comment on rebellion's end;

[23] "Angélique" from *Verse*, by permission of Alfred A. Knopf, Inc. Copyright 1934 by Adelaide T. Crapsey. Copyright 1915, 1922 by Algernon S. Crapsey.

"Yes, yes . . . Wilful and petulant but now
As dead and quiet as the others are." [24]

A short time before her death, a special-delivery letter came to her, saying that the *Century* magazine had accepted a few of her poems for early publication. Here, at last, came her first opportunity to gain public recognition as a poet. A spurt of ambition possessed her, and, as she attempted to make a collection of her poems, her strength again failed her. "It's too much," she said. "Just as I have my work, I can't do it."

Though for a while the touching prefaces that Claude Bragdon and Jean Webster had written to her single volume of *Verse* (1915) gave it the kind of recognition earned by any "human document," the actual value of her work is slowly gaining recognition on its own merits. Hers was a poetry of personal identity, which a few years later a number of women poets learned to enlarge, to publicize, to exploit, and therefore gained more notice than Adelaide Crapsey ever attained. But lacking her finesse and intensity, their more ambitious efforts have become outmoded far more rapidly than her few fine poems, and through their brief, unpretentious utterance, the rarefied spirit of her poetic impulse has survived:

> But all the dead of all the world shall know
> The pacing of my sable-sandal'd feet,
> And know my tear-drenched veil along the grass,
> And think them less forsaken in their graves,
> Saying: There's one remembers, one still mourns;
> For the forgotten dead are dead indeed.[25]

The "gentle and intense" woman who made this modest and graceful plea to our memory has not been forgotten.

[24] "To the Dead in the Graveyard Underneath My Window" from *Verse,* by permission of Alfred A. Knopf, Inc. Copyright 1934 by Adelaide T. Crapsey. Copyright 1915, 1922 by Algernon S. Crapsey.

[25] "The Mourner" from *Verse,* by permission of Alfred A. Knopf, Inc. Copyright 1934 by Adelaide T. Crapsey. Copyright 1915, 1922 by Algernon S. Crapsey.

SARA TEASDALE

Within three and four years after the birth of Sara Teasdale (1884-1933) two other poets were born in that most southern of Middle Western cities, St. Louis, Missouri, two poets whose work was so dissimilar to hers that their names can be mentioned only by way of contrast to everything she wrote. These two were Marianne Moore in 1887 and Thomas Stearns Eliot in 1888, and though between their work and Sara Teasdale's there seems more than a generation of advance in technic, subject matter, scope, and reputation, it is sometimes well to recollect that their dates of birth were within a single, and now memorable, half-decade. Though Sara Teasdale seemed always to have been a little old for her age, she also retained some of the instinctive, childlike wisdom and immaturity of those grown old too soon. One thinks of her as one of the "singers" who might well have lightened Clarence Stedman's "twilight interval" with a note of fresh, authentic "song." Like Lizette Reese, Sara Teasdale created the illusion of being born a poet or, as Virginia Woolf once wrote of Christina Rossetti, an "instinctive."

And indeed the likeness of her verse to Christina Rossetti's has more than a casual association; the direct influence of Christina Rossetti's verse may be traced throughout the poems of Sara Teasdale, and it is of no small significance that she was at work on a study of Dante Gabriel Rossetti's remarkable sister when she died in 1933. She had the same fine ear (though not with the complete subtlety of transmitting a gentle and faintly exotic music, so characteristic of Christina Rossetti's verse) and the same gift of expressing intense emotion in a quiet voice. But where Christina Rossetti's theme had been the transfiguration and sublimation of love into religious devotion, Sara Teasdale's verse substituted the experiences and emotions of feminine love for religion itself. The very charm of Christina Rossetti's poetry is the image it conveys of a temperament that suppressed the raptures of a St. Theresa within the well-bred restraints and conventions of a nineteenth-century Anglo-Catholic church. Within this subtle conflict lies the secret of Christina Rossetti's power, for in many ways she betrayed her un-English origins, and in none so poignantly as when she half disclosed her Latin temperament in the authentic voice of mystical devotion and piety. But if Sara Teasdale's earliest ideal of love and its devotion was in the image of Sappho, it was scarcely a Greek poetess at close view—and certainly not the Sappho of the French naturalists, nor the naughty poems of the 1890's.

The Sappho whom Sara Teasdale idealized, and with whom she had early identified her own poetic personality, was one of those figures who might have stepped from the chisel of William Wetmore Story, the American sculptor of the mid-nineteenth century, who after a long stay in Italy and after long contemplation of classic nudes, invested each of his mythological figures with an unmistakable air of New England chastity.

Sara Teasdale was the youngest child of middle-aged parents who seemed to have treated her with doting affection. "Anything that I wanted that my parents could get, came to me," she said, and this surfeit of uncritical devotion from her elders may partially explain her lifelong preoccupation with herself, her own health, her conscious "inner" life, her perpetual invalidism. Her family were well off and took pleasure in encouraging the tastes, desires, education, hopes, and fancies of a frail and talented girl. Before her first book, *Sonnets to Duse and Other Poems,* appeared in 1907, she had traveled widely, and she followed the course of a journey eastward as far as the European continent. Of her first book, Morton Dauwen Zabel wrote, "Sara Teasdale's early work made no pretense of being anything but the literary devotions of a talented girl whose spiritual refinement and good taste were enough to excuse the loose diction and conventional epithets with which she clothed her tributes to Duse, Guenevere, Beatrice, Sappho."

Although Sara Teasdale's lyricism from its earliest appearance in a book always created the impression of spontaneous and liquid movement, as though each poem had been improvised for the occasion of reciting it in a gentle, intimate, almost whispering voice, its artistry was of slow and erratic development. Her first four volumes, including *Love Songs,* published in 1917, showed increasing promise, but relatively small achievement. One suspects that she was the kind of poet whose critical processes (in respect to her own work) flowed on unchecked and unheeded far below the surfaces of her conscious artistry. The proof that they existed may be shown in the distinction of her later poetry as well as in her lack of confidence in completing her study of Christina Rossetti. In Sara Teasdale's case one should not hesitate to point out the obvious fact that her relationship to her work and its progress was intuitive; and one should not be afraid to say that she wrote and published the same poem many times, changing its title and shifting its musical phrasing into a number of pleasing varieties, until at last a final poem appeared which contained the best qualities of a dozen or a score of poems preceding it. Although such a method or process may have seemed prodigal, she remained so clearly within the range of her limitations and her low-pitched variations upon a few well-chosen themes were so persuasive, that one seldom questions her sensitivity or her wisdom in following out the spiral course that she pursued. Even at her third and second best, one notes the progress that she made between a first collection of *Love Songs* in 1911 and her most frequently quoted poem, "The Look," which was included in her 1915 volume, *Rivers to the Sea.* Among a group of earlier *Love Songs,* we find this urgent demand for immediate and unreserved affection:

> Brown-thrush singing all day long
>   In the leaves above me,
> Take my love this April song,
>   "Love me, love me, love me!"
>
> When he harkens what you say,
>   Bid him, lest he miss me,
> Leave his work or leave his play,
>   And kiss me, kiss me, kiss me! [26]

Today these earlier verses stand in contrast to the best and excellently tempered work of her later volumes, and however absurd her early confessions may seem to us today, they were forerunners of a flood of female self-revelations in which Edna

[26] "Love Me" from *Collected Poems.* By permission of The Macmillan Company.

St. Vincent Millay, during the 1920's, rode the crest of the wave, revelations in which no details of a love affair were spared the public, and whole schools of women poets announced proudly that they were with child. From these later movements, Sara Teasdale kept herself aloof. And she often indulged herself in the heresy of saying that she wrote to please herself, with the result that she has pleased more readers than many poets who had larger impulses in writing poetry as well as the hopes of being heard by ever-increasing audiences. "To raise esteem, we must benefit others; to procure love, we must please them," wrote Samuel Johnson in one of his *Rambler* papers. Though Sara Teasdale's object was not to benefit the human race, yet by pleasing herself, she usually managed to please others.

Within her *Rivers to the Sea,* as well as in the five volumes of verse that followed it, one can trace the gradual deepening of her music. Slowly a tone of gravity and dignity possessed it, and as her music assumed deeper qualities, images of descending dark, and autumnal sadness, and of grave and piercing self-knowledge enter a portrait that previously contained the single image of a willful young woman who had been inspired by the need to love and to be loved.

> One by one, like leaves from a tree,
> All my faiths have forsaken me.
>
> . . . . . .
>
> I have lost the leaves that knew
> Touch of rain and weight of dew.[27]

A life, such as hers, devoted to an unceasing analysis of highly sensitized personal emotion, is always guaranteed to cause eventual restlessness in an intelligent woman, and Sara Teasdale's letters, however briefly quoted in Louis Untermeyer's *From Another World,* disclosed certain active perceptions, intuitions, and flashes of common sense that indicated the critical processes at work below the smoothly rippling surfaces of her poetry. One of the attractive features of her verse was its peculiarly classical quality, a quality that permeates her best work and is a corrective to the sentimental exuberances of "The Look" and the

[27] "Leaves" from *Collected Poems.* By permission of The Macmillan Company.

bathetic simplicities of "Love Me" and "The Song for Colin." If her classicism never lost its relationship to the New England chastities of William Wetmore Story, her later poems were distinguished by their purity of diction, movement, and image—and in this interpretation of the classical spirit and its restraint we find the secret of Sara Teasdale's most subtle if not most popular charm. The first glimpse of her most enduring quality came to light in 1915.

VILLA SERBELLONI, BELLAGGIO [28]

> The fountain shivers lightly in the rain,
>   The laurels drip, the fading roses fall,
> The marble satyr plays a mournful strain
>   That leaves the rainy fragrance musical.
>
> Oh dripping laurel, Phoebus sacred tree,
>   Would that swift Daphne's lot might come to me,
> Then would I still my soul and for an hour
>   Change to a laurel in the glancing shower.

The solid facts of her biography bear a tenuous, almost unreal relationship to her poetry. In 1914 she married Ernst Filsinger, a heavy-shouldered, prosperous businessman, whose weighty and protective interest in literature included a vague and yet tender admiration for the fantasies of Walter de la Mare. Sara Teasdale herself was a tall, plain-featured woman, angular and pale; at first glance she seemed the very image of the middle-aged, overworked, conscientious, maidenly schoolmistress who still exists in the imagination of the American public. This illusion was soon dispelled by the extraordinary animation of her voice and the clear, brilliant light that seemed reflected from her pince-nez. After twelve years of marriage, she decided to live alone in a New York apartment where she limited the large circle of her acquaintances to a few friends. It was two years before this decision that her best volume of verse, *Dark of the Moon*, appeared. From then onward to 1933 there was scarcely a poem which she published that did not possess its own unpretentious charm; she had become the mistress of a style whose

28 "Vignettes Overseas, IX: Villa Serbelloni, Bellaggio" from *Collected Poems*. By permission of The Macmillan Company.

simplicity was not without a touch of austere elegance. Intimations of this latter refinement of an elegiac style, with its melancholy undertones and graceful turn of phrase, had made a tentative arrival as early as 1920 in her *Flame and Shadow,* and its beginnings may be traced through

> Let it be forgotten, as a flower is forgotten,
>   Forgotten as a fire that once was singing gold . . .
>
> .   .   .   .
>
> If anyone asks, say it was forgotten
>   Long and long ago,
> As a flower, as a fire, as a hushed footfall
>   In a long forgotten snow.[29]

The personality she had created in her poems felt that the times as well as her individual character were less youthful and less assured of an affirmative answer to her question

> After the stillness, will spring come again?

She had already written:

> I must have passed the crest a while ago
>   And now I am going down—
> Strange to have crossed the crest and not to know,
>   But the brambles were always catching the hem of my gown.
>
> .   .   .   .
>
> It was nearly level along the beaten track
>   And the brambles caught in my gown—
> But it's no use now to think of turning back,
>   The rest of the way will be only going down.[30]

Autumn had become her season and in "Arcturus in Autumn," [31] she wrote what might well be read as her valediction:

> When, in the gold October dusk, I saw you near to setting,
>   Arcturus, bringer of spring,
> Lord of the summer nights, leaving us now in autumn,
>   Having no pity on our withering;

[29] "Let It Be Forgotten" from *Collected Poems.* By permission of The Macmillan Company.

[30] "The Long Hill" from *Collected Poems.* By permission of The Macmillan Company.

[31] From *Collected Poems.* By permission of The Macmillan Company.

Oh then I knew at last that my own autumn was upon me,
   I felt it in my blood,
Restless as dwindling streams that still remember
   The music of their flood.

There in the thickening dark a wind-bent tree above me
   Loosed its last leaves in flight—
I saw you sink and vanish, pitiless Arcturus,
   You will not stay to share our lengthening night.

The four "autumn" poems written in France in 1923 are more than sufficient evidence of the final artistry her verse achieved. "Autumn (Parc Monceau)" brings to mind the formal graces of André Chénier, and indeed the poem seems to celebrate the memory of late eighteenth-century classicism that contained within its courtly, if not wholly urban, pastorals the early seeds of Continental romanticism. The poem has a purity of form and a technical brilliance that is equaled only by her "Fontainebleau," for here one rediscovers a quality in Sara Teasdale's art that is all too seldom stressed in the customary revaluations of her poetry:

Interminable palaces front on the green parterres,
   And ghosts of ladies lovely and immoral
Glide down the gilded stairs,
   The high cold corridors are clicking with the heel taps
That long ago were theirs.

But in the sunshine, in the vague autumn sunshine,
   The geometric gardens are desolately gay;
The crimson and scarlet and rose-red dahlias
   Are painted like the ladies who used to pass this way
With a ringletted monarch, a Henry or a Louis
   On a lost October day.

The aisles of the garden lead into the forest,
   The aisles lead into autumn, a damp wind grieves,
Ghostly kings are hunting, the boar breaks cover,
   But the sounds of horse and horn are hushed in falling leaves,
Four centuries of autumn, four centuries of leaves.[82]

[82] "Fontainebleau" from *Collected Poems*. By permission of The Macmillan Company.

In 1933 Sara Teasdale's death was caused by an overdose of sleeping tablets, and during that year, her last book of lyrics, *Strange Victory,* was posthumously published. These include the title poem and "In a Darkening Garden" in which the clear imagery and deepening melancholy music seem now to have foretold her end:

> All that was mortal shall be burned away,
>   All that was mind shall have been put to sleep.
> Only the spirit shall awake to say
>   What the deep says to the deep . . .[33]

Her large volume of *Collected Poems* which was published in 1937, was a book that contained over three hundred poems. If the book had been reduced to a selection of fifty titles and edited with the intelligence that had gone into George Santayana's 1922 edition of his *Poems,* Sara Teasdale's reputation would stand much higher in critical esteem than it does today.

During the years of the "poetic renaissance" which followed the publication of her first book, and the succeeding 1920's, Sara Teasdale's verse retained its associations with an earlier period in American poetry. Throughout its progress one discerns a last look backward into Stedman's "twilight interval." But if it anticipated a later school of which Edna St. Vincent Millay became the acknowledged mistress, its sensibilities also reached beyond the 1920's toward a revival of the elegiac tradition in Anglo-American verse. Not unlike the best of George Santayana's poetry, the best of Sara Teasdale's verses transcend the more facile definitions of belonging to a particular school, or to those distinctions which determine the sex of the author, or of being related to a particular nationality. It may be said that her verse had always been written in a distinctly minor key—but this definition does not modify its occasional excellence, nor the mature if muted notes of its later lyrical utterance.

The public response to Sara Teasdale's verse has always been phenomenal; her celebrity was quickly established by *Love Songs* in 1917, which was followed by public neglect during the ten

[33] "All That Was Mortal" from *Collected Poems.* By permission of The Macmillan Company.

years preceding her death in 1933. Five years later, and after the publication of her posthumous *Collected Poems,* public interest in her verse was rearoused; her book went through several editions in rapid order, and one concludes that her anonymous readers showed more discernment than the majority of her critics whose attention had been too closely held by the transitory excitements and diversions of "schools" and "movements" in American poetry.

LA COMÉDIE HUMAINE *OF E. A. ROBINSON*

> . . . I said. "Go on. The Lord giveth,
> The Lord taketh away. I trust myself
> Always to you and to your courtesy.
> Only remember that I cling somewhat
> Affectionately to the old tradition."
>
> "AVON'S HARVEST" [1] (1921)

> Time shall have more to say than men shall hear
> Between now and the coming of that harvest
> Which is to come. Before it comes, I go—
> By the short road that mystery makes long
> For man's endurance of accomplishment.
> I shall have more to say when I am dead.
>
> "JOHN BROWN" [2] (1920)

Unlikely as it may have seemed in 1900, Edmund Clarence Stedman's "twilight interval" was to produce its major poet. His presence was acknowledged by Stedman himself, but it was not until two decades had been spent in admiration of less enduring talents that the reasons for his reticence and the true values of his poetry began to be understood. From 1904 onward to the day of his death in 1935 E. A. Robinson's poetry has been subject to (one almost says "victimized by") extraordinary and erratic bursts of praise; and the praise has always been followed by longer periods of critical silence and indifference. It would be mere sentimentality to enlarge upon a general neglect of his work, and untrue to say that both the man and his poetry were consistently unappreciated; from the very beginning of his life as a poet he seemed to write for the few—and those few were as widely separate as Josephine Preston Peabody in Boston; Stedman, who had retired to his home in suburban Bronxville;

---

[1] From *Collected Poems*. By permission of The Macmillan Company.
[2] *Ibid.*

Joseph Lewis French, a battered, indigent journalist, who wrote "special feature stories" for the Sunday *World* in New York; and Theodore Roosevelt, the chief executive of the United States, in the White House. Near the close of Robinson's career in 1927, after his *Tristram,* a long narrative in verse, had been distributed by a book club, The Literary Guild, the earlier cycle of spectacular fame, an almost dangerous notoriety, reasserted itself. *Tristram* became phenomenally popular—and it was by no means the most fortunate of his longer poems. Five years after his death, Robinson's name was seldom spoken, and another period of silence has obscured the merits of his poetry.

Since his poetry is in true need of reappraisal, this is no occasion to dwell too long upon the external facts of his biography, and for those who are interested in them alone, Hermann Hagedorn's "official" life, *Edwin Arlington Robinson,* published in 1938, can be read with a moderate degree of satisfaction. Like many "official" lives, the book is not the definitive biography; Hagedorn lacked the orderly diligence of a James Boswell, but one feels that no essential details of Robinson's life have been willfully distorted, and it also seems, since a number of Robinson's friends and acquaintances are still alive, that Hagedorn accomplished his difficult assignment with a fair if unbrilliant exercise of tact and propriety. Ridgely Torrence's *Selected Letters of Edwin Arlington Robinson* is even less satisfactory; the slender volume of 178 pages seems to have been edited with a fear of what "people would say" and an unclear perception of their relationship to Robinson's poetry.

In the present instance only those biographical details which may illuminate E. A. Robinson's contribution to American poetry will receive our attention, and beyond them, Hermann Hagedorn's book should perform its service in gratifying the modified interest of the general reader.

2

Edwin Arlington Robinson was born in the little town of Head Tide in Maine in 1869, but in the following year his family moved to Gardiner, "Tilbury Town," the named and true environment of so many of his poems, which was his boyhood home and where his father became a director of a local bank.

Amy Lowell, who knew her New England with the thoroughness of native authority, once wrote of Gardiner:

I know of no place in America so English in atmosphere as Gardiner. Standing on the broad blue Kennebec, the little town nestles proudly beside that strange anomaly in an American city—the manor-house. For Gardiner, so far as custom is concerned, possessed a squire for over two hundred years. And this gentleman's house is as truly "the great house" as that in any hamlet in England. A fine Tudor mansion of grey stone with rounded bow windows, it stands on a little hill above the river and even the railroad tracks which modern commercialism has inconsiderately laid along the nearer bank cannot take away from its air of dominating dignity.[3]

It is also well to remember that if Robinson's family did not occupy a Tudor mansion, it was of the eldest New England heritage, that it numbered among its ancestors Anne Bradstreet, that it had been both distinguished and prosperous, that two generations after the Civil War, in a period when the voices of urban Chicago and New York and of the pioneer Middle and Far West sounded their echoes even in *The Atlantic Monthly*, it had produced a Robinson who recalled the accents of his "old tradition" with appropriate irony:

> Good glasses are to read the spirit through.

> And whoso reads may get him some shrewd skill;
> And some unprofitable scorn resign,
> To praise the very thing that he deplores;
> So, friends (dear friends), remember, if you will,
> The shame I win for singing is all mine,
> The gold I miss for dreaming is all yours.[4]

He had been brought up in one of those New England towns in which the very houses were "the appropriate frames for gracious mahogany, crested family silver, ivory and lacquer brought from China by seafaring ancestors." These houses were

---

[3] From *Tendencies in Modern American Poetry*, used by permission of Houghton Mifflin Company.

[4] "Dear Friends" from *Children of the Night*. By permission of Charles Scribner's Sons.

stocked with books as well as the memories of fathers and grand-fathers who had corresponded with half the learned societies of Europe, and "Tilbury Town" itself chose to honor and to com-memorate its many distinguished residents who had made their contributions to letters and the arts, and had gone out into the larger worlds of London, or Paris, or Boston, or Philadelphia, or New York.

In these surroundings during his precollege days, Robinson formed his taste in reading, and cultivated shyly but consistently a love for music; he carried the published scores of *Faust, Lucia di Lammermoor,* and *Martha* about with him and into the houses of his friends. His reading included Bryant's *Library of Poetry and Song,* Leigh Hunt, Charles Lamb, Jane Austen, Haz-litt, and Ruskin's *Sesame and Lilies*—and in his environment this seems a natural course for his early reading to take. Even his love of Dickens which he retained to the end of his life does not seem extraordinary, and his delight in Tennyson can almost be taken for granted. The unusual turn in his discriminations came with his pleasure at being invited to sit with his elders in a "literary club" to hear Ronsard or Villon or Verlaine read in the original and then promptly translated; this resembled an entry into the Lyceum circles that Ralph Waldo Emerson knew in his youth, and in the same vein Robinson's interest in poetry was stimulated by his own facility in translating Horace and Vergil, or turning the weighted periods of Cicero's orations into lines of blank verse in English. The same notes of discrimina-tion are heard in his early sonnets on Thomas Hood and George Crabbe; the reading falls frankly enough within a traditional pattern, but important variations were introduced; the tendency was toward a classical firmness of speech and moral suasion, balanced by a sudden appreciation of Verlaine, or of Wagner and Beethoven in music, or a lesser romantic poet of the early nineteenth century. If we are to trust his "Captain Craig" these choices were overlaid by a thorough rereading of the Bible and

> Wordsworth, Pope,
> Lucretius, Robert Burns, and William Shakespeare [5]

[5] "Captain Craig" from *Collected Poems*. By permission of The Macmillan Company.

and in music

> Play Handel, not Chopin; assuredly not
> Chopin.[6]

And in a letter written as late as 1917 he wrote:

> When I was younger, I was very much under the influence of Words-worth and Kipling, but never at all, so far as I am aware, under that of Browning, as many seem to believe. As a matter of fact, I have never been able to understand the alleged relationship unless it can be attributed to my use of rather more colloquial language than "poetic diction" has usually sanctioned. . . .
>
> I thought nothing when I was writing my first book of working for a week over a single line; and while I don't do it any more, I am sure that my technique is better for those early grilling exercises.[7]

But between the writing of a completed version of "Captain Craig" and Robinson's youth in Gardiner, ten years had elapsed: he had spent two years at Harvard where he showed himself far less precocious in the years 1891 to 1893 than Moody, Lodge, and Stickney, and because of the sudden collapse of his family's fortune, he had withdrawn from Cambridge to Gardiner; in his retreat he had found time to read through all of Nathaniel Hawthorne's prose and reread *The Scarlet Letter* twice; in 1896 and in 1897 he had privately published his first two books of poems, *The Torrent and the Night Before* and *The Children of the Night,* and after a brief period of oscillation between New York, Boston, Cambridge, and Gardiner, he had at last settled himself, precariously enough, in 1899 in the neighborhood of Gramercy Park, New York.

Robinson's short stay at Harvard had values which could not be determined at the time; his temperament, his habitual shyness (which afterwards contributed so hugely to the legend of his personality, and which had a resemblance to the carefully worded reticence of Henry James) had placed him at a measurable distance from his fellow undergraduates and completely obscured him from the view of his instructors. His acquaintance with William Vaughn Moody was of the slightest order and it did

---

[6] "Captain Craig" from *Collected Poems.* By permission of The Macmillan Company.

[7] Letter to L. N. Chase from *Selected Letters of Edwin Arlington Robinson.* By permission of The Macmillan Company and the author's estate.

not strike fire until a later meeting in New York. When Robinson was invited to meet the undergraduate editors of the *Advocate*, "I sat there," so he wrote afterwards, "unable to say a word." From his undergraduate days to the end of his life, he shied away from people who talked too glibly, too confidently of "literature" or of literary gossip and its ambitions; over a glass of whisky or of rum he chose less respectable companions and listened with an attention that is seldom reserved for such occasions to what they had to say. Of the courses in which he enrolled under President Eliot's elective system, perhaps only one, which was Charles Eliot Norton's "Fine Arts 3," carried its impressions into *Children of the Night,* and one almost hears Norton's fine appreciation of classical literatures in the concluding stanza of Robinson's "The Chorus of Old Men" in "Aegeus": [8]

> Better his end had been as the end of a cloudless day,
> Bright, by the word of Zeus, with a golden star,
> Wrought of a golden fame, and flung to the central sky,
> To gleam on a stormless tomb for evermore:—
> Whether or not there fell
> To the touch of an alien hand
> The sheen of his purple robe and the shine of his diadem,
> Better his end had been
> To die as an old man dies,—
> But the fates are ever the fates, and a crown is ever a crown.

Whatever advantages Robinson gained at Harvard were of a sort that yielded readily to his own character and his emotions: his going to Cambridge kept him within a circle from which he could later view New York through the eyes of one who had rightfully inherited the "old tradition" that had clung to "the little Athens" of the nineteenth century; for him the true source of the "old tradition" was Gardiner itself, but Harvard extended, however briefly, a line of continuity. The other advantage, that of leaving Harvard too soon and with the distressing circumstance of a lack of money, increased his sense of failure (which had been present throughout his efforts to find editors who were

---

[8] From *Children of The Night,* used by permission of Charles Scribner's Sons.

willing to accept his poems), and brought him to the threshold of a maturity that does not rest upon easily won academic honors; nor was it trapped and retarded by the memory of "happy days" once spent at college. If, during his stay at Harvard, he had few of those external signs of possessing talent which bring with them early rewards and transitory fame, his "invisible advance" toward poetic maturity was by no means slow; the lyrics of his first two volumes were enough to show it, and no poem written by his contemporaries at Harvard, including Moody and Trumbull Stickney, could equal in 1897 the purity of diction and the sensibility of "Luke Havergal." The poem has been reprinted in many anthologies since the day of its publication nearly a half century ago; it remains as fresh today as it ever was, and it will probably survive all schools and fashions in American poetry of the twentieth century.

We may skip if we wish that vast accumulation of fact and legend surrounding Robinson's "job," as he would have called it, as time-checker in the New York subway from the autumn of 1903 to the late summer of 1904; to the reader of Robinson's poetry, the story has the merits of taking on symbolic value: he had literally shared the darkness of an underworld that greeted his "Bewick Finzer" [9] of whom he wrote a decade later, and with Finzer he knew

> The cleanliness of indigence,
>   The brilliance of despair,
> The fond imponderable dreams
>   Of affluence,—all were there.
>
> .   .   .   .   .   .
>
> He comes unfailing for the loan
>   We give and then forget;
> He comes, and probably for years
>   Will he be coming yet,—
> Familiar as an old mistake,
>   And futile as regret.

The occasional extremes of Robinson's poverty which he faced with the same reticence with which he viewed a turn of good fortune or notoriety (for his friend Joseph Lewis French had

[9] From *Collected Poems*. By permission of The Macmillan Company.

sold a feature story of "The Poet in the Subway" to the Sunday
World) had their likeness in the current of melodrama and the
quickening contrasts of images—of lights and shadows that run
their courses through his poetry. Even in the least rewarding of
his later narratives in verse, the flagging interest of the reader is
suddenly reawakened by a flash of melodrama:

> There was a dark eruption all at once
> Of smoke and sudden flame from a tall funnel
> That leaned before it fell; and all on board
> Were singing so that Fargo on the wharf
> Could hear their sound of joy—till a dull roar
> Became a silence, and there was no ship,
> And no more sound.[10]

And it should be remembered that immediately following
Robinson's experiences in the subway came public recognition
of his gifts by Theodore Roosevelt. He was by no means unconscious of the symbolic nature of the contrast. He had written
earlier to Miss Peabody, "I was a tragedy in the beginning, and
it is hardly probable that I shall ever be anything else," and in
reference to his work in the subway, he continued, "Just what
manner of cave I may select for a time is of no importance." In
his actual meeting with the President, the superficial layers of
Robinson's shyness dropped away; he was as much at ease in
talking to Roosevelt as he was to the men who worked under
him in the subway; it was the heir of one elderly heritage in
American society meeting another on equal ground, and the
Roosevelt family, including those of the present generation, lived
outside the circle that embraces middle-class society. Like the
landed gentry of Whig persuasion in England of the eighteenth
century, the Roosevelts met their equals or those who are dis-
enfranchised by poverty with like courtesy and understanding;
instinctively, they lived up to the custom of the true aristocrat,
who meets the peasant or "failure" without constraint because
one is as much above the law as the other is below it—and Robinson shared the same understanding and privilege.

The President's recognition brought Robinson an appointment

[10] "Amaranth" from *Collected Poems*. By permission of The Macmillan
Company.

to a desk in the Custom House in Wall Street which he held from 1905 to 1909, but Roosevelt's praise of his poetry in the *Outlook* had the not unexpected result of awakening the resentment and distrust of professional critics, and their ill temper was expressed by one who wrote:

We do not dispute the President's dictum, but we suspect that he has not kept au courant with the flood of American minor verse. Had he done so, he would think twice before applying the word, "genius," to Mr. Robinson.

The only critic of the day who was properly equipped to appraise Robinson's work, Paul Elmer More, did not do so; the dramatic cycle of Robinson's notoriety had frightened him away —but the small group of Robinson's friends, and he was never without an admiring friend or two, someone who would buy him a drink, or pay a small debt secretly and in a manner not to offend his spirit of independence, at last in 1911 secured for him the privilege of staying rent-free during the summer months at the MacDowell Colony which was a few miles outside the small town of Peterborough, New Hampshire. This was a return to the simplicities of his own environment; and the wise, sympathetic, and thrifty hospitality of Edward MacDowell's widow, a concert pianist of rare sensibility and discernment, helped to create a suitable atmosphere for the writing of his poems. From this time onward the details of his biography become those of any man who is absorbed in his work and who has gained sufficient self-knowledge to extend his powers. All through his life he inspired the protective instincts of others, and it was this secret charm that had kept him afloat in the most difficult years of his life. The MacDowell Colony became his true home, but he continued to return to New York for the winter months, and on fine mid-afternoons, his tall, graceful, conservatively dressed figure could be seen in Chelsea or on 8th Street, walking briskly, weaving slightly, stripping off the heads of imaginary daisies along the curb with the end of his stick.[11]

11 For the literal-minded who may look upon the last few lines as a poetic fancy it may be explained that he was seen by one of the authors of this book exactly as it has been described.

3

In "Captain Craig," which was the first and in some respects the most important of his major poems, Robinson had found a vehicle for the expression of his major themes and observed with admirable propriety the scene around him. Here we approach the so-called problems of his "philosophy," and as we speak of them, we should take care to view them in the terms of dramatic poetry which are implicit and not as one runs through the naming of philosophic terms for their own sake. It should never be forgotten that all of Robinson's verse, whether in lyrical or dramatic narrative forms, was invested with the spirit of high and serious comedy—and such a spirit, however humane or however deeply concerned it may become with the sight of human failure and defeat, is not likely to be distracted by what Henry Adams called "conservative Christian anarchy" which had so sorely afflicted George Cabot Lodge and Trumbull Stickney. Such a spirit is likely to become critical of the "sad" attitudes that young Lodge and Stickney assumed so readily in verse:

> Miniver Cheevy, child of scorn,
>   Grew lean while he assailed the seasons;
> He wept that he was ever born,
>   And he had reasons.
>
>   .   .   .   .
>
> Miniver scorned the gold he sought,
>   But sore annoyed was he without it;
> Miniver thought, and thought, and thought,
>   And thought about it.[12]

It is significant that Robinson's Captain Craig was an elderly man (and for that matter all of Robinson's heroes were elderly men, or well past the harried stages of early middle age, whether they were variously named Merlin, or Archibald, or Isaac, or John Brown, or Mr. Flood, or even Ben Jonson) and if Captain Craig had anything to say concerning the philosophic sadness of the young, it was not complimentary:

[12] "Miniver Cheevy" from *Town Down by the River*. By permission of Charles Scribner's Sons.

> And after time,
> When we have earned our spiritual ears,
> And art's commiseration of the truth
> No longer glorifies the singing beast,
> Or venerates the clinquant charlatan,—
> Then shall at last come ringing through the sun,
> Through time, through flesh, a music that is true.
> For wisdom is that music, and a'l joy
> That wisdom:—you may counterfeit, you think,
> The burden of it in a thousand ways;
> But as the bitterness that loads your tears
> Makes Dead Sea swimming easy, so the gloom,
> The penance, and the woeful pride you keep,
> Make bitterness the buoyance of your world.[13]

Captain Craig, the ancient "failure" of "Tilbury Town," was likened by his author to Socrates; and he was a Socrates whose unknown God, like Jehovah of the Hebrews, was not witnessed in an image, and if he had a latter-day propensity for wit and ironic mirth, his resemblance to the God of the Puritan Fathers is clearly evident in his rejection of adjectives to modify his commands:

> And we have made innumerable books
> To please the Unknown God. Time throws away
> Dead thousands of them, but the God that knows
> No death denies not one: the books all count,
> The songs all count; and yet God's music has
> No modes, his language has no adjectives.[14]

Before we venture further into the moralities of Captain Craig and his invocations to the spirit of high comedy, a word should be said of his alertness in literary criticism and the excellence of the parodies that Robinson set before him in the persons of Count Pretzel von Wurzburger and Mr. Killigrew. If as Ima Honaker Herron remarked in her study of *The Small Town in American Literature* Robinson's "Tilbury Town" anticipated Edgar Lee Masters' "Spoon River," Von Wurzburger and Killi-

[13] "Captain Craig" from *Collected Poems*. By permission of The Macmillan Company.
[14] *Ibid.*

grew in "Captain Craig" also anticipated (and with greater art and skill) the arrival of Edgar Lee Masters' "Petit the Poet." Von Wurzburger's sonnet on Carmichael and the *Frogs* of Aristophanes is a beautifully tempered burlesque of the would-be sophisticated sonnet written in New York's Greenwich Village from 1900 to 1925; Von Wurzburger's sonnet belongs to that curious underworld of poetic activity in which the poet says more than he knows, and his ironies, however cleverly contrived, fall into bathos. Mr. Killigrew's lyric, "A Ballad of London," clearly reflects the work of those Americans who had read both unwisely and too well the ballads written by Tennyson, William Morris, Rossetti, and Swinburne—and it even suggests the imminent arrival of another British poet whose first book was published in 1902, coinciding with the publication of "Captain Craig"—Alfred Noyes. Captain Craig was not very gentle with Mr. Killigrew:

> I cannot say for certain, but I think
> The brown bright nightingale was half assuaged
> Before your Mr. Killigrew was born.
> If I have erred in my chronology,
> No matter,—for the feathered man sings now:
>
> " 'Yes, I go to London Town'
>   (Merrily waved the feather),
>   'And if you go to London Town,
>   Yes, we'll go together.'
>   So in the autumn bright and brown,
>   Just as the year began to frown,
>   All the way to London Town
>   Rode the two together.
>
> " 'I go to marry a fair maid'
>   (Lightly swung the feather)—
>   'Pardie, a true and loyal maid'
>   (Oh, the swinging feather!)—
>   'For us the wedding gold is weighed,
>   For us the feast will soon be laid;
>   We'll make a gallant show,' he said,—
>   'She and I together.' " [15]

---

[15] "Captain Craig" from *Collected Poems*. By permission of The Macmillan Company.

And Captain Craig concluded his commentary with:

> You are one
> To judge; and you will tell me what you think.
> Barring the Town, the Fair Maid, and the Feather,
> The dialogue and those parentheses,
> You cherish it, undoubtedly. 'Pardie!'
> You call it, with a few conservative
> Allowances, an excellent small thing
> For patient inexperience to do:
> Derivative, you say,—still rather pretty.
> But what is wrong with Mr. Killigrew?
> Is he in love, or has he read Rossetti? [16]

Captain Craig was concerned with larger matters than the quality of Mr. Killigrew's verse, but he embraced it generously within the scope of his meditations. The comedy that Captain Craig learned to regard as the fact of his existence came to him through the slow progress of self-knowledge which transcended his failure and the lives of those around him:

> Take on yourself
> But your sincerity, and you take on
> Good promise for all climbing: fly for truth,
> And hell shall have no storm to crush your flight . . .[17]

His progress, which was not unlike the progress of other characters in Robinson's poems, ran a course that lies parallel to Lambert Strether's progress in Henry James's masterpiece, *The Ambassadors;* his problems were not, of course, of precisely the same nature, but like Strether, Craig was a New Englander who saw more of the world (even if he saw much of it vicariously) than his neighbors. Craig could agree with Strether's lately-arrived-at discovery on that memorable afternoon in Paris in the sculptor Gloriani's garden—and Strether also had a habit of speaking aloud his mind to his young friends:

"Live all you can; it's a mistake not to. It doesn't so much matter what you do in particular, so long as you have your life. If you haven't

[16] "Captain Craig" from *Collected Poems.* By permission of The Macmillan Company.
[17] *Ibid.*

had that what *have* you had? I'm too old—too old at any rate for what
I see. What one loses one loses; make no mistake about that. Still, we
have the illusion of freedom; therefore don't, like me today, be without
the memory of that illusion. I was either, at the right time, too stupid
or too intelligent to have it, and now I'm a case of reaction against
the mistake. Do what you like so long as you don't make it. For it *was*
a mistake. Live, live!" [18]

Craig substituted the word "climb" for Strether's "live," but
both were vitally concerned with the "truth" of their respective
positions—and they viewed it with the customary restraint of
nineteenth-century New Englanders whose conduct had been
regulated and then set in motion by an unseen and unknown
God. Strether's young Mrs. Popcock, who, when he had failed
to rescue her brother from the toils of Paris and Mme. de
Vionnet, followed him to Europe, was not unlike a lady whom
Craig knew; at the very least, she was of the same world:

> There goes a woman cursed with happiness:
> Beauty and wealth, health, horses,—everything
> That she could ask, or we could ask, is hers,
> Except an inward eye for the dim fact
> Of what this dark world is. The cleverness
> God gave her—or the devil—cautions her
> That she must keep the china cup of life
> Filled somehow, and she fills it—runs it over—
> Claps her white hands while some one does the sopping
> With fingers made, she thinks, for just that purpose,
> Giggles and eats and reads and goes to church,
> Makes pretty little penitential prayers,
> And has an eighteen-carat crucifix
> Wrapped up in chamois-skin. She gives enough,
> You say; but what is giving like hers worth? [19]

Strether heard the reply to this kind of lady from the lips of
Mme. de Vionnet—for she had seen evil in "this dark world" and
had survived the sight of it:

"What I hate is myself—when I think that one has to take so much,
to be happy, out of the lives of others, and that one isn't happy even

[18] *The Ambassadors*, Book V, Chapter II, preface. By permission of Harper
& Brothers.
[19] "Captain Craig" from *Collected Poems*. By permission of The Macmillan
Company.

then. One does it to cheat one's self and to stop one's mouth—but that's only at the best for a little. The wretched self is always there, always making one somehow a fresh anxiety. What it comes to is that it's not, that it's never, a happiness, any happiness at all, to *take*. The only safe thing is to give. It's what plays you least false." [20]

And to this speech Craig had a corollary:

> There's yet another flower that grows well
> And has the most unconscionable roots
> Of any weed on earth. Perennial
> It grows, and has the name of Selfishness;
> No doubt you call it Love.[21]

In presenting these parallels between James and Robinson, there is no implication that they had read one another, or had in any way allowed an exchange of influences to pass between them: the point of quoting them in the present order is to show that they inhabited the same moral climate, and that both men separately held in respect the progress of self-realization and self-knowledge.

Even Robinson's frequent progress toward discovering a "light" in "darkness" has its highly sensitized presence in the last scene of James's "The Altar of the Dead" [22]—and the image is transformed to the "gap in the array," the missing candle among the others at the shrine:

He let himself go, resting on her; he dropped upon the bench, and she fell on her knees beside him, his own arm around her shoulder. So he remained an instant, staring up at his shrine. "They say there's a gap in the array—they say it's not full, complete. Just one more," he went on, softly—"isn't that what you wanted? Yes, one more, one more."

4

Many of Robinson's early critics spoke of his "gloom" and of his "pessimism" but at these points it is always better to agree

[20] From *The Ambassadors*, Book XII, Chapter I. By permission of Harper & Brothers.

[21] "Captain Craig" from *Collected Poems*. By permission of The Macmillan Company.

[22] From *Terminations*, used by permission of Harper & Brothers.

with Morton Dauwen Zabel's estimate of Robinson's position—and Zabel, by the way, was among the first to make a serious, if all too brief, contribution toward a reappraisal of Robinson's work:

> Robinson joined passion with judgment, sympathy with prudence, and a tough American loyalty with contempt for the abuses that were defiling the American heritage and giving it over to a brutal materialism that not only worsted the fine hopes of his pragmatic grandfathers, but drove him personally and by sheer revulsion away from the sideshows and vulgarizations of the affluent age around him.[23]

But what no critic has properly emphasized are the notes of wit and elegance and charm, all of which were well in keeping with the seriously mannered comic spirit that he invoked, and which permeated the best of his longer poems as well as controlled the almost faultless pace and phrasing of his shorter lyrics. If Robinson was awkward, flat, and ill at ease in writing prose, a fact which his published letters overwhelmingly testify, there is no lack of a beautifully articulated grace and wit in his poetry:

> The man Flammonde, from God knows where,
> With firm address and foreign air,
> With news of nations in his talk
> And something royal in his walk,
>
> .   .   .   .
>
> Erect, with his alert repose
> About him, and about his clothes,
> He pictured all tradition hears
> Of what we owe to fifty years.
> His cleansing heritage of taste
> Paraded neither want nor waste;
> And what he needed for his fee
> To live, he borrowed graciously.[24]

And in a deeper vein in which the emotion expressed is elegiac, the same reticence, the same classical graces are discerned:

[23] From an article on E. A. Robinson by Morton Dauwen Zabel, August 28, 1937. Used by permission of *The Nation*.

[24] "Flammonde" from *Collected Poems*. By permission of The Macmillan Company.

FOR A DEAD LADY [25]

No more with overflowing light
Shall fill the eyes that now are faded,
Nor shall another's fringe with night
Their woman-hidden world as they did.
No more shall quiver down the days
The flowing wonder of her ways,
Whereof no language may requite
The shifting and the many-shaded.

The grace, divine, definitive,
Clings only as a faint forestalling;
The laugh that love could not forgive
Is hushed, and answers to no calling;
The forehead and the little ears
Have gone where Saturn keeps the years;
The breast where roses could not live
Has done with rising and with falling.

The beauty, shattered by the laws
That have creation in their keeping,
No longer trembles at applause,
Or over children that are sleeping;
And we who delve in beauty's lore
Know all that we have known before
Of what inexorable cause
Makes Time so vicious in his reaping.

Not since the eighteenth century had any poet in English employed the arts of poetic wit with greater poise than Robinson. If his language was clipped and dry—a characteristic to which his early editors objected—and if, as Morton Dauwen Zabel has so pertinently remarked, the progress of his phrasing was "syllogistic," the formal graces of his brief elegy should not be overlooked; they return in a persistent strain throughout his many minor poems, and they lift, even at the conclusion of his least fortunate dramatic narratives, whatever seems overweighted or inappropriate. Though it is doubtful if many readers of the future will have the patience to re-endure the trials of the men and women who talk too much and meditate too often in the

25 From *Town Down by the River*. By permission of Charles Scribner's Sons.

pages of Robinson's *Tristram*,[26] the classical beauty of its last
lines are scarcely to be forgotten:

> And white birds everywhere, flying, and flying;
> Alone, with her white face and her gray eyes,
> She watched them there till even her thoughts were white,
> And there was nothing alive but white birds flying,
> Flying, and always flying, and still flying,
> And the white sunlight flashing on the sea.

5

The various lights which illuminated Robinson's poetic maturity in "Captain Craig" and which shone with increasing, if
not consistently unflickering, brilliance until the publication of
The Man Who Died Twice in 1924, were those of a latter-day
New England humanism. The softer lights and sweeter cadences
of Emerson's transcendental spirit had gone out and were stilled.
Those gifts of prophecy on which Emerson relied when he wrote

> Or say, the foresight that awaits
> Is the same Genius that creates . . .[27]

were brought to book (almost literally one might say) in Robinson's "Merlin," [28] for Merlin had been cursed by the gifts of
prophecy and his world had fallen into ruins:

> All this that was to be is what I saw
> Before there was an Arthur to be king,
> And so to be a mirror wherein men
> May see themselves
>
> .   .   .   .
>
>   but I was neither Fate nor God.
> I saw too much; and this would be the end,
> Were there to be an end.

The ancient theme of divine envy was lightly stressed; and
Merlin and the Fool, Dagonet, entered a night that resembled
as closely as the spirit of comedy can ever resemble tragedy at

[26] From *Collected Poems*. By permission of The Macmillan Company.
[27] "Fate" from *Poems of Ralph Waldo Emerson*, Houghton Mifflin Company.
[28] From *Collected Poems*. By permission of The Macmillan Company.

all the darkness that shrouded King Lear and his madness. But for us, it is significant that Robinson's Merlin did not lose his wits; and that the Fool, however dark and cold the night

> . . . heard what might have been a father's laugh,
> Faintly behind him.

The scene was characteristic of Robinson's humane temper, but in lesser figures than Merlin (who was above the lesser sins) the curse of one who hates an enemy can be resolved only by death itself—and Avon paid that price in *Avon's Harvest*. Aside from his hatred Avon remained, though middle-aged in years, a boy at a preparatory school, and Robinson, with the ease and skill of an accomplished moralist of a tradition that is not unaware of Nathaniel Hawthorne, consigned Avon to a devil of his own making.

Robinson's accomplishments in the moral arts that rejected pantheism as well as the unthoughtful hero worship of Shakespeare which had stirred so many Americans at the start of the twentieth century into writing lame blank verse, were never better expressed than in his remarkable tour de force, "Ben Jonson Entertains a Man from Stratford." Both Jonson and Shakespeare retain their stature, but Robinson happily re-created the atmospheres of *Every Man in His Humour* and of *Twelfth Night* rather than that of *Macbeth* or *Hamlet,* and within the speeches between Jonson and Shakespeare, it is well to overhear at what great distance Robinson's Shakespeare traveled from the definitions of "Nature" that had been employed by youthful poets of both the nineteenth and early twentieth century:

> "Your fly will serve as well as anybody,
> And what's his hour? He flies, and flies, and flies,
> And in his fly's mind has a brave appearance;
> And then your spider gets him in her net,
> And eats him out, and hangs him up to dry.
> That's Nature, the kind mother of us all.
> And then your slattern housemaid swings her broom,
> And where's your spider? And that's Nature, also.
> It's Nature, and it's Nothing. It's all Nothing.
> It's all a world where bugs and emperors
> Go singularly back to the same dust,

Each in his time; and the old, ordered stars
That sang together, Ben, will sing the same
Old stave to-morrow." [29]

Something very close to the sound of Shakespeare's own voice
is heard in the deftness with which it plays on the word "fly,"
and it reminds one of the same dexterity that juggled an ambiguous "will" through the lines of a famous sonnet, but Robinson's Shakespeare is one whose world has been too much with
him—and as for his retirement to the country, Robinson's Jonson
remarked, "God help him!" and then after speaking the highest
praise he could deliver, "O Lord, that House in Stratford!"

In the poems of Robinson's middle years (and these include
several of his historical portraits as well as several of his major
pieces) his language, his very art of presenting a set of phrases
in the form of a syllogism, acted as a necessary astringent to the
poetic diction of his time. In the concluding stanza of "The
Master," [30] which promises to become one of the few enduring
tributes written to the memory of Lincoln—and far too much
indifferent verse has been written in memory of his name—the
very phrasing of the lines are proof of a style that transcended
the lesser virtues of possessing "originality":

> For we were not as other men:
> 'Twas ours to soar and his to see;
> But we are coming down again,
> And we shall come down pleasantly;
> Nor shall we longer disagree
> On what it is to be sublime,
> But flourish in our perigee
> And have one Titan at a time.

The virtues that Robinson possessed were not those that found
their happiest medium in his Arthurian cycle. And as Robinson's dramatic narratives began to take on the character of
"novels in verse," his limitations in the art of telling stories for
their own sake began to be strongly felt. We may speculate, if

[29] "Ben Jonson Entertains a Man from Stratford" from *Collected Poems*.
By permission of The Macmillan Company.
[30] From *The Town Down by the River*, used by permission of Charles
Scribner's Sons.

only for a moment, as to the reasons why his Arthurian adventure became so attractive to him: First of all, it was a rich and elaborately designed shield behind which his habitual reticence could enjoy the sense of being protected and well at ease; and, perhaps, at a vantage point well removed from immediate considerations of time and place, he could create, as if he were on a holiday, the illusion of "letting himself go." And finally, although this was probably a matter of far less importance to him, the Arthurian cycle gave him an opportunity to test his wit and the astringent merits of his style against the highly gifted, loose and brilliant metrical variations through which Tennyson in the disguise of Galahad had sought the Holy Grail.

But the difficulties that Robinson encountered were not entirely of his own making. To an American, and particularly a New Englander, the active, many-sided aspects of the Arthurian myth soon present problems of their own. The Arthurian myth belongs to the northwestern isles of Europe and the European continent. Its active life, its conventions of courtly love, its sight of good and of evil, and its religious being are distinctly alien to the "old tradition" that Robinson knew. To a New Englander even its superficial details, such as dress and the most casual of its social mannerisms, tend to get in the way of seeing the picture clearly. America has always lacked its Middle Ages, and even with the resources of patient and seriously directed scholarship, it has great difficulty in reconstructing them. Among American poets, Poe alone possessed a view into the mysteries of the Gothic imagination—but in the view through the eyes of a New Englander who held to the heritage of his thoroughly Protestant beliefs with the loyalty of Robinson, the universal, the Catholic church of the Middle Ages inevitably stands between him and the object of his vision.

It is futile to argue that Robinson's Arthurian romances must not be taken literally. Of course they must not—and Robinson's Merlin properly belongs in the company of Captain Craig and the elderly Archibald. But the very naming of a place called Camelot, and of persons called Gawaine, Isolt, or Gouvernail created a heavy, slightly spurious, "literary" atmosphere that ill suited the austerities of Robinson's wit and temperament. Both the weight and rootlessness of Robinson's Arthurian devices are felt and discerned in the following lines from *Tristram:* [31]

> Tristram, the loud accredited strong warrior,
> Tristram, the learned Nimrod among hunters,
> Tristram, the loved of women, the harp-player,
> Tristram, the doom of his prophetic mother,
> Dropped like a log; and silent on the floor,
> With wild flowers lying around him on the floor—
> Wild roses for Isolt—lay like a log.

In this passage the failure is as great as Dr. Johnson's unfortunate attempt to retell the story of the virtuous Greek courtesan, Irene, who had been impetuously beheaded by Sultan Mahomet II; and the parallel grows even more deadly as one remembers that Dr. Johnson also retold his story in extremely blank and weighted verse.

But unlike Dr. Johnson's *Irene,* which failed so notoriously at the Theatre Royal in Drury Lane, Robinson's *Tristram* through the efficient distribution of The Literary Guild in 1927 reached a larger public and received more exuberant praise than any single volume of his work has known. It was rumored at the time that Robinson quietly inquired of a friend: "What is wrong with *Tristram?*" and with a characteristic intonation of mingled doubt and irony in his voice, "There's something wrong with *Tristram;* it can't be as good as I once thought it was." The sales of *Tristram* carried Robinson forward to his long-awaited economic independence; but, as he may well have suspected, the book also cut him off, even more resolutely than before, from a serious consideration of his merits at the hands of intelligent and responsible critics.

6

Though the cycle of Arthurian romances did little to increase Robinson's poetic stature, and though his novels in verse, to which he devoted so much of his time during the last ten years of his life, steered him closer to the shallows of "psychological" speculation in George Meredith's prose—and further away from

[31] From *Collected Poems*. By permission of The Macmillan Company.

the climate he shared with Henry James—it cannot be said that the writing of his longer narratives was entirely harmful. It was the kind of writing that kept him busy, that kept his hand in, as it were, toward the production and occasional felicities of many shorter poems. Of these we have the famous turn of wit that brought to a close Robinson's sonnet on New England,

> And Conscience always has the rocking chair,
> Cheerful as when she tortured into fits
> The first cat that was ever killed by Care.[32]

Memorable among them is another sonnet, "The Haunted House." And Robinson was one of four twentieth-century American poets—Robert Frost, Elinor Wylie, and E. E. Cummings are the others—who gave more to that particular lyric form, the distinction of their own speech, than they took from it:

THE HAUNTED HOUSE [33]

> Here was a place where none would ever come
> For shelter, save as we did from the rain.
> We saw no ghost, yet once outside again
> Each wondered why the other should be dumb;
> For we had fronted nothing worse than gloom
> And ruin, and to our vision it was plain
> Where thrift, outshivering fear, had let remain
> Some chairs that were like skeletons of home.
>
> There were no trackless footsteps on the floor
> Above us, and there were no sounds elsewhere.
> But there was more than sound; and there was more
> Than just an ax that once was in the air
> Between us and the chimney, long before
> Our time. So townsmen said who found her there.

Robinson's beautifully trained gift of reawakening emotion through the art of scrupulously unadorned understatement paralleled the art that his great British contemporary, Thomas Hardy, practiced; and Robinson's true contribution to poetry

---

[32] "New England" from *Collected Poems*. By permission of The Macmillan Company.
[33] From *Collected Poems*. By permission of The Macmillan Company.

written on this side of the Atlantic was comparable in quality
to Hardy's. Hardy's lyric, "The Garden Seat," [34] briefly illustrates
the resemblance:

> Its former green is blue and thin,
> And its once firm legs sink in and in;
> Soon it will break down unaware,
> Soon it will break down unaware.
>
> At night when reddest flowers are black
> Those who once sat thereon come back;
> Quite a row of them sitting there,
> Quite a row of them sitting there.
>
> With them the seat does not break down,
> Nor winter freeze them, nor floods drown,
> For they are as light as upper air,
> They are as light as upper air!

Nor can it be said that the writing of *Lancelot* in 1920 seriously retarded the final enrichment and transformation of Captain Craig into *The Man who Died Twice* in 1924. This was
the last of Robinson's poems in which the theme of human
failure is endowed with the depths of feeling and sharp turns
of wit that had been the true rewards of its author's maturity—
and something of its strength and serenity may be suggested by
reading a slightly earlier and far shorter poem, "Archibald's
Example": [35]

> Old Archibald, in his eternal chair,
> Where trespassers, whatever their degree,
> Were soon frowned out again, was looking off
> Across the clover when he said to me:
>
> "My green hill yonder, where the sun goes down
> Without a scratch, was once inhabited
> By trees that injured him—an evil trash
> That made a cage, and held him while he bled.
>
> "Gone fifty years, I see them as they were
> Before they fell. They were a crooked lot

[34] From *Collected Poems* by Thomas Hardy. By permission of The Macmillan Company.
[35] From *Collected Poems* by E. A. Robinson. By permission of The Macmillan Company.

To spoil my sunset, and I saw no time
In fifty years for crooked things to rot.

"Trees, yes; but not a service or a joy
To God or man, for they were thieves of light.
So down they came. Nature and I looked on,
And we were glad when they were out of sight.

"Trees are like men, sometimes; and that being so,
So much for that." He twinkled in his chair,
And looked across the clover to the place
That he remembered when the trees were there.

7

With *King Jasper,* the last of his long poems, Robinson's work
was finished: the "twilight interval" of his youth was far behind
him, but in 1934, another twilight of ill-health and foreboding
had begun, and something of its character colored his letter to
an old friend, Mrs. Laura Richards:

Today I have been thinking of Hitler, and of what one neurotic
fanatic may yet do to us and drag us into. It's all right to say it can't
happen, but unfortunately it can. The more I try to make a picture of
this world for the next hundred years, the more I don't like it, and the
gladder I am that I shall be out of it.[36]

Of *Amaranth,* one of Robinson's novels in verse, *The New
Republic* wrote, "a most pathetic revelation of the bitter, yet
heroic self-doubt in the mind of a poet who once struck genuine
fire, knows that he did, and fears he never will again." In his
growing illness such notices troubled him. To Ridgely Torrence
he admitted that he felt he was publishing too much. And indeed the single-volume edition of his *Collected Poems,* issued in
1937, was a book of over fourteen hundred closely printed pages.
But habit and the recurrent fears of failure, failure of the kind
that had haunted his Bewick Finzer, increased the volume of
his writing and he could not stop. He felt that he needed the
money that was now coming steadily to him from the sale of his
books, and the public that he had won through the sales of

[36] From *Selected Letters of Edwin Arlington Robinson.* By permission of
The Macmillan Company and the author's estate.

Tristram bought each new volume with an air of automatic admiration.

His illness was discovered to be cancer, and he was taken to the New York Hospital, where from a window in his room he could look out over the East River and see a corner of Welfare Island, a section of the prison itself, and its surroundings. To a friend who had admired the view, Robinson replied that he did not dare to turn his head in that direction: "I found that when I did . . . I couldn't stand it. Think of the old men down there, think of what is going on, the suffering, the crowded, dingy quarters, the loneliness. And here I am getting the utmost that can be given!" His last view of the world was of the same perspective that he saw over a quarter of a century through the eyes of Captain Craig:

> . . . yes, I have cursed
> The sunlight and the breezes and the leaves
> To think of men on stretchers or on beds,
> Or on foul floors, things without shapes or names,
> Made human with paralysis or rags;
> Or some poor devil on a battle-field,
> Left undiscovered and without the strength
> To drag a maggot from his clotted mouth;
> Or women working where a man would fall—
> Flat-breasted miracles of cheerfulness
> Made neuter by the work that no man counts
> Until it waits undone; children thrown out
> To feed their veins and souls on offal . . . Yes,
> I have had half a mind to blow my brains out
> Sometimes; and I have gone from door to door,
> Ragged myself, trying to do something—
> Crazy, I hope.—But what has this to do
> With Spring? [37]

On April 5, 1935, Robinson died, and editorials in the morning papers of the next day were filled with praise of the most distinguished poet in the America of his generation, "a man who" (as Samuel Johnson, a humanist of an earlier day, wrote of another) "had neither been enervated by applause, nor intimidated by censure or indifference."

[37] "Captain Craig" from *Collected Poems*. By permission of The Macmillan Company.

A NOTE ON STEPHEN CRANE

In 1930 when the poems of Stephen Crane (1871-1900) were reprinted and were collected for the first time between the covers of a single volume, it seemed that a final revaluation of his poetry would at last be made. Was he indeed, as had been whispered a decade before, a poetic innovator, a forerunner of the Imagists, and was he, like Emily Dickinson and Gerard Manley Hopkins whose posthumously published volumes made them seem like contemporaries to younger poets of the period, a first-rate poet? Do Crane's verses with their concise, vivid imagery, and their epigrammatic sharpness make the poetry he wrote seem more alive than when they appeared under the titles, *The Black Riders* (1895) and *War Is Kind* (1899)? In fact the moment was overripe: in 1930 it seemed ten years too late for the publication of his *Collected Poems,* since by that time a new temper and tone, quite unlike Imagism, were beginning to enter American poetry; and if Crane had been vaguely accepted as an ancestor by younger poets in 1920—and by some as early as 1916—his poems in themselves had less to offer than the technical and verbal experiments of Hopkins or the tight, oblique spirituality of Emily Dickinson. It had become clear that Crane's poetry depended too much on color and temperament, the loose and not always successful attempt at experimentation and—more than all else—on a brilliant, precocious gesture of revolt. The *Collected Poems* were reviewed with mild interest and were immediately classified as among the more notable predecessors of vers libre or (since the term had often been used loosely) the poetry of Imagism—for it was known that Miss Amy Lowell greatly admired *The Black Riders* and *War Is Kind.*

Whatever relationship Crane's verse had to Imagism and to the "poetic renaissance," including the Chicago school of Carl Sandburg and Edgar Lee Masters, for Crane was also rediscovered by Harriet Monroe, its importance as mature poetry is still debatable. One can indeed imagine Stephen Crane as a young poet (some fifteen years after his early death) contributing to Miss Monroe's *Poetry,* or to a volume of Alfred Kreymborg's *Others,* but his best talents went into his novels and short stories and it is in these and in the colorful legend surrounding his name, which had been so brilliantly interpreted by Thomas Beer in 1923, that the character of his life and work achieves an immortality. Since Crane's poetry is still referred to vaguely, and is dutifully reprinted in brief selections in anthologies of American verse, its historical importance seems pertinent and necessary. For Crane's prose and (in an infinitely more limited sense) his poetry, which was said to have been inspired by a reading of Whitman and by hearing William Dean Howells read aloud the poetry of Emily Dickinson, are among the few exceptions that gave color and life to the "twilight interval" which brought to a close the declining years of the nineteenth century. When one considers that Stephen Crane at the time of his death was a restless, isolated figure in this country, but had as his British contemporaries George Douglas Brown (author of one remarkable book, *The House with the Green Shutters*), Joseph Conrad, and an expatriated Henry James, one sees how much more fortunate he was as a novelist than as a poet. Admitting that the best sustained proof of Crane's latent poetic imagination is still to be found in the pages of his novel, *The Red Badge of Courage,* the greater body of his verse seems less dated, less affected, less "arty," and certainly less self-conscious than a number of his short stories. Even after suffering constant repetition in anthologies, the following lines from *The Black Riders* retain their freshness and their wit, their quickening penetration into psychological reality:

> In the desert
> I saw a creature, naked, bestial,
> Who, squatting upon the ground,
> Held his heart in his hands,
> And ate of it.
> I said, "Is it good, friend?"
> "It is bitter—bitter," he answered;

"But I like it
Because it is bitter,
And because it is my heart." [1]

Nor can thirty years of frequent quotation utterly destroy the elements of surprise and climactic effectiveness that are always rediscovered in reading the title poem of *War Is Kind*. But the emotions inspired by a rereading of the poem verge dangerously on the thin, almost invisible line between boyish irony and downright bathos—and many of the poems in that characteristically slender volume remind us vividly of the better poems written in youthful exuberance by Edna St. Vincent Millay and E. E. Cummings, and occasionally one also recalls the attitudes of the young Ernest Hemingway in his early poems and *In Our Time*. Stephen Crane, the handsome, melodramatic young man, with his profound curiosity concerning the nature of human guilt and fear, became a figure of spectacular prominence in the creation of a twentieth-century American legend; and one remembers, through the testimony of Ford Madox Ford (whose recollections of a long and lively career must not be accepted for their literal truth but for their flashes of an essential, one might almost say poetic, validity), how Crane took special delight in startling his English friends by gaily flashing a brace of murderous six-shooters in a drawing room and the effectiveness of that gesture is intensified and heightened if we take the trouble to remember how deeply Crane hated war and feared firearms. All this, of course, became the best-loved and best-known features of a legend surrounding the typical young and gifted American writer, a legend that some critics and a great majority of the reading public always find attractive, especially when it is accompanied by newspaper publicity.

In rereading Crane's poetry one readily admits that much of his verse seems to anticipate the characteristic economy of phrasing, lightness, and verve of a style that the Imagists claimed was a particular virtue of their art—and obviously Crane made no

[1] "The Heart" from *Collected Poems* of Stephen Crane, by permission of Alfred A. Knopf, Inc. Copyright 1922 by William H. Crane. Copyright 1895, 1899, 1926, 1929, 1930 by Alfred A. Knopf, Inc.

pretensions toward stating a poetic theory as he quickly jotted down his verses. As in his prose, he simply looked for a new means of expressing a sharp and clear reflection of his keen vision—and there are times when his verse seems to resemble the poetry of an extremely youthful Ezra Pound. We can readily compare Ezra Pound's use of the sublimated epigram with these lines taken from *The Black Riders:* [2]

> There was set before me a mighty hill,
> And long days I climbed
> Through regions of snow.
> When I had before me the summit-view,
> It seemed that my labour
> Had been to see gardens
> Lying at impossible distances.

And one also finds a sharp thrust of youthful irony and wit in:

> Friend, your white beard sweeps the ground.
> Why do you stand, expectant?
> Do you hope to see it
> In one of your withered days?
> With your old eyes
> Do you hope to see
> The triumphal march of justice?
> Do not wait, friend!
> Take your white beard
> And your old eyes
> To more tender lands. [3]

It was as though Stephen Crane were unconsciously building a bridge between the epigrams contained in Ambrose Bierce's *The Devil's Dictionary* and the early issues of the Imagist anthologies.

To those who measure date lines religiously, Stephen Crane can be said to be a poet of the twentieth century only by the slightest turn of chance (since he died almost symbolically in the first year of the century); yet it is in terms of the poetry written in the first two decades after his death that his work is best

---

[2] "XXVI" from *Collected Poems* of Stephen Crane, by permission of Alfred A. Knopf, Inc. Copyright 1922 by William H. Crane. Copyright 1895, 1899, 1926, 1929, 1930 by Alfred A. Knopf, Inc.

[3] *Ibid.,* "LXIV."

interpreted and understood. As a poet, and quite unlike the more important forerunners of the "poetic renaissance," including E. A. Robinson, Emily Dickinson, and Walt Whitman, Stephen Crane is best viewed in the light whose shadows cast historical perspectives, while the larger figures belong not only to their particular decade, but to ours and to all time.

PART II

THE "POETIC RENAISSANCE"

HARRIET MONROE
AND THE "POETIC RENAISSANCE"

It is almost impossible to speak of Harriet Monroe (1860-1936) without special reference to the hopes and aspirations of the period in which her magazine, *Poetry*, was born. In America, the years 1912 to 1918 were spoken of as the years of a "poetic renaissance," and as recently as ten years ago, instructors in schools and colleges and contributors to literary sections of the liberal weeklies glanced backward to that moment as though it were a golden age, not unlike the great days of Queen Elizabeth's England or of the Medici in fifteenth-century Florence. And as we look backward, the years of the "poetic renaissance" seem to have been of a day when magazines opened their doors widely and indiscriminately to all kinds of poetry, provided they were "advanced" and odd enough, as a time when publishers, overcome by some mysterious and unheralded compulsion, insisted upon bringing out everything or anything that remotely resembled a book of poems. The "poetic renaissance" in America also included the time when Louis Untermeyer began to edit his popular anthologies of American verse and when Carl Sandburg and Vachel Lindsay of Chicago and Springfield, Illinois, shattered the complacencies of a reading public who had grown accustomed to seeing the verse of Effie Smith, Charles Hanson Towne, and Amelia Josephine Burr appear in *Harper's, The Century*, or *Scribner's Magazine*.

To a marked degree, Harriet Monroe's little magazine, *Poetry*, founded in 1912, and edited from an unfamiliar address, 543 Cass Street, Chicago, Illinois, was actually the "poetic renaissance." The circular announcing its arrival created an air of excitement among readers of poetry that compared favorably with the publicity that attended William Butler Yeats's announcement of an "Irish Renaissance" in the 1890's. To the poets, Harriet Monroe wrote:

> *First,* a chance to be heard in their own place, without the limitations imposed by the popular magazine . . . this magazine will appeal to . . . a public primarily interested in poetry as an art, as the highest, most complete human expression of truth and beauty. *Second* . . . All kinds of verse will be considered—narrative, dramatic, lyric—quality alone being the test of acceptance. Certain numbers [of *Poetry*] may be devoted entirely to a single poem, or a group of poems by one person; except for a few editorial pages of comment and review. *Third,* besides the prize or prizes above mentioned, we shall pay contributors.[1]

Here was an offer not to be resisted, and the flame ignited by Harriet Monroe spread to other periodicals, and fanned by quickening winds of sporadic enthusiasm, it ran into far and sometimes contrary directions. In recalling the spirit, the energies released by Harriet Monroe's announcements of her magazine, one should not forget the gaiety and brightness of Alfred Kreymborg's little magazine, *Others,* published in New York, introducing a number of new poets to its readers, and edited at the risk of Kreymborg's own fragile and charming talent. Nor should one fail to recall the talk, the gossip, the stimulus to writing both prose and verse aroused by Margaret Anderson's *Little Review,* its birthplace in Harriet Monroe's Chicago, its editorial offices shifting from the Middle West to New York (wherever, in fact, Miss Anderson happened to be) and from New York to Paris.

But of all the ventures occasioned by the so-called "poetic renaissance," *Poetry* commanded a central position within them, devoting special issues of the magazine to divergent and contrasting groups of poets, and for three-quarters of an active and controversial decade, the influence of Harriet Monroe's championship of poetry "as the highest, most complete human expression of truth and beauty" was felt and echoed in editorial offices throughout the country. Her very presence in the editorial chair at 543 Cass Street created the impression that new talents in the writing of poetry could be discovered every day, and her

[1] "Poetry," Ch. 25, from *A Poet's Life.* By permission of The Macmillan Company.

career up to the inception of her magazine in 1912 seemed to have provided an education best suited to the task in which she found so much delight and perhaps an immortality in the history of American literature.

Harriet Monroe was born December 23, 1860, into a spirited, well-to-do Chicago family that had migrated from New York to the Middle West. At an early age she was sent to the Old Visitation Convent School at Georgetown, Maryland, within an hour's drive of the nation's capital, and while at that school she promised herself and God that some day she would be "great and famous." Like other young women of a generation that Henry James reflected in *The American,* Miss Monroe left convent school to make her debut into Chicago society, to visit friends and theaters in New York, to travel widely in and over Europe, assimilating sights and sounds of ancient places with the clear, quick, innocent gaze of another *Daisy Miller.* In London she met Whistler who completely charmed her and Henry James himself who "rather bored" her. Although Harriet Monroe enjoyed Europe with the same high flush of excitement with which most globe-trotting Americans of her day rediscovered everything they saw, she was not to be caught in the toils of a James heroine; through her early travels and throughout her life, she sustained the Monroe family loyalty to Chicago, and eager as she was to learn, to see, to grasp all that the large world had to offer, her desire was to bring memories of its wealth and culture home to America, to Chicago, in whose superiority she always believed.

In her candid, awkwardly written, hasty, and at last unfinished autobiography, *A Poet's Life,* published in 1938, one sees, as though looking through the wrong end of a telescope or at a roll of unprojected motion-picture film against lamp light, small and bright flashes of a young Harriet Monroe at Edmund Clarence Stedman's home in Bronxville, New York, or being introduced to Robert Louis Stevenson in a disorderly, dimly lit hotel room in Greenwich Village. The latter experience came as a shock to her romantic sensibilities: Stevenson, her hero, had looked deathly ill, deathly thin, and the room, no doubt, was clouded with cigarette smoke and unaired; his voice was a shrill whisper in a darkened room, and Harriet Monroe in a new and gay spring hat, longed for escape from the sickroom away from all thought of illness or of approaching death. The evenings at Stedman's house in Bronxville were of a kind that supplied fuel for her later activities; here an earnest, graceful, energetic, attractive young woman could take part in drawing-room discussions without fear of the dark misfortunes of all too human experience, and from Stedman himself Harriet Monroe perhaps caught fire, from his prophetic fervor and belief in the future of American poetry. At his house she met Henry Harland, who ten years later earned notoriety as the daring young editor of *The Yellow Book*. On this particular evening, Harland had praised Browning by placing him above Shelley, a declaration which horrified Harriet Monroe and caused Stedman, rushing to her defense, to say in ringing tones, "Shelley soared higher into the Empyrean."

Meanwhile, Harriet Monroe's informal education in Chicago progressed under the influence of her brilliant brother-in-law, John Wellborn Root, the architect, who taught her to value and appreciate the beginnings of an American art that was to reach maturity in the work of Louis Sullivan and Frank Lloyd Wright. It is highly probable that his influence created a background for a general appreciation of the arts, and it led to Harriet Monroe's later enthusiasms for the dance and the Russian ballet, for her delight at discovering Isadora Duncan and Pavlova, and Nijinsky's *L'Après-midi d'un faune* which she described as "timeless and modern as the rhythm of living waves." In painting, her earliest enthusiasm was wakened by Albert Pinkham Ryder, whom she sought out on visits to New York, finding his "sunlit south bedroom in a shabby boarding house," a bed in one corner, a chair or two and his "litter of masterpieces" leaning face-back against the walls. The publicity she received for the writing of "The Columbian Ode" on the occasion of the Columbian Exposition at Chicago in 1892, the connection of her family with Chicago's growth and power, her wide travels throughout Europe and the Orient, and her avowed interest in the arts paved the way for her position on the *Chicago Tribune* as art reviewer. "It was space work—Sunday reviews and a few week-day notices, with no regular salary"—but the opportunity gave Harriet Monroe a chance to prove her quickness, and she was among the first in recognizing the value of Picasso, Picabia, Maillol, Matisse, and Redon. The assignments in journalism made her particularly sensitive to gossip of "changes in the air," to new movements in art, to new names, to new ideas; and as she heard of large awards, grants, and commissions given to architects, sculptors, painters, and a few musicians, she thought of how comparatively little recognition the poet received for writing poetry. She recalled her own experience in the writing of "The Columbian Ode" as an unhappy one, for its notoriety involved a lawsuit with the *New York World* over the rights of republishing the poem, an experience which left her on the verge of a nervous breakdown, and with a growing sense of disillusionment concerning the honor and respect a poet might receive for doing honest work.

It was with the memory of this experience, and with the conviction that she was engaging her talents and forces in a memorable crusade, that Harriet Monroe applied for financial support among her friends in Chicago and in New York to maintain a magazine for the sake of poetry alone.

Although Ezra Pound was *Poetry's* first "Foreign Correspondent," writing his own motto to celebrate his approval of Harriet Monroe and her ideas—"To Hell with Harper's and the Magazine Touch"—Miss Monroe seemed to reserve her warmest admiration for the verse of Vachel Lindsay, Carl Sandburg, and Edgar Lee Masters. At a banquet given by *Poetry* in 1914 she had heard William Butler Yeats echo the modest preface to J. M. Synge's *Poems and Translations*. Yeats, speaking of the late Victorians, particularly the "over-appareled" art of Tennyson, had said:

We were weary of all this. We wanted to get rid not only of rhetoric but of poetic diction. We tried to strip away everything that was artificial, to get a style like speech, as simple as the simplest prose, like a cry of the heart.[2]

It was this aspect of the "new" poetry that made its direct appeal to Harriet Monroe, yet with her "Foreign Correspon-

[2] Introduction, p. xiii, from *The New Poetry* by Harriet Monroe and Alice C. Henderson. By permission of The Macmillan Company.

dent's'' advice, and no doubt with his repeated threats and warnings, she published T. S. Eliot's "Love Song of J. Alfred Prufrock" in 1915, and it was Harriet Monroe who first published the poetry of Wallace Stevens and was among the first to offer editorial hospitality to Conrad Aiken and Marianne Moore. But here it should be said that editors like Alfred Kreymborg accepted their work with better heart and fuller enthusiasm. The verse of Vachel Lindsay and of Carl Sandburg remained closer to Harriet Monroe's interpretation of what "new" poetry was. It seemed also to reflect her own experiment in writing "The Hotel," a long, unrhymed poem, setting down her observations at the Waldorf-Astoria in New York, and perhaps more important than all other causes in their favor, both Carl Sandburg and Vachel Lindsay seemed to reaffirm Harriet Monroe's intense loyalty to Chicago and the Middle West, and the very intonations of their verse seemed to reach into the deeper recesses of her imagination.

Harriet Monroe had few pretensions as a critic, and throughout her life she held an attitude of sharp distrust toward painters who talked too much about their art and poets who had too many theories concerning poetry. She would say, "The new poetry strives for a concrete and immediate realization of life; it would discard the theory, the abstraction, the remoteness, found in all classics not of the first order." Or she would repeat, "The artist, big or little, is in his degree a seer, and it may be that he sees deeper than the critic who is 'obsessed' by the movements of his time." Harriet Monroe had put her trust in the resources of her own imagination and intuition, and since she also possessed the gift of common sense—that rarest of all human senses—she made few mistakes in feeling or in judgment. It was in this spirit that she became a brilliant editor, willing always to accept verse that contained the "individual, unstereotyped rhythm, the surprises, and irregularities, found in all great art because they are inherent in human feeling."

To Harriet Monroe there was no lack of consistency in publishing the work of poets whose taste and intentions seemed at a far distance from her own; she had had the courage to publish the poetry of many writers long before it had become fashionable to do so, and with this knowledge and assurance, she continued to edit *Poetry* up to the date of her death in 1936. Meanwhile the early impulses and enthusiasms that had attended the founding of her magazine had begun to change their temper soon after the close of the First World War. It would not be too far-fetched to say that the "poetic renaissance" came to a final conclusion with the publication of T. S. Eliot's poem, "The Waste Land," in the November, 1922, issue of *The Dial*. From that moment onward, Harriet Monroe's position seemed to represent all the fervor, the warmth, the native quickness, and innocence that defined the hopeful attitudes of Middle Western America before the war, and readers of "The Waste Land" became aware of something from another world than that of the "new" poetry of which Miss Monroe was so ardent a champion. The unrest and the spiritual malady that had become prevalent in the large cities of Europe and of the United States seemed to speak out in voices so disturbing that it was no longer possible to ignore them, and another day beyond the period of the "poetic renaissance" had well begun.

The secret of *Poetry's* survival beyond the life of all other "little" magazines that introduced young writers to a responsive reading public was its strict adherence to Harriet Monroe's rule of paying generously for contributions. Through the subsidy of *Poetry's* guarantors, including a hundred or more of Harriet Monroe's friends in Chicago, this policy avoided the usual erratic and disproportionate rewards for writing verse that attend the dubious policy of encouraging poetry wholly by prize awards. Harriet Monroe had a more than generous enthusiasm for the actual publishing of poetry, and she did not feel that a poet was debased and his art coarsened by receiving a proportional rate of payment for each poem accepted for publication in her magazine—and in this way she offered the most subtle and practical encouragement of all.

One of the clearest portraits of Harriet Monroe's small, slight figure, her delicate features, and the bright, upward glance of her eyes behind polished pince-nez is suggested, if not re-created, in physical detail by Marianne Moore:

. . . if one may speak of Miss Monroe as if to praise, I think of her valor, her goodness to us all, her imperviousness to plebeian behavior, her affection, the subordinatingly humourous trace of indulgence—one would not call it scorn—in her attitude to suggestions bearing on literary self-protectiveness, her independence of being squired or attended upon. I recall her matter of fact "Oh, I don't think anything of rain," and on another occasion—the day before her departure for Mexico some years back—at her hotel, in a room of frigid temperature, when she had consented to rest while talking to me, "I don't believe I need a cover. Oh, if you like; I'm not used to having anyone *cover* me." I recall when she spoke, and read from her work, at the Brooklyn Institute, her somewhat skeptical proffer of literary experience and opinion, her deep uninsisted-upon eloquence as she read *The Pine at Timberline;* and despite her own belief in her mind—one dislikes the term "muse"—her air of alone-ness, her self-reliant and winning incredulity that it should be liked so very much as it was by us who heard her. Her fearless battle for art—and in art—was present for me there in a conspicuous though disclaimed laurel.[3]

It is only by an extremely selective reading of her *Chosen Poems* (1935) that one may discern the intelligence, the dignity, the grace which combined to make her personality a memorable one; again one sees her as if in glimpses behind the screen of her active life:

> I love my life, but not too well
>   To cast it like a cloak on thine,
> Against the storms that sound and swell
>   Between thy lonely heart and mine.
> I love my life, but not too well.[4]

The resiliency of her spirit was echoed best in these few lines:

> Alaska slants her shining snows,
> And India burns under the sun,
> All these my mortal eyes would see,
> All men alive are calling me;
> Yet these were all too lightly won,
> For I would go where none has gone
> To read the riddle no man knows.[5]

[3] "In Memory of Harriet Monroe," *Poetry,* December, 1936, Vol. XLIX, No. III, used by permission of *Poetry.*

[4] "Love Song I" from *Chosen Poems.* By permission of The Macmillan Company.

[5] "Plaint" from *Chosen Poems.* By permission of The Macmillan Company.

Like a true Middle Westerner, she loved her native soil, but had no aversion to dying as far away from it as possible, the more exotic and "different" the place, the better. She died at Arequipa, Peru, September 26, 1936, while attending a congress of writers, and a few months after her death, Ezra Pound, who had said, "No one more acrimoniously differed with her in point of view than I did," was to write:

The death of Harriet Monroe will be felt as a personal loss by everyone who has ever contributed to her magazine. No one in our time or in any time has ever served the cause of an art with greater devotion, patience, and unflagging kindness. . . .

The new generation of the 1930's can not measure, offhand, the local situation of 1910. An exclusive editorial policy would not have done the work of an inclusive policy (however much the inclusiveness may have rankled one and all factions).

During the twenty-four years of her editorship perhaps three periodicals made a brilliant record, perhaps five periodicals, but they were all under the sod in the autumn of 1936, and no other publication has existed in America where any writer of poetry could more honorably place his writings. This was true in 1911. It is true as I write this.[6]

6 "In Memory of Harriet Monroe" in *Poetry*, December, 1936, Vol. XLIX, No. III, used by permission of *Poetry*.

In writing of Harriet Monroe and *Poetry* some tribute must be paid to her assistant editors, many of them young poets who gave their time and labors to the magazine without payment. Among them was the critic Morton Dauwen Zabel who helped the magazine to survive in the dark period after Miss Monroe's death and who for ten years previously contributed critical articles of unequaled brilliance to the magazine. Other editors were the poets, Eunice Tietjens, Jessica Nelson North, Marion Strobel, George Dillon, Helen Hoyt, and Alice Corbin Henderson.

THE HORATIAN SERENITY
OF ROBERT FROST

Perhaps no American poet of the twentieth century has received more academic honors than Robert Frost—or has survived
them with a more evenly balanced anti-intellectual temper and
well-burnished wit. In his latter years, he has been given eighteen honorary degrees from as many colleges and universities, and
among other awards, including the first Russell Loines Memorial
Poetry Prize of 1931 at the hands of the National Institute of
Arts and Letters, he has received the Pulitzer Prize for poetry
four times, in 1924, 1931, 1937, and in 1943. Today he is probably the best-known and most readily welcome of American
poets; and he can honestly say that his numerous honors and
awards, as well as his appointments and fellowships at various
colleges, have come to him by virtue of his poetry alone.

If he may be justly considered the Horace of our day, he is one
who has lived, with admirable independence, well outside the
shadow of a Maecenas. His native shrewdness and his suburban
wit seem always to derive their qualities from an austerely tended
Sabine Farm situated "north of Boston," either in New Hampshire or in Vermont. The merits of his verse are Roman rather
than Greek, and their overtones of jealously independent rumi-
nation are more American, in the sense that they guard the inviolability of state rights, than either. His verse is by no means
unconscious of a Roman-Anglo-American heritage; it moves freely
within it, and even as recently as 1941 in a poem read before
the Phi Beta Kappa Society at Harvard University, one discovers
the following remarks:

> O paladins, the lesson for to-day
> Is how to be unhappy yet polite.
> And at the summons Roland, Olivier,
> And every sheepish paladin and peer,

Being already more than proved in fight,
Sits down in school to try if he can write
Like Horace in the true Horatian vein,
Yet like a Christian disciplined to bend
His mind to thinking always of the end.
Memento mori and obey the Lord.
Art and religion love the somber chord.
Earth's a hard place in which to save the soul . . .[1]

And the almost Roman austerities and notes of satire are heard in a later passage of the poem:

There is a limit to our time extension.
We are all doomed to broken-off careers,
And so's the nation, so's the total race.
The earth itself is liable to the fate
Of meaninglessly being broken off.
(And hence so many literary tears
At which my inclination is to scoff.)
I may have wept that any should have died
Or missed their chance, or not have been their best,
Or been their riches, fame, or love denied;
On me as much as any is the jest.
I take my incompleteness with the rest.
God bless himself can no one else be blessed.[1]

2

The external facts of Robert Frost's biography are well known, and one can find them recited at length in Gorham B. Munson's small book, *Robert Frost: A Study in Sensibility and Good Sense*. It is enough for us to know that he was born in San Francisco, March 26, 1875, of New England and Scots parentage; that shortly after his father's death in 1885, his mother and he lived with his paternal grandfather in Lawrence, Massachusetts; that his formal education was by no means regular, broken as it was by the urgencies of making a living, and after high school, reduced to a few months at Dartmouth; that after an early marriage in 1895, two years—the years 1897 and 1898—were spent at Harvard, where he specialized in the studies of Latin and Greek;

[1] "The Lesson for Today" from *A Witness Tree*. By permission of Henry Holt and Company, Inc.

that until 1905 he ran through briefly the careers of working in a factory, writing for a local newspaper, and tending a small New Hampshire farm that had been given to him by his grandfather; that in 1905 he began his long career of teaching, which was interrupted by a three years' holiday in England (1912-1915) and then resumed at Amherst in 1916. Unlike his early contemporary, E. A. Robinson—and unlike many poets before and since his arrival as a figure in the "poetic renaissance"—Frost assumed the responsibility of bringing up a family on an extremely slender income, and for us it signifies his far distance from the Bohemian and easily acquired "attitudes" in poetry that had been so eagerly welcomed by many of his later contemporaries.

To the outside world, Frost's maturity in writing verse was of extraordinarily late arrival: his almost secretly printed first book, *Twilight,* of which two copies were printed in 1894, and single poems contributed to *The Independent, The Forum,* and *The Youth's Companion* did not attract the attention of other magazine editors, nor could they, even by the wildest chance, have reached a public that had welcomed Hovey and Bliss Carman. Frost's true world was of the New England countryside; and he himself has said that he had never read a book through until he was fourteen. He has also remarked, and perhaps not too seriously, that his favorite reading as a boy was *Tom Brown's School Days*—and this book, he continued, he did not finish because he could not bear to think it had an end. From then onward he read Shelley and Keats, and a now almost forgotten mid-nineteenth-century American poet, Edward Rowland Sill, who had been born in Connecticut in 1841, had been educated at Phillips Exeter Academy and at Yale, had been appointed to a professorship in English at the University of California, and in 1882 moved back to the East where he died in 1887. The cycle of his movements bore a rough analogy to the peregrinations of Frost's childhood, but more important than the geographic distance circumscribed by his career, and his return to the East, were the simplicities of his poetic diction. It is highly probable that an attentive reading of his verse provided Frost with an example of poetic style—and that the impression was as marked as W. B. Yeats's early admiration for the verse of Lionel Johnson. In

Sill's lines, "Truth at Last," [2] one finds a far less gifted expression of those simplicities in language and emotion than is frequently found in the verses of Robert Frost:

> Does a man ever give up hope, I wonder,—
> Face the grim fact, seeing it clear as day?
> When Bennen saw the snow slip, heard its thunder
> Low, louder, roaring round him, felt the speed
> Grow swifter as the avalanche hurled downward,
> Did he for just one heart-throb—did he indeed
> Know with all certainty, as they swept onward,
> There was the end, where the crag dropped away?
>
> ·　　·　　·　　·　　·　　·
>
> 　　　　　　　　　'Tis something, if at last,
> Though only for a flash, a man may see
> Clear-eyed the future as he sees the past,
> From doubt, or fear, or hope's illusion free.

During Frost's boyhood, and indeed throughout the formative periods of his life, such simplicities as Sill's verse offered were not likely to leave a deep impression upon the minds of inattentive readers. And it is well to remind ourselves that this was a time when American millionaires and their wives had discovered touchstones of European culture by collecting snuffboxes and fans reputed to have been worn and carried by the Marquise de Pompadour or Louis XV, that this was the moment when "costume" and historical romances were read and cherished. *When Knighthood Was in Flower, If I Were King, Richard Carvel, Monsieur Beaucaire, Richard Yea-and-Nay,* and *The Forest Lovers* were the titles of novels that defined the public taste, and they expressed a desire which also included the purchase of life-size portraits painted by Gainsborough, Reynolds, Romney, and Sir Thomas Lawrence—and these were probably chosen because they seemed so well fitted to give a baronial air to the newly acquired ancestral halls that were still being built in Buffalo, Chicago, Salt Lake City, Milwaukee, San Francisco, and Grand Rapids. These reflections of popular taste have little relevance to the permanent images of culture in American life, but they do indicate, and often with deadly accuracy, the

[2] From *The Poetical Works of Edward R. Sill.* By permission of Houghton Mifflin Company.

transient, speechless, and otherwise vague longings that lie close to the heart of those who have too much money to spend, and which in turn exert their influences upon the editorial policies of popular magazines.[3] They illustrate by contrast why it was that the modest appearance in 1915 of Robert Frost's *A Boy's Will*—and this was two years later than its publication in England—was by no means spectacular. This was followed in the same year by a second book, *North of Boston,* and a third, *Mountain Interval,* in 1916. The time was then ripe and he had done well to wait. And to those who read him, the experience was like a physical and sudden return to "native soil."

To those who were conscious of or even dimly remembered Philip Freneau's lines to "The Wild Honeysuckle" that had been first published in 1786, one of Frost's early poems, "My Butterfly," which was reputed to have been written by him at fifteen, and was his first printed poem, had a familiar and yet refreshing note; two stanzas quoted from each poem will show the creation of a like atmosphere, and the first two are from "The Wild Honeysuckle": [4]

> Fair flower, that dost so comely grow,
> Hid in this silent, dull retreat,
> Untouched thy honied blossoms blow,
> Unseen thy little branches greet:
> > No roving foot shall crush thee here,
> > No busy hand provoke a tear.
>
> .   .   .   .   .   .
>
> From morning suns and evening dews
> At first thy little being came:
> If nothing once, you nothing lose,
> For when you die you are the same;
> > The space between is but an hour,
> > The frail duration of a flower.

[3] Today the "costume" novel in America has undergone a process of rejuvenation. The taste of Hollywood, great quantities of easily earned, post-Second World War money, and a desire for a quickly acquired "sense of the past" all contribute toward the commercial success of the so-called "escape" or "costume" novel. The difference between those of 1900 and those that are read today is that present versions of *When Knighthood Was in Flower* are reputed to have a more highly charged sexual content.

[4] From *The Poems of Philip Freneau,* ed. by Fred Lewis Pattee. By permission of Princeton University Press.

Thine emulous fond flowers are dead, too,
And the daft sun-assaulter, he
That frighted thee so oft, is fled or dead:
Save only me
(Nor is it sad to thee!)
Save only me
There is none left to mourn thee in the fields.

The gray grass is scarce dappled with the snow;
Its two banks have not shut upon the river;
But it is long ago—
It seems forever—
Since first I saw thee glance,
With all thy dazzling other ones,
In airy dalliance,
Precipitate in love,
Tossed, tangled, whirled and whirled above,
Like a limp rose-wreath in a fairy dance.[5]

However young Frost was when he composed "My Butterfly" (and his pastoral verses have grown far more polished and firm since that day) we have a glimpse of what were to be and still are his clear virtues and defects. "My Butterfly" "never," as Cleanth Brooks wrote of Frost's later poetry, "lapses into sentimentality, never allows itself to be grandiose, but it does not have intensity." In its youthful, pastoral vein—and here the actual age of the poet has little relevance—two brief quotations, the first from *A Boy's Will* and the second from his seventh volume, *A Witness Tree*, published in 1942 and entitled somewhat coyly "Come In," are sufficient to show that his verse is always pleasant to the ear, not difficult to the mind, and rarely dull:

I'm going out to fetch the little calf
That's standing by the mother. It's so young,
It totters when she licks it with her tongue.
I shan't be gone long.—You come too.[6]

[5] "My Butterfly" from *Collected Poems* by Robert Frost. By permission of Henry Holt and Company, Inc.
[6] "The Pasture" from *Collected Poems*. By permission of Henry Holt and Company, Inc.

Far in the pillared dark
Thrush music went—
Almost like a call to come in
To the dark and lament.

But no, I was out for stars:
I would not come in.
I meant not even if asked,
And I hadn't been.[7]

No great depths of emotion are touched here, but their economy of statement never fails to bring an adequate response. Its art lies concealed within the poem's apparent simplicity; and if it can be said that Robert Frost at his best has no pretensions whatsoever, it should be observed that as he seems to disclaim them, his art has the single pretension of that denial.

It would be difficult to weigh the value of Robert Frost's well-earned holiday in England, but it can be said that it brought him the sympathetic friendship of those who were afterwards known as "Georgian poets"—Wilfred Gibson, Lascelles Abercrombie, and Edward Thomas—and his work was also called to the attention of Harriet Monroe's "Foreign Correspondent" to *Poetry*, Ezra Pound. In lines written by Wilfred Gibson and published in *The Atlantic Monthly* in 1926, the fortunate moment of Frost's stay in England was recalled:

Do you remember the still summer evening
When in the cosy cream-washed living-room
Of the Old Nailshop we all talked and laughed—
Our neighbors from the Gallows, Catherine
And Lascelles Abercrombie; Rupert Brooke;
Elinor and Robert Frost, living awhile
At Little Iddens, who'd brought over with them
Helen and Edward Thomas? In the lamplight
We talked and laughed, but for the most part listened
While Robert Frost kept on and on and on
In his slow New England fashion for our delight.[8]

The memory of Edward Thomas, who was killed at Vimy Ridge in the First World War, was recalled by Robert Frost in

[7] "Come In" from *A Witness Tree*. By permission of Henry Holt and Company, Inc.

[8] "The Golden Room" by permission of *The Atlantic Monthly*.

his lines "To E. T." [9] which appeared in his *New Hampshire* volume in 1923:

> The war seemed over more for you than me,
> But now for me than you—the other way.
> However, though, for even me who knew
> The foe thrust back unsafe beyond the Rhine,
> If I was not to speak of it to you
> And see you pleased once more with words of mine?

With the publication of Frost's two books, *A Boy's Will* and *North of Boston,* in England before their appearance in the United States, a kinship was formed between what Edward Marsh had called "a belief that English poetry is now once again putting on a new strength and beauty" and Harriet Monroe's "poetic renaissance." Edward Marsh had expressed his confidence in the "new" poetry in the first issue of *Georgian Poetry, 1911-1912,* which was published at Harold Monro's Poetry Bookshop, situated in Bloomsbury conveniently near the British Museum. The little shop attracted young Americans, including T. S. Eliot, as well as British poets who dropped in to visit Harold Monro. Among the "Georgians," as they were called, Frost and Thomas, Gibson and Abercrombie, very nearly founded in Hertfordshire a neo-"Lake School" of poets, who bore a strong resemblance in their love of "natural beauty" and simplicity of diction to the earlier school of Wordsworth, Coleridge, and Southey. The great weakness of the "Georgians" was an uncritical acceptance of Wordsworth's language in an age when even its simplicities had become "literary" and its dullness fatal—and from them Frost, with his characteristic independence, emerged as the most enduring "Georgian" of them all. He did not relinquish a single phrase of his own speech that he had discovered in the dramatic narratives of his *North of Boston,* and of which his justly famous "The Death of the Hired Man" is an excellent illustration of what Cleanth Brooks has called "dramatic decorum."

In February of 1914 Harriet Monroe was among the first to publish the "new" poetry of Robert Frost in an appropriate

[9] From *Collected Poems.* By permission of Henry Holt and Company, Inc.

setting, which was, of course, her magazine. And in a note on Robert Frost that Harriet Monroe included in the 1932 edition of her anthology, *The New Poetry*,[10] she wrote:

> He felt, no doubt, that if he could satisfy himself that his verse presented the musical essence of his neighbors' talk, all the rest—subject, emotional motive, dexterity of technique—would be added unto him. . . . He transmutes them [his poems] almost always into a freely moving iambic measure, usually blank verse in the longer poems, and in the shorter ones rhyming couplets and stanzas. His metrical patterns are according to precedent—he tries no free-verse experiments; but there is a subtle originality, a very personal style, in his weaving of cadences over the basic metre. . . . The poet knows what he is talking about, and loves the country and the life . . . of mending stone walls, planting seed, etc. His touch upon these subjects is sure and individual, the loving touch of a specialist—we know he knows. And in the character pieces we feel just as sure of him. . . . When it comes to personal confession—to autobiography, so to speak—Mr. Frost refuses to take himself seriously. . . . This mood greets us most characteristically in *New Hampshire*. . . . New Hampshire and her poet both have character, as well as a penetrating, humorous and sympathetic quality of genius.

It must be admitted that Harriet Monroe, seated at her desk in *Poetry's* office in Chicago, viewed Frost with cooler eyes than many of the contributors to the *Recognition of Robert Frost*, a volume issued by his publishers in 1937. But her perception was no less keen, and she was quick to understand that his virtues were of a consistently traditional order. The very title of his first book published in England, *A Boy's Will*, happily recollected the refrain of Longfellow's poem, "My Lost Youth," [11] which had been suggested to the elder poet in "two lines of the old Lapland song":

> A boy's will is the wind's will,
> And the thoughts of youth are long, long thoughts.

But Frost's latter-day arrival had purged the lines of their original melancholy, and his view was taken from a "sun-burned

---

[10] 1932 ed., by Harriet Monroe and Alice C. Henderson. By permission of The Macmillan Company.

[11] From *Complete Poetical Works of Henry Wadsworth Longfellow,* Houghton Mifflin Company.

hillside" in one of the best of his early sonnets, "The Vantage
Point": [12]

> If tired of trees I seek again mankind,
>   Well I know where to hie me—in the dawn,
>   To a slope where the cattle keep the lawn.
> There amid lolling juniper reclined,
> Myself unseen, I see in white defined
>   Far off the homes of men, and farther still,
>   The graves of men on an opposing hill,
> Living or dead, whichever are to mind.
>
> And if by noon I have too much of these,
>   I have but to turn on my arm, and lo,
>   The sun-burned hillside sets my face aglow,
> My breathing shakes the bluet like a breeze,
>   I smell the earth, I smell the bruisèd plant,
>   I look into the crater of the ant.

In this poem there is subtle analogy placed between the last
three lines of the octave and the final line of the sestet; it is
lightly stressed and its true sophistication contains a promise
that is fulfilled in two later sonnets, "A Soldier" and "The Master
Speed"; but its art also tends to make the "homespun" simplicities of Frost's later and semipolitical satires seem artificial. One
admires the wit, and smiles with Frost in the closing lines of his
"New Hampshire": [13]

> I choose to be a plain New Hampshire farmer
> With an income in cash of say a thousand
> (From say a publisher in New York City).
> It's restful to arrive at a decision,
> And restful just to think about New Hampshire.
> At present I am living in Vermont.

But the art of "Home Burial" and "The Death of the Hired
Man" and the excellent conceits which delight the reader of "A
Soldier" and still another sonnet, "Acquainted with the Night,"
tend to become mere artifice in the longer poem, "New Hampshire"; in "New Hampshire" the "homespun" quality is that of
well-pressed and smartly tailored tweeds, and it creates the same
dubiously "informal" atmosphere.

[12] From *Collected Poems*. By permission of Henry Holt and Company, Inc.
[13] *Ibid.*

3

Like the Anglo-Irish poet, W. B. Yeats (and in saying this, one must not forget that there is a strain of Scots-Celtic imagination in Frost's verse which alternately bewilders and dazzles his adverse critics as well as his would-be imitators)—like Yeats, Robert Frost has learned the actor's art of wearing several "masks" with which to face the world. One is that of the whimsical child, who has grown to manhood and who invites people to "come in," to leave their weary brains behind them and call the colt in or swing on birches. In general, it should be said that American poets, from James Whitcomb Riley to Wallace Stevens and the T. S. Eliot who wrote *Old Possum's Book of Practical Cats,* are not successful in the arts of whimsey—and all stop short of the divinely inspired nonsense of Edward Lear and of Lewis Carroll. In this respect, Frost has been more successful than most—for a true touch of the irresponsible "boy's will" has entered his role. Another mask is that of the hardy, witty, New England cracker-barrel "philosopher," who was typified by Calvin Coolidge when he said, "I do not choose to run," a remark which endeared the memory of that unhappy chief executive to the intelligence and heart of the entire nation. Still another mask is that of the highly sensitized poet, who has read his Keats and has written sparely, who respects his art and seldom allows himself the luxury of being dull:

> Being the creature of literature I am,
> I shall not lack for pain to keep me awake.[14]

And finally he has assumed the mask of Horace, the Horace of "the golden mean" between extremes, who wrote his *carmina,* his odes, and particularly the first ode of his third book against the high reaches of "modern" extravagance and taste. If *A Further Range,* published in 1936, showed a slight decline in Frost's abilities, the balance was properly restored by the publication of *A Witness Tree* (1942). In "The Lesson for Today,"

[14] "New Hampshire" from *Collected Poems.* By permission of Henry Holt and Company, Inc.

he puts forward his claim to being a "liberal" and a Horatian—
and at a far distance from and more profound level than the
political liberalism that within a single generation had found
itself so sorely distressed by the presence of two world wars. In
"A Serious Step Lightly Taken" [15] Frost reminded his fellow
countrymen that their history had embraced:

> A hundred thousand days
> Of front-page paper events,
> A half a dozen major wars,
> And forty-five presidents.

In *A Witness Tree,* Frost's "vantage point" was less explicitly
regional than national, and in one sense, the slender volume of
ninety-one pages was a summary of the half-dozen earlier books
he had written. He had not relinquished his Celtic imagination
to which he paid such excellent homage in "Love and a Question," an early poem in Scots ballad form in *A Boy's Will;* and
the echo of it can be heard in the later poem, "Never Again
Would Birds' Song Be the Same," and if the actual ballad form
had been put aside, the eloquence remained. The distinction of
his phrasing had carried itself a good half-century beyond the
young poet who had read Edward Rowland Sill:

> I could give all to Time except—except
> What I myself have held. But why declare
> The things forbidden that while the Customs slept
> I have crossed to Safety with? For I am There,
> And what I would not part with I have kept.[16]

And one feels that he had employed his mother-wit to out-
trick time itself with the same intention with which the Roman
poet wished to outlive the inscriptions written in brass. Of the
national spirit that had endured three wars within his lifetime
Frost wrote:

> The land was ours before we were the land's.
> She was our land more than a hundred years
> Before we were her people. She was ours
> In Massachusetts, in Virginia,

15 From *A Witness Tree.* By permission of Henry Holt and Company, Inc.
16 "I Could Give All to Time" from *A Witness Tree.* By permission of
Henry Holt and Company, Inc.

But we were England's, still colonials,
Possessing what we still were unpossessed by,
Possessed by what we now no more possessed.
Something we were withholding made us weak
Until we found it was ourselves
We were withholding from our land of living,
And forthwith found salvation in surrender.
Such as we were we gave ourselves outright
(The deed of gift was many deeds of war)
To the land vaguely realizing westward,
But still unstoried, artless, unenhanced,
Such as she was, such as she would become.[17]

As the lines are read, one no longer questions his classic-American heritage—and the voice is the *liquida vox* of Horace.

[17] "The Gift Outright" from *A Witness Tree*. By permission of Henry Holt and Company, Inc.

EZRA POUND AND THE SPIRIT OF ROMANCE

The political activities of the Second World War in Europe have obscured the poetry of Ezra Pound, and perhaps no figure of the "poetic renaissance" which began so hopefully in 1912 stands in more drastic need of sober revaluation than the author of *Personae* and *A Draft of XXX Cantos*. Since 1924 he has lived on the Italian Riviera, and since 1935 he has been more widely known as the violent and ineffectual champion of Mussolini's regime in Italy than for any legitimate claims he may once have had upon readers of poetry in the United States. His last volume of *Cantos*, published in England in 1940, further obscured his literary reputation; in this latter volume, many of the twenty Cantos were exercises in historical rhetoric—and in several of them the overtones of Pound's political convictions were heard as one might hear the noise of static on the radio. The poet who devotes himself too strenuously to politics is often in danger of becoming an unseasonable bore; and if he becomes dependent on the fortunes of a political master, his intelligence is less well informed than the kind of knowledge that his prince or chief executive has gained. Even the hardy and coarse-grained talent of a Charles Churchill in eighteenth-century London could not withstand the reverses of political favor; his topical references soon fell "out of date," his wit became the diversion merely for specialists in eighteenth-century satire, and fifty-two years after his death, Lord Byron in a self-confessed and rare Wordsworthian mood, looked at his grave and wrote:

> . . . for I did dwell
> With a deep thought, and with a soften'd eye,
> On that Old Sexton's natural homily,
> In which there was Obscurity and Fame,—
> The Glory and the Nothing of a Name.[1]

[1] "Churchill's Grave" from *Complete Poetical Works of Lord Byron*, Cambridge ed., used by permission of Houghton Mifflin Company.

The same obscurity attends Pound's later Cantos; and unlike Churchill's rough talent, Pound's gifts, however fragmentary they may seem today, were both firm and delicate, and through dissipation in literary showmanship and political activity, the loss is proportionally greater. In the hope of clarifying an otherwise prejudiced and clouded picture we shall present a summary of Pound's contribution to the "poetic renaissance" in three panels: first his legend and its relationship to the "little" magazines of the period, then his criticism, and finally his poetry.

2

Ezra Pound was born in 1885 in Hailey, Idaho, of New England and Wisconsin heritage. His mother was distantly related to Henry Wadsworth Longfellow, and before he was two years old, he was taken to Pennsylvania and brought up in the East. In 1901, he enrolled as a special student at the University of Pennsylvania, "so that he could study what he thought important" (a characteristic gesture, even then), and in 1903 he entered Hamilton College at Clinton, New York, from which he received a bachelor's degree in 1905. During the same year he returned to the University of Pennsylvania as a fellow in Romance languages and literature and from that institution he received his master's degree in 1906. After a year of travel in France, Italy, and Spain in search of material for a thesis on Lope de Vega, he returned to America in 1907 to accept an instructorship at Wabash College, Crawfordsville, Indiana, from which he was soon released, as Fred B. Millett remarks in his *Contemporary American Authors*, "on the grounds that he was too European and too unconventional." And during the following year, in 1908, Ezra Pound, after a brief stay at Gibraltar and in Italy, began his twelve-year residence in London.

In London, guided by the friendship of W. B. Yeats and Ford Madox Ford, he was received as an American "original," the gifted, shining heir of the late James McNeill Whistler, who had died in 1903, and indeed the camera study of Pound, made by E. O. Hoppé, of London, closely resembled the portraits painted by Whistler. The tall, thin figure of Pound, seated in profile against a dark, weighted curtain could be mistaken for the brilliant American artist who had preceded him to London. Iris Barry in a lively report of "The Ezra Pound Period" which was published in *The Bookman,* New York, in October, 1931, described the position that Pound filled in London during the years of the First World War:

At that time his name stood in England along with that of the sculptor Epstein, for all that was dangerously different, horridly new. . . . Also, Pound talks like no one else. His is almost a wholly original accent, the base of American mingled with a dozen assorted "English society" and Cockney accents inserted in mockery, French, Spanish and Greek exclamations, strange cries and catcalls, the whole very oddly inflected, with dramatic pauses and *diminuendos.* . . . As literary adviser to *The Egoist* and London editor of *Poetry* (afterwards of *The Little Review*) he was forever combing obscure periodicals and tracking down new and unprinted manuscript. It was natural to him to encourage and groom young writers as though he—penniless enough himself—had been one of those patrons of the arts of whom Chesterfield spoke when he reminded his contemporaries that it was the "privilege of the privileged to assist the possessor of wit." . . . Besides the writers who flocked to him through the post there were nascent artists, sculptors, musicians to encourage, to find patrons for, to find inexpensive rooms for, to find friends for . . . to render happy by placing them in a restaurant where the shadow of the great—Yeats or Arthur Symons, perhaps—might fall fruitfully upon them. . . . So there were hundreds of letters to write, influential people to be stirred . . . hundreds more letters to write so that people inhabiting the outlying regions of culture should realize they would be foolish not to buy copies of *Prufrock* and *A Portrait of the Artist,* at a time when neither Eliot nor Joyce had an an extensive following. Something had to be done about Gaudier-Brzeska. The war had suddenly gone too far. . . . His work must be preserved. . . . Joyce in Trieste was in danger of going blind—had anything been done about that? . . . Who knew Asquith, or had any influence with anyone in the Cabinet or could persuade Lady Cunard to speak to somebody? . . . Pound . . . began signing his letters with a seal in the Chinese manner that Edmond Dulac made for him; turned from cooking dinner (one of the things he does to perfection) wrapped in a flowing and worn fawn dressing-gown to the harpsichord Dolmetsch made for him; was always striding about the streets with his head thrown back, seeing everything, meeting everybody, as full of the latest gossip as he was of excitement about the pictorial quality of the Chinese . . . or a line of Rimbaud's or Leopardi's, and never forgetting how much he disliked dons, the Elizabethan influence, the technique of Byron, or how suspicious he was about "the Greeks."

To this portrait by Miss Barry, John Gould Fletcher's autobiography, *Life Is My Song*, contributed a no less revealing detail: "The more I studied him the more I was convinced that he was a queer combination of an international Bohemian and of an American college professor out of a job."

Startling and "horridly new" as Ezra Pound's appearance in London may have seemed, James McNeill Whistler was not his single predecessor. His way had been unknowingly prepared by an earlier American, Henry Harland, who had edited *The Yellow Book* in London in 1894, whose list of contributors included Henry James, Ernest Dowson, Aubrey Beardsley, and Lionel Johnson. Through the publication of four small books of poems (*Exultations of Ezra Pound*, 1909; *Personae of Ezra Pound,* 1909; *Provença,* 1910; *Canzoni of Ezra Pound,* 1911), through his letters of advice to Miss Monroe of *Poetry* and later to Margaret Anderson who edited *The Little Review,* through his association with Wyndham Lewis who edited "the magenta-covered" *Blast,* through his friendship with Ford Madox Ford and Violet Hunt who were heirs of a Pre-Raphaelite tradition, Pound gave continuity to a standard of taste that Henry Harland had all too briefly sustained in his magazine. It could be said that Pound's activities ("London is itself a larger university, and the best specialists are perhaps only approachable in chance conversation," he once remarked) brought Henry Harland's short-lived venture "up to date." And it could also be remarked that W. E. Henley's *National Observer,* with its small circulation and its severely trained "young men," created a slightly earlier precedent for Pound's ability to marshal young writers and artists around him in something that resembled military formation. Ford Madox Ford's *The English Review* and, later, his *Trans-Atlantic Review* were contemporary periodicals of the same order. But Pound and Wyndham Lewis in founding *Blast* in 1914 set an example that was followed for many years beyond the period of the "poetic renaissance" itself. Pound's influence can be traced through the files of at least fifty "little" magazines published on both sides of the Atlantic from 1916 to 1939. All owed their debts, however indirectly the coinage may have fallen into their hands, to Ezra Pound's years of writing letters and forming literary "movements" in London. It is impossible to determine how deeply Pound was responsible for the large currency given to the names of Gérard de Nerval, Rimbaud, Jules Laforgue, Tristan Corbière, Stéphane Mallarmé, Huysmans, Gide, and Cocteau in essays published in "little" magazines which extended their list of half a hundred titles from *Blast* to James Laughlin's *New Directions Annual* for 1944; many of the names had already appeared in Arthur Symons' *The Symbolist Movement in Literature* before the twentieth century began—but if Pound seemed to be "an American college professor out of a job," he also became a minister of the arts without portfolio, eager to instruct the "passionate pilgrim" from either the United States or within the United Kingdom itself in the skills and delights of approaching Romance literatures with a knowing air.

Of the so-called literary "movements" that Pound fostered none received wider publicity than Imagism, which came to light in 1912 and achieved the dignity nineteen years later of having an entire book (*Imagism & the Imagists* by Glenn Hughes, 1931) devoted to its rise and fall. The climate that produced *Les Imagistes* deserves a few words of explanation. In London itself something very like a "rebirth" in poetic speech, style, and manner had begun to be strongly felt among young men who had come down from the universities. The "Georgian" poets who met in Harold Monro's (he who had written "Nymph, nymph, what are your beads?") Poetry Bookshop, and who had been assembled in anthologies edited by Edward Marsh, seemed to lead poetry far away from the chintz-and-horsehair intimacies of Sir Edmund Gosse's drawing room into the English countryside. The venture was a far more sedate and domestic journey than the call to the delights of Vagabondia that Bliss Carman and Richard Hovey sounded in America during the preceding decade; the "Georgians" were more decorous in pursuing their escape from both Swinburne and Victorian "respectability," and, it must be admitted, more mature. Among this group, of which Wilfred Gibson and Rupert Brooke were prominent figures, Pound quickly discovered and welcomed a fellow American, Robert

Frost, but no sooner than he recognized the "New England Eclogues" as being "infinitely better than fake," Pound returned to an earlier circle, The Poet's Club, which had held its meetings in a Soho restaurant under the spell of a young philosopher from Cambridge whose name was T. E. Hulme. Pound had been introduced to the members of the club by F. S. Flint, and when Pound arrived at the restaurant shouting his sestina: "Altaforte"—"Damn it all! all this our South stinks peace"—Flint reported that the entire café trembled. The members of the club were high-spirited talkers, and they sustained the atmosphere of after-midnight conversations held by undergraduates at college. Of the young men who frequented the club perhaps a paragraph from Wyndham Lewis's novel, *Tarr* (1918),[2] offers the best description:

A Cambridge cut disfigured his originally manly and melodramatic form. His father was a wealthy merchant at the Cape. He was very athletic, and his dark and cavernous features had been constructed by Nature as a lurking place for villainies and passions. But he slouched and ambled along, neglecting his muscles: and his dastardly face attempted to portray delicacies of commonsense, and gossamerlike backslidings into the Inane that would have puzzled a bile-specialist. He would occasionally exploit his blackguardly appearance and blacksmith's muscles for a short time, however. And his strong, piercing laugh threw A.B.C. waitresses into confusion.

This, of course, must not be mistaken for a freehand portrait of T. E. Hulme or of any other individual member of the club itself; but the atmosphere which surrounded that type of young man is convincingly presented—even the youthful and decidedly "experimental" quality of Lewis' prose adds an unconscious touch of veracity to the portrait. We can then understand how casually a discussion of the Japanese *tanka* and *haikai* took place in a Soho restaurant, and how the young philosopher, T. E. Hulme, as if to prove a point in a discussion which had lasted several hours and was probably forgotten, produced five pieces of unrhymed verse. What had begun as a half-serious private joke had an unexpected result in the closing pages of Ezra Pound's

[2] By permission of Alfred A. Knopf, Inc. Copyright 1918 by Wyndham Lewis.

book of verse, *Ripostes* (1912), in which he had inserted five poems as "the complete poetical works of T. E. Hulme," and these were prefaced by a short note of warning written in Pound's hand, "As for the future, Les Imagistes . . . have that in their keeping." To be sure, the phrase "Les Imagistes" was not unattractive, and Pound bestowed its magic (and whatever mystery it contained to the uninitiated) upon all the poetry written by his friends. He gave it to Hulme, to Richard Aldington, to F. S. Flint, to John Cournos, to Ford Madox Ford—and most importantly, and with an air of conferring a special honor upon her and her gifts, to Hilda Doolittle, "H. D."

Within a few years, several Imagist anthologies were planned and some were published. The "movement" attracted the willing co-operation of Amy Lowell from Brookline, Massachusetts, who was given strictly limited permission to spread its gospel in the United States. But it was characteristic of Pound to grow impatient of a prolonged stay within any "movement," however amusing its diversions may have been. He soon quarreled with his American representative, Miss Lowell, and as she retreated across the Atlantic to Sevenells in Brookline, Pound deserted his followers by joining forces with Wyndham Lewis in a newer "movement" that had the more exotic name of "Vorticism" to its credit. Even this brief summary of Pound's activities shows how far removed he was from the comparatively slow evolutions of the British "movement" which emanated from the shelves of Harold Monro's Poetry Bookshop; Pound displayed the instincts and mannerisms of an American pioneer in his behavior, and was ill content to rest at any spot short of an horizon that held the promise of a pre-Renaissance Europe in its view.

In 1920, as Pound prepared to leave London for Paris and the Italian Riviera, the hour of luck and good fortune which had attended the early years of his stay in England seemed to fade behind him: Hulme and Gaudier-Brzeska had been killed in battle on the fields of France; even the most enthusiastic of those who had reviewed his early books of poems, Edward Thomas, the same Thomas who had been a friend of Robert Frost, had been killed at Vimy Ridge; and the now prolonged excitement at discovering the "new" poetry had acquired a dangerously reminiscent air. As for the British public, a public that Pound perhaps had once hoped to educate, their attitude was accurately reflected in Richard Aldington's autobiography, *Life for Life's Sake* [3] (1941) and if it remembered Pound at all, it was in these unflattering terms:

> Tom Eliot's career in England has been exactly the reverse of Ezra's. Ezra started out in a time of peace and prosperity with everything in his favor, and muffed his chances of becoming literary dictator of London—to which he undoubtedly aspired—by his own conceit, folly, and bad manners. Eliot started in the enormous confusion of war and post-war England, handicapped in every way. Yet by merit, tact, prudence, and pertinacity he succeeded in doing what no other American has ever done—imposing his personality, taste, and even many of his opinions on literary England.

In Paris and at Rapallo in Italy the dissipation of Pound's energies continued. From a reading of Major Douglas' treatise on Social Credit, Pound turned to writing ill-considered pamphlets and books in praise of Mussolini's Fascist Italy. In 1939 he returned to America for a short visit during which he received an honorary degree from Hamilton College; and the opening of the Second World War found him in Italy again. In thinking of Pound's "exile" one is reminded of Henry Adams' remarks on George Cabot Lodge and Trumbull Stickney who had preceded Pound to Europe, and whose precocious gifts had been cut short by death and undue speculations upon what Adams had named "conservative Christian anarchy." During the Second World War a charge of treason against the United States obscured the latter phases of Pound's career.

3

A considerably less unhappy prospect is in view as one turns to the more serious, if lightly phrased, aspects of Pound's literary criticism, for no young writer of Pound's generation held greater promise than he who wrote *The Spirit of Romance* (London, 1910) which bore on its title page a modest statement of the book's intention: "an attempt to define somewhat the charm of

[3] By permission of The Viking Press, Inc. Copyright 1940, 1941 by Richard Aldington.

the pre-renaissance literature of Latin Europe by Ezra Pound, M.A."

Its table of contents listed essays on Arnaut Daniel, on Cavalcanti, on Montcorbier (alias Villon), on selected passages of Dante's *Divine Comedy* and the dramatic verse of Lope de Vega. There is nothing in Pound's later prose that equals the felicity of the book's Preface:

> This book is not a philological work. Only by courtesy can it be said to be a study in comparative literature. . . . I am interested in poetry. . . . Art or an art is not unlike a river. It is perturbed at times by the quality of the river bed, but it is in a way independent of that bed. The colour of the water depends upon the substance of the bed and banks immediate and preceding. Stationary objects are reflected, but the quality of motion is of the river. The scientist is concerned with all of these things, the artist with that which flows. . . . It is dawn at Jerusalem while midnight hovers above the Pillars of Hercules. All ages are contemporaneous. It is B.C., let us say, in Morocco. The Middle Ages are in Russia. The future stirs already in the minds of the few. This is especially true of literature, where the real time is independent of the apparent, and where many dead men are our grand-children's contemporaries. . . . Art is a joyous thing. Its happiness antedates even Whistler; apropos of which I would in all seriousness plead for a greater levity, a more befitting levity, in our study of the arts. . . , Good art never bores one. By that I mean that it is the business of the artist to prevent ennui; in the literary art, to relieve, refresh, revive the mind of the reader. . . . Good art begins with an escape from dulness. . . . The aim of the present work is to instruct. Its ambition is to instruct painlessly. . . . As to my fitness or unfitness to attempt this treatise: Putnam tells us that, in the early regulations of the faculty of the University of Paris, this oath is prescribed for professors: "I swear to read and to finish reading within the time set by the statutes, the books and parts of books assigned for my lectures." This law I have, contrary to the custom of literary historians, complied with. My multitudinous mistakes and inaccuracies are at least my own.[4]

What is said here has been repeated by Pound many times in *Make It New* (1935), in *A B C of Reading* (1934), *Polite Essays* (1937), and *Culture* (1938)—but the Preface to *The Spirit of Romance* was in itself a true "escape from dulness"; it employed the uses of grace and of wit, and the mention of Whistler sug-

---

[4] From *The Spirit of Romance*, J. M. Dent and Sons, Ltd., London, 1910.

gests that Pound was by no means unfamiliar with the painter's
The Gentle Art of Making Enemies. The plea for a "greater
levity" in art was decidedly refreshing because each generation
in literature so frequently mistakes dullness for seriousness, and
didactic or pious zeal for learning. Pound's Preface to his book
expressed this truism with the same glancing turn of wit that so
happily advanced the younger Bernard Shaw in his dramatic
criticism. To us who read *The Spirit of Romance* today and
since we possess some knowledge of his *Cantos* which began to
appear fifteen years later, it is of interest to observe that the
historical scheme of Pound's long poem was clearly anticipated
in "It is dawn at Jerusalem while midnight hovers above the
Pillars of Hercules. All ages are contemporaneous." (We should
also remark that the scheme was too large, too ambitious, and in
its detail, too pedantic, to enclose a poem, however long it may
become, within its frame. Obviously, the choices of "contemporaneous ages" are dependent upon the will or inclination of the
poet; within that loosely conceived scheme a poem has the license
to begin or end at any given point in "contemporaneous" time
or space; and whatever claims to formal structure it may have
are always deceptive.) Pound's early (and late) devotion to pre-
Renaissance literature has still another aspect of great interest:
with *The Spirit of Romance* he arrived in London in 1910 as a
belated member of the Pre-Raphaelite Brotherhood, but his road
had been taken by way of the North American continent and a
frequently acknowledged reading of Robert Browning. These
facts give rise to several speculations which may be taken for
what they are worth, and if they are not exaggerated in their
importance, they have true relevance to his critical prose and
his professed identities with Robert Browning and Arnaut
Daniel, the Provençal poet. The years of Pound's childhood in
the United States witnessed the rise of "Browning Clubs"
throughout the country and at their weekly or fortnightly meetings, the mysteries of *Sordello* and *The Ring and the Book* held
all the "fascination of what's difficult." Pound could not have
avoided some knowledge of these meetings, at which thousands
of women aspired to the reaches of "higher learning." We cannot
say how deeply Pound felt himself to be an "arrival" in London

from the "provinces" of North America, but we do know from his essay on Henry James (published in 1918) of his appreciation of James's "real cut at barbarism and bigotry"—and he continued his discourse with the use of a Far Western hyperbole, "by these monstrous and rhetorical brands, scorched on to their hides and rump sides." In London, Pound cultivated his Americanisms almost as violently as Joaquin Miller had in an earlier generation, and the romantic figure of the Far Western cowboy was the very image of their literary behavior, which to European eyes, always endows the "American poet" with exotic charm. The cowboy himself through his songs and ballads has a distant, slender, and yet clear relationship to the "makers" of courtly love and the troubadours. His songs are adaptations of an ancient music, overlaid with the melancholy wail of the Celtic bagpipe; and his attitude toward the lady (or the various ladies) of his choice has a heritage that extends its line from the masters and students of court music whom Pound brought back to life in *The Spirit of Romance*. The least we can say is that Pound's literary personality, however fractured it may seem upon its surface, has its own elements of extraordinary consistency.

The Spirit of Romance has evidence of the same precocity that earned Trumbull Stickney a Doctorat ès Lettres at the University of Paris in 1903, but it is extremely doubtful if Pound's intelligence would have emerged victorious over Stickney's examiners at the Sorbonne; his temperament was far too volatile, too restless, too egocentric in its investigations and discoveries to withstand the strain of a prolonged and unfriendly examination. Pound's precocity had critical overtones, and in the pronouncement of its truisms there was a proper balance (so seldom achieved in his later writings) between a concern for scholarship and critical common sense:

I have used the term "classic" in connection with Latinity: in the course of this book I shall perhaps be tempted to use the word "romantic"; both terms are snares, and one must not be confused by them. The history of literary criticism is the history of a vain struggle to find a terminology which will define something. The triumph of literary criticism is that certain of its terms—chiefly those defined by Aristotle—still retain some shreds of meaning. . . . Certain qualities and certain furnishings are germane to all fine poetry; there is no need to call them either classic or romantic. . . . The difference is neither of matter nor of paraphernalia. Seeking a distinction in the style, we are nearer to sanity, yet even here we might do well to borrow an uncorrupted terminology from architecture. Such terms as *Doric, Romanesque* and *Gothic* would convey a definite meaning, and would, when applied to style, be difficult of misinterpretation. . . . Poetry is a sort of inspired mathematics, which gives us equations, not for abstract figures, triangles, spheres, and the like, but equations for . . . human emotions . . . the spells or equations of "classic" art invoke the beauty of the normal, and spells of "romantic" art are said to invoke the beauty of the unusual.[5]

However strange Pound's criticism may have seemed to some few of his elders, there was nothing here to shock their sensibilities, except the phrase, "Poetry is a sort of inspired mathematics." And that phrase leads us to the critical affinity that Pound had discovered in his friendship with T. E. Hulme. Hulme's youthful intelligence had found itself in revolt against the utterly shabby extremes of utilitarianism into which British philosophy had fallen after the publication of John Stuart Mill's essay *On Liberty* in 1859. Hulme's mind was of a military cut; his acknowledged master was Sorel; and his semiphilosophic, semiliterary *Speculations* (which were collected and edited by Herbert Read in 1924) reflected a temperament not unlike that of an immature Stendhal. His relationships to Pound, and later to T. S. Eliot, remind one of the influence exerted by Coleridge upon Wordsworth, an influence which imposed as much harm upon the object of its attention as it did good. Wordsworth had little aptitude for assimilating Coleridge's philosophic brilliance; for a brief moment the results of Coleridge's eloquence were tonic, but beyond that moment, Wordsworth's philosophic pretensions became overweighted and pontifical. The effect of Hulme upon Pound had like results, and as Pound grew older, his critical observations tended to take on the character of Hulme's notes:

Smoothness. [wrote Hulme]
   Hate it.
  This is the obsession that starts all my theories.

[5] From *The Spirit of Romance*, J. M. Dent and Sons, Ltd., London, 1910.

Get other examples, other facets of the one idea.
Build them up by catalogue method
   (I) in science;
   (II) in sex;
(III) in poetry.

.   .   .   .   .

It is essential to prove that beauty may be in small, dry things. . . .
We introduce into human things the *Perfection* that properly belongs
only to the divine, and thus confuse both human and divine things by
not clearly separating them . . . the Middle Ages, which lacked entirely the conception of personality, had a real belief in immortality;
while thought since the Renaissance, which has been dominated by a
belief in personality, has not had the same conviction. . . . Men differ
very little in every period. It is only our categories that change. . . .
Exactly the same type existed in the Middle Ages as now. This con-
stancy of man thus provides perhaps the greatest hope of the possibility of a radical transformation of society. . . . Each field of artistic
activity is exhausted by the first great artist who gathers a full harvest
from it. This period of exhaustion seems to me to have been reached
in romanticism. We shall not get any new efflorescence of verse until
we get a new technique, a new convention, to turn ourselves loose in.[6]

These quotations from Hulme bear the marks of a tough, penetrating, inquiring mind, but the thinking is neither subtle nor is
it one that had found a well-considered point of rest within its
world; it commands rather than reflects—it makes no effort to
persuade the reader, and its effects are gained by seizing the
initiative, as though life itself were conducted by the same rules
that govern an undergraduate debating team. Its exuberance and
its youthfulness are betrayed by "a new convention, to turn ourselves loose in."

One hears an echo of T. E. Hulme's manner in Pound's thoroughly enlivening essay on Henry James; the thinking behind it
is less genuinely "tough" than Hulme's, and the prose is considerably richer in rapidly presented and vivid figures of speech, but
the didactic, nonpersuasive, note-taking manner is there; nouns
often appear without their articles, and it was as though a military command had created a scene of action and urgency:

Butler and James on the same side really chucking out the fake;
Butler focused on Church of England; opposed to him the fakers boom-

[6] From *Speculations,* used by permission of Harcourt, Brace and Company.

ing the Bible "as literature" in a sort of last stand, a last ditch; seeing it pretty well had to go as history, cosmogony, etc.[7]

Pound's exaggerated, almost "Wild West" Americanisms are also present in this short passage, but more than all else it indicates how attentively he listened to the young student of Sorel from Cambridge, and of the distance he had traveled from the persuasive, informative wit of *The Spirit of Romance* toward a "new technique." One cannot, of course, blame Hulme for "over-stimulating" Pound, for it is obvious enough that Pound's mind had a true affinity with Hulme's intelligence; though Hulme had much to say, he did not live to write his *Biographia Literaria,* and the misfortune was, that after leaving London in 1920, Pound's critical prose did not mature beyond the example presented him by Hulme.

In "A Few Don'ts by an Imagiste" (*Poetry,* Chicago, March, 1913) Pound provided the young writer, as Norman Holmes Pearson has observed, with "a fresh manual of arms"; but after 1920, and not unlike many lecturers in American colleges and universities, Pound directed too much of his criticism to an audience of unlearned youth. Though his dogmatism delighted the youthful editors of "little" magazines, the British public continued to follow the advice of *The Times Literary Supplement,* quite as if Ezra Pound or any other American poet (with the exceptions of Longfellow and Ella Wheeler Wilcox) had not existed.

4

With the same relief with which one turns from the extra-verted activities of Pound's career in London to a rereading of his criticism, one is refreshed by setting aside his criticism in favor of his poetry. No American poet (with, of course, the well-known exceptions of William Cullen Bryant who wrote "Thanatopsis" at the age of seventeen and Poe who wrote his first lines "To Helen" at twenty-two) has been more precociously gifted than Ezra Pound. One can almost say that if Poe dissi-

[7] "Henry James" from *Instigations* by Ezra Pound. Liveright Publishing Corp.

pated his gifts by the use of strong spirits and drugs, Pound's dissipations in literary showmanship, politics, and criticism were more continuously sustained than Poe's brief hours of self-indulgence, and that these dissipations, with their transitory show of merit, were nearly as destructive to Pound's poetic maturity as an immoderate use of veronal, opium, or gin. In regard to Pound's poetry, it is salutary to respect R. P. Blackmur's observation that "Mr. Pound is everywhere a master of his medium so long as the matter in hand is not his own." In a literal sense, Blackmur happened to be more often right than wrong, for many of Pound's best poems have behind them an example set by the masters of English, Provençal, Italian, Chinese, or Latin verse—and this list could be enlarged to include the masters of Greek as well as of Anglo-Saxon poetry. The trouble is that Blackmur's observation did not penetrate into the phenomenal nature of Pound's gifts, for his gifts in their sensitivity, their precocity, and their wit were distinctly fragile and were of a character that stood in contrast to the apparently bluff and "tough-minded" attitudes of Pound's literary career. A clue to the nature of Pound's true contribution to twentieth-century poetry may be found in his translation of *The Sonnets and Ballate of Guido Cavalcanti* (Boston, 1912) and a brief comparison of it with Dante Gabriel Rossetti's *The Early Italian Poets* (1861). The first comparison (or likeness) appears on the dedication page itself; Rossetti wrote, "Whatever is mine in this book is inscribed to my wife"; and what Pound wrote some fifty years later was, "As much of this book as is mine I send to my friends Violet and Ford Madox Hueffer." The original setting of the book was of a distinctly Pre-Raphaelite atmosphere, but on the second page beyond the dedication, one finds a half-title page with two lines of verse instead of the half-title; and the lines were written in Pound's characteristic manner:

> I have owed service to the deathless dead
> Grudge not the gold I bear in livery.

Whatever their origin may have been, the speech was not Rossetti's; and to clarify the nature of his relationship to the elder poet, Pound said gracefully and swiftly, "In the matter of these

translations and of my knowledge of Tuscan poetry, Rossetti is
my father and my mother."

In the translation of the sonnets, and weighing their separate
merits and flaws, Rossetti and Pound scored evenly; neither poet
gave any single sonnet the grace to stand alone and to be compared with the best of English sonnets. But among Cavalcanti's
ballate, Pound's true voice was and still is heard, and "Ballata
IX" must be regarded as one of the best of his early poems. The
quality of its grace and the freshness of its language place it
with those lyrics which are continually rediscovered among the
pastorals that Sir Philip Sidney scattered so richly between the
prose passages of his Arcadia.

> In wood-way found I once a shepherdess,
> More fair than stars was she to me seeming.
>
> Her hair was wavy somewhat, like dull gold.
> Eyes? Love-worn, and her face like some pale rose.
> With a small twig she kept her lambs in hold,
> And bare her feet were bar the dew-drop's gloze;
> She sang as one whom mad love holdeth close,
> And joy was on her face for an ornament.
>
> I greeted her in love without delaying:
> "Hast thou companion in thy solitude?"
> And she replied to me most sweetly, saying,
> "Nay, I am quite alone in all this wood,
> But when the birds 'gin singing in their coverts
> May heart is fain that time to find a lover."
>
> As she was speaking thus of her condition
> I heard the bird-song 'neath the forest shade
> And thought me how't was but the time's provision
> To gather joy of this small shepherd maid.
> Favour I asked her, but for kisses only,
> And then I felt her pleasant arms upon me.
>
> She held to me with a dear willfulness
> Saying her heart had gone into my bosom,
> She drew me on to a cool, leafy place
> Where I gat sight of every coloured blossom,
> And there I drank in so much summer sweetness
> Meseemed Love's god connived at its completeness.[8]

[8] "Ballata IX," from *The Sonnets and Ballate of Guido Cavalcanti,* Small,
Maynard and Company, Boston, copyright 1912 by Ezra Pound.

And there is the same fine quality in Pound's adaptation from Voltaire's lines "To Madame Lullin."

> You'll wonder that an old man of eighty
> Can go on writing you verses . . .
>
> Grass showing under the snow,
> Birds singing late in the year!
>
> And Tibullus could say of his death, in his Latin:
> "Delia, I would look on you, dying."
>
> And Delia herself fading out,
> Forgetting even her beauty.[9]

These are examples of Pound's particular manner of adapting verse into English; and the frequently quoted "Envoi (1919)" to his *Hugh Selwyn Mauberley* (*Personae,* 1926) was a frankly acknowledged adaptation of Edmund Waller's "Go, Lovely Rose." The same light touch made its appearance in an early sonnet, "A Virginal": [10]

> No, no! Go from me. I have left her lately.
> I will not spoil my sheath with lesser brightness,
> For my surrounding air hath a new lightness;
> Slight are her arms, yet they have bound me straitly
> And left me cloaked as with a gauze of aether;
> As with sweet leaves; as with subtle clearness.
> Oh, I have picked up magic in her nearness
> To sheathe me half in half the things that sheathe her.
> No, no! Go from me. I have still the flavor,
> Soft as spring wind that's come from birchen bowers.
> Green come the shoots, aye April in the branches,
> As winter's wound with her slight hand she staunches,
> Hath of the trees a likeness of the saviour:
> As white their bark, so white this lady's hours.

But these graces were ill suited to the expression of anger, over-weighted wit, terror, and historical commentary which were diffused so liberally through many of his seventy-one published Cantos; even in *Hugh Selwyn Mauberley,* which F. R. Leavis so respectfully admired, many of the pieces, despite their historical

---

[9] "Impressions of François-Marie Arouet (de Voltaire)" from *Lustra,* by permission of Liveright Publishing Corp.

[10] From *Personae,* by permission of Liveright Publishing Corp.

value—a value which T. S. Eliot noted as "a mine for juvenile poets to quarry"—now seem to have become period pieces, and somewhat "arty"; certainly many are less rewarding than they seemed to be twenty years ago. The prose rhythms of *Cathay* (Pound's adaptations from the Chinese), of his *Homage to Sextus Propertius* (1917) prepared his readers for the occasional felicities of his stanza form which separates one Canto from another, but the true felicities of the stanza, anticipated, so it seems in "The River-Merchant's Wife" of Rihaku in *Cathay*, and which reach a delicately balanced perfection in Cantos I and XLV were seldom achieved. One can agree with F. R. Leavis and T. S. Eliot that Pound's "new rhythms" both reflected and then invented something to be recognized as a twentieth-century sensibility in verse; and the rhetoric of the first Canto was beautifully sustained.

> "I slept in Circe's ingle.
> "Going down the long ladder unguarded,
> "I fell against the buttress,
> "Shattered the nape-nerve, the soul sought Avernus.
> "But thou, O King, I bid remember me, unwept, unburied,
> "Heap up mine arms, be tomb by sea-bord, and inscribed:
> "*A man of no fortune, and with a name to come.*
> "And set my oar up, that I swing mid-fellows." [11]

The speech came, of course, from the lips of Elpenor in the Eleventh Book of Homer's *Odyssey*, and it might well serve at some future date for Pound's own epitaph. But the loose and large scheme of the *Cantos* offered Pound too many opportunities to drift, to talk, to become willfully pedantic, or, like Landor in his *Imaginary Conversations*, to become a bore. It would seem that Pound in the years after 1920 had exhausted the wealth and abused the fine temper of his poetic gifts. If his best work seems obscure, some means should be found to republish in facsimile his first book of essays, *The Spirit of Romance*; even in the *Cantos*, fragments of a perennially youthful sensibility emerge; the gift seems harassed and battered, but its lyrical excellence is pure. One should not hesitate to say that he alone of twentieth-century poets is of proper stature to fill his defi-

[11] "Canto I" from *A Draft of XXX Cantos*, New Directions.

nition of the Inventor which he has stated so well in his study
of *How to Read:* [12]

> *The inventors,* discoverers of a particular process or of more than one
> mode and process. Sometimes these people are known, or discoverable;
> for example, we know, with reasonable certitude, that Arnaut Daniel
> introduced certain methods of rhyming, and we know that certain fine-
> nesses of perception appeared first in such a troubadour or in G. Caval-
> canti.

It is in this image that his reputation is likely to remain secure;
and it is extremely unlikely that the future will ignore (at least,
as long as poetry is read) the lyrical brilliance of his "Envoi": [13]

> Tell her that goes
> With song upon her lips
> But sings not out the song, nor knows
> The maker of it, some other mouth,
> May be as fair as hers,
> Might, in new ages, gain her worshippers,
> When our two dusts with Waller's shall be laid,
> Siftings on siftings in oblivion,
> Till change hath broken down
> All things save Beauty alone.

In these lines the unhappy moments of his *Cantos* are forgotten and within them the "charm" that he defined in *The
Spirit of Romance* is reawakened and restored.

[12] Part II, Desmond Harmsworth, London, 1931.
[13] From *Personae*, by permission of Liveright Publishing Corp.

AMY LOWELL, LITERARY STATESMAN

Those who were young in the early 1920's, and especially the aspiring young who were also interested in the reading and writing of poetry, remember the attractively bound, beautifully printed volumes of Amy Lowell's verse that were to be found on the library tables of those who had claims to be both advanced and cultured. Even the titles gave one an air of elegance and distinction—such delightful titles they were! *A Dome of Many-coloured Glass* (1912), *Sword Blades and Poppy Seeds* (1914), *Men, Women and Ghosts* (1917), *Can Grande's Castle* (1918), *Pictures of the Floating World* (1919)—and one has not named them all. For in her short career as a writer and when she died at the age of fifty-one, Amy Lowell (1874-1925) had written or rather published about seven hundred poems, had written a number of books on literary subjects, had completed a mammoth biography of John Keats, and though fatally ill, still dauntless—the mind, the will, the energy becoming keener as the too corpulent body began to fail—Amy Lowell was still planning more poems, more books. She was planning to write her autobiography, a life of Emily Dickinson was to be written, and a campaign was to be started to overcome the difficulties in the way of writing such a biography. It was true that she loved Emily Dickinson a little better than she understood her, but one is sure that the work would have been worth seeing, for like everything that Amy Lowell thought, did, or wrote it would have been filled with her own personality and energy. She was also planning to do more translations from the Chinese with Florence Ayscough, she had been planning to visit Mary Austin in the Southwest and to make a study of Indian poetry—and because her life of Keats had been rather severely treated by British reviewers, she had also planned a lecture tour of England, perhaps decided to give the critics there a piece of her mind. For Amy Lowell was one of the few Americans who had learned to put the fear of God into the English. She had discovered that effective attitude of high-handed arrogance, an indifference to the British brand of snobbery, by insisting on snobberies of her own—which was an art that John Jay Chapman had recommended to all visiting Americans. Nor was this the least of Amy Lowell's advantages in England: that she had been born to that great wealth which is even more respected and admired among effete aristocrats than in more democratic circles at home.

"Keats is killing me" she had written in a letter to John Middleton Murry, and her large body, exhausted by two surgical operations and an illness that brought with it the prospect of a third, gave way. On the morning of May 12, 1925, while looking through the many letters that always arrived with her morning mail, she suddenly felt unwell, glanced upward at her mirror, and knew her death. She saw the right side of her face drop and recognized a paralytic stroke. Thirty minutes later she was dead and the Amy Lowell legend was to begin—or rather to take on new forms.

Was she a great poet? Was Amy Lowell a poet at all? Ten years later, a young poet, Winfield Townley Scott, was to sum up what certainly became the majority opinion among his colleagues:

Her life, her career was a magnificent masterpiece. She herself must have thought it a failure, for she could not be what she most desired to be—a great poet. Her poems are the work of a woman who would have shone as extraordinary in any career, they are, even at their most expert, remarkable in the very light of their weakness, for Amy Lowell was not a poet at all.[1]

She was reputed to have said that the Lord had made her a businessman, but that she, herself, had made herself a poet; and Harriet Monroe, who had many traits in common with her, always insisted that Amy Lowell had everything but genius. Richard Aldington in his recent autobiography speaks of Amy Lowell with almost reluctant admiration: "It is the fashion now

[1] From "Amy Lowell After Ten Years" by Winfield T. Scott, in *The New England Quarterly*, VIII, Sept., 1935, by permission of *The New England Quarterly*.

to write Amy Lowell off as a society woman who would never have been heard of as a writer if she hadn't been a Lowell. That is unfair. In Amy there was something of an artist and a real esthetic appreciation." And Aldington reminds us of her enthusiasm for and support of such real artists as D. H. Lawrence and H. D.—and this at the beginning of their careers.

"Amy Lowell," wrote her biographer, S. Foster Damon, "was born with every obstacle except poverty." A child of that Lowell family who were "astonishingly indifferent to the opinions of others, who were much given to public benefactions and controversies, and who intended to be manufacturers and merchants, judges, poets, scholars and critics, and horticulturists," Amy Lowell seemed to be a summing up of all their strongest and most flamboyant qualities. Her father was described as "unmistakably a Lowell": he believed in Darwin to the end of his days and would never allow a volume of Shelley's poems to cross the threshold of his house. He took his pleasures seriously, but he preferred work to play.

Amy Lowell, his youngest child, was born at Sevenels, the great house on the Lowell estate in Brookline, Massachusetts. Sevenells was to suffuse her life and color her poetry, and with the image of it in the background, she could march out into an insecure world, charge, attack, muster her forces, issue her commands or manifestos, and then retire into her garden again, that garden of which she had once said: "I knew every tree, every rock, every flower as only children know these things." She was the spoiled and clever child of somewhat elderly parents, the sister of two distinguished and much older brothers, a cousin of the famous James Russell Lowell, and, as a child, learned to assert the remarkable personality and avid mind that seemed always to be hers alone. That personality is evident even in the letters she wrote in childhood, and sometimes there is more force in them than anything that resembles childish charm.

She was a New Englander in every thought, in every gesture, and like Harriet Monroe, she wandered through her European travels always bringing her particular section of America with her wherever she went. As a child, she had heard from her parents and older relatives much talk of the Civil War, and her childish imagination was so deeply stirred by it that years later in the Richmond Museum the feeling of childhood terror was reawakened at what she saw. She felt that the old Confederate uniforms would walk from their glass cases, and that she could feel the touch of a gauntleted hand upon her shoulder. To her the Civil War was never the memory of something that had faded into history: it was always near, and "it always seemed a war between demons and angels."

The child who could best be described by her friend, Katherine Dana, as "obstreperous" was a great reader. She liked stories about boys and girls who did things, and though there were times when she liked to escape into a world of fantasy, she very decidedly rejected everything that had been touched or elaborated by gush or whimsy. She read and reread Sir Walter Scott's Waverley Novels; she preferred Fenimore Cooper's sea stories to his Leatherstocking Tales; and another favorite was Captain Marryat's *Peter Simple*. She had developed the literary tastes of a small boy, and Jules Verne's scientific romances, Dana's *Two Years Before the Mast*, Bullen's *Cruise of the Cachelot* left their mark on her childhood and colored her imagination.

In a questionnaire to which she answered in her teens, she described her favorite heroes as Alfred the Great and Benjamin Franklin. Her "most disliked female" was Joan of Arc, whom she dismissed as being "too masculine." "What is your idea of happiness?" she had been asked, and her answer was, "To be loved." Already she was a rough, vital, strong girl, too bulky for her age and growing stout, full of tomboy mannerisms and quivering, delicate girlish sensibilities—the two elements that were to enter her poetry.

Vague, ambitious dreams possessed her and she had already written in her diary of her loneliness and her desire to be a poet. Perhaps a great deal of this yearning came from what she felt to be her physical unattractiveness as well as her consciousness of intellectual superiority. "I feel as if I must have a talent for something and I can't help thinking it is photography." Some of the schoolgirl entries are almost tragic in their pathos: "But I am ugly, fat, conspicuous & dull," she wrote, "to say nothing of a very bad temper. Oh Lord, let it be all right & let Paul love me & don't let me be a fool." She never allowed herself to become a fool, and her wit, her energy (as she became better known) gave her more friends than many a more glamorous debutante.

As a young woman, the mistress of Sevenells, and the owner of an historic name, she took part in civic activities, addressing schoolboards with a display of common sense and originality and nursing a secret passion for the stage. In 1902, after witnessing a performance of Eleanor Duse she felt herself (like Sara Teasdale after a similar experience) inspired to break into verse. It was true as she said afterwards in her curious, personal idiom that always betrayed more force than skill or grace, that the writing of this poem was the beginning of a new life, for it "loosed a bolt in my brain and I found out where my true function lay."

From then on she began writing poetry and was already beginning to revolt against her early enthusiasms for Alfred Lord Tennyson and Matthew Arnold. Her old friend, Mabel Cabot, had married Ellery Sedgwick, editor of *The Atlantic Monthly,* and it was to him that she sent four sonnets which were accepted immediately. These early sonnets appeared in August, 1910, and though it was years before the kind of verse that had made her known was written, it confirmed in her a resolution to write poetry. In this she found a lifework, an absorbing interest, an outlet for her missionary zeal, and her destiny seemed to unroll clearly before her.

When her first book appeared, she was thirty-eight years old and had been writing for ten years. Her friend, the then popular Boston poet, Josephine Preston Peabody Marks, advised Amy Lowell to send her manuscript to Houghton Mifflin, the Boston publishers, but saying with what afterward Amy Lowell thought was the sinister air assumed by our best friends toward our most cherished ambitions, that she herself did not care for poetry which had no human interest, and "why should they?"

If this advice was in the nature of a friendly warning, Amy Lowell disregarded it and sent her manuscript on to Ferris Greenslet, of Houghton Mifflin. It was, as Foster Damon says tersely, "the obvious press to select." When *A Dome of Many-coloured Glass* appeared in 1912, it was exactly the sort of book to be expected of a New England Lowell. Examining it now, more than three decades after its publication, one can agree with almost everything that had been said of it by the critics of its own time. The poems it contained were delicate, feminine, yet flat and honest; they were innocent of verbal distinction, and yet had less clumsiness and more polish than the later work written in the flush tide of her notoriety. S. Foster Damon has summed up the entire book in a single sentence: "As with the Italian primitives, the attitudes are the stock ones, but the landscape behind is fresh—the flowers are real flowers and the weather real weather."

Meanwhile, the first book opened the excitements and the fervors of the literary world to her. She was no longer Miss Amy Lowell of Sevenells, but Amy Lowell, the poet, who had published a book, and if her quick, intelligent mind (for her critical abilities always ran far beyond the reaches of her creative powers) knew that her first book was not all it should have been, she resolved to learn, to experiment, to spread her range of feeling over wider areas, to make a real test of whatever talents and abilities she felt that she possessed.

Like Harriet Monroe, she had visited the International Exhibit of Modern Art, which introduced America to everything that was then called "modern art": Brancusi's sculptures, Matisse's painting, and Duchamp's much publicized "Nude Descending a Staircase." An interest in the French Symbolist poets (not the best, for her tastes always ran to the most obvious in what was esoteric) and modern music gave her stimulus toward new ideas and theories. In the Preface to *Men, Women and Ghosts,* she wrote: "I think it was the piano music of Debussy with its strange likeness to short vers-libre poems which first showed me the close kinship of music and poetry and there flashed into my mind the idea of using the movement of poetry in somewhat the same way that the musician uses the movement of music." The impressionistic freedom, the flowing, fluctuating rhythms of vers libre seemed to open new possibilities for the art of poetry and Amy Lowell studied them carefully. Harriet Monroe's magazine,

Poetry, also added excitement and impetus to her ambitions, as it did to so many a rising poet of the period. She turned its pages eagerly and had her own poetry accepted by Harriet Monroe. Thanks to Ezra Pound a number of poets living in London were receiving publicity under the name of "Imagistes," and in *Poetry,* the poems signed by H. D., Imagist, immediately attracted Amy Lowell's attention. She felt that she had much in common with this lively group, and sailing for London in 1913, she carried a letter of introduction from Harriet Monroe to Ezra Pound. It was a case of the irresistible force meeting the immovable object, of Mahomet and the mountain coming together; great things were bound to happen and, of course, they did. The "poetic renaissance" now swung out into a full stream of achievement—and publicity.

After Amy Lowell's battle for vers libre was over (and it was over in 1922), after the corpses had been counted and the survivors decorated (they were very few in number), one felt that something had been achieved. The public had actually caught something of the general excitement felt by the poets; the dead weight of dull and academic verse (in its worst sense) had been lifted and cleared away, and an atmosphere was created in which every good poet of the period felt himself at liberty to work. Even today it is certain that every distinguished poet in both England and America, from T. S. Eliot to Archibald MacLeish, from William Carlos Williams to W. H. Auden, owes an historical debt to the memory of the Imagists.

Amy Lowell's part in that great war, her gifts for commanding the resources of newspaper publicity, her massive appearance (for she weighed over two hundred pounds), her black cigars are all too well known. Her friendships with H. D., Ezra Pound, and D. H. Lawrence kept her alert and aware of what was going on. Like Harriet Monroe, Amy Lowell had an instinct, a flair at times amounting to genius rather than a clear understanding of what the best talents of her time were doing. She admired, but was always a little afraid of Ezra Pound, she disliked T. S. Eliot, and grew uneasy whenever she read the prose and verse of D. H. Lawrence. In one of his beautiful, luminous letters filled with that desperate delicacy that Lawrence learned to use to the very rich who could be of help, he wrote to her: "How much nicer, finer, bigger you are intrinsically than your poetry is." And with that complete misunderstanding of great American intellectual and social distinctions shown by many Europeans, Lawrence wrote to his literary agent of his hopes to relieve his "ominous financial prospects." He said that he was writing a book of essays on American literature: "You may marvel at such a subject but it interests me. I was thinking of speaking to Amy Lowell about it. Her brother is the principal of Harvard and she can touch the pulse of *The Yale Review* and things like that." Of one of Lawrence's poems, Amy Lowell had written to Richard Aldington: that for "pure, far-fetched indecency, [it] beats anything I have ever seen. . . . He loses his eye about things; sometimes I think his condition is almost pathological and that he has a sort of erotic mania."

With each new book of poems, Amy Lowell's reputation increased, and if some of the better critics were silent, the furore she caused on lecture platforms, the vigor, the valor, and good sense with which she fought for the poetry of others as well as her own brought sustained applause from her large audiences. Louis Untermeyer when he met her for the first time said: "She waved no plumes and rattled no sabers, but she seemed to be advancing at the head of a victorious army." Everything around her seemed to be prospering, her work seemed to be gaining the widest possible recognition, her house seemed always to be filled with admiring friends. But from time to time, through the words or hints of friends who admired her as a person, she received a few doubts—worded delicately, of course—the intimation of something that was not overwhelming praise. D. H. Lawrence, to whom she had sent a group of her Japanese lacquer-print poems, wrote: "Do write from your real self, Amy, don't make up things from the outside, it is so saddening." Thomas Hardy (who had always been an affectionate and admiring friend) wrote to her about *Can Grande's Castle*, saying that he had not mastered her argument for polyphonic prose, "or was it prosody?" he said.

I don't suppose it is what, 40 years ago, we used to call "word-painting." Curiously enough, at that time, prose having the rhythm of verse concealed in it, so to speak (e.g., in the novels of R. D. Blackmore and others) was considered a fantastic affectation. Earlier still, when used by Lytton, it was nicknamed "the ever and anon style"—I suppose because of the rhythm in those words. . . .

I am, naturally at my age, what they call old-fashioned, and having written rhymes and metered numbers nearly fifty years ago—before you were born!—you must forgive a pedagogic tone if you find it in me. . . .

Though of course in divine poesy there is no such thing as old fashion or new. What made poetry 2000 years ago makes poetry now.[2]

Judged by these standards set down for poetry, what can we say survives of Amy Lowell? First the memory of a superb fighter, who, as Van Wyck Brooks has said, made the republic of poets rise "from the status of Haiti and become an imperial republic of the calibre of France." This remark, alas, is more prophetic than even Van Wyck Brooks thought or knew, for at the beginning of the 1940's the status of poetry appeared almost in the same sad state that it was before Amy Lowell and Harriet Monroe started their effective campaigning for the art!

Amy Lowell's imagination was vivid, often exact and always clear, and she could describe a flower, the effect of beech and of pine trees as they appeared to her sight through a heavy sunlight or an object of art with memorable vividness. Like many writers of the 1920's, like Hergesheimer, like Carl Van Vechten, like Elinor Wylie of *The Venetian Glass Nephew* (1925), Amy Lowell was, among other things, a poet of virtu, celebrating her favorite bric-a-brac, her memories of brightly costumed periods in history, and of fine furniture. Of the school to which this style of writing belongs, Amy Lowell's "Patterns" will remain as good an example as any. The poem still retains its traces of color and movement, yet one feels always that it is a portrait of an eighteenth-century scene re-created by a writer whose feet are too firmly planted in the nineteenth or twentieth century. Despite, or perhaps because of, the theatrical note which enters it, "Patterns" will remain the most representative of all Amy Lowell's more ambitious poems.

"The Sisters," a study of Elizabeth Browning and Emily Dickinson, also contains Amy Lowell's characteristic conversational

[2] From *Amy Lowell* by S. Foster Damon, used by permission of Houghton Mifflin Company.

manner and lively interest in her subject. But a lesser-known poem, "On Looking at a Copy of Alice Meynell's Poems Given to Me Years Ago by a Friend," [3] has a distinction and a delicacy she rarely attained:

> Silent the sea, the earth, the sky,
> And in my heart a silent weeping.
> Who has not sown can know no reaping!
> Bitter conclusion and no lie.
>
> .   .   .   .   .   .
>
> How strange that tumult, looking back,
> The ink is pale, the letters fade,
> The verses seem to be well made,
> But I have lived the almanac.
>
> And you are dead these drifted years,
> How many I forget. And she
> Who wrote the book, her tragedy
> Long since dried up its scalding tears.
>
> .   .   .   .   .   .
>
> I've recollected both of you,
> But I shall recollect no more.
> Between us I must shut the door
> The living have so much to do.

In this poem, saddened by human experience and loss and the passage of time, it is interesting to note that here in one of her last poems, Amy Lowell went back to the traditional metrics of her first book. This poem, which was ostensibly a poem occasioned by the rereading of Alice Meynell's poetry, is, after all, a poem about life's keenest and most painful disillusionments. It might well be entitled "On Rereading a Volume of Poetry by the Late Amy Lowell," and one can say that the spirit, the sound of the voice, the great feeling for life still remain—and we find ourselves praising her for the remarkable something that speaks best *between* rather than *in* the lines of this poem and all her poetry.

[3] From *Ballads for Sale*, by permission of Houghton Mifflin Company.

THE ISLANDS OF H. D.

If literature, as T. S. Eliot has said, must be judged by language and not by place, the poetry of H. D. has an individual, almost exotic note in our literature. She has created a world, or rather an island, that is like no one else's, an island where Hellenic temples rise, where rarefied Greek figures move in frenetic heat. Yet her early poems have worn well with the years and one can place her among the few poets who have given us a timeless vision of the beauty that all long for and that is particularly keen and strong in youth. She belongs by temperament to those who have no formal philosophy, no message that will solve the material ills of humanity, no satire on the follies of the external world; her island is a country of her own spirit and imagination.

The Greek temples of H. D. shine with a brilliant, a supernal light, their inhabitants move in a hemisphere almost too delicately sensuous, and they themselves are too modern in sensibility, too nervous in their intensity to be conventionally Attic. Theirs is not the marmoreal repose and harmony that one usually associates with figures in bas-relief on a Greek urn, for H. D.'s islands are inhabited by spirits who are possessed by that romantic neurosis, the longing for the imagined perfection of Greek attitudes and the eternal solace of the Hellenic dream that haunts the western world, and has often been the source of its finest thinking, action, and poetry. The diction, the sensibility of H. D.'s poetry are strictly modern in external tone and feeling and the poems are clean and straight. "It's straight talk, straight as the Greek!" wrote Ezra Pound to Harriet Monroe in 1912 when he first sent her H. D.'s verses.

Of all the heroines and heroes of the Imagist Movement, it is she who was, as Ford Madox Ford once said, "our gracious Muse, our cynosure, and the peak of our achievement," and she is one of the few who have survived.

It is not extraordinary that since 1911 H. D. has lived in Europe. She has been and still is the most natural of expatriates, since her work belongs to all worlds and to none. She was born in Bethlehem, Pennsylvania, in 1886 and passed most of her childhood in Philadelphia where her father was a director of the Flower Observatory. During the years that she attended Bryn Mawr College (she did not graduate), she met Ezra Pound, William Carlos Williams, and Marianne Moore, poets whose work and friendships were among the best influences upon younger writers of that time. The young girl who was already scribbling verse that she described as "lyrical in a small way," found herself when she visited France, Italy, and England in 1911 in a congenial environment. Her acquaintance with Ezra Pound was revived in London. He took her in hand as a prom-ising disciple and saw her frequently, bringing armfuls of books and excellent critical advice. Among the books he brought her were volumes of the pre-Renaissance Latin poets of which H. D. said later, "I was happy with those because the Latin was easy, yet held the authentic (though diluted) flavor of the overworked and sometimes slavishly copied Latin and Greek originals." Under the guidance of Ezra Pound's teaching and the impetus of the prescribed reading, H. D. began to write the poems that gave her name distinction, and among these were the "Hermes" and the now more than classic "Spare Us from Loveliness." Richard Aldington, who became H. D.'s husband and who was among the youngest and first to join Ezra Pound's circle of "Imagistes," has an amusing account of those now far-off days in his autobiography. It was at tea that Ezra Pound informed H. D. and Richard Aldington that they were "Imagistes," and Ezra Pound also suggested that all three of the present company write and publish a book together; ". . . it seemed the sort of thing the three musketeers would have done. But Ezra soon changed his mind. He gravely pointed out to us that he was internationally famous, while we were miserable unknowns and that consequently the whole attention of the world's press would go to his poems and ours would not even be noticed."

But with the publication of her first volume of poems, *Sea Garden* (1916), H. D. established her name and her own particular islanded glimpse of beauty. In the thirty years that have elapsed between that day and this, the poems still retain their freshness to the reader who is susceptible to the special values of H. D.'s imagination:

> Flame passes under us
> and sparks that unknot the flesh,
> sorrow, splitting bone from bone,
> splendour athwart our eyes
> and rifts in the splendour,
> sparks and scattered light.[1]

or

> Sleepless nights,
> I remember the initiates,
> their gesture, their calm glance.
> I have heard how in rapt thought,
> in vision, they speak
> with another race,
> more beautiful, more intense than this.[2]

Nor could any amount of anthologizing mar the beauty and technical brilliance of H. D.'s "Sea Gods": [3]

> But we bring violets,
> great masses—single, sweet,
> wood-violets, stream-violets,
> violets from a wet marsh.
>
> Violets in clumps from hills,
> tufts with earth at the roots,
> violets tugged from rocks,
> blue violets, moss, cliff, river-violets.
>
> Yellow violets' gold,
> burnt with a rare tint—
> violets like red ash
> among tufts of grass.

[1] "She Watches Over the Sea" from *Collected Poems of H. D.*, by permission of Liveright Publishing Corp.

[2] "The Gift" from *Collected Poems of H. D.*, by permission of Liveright Publishing Corp.

[3] From *Collected Poems of H. D.*, by permission of Liveright Publishing Corp.

We bring deep-purple
bird-foot violets.

We bring the hyacinth-violet,
sweet, bare, chill to the touch—
and violets whiter than the in-rush
of your own white surf.

The Collected Poems of H. D. were first published in 1925, and it is interesting to note that though H. D. is not one of the most publicized of contemporary poets, nor among those most talked about in contemporary reviews, this volume of her collected verse has gone into five or six editions and has continued to be read and admired by a public that has learned to appreciate the intensity and precision of H. D.'s style.

Her gifts seemed always to be drawn from the same pure source and one cannot find a time when they were ever awkward, impure, or strained.

It was not chastity that made me wild, but fear
that my weapon, tempered in different heat,
was over-matched by yours, and your hand
skilled to yield death-blows, might break

With the slightest turn—no ill will meant—
my own lesser, yet still somewhat fine-wrought,
fiery-tempered, delicate, over-passionate steel.[4]

H. D. has lived in London through the First and Second World Wars and all their dangers, and she has written of how one evening (during the First World War) she arrived home, exhausted and half-asphyxiated, after many hours in an underground air-raid shelter, to find a letter from Harriet Monroe telling her to get into the rhythm of our time, in touch with current events—to leave her Ivory Tower. "I don't know what else she said," wrote H. D., "I was laughing too much." But the Ivory Tower charge is one that every poet of her genre must learn to face from critics who read poetry in the light of literal interpretation. What she calls her *"Unexpected isle in the far seas"* remains the center of her poetic vision, and in a note on

[4] "Toward the Piraeus" from *Collected Poems of H. D.,* by permission of Liveright Publishing Corp.

poetry in *The Oxford Anthology of American Literature* she writes:

"What are the islands to me?" They are, I suppose, an inner region of defence. . . . And of memory—suppressed memory, maybe. (And what about the mother of the Muses? Mnemosene, if I remember?) Actual memory, repressed memory, desire to escape, desire to create (music), intellectual curiosity, a wish to make real to myself what is most real. . . . Times, places, dates don't seem so much to matter.[5]

In one of her later books of poems, *Red Roses for Bronze* (1931) such poems as "Triplex" and "Let Zeus Record" are in her best vein; and if other poems in this volume seem answerable to the charge of thinness, it is a poetry always unique and beautiful in form and spirit. We find a song in "Let Zeus Record, IV" [6] which is as fine as any written in our time.

> Stars wheel in purple, yours is not so rare
> as Hesperus, nor yet so great a star
> as bright Aldebaran or Sirius,
> nor yet the stained and brilliant one of War;
>
> stars turn in purple, glorious to the sight;
> yours is not gracious as the Pleiads' are
> nor as Orion's sapphires luminous;
>
> yet disenchanted, cold, imperious face,
> when all the others blighted, reel and fall,
> your star, steel-set, keeps lone and frigid tryst
> to freighted ships, baffled in wind and blast.

In April of 1943 at the Aeolian Hall in Second World War London, a poetry reading of an unusual character (since members of the royal family and the Queen herself were in the audience) included readings by the Poet Laureate, John Masefield, Arthur Waley, Edith and Osbert Sitwell, Walter de la Mare (who read "The Listener" by request), and two American poets, H. D. and T. S. Eliot. As Robert Herring wrote in *Life and Letters Today* those "in England, 'the country which cares

[5] "A Note on Poetry" from *The Oxford Anthology of American Literature*, ed. by Benét and Pearson, by permission of The Oxford University Press.

[6] From *Red Roses for Bronze*, by permission of Houghton Mifflin Company, publisher in the United States.

nothing for art,' were allowed to state their faith, one spring afternoon, at a reading to which the presence of Her Majesty, the Queen, gave the last graciousness of a May revel." But of more importance to us was the presence of two Americans, for it showed how distinctly the literary climate of London had changed since that day in 1920 when Ezra Pound left London for Paris.

In 1944 H. D. published a book, *The Walls Do Not Fall,* of forty-three poems that had been written since the beginning of the Second World War. Those signs of increased intensity which are characteristic of the recent verse written by Edith Sitwell and T. S. Eliot are readily discerned in H. D.'s new poems, and they indicate how well she has achieved (despite the actual contact of war, or because of it) the further reaches of her poetic maturity:

> Ra, Osiris, *Amen* appeared
> in a spacious, bare meeting-house;
>
> he is the world-father,
> father of past aeons,
>
> present and future equally;
> beardless, not at all like Jehovah,
>
> he was upright, slender,
> impressive as the Memnon monolith,
>
> yet he was not out of place
> but perfectly at home
>
> in that eighteenth-century
> simplicity and grace;
>
> then I woke with a start
> of wonder and asked myself,
>
> but whose eyes are those eyes?
> for the eyes (in the cold,
>
> I marvel to remember)
> were all one texture,
>
> as if without pupil
> or all pupil, dark

yet very clear with amber
shining . . .[7]

If the music of the book tends to become monotonous, the
reader is rewarded by a second or third hearing of the poem
separately; and he is also rewarded by the visual creations of a
"timeless" atmosphere which is also discerned in certain passages
of Thomas Mann's *Joseph in Egypt;* and it is in that atmosphere
that H. D.'s lines are memorable:

> We have seen how the most amiable,
> under physical stress,
>
> become wolves, jackals,
> mongrel curs;
>
> we know further that hunger
> may make hyenas of the best of us;
>
> let us, therefore (though we do not forget
> Love, the Creator,
>
> her chariot and white doves),
> entreat Hest,
>
> Aset, Isis, the great enchantress,
> in her attribute of Serqet,
>
> the original great-mother,
> who drove
>
> harnessed scorpions
> before her.[8]

There can be no doubt that a number of H. D.'s lyrics are
among the fine poetic achievements of our time; she has won
her audience within groups where the discriminating reader of
poetry will always rediscover her particular values, selecting
shorter passages from her work to be read singly and held as
one might retain a single image or a single melodic strain in
hearing a concerto. What H. D. can mean to a fellow poet is

[7] "Poem XVI" from *The Walls Do Not Fall,* by permission of The Oxford
University Press and the author.

[8] "Poem XXXIV" from *The Walls Do Not Fall,* by permission of The
Oxford University Press and the author.

best described by one well qualified to understand and appreciate her work, John Gould Fletcher:

H. D. is an inhabitant of the fabulous Golden Age, a seeker after the vanished Golden Fleece. I think of her as half-asleep in Greece while the swallows skim through the clear golden air—and the silver flute on which she set her lips makes so many a song lie silent, slipping through her fingers. Her Jason is lost, and has long since fled afar. Mirror on mirror broken by ripples, the still lake reflects the distant trees? Romantic? Classical? or American?—that nostalgia for a past that lies in clear light, for an earth unencumbered with cyclotrons and skyscrapers, where all is tall and very straight. It is H. D.'s note and we have forgotten it. We are the poorer for having forgotten.

But a quotation from H. D.'s recent book of devotional poems, *Tribute to the Angels* (1945), is the best expression of the maturity that her poetry has achieved, and of the singular richness she had discovered on her "islands." Her tribute to Our Lady, "Poem XXIX," [9] is one of the purest expressions of religious emotion in twentieth-century poetry:

> We have seen her
> the world over,
>
> Our Lady of the Goldfinch,
> Our Lady of the Candelabra,
>
> Our Lady of the Pomegranate,
> Our Lady of the Chair;
>
> we have seen her, an empress,
> magnificent in pomp and grace,
>
> and we have seen her
> with a single flower
>
> or a cluster of garden-pinks
> in a glass beside her;
>
> we have seen her snood
> drawn over her hair,
>
> or her face set in profile
> with the blue hood and stars;

[9] By permission of Oxford University Press, London.

we have seen her head bowed down
with the weight of a domed crown,

or we have seen her, a wisp of a girl
trapped in a golden halo;

we have seen her with arrow, with doves
and a heart like a valentine;

we have seen her in fine silks imported
from all over the Levant,

and hung with pearls brought
from the city of Constantine;

we have seen her sleeve
of every imaginable shade

of damask and figured brocade;
it is true,

the painters did very well by her;
it is true, they missed never a line

of the suave turn of the head
or subtle shade of lowered eye-lid

or eye-lids half-raised; you find
her everywhere (or did find),

in cathedral, museum, cloister,
at the turn of the palace stair.

THE POSTIMPRESSIONISM
OF JOHN GOULD FLETCHER

No poet has enjoyed a more dignified obscurity than John Gould Fletcher or a more subterranean and erratic reputation. The Pulitzer Prize in 1939 bestowed on his *Selected Poems* (1938) brought to public attention what had always seemed to elude it: that Fletcher was considerably more than a picturesque figure from the Imagist past, that he was continuing his work, and that the work itself was changing and still growing. John Gould Fletcher had one of the keenest intellects of the poets whom Amy Lowell gathered around her in 1917—when she was looking for disciples for her particular brand of Imagism. As widely read and as widely traveled as his fellow expatriate, Ezra Pound, his work has always lacked the lightness, the delicate, quick touch of *Exultations* and *Personae*. At his worst Fletcher has been guilty of a powerful dullness and the dignity and depth of his emotion is often marred by a surface of awkwardness and lack of finish in poetic phrasing—yet his entire work and his influence upon the literature of his time contain the rewards of seriousness and independence.

Although Fletcher has been one of the earliest and, with the exception of Ernest Hemingway, the most widely traveled of American expatriates—and had met everyone worth meeting in prewar literary Europe—he has always remained an American at heart; and in rereading the collections of his verse, one is tempted to remark that he was never more intensely American than when in Europe—a trait he held in common with Amy Lowell.

Fletcher was born in 1886, a native of Little Rock, Arkansas, and in his autobiography, *Life Is My Song* (1937), he gave an account of his family heritage which was to color his early writing and to which he has returned with greater intensity in recent years. He came from a family of wealth and of Anglo-Southern culture, and during the Civil War, his father joined the Confederate Army.

> From my father's side [wrote Fletcher], I inherited a physical frame and constitution that has been adequate to the demands put upon it by more than fifty years of living under not always easy conditions; a love for simple, honest, country folk, and for simple ways of living that has persisted despite all my sophistications; a certain streak of dour obstinacy that will not permit itself to be easily turned aside from any course once embarked upon; a love of travel and roving that is, unquestionably, the heritage of the pioneer; and a frankness in speaking out my mind that is also a marked pioneer trait. My heritage from my mother was quite different. It is from her that I trace all those aesthetic hankerings which have made me into a poet.[1]

The boy who had said of himself in youth, "I disliked Democracy," was educated at fashionable Eastern schools: at Phillips (Andover) Academy and at Harvard. Inheriting an independent income in his senior year at Harvard, he left college and took a trip to the Southwest, to Puye and Mesa Verde with an expedition from the Peabody Museum. But it was Europe that called him, as it did so many cultivated (and well-to-do) young men of his generation. In the summer of 1908, he sailed for Italy. The contrast between "the lean, spare, austere, American Southwest" and the Italian cities, "dead shells of a once magnificent heritage," baffled him in a way in which Henry James or T. S. Eliot would never have been baffled. In his slow, questioning way he asked himself over and over:

> How did it happen that so much culture, so much more than America had ever known, had once lived here and now lived here no longer? How had it come about that the Italians, once supreme in the arts, had ceased to be an art-creating people? How did it happen that the history of nineteenth-century Europe was the history of a few great, lonely individuals, from whom the mass, the mob, fell so sharply and absolutely away? I could find no answer to all these questions, or to many others.[2]

Because of this state of mind, one knows that John Gould Fletcher, despite his sensibilities and esthetic impulses, was never

[1] From *Life Is My Song*, 1937, used by permission of Farrar and Rinehart, Inc.

[2] *Ibid.*

to become the true "exile" from his native soil; the subtler values of Europe were closed to him because his heart was not with them and because his emotional strength lay elsewhere. In this he anticipated (and to some degree his work shows kinship with) the kinds of curiosity and temperament shown by Sherwood Anderson and Edgar Lee Masters—and it also explains his affinity with Amy Lowell.

For a while Fletcher felt himself to be more at home in England than in other places he had visited, and like Ezra Pound's, his arrival in London in 1909 was at a moment that seemed fortunate and promising. A. R. Orage had begun to edit *The New Age*, the Fabians had become a fashionable literary influence, and the Independent Labour Party was beginning to make itself felt: the air was alive with excitement, prophecies, hopes, forebodings. Through a friend (who happened to be a Fabian) John Gould Fletcher made the acquaintance of the dazzling Orage, who "confounded [him] with his conversational facility," and who inspired Fletcher to write poetry by asking him if he had read Walt Whitman. The young American who had been prejudiced against Whitman began to read him carefully:

I was so carried away by Whitman's robust realism, by his masterly grasp of details . . . that I immediately broke all my former allegiances to Coleridge, Keats, Byron, Shelley and Poe and began feverishly to describe the life of London in terms strongly reminiscent of his [Whitman's] own.

This experience was quickly followed by another fortunate incident—a meeting and a talk with Ezra Pound. The discussion shifted to the subject of vers libre, and rapidly became a monologue conducted by Pound with interruptions of the speaker's voice by "gesticulations and by a slight cough that came between every other word." Fletcher kept silent through bewilderment and awe and Ezra Pound, feeling that he had found another disciple, took him under his wing. When Pound learned that his fellow American in exile had published (and at his own expense) five volumes of verse in one year and was planning a sixth book, "embodying a new revolutionary theory of verbal orchestration," the elder poet must have been certain that he had discovered a man after his own heart. He at once promised to review Fletcher's work in Harriet Monroe's magazine, *Poetry*, and was as good as his word—and another poet was now launched upon a career that was to make literary history. Not that Pound and Fletcher were ever to become close friends; their temperamental differences were too great, and both had delicately nursed, well-cultivated egos. Of Ezra Pound's poetry Fletcher remarked that it was often deliberately archaic—so much so, that it repelled him; and moreover, Ezra Pound seemed a forerunner of Gertrude Stein's "Lost Generation," of whom Fletcher wrote keenly that they had learned nothing much from Europe or from America, but largely discovered their own neurotic selves. But the brief friendship stimulated both poets; they shared the feeling that both were pioneers, discoverers, educators, that some of the same impulses had brought them to Europe, and though neither would admit it, both shared the feeling of loneliness, of being away from home, and therefore welcomed a fellow American with similar tastes. Fletcher never believed that Ezra Pound seriously admired his early work. Ezra Pound's three chief aversions were superfluity of adjectives, poetic inversions, and rhetoric—all of which was summed up in Pound's hatred of the character and poetry of John Milton—and since it is to be feared that Fletcher's verse has not been entirely free of these qualities, it is not extraordinary that he felt uneasy whenever he heard Pound elaborate his theories.

When Ezra Pound left the ranks of the Imagists, and delivered the American leadership of the group over to Amy Lowell, John Gould Fletcher joined Miss Lowell's faction, and through her enthusiasm his name became known to the American public. For a long time, Fletcher's verse was praised only in the reflected light of his "Color Symphonies," which were long-drawn-out and sometimes vague attempts to capture the feeling, the mood, the spirit of postimpressionism in music and in painting. These early poems still have their admirers, but it is in "The Ghosts of an Old House," a group of poems, published among his *Goblins and Pagodas* (1916), which brought to mind the setting and atmosphere of a Southern mansion in Arkansas, that Fletcher found his true métier, and with it the themes of his latest poetry and his most enduring work. In these early and fragmentary re-creations of a lost childhood—a dark corner of a room where he is suddenly confronted with a forgotten portrait, or a cabinet filled with dusty toys—the loose and abstract improvisations of the "Color Symphonies" vanish; here all is simple, direct, and human, as if the poet had released himself from the confusions of too much theorizing, of too much speculation in esthetics, of too much mere talk about what poetry should be, and had begun to find himself. Thirteen years later, in a new preface written for his *Preludes and Symphonies* (1930), Fletcher gave further hint of the circuitous course his development had begun to take and he explained not only what he had tried to do as a poet, but the ideal of poetry that had slowly formed itself within his mind:

> The value of this book resides rather in its display of lyric temperament than in any ideas it may contain. It does not belong to that main branch that is pure folk song where are Homer and Chaucer, the authors of the *Nibelungenlied* and the *Song of Roland*. . . . Neither can it be classed with the kind of poetry that presupposes a steadily held philosophic background. . . . But perhaps there is still a third category of poetry that has nothing to justify it except its own eagerness for beauty. . . . To that kind this book belongs.[3]

All this was written at a great distance from the impulses that produced the "Color Symphonies" and the theories which surrounded them. His "Cycle of Liguria" in *The Black Rock* (1928) had already marked the change which made his *XXIV Elegies* (1935) so difficult for critics to classify. An entire generation of poetry reviewers had known Fletcher only as a member of Amy Lowell's Imagist group of poets, as a dim figure resident in London and increasingly remote; meanwhile, he had actually returned to the United States and to his native Southwest. At home his impressionism had acquired a third dimension, an historical perspective, and not a little moral force and dignity. All these mutations in Fletcher's verse were scarcely noticed, for there is nothing more exasperating for the average critic than to have had an author or an artist carefully pigeonholed, tucked away in a neat drawer, and then find that one must reshuffle

---

[3] *Preludes and Symphonies*, Macmillan, used by permission of the Author.

one's notes and readjust one's happily conceived opinions! If one test of the true artist lies in his power not to stop growing, to keep his independence, and to discover new channels for his expression, surely Fletcher has turned many of his threatened failures into successful poems. His "Elegy in a Civil War Cemetery" should make Allen Tate and other survivors of the literary Confederacy look to their laurels and his "Elegy on an Empty Skyscraper" [4] contains within its closing lines one of the fine examples of modern diction in American poetry:

> There is wide space between
> Man's topmast and his keel, and in it death
> Comes without sign or sound or stir of breath.
> No one shall fill that room, or take his place
> In it, as stowaway or come-aboard;
> Nor shall the meagre window-blind be lowered,
> Nor shall the dark be levelled by a face.

In his latest book, *South Star* (1941), Fletcher proves himself to be the most earnest and at times (when he does not allow his tendencies toward discursiveness to blur the page) he is one of the most intense of regional writers in this country. Among the shorter poems in this volume, "My Father's Watch," a poem foreshadowed by "The Ghosts of an Old House," is a memorable example of Fletcher's rediscovery of traditional metrics in the writing of poetry, and his maturity of feeling and subtlety in the uses of traditional forms finds its best expression in "The Scythe": [5]

> . . . Now scythe and well
> And hard brown hands are gone. No one at all
> Goes there on still hot days to draw aloft
> The dripping bucket on its rattling chain,
> Or lift a dipper cloudless to the brim:
> And yesterday I saw, within the house,
> Surrounded by old faces I once knew,
> How the keen scythe with its hard-whetted edge
> Had mown away the flower of lives, like grass.

[4] From *Twenty-four Elegies*. Copyright by John Gould Fletcher, 1935, and used by permission of the Author.

[5] From *South Star*, Macmillan, used by permission of the Author.

A FORMAL "OBJECTIVIST":
WILLIAM CARLOS WILLIAMS

". . . all art is necessarily objective. It doesn't declaim or explain; it presents."

> William Carlos Williams, *A Note on Poetry* (1937) [1]

Of the many poets who were supposed to owe their existence to the arrival of Ezra Pound's "Les Imagistes" and Amy Lowell's army of "free" versifiers, William Carlos Williams was the last to gain public recognition. His first book, *Poems* (1909), appeared before the "poetic renaissance" had officially begun and some three years before the mysterious term, "Les Imagistes," had been invented. The book was also published a year before Williams began his medical practice, which he has maintained ever since, in Rutherford, New Jersey, the town in which he was born on September 17, 1883. In a brief sketch of his early life and its background that Williams wrote for *The Oxford Anthology of American Literature* he remarked:

. . . my forebears seem to have been restless souls, never long in the same place. My father was born in Birmingham, England, and my mother in Mayaguez, Puerto Rico. I went to the public schools here in Rutherford, New Jersey, until I was about twelve years old, then to a New York City high school [Horace Mann], finally to the University of Pennsylvania for my degree in Medicine. Among these years was one when, with my brother, I attended a school in Switzerland [Château de Lancy in Geneva], living also in Paris for six months at that time. Later I studied Medicine at the University of Leipzig and took my internship in two hospitals in New York. Writing has been my constant companion during these years.[2]

[1] From *Oxford Anthology of American Literature*, Oxford Press, 1937. Used by permission of the Author.
[2] *Ibid.*

To his stay at the University of Pennsylvania as well as the character of his poetry, we must credit his long association with Ezra Pound whom he met at the University, Wallace Stevens who was a native of Pennsylvania whom he met in New York, and H. D. whose father was director of the Flower Astronomical Observatory at the University. The associations of regional locality (since some are accidental and others are of short duration) may be taken for what they are worth; but some degree of significance may be attached to the fact that none of these four poets is a regionalist in the usual sense of the term and some future claim may yet be made that all four represented in varying degrees a "Pennsylvania school." All four were subject to "European influences," and of the four, Williams appears to be the most firmly and determinedly rooted in an American locality, Rutherford, New Jersey, a suburb of New York.

For the most part, so completely in fact that one must search out the rare exceptions, Williams' verse has been unrhymed; in temper it has been at the furthest remove from "professional" verse; it has been protestant, yet formal, and the virtues of even his slightest pieces have been those of presenting definite objects and scenes before the eye of the reader. The details of a suburban pastoral are to be found in his lines to "The Young Housewife" from *Al Que Quiere* [3] (1917):

> At ten A.M. the young housewife
> moves about in negligée behind
> the wooden walls of her husband's house.
> I pass solitary in my car.
>
> Then again she comes to the curb
> to call the ice-man, fish-man, and stands
> shy, uncorseted, tucking in
> stray ends of hair . . .

The little portrait has the cleanliness, the freshness, the so-called "naïveté" of an American "primitive," and the same quali-

---

[3] From *Complete Collected Poems, 1906-1938,* used by permission of New Directions and the Author.

ties of neatness are seen in a poem that was published twelve years later, in 1929, "Nantucket": [4]

> Flowers through the window
> lavender and yellow
>
> changed by white curtains—
> Smell of cleanliness—
>
> Sunshine of late afternoon—
> On the glass tray
>
> a glass pitcher, the tumbler
> turned down, by which
>
> a key is lying— And the
> immaculate white bed.

This is a latter-day New England recorded by the eye and hand of a singularly alert observer; each notation has been scrupulously selected, and the entire, brilliant, almost antiseptic scene has attained the formal virtues of restraint and a thoroughly unpretentious dignity; it is simply no more or less than what it pretends to be, and one is not invited to read deeper meanings in the poem than the first sight of its words convey. Many of Williams' shorter poems have rested upon the same premise; the selection, however lightly its choices may seem to have been made, is firm; Williams has always been very much his own man, and one might almost say "his own poet." Ezra Pound in one of his *Polite Essays* observed the slow growth of Williams' poetic maturity, but the slow growth, which is so visibly reflected through the three-hundred-odd pages of *The Complete Collected Poems of William Carlos Williams* (1938) (which, by the way, was not "complete"), was turned to Williams' own advantage. Despite the fluidity of many poems and their thin if not transparent lines the impression that one gains is of a poet who has wisely accepted the laws of the pace at which he has lived, and among them "The Botticellian Trees," "Young Sycamore," "The Sea Elephant," and "The Jungle" all arrived

[4] From *Complete Collected Poems, 1906-1938,* used by permission of New Directions and the Author.

at the near perfection of an art that had earlier seemed a tentative "experiment" in vers libre. An analogy, if it is not thrust too far, exists between Williams' love lyric, "Rain," and the less clouded moments of Verlaine's impressionism, and though the "mood" that Williams has created places him at a great distance from the French Symbolist poet, the same power to suggest emotion, the same delicate control over language rather than "ideas" which so clearly distinguished the verse of Verlaine from that written by his contemporaries, may be found in the following passage from Williams' "Rain": [5]

> The trees
> are become
> beasts fresh risen
> from
>   the sea—
> water
>
> trickles
> from the crevices of
> their hides—
>
> So my life is spent
>   to keep out love
> with which
> she rains upon
>   the world
> of spring

And such an art, which in its tentative stages seems more "arty" than truly expressive, reaches its finality in Williams' characteristic little poem, "The Jungle": [6]

> It is not the still weight
> of the trees, the
> breathless interior of the wood,
> tangled with wrist-thick
>
> vines, the flies, reptiles,
> the forever fearful monkeys

[5] From *Complete Collected Poems, 1906-1938,* used by permission of New Directions and the Author.
[6] *Ibid.*

screaming and running
in the branches—

but
a girl waiting
shy, brown, soft-eyed—
to guide you
                    Upstairs, sir.

In his introduction to Williams' *Collected Poems, 1921-1931,*
published in 1934,[7] Wallace Stevens found an occasion to speak
illuminatingly of Williams, of the romantic poet in general, and
of the "anti-poetic" element in so-called "modern" poetry.
Stevens wrote:

. . . and generally speaking one might run through these pages and
point out how often the essential poetry is the result of the conjunction
of the unreal and the real, the sentimental and the anti-poetic, the
constant interaction of two opposites. This seems to define Williams
and his poetry. . . . So defined, Williams looks a bit like that grand
old plaster cast, Lessing's Laocoön: the realist struggling to escape from
the serpents of the unreal.

He is commonly identified by externals. He includes here specimens
of abortive rhythms, words on several levels, ideas without logic, and
similar minor matters, which, when all is said, are merely the diversions
of the prophet between morning and evening song. It will be found
that he has made some veritable additions to the corpus of poetry,
which is certainly no more sacred to anyone than to him. His special
use of the anti-poetic is an example of this. The ambiguity produced
by bareness is another. The implied image, as in YOUNG SYCAMORE, the
serpent that leaps up in one's imagination at his prompting, is an
addition to imagism, a phase of realism which Williams has always
found congenial. . . . But these things may merely be mentioned.
Williams himself, a kind of Diogenes of contemporary poetry, is a much
more vital matter. The truth is that, if one had not chanced to regard
him as Laocoön, one could have done very well by him as Diogenes.

In respect to the poetry of William Carlos Williams, Wallace
Stevens' last observation is by no means as casual as Stevens may
have wished his statement to appear. Williams' search for "an
honest man," as well as an instruction to others "to stand out of
my sunlight," are the kinds of truth that Williams sought in
verse. The search may at times seem wantonly naïve, and at

[7] Objectivist Press. Used by permission of the Author.

times it has resulted in incomplete and "experimental" poems, but we may be certain that Williams has never falsified his language; and he has made an ethical distinction between the uses of artifice and of art. Craftsmanship, not artifice, has been his concern, and perhaps no writer of the twentieth century has yielded so little to the temptations that mere artifice places within his path. That is why a number of Williams' poems contain a substance that is "unliterary" in the best uses of that term; some poems may be "sentimental" in Stevens' sharp and well-mannered use of the word, but whether or not the poem achieves its end, the "truth" of the poem remains unimpaired. In the image of Stevens' "Laocoön" Williams has written one of his masterpieces and one of the finest poems of his generation. It has greater density than the majority of his poems, and it illustrates what Stevens meant when he spoke of Williams' "addition to imagism," an "addition," by the way, toward which Williams leaned before "Les Imagistes" arrived:

THE YACHTS [8]

Contend in a sea which the land partly encloses
shielding them from the too heavy blows
of an ungoverned ocean which when it chooses

tortures the biggest hulls, the best man knows
to pit against its beatings, and sinks them pitilessly.
Mothlike in mists, scintillant in the minute

brilliance of cloudless days, with broad bellying sails
they glide to the wind tossing green water
from their sharp prows while over them the crew crawls

ant like, solicitously grooming them, releasing,
making fast as they turn, lean far over and having
caught the wind again, side by side, head for the mark.

In a well guarded arena of open water surrounded by
lesser and greater craft which, sycophant, lumbering
and flittering follow them, they appear youthful, rare

as the light of a happy eye, live with the grace
of all that in the mind is feckless, free and
naturally to be desired. Now the sea which holds them

[8] From *Complete Collected Poems, 1906-1938*, used by permission of New Directions and the Author.

is moody, lapping their glossy sides, as if feeling
for some slightest flaw but fails completely.
Today no race. Then the wind comes again. The yachts

move, jockeying for a start, the signal is set and they
are off. Now the waves strike at them but they are too
well made, they slip through, though they take in canvas.

Arms with hands grasping seek to clutch at the prows.
Bodies thrown recklessly in the way are cut aside.
It is a sea of faces about them in agony, in despair

until the horror of the race dawns staggering the mind,
the whole sea become an entanglement of watery bodies
lost to the world bearing what they cannot hold. Broken,

beaten, desolate, reaching from the dead to be taken up
they cry out, failing, failing! their cries rising
in waves still as the skillful yachts pass over.

The form of the poem is, of course, adapted from Dante's
famous *terza rima* of *The Divine Comedy*, but for us it is important that Williams has made it completely his own. No so-
called "traditional" poet of his time has accomplished the adaptation of a traditional form with more assurance than Williams
has employed in "The Yachts," and if Archibald MacLeish in
Conquistador has endowed the *terza rima* with brighter colors
and the speed of a lively narrative, the emotions that Williams
reawakens in the reader are of a deeper origin; and in the
progress of the poem and its control of the "real" and "unreal,"
Wallace Stevens' "Laocoön" becomes the master of his style.

The later poems of Williams, including the "Elegy in Memory
of D. H. Lawrence," define the ranges of his poetic maturity;
two quotations from his latest book, *The Wedge* (1944), illustrate the sureness with which he practiced his art:

BURNING THE CHRISTMAS GREENS [9]

Their time past, pulled down
cracked and flung to the fire
—go up in a roar

[9] From *The Wedge,* used by permission of The Cummington Press and
the Author.

All recognition lost, burnt clean
clean in the flame, the green
dispersed, a living red,
flame red, red as blood wakes
on the ash—

and ebbs to a steady burning
the rekindled bed becomes
a landscape of flame

At the winter's midnight
we went to the trees, the coarse
holly, the balsam and
the hemlock for their green

At the thick of the dark
the moment of the cold's
deepest plunge we bought branches
cut from the green trees

to fill our need, and over
doorways, about paper Christmas
bells covered with tinfoil
and fastened by red ribbons

we stuck the green prongs
in the windows hung
woven wreaths and above pictures
the living green. On the

mantle we built a green forest
and among those hemlock
sprays put a herd of small
white deer as if they

were walking there. All this!
and it seemed gentle and good
to us. Their time past,
relief! The room bare. We

stuffed the dead grate
with them upon the half burntout
log's smoldering eye, opening
red and closing under them

and we stood there looking down.
Green is a solace,

a promise of peace, a fort
against the cold (though we

did not say so) a challenge
above the snow's
hard shell. Green (we might
have said) that, where

small birds hide and dodge
and lift their plaintive
rallying cries, blocks for them
and knocks down

the unseeing bullets of
the storm. Green spruce boughs
pulled down by a weight of
snow—Transformed!

Violence leaped and appeared.
Recreant! roared to life
as the flame rose through and
our eyes recoiled from it.

In the jagged flames green
to red, instant and alive. Green!
those sure abutments . . Gone!
lost to mind

and quick in the contracting
tunnel of the grate
appeared a world! Black
mountains, black and red—as

yet uncolored—and ash white,
an infant landscape of shimmering
ash and flame and we, in
that instant, lost,

breathless to be witnesses,
as if we stood
ourselves refreshed among
the shining fauna of that fire.

And in "The Cure" [10] still another aspect of Williams' plainly
spoken and formal austerity in unrhymed verse is heard:

[10] From *The Wedge*, used by permission of The Cummington Press and
the Author.

Sometimes I envy others, fear them
a little too, if they write well.
For when I cannot write I'm a sick man
and want to die. The cause is plain.

But they have no access to my sources.
Let them write then as they may and
perfect it as they can they will never
come to the secret of that form

interknit with the unfathomable ground
where we walk daily and from which
among the rest you have sprung
and opened flower-like to my hand.

Since 1921, Williams has written several works in prose and
these include a book of essays, *In the American Grain*, two volumes of belles lettres, three novels, a translation of Philippe
Soupault's *Last Nights of Paris*, and two books of short stories.
Of these the book of essays deserves a place in the history of
American prose by the side of Gertrude Stein's *Three Lives* and
Djuna Barnes's *Nightwood;* the novels and short stories may be
considered as "works in progress" toward the control in prose
over which Williams has accomplished such excellent mastery in
his later poetry. Like Stevens, Marianne Moore, T. S. Eliot,
E. E. Cummings, H. D., and Ezra Pound, Williams has never
modified the quality of his gifts to meet the temporary demands
of commercial publication; and unlike them, his poetic maturity
has been of an almost stubborn and yet hardy growth. His
example to those poets who shall come after him is unfailingly
salutary and a sign of good health in what Wallace Stevens has
so deftly called the "corpus" of American poetry.

THE HERITAGE OF THE YELLOW BOOK
AND CONRAD AIKEN

In Conrad Aiken's early volume of critical essays, *Scepticisms,* published in 1919, one is struck by the introductory sentence of his essay on John Gould Fletcher, a poet to whom he admits a temperamental affinity. More than twenty years have passed since the essay was written, much water has run under many critical bridges, many once dazzling names are not only dim but nearly obliterated—and if that striking first sentence and paragraph arrest our attention today it is because it is a brilliant summing up, not of John Gould Fletcher's labors, but of Conrad Aiken's own peculiar position:

> Mr. Fletcher is his own implacable enemy. He has not yet published a book in which his excellent qualities are single, candid, and undivided: a great many dead leaves are always to be turned.[1]

Not that Conrad Aiken has kept silent, or has failed to labor, or—to use a more characteristic word—has failed to be "creative." He has been the "creative writer" par excellence; he has rolled up his shirt sleeves and produced some twenty volumes of poetry, five novels, and three volumes of short stories, all containing his individual virtues and his highly individual vices, glossed over with the ease of someone who has learned to write without a second glance at the sheets as they fall to the floor, and quite as though the action had been performed by an automatic hand. The failures and the never-quite-attained successes are as perceptible in his early books as in his latest—the melodious vagueness, the emphasis upon the theme of sexual adventure, reiterated in terms of the slightly soiled, amateur discussions of Freud during the 1920's, the special "artiness" of that same period which never failed to include its heritage of the 1890's from the pages

[1] *Scepticisms,* Aiken.

of Henry Harland's *The Yellow Book*. How well, how easily the thoroughly precocious Conrad Aiken of 1914 would have found a place between the covers of Harland's magazine that had come to grief (and unjustly) during the Oscar Wilde trial of 1895:

> Dead Cleopatra lies in a crystal casket,
> Wrapped and spiced by the cunningest of hands.[2]

In America the 1890's had lingered far beyond the day their time was spent in London and in Paris; and an entire wing of the "poetic renaissance," of which Conrad Aiken emerged as the most ambitious figure, vehemently revived them. Never had there appeared in American poetry so many languors and lilies and paper roses, so many "esthetic" dances and such self-conscious swaying before a tall, gilt mirror, a mirror, by the way, that might well have been designed by Aubrey Beardsley. In that dance before the mirror one recalls Aiken's *Punch: The Immortal Liar* (1921) which remarked on "how we danced and how we sang."

Time has not dealt kindly with the manner of dancing that Conrad Aiken at the age of thirty-two offered us in *Punch;* its so-called "decadence" is more amusing than frightening, and the youthful vigor with which it was pursued in jingling rhymes has lost much of its original taint of evil. In a study of Aiken's life and work in *The Melody of Chaos* by Houston Peterson (1931), there were many generalizations made that defined the period of the "poetic renaissance" as well as Aiken's place within it. The book itself has become a "period piece" and the unconscious revelations of its author's mind have an enduring curiosity value in literary history; today that innocent volume is a fascinating record of the pseudo-psychoanalytic literary criticism of the day when James Branch Cabell's *Jurgen* and Carl Van Vechten's *Peter Whiffle* were greeted with less discreet than fashionable applause.

In the simultaneous discovery of large terms like "epistemology" and "psychiatry," in the enjoyment of hearing names that brought to mind French Symbolism, the poetic uses of the word

[2] "Discordance III," from *Selected Poems*, 1930, used by permission of Charles Scribner's Sons.

"Beauty" became involved. To this movement Aiken's verse had already contributed certain valuable qualities of sensitivity and a rippling stream of lyricism:

> Music I heard with you was more than music . . .[3]

Aiken became one of the many spokesmen in a reawakened search for Beauty, and in his *Scepticisms* he chose to enter its ranks with Amy Lowell, Alfred Kreymborg, and Maxwell Bodenheim. "It is the poet's office," he wrote, "not merely to entertain, but also, on a higher plane, to delight with beauty and to amaze with understanding." Almost of necessity the newly awakened desire for Beauty was a trifle vague, and what it meant can only be guessed at. Strong men and tender women cried for it with histrionic fervor—and Sara Teasdale with simple artlessness had summed it up as well as any:

> O beauty are you not enough?
> Why am I crying after love . . .[4]

Why indeed, when it probably meant the same thing? But it also meant orange curtains and black-painted floors in New York's Greenwich Village, and these were details that could be readily associated with the facile diabolism of Aiken's volumes of verse, *The Jig of Forslin* (1916), *Punch,* and *Priapus and the Pool* (1922). It meant freely roving discussions of Freud, Havelock Ellis, and Krafft-Ebing in the same manner that Marx became a topic of conversation ten years later—and the conclusions of many hours of such talk, laughter, and speculation were stated with an air of well-considered, if not dignified, finality in Houston Peterson's *The Melody of Chaos:* "Disillusioned and fascinated by turns, we see 'sublime' passions hidden under ridiculous and revolting habits." And with these speculations, the search for Beauty also included the extramarital diversions of Iris March in Michael Arlen's popular novel, *The Green Hat*— "gallant was the word for Iris"—and perhaps, at its best, it meant a reaffirmation of faith in poetry. But it is sad to recall that the

---

[3] "Bread and Music" from *Selected Poems*, 1930, used by permission of Charles Scribner's Sons.
[4] "Spring Night" from *Collected Poems*. By permission of The Macmillan Company.

search for Beauty sometimes took form in an "artiness" which resembled the dancing of Isadora Duncan in her most robust and uninhibited period. Of that glamorous figure, H. L. Mencken, who had always been a George Babbitt at heart, but certainly not one who had ever accused himself of prudery, once said that he had no objection to the lady prancing half-naked and wildly around the stage in what had been one woman's conception of "classical art." "But why," concluded the editor of *The American Mercury,* "does she have to do it in the names of Nietzsche and Schopenhauer?"

With this side glance at the associations that Aiken's poetry brings to mind, some attention should be given to the external facts of his life and his literary activity. Our quotations are from a biographical sketch which precedes a selection of his poems in Gerald DeWitt Sanders and John Herbert Nelson's *Chief Modern Poets of England and America* (third edition, 1943): [5]

Conrad Potter Aiken, eldest of the three sons of William Ford Aiken and Anna Potter Aiken, was born at Savannah, Georgia, on August 5th, 1889. Both his parents were descended from old and prominent New England families. His father, a graduate of the Harvard Medical School, established a practice in Savannah, where he enjoyed a high reputation as physician and surgeon.

Aiken secured his early education in the Savannah public schools. From the first he evinced an interest in poetry and at nine began to write verse. In his eleventh year, his father, while temporarily deranged, killed his wife and himself. As a result of this tragedy Aiken went to live with a great aunt in New Bedford, Massachusetts. For the next seven years he attended the Middlesex School. In 1907 he entered Harvard. While an undergraduate he wrote verse and prose for the *Harvard Monthly* and the *Harvard Advocate* and was President of the *Advocate* and class poet. In his senior year he ranked high enough in scholarship to enjoy the privilege of irregular class attendance, but when he absented himself from classes for ten days to write a poem, the authorities thought he was using his privilege too freely and placed him on probation. Considering this treatment unjust, he left college and went abroad for six months, but returned the following autumn and finished with the class of 1912. . . . He made frequent trips to Europe . . . and in 1923 settled at Winchelsea, on the Sussex coast. Some months later he bought a house at Rye, within a block or two of

5 "Conrad Aiken," by permission of The Macmillan Company.

Henry James's old home, and until the outbreak of the Second World War had lived there except for two short visits to the United States in 1925 and 1933 and a lengthier one from 1927 to 1930. During the latter stay, he taught for a year, 1927-28, at Harvard. . . . From 1917 to 1919 he was an editor of *The Dial,* for which he wrote many critical articles. . . . He has edited several collections of poetry and a selection of the poems of Emily Dickinson, and is a frequent contributor to such magazines as *The New Yorker, Esquire,* and *The Atlantic Monthly.*

Conrad Aiken associated, wrote Houston Peterson, "with psychiatrists and medical men"—and no one, it is agreed, should be so narrow-minded as to disclaim friendship with men of honor in any profession. Aiken read widely, but mainly with a conscious eye on the needs of his particular temperament, which was, of course, an admirable practice, but if one judges it from the character of his writing, one would say that it tended to increase his disposition toward a lax, wandering, ruminating, partly cultivated, and perhaps self-encouraged "lazy" manner of writing verse. He had an eye for glittering metaphors in poetry, and what is so commonly called "an ear for music," but the final qualities that his gifts needed, which were those of self-discipline and self-forgetfulness, never entered his work. Throughout the vague reiterations of an all too consciously "poetic" speech in many books of prose and verse, one becomes aware that his was among the most luxuriant of fine lyrical talents ever to be squandered in America.

One of Aiken's tolerant and friendly critics, Louis Untermeyer, has expertly remarked upon the character and waste of lyrical talent in the long half narrative, half epistemological poems that Aiken included in his many volumes of verse:

Often Aiken loses himself in this watery welter of language. In trying to create a closer *liaison* between poetry and music, he places so much importance on the rise and fall of syllables that his very excess of melody defeats his purpose. His verse, thus, gains greatly on the sensuous side, but loses, in its murmuring indefiniteness, that vitality of speech which is the very blood of poetry. It is a subaqueous music, strangely like the magic of Debussy.[6]

6 From *Modern American Poetry,* ed. by Louis Untermeyer, used by permission of Harcourt, Brace and Company.

Of the longer poems, "Senlin: A Biography" (1918) [7] has the most enduring interest, and the first stanza of the second section of Book II anticipated, at a measurable distance, the overtones of T. S. Eliot's *The Waste Land:*

> It is morning, Senlin says, and in the morning
> When the light drips through the shutters like the dew,
> I arise, I face the sunrise,
> And do the things my fathers learned to do.
> Stars in the purple dusk above the rooftops
> Pale in a saffron mist and seem to die,
> And I myself on a swiftly tilting planet
> Stand before a glass and tie my tie.

But one is not surprised to find the character of Senlin so amorphous, so shadowy, so completely abstracted by his ruminations that it falls far short of any resemblance to human form. One of the reasons why Senlin failed—and his failure is repeated in all of Aiken's heroes—may be observed in T. S. Eliot's brief essay on "That Poetry Is Made with Words" in *The New English Weekly* for April 27, 1939:

> Character composed according to Freudian formulae has all the defects of the synthetic substitute; its actions are tediously predictable; it is always unconvincing and usually false. The great characters of drama and prose fiction may themselves provide material for study to psychologists; but out of the psychologists' abstractions no character can be put together.

From the "Morning Song of Senlin" we turn to another happy moment in Aiken's many *Preludes for Memnon* (1931) which overflowed one volume into another, *Time in the Rock* (1936). It can be said that the more Aiken tried to resemble Rimbaud, the more he resembled Verlaine, and the rare and best moments of his verse are distinguished by a fine turn of phrase and a graceful "dying fall" of the line. His attempts at seeming "vigorous" are always forced and histrionic; but these merits and flaws are well illustrated (and the merits have been justly admired) in his "Prelude LVI": [8]

---

[7] From *Selected Poems*, 1930, used by permission of Charles Scribner's Sons.
[8] From *Preludes for Memnon,* used by permission of Charles Scribner's Sons.

Rimbaud and Verlaine, precious pair of poets,
Genius in both (but what is genius) playing
Chess on a marble table at an inn
With chestnut blossom falling in blond beer
And on their hair and between knight and bishop—
Sunlight squared between them on the chess-board
Cirrus in heaven, and a squeal of music
Blown from the leathern door of Sainte Sulpice—

Discussing, between moves, iamb and spondee
Anacoluthon and the open vowel
God the great peacock with his angel peacocks
And his dependent peacocks the bright stars:
Disputing too of fate as Plato loved it,
Or Sophocles, who hated and admired,
Or Socrates, who loved and was amused:

Verlaine puts down his pawn upon a leaf
And closes his long eyes, which are dishonest,
And says 'Rimbaud, there is one thing to do:
We must take rhetoric, and wring its neck! . . .'
Rimbaud considers gravely, moves his Queen;
And then removes himself to Timbuctoo.

And Verlaine dead,—with all his jades and mauves;
And Rimbaud dead in Marseilles with a vision,
His leg cut off, as once before his heart;
And all reported by a later lackey,
Whose virtue is his tardiness in time.

Let us describe the evening as it is:—
The stars disposed in heaven as they are:
Verlaine and Shakespere rotting, where they rot,
Rimbaud remembered, and too soon forgot;

Order in all things, logic in the dark;
Arrangement in the atom and the spark;
Time in the heart and sequence in the brain—

Such as destroyed Rimbaud and fooled Verlaine
And let us then take godhead by the neck—

And strangle it, and with it, rhetoric.

There is a characteristic sight of felicity and facility in a "prelude" from *Time in the Rock:*

She walks
as naturally as a young tree might walk:
with no pretence: picks up her roots and goes
out of your world, and into the secret darkness,
as a lady with lifted train will leave a ballroom,
and who knows why.

Wherefor do you love her, gentlemen?
Because, like the spring earth, she is fruitfulness?
and you are seed? you need no other reason?
and she no other than her perpetual season.[9]

The austerities of E. A. Robinson, or the happily poised restraint of Robert Frost, or the wit with which both poets were
endowed are absent here. Yet Aiken's poetic gifts are to be found,
scattered and abandoned, through many pages of dull verse; his
dissipation of talent was as marked as the earlier dissipation of
the finer art and more intelligently inspired gifts of Ezra Pound.
A hidden warning of Aiken's weakness and the distractions on
which it fed may be discovered in the Introduction to his *Scepticisms*. He had spoken of the position of the poet in respect to his
contemporaries:

It is cut-throat competition, a survival of the fittest. We lose no
opportunity to praise our own sort of work, or to condemn that sort
which we consider dangerous.

This may well be a youthful and honest criterion for criticism,
but it is not likely to sustain the gifts, or to lead the way toward
the esthetic discrimination, of a mature poet. The answer to it
may be found in Thomas Mann's essay on "Richard Wagner and
the Ring of the Nibelungen" in *Decision*, January-February,
1942, in which he said:

Indeed, it is probable that objective recognition of the claims of
another's art is hardly characteristic of the artist's active and struggling
years. "Beautiful," says Kant, "is that which gives us disinterested
pleasure." And very likely no performance of another can give quite
disinterested pleasure to him upon whom it is laid to achieve the
height of beauty himself. At least not until he has quite reached his

[9] "Prelude LXXXV" from *Time in the Rock*, used by permission of
Charles Scribner's Sons.

goal. For only then is his praise free from the need to flatter himself, to defend and strengthen his own position.

There is no evidence of that kind of wisdom in anything that Conrad Aiken has written, either in verse or prose. Certainly, a recent sonnet sequence, *And in the Human Heart* (1940), shows none of the poetic maturity that we may have hoped for in 1921; the familiar sights of "chaos" and the "void" remained quite as they seemed to him in earlier days, and if anything, the language of the sonnets was more abstracted, more relaxed, more sonorous than the shapeless and "watery" speech of his semipsychiatric, semiepistemological ruminations in verse:

> If the void sunders downward, let us fall,
> nethermost whistling Nothing there to find—
> these but our nightmares, our own dragons, all,
> who through the chaos but extend the mind.[10]

"Death among violins and paper roses" still played a leitmotiv through Conrad Aiken's verse; nor have the awards that he has won, the Shelley Memorial Award, 1929, the Pulitzer Prize for his *Selected Poems* in 1930 (and these were given more deservedly to him than to many recipients of similar honors), served to endow him with the assurance and strength to build beyond the moment when Aldous Huxley wrote in *The Nation and Athenaeum* (London, 1920):

Mr. Aiken possesses many poetical merits. He has a flow of language that is refreshing in this age of meagrely trickling springs. . . . But he has the defects of his qualities. His facility is his undoing. . . . He runs along like Wordsworth's hare in 'The Leech-Gatherer,' in a rainbow mist of his own making. . . . But a mist, however iridescent, is always a mist; and after running along at Mr. Aiken's side for a hundred pages or so one begins to long for clarity and firmness, for a glimpse of something definite outside this golden haze. . . . If Mr. Aiken is to be more than an agreeable maker of coloured mists he will have to find some new intellectual formula into which to concentrate the shapelessness of his vague emotions.

10 Sonnet sequence from *And in the Human Heart,* used by permission of Duell, Sloan & Pearce, Inc.

THREE MIDDLE WESTERN POETS:
MASTERS, LINDSAY, AND SANDBURG

EDGAR LEE MASTERS

When on March 1, 1914, William Butler Yeats spoke in Chicago of a poetic style "like speech, as simple as the simplest prose, like a cry of the heart," his audience was half prepared to recognize that style and to believe that they had made a like discovery of the "new" poetry. If regionalism in Ireland had anticipated by a few short years a similar movement in the American Middle West, the moment of its birth in the Abbey Theatre was no less exciting than the almost simultaneous arrival of three Middle Western poets, Edgar Lee Masters, Vachel Lindsay, and Carl Sandburg. The Chicago audience and their th ee poets would have heartily accepted a definition of poetry set down as early as 1908 by Yeats's fellow countryman, J. M. Synge:

> In these days poetry is usually a flower of evil or good; but it is the timber of poetry that wears most surely, and there is no timber that has not strong roots among the clay and worms.
> Even if we grant that exalted poetry can be kept successful by itself, the strong things of life are needed in poetry also, to show that what is exalted and tender is not made by feeble blood. It may almost be said that before verse can be human again it must learn to be brutal.[1]

The eldest of the three poets—and none of the three was under thirty at the moment when Chicago and *Poetry* magazine announced their arrival on the scene—was Edgar Lee Masters. In the controversy that greeted Edgar Lee Masters' *Spoon River Anthology* (1915) readers of poetry in the United States were delighted to find short, dramatic verses that were "like speech, as

[1] Preface to "Poems" from *Works of John M. Synge,* Vol. II, used by permission of Random House, Inc.

simple as the simplest prose," and that the entire book could be read with the facility that they enjoyed in reading a popular novel. The verses were monologues spoken from the tombstones of a small Middle Western town, and they recited the brief joys, the gossip, the frustrated ambitions, the griefs, the ironies of a community that had once thrived, but had been left in a condition of Protestant unrest, and had been cheated in its hopes of nineteenth-century "progress."

While Amy Lowell lectured to women's clubs on the virtues of vers libre, a larger public had made its own discovery of "free verse" in the unrhymed monologues of Edgar Lee Masters' *Spoon River Anthology*—and the discovery seemed to be one of greater relevance to a national literature because abstract theories and manifestoes of writing verse had acquired a local habitation and the familiar sound of American family names. The half-ironic warnings that "man is mortal" which emanated from the shadows of Masters' Spoon River churchyard were spoken in terms of a direct antithesis to the happy countrymen and children of James Whitcomb Riley's Hoosier lyrics; it was as though thousands of restless, defeated, anonymous souls had suddenly found their voices, and an equal number of "Aunt Marys," "Orphan Annies," "Raggedy" men, and "Uncle Sidneys" had lost their innocent smiles and tears.

What the "dead souls" of Spoon River had to say implied the same experiences, the same beliefs, the same bewildered sense of loss that defined the causes of material success and failure in the novels of Theodore Dreiser. By a turn of good fortune Masters' *Anthology* appeared at the very moment when the voices of his Spoon River Valley were most likely to be heard.

Edgar Lee Masters was born in Garnett, Kansas, on August 23, 1869, and readers of his autobiography, *Across Spoon River* (1936), will not fail to recognize in him an archetype of the zealously independent, slowly maturing, Middle Western American of his generation. With his fellows he shared the same general, hard-earned pragmatic beliefs and disillusionments. His early readings included the poetry of Bryant, Keats, Shelley, and Byron and the prose of Herbert Spencer's *First Principles*. To these foundations of a semiliterary culture, the speeches of Robert Ingersoll and of William Jennings Bryan were added; and today one can hardly overestimate the evangelical power that Ingersoll and Bryan exerted within the imaginations of young men who looked for their salvation beyond the horizons of the Congregational and Baptist Church suppers, the public high school, and the small-town, Middle Western college. For those who did not leave the Middle West for study in an Eastern university, the difficult and cross-grained virtues of self-education retained their hold, and with them came the well-grounded strengths and weaknesses of "making one's own way," and as if to counterbalance the weight of a material or "scientific" philosophy, came the adventurous, and often vicarious, yearning for distant places, a youthful "nostalgia" for "the glory that was Greece, the grandeur that was Rome." Rather more than a hint of these fluid and yet persistent speculations and desires is to be found in the pages of Masters' autobiography:

> If I needed anything I needed wise eyes to see what I was and to guide me. . . .—Did Keats have more time than I had? I suspect that he did not. But he had far more inspiring friends, and far richer cultural influences about him than I had. . . . What I wrote reflected my prison, my unhappiness. . . . These words are in no sense an apologia. I am merely setting down my circumstances, and without sparing myself. I was the chief influence in my own career. Americans do not come to a possession of their gifts as early as English writers do, and I was an American, and circumstanced with the most characteristic conditions of American life.[2]

These reflections were revived by Masters' memory of the year 1906, when he was a man of thirty-seven, and his imagination had been inspired by the idea of writing his *Spoon River Anthology* in the form of an extended work in prose, a long novel, that was to embrace the interwoven lives of people whose misadventures were circumscribed by the larger destiny of a small town in Illinois. Fortunately, the work in prose was never written, but the idea came to life again eight years later when at the prompting of his friend, William Marion Reedy, Masters agreed

---

[2] From *Across Spoon River*, copyright, 1936, by Edgar Lee Masters, and reprinted by permission of Farrar & Rinehart, Inc.

to write his book in verse and to contribute his Spoon River monologues to the pages of *Reedy's Mirror.*

The candid, awkward recital of his life in *Across Spoon River* provides an environment for the writing of Masters' *Anthology:* his family, as it moved from Kansas to Illinois, shared the memories of a generation that knew the conflicts of the Civil War, the fables and legends which had accumulated around the name and figure of Abraham Lincoln, and the fair prospects as well as the disillusionments of an American postwar economy. Most of Masters' boyhood was spent in Lewistown, Illinois, and the variety of his early experiences included work in a printing office, writing verse for Chicago newspapers, a brief attendance at Knox College, a clerkship in his father's law office, and an ill-paid job of collecting bills for the Edison Company in Chicago. Between 1898 and 1914 he had published three books of verse and had written a half-dozen plays, all of which were notably unsuccessful and generally ignored—but by the time he had consented to write his *Spoon River Anthology* for the pages of *Reedy's Mirror,* he was well known and respected as an able and prosperous Chicago lawyer. As he turned to the writing of his *Anthology,* all the self-acquired learning, the suppressed energies and observations, all the subconscious processes of his imagination that had slept within him for many years seem to have been released; the writing of the book seems to have produced in him the same trancelike state that W. B. Yeats has described in his own autobiographies, and it is not surprising to learn that soon after the manuscript of the *Spoon River Anthology* had been sent to the publishers, its author collapsed and was dangerously ill. Harriet Monroe, of *Poetry,* read and corrected the final proofs of the book, and after its publication the book's notoriety destroyed Masters' law practice in Chicago— for who would trust a lawyer who had written an eminently notorious book of poems in "free verse"?

The phenomenon was one that could not be repeated, as the many volumes of verse and prose that followed *Spoon River* testify; Masters' poetic gifts had expended their energies and their perceptions in the eloquent lines of "The Hill," in the frequently quoted "Anne Rutledge," and the lesser-known "Thomas Trevelyan": [3]

> Reading in Ovid the sorrowful story of Itys,
> Son of the love of Tereus and Procne, slain
> For the guilty passion of Tereus for Philomela,
> The flesh of him served to Tereus by Procne,
> And the wrath of Tereus, the murderess pursuing
> Till the gods made Philomela a nightingale,
> Lute of the rising moon, and Procne a swallow!
> Oh livers and artists of Hellas centuries gone,
> Sealing in little thuribles dreams and wisdom,
> Incense beyond all price, forever fragrant,
> A breath whereof makes clear the eyes of the soul!
> How I inhaled its sweetness here in Spoon River!
> The thurible opening when I had lived and learned
> How all of us kill the children of love, and all of us,
> Knowing not what we do, devour their flesh;
> And all of us change to singers, although it be
> But once in our lives, or change—alas!—to swallows,
> To twitter amid cold winds and falling leaves!

In "Petit the Poet" and in "The Village Atheist" the historical veracity of the portrait is of greater interest than the verse itself; but since Masters' "Atheist" is far more perceptive than any similar attempts to present the same character in American fiction, Masters needs no defense and certainly no apology for having written the following lines:

> Ye young debaters over the doctrine
> Of the soul's immortality,
> I who lie here was the village atheist,
> Talkative, contentious, versed in the arguments
> Of the infidels.
> But through a long sickness
> Coughing myself to death
> I read the *Upanishads* and the poetry of Jesus.
> And they lighted a torch of hope and intuition
> And desire which the Shadow,
> Leading me swiftly through the caverns of darkness,
> Could not extinguish.

[3] From *Spoon River Anthology*, The Macmillan Company. By permission of the Author.

> Listen to me, ye who live in the senses
> And think through the senses only:
> Immortality is not a gift,
> Immortality is an achievement;
> And only those who strive mightily
> Shall possess it.[4]

A second volume of Spoon River monologues, *The New Spoon River,* appeared in 1924; and as if to prove that both volumes of Spoon River had a justifiable precedent in, as well as the influence of, a wide reading that included translations of Greek literature, to say nothing of .Dante's *La Divina Commedia,* Masters wrote an essay, "The Genesis of Spoon River," for the readers of H. L. Mencken's magazine, *The American Mercury.*[5] A quotation from the essay illustrates the broad scope of its author's intentions in writing the work that had changed his profession and had brought him fame.

There are two hundred and forty-four characters in the book, not counting those who figure in the Spooniad and the Epilogue. There are nineteen stories developed by interrelated portraits. Practically every ordinary human occupation is covered, except those of the barber, the miller, the cobbler, the tailor and the garage man . . . and all these were depicted later in the *New Spoon River.* What critics overlook when they call the Anthology Zolaesque, and by doing so mean to degrade it, is the fact that when the book was put together in its definitive order, . . . the fools, the drunkards, and the failures came first, the people of one-birth minds got second place, and the heroes and the enlightened spirits came last, a sort of Divine Comedy, which some critics were acute enough to point out at once.
The names I drew from both the Spoon river and the Sangamon river neighborhoods, combining first names here with surnames there, and taking some also from the constitutions and State papers of Illinois.

Within the past quarter of a century Masters has written at least fifteen books of verse, seven novels, five biographies, including a life of Vachel Lindsay and a history of Chicago; throughout all his writing, no matter how uneven its quality may be, the merits of sincerity and of courage are always to be found. Of his narrative poems, *The Domesday Book* (1920) and

---

[4] "The Village Atheist" from *Spoon River Anthology,* The Macmillan Company. By permission of the Author.
[5] January, 1933, used by permission of the Author.

its sequel, *The Fate of the Jury* (1929), are the best-known, if somewhat disheartening, examples of his later style. Both books were "novels in verse," rather than poems, and in fairness to Masters' intentions and actual accomplishments, it should be observed that the heroine of his two novels in verse, a young woman of the First World War generation, anticipated and paralleled the misadventures of Eugene O'Neill's heroines on the stage whose choice of many love affairs and of lovers showed less discrimination than their experiences warranted.

Today, and largely because of the position he attained through the success of the *Spoon River Anthology*, Masters justly commands the respect of those who admire the semibelligerent and independent attitude with which he faced the world, and not unlike his, contemporary, Theodore Dreiser, his merits have the sturdy, if often graceless exterior, of what is sometimes referred to as "American Gothic."

In an interview written by Robert van Gelder in the New York *Times*, February 15, 1942, one hears the forthright, opinionated convictions of a man whose contribution to the regional literature of the Middle West has survived the controversies and distractions of the "poetic renaissance":

As for other modern poets, Mr. Masters continued, they are worthless and he cannot make anything of them at all. "They have no principles, no individuality, no moral code and no roots. . . ."

"What are your roots?" [van Gelder asked].

"The America of Jefferson—of Jeffersonian democracy. I date back a long time. I believe in an America that is not imitative, that stands alone, that is strong." . . . Bitterly opposed to the "Lincoln myth," and arguing that Lincoln was hypocritical, slow-witted, vindictive and cold, Mr. Masters is convinced . . . that "Americans are provincial." On the other hand, "I am a Hellenist. . . . The great marvel of the world is Greek civilization. They thought in universals, as did the Elizabethans. We are provincial in our thoughts. . . .

"Some one should write an article on America's Cinderella complex and the many men it has destroyed. The man in the country dreaming of being the guest of honor at a city banquet. The Cinderella complex—the destroyer of virility, of sound workmanship and honest thought. William Dean Howells—do many people think of him now?"

"Probably not very often, he had that Cinderella complex." [6]

[6] By permission of Robert van Gelder.

VACHEL LINDSAY

The most highly gifted poet of Harriet Monroe's "Middle Western School" was Nicholas Vachel Lindsay, who was born November 10, 1879, in Springfield, Illinois, and died by his own hand "harassed by debts and the sense of defeat" in the house where he spent his boyhood in Springfield, December 5, 1931. Like Masters' *Spoon River Anthology,* his poetry had the artless character of seeming phenomenal, but it remains a phenomenon of unusual purity, and perhaps of enduring life. And it is entirely probable that future readers will regard it with something of the awe which they reserve for the handful of lyrics that Edgar Allan Poe had left behind him and something of the delight with which the nonsense verses of Edward Lear are perennially revived. To reread the large volume of his *Collected Poems* (1925) is a cheerless task, for Lindsay was certainly no critic of his own gifts; his verse, schooled as it was in the rhythms and brasses of the Moody and Sankey hymnals, often ran into a maudlin, self-hypnotic repetition of identical words and phrases, and Lindsay, possessed by the cult of child-worship, was never able to discern that invisible line where his fancies ended and the true work of his imagination began. One concludes that he was as fragmentary a poet as Hart Crane became in a later generation, and if anything his gifts were more directly inspired and less contaminated by the incongruities of the environment which surrounded them. Lindsay's "I Heard Immanuel Singing" [7] is one of the most extraordinary of American "spirituals" and it deserves a place, on its poetic merits alone, in the near company of Christopher Smart's "Song to David":

> I heard Immanuel singing
> Within his own good lands;
> I saw him bend above his harp.
> I watched his wandering hands
> Lost amid the harp-strings;
> Sweet, sweet I heard him play.

[7] From *Collected Poems of Vachel Lindsay.* By permission of The Macmillan Company.

His wounds were altogether healed.
Old things had passed away.

All things were new, but music.
The blood of David ran
Within the Son of David,
Our God, the Son of Man.
He was ruddy like a shepherd.
His bold young face, how fair.
Apollo of the silver bow
Had not such flowing hair.

I saw Immanuel singing
On a tree-girdled hill.
The glad remembering branches
Dimly echoed still
The grand new song proclaiming
The Lamb that had been slain.
New-built, the Holy City
Gleamed in the murmuring plain.

The crowning hours were over.
The pageants all were past.
Within the many mansions
The hosts, grown still at last,
In homes of holy mystery
Slept long by crooning springs
Or waked to peaceful glory,
A universe of Kings.

He left his people happy.
He wandered free to sigh
Alone in lowly friendship
With the green grass and the sky.
He murmured ancient music
His red heart burned to sing
Because his perfect conquest
Had grown a weary thing.

No chant of gilded triumph—
His lonely song was made
Of Art's deliberate freedom;
Of minor chords arrayed
In soft and shadowy colors
That once were radiant flowers:—

The Rose of Sharon, bleeding
In Olive-shadowed bowers:—

And all the other roses
In the songs of East and West
Of love and war and worshipping,
And every shield and crest
Of thistle or of lotus
Or sacred lily wrought
In creeds and psalms and palaces
And temples of white thought:—

All these he sang, half-smiling
And weeping as he smiled,
Laughing, talking to his harp
As to a new-born child:—
As though the arts forgotten
But bloomed to prophesy
These careless, fearless harp-strings,
New-crying in the sky.
"When this his hour of sorrow
For flowers and Arts of men
Has passed in ghostly music,"
I asked my wild heart then—
What will he sing to-morrow,
What wonder, all his own
Alone, set free, rejoicing
With a green hill for his throne?
What will he sing to-morrow,
What wonder all his own
Alone, set free, rejoicing,
With a green hill for his throne?

The poet who wrote these lines (and they were completed in 1909) had an unworldly temperament not unlike Smart's who sank to his knees and prayed aloud in the streets of eighteenth-century London; the good people of London thought Smart was mad, and citizens of Springfield, Illinois, believed that Lindsay was at least "half cracked"; and in defining the character of Lindsay's devotion to poetry, which carried him, a tall, sandy-haired man, in a store-bought, ill-fitting, blue serge suit, singing and shouting, onto the platforms of American lecture halls, it is well to remember Samuel Johnson's remarks on Smart's "madness":

Madness frequently discovers itself merely by unnecessary deviation from the usual modes of the world. My poor friend Smart showed the disturbance of his mind by falling upon his knees, and saying his prayers in the street, or in any other unusual place. Now, although, rationally speaking, it is greater madness not to pray at all than to pray as Smart did, I am afraid there are so many who do not pray, that their understanding is not called in question.

And later, Johnson continued with:

His infirmities were not noxious to society. He insisted on people praying with him; [quite as Lindsay tried to draw his audiences into chanting with him the refrains of his poems] and I'd as lief pray with Kit Smart as any one else.[8]

The citizens of Springfield—or, for that matter, the people of the United States—were no more accustomed to reading or hearing poetry read in the terms in which Lindsay wrote and recited it than eighteenth-century Londoners were accustomed to praying in Christopher Smart's fashion. Lindsay's platform appearances were not conceived as devices in showmanship; they were grave and noisy, and once their novelty had become shopworn, and Lindsay himself seemed like a ruddy-faced farmer's boy who had become middle-aged, the performance became embarrassing in its artlessness, and not in the least conducive to the placid or half-patronizing enjoyment that is required for the successful tour of the poet before the audiences of American poetry societies and their affiliated women's clubs. Lindsay could not be tolerated as an attractive celebrity from overseas: he was not the Irish poet, "Æ," (George Russell), or even W. B. Yeats, or the handsome, brown-skinned, full-bearded East Indian, Rabindranath Tagore; he was neither picturesque, nor conventionally exotic, and in his latter years, his figure was, if anything, a shade too familiar, and far too much like someone who had lived all his life on Main Street in a small town, and had now, somehow, "gone wrong."

Although Lindsay's boyhood was far more strictly dominated by his mother's concern for "art" than Edgar Lee Masters', it was shaped by many of the same elements at work in a Middle

---

[8] From Boswell's *Life of Johnson*, Vol. I, used by permission of Charles Scribner's Sons.

Western environment. He was the son of Dr. Vachel T. Lindsay, a practicing physician of Springfield, and the plans for his education, though earnestly pursued, were made up of several false starts and changes. After his academic failure at Hiram College, Mrs. Lindsay, a Campbellite, had convinced herself that her son was not a poet; she was all too sure that he had not been born a writer, and in her mind, poets were not made but born, and she decided that he was destined to become "an artist," "a Christian cartoonist," "a warrior of God," "a soul in search of beauty." In Lindsay's preface to the 1925 edition of his *Collected Poems* there is ample, and perhaps disastrous, proof that he half believed her; and in his efforts to explain the meaning, the earnest, if not always serious, content of his poetry, he wrote vaguely of Swedenborg and of the "Mystic" city of Springfield, Illinois, a "Springfield of Visions" which, in a fanciful display of scrolls and flourishes in pen and ink, he called his "Map of the Universe." The drawing was reproduced as the frontispiece to his *Collected Poems* as well as an illustration for his rhapsodic work in prose, *The Golden Book of Springfield* (1920). He had visited Europe in the company of his parents, he had studied painting at the Art Institute of Chicago, and at the Chase School in New York; he had read fervently in the poetry of Poe and of Swinburne and Rossetti; and he had spent several years "trading" his rhymes for bread and lodging across the United States from New York to San Francisco. In January, 1913, Harriet Monroe published his poem "General William Booth Enters into Heaven" in *Poetry,* and during the same year, his first book of verse was published with "General William Booth" as the title poem. Since 1905, he had been printing individual poems on cards and broadsides, and a few had been issued as pamphlets, but it was not until he had received encouragement from Harriet Monroe, and his book the imprint of a New York publisher, that he came into a notoriety which so closely resembled fame.

The success of "General William Booth" inspired the aging William Dean Howells to speak of it as a "fine, brave poem . . . that makes the heart leap," while the highly respectable and cautious *Review of Reviews* said tersely, "It is perhaps the most remarkable poem of a decade." With this recognition, Lindsay delivered himself over to the American lecture-hall public of the hour, and from its applause he gained the confidence and the renewals of nervous energy to write "The Congo," "The Santa Fé Trail," "The Chinese Nightingale," "Bryan, Bryan, Bryan, Bryan," and "John L. Sullivan," which were readily accepted as his masterpieces. In the company of his mother he made an equally triumphant tour of England, and the British public welcomed him with the same delight and curiosity that it had bestowed on the earlier tours of Bret Harte, Joaquin Miller, Artemus Ward, and Mark Twain—but this source of inspiration had within it all the evils of a pleasant dream that shifts without warning into a prolonged nightmare; the lecture hall also became his means of livelihood, and when, after his marriage in 1925, and he had assumed the responsibilities of raising a family, he found that his earlier stimulus for writing verse had failed him, he was faced with dwindling audiences and the prospects of actual starvation.

The gifts which Lindsay possessed were not of a kind that gathered strength as he attempted to mature, nor could he transform those realities which he saw with the clear and direct gaze of a child into the symbols and portents of adult life; from his mother he had acquired a fantastic, almost fanatical loyalty to the Anti-Saloon League, and he wrote verses of great charm to celebrate his devotion to that cause:

> There's a snake on the western wave
> And his crest is red.
> He is long as a city street,
> And he eats the dead.
> There's a hole in the bottom of the sea
> Where the snake goes down.
> And he waits in the bottom of the sea
> For the men that drown.
>
> This is the voice of the sand
> (The sailors understand)
> "There is far more sea than sand,
> There is far more sea than land.
>   Yo . . . ho, yo . . . ho."

He waits by the door of his cave
While the ages moan.
He cracks the ribs of the ships
With his teeth of stone.
In his gizzard deep and long
Much treasure lies.
Oh, the pearls and the Spanish gold . . . .
And the idols' eyes . . . .
Oh, the totem poles . . . the skulls . . .
The altars cold . . .
The wedding rings, the dice . . .
The buoy bells old.[9]

And for himself he held to his long admiration for "The Boy
Orator," William Jennings Bryan—but he also held in confused
reverence, and with a characteristic lack of discrimination, the
names of George Washington, Andrew Jackson, Robert E. Lee,
Abraham Lincoln, Whitman, Emerson, Altgeld, Johnny Appleseed, and Mary Pickford. In his fancy many of these figures had
the archaic charm of cigar-store Indians, but whenever his imagination actually touched them, they suddenly sprang to life within
a world that was singularly unliterary and appropriate for their
being, and within it we find his "Flower-Fed Buffaloes": [10]

The flower-fed buffaloes of the spring
In the days of long ago,
Ranged where the locomotives sing
And the prairie flowers lie low:—
The tossing, blooming, perfumed grass
Is swept away by the wheat,
Wheels and wheels and wheels spin by
In the spring that still is sweet.
But the flower-fed buffaloes of the spring
Left us, long ago.
They gore no more, they bellow no more,
They trundle around the hills no more:—
With the Blackfeet, lying low,
With the Pawnees, lying low,
Lying low.

[9] "The Sea Serpent Chantey" from *Collected Poems of Vachel Lindsay*. By
permission of The Macmillan Company.
[10] From *Going to the Sun*, used by permission of D. Appleton-Century
Company.

For ten years Lindsay continued his strenuous tours of the country, which crossed the same territory that James Whitcomb Riley traveled twenty years before him, and the shouting of "The Congo" and the recitation of "Factory Windows Are Always Broken" [11] left his audiences less reassured of their security, if not, on occasion, less amused:

> Factory windows are always broken.
> Somebody's always throwing bricks,
> Somebody's always heaving cinders,
> Playing ugly Yahoo tricks.
>
> Factory windows are always broken.
> Other windows are let alone.
> No one throws through the chapel-window
> The bitter, snarling, derisive stone.
>
> Factory windows are always broken.
> Something or other is going wrong.
> Something is rotten, I think, in Denmark.
> *End of the factory-window song.*

As Jean Cocteau once remarked, the true poet wishes less to be admired than to be believed, and it was Lindsay's misfortune never to inspire confidence and ultimate conviction among audiences who had at first cheered him and then grew weary of the middle-aged, strained, half-serious child's play that he enacted before their eyes.

Among Lindsay's erratic gifts was a felicity of epithet and with it his remarkable "Bryan, Bryan, Bryan, Bryan" [12] attains a memorable quality that transcends its half-forgotten names; the theme of the poem was, of course, as old as François Villon's ancient question, "Where are the snows of yesteryear?"

> Where is McKinley, Mark Hanna's McKinley,
> His slave, his echo, his suit of clothes?
> Gone to join the shadows, with the pomps of that time,
> And the flame of that summer's prairie rose.
>
> .   .   .   .

[11] From *Collected Poems of Vachel Lindsay*. By permission of The Macmillan Company.
[12] *Ibid.*

Where is Roosevelt, the young dude cowboy,
Who hated Bryan, then aped his way?
Gone to join the shadows with mighty Cromwell
And tall King Saul, till the Judgment day.

. . . . .

Where is that boy, that Heaven-born Bryan,
That Homer Bryan, who sang from the West?
Gone to join the shadows with Altgeld the Eagle,
Where the kings and the slaves and the troubadours rest.

And from this he turned to the glorified light verse of his
"Simon Legree—A Negro Sermon," [13] which was by far the best
thing of its kind in English since Richard Harris Barham under
the pseudonym of "Thomas Ingoldsby, Esquire" presented *The
Ingoldsby Legends*:

He beat poor Uncle Tom to death
Who prayed for Legree with his last breath.
Then Uncle Tom to Eva flew,
To the high sanctoriums bright and new;
And Simon Legree stared up beneath,
And cracked his heels, and ground his teeth:
And went down to the Devil.

He crossed the yard in the storm and gloom;
He went into his grand front room.
He said, "I killed him, and I don't care."
He kicked a hound, he gave a swear;
He tightened his belt, he took a lamp,
Went down cellar to the webs and damp.
There in the middle of the moldy floor
He heaved up a slab; he found a door—
And went down to the Devil.

. . . . .

And the Devil said to Simon Legree:

"I like your style, so wicked and free.
Come sit and share my throne with me,
And let us bark and revel."

And there they sit and gnash their teeth,
And each one wears a hop-vine wreath.

[13] From *Collected Poems of Vachel Lindsay*. By permission of The Macmillan Company.

> They are matching pennies and shooting craps,
> They are playing poker and taking naps.
> And old Legree is fat and fine:
> He eats the fire, he drinks the wine—
> Blood and burning turpentine—
> > *Down, down with the Devil;*
> > *Down, down with the Devil;*
> > *Down, down with the Devil.*

Lindsay wrote several books in prose, all of which are curiosities of literature: his study, *The Art of the Moving Picture* (1916), paralleled in one of its chapters Ezra Pound's interest in the Chinese written character, and while Pound went for instruction to the Fenollosa manuscripts, Lindsay in his painstaking fashion studied the Egyptian *Book of the Dead,* and speculated on the hieroglyphic of Osiris. His instructions in *A Handy Guide for Beggars* (1916) [14] were characteristic of the standard of living he held in mind and of his unworldliness:

(3) Have nothing to do with money and carry no baggage;
(4) Ask for dinner about quarter after eleven;
(5) Ask for supper, lodging and breakfast about quarter of five;
(6) Travel alone;
(7) Be neat, deliberate, chaste and civil;
(8) Preach the Gospel of Beauty.

The purity of Lindsay's devotion to his cause of writing verse and to his "Mystic" Springfield, as well as the misfortune that resulted in his suicide, reminds one of the calm, reflective words that Samuel Taylor Coleridge once addressed to his friend, Charles Lamb: "I look upon you as a man called by sorrow and anguish and a strange desolation of hopes into quietness, and a soul set apart and made peculiar to God." It is in those words, and not in the language of the flamboyant elegy that Lindsay once wrote in memory of John P. Altgeld, that Lindsay's own epitaph deserves to be written.

CARL SANDBURG

Carl Sandburg's *Chicago Poems* were published in 1916, and perhaps the best description of the time and place which re-

[14] By permission of The Macmillan Company.

ceived them with so much enthusiasm and applause is contained in Sherwood Anderson's *Memoirs* (1942); [15] as he recollected his adventures in Chicago, Anderson wrote:

> Lucian Cary came to Margy's house. I went with her and Ben Hecht to a town down state where Ben, then a star reporter on the *Daily News,* was covering a murder trial and a hanging. . . .
>
> It was during that summer that I met Carl Sandburg. I was introduced to him by Ben Hecht and we went for a long afternoon's walk through the factory district on Chicago's West Side. . . . Ernestine Evans . . . was there. . . . She brought Robert Lovett to her rooms. Llewellyn Jones came. Through Ben Hecht I also met Henry Justin Smith of the *News,* Burton Rascoe, then doing books for the *Tribune,* and Lewis Galantiere, who was to become a lifelong friend. We were all from the Middle West. We were all full of hope.
>
> It was the time in which something blossomed in Chicago and the Middle West. Dreiser from Terre Haute in Indiana had written and published *Sister Carrie* and Norris who already had written *McTeague* was fighting for Dreiser as Dreiser later was to fight for me, and had been joined in his fight by Francis Hackett, Floyd Dell, Henry Mencken and others. Edgar Lee Masters had written his *Spoon River Anthology;* down the state Vachel Lindsay was shouting forth his stirring verses; Sandburg was writing his magical *Chicago Poems;* and Margaret Anderson, still working as editor on some church paper, was soon to break loose and start her *Little Review. . . .*
>
> All over the country indeed there was an outbreak of new poets. Something which had been very hard in American life was beginning to crack, and in our group we often spoke of it hopefully. And how exciting it was. Something seemingly new and fresh was in the very air we breathed— So there I was, a little under the wing of Margy, who knew so well all of these to me so wonderful people. She was untiring, working all day as a reporter and ready every evening for any kind of adventure with the rest of us. She would run out to arrange for gin and sandwiches and then seat herself on a low bed at the side of the room. She would put flowers in her hair and we others would gather about, Mike Carmichael of the flowing red beard serving the drinks, some woman of the party, Eunice Tietjens or Mrs. Lucian Cary, seeing that we were supplied with sandwiches, the rest of us—and we were often as many as twenty—sitting about on the floor.
>
> What ho! for the new world.

And it was indeed a "new world" that welcomed an easy, half Bohemian, half journalistic fraternity; the ease of the "home-

[15] Harcourt, Brace. Copyright 1942 by Eleanor Anderson. Reprinted by permission of Eleanor Anderson.

spun" social manner was almost an affectation; and within an hour everyone felt extremely democratic and American, celebrating the warmth of sentiment so facilely aroused by addressing one another by the first name.

Part of the "new world" was significantly expressed in Carl Sandburg's poem, "Chicago": [16]

> Hog Butcher for the World,
> Tool Maker, Stacker of Wheat,
> Player with Railroads and the Nation's Freight Handler;
> Stormy, husky, brawling,
> City of the Big Shoulders:

They tell me you are wicked, and I believe them; for I have seen your painted women under the gas lamps luring the farm boys.

And they tell me you are crooked, and I answer: Yes, it is true I have seen the gunman kill and go free to kill again.

And they tell me you are brutal, and my reply is: On the faces of women and children I have seen the marks of wanton hunger.

And having answered so I turn once more to those who sneer at this my city, and I give them back the sneer and say to them:

Come and show me another city with lifted head singing so proud to be alive and coarse and strong and cunning.

In these lines, J. M. Synge's remarks, quoted by Yeats, have a literal application: "It may almost be said that before verse can be human again it must learn to be brutal"; and Sandburg's contribution to a regional literature was not unlike the contribution made by Synge when he wrote *The Playboy of the Western World.* Everything that Sandburg has to say can be understood quickly and at a first reading, and a testimony of the ease with which his verse has been read is found in the fact that an entire generation of high-school children have had their introduction to the poetry of the "poetic renaissance" through the flowing rhetoric and rhythms of his unrhymed verses. In the mid-twentieth century, Sandburg was perhaps the last valiant exponent of the kind of "free verse" that had been rediscovered with so much excitement among those who listened to Amy Lowell's lectures on vers libre. In the preface to a single-volume new edition of

[16] From *Chicago Poems,* used by permission of Henry Holt and Company, Inc.

his *Smoke and Steel, Slabs of the Sunburnt West, Good Morning, America* [17] (1942), Sandburg wrote:

> Recently a poet [the poet was Robert Frost] was quoted as saying he would as soon play tennis without a net as to write free verse. This is almost as though a zebra should say to a leopard, "I would rather have stripes than spots," or as though a leopard should inform a zebra, "I prefer spots to stripes. . . ."

With this bit of zoological fancy and characteristically shrewd humor, Sandburg continued:

> The arguments against free verse are old. They are not, however, as old as free verse itself. When primitive and prehistoric man first spoke with cadence or color, making either musical meaning or melodic nonsense worth keeping and repeating for its definite and intrinsic values, then free verse was born, ages before the sonnet, the ballad, the verse forms wherein the writer or singer must be acutely conscious, even exquisitely aware, of how many syllables are to be arithmetically numbered per line.
>
> The matter should not be argued. Those who make poems and hope their poems are not bad may find readers or listeners—and again they may not. The affair should rest there.

And as one rereads Sandburg's verse, which has an easy rhythm of speech that he had made his own, all talk of "literary" influence and of protracted "literary" argument does seem irrelevant. What his verse reflects is first of all the life and movement of a large Middle Western city that has been observed by a skilled reporter, and the larger world outside the city flows through the verses with the same urgency, the same vivid rhetoric, and often with the same speed with which the teletype communicates its news to the city desk of a metropolitan newspaper. Often enough, the verses were brief editorials, and others were abbreviated "human-interest stories," which were told with an expertly placed touch of pathos, or derisive and sometimes heavily pointed criticism of social evils. In a half fanciful, half hortatory mood Sandburg instructed the spring grass to rise:

> Spring grass, there is a dance to be danced for you.
> Come up, spring grass, if only for young feet.
> Come up, spring grass, young feet ask you.

[17] From preface, 1941, used by permission of Harcourt, Brace.

Smell of the young spring grass,
You're a mascot riding on the wind horses.
You came to my nose and spiffed me. This is your lucky year.

Young spring grass just after the winter,
Shoots of the big green whisper of the year,
Come up, if only for young feet.
Come up, young feet ask you.[18]

We do not know, of course, if the grass responded to such encouragement, but we can assume that it did, and that even in a city park, the seasonal shoots of green made their appearance. In Sandburg's verse the corn laughs, the cities brood, and when Sandburg visited New Hampshire, he came away with "a little handkerchief bundle of remembers"—all of which was, of course, on the far side of whimsy. Of the many American poets who have attempted to be whimsical with dubious results, or have written books for children, Sandburg was among the few who had been commercially successful; the best of his children's books are *Abe Lincoln Grows Up*, a selection made from his *Abraham Lincoln: The Prairie Years*, in 1928, and a selection from his verse, *Early Moon*, which was published in 1930.

A sympathetic and brief commentary on Carl Sandburg and his verse has been written into a preface to his *Selected Poems* (1926) [19] by the British liberal journalist, Rebecca West:

He was born of Swedish parentage in Galesburg, Illinois, in 1878. At the age of thirteen he left school and began driving a milk wagon. He subsequently became a bricklayer and a farm labourer on the wheat-growing plains of Kansas . . . he became an hotel servant in Denver, a coal-heaver in Omaha . . .

And to these biographical facts Fred B. Millet in *Contemporary American Authors* [20] has added:

In 1898, when he was a house painter's apprentice in Galesburg, he entered the Spanish-American War and served for eight months in Porto Rico with the Sixth Illinois Infantry. In the army a friend from Lombard College in Galesburg interested him in improving his neces-

[18] "Spring Grass" from *Good Morning, America,* used by permission of Harcourt, Brace.
[19, 20] By permission of Harcourt, Brace.

sarily limited educational background; and when he returned from war he entered the college. He earned his way by work as tutor, bell ringer, and janitor, and was captain of the basket-ball team. . . .

After college and a period of business experience he entered politics and journalism in Milwaukee, where he was an organizer for the Social-Democratic party and from 1910 to 1912 was secretary to the mayor. Moving to Chicago, he became associate editor of the *System Magazine* (1913) and helped N. D. Cochran with an experimental tabloid, the *Daybook*. . . . It ceased publication in 1917, and Sandburg joined the staff of the *Daily News.*

Rebecca West continued with:

He can describe the inner life of the eager little girls who leave small towns and come to Chicago. . . . He can describe the inner life of the strong young men who wander about the vast land, proud and yet perplexed; proud because they are lending their strength to the purposes of a new civilization, perplexed because they do not know what it is all about.[21]

She went on to describe Sandburg's interest in singing songs and how skillfully he had mastered the art of accompanying them on the banjo and the guitar; and Sandburg's official biographer, Karl Detzer, in his book, *Carl Sandburg: A Study in Personality and Background* (1941), also wrote of his ability to be a "wandering minstrel with a frayed shirt collar and an old guitar, this one-time movie reviewer, dishwasher, door-to-door salesman, harvest hand, bootblack, hobo"—but one still concludes that in actuality Sandburg was never the "hobo" that he appeared to be. His performances with a guitar were far more artful than the strenuous entertainment with which Lindsay strove to attract his audiences; obviously Sandburg enjoyed the singing of the American folk songs he had collected, and the atmosphere of relaxation that he created was conveyed to those who heard him sing. This was an accomplishment that he turned to advantage when he published his own selection of American songs in *The American Songbag* (1927) and the book was received with the same enjoyment that he probably had in editing it.

Well-poised and experienced, Sandburg succeeded in creating a unified literary personality with which he provided an atmosphere for his verses; the verses themselves may often contradict

21 Preface from *Selected Poems*, used by permission of Harcourt, Brace.

one another, and even much of the slang that can be found within them had the misfortune of falling rapidly "out of date," but the rhythmical unity of his verse (which is not far unlike the unified cadence of Sherwood Anderson's prose) holds together the many disparate fragments of Americana, which were produced almost as a tour de force between the covers of his *The People, Yes* (1936). Old jokes, tall stories, Pullman-car confidences and views, editorial comments on the rich and the poor, proverbs, and the kind of knowledge that can be gained by reference to the files of *The World Almanac* were thrown and heaped together half humorously, half gravely. Sandburg himself was not to be trapped by any solemn or unguarded statement; the reply was always "The people, yes," "Ai! ai! the sleepers wake!" and "The people will live on," all of which were oracular and certainly indisputable pronouncements.

But the more serious concern of Sandburg's imagination has always been related to the glimpses of historical episodes in his verse and a monumental biography of Abraham Lincoln. Two volumes of *Abraham Lincoln: The Prairie Years* appeared in 1926; and four other large volumes, *The War Years*, appeared in 1939, and the latter received the Pulitzer Prize for biography. It is in the great wealth of mythology and fact surrounding the name of Lincoln that Sandburg seemed most genuinely "at home"—and at least four poems, "Cool Tombs," "Shenandoah," "Grass," and "Old Timers," show Sandburg's true affinity with his subject and his abiding interest in the importance of the Civil War; his happiest moments are in the following lines:

> When Abraham Lincoln was shoveled into the tombs,
>   he forgot the copperheads and the assassin . . .
>   in the dust, in the cool tombs [22]

and in

> And I drove a wagon and team, and I had my arm shot off
> At Spotsylvania Court House.
>
> I am an ancient reluctant conscript.[23]

[22] "Cool Tombs" from *Cornhuskers*, used by permission of Henry Holt and Company, Inc.

[23] "Old Timers" from *Cornhuskers*, used by permission of Henry Holt and Company, Inc.

and in "Grass": [24]

> Pile the bodies high at Austerlitz and Waterloo.
> Shovel them under and let me work—
>> I am the grass; I cover all.
>
> And pile them high at Gettysburg
> And pile them high at Ypres and Verdun.
> Shovel them under and let me work.
> Two years, ten years, and passengers ask the con-
>> ductor:
>>> What place is this?
>>> Where are we now?
>
>> I am the grass.
>> Let me work.

In these lines Sandburg's hortatory manner had an air of historical authority and his familiarity with the subject seems
entirely justified and appropriate. It was also justified by his
own experience in two wars, the first as a soldier in the Spanish-
American War, the second as a war correspondent in the First
World War, or rather as a special-feature writer stationed at
Stockholm in which he saw, according to his biographer, Karl
Detzer, the beginnings of "the Communist experiment" across
the Baltic and he had a particular interest in Sweden, not only
as the birthplace of his parents, "but because it was the home of
the European co-operative movement."

In Carl Sandburg the "poetic renaissance," as Chicago knew
it, had rounded to a full circle. Sandburg was one of the two
poets—the other was Vachel Lindsay—in whom Harriet Monroe
of *Poetry* felt the deepest confidence and pride of discovery, and
today it seems that the gifts and temperaments of the two men
complemented one another. If Sandburg entered the peripheries
of Chicago's Bohemia and arrived at its center whenever he felt
the need of relaxation, his more serious activities and the responsibilities of bringing up a family imposed a discipline upon
his life that is not to be confused with the work or lack of work
done by lesser members of the group. If Lindsay was unworldly
in his conduct, and often childlike in the perceptions of his

[24] From *Cornhuskers*, used by permission of Henry Holt and Company, Inc.

poetry, Sandburg's observations were schooled in the experiences of political organization, of easy contact with the world around him, of maintaining his independence while apparently moving with the crowd. Like Robert Frost, his only pretension has been the seeming lack of all pretensions whatsoever; and under the loose, wandering, apparently half-bewildered exteriors of his verse, a shrewd and a not too tolerant strain of a Protestant attitude exists. In English literature it is the heritage of John Bunyan's *Pilgrim's Progress,* and in Sandburg the strain is more probably in the direct line of his Swedish heritage, and the best description of it is in his own words:

> I can take off my shirt and tear it,
> and so make a ripping razzly noise,
> and the people will say,
> "Look at him tear his shirt."
>
> I can keep my shirt on.
> I can stick around and sing like a little bird
> and look 'em all in the eye and never be fazed.
>   I can keep my shirt on.[25]

Much has been written of Whitman's influence on Sandburg's verse, but as one rereads the best of Sandburg's poetry, its rhythms owe a greater debt to the cadences of Lincoln's "Gettysburg Address" than to any other source in literature, and it is highly probable that a "Sandburg" would have arrived even if Whitman had never existed. If Sandburg's realistic observations in verse have their true precedents in the journalistic exercise of his talent, their influence upon the work of other poets and of American novelists should not be underestimated: traces of Sandburg's skill in observing realistic detail are discoverable in Archibald MacLeish's *Frescoes for Mr. Rockefeller's City,* in John Dos Passos' historical interludes which separate the narrative passages of his trilogy, *U.S.A.,* and in the so-called "newsreels" of the same work, which stress in the selection of fragmentary quotations from newspaper headlines and catchwords, the particular moments in time through which the narrative takes its course. Sandburg's long and sustained interest in the Lincoln legend also

---

[25] "Shirt" from *Smoke and Steel,* used by permission of Harcourt, Brace.

anticipated in its devotion to historical background and verisi-
militude the writing of Stephen Vincent Benét's long narrative
in verse of the Civil War, *John Brown's Body,* and it can be said
that in all these, and in his own fashion, Sandburg prepared the
American public to accept the work of a younger generation.

In 1928 he was Phi Beta Kappa poet at Harvard, and he has
received honorary degrees from Lombard College, Knox College,
and Northwestern University. After a period of six years' retirement during which he completed his *Abraham Lincoln: The
War Years* in 1939, he resumed his journalistic career as a
columnist for a Chicago tabloid, and a collection of his later
sketches in verse and prose appeared in a volume, *Home Front
Memo* (1943).

PART III

THE 1920'S

DONALD EVANS: PREFACE TO THE 1920'S

There is a morbid pleasure in store for the literary historian when in reading among faded volumes of verse and forgotten names, he comes upon a name and a book that even in failure, even in oblivion, still has some signs of life. It is like finding what seemed to be a corpse still faintly breathing among the unburied dead, and the pathos and surprise are deepened when one sees in the almost extinguished features a face and an expression however fleeting that are unmistakably familiar: for Donald Evans' (1885-1921) work and name now serve to remind us only of others that came after, and are now famous and honored. Little if any of Donald Evans' poetry was read a decade after his early death; today his books are difficult to obtain and are out of print, and in his lifetime they were published by an obscure publisher and bookseller, Nicholas Brown, of Philadelphia and New York. In rereading these thin, almost privately printed books of verse, one is struck by a peculiar fact: for if Evans may be listed among the failures (and he thought of himself as a failure throughout his short career), it is not among the dull, the heavy, indistinguishable dead that he belongs.

Donald Evans' life held small triumphs and large frustrations, and when in 1921 he died (reputedly by his own hand) it appeared a fitting end to a career that seemed so ineffectual, tortured, so maladjusted to the world it faced and could not hope to conquer. He was born and educated in Philadelphia and was well known in New York's Greenwich Village (this was before Edna St. Vincent Millay and Floyd Dell and a flood of Middle Western *émigrés* were to give it full publicity) as the leader of a band of "esthetes" among whom were Wallace Stevens, Walter Conrad Arensberg (the author of two or three fine poems), Witter Bynner, Carl Van Vechten, Muriel Draper, Kenneth MacGowan, Pitts Sanborn, Gilbert Seldes, and others, some of whose names are now shadowy memories but were once well known in theatrical and literary circles. Among his acquaintances and friends were also Mabel Dodge and Gertrude Stein—and to the former, he wrote two of his best "Sonnets from the Patagonian"—and it is now remembered to his credit that he was the "Claire Marie" who published Miss Stein's *Tender Buttons* at "Three, East Fourteenth Street," New York, in 1914.

With all his love of elegance (and one story was told of how he rented a high-ceilinged front parlor and placed, with curtains drawn, a stone sundial in it, under a glaring Mazda lamp) and of opulent gestures, borrowed from the 1890's, he seems to have lived a life of dull jobs, requiring long hours of hard, uncongenial labor. At one time he had been music critic of the *New York Globe,* but his later years were spent in grinding out editorials for a garment-trade journal. In 1918 he wrote, making wistful advances to Amy Lowell:

> Because I have always been an honest citizen making a decent living in straight-forward newspaper work, 10-12 hrs. daily for thirteen years, I have perhaps in my poetry been a little too conscious of the poet, and in an imagined need provided him with a shield of artificiality which he never requires. When among intelligent people I think I pass for being simple, unaffected, modest, but there are so many pretentious bores and big-wigs one must meet and live with . . . that to keep alive it has sometimes seemed necessary to be a shock-distributor.[1]

It was as a distributor of shocks, as a champion against the commercialized dullness of a hypocritical morality and in revolt against the flabby sentiments of popular magazine verse—as well as the shoddiness of its techniques—that Donald Evans' early poetry was written. Belated hints and fragments of twentieth-century European culture began to appear as names and titles of books in Greenwich Village, and if it reached New York by way of such doubtful documents as the latter Russians wrote, in works of ambiguous merit such as *Sanine,* or Andreyev's *The Seven That Were Hanged,* or the last dregs of Arthur Symons' coterie in Paris and London—or at its very worst in the influences emanating from the naïve naughtiness and bad taste of Edgar Saltus, as

---

[1] *Amy Lowell* by S. Foster Damon, used by permission of Houghton Mifflin Company.

well as the now forgotten verse of Benjamin de Casseres and George Sylvester Viereck with its unconsciously amusing Satanism—at its best the moment produced the critical writing of James Gibbons Huneker, whose syndicated articles on painting, music and belles lettres were read in Sunday supplements of newspapers throughout the country.

Donald Evans' first book, *Discords* (1912), aroused an interest among some few reviewers because of its sexual references—which were intended to shock its readers and evidently did—but on re-reading them today the poems seem to glow with a spiritual rather than physical fervor. His *Two Deaths in the Bronx* (1916) received the same fate of faint praise and blame, and though it is a book of many brilliant promises and innovations, the majority of its poems must be counted as failures. In poems such as "For the Haunting of Mauna," "Dinner at the Hotel de la Tigresse Verte," "Mary Douglas Bruiting the Beauty of the Hands of Monsieur Y.," "Rouge for Virgins" (the titles best describe the poems) we see traces of the manner which was afterward to take form and to become distinguished in a poet like Wallace Stevens; and in another poem (this time unfortunately titled "Frail Phrases" [2]) Evans drew a portrait of a "chatoyant Mrs. Ashleigh Norwood" (who seems not unlike a re-creation of an early, none too good, and unwritten poem by T. S. Eliot):

> She gave him greeting out of her suave prides,
> Her inviolate charm and her renewing beauty,
> And he forgot the profaning of the phrases
> Under the assonances of her invictive personality.
> "Will you ride with me?" she asked, and he,
> Pointing to the other hansom abreast hers, parleyed:
> "With you, or in that?"
>
> "Oh, with me," sloped her answer,
> "The other hansom conveys my emotions—
> I carry with me only my powder puff."
> Flushed he hung on her pause, and held
> The silence, tasting her valorous words;
> Then he bade the driver make on, bowing low
> As she was drawn out of sight.

•   •   •   •   •   •   •

2 From *Two Deaths in the Bronx*, published by Frank-Maurice.

"Perishable women! Frail phrases!"
Then as he let drop his chin upon his breast
He thought of the long-entombed praise of the printer
When he looked for the first time
On Mrs. Norwood's portrait:
"And she might have killed an Emperor of France."

If a few of Donald Evans' poems exhibit true sensibility, an instinct for an accurate use of words, and a sharp wit, one often feels, as in this poem, that too frequently (to quote another poem) he is one

. . . who lusts uncomforted
To kiss the naked phrase quite unaware.[3]

Perhaps the years of drudgery in journalism had enervated his poetry and blunted the promise that he once held in achieving a fine style; in any case, his *Ironica* (1919) shows a loss of brilliance, and though a few poems in the volume hint of interesting subject matter, as well as further innovations, diffusion and a slovenliness of phrasing—as well as a pointless scattering of his wit—seem to have overwhelmed the brightest of his intentions.

Sonnets from the Patagonian (1918) was his best known book, and in some respects it still remains the best of his five books. It brought him a modicum of fame and a greater critical notice than he has received before or since. In six weeks' time every poem in the book had been quoted in reviews, and had been praised or blamed. To a generation of younger reviewers *Sonnets from the Patagonian* seemed to represent all that was European and elegant, the more so, because it contained precisely the same exotic, slightly erotic flavor that was to find expression in the first imitation-leather-bound selection of books chosen for Albert Boni's and Horace Liveright's "Modern Library," that "Modern Library" (still being selected and published for another generation and its tastes) which first helped to spread widely in America the fame of George Moore's *Confessions of a Young Man*, Flaubert's *Madame Bovary*, Gautier's *Mademoiselle de Maupin*, and similar, if less excellent, volumes, which combined the graces of

[3] "En Monocle" from *Sonnets from the Patagonian*, published by Frank-Maurice.

style with something dimly approaching pornography. Of Donald Evans, *The Nation* (London) commented:

Mr. Evans, we suspect, is accounted a desperate fellow in America. It is the fatality of that fresh and ingenious land to be pricked, shocked, and stimulated by the sensations which do not arouse so much as a wink from us jaded Europeans. There is something childlike, radiant and captivating about a country which still shudders for instance at the invasion of Futuristic buccaneers. . . . He [Donald Evans] is the happiest blend of the free verse . . . glass of green water (colored by the absinthe school) and the *Yellow Book,* the whole sauced by a sardonic treatment of life, sordidly and entrancingly vicious.

It must be admitted that Donald Evans' premonitions of evil seem to spring from shallower sources than those discovered and realized by poets of deeper sensibility, yet the premonitions are genuine enough and seem to foretell the disaster which brought his life and career to an early end. Whatever sense of evil existed in *Sonnets from the Patagonian,* one finds it more deliberately sought after than in the work of the far greater Baudelaire of whose *Fleurs du mal* it might be said that in this country it was frequently interpreted by those who clutched the flowers and only half understood the evil—and it is also clear that Donald Evans, however tortured, however fatally possessed, could never have been another Baudelaire or Poe.

It can be well imagined that future historians of American poetry will reread the *Sonnets from the Patagonian* for their documentary interest, for their minute, sharp sketches of New York's intellectual, artistic, and social life in the period before and during the First World War. If the same can be said of Ezra Pound and of Conrad Aiken, it is also true that Evans was a figure in a large, inchoate movement, the exiles-at-heart, who whether they were at home, or in London, or on the European continent, expressed their emotions in the same tone of voice and with the same gestures of loss and restlessness. Donald Evans' sonnet, "In the Vices," [4] reminds one of a half-dozen "exiled" poets of the period, and with them of a brighter, flashier, less sophisticated E. A. Robinson:

[4] From *Sonnets from the Patagonian,* published by Frank-Maurice.

Gay and audacious crime glints in his eyes;
And his mad talk, raping the commonplace,
Gleefully runs a devil-praising race,
And none can ever follow where he flies.
He streaks himself with vices tenderly;
He cradles sin, and with a figleaf fan
Taps his green cat, watching a bored sun span
The wasted minutes to eternity.

Once I took up his trail along the dark,
Wishful to track him to the witches' flame,
To see the bubbling of the sneer and snare.
The way led through a fragrant starlit park
And soon upon a harlot's house I came—
Within I found him playing at solitaire!

The sonnets also remind one of the tone that was to become fashionable in the 1920's, particularly in the magazine *Vanity Fair,* many of whose attitudes are still sustained (and brought up to date) in the pages of *Vogue, Harper's Bazaar,* and *The New Yorker.* The "Two Portraits of Mabel Dodge" seem filled with minor touches of charm and wit and recall with extraordinary vividness the moment of their composition:

Her pampered knees fell under her keen eye
And it came to her she would not go mad.
The gaucheries were turning the last screw,
But there was still the island in the sea,
The harridan chorus of eternity

. . . .

She tried to rouge her heart, yet quite in vain.
The crucifix danced in, beribboned, gay,
And lisped to her a wish for the next waltz.[5]

And one finds a felicitous turn of phrasing in a group of sonnets under the title, "Portrait of Carl Van Vechten," [6] and dedicated to Gertrude Stein in which Evans wrote the following lines:

He had bowed his head in sorrow at his birth,
For he had said long ere he came to earth
That it was no place for a gentleman.

. . . .

[5] "The Last Dance at Dawn" from *Sonnets from the Patagonian,* published by Frank-Maurice.
[6] From *Sonnets from the Patagonian,* published by Frank-Maurice.

And when they called him cad he found release—
He felt he had used the finest snub of all.

There is a rare and curious pamphlet in the New York Public Library called *The Art of Donald Evans,* written shortly before his death, in which a "Cornwall Hollis" describes Evans as "a tall, dark slender man about thirty-five. . . . In his private life his correctness is almost a vice, self-conscious to an absurd degree. He asks no special privileges from society because he is an artist. He would deny indignantly that he is 'artistic.'" And he is further described as appearing at first glance more like "a surgeon with a passion for experimentation" than a poet. He is quoted as saying: "I fear I am too much of a male to find my interests in the men's smoking room." This entire attitude has grown familiar to us through the anti-Bohemian revolt that began in the late 1920's and continued with the social realists of the thirties who almost felt it their duty to apologize for being known as "artists" at all.

Perhaps the best and certainly most enduring expression of the attitude toward which Evans groped—even to the statement of an esthetic and the realization of a literary personality—may be found in Wallace Stevens's "Le Monocle de mon Oncle." The process can only be described as groping or dimly feeling his way through the pages of his last book, *Ironica;* and in reading his sonnet "Failure at Forty," there is good reason to believe that the poem reflected his personal sense of loss and that he felt his own limitations keenly and not without despair. Even then his small literary reputation had begun to fade. In a letter to Arthur Davison Ficke, who had sent her a volume of Evans' poems, Amy Lowell wrote tersely: "They are merely 1890 gone mad." And when Evans was in training at Camp Crane, Allentown, New Jersey, in the spring of 1918, someone had sent him a few volumes of Amy Lowell's verse—out of loneliness and out of that eclectic taste that inclined him to be sympathetic to anything that seemed "modern" at the moment, Evans wrote to Amy Lowell an enthusiastic appreciation of her work. The correspondence was both pathetic and amusing—and for us today, it is instructive of what were two hopelessly divergent tendencies of that hour. Amy Lowell was naturally suspicious: "It is most satisfactory," she wrote, "to know that after living exclusively with my work, you still find it interesting." And again she wrote with characteristic bluntness: "You see, I am such an elderly person that I lived during the 90's. My twenty years saw the annual reappearance of *The Yellow Book* and those 'mauve joys' and 'purple sins' were the very 'latest thing,' so I must be pardoned for finding their manner very dusty." Miss Lowell then went on to admit that Evans' object and manner was in part a "search for Beauty," but she continued in her inimitable and most charming Lowellese to say that she too hunts for Beauty yet ". . . I do not seem to have to hunt for it down back alleys." And again she gave vent to what may well have been a justified suspicion—that Evans had little genuine liking for her poetry: "Sometimes I wonder why you like my work? . . . You remind me a little of a man who has stuck a monocle in his eye for effect and afterwards is afraid to take it out because of a kind of *mauvaise honte,* a dread lest the change be commented upon. *Courage mon enfant! En avant!* Break the monocle and go ahead!"

This was, of course, the voice of unusually clear-headed sanity, of that common sense that is reasonable to the point of madness. Amy Lowell's intellect was not of the finest in foreseeing all aspects of future tendencies in poetry, but she knew and was often the voice of the sensible opinion of the moment.

In the writing of poetry Evans had failed and knew it, but as a literary figure, however dim and shadowed it may be, his image has lasted longer than Amy Lowell believed it would. It is not beyond the range of possibility that Wallace Stevens * has built a successful esthetic on what Evans had attempted and failed to realize; and it was all too clear that Evans in the particular limitations of his gifts lacked taste and knowledge. In another direction a certain aspect of Evans' literary mannerisms and inten-

* Although the first edition of Wallace Stevens' *Harmonium* did not appear until 1923, Stevens' verse was published in *Poetry* (Chicago) as early as 1914. There seems to be evidence of "cross-influences" at work between the early poems of Wallace Stevens and the less well-poised, less gifted writings of Donald Evans; at the very least, there seems to be a strong temperamental affinity between them.

tions were only too well expressed in the pastiche novels of Elinor Wylie, in the expensive-lingerie and old-furniture school of Joseph Hergesheimer's most florid period—and most conclusively in the once fashionable novels of Carl Van Vechten. In America Evans' verse very nearly anticipated and almost brought to light a rediscovery of wit and sensibility, but through want of poetic intelligence, taste, and character, his auguries of promise remained fragmentary and unfulfilled.

2

It will be observed in the following pages of our history that the order is by no means strictly chronological, but we wish to reassure our readers that our presentation of individual figures within each chapter is not purely arbitrary. In literature, and particularly as one reads poetry, divisions of time, of sex, of race, and of geographical regions are, more often than not, of superficial and transitory value. But as history becomes foreshortened to a mere quarter of a century, schools and groups of poets move more conspicuously into view. Their chronological order cannot be determined by dates of birth alone, but rather by the historical precedence in which their poetry, their literary personalities, and the publication of their books, as well as the arrival of their particular school or movement, gained public recognition.

The "poetic renaissance" did not reach its end abruptly in the early 1920's, and although its principal figures and "inventors" were well established by that date, its criteria, including a fading heritage of the 1890's in the Bohemian activities of American writers, lingered on and were transformed into the excesses of what F. Scott Fitzgerald so fondly called "the Jazz Age." It was not until 1922 when T. S. Eliot's *The Waste Land* appeared in the pages of *The Dial* that a slight change in climate and poetic temperament could be discerned. But naturally enough, whatever changes in poetic speech and manner were taking place, their actual presence was not generally known. At the very moment when *The Waste Land* created a spectacular controversy among critics and reviewers of poetry, the literary personality of

Edna St. Vincent Millay almost completely filled the scene. And it was not until the end of the decade—and the period was remarkably prolific in the writing and publication of verse—that the importance of Eliot's contribution to contemporary literature was acknowledged and recognized. This explains the order we have chosen in the following section, which places Edna St. Vincent Millay first and Eliot last, and between them a similar order of precedence may be observed.

Today many critics who have advanced to middle age review the 1920's with an almost nostalgic air, with something, let us say, that recalls the note of yearning expressed so memorably by Longfellow when he wrote:

> My heart goes back to wander there,
> And among the dreams of the days that were,
>   I find my lost youth again.[7]

But these values are, of course, quite as deceptive as an unripe enthusiasm for the present tense and an overripe concern for those platitudes of literary discourse which as E. E. Cummings so cheerfully reminds us, "are not to be resharpened." Almost none of the figures in the following chapters is unfamiliar to the reader of contemporary American poetry; and each, we hope, has been presented in the light of a renewed and welcome introduction.

[7] "My Lost Youth" from *Poems of Henry Wadsworth Longfellow*, used by permission of Houghton Mifflin Company.

EDNA ST. VINCENT MILLAY
AND THE POETRY OF FEMININE REVOLT
AND SELF-EXPRESSION

As if he had anticipated (and certainly this was not among his intentions) the arrival of Edna St. Vincent Millay in the New York that was captured by her charms in 1920, Henry James sat down in 1897 to write an extended review of the letters of George Sand. The task was a formidable one, but he was more than equal to it, and it became so congenial to his insights and speculations that he resumed it with evident pleasure in 1899 and 1914. The long essay was among the best of James's critical studies for he had found (as he had discovered earlier in *The Tragic Muse*) a phenomenon and a heroine much to his liking. Today the reader of both Edna St. Vincent Millay's poetry and James's essay can revive for his own pleasure something of the original impact—and "impact" is scarcely a strong enough word to describe it—that had been felt by her earliest admirers. As one reads James's essay, few substitutions are necessary: since Miss Millay's gifts in verse were frequently histrionic, the word "actress" should be substituted for "journalist," but it should also be remembered that not even the arts of journalism were outside Millay's province:

It was not in the tower of art that George Sand ever shut herself up; but I come back to a point already made in saying that it is in the citadel of style that, notwithstanding rash *sorties,* she continues to hold out. . . . George Sand is too inveterately moral, too preoccupied with that need to do good which is in art often the enemy of doing well. . . . She had in spite of herself an imagination almost of the first order, which overflowed and irrigated, turning by its mere swift current, without effort, almost without direction, every mill it encountered. . . . For the case was definitely a bold and direct experiment, not at all in "art," not at all in literature, but conspicuously and repeatedly in the business of living; so that our profit of it is before anything else that it was conscious, articulate, vivid—recorded, reflected, imaged. The subject of the experiment became also at first hand a journalist—much of her work being simply splendid journalism—commissioned to bring it up to date. She interviewed nobody else, but she admirably interviewed herself, and this is exactly our good fortune. . . . Her masterpiece, by a perversity of fate, is the thing she least sat down to. It consists—since she is a case—in the mere notations of her symptoms, in help given to the study of them.[1]

And with a lighter touch James noted a similar phenomenon in the description of Miriam, his heroine of *The Tragic Muse;* [2] the love of the theater, which was shared alike by Miss Millay and her admirers, makes James's description of Miriam, who was an actress, singularly appropriate:

But the great thing, to his mind and, these first days, the irresistible seduction of the theatre, was that she was a rare incarnation of beauty. Beauty was the principle of everything she did and of the way, unerringly, she did it—an exquisite harmony of line and motion and attitude and tone, what was the most general and most characteristic in her performance. Accidents and instincts played together to this end and constituted something which was independent of her talent or of her merit . . . which in its influence . . . was far superior to any merit and to any talent.

In these two descriptions James brought to light the essential qualities which are so difficult to define in the poetry of Miss Millay and in its meaning to the members of her generation; and in those terms, and to the average reader of poetry, to the teacher of poetry in secondary schools and in colleges, to the reviewer on every newspaper or weekly periodical that carried popular weight, the name of Edna St. Vincent Millay was a definition of poetry itself. To recite:

> What lips my lips have kissed, and where, and why,
> I have forgotten . . .[3]

[1] "George Sand" from *Notes on Novelists* by Henry James, used by permission of Charles Scribner's Sons.

[2] Used by permission of Houghton Mifflin Company.

[3] "What Lips My Lips Have Kissed" from *The Harp-Weaver and Other Poems,* published by Harper & Brothers. Copyright, 1920, by Edna St. Vincent Millay.

or

Euclid alone has looked on Beauty bare . . .[4]

or

My candle burns at both ends;
It will not last the night; [5]

or

O world, I cannot hold thee close enough! [6]

was sufficient to prove that one was not tone deaf to the personality, the charms, the aspirations, the candor, the siren utterances of poetry written after 1900. To those who read *Renascence*
(1917), *Second April* (1921), *A Few Figs from Thistles* (1922),
The Harp-Weaver and Other Poems (1923) here was verse that
rhymed and held familiar cadences; but more important than
the facile rhyming, with its overtones that have been heard in
American poetry since Thomas Moore sang his *Irish Melodies,*
was the creation of a literary personality that was as vivid as
the wayward and mythical "Dark Lady of the Sonnets" who in
the person of Katharine Cornell flashed across the Broadway
stage in Clemence Dane's extremely blank-versed and noisy play,
Will Shakespeare. But Miss Millay's creation also combined the
image of what Carol Kennicott in Sinclair Lewis' *Main Street*
wished to be with the heroines of F. Scott Fitzgerald's *This Side
of Paradise* and Floyd Dell's *Mooncalf.* The performance was, to
say the least, theatrical; and Miss Millay's verses intoned the full
expression of what the emancipated young woman of 1920 had
to say: every attitude of her social and sexual revolt against the
proprieties of an earlier generation was caught and crystallized;
her freedom with lovers, real or imaginary; her reaches toward
"beauty" in the names of Euclid, Sappho, Catullus, Vergil, Shake-

[4] "Euclid Alone Has Looked on Beauty Bare" from *The Harp-Weaver and
Other Poems,* published by Harper & Brothers. Copyright, 1920, by Edna St.
Vincent Millay.

[5] "First Fig" from *A Few Figs from Thistles,* published by Harper & Brothers. Copyright, 1918, by Edna St. Vincent Millay.

[6] "God's World" from *Renascence and Other Poems,* published by Harper
& Brothers. Copyright, 1917, by Edna St. Vincent Millay.

speare, Beethoven, Pan, Bluebeard, or God Himself; her interpretations of social wrongs and pities; her love of "dressing up"
for grand occasions; her childishness and her sudden, precocious
gestures of being no mere girl at all, but a woman who had
already grown weary of sin.[7] And it must be confessed that no
American novelist of the period has portrayed the young woman
whose archetype was George Sand and who lived in the New
York of 1920 half as well as Miss Millay presented her little
heroine.

But Miss Millay's creation did not spring in the year of 1920
like the patroness of urban arts, Athena, full-grown at twenty-
eight, from the head of Zeus. While a student at Vassar College,
from which she graduated in 1917, she won an intercollegiate
poetry contest, and had been the center of a literary controversy
in 1912 because her poem, "Renascence," did not win an award
offered by *The Lyric Year,* an anthology edited by Ferdinand
Earle and in which the poem, "Renascence," appeared among
poems written by Orrick Johns (the unlucky winner of that contest), Richard Le Gallienne, Bliss Carman, George Edward Woodberry, Vachel Lindsay, Louis Untermeyer, William Rose Benét,
Joyce Kilmer, and John Hall Wheelock. The impressive list of
names of elder poets insured the maximum publicity for the controversy that followed the publication of the anthology—and the
introduction of a new personality in the image of a pretty and
young woman completely disarmed the critics and reviewers.

It would be tedious to dwell at length on the fact that the
sonnets written by Edna St. Vincent Millay's heroine more closely
resembled the love sonnets of Elizabeth Barrett Browning than
those of Shakespeare, or that the metrics, rhymes, and exhorta-
tions of "Renascence" itself seemed to parallel the evangelical
fervor of John Masefield's *The Everlasting Mercy,* which had
been received with so much enthusiasm in 1911, or to insist, with

[7] Mr. Carl Van Doren in his *Three Worlds* (1936) says: "The early
poems of Edna Millay are the essence of the Younger Generation. Ask the
romantic Younger Generation what it demanded and it answered: to be free.
Ask it free for what, and it did not answer, but drove faster, drank more,
made love oftener. When it came to the sterner time after 1929 it had to give
up its habits or else seem like an elderly beau amusing to the youngsters.
The youngsters now condescend to the 1920's as to an age of amateurs."

ill-natured dogmatism, that the verses written by the attractive
heroine who had made her theatrical debut on the stage of the
Provincetown Players in Greenwich Village in New York, and
who acted in early productions of the Theatre Guild, seemed,
more often than not—and after a reading of Rupert Brooke's
verses—to be a literary exercise in the release of feminine emotion. Without that release, the heroine would never have existed;
without her confessions of faithlessness, without her assurance
that she drank and lived "what has destroyed some men," without her conviction that "Love has gone and left me and I don't
know what to do," without such lapses in taste as "the soft spit-
ting snow," without her admission that "I drew my hate from
out my breast/And thrust it in the ground," obviously the young
woman would not have been the phenomenon she was—emancipated surely, but her virtues demanded the presence of youth,
and her faults needed the hopeful tolerance that is so often
claimed and exacted by attractive young women from bewildered
and broad-minded parents. Even in these details, Miss Millay's
heroine delighted her elder critics and young admirers—and a
dimmed and equally fictional reflection of the type of young
woman she was appeared in Edmund Wilson's novel, *I Thought
of Daisy* (1929).[8]

Unfortunately, but no less humanly, Miss Millay's creation
had her darker moments, which resembled, more than all else,
the scene in Nathaniel Hawthorne's fable, *Mrs. Bullfrog*,[9] describing the sudden transformation of the lovely Mrs. Bullfrog:

I had scrambled out of the coach and was instinctively settling my
cravat, when somebody brushed roughly by me, and I heard a smart
thwack upon the coachman's ear.

"Take that, you villain!" cried a strange, hoarse voice. "You have
ruined me, you blackguard! I shall never be the woman I have been!"

And then came a second thwack, aimed at the driver's other ear; but
which missed it, and hit him on the nose, causing a terrible effusion of
blood. Now, who or what fearful apparition was inflicting this punishment on the poor fellow remained an impenetrable mystery to me. . . .

[8] In the character of Rita Cavanagh.
[9] Modern Library Giant edition, Random House, edited by Norman
Holmes Pearson.

Who could the phantom be? The most awful circumstance of the affair
is yet to be told: for this ogre, or whatever it was, had a riding habit
like Mrs. Bullfrog's, and also a green silk calash dangling down her
back by the strings.

An indication that a noisy heroine expressed an ideal of conduct made an early appearance in "Renascence":

> The sky, I said, must somewhere stop . . .
> And—sure enough!—I see the top!
> The sky, I thought, is not so grand;
> I 'most could touch it with my hand!
> And reaching up my hand to try,
> I screamed, to feel it touch the sky.
>
> I screamed, and—lo!—Infinity
> Came down and settled over me;
> Forced back my scream into my chest;
> Bent back my arm upon my breast . . .[10]

And as time progressed it produced such commands as

> Detestable race, continue to expunge yourself, die out.
>
> .   .   .   .
>
> Convert again into putrescent matter drawing flies
> The hopeful bodies of the young . . .[11]

and such observations as

> A stuffless ghost above his struggling land,
> Retching in vain to render up the groan [12]

and

> From the wound of my enemy that thrust me through
>   in the dark wood
> I arose; with sweat on my lip and the wild woodgrasses
>   in my spur [13]

[10] "Renascence" from *Renascence and Other Poems,* published by Harper
& Brothers. Copyright, 1917, by Edna St. Vincent Millay.

[11] "Apostrophe to Man" from *Wine from These Grapes,* published by
Harper & Brothers. Copyright, 1934, by Edna St. Vincent Millay.

[12] "Two Sonnets in Memory of Sacco and Vanzetti, Sonnet II" from *Wine
from These Grapes,* published by Harper & Brothers. Copyright, 1934, by
Edna St. Vincent Millay.

[13] "Aubade" from *Wine from These Grapes,* published by Harper &
Brothers. Copyright, 1934, by Edna St. Vincent Millay.

and

> And weep, with your knuckles in your mouth, and say Oh, God!
>   Oh, God! [14]

and

Never when worked upon by cynics like chiropractors having grunted
   or clicked a vertebra to the discredit of these loves.[15]

And the phenomenon became even less convincing and less
attractive when it addressed the following remarks to "The
Fledgling": [16]

> So, art thou feathered, art thou flown,
> Thou naked thing? . . .
>
> .   .   .   .
>
> Shall I no more with anxious note
> Advise thee through the happy day,
> Thrusting the worm into thy throat,
> Bearing thine excrement away?

The transformation was, to say the least, an unlovely one; and
the talent which in *A Few Figs from Thistles* inspired most of
the arch cynicism of Dorothy Parker's light verse and Samuel
Hoffenstein's *Poems in Praise of Practically Nothing* spoke grace-
lessly and flatly in *Conversation at Midnight* [17] (1937):

> When they had left the room
> Merton said, "Awfully nice fellow, Anselmo, I think."
> "Swell guy," said Pygmalion.
> John said, "Don't you think we all ought to go home?"
> "Hell, no," said Pygmalion. "Where's my drink?"

Certainly these lines were what Henry James would have called
mildly and appropriately enough "rash *sorties*" that had been

[14] "Childhood Is the Kingdom Where Nobody Dies" from *Wine from
These Grapes*, published by Harper & Brothers. Copyright, 1934, by Edna St.
Vincent Millay.

[15] "Modern Declaration" from *Huntsman, What Quarry?* published by
Harper & Brothers. Copyright, 1933, 1934, 1936, 1937, 1938, 1939, by Edna
St. Vincent Millay.

[16] From *Wine from These Grapes*, published by Harper & Brothers. Copyright, 1934, by Edna St. Vincent Millay.

[17] Published by Harper & Brothers. Copyright, 1937, by Edna St. Vincent
Millay.

made at some distance outside "the tower of art"; but in the meantime, the personality that they represented had in 1925 written on commission from the Metropolitan Opera Association, a lyric drama, *The King's Henchman,* with music by Deems Taylor, and it received in 1923 the Pulitzer Prize for *The Harp-Weaver and Other Poems.*

By 1937 Millay's phenomenal young woman, who like James's George Sand had so "admirably interviewed herself," was no longer favored by her critics, and with the exception of Edmund Wilson in the pages of *The New Republic,* whose taste in verse had been formed during the period when *A Few Figs from Thistles* had become a touchstone of poetic excellence in America, the young woman began to receive unlaudatory press notices. Louis Untermeyer who had consistently made the best selections of her verse in his anthologies wrote of her *Conversation at Midnight:*

> . . . she can create neither real controversy nor actual character . . .
> she falls back upon clichés of thought as well as stereotypes of expres-
> sion. . . . She has written more uneven books, but, in all fourteen
> volumes, she has never been so insistently discursive and so consistently
> dull.[18]

2

Today it requires patience and industry to unearth felicitous passages from her many volumes of what seemed to be spontaneously written verse; her sonnets were not of the quality in which, as Genevieve Taggard once wrote, "immortality is here defined, served and achieved," and a serious, illuminating, if somewhat painful, analysis of what was wrong with Miss Millay's sonnets in general may be found in a discussion of "Euclid Alone Has Looked on Beauty Bare" by Elizabeth Drew and John L. Sweeney in their *Directions in Modern Poetry* (1940). In a "Memorial to D. C." [19] the impression of ease and artlessness which delighted Edna St. Vincent Millay's early critics still retains its freshness and charm:

[18] From *Modern American Poetry,* used by permission of Harcourt, Brace.
[19] From *Second April,* published by Harper & Brothers. Copyright, 1918, 1920, 1921, by Edna St. Vincent Millay.

Cherished by the faithful sun,
On and on eternally
Shall your altered fluid run,
Bud and bloom and go to seed:
But your singing days are done;
But the music of your talk
Never shall the chemistry
Of the secret earth restore.
All your lovely words are spoken.
Once the ivory box is broken,
Beats the golden bird no more.

And the same felicity in clear, firm outline may be found in the fortunately titled lines, "The Cameo": [20]

Forever over now, forever, forever gone
That day. Clear and diminished like a scene
Carven in cameo, the lighthouse, and the cove between
The sandy cliffs, and the boat drawn up on the beach;
And the long skirt of a lady innocent and young,
Her hand resting on her bosom, her head hung;
And the figure of a man in earnest speech.

Clear and diminished like a scene cut in cameo
The lighthouse, and the boat on the beach, and the two shapes
Of the woman and the man; lost like the lost day
Are the words that passed, and the pain,—discarded, cut away
From the stone, as from the memory the heat of the tears escapes.

O troubled forms, O early love unfortunate and hard,
Time has estranged you into a jewel cold and pure;
From the action of the waves and from the action of sorrow forever
    secure,
White against a ruddy cliff you stand, chalcedony on sard.

The musical talent that guided these lines was something that could be called "a Celtic ear," and between the lines, one almost hears the wail of the Irish bagpipe. To the New England landscape (for Millay was born in Rockland, Maine, February 22, 1892) she seems to have written the following poem, but even here, "Earth" bears a likeness to the young woman of 1920 who so easily dominated the wills and passions of her admirers.

[20] From *Buck in the Snow*, published by Harper & Brothers. Copyright, 1928 by Edna St. Vincent Millay.

THE RETURN [21]

Earth does not understand her child,
　Who from the loud gregarious town
Returns, depleted and defiled,
　To the still woods, to fling him down.

Earth can not count the sons she bore:
　The wounded lynx, the wounded man
Come trailing blood unto her door;
　She shelters both as best she can.

But she is early up and out,
　To trim the year or strip its bones;
She has no time to stand about
　Talking of him in undertones

Who has no aim but to forget,
　Be left in peace, be lying thus
For days, for years, for centuries yet,
　Unshaven and anonymous;

Who, marked for failure, dulled by grief,
　Has traded in his wife and friend
For this warm ledge, this alder leaf:
　Comfort that does not comprehend.

3

It was not surprising that the phenomenal success of Edna St. Vincent Millay's heroine encouraged and inspired imitators, most of whom showed a tendency to emulate the hortatory gestures of her lines beginning with "Down, you mongrel, Death!" in verses called "The Poet and His Book." This peculiar mannerism was adopted by young poets of both sexes, and as newly acquired political convictions entered the language of verse, the mannerism became more pronounced, and if anything, a shade more hysterical in proclaiming its beliefs, whether to the right or left or to no political associations at all.

The example set by Millay in following fashionable opinion

[21] From *Wine from These Grapes,* published by Harper & Brothers. Copyright, 1934, by Edna St. Vincent Millay.

as it was expressed in the pages of *Vanity Fair* or the liberal weeklies or the *Masses* held a not unnatural attraction for young women; a veritable maiden choir arose in the wake of Millay's rapid progress, caught the public ear, and in most cases dwindled into the feeble strains of an undistinguished maturity.

Among the best known of the women who shared a lesser measure of Edna St. Vincent Millay's favor with the public and whose sensibilities somewhat approached Miss Millay's own was Genevieve Taggard. Her first book, *For Eager Lovers* (1922), showed an authentic, slight, but fragile lyric gift, which was never as fully disciplined as it was once thought, but altogether charming. Since then and through the titles of many succeeding volumes, including *Words for the Chisel* (1926), *Traveling Standing Still* (1928), *Calling Western Union* (1936), she has, and not without genuine fervor, traveled through many styles, and has been cheerfully willing to embrace causes for the betterment of mankind. Her effects in verse have been more often experimental than fortunate; from the dreamy candor of her "The Enamel Girl," [22] one of her earliest and most admired pieces, she turned in 1933 to a less happy venture of addressing an American workman dying of starvation. Brief quotations from the two poems will serve to illustrate the experimental character of her verse:

> Fearful of beauty, I always went
> Timidly indifferent;
>
> Dainty, hesitant, taking in
> Just what was tiniest and thin;
> .   .   .   .
> Fond of arts and trinkets, if,
> Imperishable and stiff
> .   .   .   .
> With one caress, with one kiss
> Break most fragile ecstasies . . .

[22] From *Traveling Standing Still*, reprinted by permission of Alfred A. Knopf, Inc. Copyright 1922 by Alfred A. Knopf, Inc.

Now terror touches me when I
Dream I am touching a butterfly.

In her later, more vigorous, less formal verses, she intoned an artificial or, rather, an unconvincing cheeriness in advancing the causes of social revolt:

Swell guy, you got to die.
                    Did you have fun?
I guess we know you worked.
                    I guess we saw you.
It got you just the same.[23]

If these lines fill us with more embarrassment than pity and seem strangely reminiscent of Miss Millay's less happy moments in *Conversation at Midnight,* it is because the language, the technique, the poet herself were not by temper and discipline within clear range of their grim subject matter. In justice to Genevieve Taggard it should be said that many poets of the period also felt it their duty to write poems for and about the proletariat in a manner which they fondly imagined was the very language of the workers.

Genevieve Taggard was also the author of an interpretation of *The Life and Mind of Emily Dickinson* (1930); the book had its moments of insight and it was well received, but since then it has been superseded by George F. Whicher's more sober, and perhaps definitive, study (1941) of the New England poet's life and work. In her verse Miss Taggard's work was always at its best when the theme was personal and her talents for simple verbal melodies were frequently employed. It was as a writer of wide sympathies and warm feelings that her verses carried their greatest claim to the attention of her readers.

The virtues of esthetic and emotional maturity came uneasily, sadly, almost unwillingly to Miss Millay and the members of her school. This weakness became obvious long before the early enthusiasms of her vogue began to fail, and it was betrayed by an overindulgence of commands in verse which echoed:

[23] "To an American Worker Dying of Starvation" from *Calling Western Union,* used by permission of Harper & Brothers.

> *Sexton, ply your trade!*
> *In a shower of gravel*
> *Stamp upon your spade!* [24]

It was apparent even in the poetry of Louise Bogan who has written more about the virtues of craftsmanship than any other member of the group (for she wrote bright and terse reviews of poetry in *The New Yorker*), and who was more literary, if not less personal, in her references. Miss Bogan published her first book, *Body of This Death*, in 1923, which was at the height of a popular rediscovery of Emily Dickinson and the merits of the seventeenth-century "metaphysical" poets. Among many lesser poets of the 1920's, the avowed practice of "chiseling" verse, of pruning and perfecting English metrics, took on the air of being a manifesto, and perhaps its goal dimly paralleled the French Parnassians of the middle nineteenth century, who also revolted against the unbridled romanticism of their predecessors. In this country "words for the chisel" (the literal title of one of Genevieve Taggard's books) became a substitute for Gautier's *Emaux et Camées* and his famous lines:

> Oui, l'œuvre sort plus belle
> D'une forme au travail
> Rebelle,
> Vers, marbre, onyx, émail.[25]

Less adventurous than Miss Taggard, Louise Bogan held far more closely (shall we say?) to the fixed ideal of the hammer and the chisel, and less to the looser phrasing of Miss Millay. A fierce, almost frightening, rhetoric and an unguarded love of passionate pagan sentiment seemed to overwhelm her verse, especially in its later phases. As one rereads Louise Bogan's *The Sleeping Fury* (1937) one is impressed by a tone of voice which more closely resembles that of a lady "Commando" than of Gautier:

> Face them. They sneer. Do not be brave.[26]

. . . .

[24] "The Poet and His Book" from *Second April*, published by Harper & Brothers. Copyright, 1918, 1920, 1921, by Edna St. Vincent Millay.

[25] "L'Art" from *Emaux et Camées*, Editions Nilsson, Paris.

[26] "Exhortation" from *The Sleeping Fury*, 1937, used by permission of Charles Scribner's Sons.

> Now, you great stanza, you heroic mould,
> Bend to my will, for I must give you love: [27]
>
> .   .   .   .   .   .
>
> Drink Wexford ale and quaff down Wexford water
> But never love.[28]
>
> .   .   .   .
>
> It is yourself you seek
> In a long rage.[29]

And the echo of Millay's voice is heard in the following two lines from the same poem:

> Strangers lie in your arms
> As I lie now.[29]
>
> .   .   .   .

or

> But you, fierce delicate tender touch,
> Betrayed and hurt me overmuch,
>
> For whom I lagged with what a crew
> O far too long, and poisoned through! [30]

Not unlike Genevieve Taggard, Louise Bogan was at her best whenever her speech became less strained and violent, and in "M., Singing," [31] she had probably written her least pretentious lyric.

> Now, innocent, within the deep
> Night of all things you turn the key,
> Unloosing what we know in sleep.
> In your fresh voice they cry aloud
> Those beings without heart or name.

[27] "Single Sonnet" from *The Sleeping Fury*, 1937, used by permission of Charles Scribner's Sons.

[28] "Hypocrite Swift" from *The Sleeping Fury*, 1937, used by permission of Charles Scribner's Sons.

[29] "Man Alone" from *The Sleeping Fury*, 1937, used by permission of Charles Scribner's Sons.

[30] "Spirit's Song" from *The Sleeping Fury*, 1937, used by permission of Charles Scribner's Sons.

[31] From *The Sleeping Fury*, 1937, used by permission of Charles Scribner's Sons.

Those creatures both corrupt and proud,
Upon the melancholy words
And in the music's subtlety,
Leave the long harvest which they reap
In the sunk land of dust and flame
And move to space beneath our sky.

Perhaps the most distinguished—and certainly her gifts were more individual—of the poets who inherited the flaws and merits of the example placed before them by Miss Millay, was Hilde-garde Flanner. To the general public her name was less well known than either Louise Bogan's or Genevieve Taggard's, but among discriminating readers of poetry it held a secure and highly respected position. The reasons for her particular emi-nence as well as her lack of general recognition are not difficult to define: her language was less spectacular than that spoken by her immediate contemporaries, less "commanding" in tone, and her fourth volume, *Time's Profile* (1929), a book of 156 pages, unhappily diffused, rather than intensified, those qualities that had given her verse distinction. It was then fashionable to list all love lyrics and all verse inspired by all varieties of religious emotion under the heading of "metaphysical" verse, and Flan-ner's collection of poems was not enhanced by the fashionable claims and catchwords of the day. But in that collection seven "Sonnets in Quaker Language" [32] retain their charm and grace and deserve to be better known:

I

Thee is obscured, beloved, as though I
Beheld thy body through a ghost between.
What death of other lovers, and what cry
Of other deaths and loves here intervene?
Is it thee carries, like old ambergris,
The sweet, tenacious presence of the dead,
That, like a wind about us, memory
Disturbs the dust thee once thought buriéd?
Or is it I who veil a wakeful ghost
Within the haunted distance of my eyes,
And am forever the unearthly host
Unto a thing long dead that never dies?

[32] From *Time's Profile*, Macmillan, by permission of the Author.

Thee kiss me through a ghost! and so inter
All past loves in a radiant sepulchre.

VII

I know not where thee sleeps to-night, my love.
"Far up into the mountain," so thee said.
I only know some purple height above
Is the moon's camping-ground and thy cool bed.
Elate upon dark altitude thee lies
With the abundant sky spread over thee.
The stars are multiplied within thy eyes,
The sum of night reduced to filigree.
My heart has followed thee and should thee hear
A little step ascend ·the wilderness
It is perhaps the light boot of the deer,
Or should it stumble thee can surely guess.
May thee be folded from all mountain harm
And dream of waking upon love's quiet arm.

A later group of Hildegarde Flanner's poems, *If There Is Time*, which was published in 1942, had less poise than her Quaker sonnets, and in the overtly conscious line

The ugly female laughter of a hawk.

one hears the familiar speech of mistaken candor and false vigor with which Miss Millay "screamed," and Mrs. Bullfrog became an "apparition" that was unlovely to the sight of her distracted husband, and Miss Bogan went out of her way to court the dubious charms of a sleeping fury.*

4

As we may have said before, "imitation is the severest criticism" of any poet's work; and yet poets can scarcely be blamed for the ineptitudes of those who follow them. Among her admirers and imitators Edna St. Vincent Millay's creation of the emancipated young woman still dominates the early years of the 1920's in American poetry, and we know her faults perhaps too

---

* This may be described in D. G. Rossetti's phrase when he spoke of Elizabeth Barrett Browning and her imitators as those who assumed a "falsetto masculinity."

well. How clearly her gifts excelled the talents of her followers
is shown in one of the best poems in *The Buck in the Snow*
(1928) which will probably take its place as the most distinguished of her many volumes:

THE HARDY GARDEN [33]

Now let forever the phlox and the rose be tended
Here where the rain has darkened and the sun has dried
So many times the terrace, yet is love unended,
    Love has not died.

Let here no seed of a season, that the winter
But once assails, take root and for a time endure;
But only such as harbour at the frozen centre
    The germ secure.

Set here the phlox and the iris, and establish
Pink and valerian, and the great and lesser bells;
But suffer not the sisters of the year, to publish
    That frost prevails.

How far from home in a world of mortal burdens
Is Love, that may not die, and is forever young!
Set roses here: surround her only with such maidens
    As speak her tongue.

Her virtues were those of an effortless, seemingly artless charm
of youth, and of lightly touched and quickly dispelled sorrow;
to many readers Miss Millay's verse will probably hold the same
enjoyment that Elizabeth Barrett Browning's verses held for
nearly a half century, and because of its youthful insights and
improvisions, it will probably introduce other generations of
girls and young women to the phenomena of an adolescent self-
discovery in terms of poetry.

[33] From *The Buck in the Snow*, published by Harper & Brothers. Copyright 1928 by Edna St. Vincent Millay.

ELINOR WYLIE AND LÉONIE ADAMS:
THE POETRY OF FEMININE SENSIBILITY [1]

ELINOR WYLIE

Elinor Wylie, who was born September 7, 1885, and died in New York December 16, 1928, was not a precocious poet, and her publications, like the brilliant, public events of her career, were timed with art; she appeared before her readers as the finished artist, correct and polished. Her second book, *Nets to Catch the Wind,* 1921, was published when Mrs. Wylie was in her thirties and its appearance quickly established her reputation. (In 1912 her first book of poems, *Incidental Numbers,* a private edition of sixty copies with the author's name withheld from the title page, was printed in London.) Unlike Edna St. Vincent Millay, Mrs. Wylie did not choose to conduct her education in public: refinement and fastidiousness were among the chief characteristics of the legend built around her name and among her chief literary influences were Lionel Johnson, Walter Savage Landor, and Thomas Love Peacock, all writers who combined the imaginative warmth of the Romantic Movement with the decorum, the restraint, the rhetorical elegance of the eighteenth century. It has been said that she had been influenced by the poetry of W. B. Yeats, but if this is true, her work reflected Yeats's poetry whenever it seemed to be most notably influenced by his early friend and contemporary, Lionel Johnson. From John Donne, she, like many young writers of the 1920's,

[1] Some of the best women prose writers may be placed in this category. Certainly in modern times Virginia Woolf, Katherine Mansfield, Dorothy Richardson, Elizabeth Bowen, Eudora Welty, Katherine Anne Porter may be said to form what may be called (and not in their dispraise) a school of feminine sensibility which approaches the delicate, sometimes minor but far from insignificant poetry written by some women who have adopted poetry as their medium. A similar preoccupation with style can be noted.

acquired subject matter and "metaphysical" attitudes, rather than the qualities of his vigorous intellect, the depth of his insight, and his masculinity. From Shelley (whom she romanticized all her life and seemed to have loved for the wrong reasons, always loving rather than understanding him) the chief influence came through his letters with their boyish mixture of eighteenth-century diction and Romantic sensibility. In fact it might be said of her lifelong passion for Shelley that, unlike Amy Lowell's patient, humble, almost maternal devotion to Keats's memory, hers was a passion of self-identity. She re-created Shelley in her own image, and with this vision before her as she sat down to write, she half convinced herself that she *was* Shelley, writing the poems that he would have written—if he had been a beautiful woman and a poet, living as she lived, and writing in the 1920's. She also wrote as if to please the minds of Walter Savage Landor and Thomas Love Peacock—and if Landor's personal relationship to Shelley may be reduced to a bowing acquaintance on the streets of Pisa, and if Peacock's memoirs revealed the young poet in the light of half cynical, half affectionate regard, these men were the most fastidious and (in an intellectual and esthetic sense) the most respectable of Shelley's friends and contemporaries.

No woman (especially in the 1920's—and Edna St. Vincent Millay shows only too well the dangers of that period) could have chosen finer models than Peacock and Landor, for both were men of the world, men of wit and intellect, and what is even more important, both were fastidious and brilliant writers. There is considerable evidence that Elinor Wylie took their virtues to heart and in so doing avoided the pitfalls and temptations of many women writers. As early as 1854, a Mr. George Bethune, who edited a popular anthology containing the best selections he could find of all the Englishwomen writing poetry, from the Duchess of Newcastle to Elizabeth Barrett Browning, and who had made a wide study of his subject, wrote sadly:

The prominent fault of female poetical writers is an unwillingness to use the pruning knife and the pumice-stone. They write from impulse and as rapidly as they think. The strange faculty, which women have, of reaching conclusions (and, in the main, safe conclusions) without the slow process of reasoning through which men have to pass; the strong moral instincts with which their nature is endowed, far above that of the other sex; their keen and discerning sensibility to the tender, the beautiful and luxuriant render them adverse to critical restraint.

If one puts aside the comments on the strong moral instincts of women (since in the 1920's many who had them were careful to disguise them or to call them something else), Elinor Wylie was almost completely free of these particular defects in Mr. Bethune's female Muse. Because it lacked these flaws, her work was a memorable example to her immediate contemporaries; it set a standard and a taste whose influence should not be under-estimated, and even today, one rediscovers the imprint of its mark upon the verse written by her followers. Such an influence (for she, like Miss Millay, became headmistress of a literary school) is often the direct result of a powerful or attractive personality—and the personality with which Elinor Wylie faced the world was so passionately self-obsessed, sharp, and self-pene-trating that it took on (like all transfigurations of true love) an almost impersonal air. It was as though she had seen her face in the mirror and found it so compelling and beautiful that the self-image was reflected everywhere. Even in her portrait of a painter (and it would be Velásquez!) there is a double image of a beautiful and arrogant woman, disguised as a painter lean-ing from his studio window, and a Castilian gentleman walking down the street. The emotion in the scene is completely self-absorbed and completely feminine:

> He burnt the rags in the fireplace
> And leaned from the window high;
> He said, "I like that gentleman's face
> Who wears his cap awry."
>
> This is the gentleman, there he stands,
> Castilian, sombre-caped,
> With arrogant eyes, and narrow hands
> Miraculously shaped.[2]

If Elinor Wylie's self-absorption may be defined in terms of what the eighteenth century called a "ruling passion," like all

[2] "Castilian" from *Collected Poems*, by permission of Alfred A. Knopf, Inc. Copyright, 1932, by Alfred A. Knopf, Inc.

overwhelming and consuming emotions it carried with it the conviction of having an importance beyond the mere reflection in a glass; and she conveyed her "passion" with all the art her skill could master. To this day we have unconsciously amusing parodies of her style, poems that speak of proud boys running in the wind, poems of equally proud, fastidious, well-dressed, good-looking women who yearn to possess the "hard heart of a child," to own things that contain the qualities of quicksilver and of crystal—but it is the attitude and not the essence that her imitators have caught—and she, like many a good artist before her, cannot be held responsible for all the inept vanities and empty gestures of the school which followed her. Carl Van Doren defined one of her more valuable characteristics when he said, "She respected the passions and she respected mind and manners," and this form of respect—in her case, self-respect— was as rare twenty-five years ago as it is today, and those who have it are seldom shoddy craftsmen.

Her novels were, as H. Lüdeke, a Dutch commentator, wrote, limited to "a dream world, a dream-perfume distilled from literature," a world which was perhaps best achieved and created in the early poetry of Edith Sitwell. Too many literary fancies and vanities employed Elinor Wylie's moments as she composed her prose romances. But where was the form into which the essence of her personality could find hope of an endurance beyond the moment of creation? what form could contain the perishable mood, the willful mannerism? what air could keep the grass green in that artful, seemingly artificial, world, could keep the strange, metallic, blown-glass flowers blooming? The answer may be found in her poetry.

Her posthumously published *Collected Poems* containing her four books of poems between the covers of a single volume appeared in 1932. The book was edited by her husband, William Rose Benét, and his preface, unlike most pieces written on such occasions (one has only to remember the ghoulish figure of J. Middleton Murry over the remains of Katherine Mansfield) is an excellent tribute to Mrs. Wylie's memory, informal, light in texture, and yet sustained by dignity. The span of Elinor Wylie's professional writing lasted for the comparatively short space of seven or eight years—and in fashion or out, her poems have retained all that a brief moment in prose letters had to say.

The external world that Elinor Wylie's poetry reflected in the public mind was of Washington, D. C., and New York society in which Mrs. Wylie had been a conspicuous figure, and probably the most innocent betrayal of the milieu was in a story of her life written by her sister, Nancy Hoyt, *The Portrait of an Unknown Lady* (1935). There, the buying of an expensive pair of silver slippers, or a gown to be worn at a literary soirée, or the acquisition of a Shelley autograph were placed on the same level as the writing of a fine poem or the last scene of an unhappy love affair. The poet herself cannot be blamed for the revelations contained in a biography, but if one reads another record of the period by one of the most intelligent members of a group that moved in the same literary orbit, one is again struck by Nancy Hoyt's artless accuracy: for Edmund Wilson's *I Thought of Daisy* re-creates the same moral climate and confusion of values—and will no doubt cause a future historian of our time, of our literary life and its morals and manners, the same amusement and distress.

Elinor Wylie (unlike many of her friends and imitators) was born into a scene of social activity that Henry James or Edith Wharton or Amy Lowell of Sevenells would have understood, and here, one may truly add, "that she lived as she wrote and wrote as she lived." Rarely in literary history have a personality and the actual details of living been so completely unified. "Elinor was accustomed to reading the best books, wearing the nicest tea-gowns, and living the most quiet of quiet lives"—wrote Nancy Hoyt, but again one must add that the "quiet life" had almost come to an end the moment Elinor Wylie became a literary figure of some consequence. She displayed her aloofness to large and admiring groups of what were then known quaintly as "sophisticates" in New York literary society, and her beauty, her temperament, her romantic domestic history had already preceded her. She appeared at Poetry Society dinners attired with a *chic* until then unknown to literary ladies, or walked into poetry recitals of the MacDowell Colony Club reading badly in a shrill voice that was said to have resembled Shelley's—but dressed to perfection, looking, as Carl Van Doren remarked, "like the white queen of a white country," and she entertained at her apartment in New York's 9th Street in an exquisitely furnished room, "dominated by its memorable silver mirror." Her poems, as each slim volume appeared, furthered the atmosphere of glamour surrounding her name to an increasing public, and her novels, which made solid sums of money and were published in an amazingly rapid progression, sustained the legend of the hand that wrote:

> O, she is neither good nor bad,
> But innocent and wild! [3]

and

> Five-petalled flame, be cold:
> Be firm, dissolving star:
> Accept the stricter mould
> That makes you singular. [4]

Among those with whom she had lived before her marriage to William Rose Benét in 1923, her devotion to poetry was singular enough, but the sense of doom that was so memorably expressed in the concluding sonnet of her posthumously published *Angels and Earthly Creatures* (1929) had its analogy to one of the closing scenes in Edith Wharton's masterpiece, *The House of Mirth*, that novel of fashionable New York society whose heroine, Lily Bart, lived within the same moral and social environment that Mrs. Wylie had inhabited. And though Mrs. Wylie's character and temperament were as clearly self-realized as Lily Bart's were vague and immature, their sensibilities were of like depth and quality; and Elinor Wylie was as fine an artist in the writing of her sonnets as Edith Wharton was a true mistress of her art in writing prose. The analogy is one in which premonitions of disaster are also of like depth and quality; and the very details of dress, their emotional im-

---

[3] "Beauty" from *Collected Poems*, by permission of Alfred A. Knopf, Inc. Copyright, 1932, by Alfred A. Knopf, Inc.

[4] "Address to My Soul" from *Collected Poems*, by permission of Alfred A. Knopf, Inc. Copyright, 1932, by Alfred A. Knopf, Inc.

portance to Lily Bart, created an atmosphere which was far better suited to express the sense of loss that was conveyed in the sonnets of *Angels and Earthly Creatures* than any recital of biographical facts and their relationship to Elinor Wylie's poetry:

The remaining dresses, though they had lost their freshness, still kept the long unerring lines, the sweep and amplitude of the great artist's stroke, and as she spread them out on the bed the scenes in which they had been worn rose vividly before her. An association lurked in every fold: each fall of lace and gleam of embroidery was like a letter in the record of her past. She was startled to find how the atmosphere of her old life enveloped her. But, after all, it was the life she had been made for: every dawning tendency in her had been carefully directed toward it, all her interests and activities had been taught to centre around it. She was like some rare flower grown for exhibition, a flower from which ev ry bud had been nipped except the crowning blossom of her beauty.

Last of all, she drew forth from the bottom of her trunk a heap of white drapery which fell shapelessly across her arm. It was the Reynolds dress she had worn in the Bry *tableaux*. It had been impossible for her to give it away, but she had never seen it since that night, and the long flexible folds, as she shook them out, gave forth an odour of violets which came to her like a breath from the flower-edged fountain where she had stood. . . . She put back the dresses one by one, laying away with each some gleam of light, some note of laughter, some stray waft from the rosy shores of pleasure. She was still in a state of highly-wrought impressionability, and every hint of the past sent a lingering tremor along her nerves.[5]

The note that Edith Wharton touched so clearly was elegiac, and in the concluding paragraphs of her novel, the appropriately brief scene after Lily Bart's death, one has a glimpse of the same moment that Elinor Wylie felt so surely before her own untimely death. Lily Bart's lover had come to her rooms.

It was this moment of love, this fleeting victory over themselves, which had kept them from atrophy and extinction; which, in her, had reached out to him in every struggle against the influence of her surroundings, and in him, had kept alive the faith that now drew him penitent and reconciled to her side.

He knelt by the bed and bent over her, draining their last moment

[5] From *The House of Mirth* by Edith Wharton, used by permission of Charles Scribner's Sons.

to its lees; and in the silence there passed between them the word which made all clear.[6]

And this last scene was re-enacted in the last eight lines of her last sonnet, a sonnet of sixteen lines, for which she had a precedent in Meredith's sixteen-line sonnets in his sequence, *Modern Love:*

> And let us creep into the smallest room
> That any hunted exile has desired
> For him and for his love when he was tired;
> And sleep oblivious of any doom
> Which is beyond our reason to conceive;
> And so forget to weep, forget to grieve,
> And wake, and touch each other's hands, and turn
> Upon a bed of juniper and fern.[7]

Throughout her later work there is a quality not common to lyric poetry that moves as easily as hers and that quality is best described in terms of poetic intelligence and wit. Her intelligence was of a sort that implied the uses of self-conscious art: hers was the expression of a larger movement toward conscious artistry in poetry, a movement which at its best includes such diverse figures as Conrad Aiken and T. S. Eliot and the later William Butler Yeats. And since formality was among the laws by which she lived, the sonnet became the means by which her world of bright objects, chamber music, and self-identified emotions took fire, and in her last sonnet sequence discovered its most fortunate and enduring form.

Nor after one has praised her sonnets, should one fail to mention once again her gifts for re-creating verbal music, her sharp and clearly discerning ear. Many of Elinor Wylie's shorter lyrics bear testimony to this feeling for music and it is one of the reasons why her poems were often reread and are still read with pleasure. One of the most subtle and technically adroit of her later poems—which contains her characteristic music at its best and which illustrates her art in reiterating her major theme—is

[6] From *The House of Mirth* by Edith Wharton, used by permission of Charles Scribner's Sons.

[7] "Angels and Earthly Creatures" from *Collected Poems,* by permission of Alfred A. Knopf, Inc. Copyright, 1932, by Alfred A. Knopf, Inc.

"Chimaera Sleeping." [8] Since the poem is rarely quoted in anthologies, it deserves complete quotation here:

Ah, lovely thing, I saw you lie
Within a beam of the sun's eye,
Where falling light and flying shade
Were bound together in a braid
Made of sky and earth colour:
Leaves blew over the forest floor:
The shadows were their noonday least.
I knew you neither man nor beast,
Nor god, nor rebel angel lost,
But that foreknown and holy ghost,
Beauty's pure pathetic shape;
The trap I never shall escape;
The heavenly bait; the honey breath
Issuing from the jaws of death.
So I approached, bereft of power,
And saw the pattern of a flower
Which moved in light and clearly shone
Under the arch of your breast-bone:
I saw a flower of white and green
Growing where your heart had been,
And grass obscured and dimly lit
As though a stream flowed over it:
Yea, through your body pale as glass
I saw the petals of the grass
Wave in the wind and softly stir
As seaweed under seawater.
You lay forlorn, hollow and thin
As a serpent's winter skin
From which his life of fiery gold
Has crawled away and left it cold:
And through your cold transparent flesh
The grass grew delicate and fresh;
I saw its blades, exact and plain
Through the blank crystal of your brain:
And nothing remained of fear and grief
Save the clear air and the green leaf;
And these the wind hath power to move;
And nothing there remained of love.
Then sorrow and joy dissolved my clay
To see you thus, and far away;

[8] From *Collected Poems*, by permission of Alfred A. Knopf, Inc. Copyright 1932, by Alfred A. Knopf, Inc.

Your body laid upon the lawn;
Your spirit fled like a fox or fawn;
Your body consumed to silver ash
Whence passed the soul of the lightning flash;
Whence passed the lightning's living blood:
And I pursued you from the wood,
And, as I followed on, I wept
To leave the thicket where you slept.

To all who wrote in her genre during the first half of the 1920's in America (and the list would include those novelists whose accomplishments brought to transitory life the dreams and aspirations of the forgotten Donald Evans), Elinor Wylie's poetry became the very personification of their art; their intentions were endowed with a brittle, and yet unmistakable, distinction, and their desires were cast into a form that is most likely to endure.

LÉONIE ADAMS

When Léonie Adams' two books of poetry appeared, *Those Not Elect* (1925) and *High Falcon* (1929), critics and reviewers turned with relief from the poetry of feminine self-identity to welcome a poet of personal reticence whose verses held great charm. As at this particular moment critics were much preoccupied with discussing the merits of twentieth-century neometaphysical poetry, Léonie Adams' verse was put into the company of Vaughan's and Herbert's poetry; and she was spoken of as being both a "metaphysical" poet and a "mystic." For the purpose of clarifying an obscure discussion, the present authors ask the indulgence of their readers as they set aside the charms of Léonie Adams' verses to present a brief history of the term "metaphysical" and its meaning to those who reviewed or criticized poetry during the 1920's.

In the 1920's it was obvious that the word "metaphysical" had undergone a transformation from the day that Samuel Johnson used it as a term of unfavorable criticism in his "Life of Abraham Cowley." Although Johnson's remarks have been famous for almost two hundred years, it is best in matters of this kind to move slowly and to remind ourselves of what Johnson actually said:

The metaphysical poets were men of learning, and to show learning was their whole endeavour; but, unluckily resolving to show it in rhyme, instead of writing poetry they only wrote verses, and very often such verses as stood the trial of the finger better than of the ear; for the modulation was so imperfect, that they were only found to be verses by counting the syllables.[9]

In other words, Johnson belonged to the "new order" of critics who acknowledged Dryden as their master; and he was careful to show that he had rejected the "singularities" of seventeenth-century poetry, its irregular laws of spelling and of syntax as well as the conflicts of its diction and its imagery, and while he confessed that Donne had "wit," it was clear that Donne's poetry, as Johnson read it, did not possess the smoothness, the formal grace and dignity of Pope's "numbers." Now, we must not forget that Johnson, with his characteristic sanity and good sense, was primarily a critic of moralities, and that his standards for humane values in literature were those which conformed to the theology of the Anglican church—and here a few words from T. S. Eliot in his *For Lancelot Andrewes* (1928) are particularly helpful. Eliot wrote, "Devotional poetry is religious poetry which falls within an exact faith and has precise objects for contemplation"; and whatever else may be said of Johnson's point of view in criticism, it was consistently devotional, and it mistrusted all variations of manner and of content from the then well-established order of Anglican faith. Even Donne's "Holy Sonnets" [10] with their lines

> Batter my heart, three person'd God; for, you
> As yet but knocke, breathe, shine, and seeke to mend

presupposed too violently an element of doubt within its statement of conversion to the Faith; and, if not overtly heretical, it was certainly unserene. We can then well understand why Johnson's "metaphysical" became an emphatic term of disapproval.

All the reasons why the word "metaphysical" acquired attrac-

[9] From *The Life of Abraham Cowley* by Samuel Johnson, Vol. I, of Lives of the English Poets, Everyman Edition, E. P. Dutton.
[10] "Holy Sonnet XIV," from *Poetry of John Donne*, Oxford University Press.

tive qualities in American poetry of the twentieth century need not be too obscure; and at least two of them may be advanced in general observation. In the contribution of a brief essay, "Donne in Our Time," to *A Garland for John Donne,* edited by Theodore Spencer (1931), T. S. Eliot fixed the dates of his own "experience within the terms of this paper" as "roughly 1906-1931," and his estimate coincided with the slow but seemingly rapid rise to eminence of Donne's name during the 1920's, and which was later to reach its widest popular distribution when Ernest Hemingway quoted a phrase from one of Donne's sermons as the title of his novel, *For Whom the Bell Tolls,* in 1940, a work which even by the widest stretches of human imagination, could scarcely be called "metaphysical." We must first agree with T. S. Eliot that Professor Briggs at Harvard read Donne aloud with "great persuasiveness and charm," and to this we should add that Professor R. E. N. Dodge, that excellent authority on Edmund Spenser, continued Professor Briggs's services to Donne with perspicacity and wit at the University of Wisconsin. In 1912 Herbert J. C. Grierson, Chalmers Professor of English Literature in the University of Aberdeen, published his definitive edition of *The Poems of John Donne,* and from these observations we have evidence of a widely spread revival of interest in Donne's poetry (which was later to include the poetry of all the "metaphysicals") within the colleges and universities.

Another reason for a renewed appreciation of John Donne is less clearly dependent upon the excellence of Grierson's timely edition of his poems, and in stating it we must allow ourselves a limited, and yet not too closely restricted, area for speculation. If we assume that Matthew Arnold's "Dover Beach" anticipated, however tentatively, however unconsciously, an era of religious doubt which gave the closing years of the nineteenth century an overtone of elegiac sensibility, we arrive at a renewed awareness to the elegiac notes which were sounded throughout the span of seventeenth-century poetry. The seventeenth century in England included significantly Cromwell's rebellion, Hobbes's materialism, the founding of the Royal Society, the downfall of Archbishop Laud, and the re-establishment of the Anglican church, and these circumstances have an analogy to the active contradictions of renewed discoveries in science and disillusionments in both science and religion which took place in America during the first quarter of the twentieth century. What had seemed "abounding" in "conceits," "medicinal," "far-fetched" to Johnson's eye seemed appropriate to the temper and the very texture and speech of twentieth-century poetry. The coming of the First World War, its progress, and its continuation into the present decade restored the presence of death that had its image in the engraving of John Donne's figure in a shroud.

It can be assumed that during this quarter of a century the names of Johnson's metaphysical poets became well known, but we are not prepared to say how profoundly their poetry was read and understood. We know that T. S. Eliot, F. R. Leavis, and Herbert J. C. Grierson and several of his associates in England and John Crowe Ransom and Cleanth Brooks in this country wrote with nice discrimination of seventeenth-century values in poetry, and in respect to it maintained an excellent level of scholarship. Meanwhile in the middle 1920's the word "metaphysical" was given to poets and their poetry as a word of encouragement and praise, and this was done with the same cheerful and benign air of generosity with which Ezra Pound a few years earlier bestowed the title of "Les Imagistes" upon his friends. In 1929 an anthology of "metaphysical" verse appeared which included selections from the poetry of Léonie Adams, E. E. Cummings, Elinor Wylie, Louise Bogan, Carl Sandburg, T. S. Eliot, Rupert Brooke, Hart Crane, Mark Van Doren, Allen Tate, Robert Frost, Edna St. Vincent Millay, Wallace Stevens, and Marianne Moore! What had once been "mystical" or "pantheistic" or "transcendental" had suddenly become "metaphysical" in the minds of critics, and it seemed as though all the world were metaphysical to those who had presumably read John Donne and Andrew Marvell. The contemporary poets who had been advanced under this revived classification were not to be blamed, for obviously the fashionable word, "metaphysical," had been inflated to the bursting point. And though the rough analogy of twentieth-century poetry to the lyricism of the seventeenth century remained what it had been in 1920, "metaphysical" poetry as an esoteric claim to praise collapsed; by 1936 "public speech" and "social poetry" held the center of attraction, and to be "metaphysical" became again a quality that was not above reproach.

Actually the neometaphysical poets of the twentieth century were writers of a distinctly different temper from their seventeenth-century predecessors—with the exception of T. S. Eliot, they were not deeply concerned with the emotional conflicts and the problems of religious doubt and conversion—and they were of course at a greater distance in time and feeling from the strains of court music that had been heard in the "airs" of Thomas Campion. The lesser poets of the 1920's in America quickly reduced what had been called a "metaphysical" vocabulary to what now seems to have been no more than "the blood, the bone, and the brain school," for the frequent reiteration of "bone, blood, and brain" in lines of verse was their only legitimate claim to having once read the poetry of Emily Dickinson and John Donne.

As one rereads the poetry of Léonie Adams it is more seemly to agree, and certainly more pertinent, that at her best she was more unworldly than metaphysical. Seventeenth-century philosophy, learning, irony, and religious "enthusiasm" as well as the conflicts of scientific observation and theological wit are singularly absent from her work, nor do her lines revive the strains of seventeenth-century music. Her "keepings" (as Gerard Manley Hopkins would have called them) were of Hopkins, Walter de la Mare, and John Crowe Ransom—and in her poem, "The Mount," her cadences and metrics resemble, if anything, a variation in lyrical verse that had acquired distinction in the poetry of W. B. Yeats's middle years. All this is said not to dispraise the charm of Léonie Adams' gifts, but to define their character with greater accuracy than her earlier critics have done.

John Crowe Ransom's "Antique Harvesters," the most sensitive of his finer poems which appeared in his *Two Gentlemen in Bonds* [11] (1927) contained the following lines:

[11] By permission of Alfred A. Knopf, Inc. Copyright, 1927, by Alfred A. Knopf, Inc.

We pluck the spindling ears and gather the corn.
One spot has special yield? "On this spot stood
Heroes and drenched it with their only blood."
And talk meets talk, as echoes from the horn
Of the hunter—echoes are the old men's arts,
Ample are the chambers of their hearts.

Here come the hunters, keepers of a rite.
The horn, the hounds, the lank mares coursing by
Straddled with archetypes of chivalry;
And the fox, lovely ritualist, in flight
Offering his earthly ghost to quarry . . .

And from Léonie Adams' *High Falcon* we have two parallels
to Ransom's "Antique Harvesters," one from "The Moon and
Spectator," and the second from "Ghostly Tree," and from
these it is not unreasonable to assume that Ransom shared with
Hopkins and de la Mare her highest esteem and the position
of a master:

The moon, that chill frame, I saw enact
Her rite commemorative of a bound ghost,
And thought of a night wildly born, outliving storm,
And its tears lost.[12]

O beech, unbind your yellow leaf, for deep
The honeyed time lies sleeping, and lead shade
Seals up the eyelids of its golden sleep.
Long are your flutes, chimes, little bells, at rest,
And here is only the cold scream of the fox,
Only the hunter following on the hound;
While your quaint-plumaged,
The bird that your green summer boughs lapped round,
Bends south its soft bright breast.[13]

And again it was as though the closing stanzas of "Antique
Harvesters," with their mention of death and "the Proud Lady,"
had brought to Léonie Adams' mind the title of one of her best-
known poems, "Death and the Lady"; the theme and charms of
her poem recalled Matthias Claudius' *Der Tod und das Mädchen*,

[12] "The Moon and Spectator" from *High Falcon*, by permission of The
John Day Company.
[13] "Ghostly Tree" from *High Falcon*, by permission of The John Day
Company.

a lyric which in its haunting echoes and refrains found an appropriate parallel in the music written for it by Franz Schubert; certainly, Léonie Adams' re-creation of her world had a closer kinship to the revivals of a Gothic imagination in the poetry of the early and late nineteenth century than it had to metaphysical poetry in the sense in which Samuel Johnson defined the term.

DEATH AND THE LADY [14]

Their bargain told again

Death to the Lady said,
While she to dancing-measure still
Would move, while beauties on her lay,
Simply as dews the buds do fill,
Death said: "Stay!
Tell me, Lady,
If in your breast the lively breath
May flicker for a little space,
What ransom will you give to Death,
Lady?" he said.
"Oh not one joy, Oh not one grace,
And what is your will to my will?
I can outwit parched fancies still,"
To Death said the Lady.

Death to that Lady said,
When blood went numb and wearily,
"In innocency dear breath you drew,
And marrow and bloom you rendered me,"
She said, "True."
"How now, Lady?"
"My heart sucked up its sweet at will,
Whose scent, when substance' sweet is past,
Is lovely still, is lovely still,
Death," she said.
"For bones' reprieve the dreams go last.
Soon, soon your flowery show did part,
But preciously I cull the heart."
Death said to the Lady.

Death to that Lady said,
"Is then not all our bargain done?
Or why do you beckon me so fast,
To chaffer for a skeleton

14 From *Those Not Elect*, by permission of The John Day Company.

Flesh must cast,
Ghostly Lady?"
"For, Death, that I would have you drain
From my dead heart the blood that stands
So chilly in the withered vein,
And, Death," she said,
"Give my due bones into your hands."
"Beauties I claim at morning-prime,
But the lack-luster in good time,"
Death said to the Lady.

The frequent use of the word "sweet," the "so sweet pain,"
and the adjective "cold," even the sound of her "airy shell" spoke
of her mingled debt to and careful, attentive readings in the
poetry of de la Mare and Gerard Manley Hopkins. And Léonie
Adams' "Kennst Du Das Land" [15] revived for readers of poetry
in 1929, less profoundly of course, but with unmistakable grace
and charm, the Gothic world of imagination that Poe had
discovered an hundred years before Miss Adams' *High Falcon*
had its proofs corrected and sent to the printer:

No, I have borne in mind this hill,
For once before I came its way
In hours when summer held her breath
Above her innocents at play;
Knew the leaves deepening the green ground
With their green shadows, there as still
And perfect as leaves stand in air;
The bird who takes delight in sound
Giving his young and watery call,
That is each time as if a fall
Flashed silver and were no more there,
And knew at last, when day was through,
That sky in which the boughs were dipped
More thick with stars than fields with dew;
And in December brought to mind
The laughing child to whom they gave
Among these slopes, upon this grass,
The summer-hearted name of love.
Still can you follow with your eyes,
Where on the green and golden ground
The dancers will not break the round,

15 From *High Falcon,* by permission of The John Day Company.

The beechtrees carved of moonlight rise;
Still at their roots the violets burn,
Lamps whose flame is soft as breath.
But turn not so, again, again,
They clap me in their wintry chain;
I know the land whereto you turn,
And know it for a land of death.

It was not without misgiving and a sense of disquiet that sympathetic readers of Léonie Adams' verses—and this after a silence since 1929 which had been broken only by a poem, *This Measure*, published in a limited edition in 1933, and rare appearances in *Poetry* and *The New Republic*—discovered the following statement by her in Fred B. Millett's *Contemporary American Authors* [16] (1940):

I sometimes feel that poetry at present like other things is about to undergo the kind of variation that amounts to the leap to a new genus. I was first preoccupied with sound patterns—that took me to the seventeenth century—then I recognized the necessity for the more modern preoccupation with images which should not be gathered along the way of discourse or meditation, but assumed before starting out, like apparel, or entered into as a world. I have been silent a long time because I am now grappling with the limitations of the lyric.

The statement was certainly ill advised, and in respect to the writing of poetry, naïve. Lyric forms are limited only by the resources and talents of the poet who employs them; a lyric is either written or it remains undone, and during the past fifteen years, traditional lyric forms have been employed with individual variation and distinction by a large number of poets, including E. E. Cummings, Robert Frost, T. S. Eliot, Edith Sitwell, W. H. Auden, Dylan Thomas, and Henry Treece—and there was, of course, no evidence of their "grappling with" the form itself, its limitations, its subject matter, or the very language with which their poems had been written.

From this statement one returns (as her critics turned in 1925 and 1929) to the rediscovery of the small, Gothic, yet distinct and delightful world of Miss Adams' imagination; and it is more than likely that some five or six of her lyrics will continue to be enjoyed by the readers of popular anthologies of verse.

[16] By permission of Harcourt, Brace.

"THE ROMANTIC TRADITIONISTS":
WILLIAM ELLERY LEONARD,
LOUIS UNTERMEYER, ROBERT HILLYER,
AND MARK VAN DOREN

In this chapter the poets who are included under the title of one of Allen Tate's poems can scarcely be called a school or a movement, nor is it certain that Tate's poem itself refers to them. But the title does serve as a happy means of giving their poetry and verse a place within this volume, and Leonard's and Untermeyer's verses move as far left of center as Hillyer's and Van Doren's move to the right. The area represented by "romantic traditionists" has been a large one in American poetry; and it could be stretched to include the poetry of William Rose Benét, but in his case it seems more fitting that it be considered in the same chapter that treats of his brother's work, the poetry of Stephen Vincent Benét; both brothers shared an historical imagination and both were consciously "American" in the sense that the figures in the present chapter were not, and we need not remind our readers that all classifications tend to break down beyond certain established limits. And for our immediate purpose "romantic traditionists" implies an academic quality as well as certain romantic tendencies, which were largely those of language, and which define the poetry of the four poets in this chapter.

2

William Ellery Leonard was born in Plainfield, New Jersey, January 25, 1876; and he died in 1944 at Madison, Wisconsin, where since 1906 he had been a member of the English department, first as an instructor and latterly as a professor, in the University of Wisconsin. He was of New England heritage and the son of a clergyman and journalist; he attended Boston University on a scholarship, and after he graduated from that institution in 1898, he went to Harvard where he received his master's degree in 1899. Not unlike his immediate contemporaries, George Cabot Lodge and Trumbull Stickney, Leonard was a brilliant linguist, and his talent for acquiring languages guided him to Europe where he furthered his studies at Göttingen and at Bonn, traveled extensively in Germany and in Italy, and returned to this country to complete his graduate work and to receive his doctor's degree in New York at Columbia. But quite unlike Lodge or Stickney, his early years were marked by the necessity of earning a living; his graduate studies were interrupted by teaching in secondary schools, and after he left Columbia, he took a position in Philadelphia as an editor of a dictionary which remained incompleted and was never published. His autobiography, *The Locomotive-God* (1927), which was a painful and not too trustworthy effort at self-psychoanalysis, and his selected poems, *A Son of Earth* (1928), which were so arranged that they attempted to provide the reader with an autobiography in verse, were in effect a new Childe Harold's pilgrimage for those who had read his *Two Lives* (1922 and 1925). *Two Lives* had been written in 1913, had been privately printed nine years later, and in 1925 it was received as a sonnet sequence which rivaled in its candor and its dramatic revelations of domestic misfortunes (for Leonard's first wife had lost her mind and then committed suicide) George Meredith's *Modern Love*. Both critics and educators, including Bliss Perry, Van Wyck Brooks, H. L. Mencken, and J. E. Spingarn, highly praised the merits of *Two Lives,* and indeed the notoriety of that work overshadowed the more lasting values of Leonard's translations of Lucretius' *On the Nature of Things* (1916), *Beowulf* (1923), and fragments of Sappho which were included under the title "An Ægyptian Papyrus," among his selected poems in 1928.

The publication of Leonard's novel in sonnets coincided with the publication of Sherwood Anderson's *Many Marriages* (1922) and both its enthusiastic reception and its brief notoriety are partially explained in Harlan Hatcher's *Creating the Modern American Novel* (1935); Anderson and Leonard were exactly the same age; both men had known relative poverty and obscurity in youth; both made a late arrival into public recognition, and at the time of their arrival on a scene that welcomed a candid discussion of sex and its misfortunes in the loose jargon of what was believed to be "Freudian psychology," both men had very nearly exhausted their energy in "finding themselves"—which is the fate of so many writers who in youth had found the world a difficult place in which to earn a living, and whose temperaments remained ill adjusted to the shocks of worldly disillusionment. Hatcher wrote:

Both Sherwood Anderson and America grew more sex-conscious as the third decade of the century unfolded. The frontiersman's fear of sex, his naïve madonna-worship of the pure and inviolate female, and the tragi-comic effects of these attitudes upon his conduct, were present in Sherwood Anderson's *Poor White* (1920). In *Many Marriages* these elements overshadow every other. The novel appeared in 1922 when the sex theme was nearing the height of its popularity, and no doubt that fact is partially responsible for the overemphasis and the resulting failure of *Many Marriages*.[1]

Two Lives, with its story of the bewildered and scholarly poet, who faced the terrors of living with an afflicted wife, shared the same sensational appeal and the same failure that met Anderson's *Many Marriages;* and today the book seems less tragic than pathetic or naïve.

At the University of Wisconsin, Leonard's presence, his tall, gray-clad figure with its shock of white hair, and his loosely knotted "Windsor" bow tie, whose Bohemian, almost Byronic, negligence was an attractive contrast to the formal, if decidedly unpedantic, manner of his speech and appearance, created an "atmosphere" to all undergraduates who were interested in poetry. It is doubtful if any university lecturer of his day—and it must be remembered that Barrett Wendell and Irving Babbitt were his contemporaries—excelled him in the teaching of comparative literatures. Those students who survived the severe discipline of his seemingly innocent course in Anglo-Saxon, which included comparative studies of Greek, Hebrew, Sanskrit, Latin, and Icelandic literatures as well as the literature which gave a

---

[1] "Sherwood Anderson" from *Creating the Modern American Novel* by Harlan Hatcher, used by permission of Farrar & Rinehart, Inc.

title to the course, emerged with a renewed respect for the power
of language and its relationship to poetry. Few students escaped
the influence of his Germanic training in philology, or the
severity of manner which he probably inherited from Kittredge
at Harvard, under whom he studied for his master's degree. The
course was ill attended, for it demanded from its students an
almost selfless devotion to poetry and a Puritan toughness of
fiber to withstand Leonard's oral examinations.

In his own translation of Lucretius, Leonard's standards were
no less exacting; the translation into English verse was at times
crabbed and turgid, and at other times overweighted by the
force of Anglo-Saxon periods and cadences; yet the entire work
remains firm and solid, and few translations of equal length into
English verse are of equally high quality and cumulative power.
It was as though the anonymous author of *Piers Plowman* had
undertaken the task of translating the darkened, smoky speculations of the great Roman poet into his own language, and
Leonard had modified that speech into passages of blank verse
which could be read and understood by the twentieth-century
reader.

Something of the translation's strange, if overly weighted,
felicity is in the lines of the sonnet that Leonard inscribed to
Lucretius in the summer of 1912 at Madison, Wisconsin:

> . . . if to have caught
> Thy splendour, and thy pathos, and thy song
> (Thy hand upon my shoulder, Master, long
> From room to aery room) avail me aught,
>
> Then not without some scope of thy old truth,
> Then not without some ring of thy old worth,
> My sturdy voice of still unconquered youth
> Hath in an unknown tongue reported thee
> Unto a Continent of thy dear Earth . . .
> To thee unknown, beyond an unknown sea.[2]

Like Trumbull Stickney, Leonard caught and held in fragments of his best poetry the elegiac note in twentieth-century

[2] *On the Nature of Things* by Lucretius, trans. by W. E. Leonard, from
Everyman's Library, used by permission of E. P. Dutton & Co., Inc.

verse; and among his new versions of well-known Sapphic fragments, the following lines were written:

> Death shall be death forever unto thee,
> Lady, with no remembrance of thy name
> Then or thereafter; for thou gatherest not
> The roses of Pieria, loving gold
> Above the Muses. Even in Hades' House
> Wander thou shalt unmarked, flitting forlorn
> Among the shadowy, averted dead.[3]

Leonard's ventures into light verse, *Aesop and Hyssop* (1912),
and his political verses, *The Lynching Bee* (1920), were far less
happy, and at their best the verses to Tom Mooney, "A War
Movie," and "The Lynching Bee" itself echoed the strains of
Vachel Lindsay's "The Congo." In academic circles, Leonard's
name will probably survive because of his two studies in prose:
his *Socrates* (1915) and his *La Métrica del Cid* (1931). Leonard's
rhetoric was of a latter-day romantic order, but whenever it
became inspired by a subject less overtly and consciously personal than his autobiographies in verse and prose, a happier
expression of that rhetoric paid its debt to Rome. To the Middle
West, Leonard brought his associations of a New England
heritage, which included a Protestant-Abolitionist spirit that
had turned against itself in violent self-criticism of its despised
"Puritanism" and prudery—and in Leonard's case it achieved
serenity only as it recalled images of Rome, or had been subjected to the austerities of scholarship. To a colleague who had
died in Rome, Leonard wrote "The Latin Scholar," [4] and though
the overtones of a nineteenth-century rhetoric are still heard, the
deeper and pervading spirit of Leonard's identity with New England's classical heritage also finds its voice:

> Friends whose own griefs had borne the heaviest stroke
> Best saw into his eyes, but never spoke . . .
> Lover of children, pictures, books, and flowers,
> Art was for him man's life, man's life an art,

[3] "An Ægyptian Papyrus—some fragments of Sappho of Lesbos, 600 B.C."
from *A Son of Earth*. Copyright, 1928, by The Viking Press, Inc.

[4] From *A Son of Earth*. Copyright, 1928, by The Viking Press, Inc.

Gracious of step and voice in hall or home . . .
He once brought Vergil to these lakes of ours,
But Vergil, kinsman of his gentle heart,
Took him forever from us back to Rome.

3

In 1919 Louis Untermeyer issued the first of his now famous anthologies of *Modern American Poetry,* of which Allen Tate in compiling a selected list of recent American poetry and poetic criticism to be sent to Soviet Russia "as a sign of good will from the U. S. State Department from the Library of Congress" (1943) remarked, "Still the best omnibus anthology of contemporary American poetry." The anthologies were then in their sixth revised edition, and indeed no one since Stedman had shown a more disinterested knowledge of the subject, or greater skill in keeping what might well have dropped into a mere repetition of academic choices a source of lively interest and well-modulated authority. Among the critics and reviewers of American poetry in the 1920's Untermeyer was the first to recognize the importance of the anthology in voicing a critical survey of his chosen field. Of his method in revising new editions Robert Hillyer wrote in his *A Letter to Robert Frost* (1937): [5]

> Taste changes. Candid Louis Untermeyer
> Consigns his past editions to the fire;
> His new anthology, refined and thrifty,
> Builds up some poets and dismisses fifty.
> And every poet spared, as is but human,
> Remarks upon his critical acumen.

If Untermeyer's anthologies have survived the moments of their original compilation it is because they have provided the public with an appreciation of modern poetry without the usual interference of literary warfare and clique discriminations. Like Harriet Monroe's when she edited *Poetry,* Untermeyer's value as an editor was to represent all schools of verse, and never to permit a poem or his own commentary on it to appear dull or

[5] By permission of Alfred A. Knopf, Inc. Copyright, 1936, by Robert Hillyer.

witless; and in this respect it is difficult to overestimate his wisdom (with time passing between successive editions of his anthologies) in dropping certain poets and reinforcing earlier selections.

The popularity of his anthologies quickly and unjustly overshadowed Untermeyer's true gift in the writing of light verse. In his parodies and satires he maintained the highest standards of a tradition that stemmed from his readings in Heine, Horace, and W. S. Gilbert, and in exercising that gift, he raised the standards of what the early nineteenth century knew as "the school of New York wits." In New York and during the 1920's, a revival of light verse took its impetus from the successes of Edna St. Vincent Millay's *A Few Figs from Thistles*, Dorothy Parker's *Enough Rope* (1926), Franklin P. Adams' *So Much Velvet* (1924), and the revival continued in Christopher Morley's *Translations from the Chinese* (1933) and in *Free Wheeling* (1931) by Ogden Nash. Of the entire group, Nash was the most topical and fluent, but it is doubtful if his urban uses of slang and breakneck rhymes would have existed without the examples set before him in E. E. Cummings' lighter verses. At first reading Nash's verse was both clear and gay, but on second reading its devices become a shade too obvious—and a third reading completely removes the element of surprise.

Untermeyer's wit in verse was of a more enduring order; and as he wrote a mock love song [6] (with a volume of Heine) none of his contemporaries could administer a *coup de grace* in a final stanza with half the ease and polish that he employed:

> Prayers are not what you want. I see
> That, when all other beauty fails,
> You will not alter, you will be
> As fair and young—and hard as nails.

It was indeed his identity with Heine that gave so many of his parodies an air of being written not for the moment alone but from a point outside and above the literary quarrels and adven-

---

[6] "So Rein Und Shön" (With a volume of Heine) from *Selected Poems and Parodies of Louis Untermeyer*, by permission of Harcourt, Brace.

tures of the day; —*and Other Poets* (1917) and *Including Horace* (1919) seem to have combined the felicities of a W. S. Gilbert with a hardy and well-sharpened edge of twentieth-century urban wit. His lines adapting Horace's Book I: Ode 23 to an exercise in hidden rhyme illustrated his gift in presenting a parody without an immediate and contemporary poet in view. It was done, one suspects, for the joy of writing it, and the reader is given another clue as to why the best of Untermeyer's satires in verse were purged of the so-called "personalities" and lapses in taste which so frequently marred the work of lesser satirists. The first stanza of the parody shows the Gilbertian lightness of Untermeyer's gift:

> Though all your charms in a sweet disarray,
>   Chloë, have won me, you shun me as though
> I were a tiger that searches for prey,
>   I would not hurt you, your virtue is so
> Glowing that passion is melted away.[7]

Not all of Untermeyer's parodies are of equal quality, and many of them (which is a reason why they are not better known) demand a greater knowledge of the verse that Untermeyer has satirized than the general reader of contemporary poetry can supply, but it is likely that the parodies on A. E. Housman, on Edgar A. Guest, the newspaper poet, and on the *terza rima* that Archibald MacLeish used so effectively in his *Conquistador* will remain the best of their kind in American poetry, and in the parody of *Conquistador,* Untermeyer retold a story from the nursery rhymes of Mother Goose:

> And this little pig had none—not for love nor the paying—
> Dust in his corded throat: and the knife above it:
> And the quick slit under the jaw: and he took it bravely . . .[8]

Untermeyer's adaptations of Heinrich Heine's poems (1917, 1923, 1937) into English will probably remain the most impres-

---

[7] "To Chloë" from *The Selected Poems and Parodies of Louis Untermeyer,* by permission of Harcourt, Brace.

[8] "Archibald MacLeish" from *The Selected Poems and Parodies of Louis Untermeyer,* by permission of Harcourt, Brace.

sive tribute to Heine's memory that the present century will yield in English and certainly Untermeyer's wit has rescued some five hundred of Heine's shorter poems from the curse of dullness which obscured even the best intentions of his earlier translators.

Louis Untermeyer was born in New York October 1, 1885, and as he has written of himself in a note in' the sixth edition of his *Modern American Poetry* [9] (1942):

> He attended the De Witt Clinton High School, but his failure to comprehend the essentials of geometry prevented him from graduating. In his youth his one ambition was to be a composer. . . . In 1923 he retired from business and, after two years of study abroad, returned to America to devote himself entirely to literature. . . . He became "poet in residence" at various universities. His lectures brought him into every state of the Union except South Dakota.

'He was the author of nine books of verse, the best of which was *The Selected Poems and Parodies of Louis Untermeyer* (1935), and in that volume the quality of the poems written in lighter measures hold a position (though they do not pretend to do so) of more originality than those that were apparently conceived at graver moments. His only flaw as a self-critic has been an inability to take his seemingly unserious verse with the seriousness that it deserved. He has been the editor of at least a dozen anthologies of verse, and the author of five books in prose on American poetry, and to these he has added his autobiography, *From Another World* (1939). In Fred B. Millett's *Contemporary American Authors* [10] he wrote:

> My general attitude seems to be "centrist." While I appreciate the value of tradition, I applaud the validity of experiment. . . . If I had to choose either—a choice which, thank God, has not yet been forced upon me—I would go over unhesitatingly to the radicals and experimenters, even though I am by nature a son of Libra, and hence a hesitating Liberal.

The note of candor and the half-ironic pun on Libra were characteristic of his manner; and those who wish to rediscover his true poise and value will return to some of the critical com-

[9] From fifth edition, by permission of Harcourt, Brace.
[10] By permission of Harcourt, Brace.

mentaries in his anthologies, his translations of Heine, and his own light verse, which is inimitable.

4

For the past twenty years it has been an easy matter to under-estimate the poetic gifts of Robert Hillyer—but this does not mean that his work has lacked recognition (for his *Collected Verse* received the Pulitzer Prize in 1934 and his position as Boylston Professor of Rhetoric and Oratory at Harvard since 1937 cannot be described as one that has been obscure). Yet as one rereads his seventh book of verse, *The Seventh Hill*, which was published in 1928, there is the renewed delight that resembles the finding of unknown verses written by a familiar name. The majority of Hillyer's verses bore a relationship, and not always a happy one, to the latter-day British "Georgian" poets, Edmund Blunden and Siegfried Sassoon, whose writings in both prose and verse have been fluent, bland, aware of technical devices, careless in diction, and on rare occasions, memorable. It might be said that this general relationship describes the external qualities of Hillyer's verse—those moments at which it substituted personal candor for the more difficult virtues of seeking truth and allowed the sonnet to flow through its fourteen lines, observing as it did so, the usual pleasantries or discomforts of seasonal change in language that repeats anticipated phrases and the usual rhymes. But this does not describe two singular merits of Hillyer's verse; one is its true affinity at its best with the shorter poems of Robert Bridges, and the other the independent, characteristic play of wit that is to be found in his *A Letter to Robert Frost and Others* (1937). As far as sensitive readers of lyric poetry are concerned, the first merit was the more important, for its quality has been a rare one in twentieth-century American poetry, and it is why Hillyer's slender volume, *The Seventh Hill*, becomes the object of a rediscovery. The gift that Hillyer possessed was an extremely sensitive ear for verbal music, a gift that, however "literary" its speech may be, never fails to delight the reader, for among the best of Hillyer's lyrics the clear strains of sixteenth-century music were revived and were sounded with the mastery that conceals its art:

> .   .   .   .   .   .
> Let the nightingale in vain
> Lift his amorous refrain,
> Let the dying reedy swan
> Cease her prothalamion.
> They are sunk in such a bliss
> Deep as old Atlantic is.
> End our song and come away
>   (come away)
> Music hath no more to say.[11]

This was "chamber music" in the same sense that James Joyce's shorter lyrics were *Chamber Music* and *Pomes Pennyeach*. And another lyric from the same volume, *The Seventh Hill*, was still another "pastoral":

> So ghostly then the girl came in
> I never saw the turnstile twist
> Down where the orchard trees begin
> Lost in a reverie of mist.
>
> And in the windless hour between
> The last of daylight and the night,
> When fields give up their ebbing green
> And two bats interweave their flight,
>
> I saw the turnstile glimmer pale
> Just where the orchard trees begin,
> But watching was of no avail,
> Invisibly the girl came in.
>
> I took one deep breath of the air
> And lifted up my heavy heart;
> It was not I who trembled there
> But my immortal counterpart.[12]

In rereading all of Robert Hillyer's verse one has the impression of a fine poetic sensibility and wit that, not unlike Conrad

[11] "Pastoral II" from *Collected Poems*, by permission of Alfred A. Knopf, Inc. Copyright, 1933, by Robert Hillyer.

[12] "Pastoral VII" from *Collected Poems*, by permission of Alfred A. Knopf, Inc. Copyright, 1933, by Robert Hillyer.

Aiken's more spectacular display of talent, have been wasted or diffused and squandered. The wit of Robert Hillyer's heroic couplets in his *A Letter to Robert Frost* is of rare accomplishment—and its critical candor reminds one of James Russell Lowell's *A Fable for Critics,* and much of it seems to have been written in the same high-spirited vein. Granting Hillyer's intentions to emulate the Horace that Pope adapted in his famous "Epistle to Dr. Arbuthnot," Hillyer's conclusions lacked classical firmness and poise; and the same weaknesses are to be discovered among his less fortunate lyrics in which stanzas could be arbitrarily transposed or final stanzas omitted without loss—or as he confessed,

> Like Johnson's friend, I woo philosophy,
> But cheerfulness creeps in in spite of me.[13]

Robert Hillyer was born June 3, 1895, in East Orange, New Jersey, and during the 1920's he was among the most precociously gifted literary figures in America. His first book of verse, *Sonnets and Other Lyrics,* was published in 1917, the year he graduated from Harvard. From 1920 to 1921 and through a fellowship awarded by the American-Scandinavian Foundation, he studied at the University of Copenhagen. In 1932 he published a novel, *Riverhead,* which became a "best seller" and received critical praise for the imaginative insights and sensitivity of its prose; and his introduction to a volume which contained the collected poems of both John Donne and William Blake was distinguished by its critical ease and scholarly excellence.

5

Mark Van Doren's verses have long been associated with several divergent schools in twentieth-century American literature, but it is more than likely that the best of his work will come to rest slightly "right of center" which was the position that he held on the editorial staff of the liberal weekly, *The Nation,* from 1924 to 1928. These were the years that he published his first two books of verse, *Spring Thunder* (1924) and *Now the Sky*

13 From *A Letter to Robert Frost,* by permission of Alfred A. Knopf, Inc. Copyright, 1936, by Robert Hillyer.

(1928), and most critics have agreed that much of his inspiration in writing verse stemmed from an influence, then widely felt, of the poetry of Robert Frost. His own poetic character was less easy to define, but Van Doren was by very temperament and disposition a relaxed and facile writer of both prose and verse; and indeed his large and generous labors as an editor and reviewer, as a novelist and lecturer and critic, and writer of books for children create an analogy to that nearly forgotten man of letters in early nineteenth-century England, Robert Southey, who became poet laureate, was Wordsworth's sympathetic friend, and who was also a true friend of Walter Savage Landor.

Van Doren's narrative romances in verse, *Jonathan Gentry* (1931) and *The Mayfield Deer* (1941), bear a resemblance to Southey's *The Curse of Kehama* and *Roderick*—if one can conceive of Southey being born as Mark Van Doren was in Illinois, June 13, 1894, and subject to the same environment and education of a twentieth-century American writer. Neither *The Curse of Kehama* nor *Jonathan Gentry* were fortunate experiments in the writing of narrative verse, but both seem to have been earnest and sincere in their effort to supply the public with the kind of verse it cared to read; and *Jonathan Gentry* suffered from lapses in taste and infirm writing:

> Click, click, clickety click, clickety clickety click, click.
> He listened, and it told him of a bullet singing true.
> Click, click, click, click, clickety clickety click,—
> Click, and one was coming home instead of two, of two.[14]

Verses such as these went on for seven stanzas in the narrative. And the narrative, which embraced a family chronicle and references to the American Civil War, also contained snatches of songs:

> Tom, Tom, the son of a gun,
> Stole my gal and away he run.
> I'm Tom, too.
>
> Stranger, do you chew? [15]

[14] "Jonathan Gentry" from *Collected Poems*, by permission of Henry Holt and Company, Inc.
[15] *Ibid.*

Jonathan Gentry came to a close with the following commentary in verse:

> Over the mountains, boys,
> And down the river middle,
> Won't learn nothin' new,
> Hey diddle diddle.
> Adam and Eve,
> They dig and spin
> Till the Lord he's tired
> And turns 'em in.[16]

A far more successful venture in the writing of verse at length was Van Doren's *A Winter Diary* [17] (1935) and the literary personality that it conveyed to the reader had a slightly awkward, domesticated, boyish charm; quite as Robert Southey, a century before him, celebrated the joys of eating gooseberry tarts, so Van Doren in New England wrote of

> Dark, horny Hubbards that will slice in half
> And come with pools of butter as we laugh,
>
> .   .   .   .
>
> Firm corn, and tapering carrots, and the blood
> Of beets complete the tally of saved food;
> Yet over in a corner, white and square,
> Is the big bin with our potato-share.
> Then seven barrels of apples standing by.
>
> .   .   .   .
>
> The Baldwins to be eaten, and the Spies;
> But Greenings are for betty and for pies.
>
> .   .   .   .
>
> And suddenly we smell a breakfast waiting:
> Bacon and yellow eggs; or, alternating,
> Buckwheat cakes with butter for anointing . . .

This was not distinguished verse, but it was hearty in the naming of food that growing children enjoy. And the same boyish heartiness and vigor entered a lyric that took its images from the so-called "metaphysical" school:

---

[16] "Jonathan Gentry" from *Collected Poems,* by permission of Henry Holt and Company, Inc.

[17] From *Collected Poems,* by permission of Henry Holt and Company, Inc.

Strike then the rusted strings.
Pound, pound the sluggard voice.
And bid deposéd kings
With our poor selves rejoice.

    · · · · · ·

Pour liquor that will widen
The skull's already smile.
The darkness we have died in,
Let it be red awhile.

    · · · · · ·

Ha! and now we gather.
Ho! and now we part.
Let every bone be lather,
Next to the fiery heart.[18]

Perhaps the best of Van Doren's verses in a similar vein was "Spectral Boy": [19]

I told you I would come, he said,
I told you with these very eyes.
Be not ashamed. The grave is deep,
And terror in it dies.

If in these circles that you see
There is the old, the child's alarm,
It does not live to startle you,
Or work the pulse's harm.

It was not gathered underground,
It was not freed upon a day,
Except that something might come home
Of the whipped soul, and stay.

Except the fever, all is here.
My deathless part, my fear, returns.
Be not ashamed. The grave is cold.
Nothing in it burns.

I have not suffered since I died,
Though I have lain with eyes as round
As when you fixed them; but enlarged,
Some days, from lack of sound.

---

[18] "Strike the Rusted Springs" from *Collected Poems*, by permission of Henry Holt and Company, Inc.
[19] From *Collected Poems*, by permission of Henry Holt and Company, Inc.

And so there fell to me an hour
Of utter quiet; then I rose,
And am revisiting old Time,
Before his close.

Was I not washed and buried well?
Why this desire, why this research
For time and wrath? Be still, I beg!
What now? This twitch and lurch—

You would escape me, but I swear
I was not sent to punish you.
I came alone, that fear might form
Once more on me like dew.

No longer groan and hide your hands.
This thing I seek is chill and sweet.
Be not ashamed. The grave is pure.
No horror now. No heat.*

These lines were decidedly more fortunate than the instruction to "Pound, pound the sluggard voice," for the voice is always difficult to "pound," and it is still more awkward for the human voice to make a noise that resembles "pounding." But in rereading Van Doren's verse, one must accept it or reject it without demanding precision of language, or of music, or of meaning. Van Doren's verse was always happiest when one asked least of it; and in a homely and domesticated rephrasing of Robert Herrick's "The Argument of his Book," Van Doren wrote:

I sing of ghosts and people under ground,
Or if they live, absented from green sound.

.   .   .   .

I am in love with joy, but find it wrapped
In a queer earth, at languages unapt;

.   .   .   .

I sing of men and shadows, and the light
That none the less shines under them by night.
Then lest I be dog enemy of day,
I add old women talking by the way;
And not to grow insensible to noise,
Add gossip girls and western-throated boys.[20]

[20] "The End" from *Collected Poems,* by permission of Henry Holt and Company, Inc.

In 1940 Van Doren's *Collected Poems, 1922-1938* received the Pulitzer Prize, and since the middle of the 1920's Van Doren has been a popular teacher at Columbia University and lecturer at the New School for Social Research in New York. He has been the editor of several anthologies, of which *An Anthology of World Poetry* (1928) and *American Poets, 1630-1930* (1932) were the best known. Of the many books in prose and verse that Van Doren has written his most distinguished and mature volume was his admirable collection of brief essays on Shakespeare. In presenting his *Shakespeare* (1939) he persuasively reminded the American public that Shakespeare was, above all things, a poet.

MARIANNE MOORE: THE GENIUS
OF THE DIAL

In re-creating the hour that produced the early poems of
Marianne Moore, it is well to recall the existence of a magazine
that she edited from 1925 to 1929. In those days *The Dial* was
far more than a monthly publication of highly sustained literary
values; it was an institution, which, not unlike a college or a
university, became a school for younger writers, and its position
overshadowed the hitherto undisputed eminence of *The Atlantic Monthly*. Its circulation was small, and in some respects its
editorial policy emulated the character of Ezra Pound's and
Wyndham Lewis's *Blast* and Margaret Anderson's *The Little
Review*. To the general public it maintained an almost frightening "esoteric" front, which was modified by its conservative
exterior, for like W. E. Henley's periodicals of late nineteenth-
century England, *The Dial* of New York's 1920's paid its respects
to tradition through the austere and formal excellence of its
taste in typography. For a further description of *The Dial*, the
appearance of its offices, and its historical value, we quote
Marianne Moore's memoirs of *The Dial*, including an appropriate editorial foreword, as they were published in the December, 1940, issue of *Life and Letters To-Day* (London):

[The Dial, *founded in 1840 with Margaret Fuller as editor, Emerson
as next editor, and Oliver Wendell Holmes, Hawthorne, and others as
contributors, was discontinued after four years. In 1880 it was re-estab-
lished by Francis F. Browne, of Chicago, but in 1917 there was a change
in editorial policy; the publication offices were moved to New York and
as a fortnightly with socially analytical and humanitarian emphasis, it
was varyingly edited, first by George Bernard Donlin, then by Robert
Morss Lovett; with Thorstein Veblen, Helen Marot, Randolph Bourne,
Van Wyck Brooks, Harold Stearns and others as contributing editors.
In 1920 it was refashioned and brought out as a non-political monthly
of "art and letters" by Scofield Thayer, Editor, and J. S. Watson, Presi-*

dent; with Lincoln MacVeagh as Treasurer, and was entitled The Dial,
*The Dial Publishing Company Inc. being the full title, as it had been
of the fortnightly* Dial. *The Dial Press, it might be noted, was not
synonymous with it, but a separate organization. Then with Stewart
Mitchell as Managing Editor, followed by—though not always with the
same title—Gilbert Seldes, Alyse Gregory, Kenneth Burke, and Marianne
Moore—it was discontinued with the July issue,* 1929.]

As growth-rings in the cross section of a tree present a contrastingly
differentiated record of experience, successive editorial modifications of
a magazine adjoin rather than merge; but the later *Dial* shared, or
thought it shared, certain objectives of its predecessors. It is that *Dial*
which I know best, and when I think of it recollections spring up of
manuscripts, of letters, of people.

I think of the compacted pleasantness of those days at 152 West 13th
Street, and the three-storey brick building with carpeted stairs, fireplace
and white mantelpiece rooms, business office in the first storey front
parlour, and of plain gold-leaf block letters, *The Dial,* on the windows
to the right of the brown stone steps leading to the front door. . . .

I recall the condensed but explicit anatomy of duties with which the
office was provided; and despite occasional athletically protesting editorial reciprocities, the inviolateness—to us—of our "contributing editor-
critics," Gilbert Seldes (The Theatre), Henry McBride (Modern Art);
Paul Rosenfeld and then Kenneth Burke (Music). Almost recklessly
against the false good, they surely did represent *The Dial* in "encouraging a tolerance for fresh experiments and opening the way for
a fresh understanding of them."

However "esoteric" its front may have been to the general
public, *The Dial* continued the services of *The Little Review*
with greater and more nicely balanced authority; its pages contained chapters of W. B. Yeats's autobiographies, letters on literary events in Germany that had been written by Thomas
Mann, one of George Moore's later novels, *Héloïse and Abélard,*
ran its serial length between its covers, and T. S. Eliot contributed a London letter. In respect to poetry, *The Dial's* awards of
two thousand dollars each were presented with rare discernment
for true merit, and rarer still, the awards were given to poets,
who at the moment of receiving them were in actual need of
money and further encouragement for the progress of their work.
In 1922, T. S. Eliot's *The Waste Land* received *The Dial* award;
in 1924 Marianne Moore's second book of poems, *Observations,*
received it; in 1925 it was given to E. E. Cummings; in 1926 to

William Carlos Williams; and in 1927 to Ezra Pound. In all these instances, the award reflected honors on the magazine itself; and like *Poetry's* Helen Haire Levinson Prize, such awards came to the poet with the honors of having received practical recognition from a source that had true standards to maintain.

The Dial, which from its revival in 1920 had been a generously subsidized magazine, came to the end of its career in 1929; and among the contributors to its last issue was Joseph Ferdinand Gould, a New England wit from Boston, who at Harvard had been the contemporary of Walter Lippmann, Conrad Aiken, and John Reed, who was the friend of E. E. Cummings, and who during the 1920's brilliantly disguised himself as a Greenwich Village Bohemian in New York without loss to his Boston heritage or the quality of his sturdily provincial New England wit. As the offices of *The Dial* closed, and the "plain gold-leaf block letters" of its name faded from the brownstone house in West 13th Street, Gould wrote:

> Who killed The Dial?
> "I," said Joe Gould,
> "With my inimitable style,
> I killed The Dial."

But of course Gould's claims could have been made by any or all of *The Dial's* contributors during the ten years of its revival, and the magazine had performed its services to American literature with a longer lease of life than most of the "little magazines" which during the preceding decade had bravely "died to make verse free." The plain fact of the matter was that *The Dial's* handsome subsidy had been withdrawn. A new decade was at the threshold, and *The Dial* had honorably discharged its responsibilities.

2

POETRY [1]

I, too, dislike it: there are things that are important beyond all
    this fiddle.
Reading it, however, with a perfect contempt for it, one dis-
    covers in
it after all, a place for the genuine.

[1] From *Selected Poems*, 1935. By permission of The Macmillan Company.

> Hands that can grasp, eyes
> that can dilate, hair that can rise
>   if it must, these things are important not because a
high-sounding interpretation can be put upon them but because
>   they are
>   useful. When they become so derivative as to become unintelligible
>   the same thing may be said for all of us, that we
>   do not admire what
>   we cannot understand . . .

wrote Marianne Moore. Since then her commentary on poetry
has become justly famous, for the poem on poetry spoke her
mind, and her mind released as fine a discrimination in the arts
of literary wit as any critic has shown in twentieth-century literature. The poem also illustrated by example the nature of Miss
Moore's gift, which was a gift of employing prose cadences with
the aid of rhyme. In his introduction to Marianne Moore's
Selected Poems [2] (1935) T. S. Eliot wrote:

> Miss Moore's poetry, or most of it, might be classified as "descriptive"
> rather than "lyrical" or "dramatic." Descriptive poetry is supposed to
> be dated to a period, and to be condemned thereby; but it is really
> one of the permanent modes of expression. In the eighteenth century—
> or say a period which includes *Cooper's Hill, Windsor Forest,* and
> Gray's *Elegy*—the scene described is a point of departure for medita-
> tions on one thing or another.

Eliot's mention of Pope's "Windsor Forest" brought an appropriate eighteenth-century association to the qualities of Miss
Moore's wit. To observe and then to comment briefly, as though
she had added a footnote to her discovery, were among the completely disarming qualities of Marianne Moore's style—and the
footnote was usually credited to the *New York Times,* or the
Illustrated London News, or *Strange Animals I Have Known,* or
Tolstoy's *Diary,* or stray paragraphs from the casual reading that
the world so thoughtlessly absorbs over coffee and toast at the
breakfast table. This was wit of a unique and highly polished
order, and Marianne Moore's candor in setting her footnotes between quotation marks and listing their sources in an appendix
to her books gave still another turn to an ingeniousness which
dispels mystery and doubt.

[2] By permission of The Macmillan Company.

But above and beyond Marianne Moore's method of writing verse, which she had explained and presented with far more clarity and precision than many of her critics, was the air of courtesy and good breeding with which she offered her particular observations to the world—and these were offered at a time when poets and critics alike feared to admit the existence of something that they contemptuously called "good manners" in civilized and adult society. The rule was then to fear "gentility" in American poetry and to cultivate a familiar "we boys" manner of address that was supposed to represent the spirit of American democracy. It was forgotten that American democracy also implied respect for individual distinction, and a habit grew in which even figures from the classic American past were referred to by their Christian names. Two figures of irreproachable dignity and reticence in their private lives received rather more than their share of posthumous familiarity: Longfellow became "Henry" and Emily Dickinson "Emily," and at a moment of still greater intimacy and freedom, she became that "little tippler in the sun." Of course, little harm had been done to poetry itself; and in the case of Marianne Moore's poetry, it was both refreshing and clear that she offered her readers the implied compliment of being civilized, self-respecting, and adult human beings, and the tone in which she addressed them was not unlike the same compliment that Samuel Johnson bestowed upon his "common reader."

Of the physical objects discovered among Marianne Moore's observations, which were a great number of small animals and fish (and the jerboa might well be taken as her heraldic beast), one cannot improve on T. S. Eliot's description of the way she has brought them to the reader's eye:

So, in her amused and affectionate attention to animals—from the domestic cat, or "to popularize the mule," to the most exotic strangers from the tropics, she succeeds at once in startling us into an unusual awareness of visual patterns, with something like the fascination of a high-powered microscope.[3]

[3] From T. S. Eliot's Introduction to *Selected Poems*, 1935. By permission of The Macmillan Company.

That "fascination" accurately describes the enjoyment that the reader always shares as he turns the pages of her volumes, including *What Are Years?* (1941)—but naturally Marianne Moore did not pretend to give us everything that the word "poetry" implied. The fine prose cadences that she employed, which seem to have stemmed from a sensitive reading of Anthony Trollope's novels and Henry James's prose of his "middle period," the period in which he wrote *The Tragic Muse,* those cadences which were accented by what Eliot called Marianne Moore's "*light rhyme,*" do not always succeed in enclosing the minutiae of her observation in a long poem. The minutiae do not, as Eliot feared, irritate the eye of Marianne Moore's reader, but they do tend to create smaller unities within a longer poem that overcome or break through the larger unit of the poem itself, and the poem becomes one in which the sum of its parts is greater than the whole. And this defect raises its multiple tentacles in "An Octopus," in "Marriage," and in "The Plumet Basilisk," and among Marianne Moore's later poems, "The Pangolin." In these instances the sensitive commentary that Marianne Moore offered her readers tended to drift in the direction of becoming an editorial; and an editorial, however engaging, however intelligent it may be, remains, as Wallace Stevens might well have phrased it, on an "anti-poetic" level in poetry. In these the various themes that Marianne Moore may have had in mind were either lost or placed within the editorial portions of the poem. Even Eliot confessed his difficulty in finding the "subject matter" of "The Jerboa," and then concluded with a fine sense of judgment that whatever subject matter allows us the most powerful and most secret release is a personal affair.

All this is, perhaps, another way of saying that the formal elegance that Marianne Moore achieved in her choice of language was not always achieved in the completion of an entire poem; and when she was at her second best we must be content to enjoy fragments of her world as they seem to have been observed through the eye of a microscope. Marianne Moore was always happiest in her shorter poems, poems in which her light rhymes were clearly heard, and therefore supplied in themselves

the metrical unity that is always required in the completion of
a poem for its own sake, and among these "No Swan So Fine"
is a beautiful example:

No Swan So Fine [4]

'No water so still as the
        dead fountains of Versailles.' No swan,
with swart blind look askance
and gondoliering legs, so fine
        as the chintz china one with fawn-
brown eyes and toothed gold
collar on to show whose bird it was.

Lodged in the Louis Fifteenth
        candelabrum-tree of cockscomb-
tinted buttons, dahlias,
sea-urchins, and everlastings,
        it perches on the branching foam
of polished sculptured
flowers—at ease and tall. The king is dead.

and "What Are Years" is still another:

What Are Years [5]

What is our innocence,
what is our guilt? All are
        naked, none is safe. And whence
is courage: the unanswered question,
the resolute doubt,—
dumbly calling, deafly listening—that
in misfortune, even death,
        encourages others
        and in its defeat, stirs

        the soul to be strong? He
sees deep and is glad, who
        accedes to mortality
and in his imprisonment, rises
upon himself as
the sea in a chasm, struggling to be
free and unable to be,
        in its surrendering
        finds its continuing.

[4] From *Selected Poems*, 1935. By permission of The Macmillan Company.
[5] From *What Are Years?* By permission of The Macmillan Company.

So he who strongly feels,
behaves. The very bird,
        grown taller as he sings, steels
his form straight up. Though he is captive,
his mighty singing
says, satisfaction is a lowly
thing, how pure a thing is joy.
        This is mortality,
        this is eternity.

And the unities of theme, imagery, and metric were memorably
intensified and sustained in Miss Moore's "Sun!"

"SUN!" [6]

Hope and Fear—those internecine fighters—accost him.

"No man may him hyde
From Deth holow-eyed;"
This, for us mortal truth, for us shall not suffice.
You are not male or female, but a plan
Deep-set within the heart of man.
Splendid with splendor hid you come, from your Arab abode,
A fiery topaz smothered in the hand of a great prince who rode
        Before you, Sun—whom you outran.
        Piercing his caravan.

O Sun, you shall stay
With us. Holiday
And day of wrath shall be as one, wound in a device
Of Moorish gorgeousness, round glasses spun
To flame as hemispheres of one
Great hourglass dwindling to a stem. Consume hostility;
Employ your weapon in this meeting-place of surging enmity!
        Insurgent feet shall not outrun
        Multiplied flames, O Sun.

"Sun!" was not characteristic of Marianne Moore's later manner; but like her poetry at its best, its formal graces extended
throughout the area of the poem; we are certain that the poem
is self-contained and complete, and that its life is independent
of its author's mannerisms and critical commentaries. An

[6] From *Poems*, published by The Egoist Press, London. By permission of
the Author.

example of Marianne Moore's courtesy and poise may be found in "Silence" and in it her wit paid its respect to her readers with salutary advice.

3

Since the present chapter opened with a passage of Marianne Moore's prose, and since the qualities of her prose at its best are second only to the charms of her poetry, it is a pleasure to quote her notes on a group of photographs of Anna Pavlova which appeared in *Dance Index;* and it could be said that Marianne Moore described the character of her own esthetic in the following paragraph:

"The stage is like a magnifying glass. Everything tends toward exaggeration," and as in music, sensibility avoids use of the pedal, so with Pavlova, humor, esprit, a sense of style—and also a moral quality—made it impossible for her to show off, to be hard, to be dull; the same thing that in life made her self-controlled so that she was not a prison to what she prized; so that her punishment for what she deplored, was apartness from it. "Her dancing," says Mr. Beaumont, quoting a French writer, "was 'la danse de toujours, dansée comme jamais,—' the dance of everyday as it was never danced before"; and speaking of the "Gavotte" danced to "The Glowworm" music by Paul Lincke, nothing could be more ordinary from the viewpoint of both choreography and music, yet she made it into a delicious miniature of the Merveilleuse period.[7]

Marianne Moore was born in St. Louis, Missouri, on November 15, 1887, and she received her bachelor's degree at Bryn Mawr in 1909. For four years (1911 to 1915) she taught stenography in the government Indian school at Carlisle, and in 1921, her friends, H. D. and "Bryher," Mrs. Winifred Macpherson, published her first book of poems. Her rules of living had been those of quiet austerity and reticence, and of her it should be said, as Samuel Johnson once wrote of Sir John Denham, she was "one of the writers that improved our taste, advanced our language, and whom we ought therefore to read with gratitude."

[7] From "Notes on the Accompanying Pavlova Photographs," Vol. III, No. 3, March, 1944, by permission of *Dance Index.*

THE HARMONIUM OF WALLACE STEVENS

> And although my mind perceives the force behind the moment,
> The mind is smaller than the eye.
>
> "A Fish-Scale Sunrise," from *Ideas of Order* (1936)

Since the publication of his first edition of *Harmonium* in 1923, Wallace Stevens has been the James McNeill Whistler of twentieth-century American poetry. It could be said that Whistler had been Stevens' true predecessor; and the analogy applies not to their biographies but to the qualities of their art. Whistler was as fine a rhetorician in his painting (that is, if painting can be said to have a rhetoric) as Stevens was a poet, and the analogy can be extended even further. The true subject matter of Whistler's painting was a formal elegance that had combined its graces with those of plastic brilliance; and that was why even the fashionable canvases of his fellow American and fellow expatriate in London, John Singer Sargent, if placed alongside of Whistler's portraits seem comparatively "commercial," a trifle shoddy, and certainly meretricious. There was a coarse strain in Sargent that had been suppressed and yet could not be fully glossed; and this coarsened strain, or taint, or fiber gave him an almost muscular contact with the successful, newly rich, fashionable members of society who sat before him to have their portraits "taken." Whistler did not possess the same coarse strain, and he remained, despite his notoriety, a "painters' painter" in much the same fashion that Stevens, in a latter day, remained a "poets' poet." The painter who successfully controverted John Ruskin in a court of law and who wrote *The Gentle Art of Making Enemies* was a man of wit with an eye and an ear for legal logic, and so was Wallace Stevens. And both men had their "chromos" (which was, of course, one of the penalties of fame). During the very years that "Whistler's Mother" became an engraving on a United

States postage stamp, Wallace Stevens' "Peter Quince at the Clavier" became a "best-loved" choice among anthologists of twentieth-century American poetry.

2

Before we speak of Wallace Stevens' poetry directly, a word should be said of its high reputation among critics of its day. For the past fifteen years his poetry has been the occasion for a great quantity of excellent talk in critical reviews, and it is to Stevens' credit that he stimulated his critics to exercise their brains in searching out the superlatives of praise. His poetry drove them into many curious fields of speculation, and then, once they were well on their way, it leaped ahead, leading them in small and closely herded droves into the bogs of metaphysical discussion. As a tribute to Stevens' gifts and their accomplishments, and in particular, his wit, which had been exemplified in his "The Comedian as the Letter C," all this has been a gratifying spectacle, and one may suppose that Wallace Stevens, in his quiet fashion, has enjoyed it. Since the earliest publication of his work in Harriet Monroe's *Poetry* in 1914, Stevens successfully created an atmosphere of high and brilliantly serious comedy wherever his poems have appeared, and if since 1931 his poetry at its second best has shown a tendency to grow more diffuse with the passage of time, its sensibility remained untarnished, and its rhetoric continued to refresh the eye and ear.

The strange question that has been so often raised concerning Wallace Stevens' verse is one concerning its philosophy. Can we hook ladders, as it were, to Stevens' Prester John's balloon, float among the stars, which are now named by the striking titles of Stevens' poems, such as "The Paltry Nude Starts on a Spring Voyage," "Lions in Sweden," "Anglais Mort à Florence," "The Woman that Had More Babies than That"—and then expect to land on a terrain peopled by Zeno, Plotinus, Socrates, William James, and Professor Whitehead? The sensible answer would be "No!"; and it should be an unhesitating one and final. If one makes allowances for a difference of some two thousand years, one becomes convinced that Wallace Stevens was one of those who were kept in mind when Plato excluded poets from his ideal republic. In saying this we do not mean that Stevens' poetry has lacked intelligence, or has been without the evidence of a finely tempered and inquiring mind beneath the surface of its skeptical appraisal of the world—but in reading Stevens' verse a distinction should be made between a so-called "intellectual poetry" and the kind of poetry that employs to the utmost the resources of poetic intelligence and wit. This distinction is one of particular relevance to the majority of Stevens' verses, because a number of them made use of terms that had their origin in the language of philosophic discourse; and one might almost say that Stevens has always permitted himself to ruminate at large on the lack of order in the world that remained outside his range of vision. His true wisdom, his rightness, his precision were always related to objects that were close at hand. In *Ideas of Order* (1936) he identified the future harmonies of the world with skepticism:

> Too many waltzes— The epic of disbelief
> Blares oftener and soon, will soon be constant.
> Some harmonious skeptic soon in a skeptical music
>
> Will unite these figures of men and their shapes
> Will glisten again with motion, the music
> Will be motion and full of shadows.[1]

But Stevens' skepticisms should not be advanced as his prime excuse for being; they should be accepted only in so far as they exist within the poem for the poem's sake; we may admire the wit and the sensibility that gave them poetic meaning—and we may even add them to our own store of critical observations on the world around us—but to regard them as the expression of a "philosophy," or as a means of living in the sense that creates or furthers a philosophic system—that is another matter. And if we subjected Stevens' poetry to that test, it would be less firm than Alexander Pope's magnificent patchwork of theology, aphorisms, and ideas which came to the surface of his memorable poem, *An Essay on Man*.

It is to be hoped that these remarks do not retard an enjoy-

---

[1] "Sad Strains of a Gay Waltz" from *Ideas of Order*, by permission of Alfred A. Knopf, Inc. Copyright 1935, 1936, by Wallace Stevens.

ment of Wallace Stevens' poetry. The fact that Wallace Stevens' poetry contained critical observations of the thoroughly American, pragmatic world which surrounded it should not have occasioned much surprise; but a thinking poet (and for this we may be grateful) does not necessarily become transformed into a philosopher. When Wallace Stevens' verse speaks charmingly of angels and of rabbins and "the flat historic scale," it does so in a manner that does not anticipate a supplementary volume to Professor Whitehead's study of *Process and Reality*. One should be happy to read the half-dozen volumes of his verse as though their author were a poet of heightened sensibility who possessed an appreciation of the comedy which existed and still exists in a civilized milieu.

In "The Pleasures of Merely Circulating" [2] one assumes Stevens was not above enjoying one of his own jokes, and in its final stanza we hear the strains of an imperfectly tuned hurdy-gurdy:

> Mrs. Anderson's Swedish baby
> Might well have been German or Spanish,
> Yet that things go round and again go round
> Has rather a classical sound.

In his lighter verses, and in an order of descending values, one would like to find fewer of Wallace Stevens' "Hurroos" and "da da doos" which are harmless expletives, but they create an atmosphere that is a shade too consciously *chi-chi* and they cross the invisible border line between seeming "smart" and fashionably attired into an area of minor verse which has a knowing air and yet is coy. But these lapses in taste do not seriously distract the reader's attention from the more enduring qualities of Wallace Stevens' wit.

3

In his six books of verse, the two *Harmoniums* (1923 and 1931), *Ideas of Order* (1936), *The Man with the Blue Guitar* (1937), *Parts of a World* (1942) and *Notes Toward a Supreme Fiction* (1942), there are many fine pieces and at least a dozen

[2] From *Ideas of Order*, by permission of Alfred A. Knopf, Inc. Copyright 1935, 1936 by Wallace Stevens.

excellent poems. If they have not been appreciated by the general public, it is because a number of them were "studio pieces," which is not to say that they were composed within an "Ivory Tower," but that their speech, as in *The Man with the Blue Guitar,* approximated studio "shop talk," the speech of poets who are concerned with problems of verbal expression, of its relationship to subjective being or fantasy, and its larger relationship to the world outside—which does not care whether the guitar is blue or green or red, and if the public hears its music it is either pleased or dissatisfied. But beyond these ruminations, what is that element of delight that reawakens the eye and ear in the best of Wallace Stevens' poetry, that rewards even the most indifferent reader of verse who happens to glance through or down the table of contents that lists the titles of his poems? One source of freshness and of delight is that Stevens' wit has been derived from what seems to be a careful and highly selective reading of French poetry from Baudelaire to Laforgue and Corbière. The oriental images which appear so tastefully presented in Stevens' verses belong to a French origin rather than one that can be traced directly to the King James Version of the Bible, and one associates the texture of their fabric with the imagery of Flaubert's *Salammbô*. If, as Marianne Moore has remarked in her suggestion that a relationship exists between T. S. Eliot and Stevens, that we had "better say each has influenced the other," certainly Stevens has drawn more from his readings among the Symbolists than Eliot has. And indeed Stevens seems to have adapted the poetry of his French masters into English with something of the same felicity, the same independence, the same ease with which British poets of the early seventeenth century, including Robert Herrick, adapted the love elegies of Ovid to their own means of expression. That was why Stevens' Peter Quince saw his Susanna in the reflected light of a mirror whose frame might well have been designed by Aubrey Beardsley, rather than a figure whose beauty stood against a darkened background of a seventeenth-century text (and a moral one) of the Old Testament:

> Anon, their lamps' uplifted flame
> Revealed Susanna and her shame.

And then, the simpering Byzantines
Fled, with a noise like tambourines.[3]

How closely Stevens followed his French masters and then re-created them with a distinction quite his own is illustrated in his:

THE WORMS AT HEAVEN'S GATE [4]

Out of the tomb, we bring Badroulbadour,
Within our bellies, we her chariot.
Here is an eye. And here are, one by one,
The lashes of that eye and its white lid.
Here is the cheek on which that lid declined,
And, finger after finger, here, the hand,
The genius of that cheek. Here are the lips,
The bundle of the body and the feet.

.   .   .   .   .   .

Out of the tomb we bring Badroulbadour.

There had been nothing quite like this in American poetry of the nineteenth century that stemmed from a British heritage; but it would have been familiar enough to any cultivated resident of Paris who had read his Baudelaire and his Rimbaud and his Laforgue, and who was calmly awaiting the turn of the old century into the twentieth.

The linear grace of "Last Looks at the Lilacs" [5] is not unlike the grace that Whistler learned in his observation of Japanese prints; and the drawing under the impressionistic strokes of the brush is quite as firm:

And say how it comes that you see
Nothing but trash and that you no longer feel
Her body quivering in the Floréal

Toward the cool night and its fantastic star,
Prime paramour and belted paragon,
Well-booted, rugged, arrogantly male,
Patron and imager of the gold Don John,
Who will embrace her before summer comes.

[3] "Peter Quince at the Clavier," from *Harmonium*, by permission of Alfred A. Knopf, Inc. Copyright 1923 by Alfred A. Knopf, Inc.
[4] From *Harmonium*, by permission of Alfred A. Knopf, Inc. Copyright 1923, 1931 by Alfred A. Knopf, Inc.
[5] *Ibid.*

Two examples, as well as two aspects, of Stevens' characteristic style may be found in the next to the last section, "A Thought Revolved," in *The Man with the Blue Guitar;* the first illustrates Stevens' wit as it reburnishes the ancient surfaces of Plato's world of ideas, and it is perhaps the best brief example of Stevens' tendency to ramble at large among generalities; the second is a far better poem—its rhetoric is magnificently sustained, its images are directly presented, yet none takes precedence above the other, the poem is self-contained, and one feels that all praise of it becomes gratuitous:

MYSTIC GARDEN & MIDDLING BEAST [6]

The poet striding among the cigar stores,
Ryan's lunch, hatters, insurance and medicines,
Denies that abstraction is a vice except
To the fatuous. These are his infernal walls,
A space of stone, of inexplicable base
And peaks outsoaring possible adjectives.
One man, the idea of man, that is the space,
The true abstract in which he promenades.
The era of the idea of man, the cloak
And speech of Virgil dropped, that's where he walks,
That's where his hymns come crowding, hero-hymns,
Chorals for mountain voices and the moral chant,
Happy rather than holy but happy-high,
Day hymns instead of constellated rhymes,
Hymns of the struggle of the idea of god
And the idea of man, the mystic garden and
The middling beast, the garden of paradise
And he that created the garden and peopled it.

For the most part, this' is fine studio conversation; it is adroit, and in American poetry it is refreshingly singular; and it recalls something of the atmosphere that Mallarmé created on those evenings when he allowed younger writers to sit at his feet in deference to what he had to say—but it remains a conversation to be understood by the aspiring artist or the young literary critic.

[6] From *The Man with the Blue Guitar,* by permission of Alfred A. Knopf, Inc. Copyright 1935, 1936 by Wallace Stevens.

In the following poem the speech is no less characteristic but the studio seems happily forgotten:

ROMANESQUE AFFABULATION [7]

He sought an earthly leader who could stand
Without panache, without cockade,
Son only of man and sun of men,
The outer captain, the inner saint,

The pine, the pillar and the priest,
The voice, the book, the hidden well,
The faster's feast and heavy-fruited star,
The father, the beater of the rigid drums,

He that at midnight touches the guitar,
The solitude, the barrier, the Pole
In Paris, celui qui chante et pleure,
Winter devising summer in its breast,

Summer assaulted, thundering, illumed,
Shelter yet thrower of the summer spear,
With all his attributes no god but man
Of men whose heaven is in themselves,

Or else whose hell, foamed with their blood
And the long echo of their dying cry,
A fate intoned, a death before they die,
The race that sings and weeps and knows not why.

It should be said that "celui qui chante et pleure"—the one who sings and weeps—was at once a more direct statement and one of broader human relevance than Stevens' "poet . . . among cigar stores," and the same fortunate phrasing was to be found in his "To the One of Fictive Music," which has been so frequently quoted by anthologists. A word should be said concerning two versions of Stevens' "Sunday Morning"—the first of which appeared in *Poetry* in 1915 and the second in his *Harmonium* of 1923; the second is a poem of eight stanzas, the first is one of five—and the rearrangement of the order in which the stanzas followed one another produced two totally different aspects of

[7] From *The Man with the Blue Guitar*, by permission of Alfred A. Knopf, Inc. Copyright 1935, 1936 by Wallace Stevens.

the scene. Even today the first version seems to end on a more decisive note, and its last four lines seem to enclose the entire poem.

> They shall know well the heavenly fellowship
> Of men that perish and of summer morn.
> And whence they came and whither they shall go
> The dew upon their feet shall manifest.[8]

In many of Stevens' poems there was a tendency to place the poem itself within a frame of editorial commentary, which was advanced, so one believes, for the sake of logical clarity—but one also feels that Stevens' effort toward logical consistency is oftener than not an afterthought, that he has not been content to let the poem stand for its own sake, and that after writing it he has tried to make it serve a general theme that may or may not have been related to the poem. In his *Notes Toward a Supreme Fiction* (1942) Stevens continued the speculations that began with "To the One of Fictive Music" and extended through *The Man with the Blue Guitar* and *Parts of a World*. In this volume and not unlike MacLeish and William Carlos Williams, Stevens paid his respects to the *terza rima;* and in one poem if one drops the opening and closing stanzas which seem to surround it almost fortuitously with what he himself would call an "anti-poetic" apology for its being, a poem of singular beauty and richness comes to light.

> I am the spouse. She took her necklace off
> And laid it in the sand. As I am, I am
> The spouse. She opened her stone-studded belt.
>
> I am the spouse, divested of bright gold,
> The spouse beyond emerald or amethyst,
> Beyond the burning body that I bear.
>
> I am the woman stripped more nakedly
> Than nakedness, standing before an inflexible
> Order, saying I am the contemplated spouse.
>
> Speak to me that, which spoken, will array me
> In its own only precious ornament.
> Set on me the spirit's diamond coronal.

[8] "Sunday Morning," by permission of *Poetry* Magazine, Vol. VII, 1915.

Clothe me entire in the final filament,
So that I tremble with such love so known
And myself am precious for your perfecting.[9]

It was gratuitous for Stevens to repeat (as he has done) that
art is analogous to life—and on occasion, "life [as Oscar Wilde
phrased it] is an imitation of art." Stevens' best poems have fully
demonstrated both aspects of that now somewhat elderly and
bearded paradox.

Wallace Stevens was born in Reading, Pennsylvania, in 1879;
he was educated at Harvard and the New York Law School, and
since 1934 he has been vice-president of the Hartford Accident
and Indemnity Company. Like Marianne Moore's, his relationship to "public life" is one of admirable reticence and dignity.
His poetry received the Helen Haire Levinson Prize from *Poetry*
in 1920, and in 1936 *The Nation's* poetry award, and in December, 1940, *The Harvard Advocate* devoted an entire issue to a
discussion of Stevens' verse. If in pre-First World War London
Ezra Pound visibly emulated Whistler's mannerisms, Stevens in
a later decade continued, and perhaps has endowed with greater
endurance in literary forms, those qualities of elegance and wit
which have been discerned in Whistler's canvases, and as one
pays the tribute of appreciation to Whistler's painting and
Stevens' poetry, it is true that the

. . . mind perceives the force behind the moment,
The mind is smaller than the eye.[10]

[9] "It Must Be Abstract" from *Notes Toward a Supreme Fiction,* by permission of the Cummington Press and Wallace Stevens.
[10] "A Fish-Scale Sunrise" from *Ideas of Order.* By permission of Alfred A.
Knopf, Inc. Copyright 1935, 1936 by Wallace Stevens.

THREE POETS OF BRATTLE STREET:
E. E. CUMMINGS, JOHN WHEELWRIGHT,
DUDLEY FITTS

When in 1923 E. E. Cummings' first book of poems, *Tulips and Chimneys*, appeared, it gained almost overnight an "esoteric" reputation. Its typographical innovations, its lower-case "i's," its uses of parentheses, its "thys" and "thous" created an atmosphere that critics viewed as seeming to be "revolutionary," subjective or merely willful, "private," and very gay. It was also clear that the poems were written by the same hand and by the same poetic intelligence that gave life and energy and wit to a short, autobiographical narrative of the First World War, *The Enormous Room* (1922). However far E. E. Cummings traveled (which was substantiated by a second autobiographical narrative of a trip to Soviet Russia, *Eimi*, published in 1933), and he has lived in New York for nearly twenty years, it was certain that everything he wrote retained its "Harvard accent." And not unlike Amy Lowell's verse and prose, Cummings' poetry carried Cambridge, Massachusetts, with it wherever it went:

> my uncle Ed
> that's
> dead from the neck
>
> up is led all over
> Brattle Street by a castrated pup.[1]

For E. E. Cummings, the son of Edward Cummings (who had taught English at Harvard and who was minister of the Old South Church in Boston), was born in Cambridge in 1894.

[1] #140 from *Collected Poems,* published by Harcourt, Brace and Company. Copyright, 1923, 1925, 1931, 1935, 1938, by E. E. Cummings.

To some readers, Cummings' lighter verses may have seemed
to be a virtual deflowering of New England; actually they extended the life of an area that had its precincts marked by the
proximity of Boston's State House, Harvard University, the
Charles River, the Field of Lexington and Concord's bridge.
Even Cummings' typographical devices (with their grammatical
and private jokes) could have existed only within a world in
which academic rules and standards of personal conduct were
thoroughly established. No American poet of the twentieth century has ever shown so much implied respect for the conventions
of his milieu through conscious blasphemy as E. E. Cummings.
If Cummings' verse seemed "revolutionary" and radical (which
it was in the sense that its wit was concerned with the roots of
syntax and grammar) it was because its life was and still is so
completely surrounded by conventions:

> the first president to be loved by his
> bitterest enemies" is dead
>
> the only man woman or child who wrote
> a simple declarative sentence with seven grammatical
> errors "is dead"
> beautiful Warren Gamaliel Harding
> "is" dead
> he's
> "dead"
> if he wouldn't have eaten them Yapanese Craps
>
> somebody might hardly never not have been unsorry, perhaps [2]

If one does not take for granted the existence of ritual and
the establishment of laws, which may be theological or legal or
grammatical, all blasphemy, and all breaking of the law, becomes a meaningless exercise. This is a truism (and a convention) that has been clearly recognized and advanced in the
majority of E. E. Cummings' lighter verses; and in his blasphemy
Cummings created a world through which a perennially young,
handsome, "alive," "becoming" poet moved. The personal convention that Cummings established within a larger area had

[2] #200 from *Collected Poems*, published by Harcourt, Brace and Company.
Copyright, 1923, 1925, 1931, 1935, 1938, by E. E. Cummings.

338 *A History of American Poetry*

certain well-cut boundaries not unlike those that are indicated by the colors of blue, pink, and green on a schoolroom map. One was that of the Harvard graduate who kept alive the friendly rivalry with Yale:

> one thought alone: to do or die
> for God for country and for Yale [3]

Another was a candid distrust of elderly people and of "foreigners." The dislike of the elderly extended from "the Cambridge ladies who live in furnished souls," the bearded figures of nineteenth-century American poets, including "William Cullen Longfellow," and "Henry Wadsworth Bryant" to the entire line of Presidents of the United States from "Wouldwoe Washington" to "Clever Rusefelt." Of "foreigners" the dislike was even more frankly expressed; the French were not praised in *The Enormous Room,* and the Russians were not approved of in *Eimi,* and the "bretish" were also banned from Cummings' young man's (if not Plato's) republic. The positive aspect of the convention was the inviolability of the relationship of one young man to one young woman, "Girlboys may nothing more than boygirls need," and as this relationship took place, all other "girls" and all other "boys," no matter what their names were, or what their pretensions were, or what their worldly positions may have been, dropped to the level of inanimate life—they became "dolls" or mere nouns graced with unflattering, and often enough, unprintable adjectives. In other words, Cummings wrote excellent love lyrics, lyrics which contained all the compliments that a young woman would like to hear, and such compliments also enhanced the figure of a perennially youthful lover who would go to war against any and all of the conventions that were outside of or that threatened to impede or to divert the course of courtly love.

What Cummings' verse presented at its center was a revitalized image of the "romantic traditionist" of whom we have spoken in an earlier chapter; and theoretically his verse was not far removed from the kind of verse his predecessors wrote. In prac-

---

[3] #149 from *Collected Poems,* published by Harcourt, Brace and Company. Copyright, 1923, 1925, 1931, 1935, 1938, by E. E. Cummings.

tice, however, his poetry was far more unified than theirs; its speech was fresher and was addressed directly to a generation that had shared the diversions and excitements of F. Scott Fitzgerald's "Jazz Age." It was a generation that held great, and largely sentimental, regard for the kind of youthful experience it had enjoyed in Paris, and which accepted as its "true confession" Ernest Hemingway's novel, *The Sun Also Rises* (1926). The girls and young women in Cummings' second book of poems, *&* (1925), are drawn from the same models who sat for Hemingway's *The Sun Also Rises* and John Dos Passos' *1919:*

> my girl's tall with hard long eyes
> as she stands, with her long hard hands keeping
> silence on her dress, good for sleeping
> is her long hard body filled with surprise
> like a white shocking wire, when she smiles
> a hard long smile it sometimes makes
> gaily go clean through me tickling aches,
> and the weak noise of her eyes easily files
> my impatience to an edge—my girl's tall
> and taut, with thin legs just like a vine
> that's spent all of its life on a garden-wall,
> and is going to die. When we grimly go to bed
> with these legs she begins to heave and twine
> about me, and to kiss my face and head.[4]

The poem was, properly enough, a sonnet, freshly written and with full respect paid to traditional form. And though it is by no means the best of Cummings' many sonnets it illustrates his command of formal excellence within an established tradition of lyric verse as well as his ability to portray the kind of girl, and indeed the heroine, who engaged the attention of his contemporaries. One might go on to say that the young women of Hemingway's early stories and of Dos Passos' novels were mindless, and were articulate only when they were performing their ultimate and primary functions within the embraces of their lovers. Not without self-conscious—and it must be admitted boyish—cruelty, but with greater wit, Cummings presented a Hemingway heroine in Effie:

[4] #66 from *Collected Poems*, published by Harcourt, Brace and Company. Copyright, 1923, 1925, 1931, 1935, 1938, by E. E. Cummings.

cross the threshold have no dread
lift the sheet back in this way.
here is little Effie's head
whose brains are made of gingerbread [5]

But if Cummings' verse could show discourtesy to more than several young women of its day, its recurrent theme remained that of courtly love:

All in green went my love riding
on a great horse of gold
into the silver dawn.

four lean hounds crouched low and smiling
the merry deer ran before.

Fleeter be they than dappled dreams
the swift sweet deer
the red rare deer.

Four red roebuck at a white water
the cruel bugle sang before.

Horn at hip went my love riding
riding the echo down
into the silver dawn.

four lean hounds crouched low and smiling
the level meadows ran before.

Softer be they than slippered sleep
the lean lithe deer
the fleet flown deer.

Four fleet does at a gold valley
the famished arrow sang before.

Bow at belt went my love riding
riding the mountain down
into the silver dawn.

four lean hounds crouched low and smiling
the sheer peaks ran before.

[5] #58 from *Collected Poems*, published by Harcourt, Brace and Company. Copyright, 1923, 1925, 1931, 1935, 1938, by E. E. Cummings.

Paler be they than daunting death
the sleek slim deer
the tall tense deer.

Four tall stags at a green mountain
the lucky hunter sang before.

All in green went my love riding
on a great horse of gold
into the silver dawn.

four lean hounds crouched low and smiling
my heart fell dead before.[6]

The lyrical accomplishment here is such that one can compare
it only with Ezra Pound's fine and memorable adaptations from
the Provençal poets and from Cavalcanti. And there has always
been a more abiding temperamental affinity between Pound's
lyricism and that of Cummings than there has ever been between the *Cantos* of Ezra Pound and the later poetry of T. S.
Eliot.

The theme was crossed by still another sonnet that was a farewell to Paris of the 1920's and it has an alcoholic, barrel-organ
note that echoes through its lines:

goodby Betty, don't remember me
pencil your eyes dear and have a good time
with the tall tight boys at Tabari'
s,keep your teeth snowy, stick to beer and lime,
wear dark, and where your meeting breasts are round
have roses darling, it's all i ask of you—
but that when light fails and this sweet profound
Paris moves with lovers, two and two
bound for themselves, when passionately dusk
brings softly down the perfume of the world . . .[7]

The poem says very nearly everything that many American
novelists of the period had to say, and it has the advantage of
saying it with greater art and in fewer words. It is avowedly and

[6] #6 from *Collected Poems*, published by Harcourt, Brace and Company.
Copyright, 1923, 1925, 1931, 1935, 1938, by E. E. Cummings.
[7] #35 from *Collected Poems*, published by Harcourt, Brace and Company.
Copyright, 1923, 1925, 1931, 1935, 1938, by E. E. Cummings.

shamelessly sentimental, but one is certain that the character
who speaks it is the uninhibited and gifted brother of one who
had

> one thought alone: to do or die
> for God for country and for Yale
>
> above his blond determined head
> the sacred flag of truth unfurled,
> in the bright heyday of his youth
> the upper class American
>
> unsullied stands, before the world: [8]

In another poem the theme of courtly love continued with

> you shall above all things be glad and young.
> For if you're young, whatever life you wear
>
> it will become you; and if you are glad
> whatever's living will yourself become.
> Girlboys may nothing more than boygirls need:
> i can entirely her only love
>
> whose any mystery makes every man's
> flesh put space on; and his mind take off time
>
> that you should ever think, may god forbid
> and (in his mercy) your true lover spare:
> for that way knowledge lies, the foetal grave
> called progress, and negation's dead undoom.
>
> I'd rather learn from one bird how to sing
> than teach ten thousand stars how not to dance [9]

Any attempt to translate this poem into prose or into words
that are other than its own soon approaches the danger of becoming ridiculous; but among the more important things that
the poem had to say was its implied compliment to a lady whose
physical attraction and beauty were in her lover's eyes so great
that they transcended all thought of thinking—and the compliment was paid in the manner of a sixteenth-century lyricist. The

[8] #149 from *Collected Poems*, published by Harcourt, Brace and Company.
Copyright, 1923, 1925, 1931, 1935, 1938, by E. E. Cummings.
[9] #315 from *Collected Poems*, published by Harcourt, Brace and Company.
Copyright, 1923, 1925, 1931, 1935, 1938, by E. E. Cummings.

poem is not particularly subtle, but it is properly witty, and if not overly complex (for any girl can feel its implications), it is also properly and, in a courtly sense, elaborate. A lighter phrasing of the same compliment may be found in

> mr youse needn't be so spry
> concernin questions arty
>
> each has his tastes but as for i
> i likes a certain party
>
> gimme the he-man's solid bliss
> for youse ideas i'll match youse
>
> a pretty girl who naked is
> is worth a million statues [10]

The speech of the poem has its proper Harvard twang as it imitates in broad burlesque the speech of the American "comic strip"; the words are to be recited in a would-be "tough-boy" manner from the left side of the mouth, and the compliment is paid with all the appropriate gestures—and the charm—of a well-bred undergraduate.

In still another poem Cummings wrote:

> my sweet old etcetera
> aunt lucy during the recent
>
> war could and what
> is more did tell you just
> what everybody was fighting
>
> for
>   .   .   .   .   .
>   my
> self etcetera lay quietly
>   .   .   .   .   .
>
> (dreaming,
> et
>   cetera, of
> Your smile
> eyes knees and of your Etcetera) [11]

---

[10] #133 from *Collected Poems*, published by Harcourt, Brace and Company. Copyright, 1923, 1925, 1931, 1935, 1938, by E. E. Cummings.
[11] #148 from *Collected Poems*, published by Harcourt, Brace and Company. Copyright, 1923, 1925, 1931, 1935, 1938, by E. E. Cummings.

Which seemed to be a brilliant adaptation into Harvard English of John Wilmot's "Et Cætera":

> Yet hugg'd me close, and, with a Sigh, did say,
> Once more, my Dear, once more, Et Cætera.[12]

In this vein Cummings' poetry has never found a happier expression than in his *1 × 1* (1944); and such lyricism is always rare in any period:

> "sweet spring is your
> time is my time is our
> time for springtime is lovetime
> and viva sweet love"
>
> (all the merry little birds are
> flying in the floating in the
> very spirit singing in
> are winging in the blossoming)
>
> lovers go and lovers come
> awandering awondering
> but any two are perfectly
> alone there's nobody else alive
>
> (such a sky and such a sun
> i never knew and neither did you
> and everybody never breathed
> quite so many kinds of yes)
>
> not a tree can count his leaves
> each herself by opening
> but shining who by thousands mean
> only one amazing thing
>
> (secretly adoring shyly
> tiny winging darting floating
> merry in the blossoming
> always joyful selves are singing)
>
> "sweet spring is your
> time is my time is our
> time for springtime is lovetime
> and viva sweet love" [13]

[12] "Et Cætera, A Song" from *The Poetical Works of John Wilmot, Earl of Rochester,* ed. by Quilter Johns, Haworth Press, London.

[13] From *1 × 1*, published by Henry Holt & Company. Copyright, 1944, by E. E. Cummings.

All these were written (so it seems) in the same spirit that graced the songs and speeches of the *commedia dell' arte,* which traveled up from Italy in the sixteenth century to entertain the peoples of the rest of Europe. And it has been said that the *commedia dell' arte* (and in this respect its relationship to Cummings' poetry is pertinent) was an ancestor of the American stock-company burlesque show. The characters who speak or are referred to in Cummings' verses might well have been reciting the traditional roles that the *commedia dell' arte* provided four centuries ago; and the devices that the verses themselves employ, the almost manual skill of transposed words, phrases, and of rhymes, have the same quality that we enjoy when we witness a performance of Charles Chaplin in his early films or one given by Robert Edward (Bobby) Clark in a musical revue. And Cummings has always been careful never to permit the central figure of his young lover to slip into the unwitting fatuousness of middle age.

2

When John Donne wrote

For Godsake hold your tongue, and let me love [14]

he expressed that feeling of impatience that Cummings betrayed so often against the world (which included highly advertised products, advertising slogans, politics, and wars) and which existed outside the being of a youthful lover and his lady. It was from this center that the great majority of his critical remarks were addressed. The terms that Cummings used were obviously those of burlesque rather than satire, for satire has a moral aspect that seldom entered Cummings' verse, and for a definition of it we need go no further than a statement that James Laver made in a new edition of Charles Churchill's *Poems* [15] (1933):

. . . as the nineteenth century advanced the satirical element in English poetry grew smaller and smaller. It has not yet recovered its place therein, for the satirist needs both irreverence and strong moral con-

[14] "The Canonization" from *The Poems of John Donne,* published by Oxford University Press.
[15] Edited by John Laver, published by Viking Press.

viction, and the Victorian age had the second without the first, while the modern period has the first without the second.

The world of Cummings' conventions is too small to admit the presence of a complete moral order, but it has within it the clear (and one almost says courageous) recognition that a Christian faith exists in twentieth-century America. The best expression of that truth may be found in Cummings' elegy [16] written in memory of his father, and in scattered references in several of his poems—but Cummings' irreverence always had a wider application than his blasphemy.

As in the reading of Wallace Stevens' poetry, so in reading E. E. Cummings' lighter verses, a distinction should be made between the two words, "intellect" and "intelligence"; Cummings' verse has invention and poetic intelligence and wit, but the central figure within it, or its hero, who seems to speak the lines of Cummings' love songs, is always presented as a violent anti-intellectual: "Hearts being sick, Minds nothing can," it says—and there, as far as the verse is concerned, the matter ends. Some few of Cummings' critics, and in particular R. P. Blackmur in his book, *The Double Agent* (1935), were evidently in no mood to enjoy a revival of the *commedia dell' arte* at a stone's throw from Boston Common, and it should be admitted that there are moments when Cummings' verses are all too coy and arch.

In the same spirit in which Cummings wrote his poetry—and with the same themes presented within it and with much of the same art—he wrote a play, *Him* (1927), which was successfully produced at the Provincetown Theatre in New York in the late 1920's. This was followed by a beautifully composed ballet (a burlesque of *Uncle Tom's Cabin*), *Tom,* in 1935.

The entire question of Cummings' maturity in the writing of his poetry has been and still remains a private matter. In the light of Cummings' accomplishments and in the recognition of the boundaries or limits that they have circumscribed, it is very nearly an impertinence for anyone to tell him to "grow up," for one must not forget that he is one of the finest lyric poets

[16] #34 *50 Poems* by E. E. Cummings, Duell, Sloan and Pearce.

of all time. Some eight years after its publication in 1938, Cummings' *Collected Poems* has a popularity that could almost be described in terms of being a subterranean "best-seller"—its appeal to younger readers of poetry (as well as to those who "stay young") is of a kind that looks as though it would endure for many years to come; its lyrical graces and its inventive turns of wit are of an order that transcend its moments of boyish cruelty and juvenile preoccupations.

3

In American poetry of a latter-day New England and in a Boston that Amy Lowell and E. E. Cummings knew, no picture of the time and place can be made complete without reading the strictly occasional poetry of John Brooks Wheelwright. Wheelwright was born in Milton, Massachusetts, in 1897, the son of Edmund Wheelwright, an architect, and was a descendant of the Reverend John Wheelwright, who was one of the founders of Wells, Maine, and of Exeter, New Hampshire. He was educated at the Fay School at Southboro and at St. George's School, Newport, Rhode Island, and at Harvard College from which he received his bachelor's degree in 1920. He followed his father's interest in architecture, and after he left Harvard he spent a year and a half in Florence, Italy, and then returned to Boston to further his study in architectural design at the Massachusetts Institute of Technology. Poetry, politics of a radical left persuasion, architecture, and the Episcopalian Church were at the centers of his faith and life—and his respects were paid to all four, which he seemed to regard as "activities" in much the same sense that Amy Lowell discovered her avocations in the writing of vers libre and accepting engagements to lecture on it from public platforms. Like Amy Lowell, Wheelwright also possessed a "flair" for showmanship and the ability to create a personal legend. It was rumored that he mounted a soapbox one evening in a dinner jacket with a red carnation in the buttonhole of its lapel to lecture on socialism in Boston Common. And during the early 1930's it was also said that he walked down Beacon Street in Boston with signboards slung across his shoulders, which bore the legend in large letters, front and back: FREE TROTSKY.

But behind the legend which he so devotedly inspired was a slender figure in ill-fitting "American business suits" of clothes, who had a fine head with a nearly "hawklike" nose, thin lips, and slightly slanted, narrowed eyes—and those who saw him regretted that an accident of time (a disparity of over an hundred years) precluded his sitting for a portrait by Charles Willson Peale. For John Wheelwright in appearance and manner was a pre-Revolutionary Bostonian of radical convictions; and the quality of his wit in conversation as well as in letters that he wrote to friends was of an eighteenth-century order. His concern for the "class struggle" of which there was so much talk among younger writers of the 1930's was seriously motivated, but it also had much of the same ardor and temper that James Boswell revealed in his concern for the affairs of Corsica; in mind and heart its motives were disinterested, and not without prophetic insight, yet all its "dialectical materialism" remained untouched by matters of human or physical reality.

Perhaps his more immediate ancestors can be found in the remains that have been left us of George Cabot Lodge's poetry and of Trumbull Stickney's, and the precedent is not one of kind (for Wheelwright's verse had totally different sources and intentions) but in the diversions of its energy to ideas and to distinctly "extrapoetic" activities. As Stickney's energies had been diverted to scholarship, and Lodge's to an eager reading of Schopenhauer, in like manner Wheelwright's energies were divided between reading Trotsky's *Literature and Revolution* and the writing of a *Critical History of Architecture in the United States*, a work that was left unfinished at the time of his death. His three books of verse, *Rock and Shell* (1933), *Mirrors of Venus* (1938), and *Political Self-Portrait* (1940), were not the products of a so-called "minor" poetic intelligence and imagination, but they were deeply fractured by divergent impulses—and the wonder was that Wheelwright found the time to write poetry at all. Very nearly all of Wheelwright's verses lacked the presence and the unforced control of a "melodic ear," and unlike Marianne Moore, he had yet to find a "light rhyme" or its equivalent with which to define his particular art of writing verse. Some of his effects were "experimental" and inventive, others seem to have been studiously premeditated, still others had an air of seeming accidental, and the great majority were dominated by a prose rhythm that had yet to achieve its maturity. But at the center of the verse where a number of Wheelwright's epigrams remained half-formed and half-concealed, a personality that had created its own speech emerged: the speech was often critical and it welcomed controversy, and it was persistent in its effort to write poetry with ideas and not with words:

> Marble lyres mark
>   Where minor singers slumber,
> And glistering night weeps
> On willows above their graves;
> But a wordless wind sweeps
>   Over the solid dark
> As over Sappho's waves
>   Of keen thinkers without number.
> The weakling who has known
>   A small grief has his meekness.
> They who can teach and show
>   Know words he never names
> Who sweeps the sobbing bow,
>   Whom Pity quickly claims.
> Pity the strong alone
>   Who seldom show their weakness,
> Whose hearts break with no sign
>   But withered lips and tresses,
> Who know, if sounding cord
>   To all their thought were given,
> If they trod out the wine
>   Longed for, from memory's presses,—
> The dissonances, poured
>   Would sour their own heaven.[17]

These lines might well be read as Wheelwright's antistrophe to E. E. Cummings' love songs which so strenuously and with so lyrical an art denied the uses of the intellect. But like Cum-

---

[17] "Mossy Marbles" from *Rock and Shell*, by permission of Bruce Humphries, Inc. Copyright, 1933, by John Wheelwright.

mings, Wheelwright was highly skilled in the writing of prepara-
tory-school and Boston slang:

> I remember how I said to Pa
>
> .   .   .   .
>
> how it was my belief how, someday, there would be:
> no thundering El, nor rumbling Sub; no chu-chus; up-chuck alleys [18]

and as Wheelwright wrote it, it was scarcely poetry at all, and
one is fairly certain that Wheelwright did not intend it to be.
His remarks on the ghost of Amy Lowell were of the same nature,
but they had the advantage of seeming to be a colloquy between
two urban New Englanders who viewed one another with not
unkindly but neighborly distrust:

> Our road forked; and she took one tine; and I took the other; and
>   waste-lot Delta ragweed (fenced by granite posts and hickory rails
>   set diamond-wise) widened its wedge between.
> But I turned for "Good-bye" to Amy Lowell, Biggest Traveling One-
>   Man Show since Buffalo Bill caught the Midnight Flyer to contact
>   Mark Twain:
> "One would be inclined, at moments, to doubt the entire death!" I
>   shouted.
> Grinning from ear to ear, she shouted back: "Mr. Brooks, you are per-
>   fectly right;—one would be." [19]

And it was once said of Wheelwright that he interrupted one
of Amy Lowell's public lectures which attempted to explain the
technique of writing vers libre with the question: "Miss Lowell,
how do you write poetry if you haven't got anything to say?" It
was also said that Amy Lowell could not supply a ready answer.

It was in this vein, when he was talking to the ghost of Amy
Lowell or to his distantly removed friends, that Wheelwright's
Bostonian accent took on the air of authority. His best poems,
however, were "Ave Eva" and "Train Ride," and of the first
poem he wrote: "In 'Ave Eva' Yesod appears as the character of
Mother Eve and Malkuth as the character of Satan, whose flesh
is clothed in four colors of the Veil of the Temple . . . azure

---

[18] "A Small Prig in a Big Square" from *Selected Poems*, 1941 (Poet of the
Month), by permission of New Directions.
[19] "Dinner Call" from *Selected Poems*, 1941 (Poet of the Month), by permission of New Directions.

for Air; purple for Water; flaxen for Earth; and scarlet for Fire,—
together with the gooseberries, strawberries, and roses from the
1629 Journal of Pastor Higginson . . ."

Wild strawberries, gooseberries, trampled;
sweet single roots torn; I hoofed to a ground
where a woman sat, weeping over a wounded bird.
"O silent woman, weeping without tears;
"O weeping woman, silent on this ground
"more withered than the barren; may I not help you heal
"the suffering of this wounded bird?" I said.

"But let your hand first mend the axle of this wheel,
"O scarlet-handed, azure-eyed," she answered.
"Let your eyes find the balance of these scales
"fashioned from two of my sons' brain-pans."

"Woman with scale and wheel and wounded bird
"more disconsolate than a child with broken toys;
"first, I beseech you, uncripple this wounded bird
"whose sufferings give to the mute universe
"measure of its own pain." With no reply
the frightened woman, more frightened, for an answer
dropped her frightened eyes to the unanswering
eyes of a third skull between her feet. Then I commanded:

"Get up. There are more skulls hid than the three
"skulls seen. Get going on your business!"

"You flaxen-faced and purple-lipped!" she cried,
"My business is to gather up my strength;
"my purpose is to mend the axle and the hub;
"and my intent, to find the balance of the scale."

"And . . . were the balance trued, were Adam's
"dust, which was your dearest flesh and blood,
"sifted over Abel's hunger-murdered eyes,—
"should the scale tip; my apposite pan
"I would then load with the bones of the warring hordes
"of goodly Abel's brothers, Cain and Seth . . .
"Leave your gray ground, Eve, go along with me."

"Satan," she said, "when my car moves I move.
"And the bird will fly. Its flight will heal its wing.
"I, and my best sons, Cain and Seth, require
"them who wish the bird healed mend my car.

"The bird cannot be healed except by flight.
"And when I move and my car mows the roses,
"let dust and bone and mold slowly close
"Abel's insatiate, unanswering eyes,—
"you azure-eyed, you flaxen-faced, purple-lipped and scarlet-handed!
"The bird will fly. Its flight will heal its wing."

Then I departed as I came, tearing roses
and trampling the gooseberries and strawberries.[20]

The rhetoric of this poem and its imaginative insight are of a quality that owe their strength to the heritage that produced a Reverend John Wheelwright as well as a John Brooks Wheelwright of a latter-day Boston. The colloquy between Satan and Eve was written in terms of that heritage, and it was a conversation that, if Hawthorne could have overheard it, he would have understood. In every respect this poem was immeasurably better than any of the so-called "socially conscious" poems that Wheelwright wrote. And in Wheelwright's "Train Ride" there is a particularly felicitous passage in the last nine lines. The line in italics was "a slogan," so Wheelwright wrote, "of the elder Liebknecht," but the lines also deserve to be read for their felicity of diction and for their ability to create the presence of an historical imagination at work within them:

> All Poetry to this not-to-be-looked-upon sun
> of Passion is the moon's cupped light; all
> Politics to this moon, a moon's reflected
> cupped light, like the moon of Rome, after
> the deep wells of Grecian light sank low;
> *always the enemy is the foe at home.*
> But these three are friends whose arms twine
> without words; as, in a still air,
> the great grove leans to wind, past and to come.[21]

All of Wheelwright's books (with the exception of his posthumously issued *Selected Poems* in a booklet in 1941) were published at his own expense by a small Boston publishing house, and not unlike Vachel Lindsay in an earlier generation, Wheel-

[20] "Ave Eva" from *Selected Poems*, 1941 (Poet of the Month), by permission of New Directions.
[21] "Train Ride" from *Selected Poems*, 1941 (Poet of the Month), by permission of New Directions.

wright distributed pamphlets of *Masque with Clowns*, "poems for a dime," and read his verse aloud before variegated groups of people: "working-class" groups and at the Boston Adult Education Center, Harvard and Tufts Colleges, and at meetings of the New England Poetry Society.

On Monday, September 16, 1940, the New York *Times* contained the following notice of Wheelwright's death:

Special to THE NEW YORK TIMES

BOSTON, Sept. 15.—John B. Wheelwright, 43, a poet of this city, was fatally injured early today by an automobile in the Back Bay. He died on the way to a hospital.

The driver, John A. Lewis, 36, of Bristol, R. I., was arrested later on a charge of drunkenness.

Wheelwright's mature life as a poet had just begun and his death seemed to have been caused by an unusually stupid and certainly unforeseen accident. In verse (and there were others) the best tribute to Wheelwright's memory was Robert Fitzgerald's "Portrait" in his volume of poems *A Wreath for the Sea* [22] (1943):

To place the precisely slippered toes
With meditation on each stair;
To hold his lurking counterpose
Of anger, smiling to play fair;

To balance with his glittering sea-
Eyes the fragility of bone,
Slender and gaunt as a winter tree—
Studied all grace, and so his own.

To be cat-eyed, slit-eyed, to catch
Astringent nets of namby creatures,
That with articulate despatch
He skewered with their pamby teachers;

To note in the cold Boston bay
The flouncing light on the clean arches;
To know with exact hate the way
A faking builder stuffs and starches;

[22] Arrow Editions, by permission of New Directions.

To stand amid his Where and Whence
With verse in never-ending bout,
To figure some unworldly sense
And keep the melodic nonsense out;

To write a sterner myth than Tate's
Or that of Cummings or of Crane—
Owned and disowned the Concord gates
And Cousin Brooks' sweet terrain.

But saw the heads of death that rode
Within each scoundrel's limousine,
Grinning at hunger on the road
To incorporate the class machine;

And saw the tower of the poor,
Lonely, ignoble, noisy, blind,
With that great Cross upon the tower.
Fantasy drove him out of mind.

Yet upward in LaFarge's flame
His saviour twisted, and does still;
The true line comes as once it came
To masculine Homer's steady will;

Control and Charity of the just,
And their wild laughter flung at night,
Commemorate his death, his dust,
His gaiety. John Wheelwright.

4

A near contemporary of Wheelwright at Harvard, who was six
years younger than he and a native of Boston, who as a boy had
been taught to be quick and learned in both Latin and Greek,
was Dudley Fitts. The poet in Fitts was more often than not
concealed behind his adaptations into English from the Greek
and Latin, which he seemed to carry before him as a shield—to
protect, perhaps, and to keep alive the sensibility and wit which
never failed to delight the sensitive reader of poetry. Fitts's sensibility in poetry was not one of possessing a "melodic ear" but
rather one of tonal propriety and grace; his verse, whether it was
written in imitation of the ancients as in his *One Hundred Poems*

from the Palatine Anthology (1938) or in a collection of forty-
nine *More Poems from the Palatine Anthology* (1941), or in a
selection of his own *Poems 1929-1936* (1937) moved with formal
elegance within the traditions that inspired it. Like Wheelwright's and Cummings', Fitts's language was Boston English;
some few of its external mannerisms had, let us say, acquired
certain "influences" from the Ezra Pound of *Hugh Selwyn
Mauberley* and *Homage to Sextus Propertius* as well as T. S.
Eliot's *The Waste Land*—but these were superficial accretions
and they are not to be confused with the true and distinct qualities of wit that Fitts possessed. Fitts's imitation of Lucilius with
its new title, "A Valentine for a Lady," illustrates how much
advice Fitts may have taken in reading Pound and how distinctly he remained his own master, as it were, on New England
soil:

> Darling, at the Beautician's you buy
> Your [a] hair
>   [b] complexion
>   [c] lips
>   [d] dimples, &
>   [e] teeth.
> For a like amount you could just as well buy a face.[23]

The classical joke was brilliantly refreshed; and the economy
of classical phrasing was retained. In a Commentary at the end
of his *One Hundred Poems from the Palatine Anthology*[24] he
remarked (and his position was counter to that of "the Romantic
Traditionists" whom we have discussed in an earlier chapter):

I must confess that I have never been able to understand the praise
generally awarded William Johnson Cory's version of Kallimachos'
famous elegy:

> *They told me, Heraclitus, they told me you were dead.*

Indeed, this particular jingle seems to me to illustrate admirably what
so often happens to a translator when he undertakes one of the epigrams. Possibly it is the fault of the elegiac couplet itself: the dactylic
rhythm is deceptive and beguiling, and the form's extreme concentra-

[23] "A Valentine for a Lady" from *One Hundred Poems from the Palatine
Anthology,* by permission of New Directions and the Author.
    [24] By permission of New Directions and the Author.

tion, suggesting immediately a pair of dainty quatrains or, worse, the neo-Swinburnian canter, very easily results in triviality. Whatever the reason, too many of the English translations are little more than competent *vers de société:* the plangent cadences of the Greek have gone over into something ludicrously reminiscent of a Savoy Opera patter-song. It is significant, too, that this same *reductio ad pistrinam* impairs, though less seriously, the ordinary translations of Horace.

On these remarks only one further observation may be made, and that is that the authors of the "Savoy Operas"—W. S. Gilbert and Sir Arthur Sullivan—probably held the example of Aristophanes in mind, and that in doing so, they effected a double parody, one of reference to their own day and one that amounted to a conscious burlesque of a classical tradition in comic dramatic verse. But Fitts's sensibility and wit were as distinctly of a twentieth-century order as Gilbert's and Sullivan's had been Victorian.

The lightness of Fitts's "Valentine for a Lady" was balanced by his version of Leonidas of Tarentum's "Epitaph for a Sailor": [25]

> These were my end: a fierce down-squall from the east,
> And night, and the waves of Orion's stormy setting:
> And I, Kállaischros, yielded up my life
> Far on the waste of the lonely Libyan sea.
>
> And now I roll with the drifting currents, the prey
> Of fishes:
>   and this gravestone lies
> If it says that it marks the place of my burial.

The clean diction, the sense of classical restraint, the finely balanced periods and rhythms place Fitts's adaptations of the Greek anthology in a world far removed from the far more clumsy, thickly worded, unrhymed verses of Edgar Lee Masters' *Spoon River Anthology.* But of course Fitts retained his proximity to the classical example, while Masters did not—and Fitts had the advantage, which was probably not consciously employed, of being like Cummings in the shadow of what once had been the "little Athens of America," Boston itself. Fitts's verse was well placed, if at times too sparely, within that heritage; in

[25] From *One Hundred Poems from the Palatine Anthology,* by permission of New Directions and the Author.

his own poems Fitts's sensibility to an elegiac spirit and its form
is shown in the last lines of his "Retreat": [26]

> (Shiloh, Malvern Hill: you,
> long after drum and rain, you, shored
> from winter in sleepy death, you, lover
> of Purcell and the warm strings,
>   you beautiful and old.)

Few poets of Fitts's generation have invoked the memories of
the Civil War with greater art, and none with finer delicacy of
feeling and emotional restraint. The same qualities are to be
found in his sonnet, "Fifth Anniversary": [27]

> Now I can not even remember you,
> here at your hearth, drowsing in your chair,
> dreaming you out of silence (old winds renew
> old riddles: wet boughs in the wind).
>   Out there,
> lonely out there, you too—tell me, is your door
> so subtly locked? are your new windows barred?
> is it so cold in your house? is your
> bed, like mine, so loveless now, so hard?
>
> The worlds revolve. Sir in that aftercold
> wandering, drawn by dark wind and star-motion,
> could any love of mine touch you, then old
> dreams were more than dream or dreaming-passion
> to me, frail five-years-dead!
>   who stare away
> (poor Ghost!) the long night and the longer day.

In a lighter vein (one in which it was singularly appropriate
for Fitts to edit *An Anthology of Latin American Poetry* in 1942)
Fitts wrote his "Homage to Rafael Alberti": [28]

> Rafael, in your Cádiz, white against blue quadrate,
> In your District of Angels, Cádiz,
> If there is cadence of wind or sun, bells
> Toll it, record it; and you
> Translate the liquid characters as they run.

[26] From *Poems 1929-1936*, by permission of New Directions and the Author.
[27] *Ibid.*
[28] *Ibid.*

The shudder of rain on the roofs is rain only,
Rain, rain only; but within the rain your Angels—
Informing rain and roofs and the stippled entries,
The wine-shop cats crouched in the sweet dust of wine,
Shell, wire, langosta, razorblade, musty files—
Move hugely, quiet; and your stricken eyes
Mark the santoral-sinew pulsing there,
Throbbing,
　　　　　Angel-rain, Angel-world, meaning-of-Angels,
Ladder of Cádiz, hallow-of-Angels-latent,
The delicate armies, inward fire white,
Alleluyas of glass and bell, for ever bright.

And Fitts's "Priam"[29] has the same finely textured rhetoric in still another vein:

The stars marched down with lightning to the sea
And all my lances gathered in the night.
Three angular horns: I have heard them sound the fall
Of venerable kings.
Three tapers wavering: and the distant
Cry of my name threefold on a dark shore.

It was in this directly classical vein that Fitts in collaboration with Robert Fitzgerald wrote English versions of *The Alcestis of Euripides* (1936) and *The Antigone of Sophocles* (1939) and these two volumes were soon recognized as being among the best of twentieth-century adaptations of classical drama into English verse. The merits of Dudley Fitts's own verse have been overshadowed by the more generally accepted merits of the verse that he has offered "as a translation"; actually the true merits of both are of the same quality; but it may be counted a misfortune that he did not permit more of his own wit and sensibility to be more clearly associated with his name. His verse as it appeared in a single volume, *Poems 1929-1936,* seemed less complete than it should have been, but if it is viewed in the same light in which one reads his English versions of the Palatine Anthology, a sense of balance is created, and even today it is to be hoped that a single volume which contains selected translations as well as additional poems will one day be issued to represent the measure of Dudley Fitts's contribution to contem-

[29] From *Poems 1929-1936,* by permission of New Directions and the Author.

porary American poetry. Since 1926, Dudley Fitts has been an instructor of English at Choate and latterly at Andover Academy.

5

In respect to poetry and during the first half of the twentieth century the brevity (and perhaps the hint of a renewed twilight) of New England's "Indian Summer" now seems to have been a less fortunate, and certainly less accurate, description of Boston's climate than it may have seemed in 1920, or even as recently as in 1940, when Van Wyck Brooks found *New England: Indian Summer* a happy title for his genial sketches in historical criticism. In a sense Cummings, Wheelwright, and Fitts were salutary "regional" poets; each retained in a healthy and characteristically Bostonian fashion his own independence, and obviously the independence was such that the presence of one did not unduly influence or compromise the other. Of the three Wheelwright was the most "experimental," but the poetry of all three owed a profound debt to Boston's heritage, to its conventions, to the proximity of Harvard, to the traditional aspects of English poetry, and to the language which is still spoken in the neighborhood of Brattle Street.

JOHN CROWE RANSOM, ALLEN TATE,
ROBERT PENN WARREN,
AND A NOTE ON LAURA RIDING

"O Trade! O Trade! would thou wert dead!
The Time needs heart—'tis tired of head:
We're all for love," the violins said.
Sidney Lanier, "The Symphony" (1875) [1]

"Love sows, and lovers reap anon—and he
Is blind, and scatters baleful seed that bring
Such fruitage as blind Love lacks eyes to see!"
James Branch Cabell, *Chivalry* (1909) [2]

For the historian of American poetry it is sometimes difficult to place in orderly perspective the work of certain poets who have freely indulged themselves in "group activities." And in no case is that difficulty more distracting than in an evaluation of the poetry written by John Crowe Ransom, Allen Tate, and Robert Penn Warren. What these poets have actually written has been clouded by a smoke screen of several ventures, the first a little magazine called *The Fugitive,* edited in Nashville, Tennessee, from 1922 to 1925, which was followed by a movement called "agrarianism" and a generously subsidized literary quarterly, *The Southern Review,* edited at Baton Rouge, Louisiana, by Charles Pipkin, Cleanth Brooks, and Robert Penn Warren, from 1935 to 1942, and latterly, the *Kenyon Review,* another literary quarterly, founded and edited at Kenyon College, Gambier, Ohio, by John Crowe Ransom in 1939, in which the principles of "agrarianism" seem to have been displaced by something that could properly be called "neoscholasticism." In

---

[1] From *Poems of Sidney Lanier,* by permission of Charles Scribner's Sons.

[2] "The Sestina" from *Chivalry,* by permission of Robert McBride & Company and the Author.

method of critical procedure and in group organization the various publications and "movements" in which the same writers appeared and assumed an almost military leadership (for a favored word in their critical articles on poetry was "strategy") a great debt was owed to the earlier activities of Ezra Pound and T. E. Hulme in London. The wonder was that time was found for writing poetry at all; and in consideration of the poetic gifts that were and still are possessed by Ransom and Tate, the example set by their "group activities" (which has been a diversion of notable historical interest) is one that Veblen would have described as another aspect of the American phenomenon of "conspicuous waste." In this case the "waste" was one of poetic intelligence and wit that had been diverted to the secondary excitements of editing magazines, of marshaling critical forces in unnecessary self-defense, of undue speculations in esthetic problems—all of which served to dissipate and to distract the excellent temper of the poetry that had made its presence felt in John Crowe Ransom's *Chills and Fever* (1924), *Two Gentlemen in Bonds* (1927), and in Allen Tate's *Selected Poems* (1937).

It is only fair to say that the self-consciously "reactionary" poets of the South (for Ransom was born in Pulaski, Tennessee, in 1888, Tate in Winchester, Kentucky, in 1899, and Warren in Guthrie, Kentucky, in 1905) were no more military and considerably more mature in their fondness for critical "strategy" than their contemporaries of liberal and left persuasion. Even as recently as September 11, 1944, Malcolm Cowley in the pages of *The New Republic* wistfully, unguardedly, and naïvely wrote of Robert Frost:

He is being praised too often and with too great vehemence by people who don't like poetry. And the result is that his honors shed very little of their luster on other poets, who in turn feel none of the pride in his achievements that a battalion feels, for example, when one of its officers is cited for outstanding services.

The image of poets writing in "battalions," and probably chanting their verses to the sound of feet in lockstep, was indeed an unfortunate picture and one that did not leave much hope for individual distinction in poetry. The image was probably a slip of the pen or the unconscious reflex of ten fingers striking the keys of a typewriter, but the device of thinking of poetry being written in the same way as military commands are to be followed is clear enough. The truth is that actual poetry has never been written in that fashion; and one cannot conceive of even so public-spirited a poet as John Milton shouting out as he composed them the stanzas of *Lycidas* in unison with some two hundred of his comrades. One would also like to ask how Milton's *Samson Agonistes* could have shed "luster" on Marvell's "Horatian Ode," since they were totally different poems and each distinguished in its own right, or how Marvell's "To his Coy Mistress" cast its reflected glory on Milton's sonnet on his deceased wife.

It is better for the historical critic to disentangle the merits of the Southern poets from their more immediate affiliations and to treat them as individually gifted writers who responded to and frequently against (and in that sense, they were truly "reactionary") the limitations, the depth, and the richness of a Southern, and almost strictly regional, heritage.

2

Since John Crowe Ransom was the most mature, and perhaps, even now, the most gifted of the three, his poetry deserves the first consideration. The facts of his biography, which need not be given too much consideration here, have some slight relevance to his poetry. His father was a minister and his granduncle had been active in the founding of the Ku Klux Klan. In 1909 he graduated from Vanderbilt University, and continued his education (since he had been sent as a Rhodes Scholar) at Christ Church, Oxford, where he received in 1913 a bachelor's degree in the classics and in mathematics. The memory of this latter experience may be noted (for whatever it may be worth) in the last four stanzas of his "Philomela," the concluding poem of his volume, *Chills and Fever:* [3]

[3] Reprinted by permission of Alfred A. Knopf, Inc. Copyright, 1924, by Alfred A. Knopf, Inc.

I went out to Bagley Wood, I climbed the hill;
Even as the moon had slanted off in a twinkling,
I heard the sepulchral owl and a few bells tinkling,
There was no more villainous day to unfulfil,
The diuturnity was still.

Up from the darkest wood where Philomela sat,
Her fairy numbers issued. What then ailed me?
My ears are called capacious but they failed me,
Her classics registered a little flat!
I rose, and venomously spat.

Philomela, Philomela, lover of song,
I am in despair if we may make us worthy,
A bantering breed sophistical and swarthy;
Unto more beautiful, persistently more young
Thy fabulous provinces belong.

The wit in the poem transcends its biographical interest; more than all else it is a refreshingly ironic colloquy with the famous nightingale; and the respects to her fame and her longevity were paid in a fashion that is not unlike a chivalrous compliment spoken to a beautiful woman. But the observation can be made that the lines also denote the presence of a disenchanted speaker, one who has heard Philomela with his own "capacious" ears, and has registered his disappointment and perhaps the difference of his own "bantering breed" from those who heard her earlier and who were "persistently more young." The general character of the disenchanted speaker was not unlike that of an elder Southern writer, James Branch Cabell, of Virginia, who wrote his volumes of short stories that were interspersed with verses, *Gallantry* in 1907 and *Chivalry* in 1909. Ransom's sonnet "The Tall Girl" with its play of forces between the "Queens of Hell" and the "Queen of Heaven," "a fine motherly woman," had within it much of the same spirit of irony that Cabell practiced with so much skill in his facile, Swinburnian verses and in his gracefully phrased and somewhat overtly polished prose:

The cornerstone of Chivalry [so Cabell wrote] I take to be the idea of vicarship: for the chivalrous person is, in his own eyes at least, the child of God, and goes about this world as his Father's representative in an alien country. . . . Questionless, however, the Chivalrous attitude does not very happily fit in with modern conditions, whereby the self-elected obligations of the knight-errant toward repressing evil are (in theory at all events) more efficaciously discharged by an organized police and a jury system.[4]

Ransom had the same distrust of what he called "moralism" in poetry in his volume, *The New Criticism* (1941), and one gains the impression that the novelist, Cabell, and the poet, Ransom, have inhabited the same world, a world in which the elder figure of disenchantment haunts the younger who would hastily disclaim the gifts of smoothness in prose and verse—with their hint of sophistry—that the elder Southerner possessed. Cabell's facility was, of course, his own undoing, and in that respect he remained a horrid, if not completely terrifying, example to younger writers who lived within the same cultural tradition, who avoided (as Cabell did not) a too assiduous devotion to the novels of Anatole France and the poetry of Swinburne, and yet faced the same problems of Southern chivalry—a heritage which in itself presented the ironic conflicts of neoclassicism and romantic behavior. Cabell's *The Rivet in Grandfather's Neck, A Comedy of Limitations* (1915), a realistic novel, which was fortunately remote from his fanciful land of "Poictesme," still remains among the best of ironic commentaries in prose on the so-called "modern" South. The presence of a neoclassical architecture (a beauty which carried with it a neofeudal plantation economy and its evocative memories of a Civil War and the "Reconstruction"), a love of Latin learning, which in its modern aspect became French or Italian, are all parts of what might be called a Southern "complex" and are in its literature. For the gifted poet the "complex" has an appropriate density and richness of texture that cannot be ignored—it is too rich, too lush, almost too overwhelming in its accretions of meaningful details.

Whatever the so-called "content" of Southern poetry may have been, the center of its concern seems to spin within a vortex of the classical-romantic contradictions, and in Ransom's poetry in

[4] "The Demi-Urge" from *Beyond Life*, by permission of Robert McBride & Company and the Author.

particular, scientific observation (which was probably spurred by his interest in mathematics at Christ Church) and a deeply realized, if skeptical, attitude toward religious values were added to the other contradictions which in their raw state existed within the very nature of his environment. Two other biographical circumstances may have contributed toward a reason why the best of Ransom's poems were never entirely submerged by Southern provincialism. One was his experience as a first lieutenant in the field artillery in the 1914-18 World War, the other was the fact that some few of his early verses were published by Christopher Morley (who had been a Rhodes Scholar from Maryland at New College, Oxford, at the time Ransom was at Christ Church); and Morley introduced Ransom's verse to the readers of the two popular columns which he edited, the "Chafing Dish" in the *Philadelphia Public Ledger* and the "Bowling Green" of the *New York Evening Post*. Such circumstances cannot fully explain the reason why a worldly temper, or something that Mark Van Doren described as "peppering his diction with fresh, realistic words," had entered Ransom's poetry, but it was clear that however strongly Ransom's poetry held to its associations of the South, it could not accept without question a Southern "credo" and a Southern faith. The conflict created something that resembled, or at least had an affinity to, the "metaphysical" character of seventeenth-century verse. "Realistic words" and thoroughly skeptical, "scientific" observations were placed in opposition to the usual expressions of emotion:

> Better to walk forth in the murderous air
> And wash my wound in the snows; that would be healing;
> Because my heart would throb less painful there,
> Being caked with cold, and past the smart of feeling.[5]

And in "Armageddon" (which was described in the language and imagery of a tournament with much of the same ironic spirit with which Cabell wrote his *Chivalry*) Christ and Antichrist were at war; it was a poem in which "the Wolf said Brother to the Lamb" and in which

[5] "Winter Remembered" from *Chills and Fever*. Reprinted by permission of Alfred A. Knopf, Inc. Copyright, 1924, by Alfred A. Knopf, Inc.

Antichrist and the armies of malfeasance
Made songs of innocence and no bloodshed.[6]

But however sharply the contrasts and likenesses of faith and antifaith were defined, Ransom's poetry remained at some distance from the religious temper of Donne's verse in his "Holy Sonnets"; Ransom's verse was "metaphysical" only in the sense that its so-called scientific observations were genuinely (and ironically) at war with an elder poetic convention of accepting Keats's nightingale and all the values of romantic poetry. "Blackberry Winter," [7] which is among the finest of Ransom's lyrics, illustrates the nature of a poetry that conveyed the graces of a half Cavalier, half romantic music and yet said farewell to them:

> If the lady hath any loveliness, let it die.
> For being drunken with the steam of Cuban cigars,
> I find no pungence in the odour of stars,
> And all of my music goes out of me on a sigh.
>
> But still would I sing to my maidenly apple-tree,
> Before she had borne me a single apple of red;
> The pictures of silver and apples of gold are dead;
> But one more apple ripeneth yet maybe.
>
> The garnished house of the Daughter of Heaven is cold.
> I have seen her often, she stood all night on the hill,
> Fiercely the pale youth clambered to her, till—
> Hoarsely the rooster awakened him, footing the mould.
>
> The breath of a girl is music—fall and swell—
> The trumpets convolve in the warrior's chambered ear,
> But I have listened, there is no one breathing here,
> And all of the wars have dwindled since Troy fell.
>
> But still I will haunt beneath my apple-tree,
> Heedful again to star-looks and wind-words,
> Anxious for the flash of whether eyes or swords,
> And hoping a little, a little, that either may be.

Ransom's lyrical gifts were far beyond those of any Southern poet of his day; the weakness of the Fugitives in general was a

[6] "Armageddon" from *Chills and Fever*. Reprinted by permission of Alfred A. Knopf, Inc. Copyright, 1924, by Alfred A. Knopf, Inc.

[7] From *Chills and Fever*. Reprinted by Alfred A. Knopf, Inc. Copyright, 1924, by Alfred A. Knopf, Inc.

lack of sensibility to verbal music, but this weakness was not shared by the best of Ransom's poetry. Truly enough he "reacted" against those extremes of Swinburnian facility that had been revived by James Branch Cabell as well as the unfortunate preoccupation with music for its own sake (and with small respect for verbal meaning and intelligence) which had vitiated so much of the poetry written by Sidney Lanier. Lanier, who was perhaps the most important of Ransom's literary "ancestors" in the South, whose sentiments were certainly "agrarian," who was, if anything, more "regional" than the most "regional" of the Fugitives, had a bad eye and ear for diction. In respect to poetry written south of the Mason-Dixon line, this latter flaw stood for correction and was absent from John Crowe Ransom's verse—and it is not improbable that the very existence of Ransom's two volumes of poetry, *Chills and Fever* and *Two Gentlemen in Bonds,* set a high standard and approved a respect for poetic diction that had long been lacking in verse that owed its debt to a Southern heritage.

Such poems as "Blue Girls," "Piazza Piece," and "Here Lies a Lady" (from a line of which *Chills and Fever* took its title) were widely and deservedly quoted by anthologists. The virtues of these particular lyrics were close to those of the highest standards set for light verse in English; and it was impossible to read them without admiring their metrical brilliance and the quality of their ironic wit—but the most successfully ambitious of nearly two hundred short poems that John Crowe Ransom has permitted himself to print is "Antique Harvesters." The poem is Ransom's masterpiece; and no poem written in the twentieth century by one who self-consciously paid homage to a Southern culture and environment equals its power to yield fresh meanings after numerous rereadings. After its appearance in *Two Gentlemen in Bonds* in 1927, the poem went through mutations which made (one would say) another poem of it in the 1936 and 1942 editions of Louis Untermeyer's *Modern American Poetry.* An entire stanza was added to the poem at its close; and the third line of its fourth stanza contained a verbal change with the addition of the word "quaint." One cannot, of course, paraphrase either version of the poem, but one can quote its stage direction: "Scene: Of the Mississippi the bank sinister, and of the Ohio the bank sinister," and then remark that the latter version is superior to the earlier. And it is also safe to assume that "our Lady" of the poem has her origins in the ancient fables and myths of harvesting the earth, and that Ransom has succeeded in giving her a habitation and a name.

It is of further interest to observe that beneath the lyrical overtones of Ransom's verse a coarse and heavily fibered strain exists; his ironic "Survey of Literature" [8] uncovers it:

> And for precious John Keats,
> Dripping blood of pickled beets.

And it is also present in "Amphibious Crocodile," in "Dog," and in "Fresco"; a harsh, ironic note enters their nearly doggerel metrics; the effects seem to be well deliberated, but the objects of his ridicule are momentarily crushed rather than dispelled by wit. One can defend these verses by saying that Ransom stood against artificial smoothness in writing and a false urbanity; but the fact remains that the results were unconvincing and unsuccessful—and that their very jokes betray concerns of private and provincial interest, which are understood and perhaps enjoyed by a few friends, but are of little consequence to general readers of poetry. If the public has neglected the ironic situations that Ransom presented in his sequence of twenty sonnets, "Two Gentlemen in Bonds," which gave a title to his second volume of verse, it was because its range of reference had been too strictly limited within the larger world of James Branch Cabell's novel, *The Rivet in Grandfather's Neck*. There is better writing in some few lines of the sonnets than can be found in all of Cabell's prose, but these must be sought out by the patient reader, and his rewards are those of fragmentary value. If in America the majority of those who read poetry were men, it is likely that the coarser strain in Ransom's verses as well as his ironic wit that turns its edge against courtly love and the

---

[8] From *Chills and Fever*. Reprinted by Alfred A. Knopf, Inc. Copyright, 1924, by Alfred A. Knopf, Inc.

arts of chivalry would find a larger number of readers to appreciate them. But as Henry Adams noted in 1911, the number of men who read, or care to listen to poetry read, is small; and this phenomenon, combined as it is with Ransom's intractable temper in his verse, has served to make him the leader of an extremely small group of admirers. Because he has devoted so much of his time since 1927 to the writing of three books of criticism, *God without Thunder* (1930), *The World's Body* (1938), *The New Criticism* (1941), something very like a dissipation of his poetic gifts seems to have taken place. Unlike the articles written by his followers, the quality of his prose in criticism has not suffered all the disasters which have trapped the devotees of a neoscholastic school of criticism—and one might almost say that Ransom has been too fine a poet to allow his prose to echo the jargon of a neoscholastic, neophilosophic school. If he has failed to take T. S. Eliot's warning to the poet, which was called "A Commentary: That Poetry Is Made with Words" in the pages of *The New English Weekly* for April 27, 1939:

> The two most dangerous subjects of study for the poet—I think, the only subjects that are always dangerous for him—are esthetics and psychology. Whether a poet can afford to interest himself in other abstract and philosophical studies is an individual matter: there are conspicuous instances of the good use of such an aliment. But abstract studies which turn upon the practice of his own art are a very different matter. The danger of esthetics is that it may make us conscious of what operates better unconsciously . . .

he has also kept his prose and the quality of his intelligence at a measurable distance from that of another writer who wrote in his attempt to discuss the poetry of T. S. Eliot and Garcia Lorca in *The American Bookman* for Winter, 1944, of "the objective correlative." The following statement appears to be a single sentence:

> In any case, association will not explain the process of choice, since the poet is not really choosing one image as against another because the former happens to correspond to a pre-existing feeling; what he is doing is creating imagery and conceiving novel situations, and association cannot explain the pat congruity that exists from the very first moment of conception between our symbol and the feelings or emo-

tions which, outside of their symbolic embodiment, the artist neither understood nor could define.[9]

One does not doubt the seriousness of the writer's intention, but the result is a jargon that tends to discourage the intelligent reading and understanding of poetry, however excellent it may be. Another quotation, equally serious in its intentions, and more scholastic in its language than philosophic, may be found in the Summer, 1944, issue of the *Kenyon Review*. The effort here was to deal with technical matters in writing verse, but the results, as they attempted to illuminate the character of Gerard Manley Hopkins' poetry—and its sprung rhythms—were, to say the least, unfortunate:

> That its identity with the age-old dipodic measures of English poetry has not been widely understood is due partly to the poet's own contradictory utterances, partly to the somewhat primitive state of metrical knowledge in his own time, partly to his inherent conservatism of linear and stanzaic forms, and partly to his free, uncadenced, and unbalanced handling of the rhythm itself. His inability to recognize the time-marking role of secondary stress inevitably confused and thwarted all attempts at explanation.[10]

One is certain only that the author of such prose was regrettably tone deaf; and that however industrious he may have been in the naming of "alexandrine," "dipodic trimeters," "tetrameters," and "the normal length of the English dipodic long line," his total understanding of a poem in reading it aloud was likely to be faulty.

It is certainly not too much to say that these excursions into what has been fondly regarded as an "analysis of poetry" are dangerous ventures for any poet. Ransom's proximity to the scene of such labors increases the miracle of his survival as well as the endurance of the verse that he has allowed himself to publish at infrequent intervals. The tone of his "Address to the Scholars of New England" (which was the Harvard Phi Beta Kappa Poem of June 23, 1939) was harsh and dry; the poem

[9] Eliseo Vivas, "The Objective Correlative of T. S. Eliot," by permission of *The American Bookman*, Winter, 1944.

[10] Harold Whitehall, "Gerard Manley Hopkins," by permission of the *Kenyon Review*, Summer, 1944.

possessed formal distinction and its critical attitude toward New England and "the youngling bachelors of Harvard" was salutary—and one was reassured that the poet who wrote its lines held to an austerity of speech that was both mature and admirable. But the poem as poem lacked the wit and contact with the world that made Robert Frost's "The Lesson for Today" (which was read on a like occasion at Harvard in 1941) memorable. The elder poet was by no means as strict in the terms of his semiphilosophic discourse as Ransom seemed to be and in contrast to Ransom's "Address," his speech in verse seemed positively rakish. But Frost's knowledge of the world was carried with it—and he did not forget (as indeed he could not, being the kind of poet he was) that his speech was above all things a dramatic poem, a thing of art in which all outward signs of effort should be happily concealed. And in contrast to Frost's poem, Ransom's "Address" was very nearly tongue-tied by an historical and an overtly scholastic authority.

One must return to other aspects of Ransom's verse to find its true felicity, to his "Spectral Lovers" in his volume *Chills and Fever,* and to the last two lines of a later poem, "Painting: A Head": [11]

> To spread the hyacinthine hair and rear
> The olive garden for the nightingales.

Although Ransom in his "Address to the Scholars of New England" spoke of a "metaphysic" that makes Earth and Heaven one, and though some of his verse has justified its affinity with certain poets of the "metaphysical" school of the seventeenth century, Ransom's poetry seems to have developed an even stronger affinity with the strains of John Dryden's odes and satires. Ransom's verse lacks the weight and polish of Dryden's masterpieces, nor has it the advantage of Dryden's rich production, which included the sustained art of writing *All for Love*—but in the light of Ransom's influence upon his followers and in his effort to create and to impose an orderly system of criticism upon them,

[11] From *Selected Poems.* Reprinted by permission of Alfred A. Knopf, Inc. Copyright, 1924, 1927, 1934, 1945, by Alfred A. Knopf, Inc.

it is not unfortunate to think of him as the John Dryden of contemporary Southern literature.

3

> Do not the scene rehearse!
> The perfect eyes enjoin
> A contemptuous verse;
> We speak the crabbed line.
>
> Allen Tate, "To the Romantic
> Traditionists" [12] (1934)

As one turns from the poetry of John Crowe Ransom to Allen Tate's *Selected Poems,* another beginning to this chapter should be made. As one reads Tate's "crabbed" lines one thinks more of Poe and of Lanier than of James Branch Cabell, for Poe and Lanier seem to represent the centers toward which Tate's poetry has moved and then violently rejected, quite as though it had been informed of a strong polar attraction and had strained its effort in an opposite direction.

On August 7, 1875, Sidney Lanier wrote a letter of gratitude to Bayard Taylor, who had been one of the few men of letters of that day to take an interest in Lanier's extraordinary, and perhaps misguided and thwarted, talent.

> I could never describe to you what a mere drought and famine my life has been, as regards that multitude of matters which I fancy one absorbs when one is in an atmosphere of art, or when one is in conversational relation with men of letters, with travel, with persons who have either seen or written or done large things. Perhaps you know that with us of the younger generation in the South since the war pretty much of the whole of life has been merely not dying.[13]

"Merely not dying" was a complaint that many a Southerner could have made for several decades after Lanier's death. Before the Civil War and with the exception of Poe, and though it had a literary magazine or two, the South did not seem as lively in its appreciation of the arts as the more industrial and less con-

[12] From *Selected Poems,* by permission of Charles Scribner's Sons.
[13] Preface from *Poems of Sidney Lanier,* by permission of Charles Scribner's Sons.

ꞏsciously aristocratic North. When New England with Boston and Harvard at its center became absorbed in German literature and philosophy, the South in its oratory and its literary tastes seemed to reflect the more florid aspects of Sir Walter Scott's Waverley Novels and the romances of Bulwer-Lytton—and in poetry, the all too obviously sweet lyricism of Tom Moore. Henry Timrod and Paul Hamilton Hayne were figures among the lesser Southern poets, and after Lanier's death, the arrival of a poet such as Madison Cawein was anything but a heartening example.

Much, if not all, of the "reactionary" spirit in Tate's poetry and in his *Reactionary Essays on Poetry and Ideas* (1936) seems to have sprung from a recoil against the "merely-not-dying" attitude in Southern literature as well as its lushly sentimentalized romanticism; the reaction was in itself very nearly a romantic gesture, but it gave spirit and verve to his participation in editing *The Fugitive* and it provided a surplus of the restless energy that aimed at perfection in the ten years, 1926 to 1936, in writing and rewriting his "Ode to the Confederate Dead." He had been educated at Georgetown University and the University of Virginia and he received his bachelor's degree, *magna cum laude,* in 1922 at Vanderbilt University, and six years later, his first book of poems, *Mr. Pope and Other Poems,* appeared. With the exception of his two biographies, *Stonewall Jackson* (1928) and *Jefferson Davis* (1929), and a novel, *The Fathers* (1938), it seemed impossible for Tate's writing to be dull; in verse and in criticism it could be both inept and awkward, but it remained untouched by the slightest taint of mediocrity, and it wisely avoided the pitfalls of neoscholasticism. What Tate's verse lacked was the presence of a "melodic ear," but this lack was balanced, or rather compensated, by the evidence of a concentrated energy within its lines, and the nature of the craftsmanship he practiced is illustrated by four lines from his verses on "The Subway": [14]

> Harshly articulate, musical steel shell
> Of angry worship, hurled religiously
> Upon your business of humility
> Into the iron forestries of hell.

[14] From *Selected Poems,* by permission of Charles Scribner's Sons.

And another aspect of Tate's disquieting and yet salutary art may be found in the first two stanzas of "Idiot": [15]

> The idiot greens the meadows with his eyes,
> The meadow creeps implacable and still;
> A dog barks, the hammock swings, he lies.
> One two three the cows bulge on the hill.
>
> Motion that is not time erects snowdrifts
> While sister's hand sieves waterfalls of lace.
> With a palm fan closer than death he lifts
> The Ozarks and tilted seas across his face.

The metrics of the two stanzas seem strained and forced, but concentration of what is seen, and the placing of objects before the eye in quickening succession generate their own excitement. The lines are by no means graceful, but they compel attention, and are memorable in the sense that they retain their hold upon the reader's imagination.

The concentration of imagery that Tate achieved in "The Idiot" had its parallel in Hart Crane's "Black Tambourine": [16]

> Æsop, driven to pondering, found
> Heaven with the tortoise and the hare;
> Fox brush and sow ear top his grave
> And mingling incantations on the air.

This particular affinity was, of course, still another "reaction" against the South, for Tate in the early 1920's came east to New York. As Philip Horton in his *Life of an American Poet, Hart Crane* [17] wrote:

From Nashville, Tennessee, came Allen Tate in full flight from the provincial isolation of the South, very much as Crane had fled from Cleveland. After two years of stimulating correspondence which according to Tate in his essay in *Poetry*, July 1932, on Hart Crane and the American Mind, had begun in 1922 the two were at last able to exchange ideas and criticisms of each other's work directly.

Briefly, both exchanged "influences" upon one another's verse, and probably through Ezra Pound's and T. S. Eliot's professed

[15] From *Selected Poems,* by permission of Charles Scribner's Sons.
[16] From *Collected Poems of Hart Crane,* by permission of Liveright Publishing Corporation.
[17] By permission of W. W. Norton & Company.

interest in Laforgue and Corbière (an intelligence which had been distributed in New York through the pages of Margaret Anderson's *The Little Review, The Dial,* and T. S. Eliot's newly founded magazine, *The Criterion,* edited in London) Tate and Crane also exchanged their readings in French Symbolism.

In the early 1920's the South still lacked its "atmosphere of art" and its "conversational relation with men of letters" that Lanier had observed in 1875. Its arts, as Donald Davidson wrote in *Poetry,* in May, 1932, "in times past took another direction than poetry: They were the eighteenth century arts of dress, conversation, manners: or, I might add, of architecture, handicraft, oratory, anecdote."

And it was clear that Tate in New York, and later on in France, from 1928 to 1930, did not wish to share the provincialism that had been forced upon Lanier. There are qualities of a "fierce latinity" and a restlessness in Tate's poetry that distinguished it from the kind of verse that had been written by his Southern predecessors and his contemporaries. His rhetorical gestures in his "Ode to the Confederate Dead" were Roman, overly weighted perhaps, and certainly didactic. The lines of the poem conveyed the impression of a full-dress military uniform being worn, and not naïvely, but with a sense of half-romantic ardor and with a half-ironic splendor. Few poets have been less highly conscious of "making" poetry than Tate, and in his writing of his "Ode to the Confederate Dead," he confessed in a preface to his *Selected Poems:* "I have repeatedly asked other poets to help me with this poem, which I felt was beyond my powers. In 1931 Mr. Robert Penn Warren contributed one line, in my opinion its best"—which was admirable in giving credit where credit was due, but the original lines that give life to Tate's effort at perfection are:

> In the ribboned coats of grim felicity [18]

and

> The gentle serpent, green in the mulberry bush.[18]

[18] "Ode to the Confederate Dead" from *Selected Poems,* by permission of Charles Scribner's Sons.

And one is disturbed and not reassured by Tate's concern in building hugely upon a poem much of which the writer feels must be sustained by abstract argument. The poem presumed to carry too much weight and too many things at once: the memory of the Civil War, of philosophy and metaphysics, of autumn's season of the year, of the "furious murmur" of "chivalry"—all of which was interesting enough but unevenly composed.

The truth was that Tate was a notoriously uneven poet, and if one of his friends remarked that his "Sonnets of the Blood" were "among the worst sonnets in the English language" one can understand, but not entirely concur with, the friend's mood of genuine despair. There are worse sonnets in the English language—and they are the totally mediocre sonnets that have been written by thousands of versifiers. The majority of Tate's sonnets think aloud and often awkwardly; they have the speech of critical abstraction and little music—except the homage paid to an obligatory rhyme—but they reward the reader with an occasional observation, and a hard-won and brilliant image of seasonal change or of classical reference, "Call it the house of Atreus where we live," or a phrase that seems to express a withheld and controlled rhetoric of dignity and anger.

Tate's virtues were scarcely those of lyrical persuasion and grace of movement, but were those of masculine force and difficult poetic achievement; in reading many of his poems one gains the impression of verbal honesty and a poetic insight that had been too often distracted by the proximity of critical ideas, and such distraction was not unhappily conveyed in the last stanza of his tribute to Alexander Pope:

> What requisitions of a verity
> Prompted the wit and rage between his teeth
> One cannot say: around a crooked tree
> A moral climbs whose name should be a wreath.[19]

The poem was as Hart-Crane-like in its phrasing as "Idiot," but it had an air of critical decision that was Tate's own, an

[19] "Mr. Pope" from *Selected Poems,* by permission of Charles Scribner's Sons.

air of knowing its own mind and its intentions. Tate's self-imposed manner of writing produced many fine and memorable passages of verse, but few, a very few, fully rounded and completed poems—and at their best they were of an elegiac strain in twentieth-century poetry. His elegy to Jefferson Davis was among them, and so was his "Aeneas at Washington," and not the least of these was "The Mediterranean," which has been frequently quoted in anthologies. It has been among Tate's virtues as a poet never to rest too long upon his laurels; and despite the wide, just, and devoted recognition that his verse has received in this country and in England, he has not been content to repeat himself or, like other well-established poets of his generation, to write unconscious parodies of his earlier successes. In 1943 he published a characteristic and not wholly fortunate adaptation of the *Pervigilium Veneris* into English verse. Tate's "fierce latinity" of which he wrote so well in his "Ignis Fatuus" was re-illuminated, and the character of his translation (which was not happily suited to celebrating the Eve of St. Venus and the joys of love and spring) is more truly represented by two stanzas of his "Ignis Fatuus" [20] itself:

> In the twilight of my audacity
> I saw you flee the world, the burnt highways
> Of summer gave up their light: I
> Followed you with the uncommon span
> Of fear-supported and disbursed eyes.
>
> . . . . . .
>
> High in the hills, by what illuminations
> Are you intelligible? Your fierce latinity
> Beyond the nubian bulwark of the sea
> Sustains the immaculate sight.

Few American poets of the twentieth century and certainly no poet of the South has been in such complete command of a semineoclassic vocabulary, which was of a kind that bore a relationship to the eighteenth-century British poet, William Collins, to whom Tate paid tribute when he wrote a variation on Collins' "Ode to Fear." The first stanza of Tate's "Ode to Fear" [21] had

---

[20] From *Selected Poems*, by permission of Charles Scribner's Sons.
[21] *Ibid.*

an excellence that was not sustained by the rest of the poem, and it deserves quotation with the best of Tate's poetry:

> Let the day glare: O memory, your tread
> Beats to the pulse of suffocating night—
> Night peering from his dark but fire-lit head
> Burns on the day his tense and secret light.

It was as though Tate had written the entire poem in the first four lines, and the following five stanzas seem to arrive as a stilted anticlimax to the powerful rhetoric of the first four lines. Among the best of Tate's longer poems was his four "Seasons of the Soul" which appeared in John Crowe Ransom's the *Kenyon Review* for Winter, 1944. The poem had its infirm lines, its crude and floundering phrases, such as "combustible juice," and "Jack-and-Jilling seas," but the poem was proof of Tate's poetic maturity as well as renewed evidence of Tate's salutary influence upon American poetry of the 1920's, for Tate upheld the standards of a classical tradition in poetry as it opposed the witless and irresponsible extremes of "experimentation" for its own sake. The last three stanzas of the last and fourth section of the poem, of which the subject is fire, contain a sustained felicity that is far beyond anything Tate has written:

> It burns us each alone
> Whose burning arrogance
> Burns up the rolling stone,
> This earth—Platonic cave
> Of vertiginous chance!
> Come, tired Sisyphus,
> Cover the cave's egress
> Where light reveals the slave,
> Who rests when sleeps with us
> The mother of silences.
>
> Come, old woman, save
> Your sons who have gone down
> Into the burning cave:
> Come, mother, and lean
> At the window with your son
> And gaze through its light frame
> These fifteen centuries
> Upon the shirking scene

Where men, blind, go lame;
Then, mother of silences,

Speak, that we may hear;
Listen, while we confess
That we conceal our fear;
Regard us, while the eye
Discerns by sight or guess
Whether, as sheep foregather
Upon their crooked knees,
We have begun to die;
Whether your kindness, mother,
Is mother of silences.[22]

4

In John Crowe Ransom's *Chills and Fever* there was a poem, "A Plea in Mitigation," [23] which tells us something of the character and the aims and ambitions of the little magazine of Southern verse that was called *The Fugitive*. In his manly fashion, Ransom spoke for himself, but through his lines one gains a perspective on the entire group:

Anatomy, that doled my dubious features,
Had housed within me, close to my breastbone,
My daemon, always clamouring, Up, Begone,
Pursue your gods faster than most of creatures!

And if an alien, hideously at feud
With those my generation, I have reason
To think to salve the fester of my treason:
A seven of friends exceeds much multitude.

From the foreword of the anthology, *Fugitives*,[24] we may conclude that "a seven of friends" were those mentioned in the following paragraph:

Originally there were seven friends—Donald Davidson, James Marshall Frank, Sidney Mittron-Hirsch, Stanley Johnson, John Crowe

[22] "Seasons of the Soul" from *The Winter Sea*. By permission of the Author and the Cummington Press.

[23] Reprinted by permission of Alfred A. Knopf, Inc. Copyright, 1924, by Alfred A. Knopf, Inc.

[24] From *Fugitives: An Anthology of Verse*, copyright 1928 by Harcourt, Brace.

Ransom, Alec B. Stevenson, and Allen Tate. These men, or most of them, had been meeting often for some years at the home of James Marshall Frank and Sidney Mittron-Hirsch, where they talked about poetry and philosophy. In the autumn of 1921 they became interested in the writing of poetry, and after a while their poems and the criticism of them became the chief object of their meetings which were now held regularly. Manuscripts piled up so rapidly that upon the suggestion of Sidney Mittron-Hirsch, which everybody else naturally fell in with, the group decided to start a poetry magazine as a cooperative undertaking. The first issue came out in April, 1922. There was no editor. Poems were chosen by ballot. The authors hid themselves under pen-names.

The atmosphere in the drawing room of a house in Nashville, Tennessee, must have held the youthful charm of a room in a Greek-letter supper club at an American university; and as Ransom's poem seems to bear witness, the same oaths of loyalty were sworn, and the same communal spirit prevailed within a small circle, which had the attraction of a secret society that had decided to make its talents known to the wide and busy, and perhaps unfriendly, world. The anthology itself contained selections from the verse of Donald Davidson, William Yandell Elliot, James Marshall Frank, Stanley Johnson, Merrill Moore (who afterwards became notorious through publishing a thousand sonnets in a single volume), John Crowe Ransom, Laura Riding, Alec Brook Stevenson, Allen Tate, Robert Penn Warren, and Jesse Wills. With the exception of Ransom, Tate, and Warren, the group produced no poets who developed beyond the usual display of a youthful interest in literature and an equally youthful desire to write verse—but in Laura Riding, an often entertaining and, at times, a colorful writer of prose emerged. And from her writings in prose one gathers that she was a vivid and aggressive literary personality.

Laura Riding (who was born in New York in 1901) was among the American "expatriates" who went to Europe to live in the middle of the 1920's, and she left for Europe from Nashville, Tennessee. In Philip Horton's life of Hart Crane, one reads of her befriending Crane in London, and from her collaborations with Robert Graves, one assumes that she admired Graves's verse, and formed a union between Ransom's and Tate's group in Tennessee with slightly insurgent, but otherwise thoroughly re-

spectable groups of writers in London and in Paris. Quite as
Oscar Wilde in an earlier generation became an ambassador of
the British Pre-Raphaelites on his lecture tours in America, so
Laura Riding became an unofficial and unacknowledged emis-
sary of the Nashville Fugitives in postwar Europe. She had the
ability to create a lively personal legend, and it was rumored
that in her house in Deya, Majorca, where she lived until the
Spanish Civil War broke out in 1936, the following inscription
was written in large gold letters on her bedroom wall: "God is
a Woman."

In 1938 Laura Riding published her *Collected Poems,* a volume
of 477 pages of experimental verse, and which contained the industrious product of some twelve years of setting down on paper
whatever she had in mind. Her preface to the reader was an
eloquent personal document in which she quoted W. H. Auden
as saying that she was "the only living philosophical poet." The
verse itself was far less rewarding than her instructions to the
reader; and despite the number of attractive titles, such as "The
Vain Life of Voltaire," [25] it was all too obvious that her verses
lacked imagination, verbal discipline, and the presence of an ear
that could guide the rhythmical progress of a poem:

> Voltaire in haste sought the Devil,
> Who refused him in haste
> As too haunted, too equal.
>
> . . . . . .
>
> Epilogue is epigram
> For any man whose anagram
> Meant too much. For all such
> Should be one crutch
> Held under the nose
> Instead of rose.

Which, no matter how carefully one rereads the lines, remains
the work of an industrious, earnest, and ungifted amateur. John
Brooks Wheelwright in a review of Laura Riding's verse for
Poetry, August, 1932,[26] said all that could justly be said of her
experiments in writing:

[25] From *Collected Poems,* by permission of Random House, Inc.
[26] Reprinted by permission of *Poetry.*

The labor of un-thinking and un-writing which Gertrude Stein and E. E. Cummings have done for poetry is by no means completely done. But even their energy flickers at times, and in their followers the purpose seems to have given way to the means. . . . Laura Riding rests along a line of literary development. The development has always been too literary. Among Miss Riding's happiest works are those wherein she contrives to give the sensation which we get from reading Sapphic fragments, but this is an evasive technical device, like that of building ruins or sculping shattered statues . . . she has, as she says, a whole dictionary of un-words; but it is the syntax which she has not mastered. Most of her poems are too long, and while most of them are not clear enough, many, like The Nightmare with its unnecessary signposts, are too clear. It is conscious thought that she has not thought about.

But the lack of discipline as well as the lack of a gift for writing verse did not prevent Laura Riding (in collaboration with Robert Graves) from writing a thoroughly entertaining, informative and shrewd little book of criticism, *A Pamphlet against Anthologies,* which found a small audience among those writers who were young in 1928. The little book created the atmosphere of a literary holiday; it was a counterblast against established reputations and editors; it misread and misinterpreted the poetry of W. B. Yeats—but its air of irreverence toward most of the poets named within its pages was gay and salutary. The book set to one side the platitudes of nineteenth-century criticism of poetry, and in its closing chapter, it mentioned with respect the *Georgian Poetry* anthologies (which had included the early verse of Robert Graves) and *Fugitives* (which numbered among its contributors Miss Riding).

Even as recently as 1943, the original loyalties of the Fugitives group remained unbroken. When Allen Tate served his appointment to the Chair of Poetry in the Library of Congress at Washington, D. C., with characteristic chivalry and tact, he remembered Laura Riding. In a selected list of recent American poetry and poetic criticism, which the State Department asked to be compiled for the purpose of sending books, "a token of cultural good will," to Soviet Russia, Tate wrote the following comment on Laura Riding's *Collected Poems:*

Great creative energy and inventiveness in language have made Miss Riding one of the most individual poets of our age.

And not since Poe spoke in great praise of the verses written by Mrs. Welby and Miss Mary A. S. Aldrich has the South witnessed a more courteous appraisal of a woman writer by a gifted poet.

5

Robert Penn Warren was the youngest, and in some respects the most promising, of those who gave distinction to the *Fugitives* anthology of 1928. He graduated from Vanderbilt University in 1925, and he continued his postgraduate studies at the University of California, at Yale, and as a Rhodes Scholar at Oxford, where he received a degree of bachelor of letters in 1930. In an academic sense, his career was remarkably precocious, and he showed an equal brilliance and facility in his editorial labors, for he served as one of the editors of *The Southern Review* and as an advisory editor of the *Kenyon Review;* in 1929 he published a biography of John Brown and edited during the following decade—two in collaboration with Cleanth Brooks—several text-books on verse and prose. To these he added the writing of two novels, *Night Rider* (1939) and *At Heaven's Gate* (1943), both of which were highly praised by reviewers of fiction. He contributed critical articles to the magazines, and if his critical prose showed little depth of insight, his judgments were uniformly reasonable and discreet. Not since Mark Van Doren edited the literary section of *The Nation* in the middle 1920's had there been a young writer who with like ease seemed so decisive, sensible, and careful to praise other writers, who at the moment were rising in critical esteem.

By 1942 Warren was well established as one of the most distinguished poets of his generation in America as well as in the South, and reviewers in the liberal weeklies as well as those who wrote for the literary quarterlies combined to praise a pamphlet of *Eleven Poems on the Same Theme* and the memory of his *Thirty-six Poems* (1935). In 1944 he published his *Selected Poems 1923-1943*, which gave readers of his verse an opportunity to evaluate its merits and its flaws. In this book, as in Tate's *Selected Poems*, an "Ode to Fear" made its arrival, with its refrain taken from the "Lament for the Makaris" of William

Dunbar, that all too little known and lively Scots poet of the late fifteenth and early sixteenth centuries—and the Latin refrain was a happy choice. Unfortunately, the poem itself reflected more of the extraverted energies of Louis MacNeice, a young British poet of the 1930's, than the wit and sensibility of Dunbar, and one feels that it had been done merely as a freehand exercise in writing verse. Something of the same insensitivity attended the impression left by the long poem which opened the volume of *Selected Poems,* "The Ballad of Billie Potts," a poem which made a dubious use of Kentucky dialect with interludes of verse that had been written as though they were stilted and unconscious parodies of T. S. Eliot's "Burnt Norton." And one felt strongly that an effort had been made to combine the effects of Eliot's *Four Quartets* with the popular successes of Jesse Stuart's novels and the stage version of Erskine Caldwell's *Tobacco Road.* The experiment was not a happy one.

At its best the promise of Robert Penn Warren's talent for writing verse remained what it was in the *Fugitives* anthology— and it was reinforced by the inclusion of a poem, "Bearded Oaks," in his *Selected Poems.* Warren's true gifts seem to be those of writing half meditative, half descriptive verses, which incidentally recall the physical atmosphere and the psychological environment of the South, and for that reason "Bearded Oaks" is a far more successful poem than his pretentious and overtly conscious literary exercises. Warren, like many others of the *Fugitives* anthology, lacked Ransom's excellently tuned and "capacious" ear, which detected the flaws in the song that Philomela sang.

From Warren we must for the present rest content with his "Bearded Oaks": [27]

> The oaks, how subtle and marine,
> Bearded, and all the layered light
> Above them swims; and thus the scene,
> Recessed, awaits the positive night.
>
> So, waiting, we in the grass now lie
> Beneath the languorous tread of light:

[27] From *Selected Poems,* by permission of Harcourt, Brace and Company.

The grasses, kelp-like, satisfy
The nameless motions of the air.

Upon the floor of light, and time,
Unmurmuring, of polyp made,
We rest; we are, as light withdraws,
Twin atolls on a shelf of shade.

Ages to our construction went,
Dim architecture, hour by hour:
And violence, forgot now, lent
The present stillness all its power.

The storm of noon above us rolled,
Of light the fury, furious gold,
The long drag troubling us, the depth:
Dark is unrocking, unrippling, still.

Passion and slaughter, ruth, decay
Descend, minutely whispering down,
Silted down swaying streams, to lay
Foundation for our voicelessness.

All our debate is voiceless here,
As all our rage, the rage of stone;
If hope is hopeless, then fearless fear,
And history is thus undone.

Our feet once wrought the hollow street
With echo when the lamps were dead
At windows, once our headlight glare
Disturbed the doe that, leaping, fled.

I do not love you less that now
The caged heart makes the iron stroke,
Or less that all that light once gave
The graduate dark should now revoke.

We live in time so little time
And we learn all so painfully,
That we may spare this hour's term
To practice for eternity.

This was obviously far better than the lines from "Billie Potts," [28] which paralleled equally unfortunate lines in Mark Van Doren's "Jonathan Gentry":

[28] From *Selected Poems*, by permission of Harcourt, Brace and Company.

"But not too early fer hit's my aim
To git me some fun 'fore they know my name,
And tease 'em and fun 'em, fer you never guessed
I was Little Billie what went out West."

Which was verse that, however amused the author may have been in writing it, fails to convey enjoyment to the reader, and soon wearies both the eye and ear.

Warren, at the time of publishing his *Selected Poems,* had yet to write a poem that holds the attention of the reader as well as Ransom's "Antique Harvesters," and he had yet to master his talents for writing verse of a quality that produced Tate's "The Mediterranean," "Aeneas at Washington," and "Seasons of the Soul." But it should be said that the small group of poets who contributed to the pages of the *Fugitives* anthology offered good health and a corrective to a cultural climate that in the generation before them gave popularity to such poets as Madison Cawein, led James Branch Cabell to an ironic and misguided journey in the direction of his "Poictesme," and in the "nameless motions of the air," ignored the causes of Lanier's failure and sentimentalized the presence of his genius.

THE NEGRO POET IN AMERICA

Of all national and distinctly racial groups of people who came to America, the Negro is among the eldest, and it is therefore not surprising that the literature which bears his name is less "primitive," less "childish," and less "naïve" than it has been commonly supposed. In John Lomax' compilation of folk songs and in Carl Sandburg's *American Songbag* he has been rightfully regarded as a master of folk art; and disguised by anonymity he has enjoyed a freedom and an inventiveness of expression that has not been shared by the Negro poet whose name appears on the title page of a new book. The moment his name appears he begins to share a number of complex, contradictory, and distracting responsibilities; and for nearly a hundred years every political party in America, and one should be careful to say, in the North and South alike, has taken advantage of his situation. Pathos and self-pity have been his shield and his internal weakness, and only among such able Negro leaders as James Weldon Johnson do we find a clear-minded and just appraisal of the Negro's contribution to American poetry. Johnson's anthology, *The Book of American Negro Poetry* (1922), contained a selection from the work of some thirty Negro poets and Countee Cullen's selection from the work of thirty-eight Negro poets five years later served as an introduction to the nature and scope of a poetic literature written by the North American Negro during the twentieth century.

Both anthologies opened (and not without reason) with selections from the verses of Paul Laurence Dunbar, who was born in Dayton, Ohio, in 1872, and died in the city of his birth in 1906. Of all twentieth-century American Negro poets Dunbar was perhaps the best known, and in the sense that James Whitcomb Riley was heard, read, and applauded, the most popular.

Of his verse in dialect (which like Riley's seemed to stem from a reading of James Russell Lowell's *Biglow Papers*) William Dean Howells wrote:

> In nothing is his essentially refined and delicate art so well shown as in these pieces, which, as I ventured to say, described the range between appetite and emotion, with certain lifts far beyond and above it, which is the range of the race. He reveals in these a finely ironical perception of the Negro's limitations, with a tenderness for them which I think so very rare as to be almost quite new. I should say, perhaps, that it was this humorous quality which Mr. Dunbar had added to our literature, and it would be this which would most distinguish him, now and hereafter.[1]

It was plain that Howells wrote with the warmest of good intentions, and these remarks along with others were published as an introduction to Dunbar's *Lyrics of Lowly Life* in 1896. But aside from the observation that Dunbar's art was "essentially refined and delicate" Howells' introduction had far less reality and perception than James Weldon Johnson's critical commentaries on and reminiscences of Paul Laurence Dunbar and his poetry:

> When I first met him he had published a thin volume, "Oak and Ivy," which was being sold chiefly through his own efforts. "Oak and Ivy" showed no distinctive Negro influence, but rather the influence of James Whitcomb Riley. . . . He talked to me a great deal about his hopes and ambitions. In these talks he revealed that he had reached a realization of the possibilities of poetry in the dialect, together with a recognition of the fact that it offered the surest way by which he could get a hearing. Often he said to me: "I've got to write dialect poetry; it's the only way I can get them to listen to me." I was with Dunbar at the beginning of what proved to be his last illness. He said to me then: "I have not grown. I am writing the same things I wrote ten years ago, and am writing them no better." His self-accusation was not fully true; he had grown, and he had gained a surer control of his art, but he had not accomplished the greater things of which he was constantly dreaming; the public had held him to the things for which it had accorded him recognition. . . . As a man, Dunbar was kind and tender. In conversation he was brilliant and polished. His voice was his chief charm, and was a great element in his success as a reader of his own works. In his actions he was as impulsive

---

[1] Introduction to *Lyrics of Lowly Life* by Paul Laurence Dunbar. Reprinted by permission of Dodd, Mead & Company, Inc.

as a child, sometimes even erratic; indeed, his intimate friends almost looked upon him as a spoiled boy. He was always delicate in health. Temperamentally, he belonged to that class of poets who Taine says are vessels too weak to contain the spirit of poetry, the poets whom poetry kills . . .[2]

It can be said of Dunbar that where Riley grew complacent, and accepted his fame as a just reward for his talents, the Negro poet grew more disquieted; he probably saw his own position in relationship to writing poetry with a keener sense of reality and less cynicism than those with which the "Hoosier Poet" perceived his place in respect to writing "dialect" poetry. In Dunbar's humility and pathos, there is a note of something that is almost frightening. Most of his verse was admittedly "magazine verse" of the period, and certainly it was of a kind that editors were glad to accept and to publish. Obviously, Dunbar had read Robert Burns as well as Riley—and he had also read the minor British poets of the day, including Austin Dobson and Andrew Lang, who had found great favor with editors of American periodicals. His facility in writing verse carried what might have been no more than a harmless imitation of "popular favorites" into an accelerated decadence of all the minor verse that filled the empty spaces between nonfiction articles and the short stories in widely circulated magazines:

> I cast my bread upon the waves
>   And fancied then to await it;
> It had not floated far away
>   When a fish came up and ate it.[3]

And for a moment the cliché was dispelled by a minute flash of wit and the presence of reality; and there was no compromise with the expression of pathos, humility, and even terror, which seemed to flow between rather than in the following lines:

> Let me close the eyes of my soul
>   That I may not see
> What stands between thee and me.

[2] From *The Book of American Negro Poetry*, ed. by James Weldon Johnson, by permission of Harcourt, Brace and Company.

[3] "After Many Days" from *Complete Poems*. Reprinted by permission of Dodd, Mead & Company, Inc.

> Let me shut the ears of my heart
>   That I may not hear
> A voice that drowns yours, my dear.
>
> Let me cut the cords of my life,
>   Of my desolate being,
> Since cursed is my hearing and seeing.[4]

And as if to prove that his poems in a so-called "humorous Negro dialect" were false, with equal facility he wrote verses in an "Irish brogue":

> Tim Murphy's gon' walkin' wid Maggie O'Neill,
>   O chone! [5]

To get a hearing was his purpose, and one remembers that his remarks to James Weldon Johnson were not lightly said: "I've got to write dialect poetry; it's the only way I can get them to listen to me."

Another Negro poet who was born in Ohio was James Edwin Campbell. His life was devoted to journalism in Chicago; he was by no means as widely known as Dunbar, and Johnson in his biographical index of authors in *The Book of American Negro Poetry* was uncertain as to the dates of Campbell's birth and death. In the few verses of Campbell's writing that Johnson quoted, the lines in dialect reveal a more genuine and deeper reach into the imaginative life of the North American continent than any of the many verses that crowd the double columns of *The Complete Poems of Paul Laurence Dunbar*. Today Campbell's verses have almost the same anonymity that gave life to the Negro work songs and spirituals:

> Salvation's light comes pourin' down—
> Hit fill de chu'ch an' all de town—
> Why, angels' robes go rustlin' 'roun',
> An' hebben on de Yurf am foun',
> When ol' Sis' Judy pray.[6]

[4] "Despair" from *Complete Poems*. Reprinted by permission of Dodd, Mead & Company, Inc.

[5] "Circumstances Alter Cases" from *Complete Poems*. Reprinted by permission of Dodd, Mead & Company, Inc.

[6] "When Ol' Sis' Judy Prays" from *The Book of American Negro Poetry*, ed. by James Weldon Johnson, by permission of Harcourt, Brace and Company.

And the same quality enters Campbell's "De Cunjah Man," [7] which despite its artificial devices of writing in dialect has its moment of imaginative validity, and one feels that the poem in its own right has greater importance than its author:

> Me see him stan' de yudder night
> Right een de road een white moon-light;
> Him toss him arms, him whirl him 'roun',
> Him stomp him foot urpon de groun';
> De snaiks come crawlin', one by one,
> Me hyuh um hiss, me break an' run—
>   De Cunjah man, de Cunjah man,
>   O chillen, run, de Cunjah man!

Within his limitations Campbell achieved a rare objectivity in writing verse, and his comparative lack of fame was probably an advantage that he held over the readily patronized talents of Dunbar.

William Stanley Braithwaite was born in Boston, Massachusetts, in 1878. As an editor of the literary section of the *Boston Evening Transcript,* he refused to allow questions of racial discrimination to modify his opinions; his anthologies of English verse, which were published in a series that extended from Elizabethan times through the reign of George IV, were models of informative, unpretentious, scholarly, and decorous compilation. And perhaps no man of letters in America during the period between 1900 and 1912 was better informed in a general knowledge of English verse than he. As James Weldon Johnson wrote of him in 1922,

. . . he stands unique among all the Aframerican writers the 'United States has yet produced. He has gained his place, taking as the standard and measure for his work the identical standard and measure applied to American writers and American literature. He has asked for no allowances or rewards, either directly or indirectly, on account of his race.[8]

---

[7] From *The Book of American Negro Poetry,* ed. by James Weldon Johnson, by permission of Harcourt, Brace and Company.
[8] *Ibid.*

In this respect one must not underestimate his strength of moral character and courage, and Johnson's appreciation of his merits was one that reflected honor upon both writers. Johnson went on to say:

> Mr. Braithwaite is the author of two volumes of verses, lyrics of delicate and tenuous beauty. . . . But his place in American literature is due more to his work as a critic and anthologist than to his work as a poet. There was still another role he has played, that of friend of poetry and poets. It is a recognized fact that in the work which preceded the present revival of poetry in the United States, no one rendered more unremitting and valuable service than Mr. Braithwaite.[9]

Of Dunbar's and Braithwaite's immediate contemporaries, James Weldon Johnson himself, who was born in Jacksonville, Florida, in 1871, was the most distinguished figure, and the only American Negro poet of the twentieth century who achieved poetic maturity. He had the good fortune not to be a precocious writer, and while he remained self-conscious and aware of his responsibilities to his race, he was also aware of those less obvious responsibilities which came to him in maintaining his dignity as a writer. His *The Autobiography of an Ex-Colored Man* (1912) is a prose document of a kind that deserves to be placed on the same shelf that should be reserved for the British poet W. H. Davies' *The Autobiography of a Super-Tramp* (1906). Of the two books, Johnson's is perhaps the more sophisticated, and unlike most literature of its kind, the quality of its prose merits respect. After Johnson graduated from Atlanta University in 1894, he furthered his education by the study of law and was admitted to the bar in Florida in 1897. Meanwhile he had been principal of the Stanton Central Grammar School for Negroes in Jacksonville, Florida. In 1901 he moved to New York, and in collaboration with his brother, J. Rosamond Johnson, a singer, wrote songs that achieved celebrity on the Broadway stage. After taking a master's degree and attending Columbia University for three years, Johnson was appointed United States Consul to Puerto Cabello, Venezuela, in 1906, and he continued

[9] From *The Book of American Negro Poetry*, ed. by James Weldon Johnson, by permission of Harcourt, Brace and Company.

his services as a United States consul by accepting another appointment to Corinto, Nicaragua, in 1909.

His first book of poems, *Fifty Years, and Other Poems,* appeared in 1917, and though the quality of verse was often marred by occasional clichés in phrasing, such individual poems as "The White Witch" (which has been frequently quoted in anthologies of American verse) shows the presence of a gifted poetic imagination. And no single book of poems written by a Negro in America equaled the dignity and restraint of his seven sermons in verse, *God's Trombones* [10] (1927). Of these the first sermon, "The Creation," in unrhymed verse, was the most successful. The six poems which followed it were less so because their closing lines seemed to lack the required note of finality that was so distinctly heard in the last lines of the first poem:

> Then into it He blew the breath of life,
> And man became a living soul.
> Amen. Amen.

In his latter years, Johnson became a widely known publicist and was a Visiting Professor of Creative Literature at New York University. In 1933 he was awarded the W. E. B. Du Bois Prize for Negro Literature and he was a member of the Academy of Political Science and the Ethical Society. On June 26, 1938, he was killed in an automobile accident, near Wiscasset, Maine, and among the honorary pallbearers at his funeral were Colonel Theodore Roosevelt, Deems Taylor, and Carl Van Vechten, whose presence signified a national tribute to the most distinguished Negro writer of his day in America.

In the younger generation of Negro poets who came into prominence after Johnson had established his reputation as a publicist and the author of a first book of poems, none had greater promise than Claude McKay, who was born in Jamaica, West Indies, in 1890. In 1922, his third book of poems, *Harlem Shadows,* with an introduction by Max Eastman, appeared. At that time McKay belonged to a group of younger American writers whose political ideas were semi-Marxian and whose con-

[10] By permission of The Viking Press. Copyright, 1927, by The Viking Press, Inc.

duct, so admirably described by Mabel Dodge in her *Movers and Shakers* (1936), was wholly Bohemian. The group included Edna St. Vincent Millay, John Reed, Max Eastman, and Floyd Dell, and it contributed verses and prose to *The Liberator* (of which Eastman was an editor). All felt the influence of Rupert Brooke's "The Great Lover," [11] and beneath the surfaces of political excitement, the following lines from Brooke's poem were remembered and emulated:

> O dear my loves, O faithless, once again
> This one last gift I give: that after men
> Shall know, and later lovers, far-removed,
> Praise you, "All these were lovely"; say, "He loved."

No poet in America more clearly reflected the immediate effects of Brooke's widely distributed influence than McKay; and in McKay's verses, Brooke's diction and imagery (and without the loss of personal charm) acquired tropical heat and coloring. McKay's talents, even in their earliest expression, were overripe, and his facility in writing verse probably exhausted his resources before he could find a mature and memorable expression of them. McKay's lyrical gifts were genuine, and were perhaps of a higher quality than he realized; and it is to be regretted that his later ventures in writing were devoted to semiautobiographical romances in prose.

A less spectacular gift than McKay's but one of greater purity in language and emotion was possessed by Jessie Redmon Fauset, who was educated in the public schools of Philadelphia and at Cornell University, and who traveled extensively in Europe. For several years, Miss Fauset was literary editor of *The Crisis,* and though she insisted that all her life she had "wanted to write novels and have had one published," her contributions in verse were of a character that reminds one of a less mature Sara Teasdale. Although her accomplishments in verse were slight and unpretentious, it is not unlikely that a few of her occasional verses will in more fortunate times anticipate the sensitive and,

---

[11] From *Collected Poems.* Reprinted by permission of Dodd, Mead & Company, Inc.

it is to be hoped, thoroughly unpatronized qualities of Negro verse.

Langston Hughes's first book of verse appeared in 1926 with an introduction by Carl Van Vechten. Of Hughes, Van Vechten wrote:

Born on February 1, 1902, in Joplin, Missouri, he had lived, before his twelfth year, in the City of Mexico, Topeka, Kansas, Colorado Springs, Charlestown, Indiana, Kansas City, and Buffalo. He attended Central High School, from which he graduated, at Cleveland, Ohio, while in the summer, there and in Chicago, he worked as delivery- and dummy-boy in hat stores. In his senior year he was elected class poet and editor of the Year Book.[12]

Van Vechten continued his introduction with a further list of Langston Hughes's travels, which included journeys to Europe and Africa, and the character of Hughes's adventurous, restless, wandering life was reflected in his novel, *Not Without Laughter* (1930), his short stories, and his autobiography. Hughes's talents for writing verse were discovered by Vachel Lindsay, who, on one of his lecture tours through the United States, met the young Negro poet who was then a busboy in a Washington hotel. Lindsay's encouragement, as well as Jessie Fauset's acceptance of Hughes's early verses for the pages of *The Crisis,* led to the publication of his first book, *The Weary Blues.* The verse of Lindsay and of Carl Sandburg left its impress upon the external appearance of Hughes's lively and extraverted portraits of Harlem café life. In *The Weary Blues,* in *Fine Clothes to the Jew* (1927), and in *Shakespeare in Harlem* (1942) Hughes caught and projected scenes of urban Negro life that were as melodramatic and as vivid as Erskine Caldwell's scenes of misadventure in the lives of the "poor Whites" that were enacted upon the Broadway stage for seven years in *Tobacco Road. The Weary Blues* and *Fine Clothes to the Jew* held the attention of the public in much the same fashion and, it is to be feared, for some of the same reasons for which *Tobacco Road* enjoyed its long run in the vicinity of Times Square. Hughes's sketches in verse with their undertones

12 Introduction by Carl Van Vechten to *The Weary Blues* by Langston Hughes. By permission of Alfred A. Knopf, Inc. Copyright, 1927, by Alfred A. Knopf, Inc.

of bitterness, humor, and pathos were of a kind that awakened the sensibilities of the well-meaning social worker rather than the serious reader of poetry. Like Dunbar, who had been encouraged to write "in dialect," Hughes's verses seem to have been written in a latter-day formula of night-club songs and social protest, which were almost certain to attract fashionable curiosity and patronage, but did not leave a deep or lasting impression upon their readers. Hughes's readers had been entertained, and sometimes shocked, by scenes of a brutalized and amoral life in Harlem, but Hughes's characters lacked the dignity and poise that were implied in James Weldon Johnson's Negro sermons, and that loss vitiates Hughes's avowedly light verses in *Shakespeare in Harlem.*

Far more studiously and gravely inclined were Countee Cullen's verses in *Color* (1925). Cullen was born in New York in 1903,[13] and was the adopted son of a minister of the Salem Methodist Episcopal Church which he had founded in 1902. Cullen attended New York University and he received his master's degree in English Literature at Harvard in 1926. In sensitivity and in his devotion to literature, Cullen followed in the footsteps of William Stanley Braithwaite, and if his own verse was not always successfully written, like Jessie Fauset he upheld a standard for Negro verse that was not modified by racial distinctions and which showed maturity of taste and of judgment in an anthology of Negro verse, *Caroling Dusk* (1927). Another poet whose education and general background has made a definite, and at present immeasurable, contribution to Negro literature was Sterling A. Brown. Brown was born in Washington, D. C., in 1901, and received his master of arts degree at Harvard in 1923. If it can be said that Cullen continued his writings in the direction of Braithwaite's verse, it can also be said that Brown extended the work that had been so well begun by James Weldon Johnson. Quite as Johnson gave new life to the Negro "spirituals" in his *God's Trombones,* Brown turned his attention to a revival of the Negro work song in his *Southern Road* (1932). He has yet to achieve the dignity in verse that Johnson accomplished, but

[13] Cullen died in New York January, 1946.

his gifts, like Johnson's, seem to be those of a late maturity, and from 1923 onward the seriousness as well as the depth of his intentions has remained unquestioned.

In 1942 the Yale Series of Younger Poets, edited by Stephen Vincent Benét, published a first book, *For My People,* by Margaret Walker, which received high praise and wide recognition. Margaret Walker was born in Birmingham, Alabama, in 1915, and was educated at Northwestern University and at the University of Iowa from which she received her master's degree in 1940. Like Brown's her interests have been academic and they have led to her accepting a professorship in English at Livingstone College, Salisbury, North Carolina. As in an earlier decade Langston Hughes's verse carried its debt to Carl Sandburg's *Chicago Poems,* so in *For My People* Margaret Walker's verses held an external relationship to Archibald MacLeish's *Public Speech* (1936). Many of the verses were written as though they were spoken in public and from a raised platform in a large amphitheater—and they seemed to express the racial and political temper of the 1930's in American verse. Probably the most enduring promise of the volume can be found in its unrhymed sonnets, for these have been less urgently affected by the demands of a moment in which many lesser poets of the decade felt that "public speech" should be their sole concern in writing poetry.

It was not without wisdom that the elder generation of Dunbar, Johnson, and Braithwaite saw the figure of the Russian poet, Alexander Pushkin, as a distant end in view for their accomplishment. Pushkin was known to have had Negro blood in his veins, but that accident of birth had not adversely modified the quality of his poetry. The American Negro has no facile means of solving the problem that a gift for writing poetry places before him; yet Pushkin's example is not to be lost sight of. And the obvious fact that the Negro writer in the United States is, above all other considerations, the product of a North American environment should not be forgotten.

ROBINSON JEFFERS
AND THE BIRTH OF TRAGEDY

In 1925, when his fourth book, *Roan Stallion, Tamar, and Other Poems,* appeared with the imprint of a commercial publisher's name on its title page, the American public discovered Robinson Jeffers as its major poet of the Pacific Coast. Subconsciously, and also in a superficial sense, the public had been well prepared to receive him. At that moment no dinner conversation was complete without mention of Freud or Gertrude Atherton's novel, *Black Oxen* (1923), with its theme of sexual rejuvenation through glandular surgery, and Eugene O'Neill's new play, *Desire Under the Elms* (1925). Jeffers' fable in unrhymed verse of the woman whose name was California and of the roan stallion, was the latest arrival among those who enjoyed a further excuse for using a newly learned Freudian vocabulary. If this latter enjoyment in reading Robinson Jeffers' narrative poems was less profound than serious critics of poetry wished it to be, it had the charm of being provocative—and the very mention of Robinson Jeffers' name carried with it the aura of a phenomenal popular success and notoriety.

In the eyes of the public (many of whom seldom read poetry) good fortune had attended *Roan Stallion,* for the book was greeted with the same "shock of recognition" that had been reserved for Sherwood Anderson's *Dark Laughter* (1925), Joseph Hergesheimer's *Cytherea* (1922), D. H. Lawrence's *The Rainbow* (1915), and James Branch Cabell's *Jurgen* (1919). If Jeffers' intentions were often misunderstood (as indeed they were), *Roan Stallion* and subsequent volumes of verse, *The Women at Point Sur* (1927), *Cawdor* (1928), and *Dear Judas* (1928), received sufficient attention to make his name well known. No poet of Jeffers' generation in America enjoyed a more widely spread and quickly acknowledged fame.

However fortunately Jeffers' fourth book reached a public that seemed rather more than willing to accept its violence and to speculate upon its relevance to Freudian psychology, the preparation for its arrival in America was of an earlier origin than the vogue of what was then called "sexual realism in the novel." That preparation had begun when George Cabot Lodge, "Bay" Lodge, had reviewed in 1896 his pursuit of philosophic speculation in Berlin. Henry Adams' "Young Savage" had turned to the teachings of Schopenhauer at their source, and however dimly he may have perceived it, he had had his vision of a "Götterdämmerung." Even as recently as 1934, his presence was recalled in Edith Wharton's memoirs, *A Backward Glance*,[1] and his shadowy stature had lost none of its significance. Mrs. Wharton wrote:

> Bay Lodge . . . was one of the most brilliant and versatile youths I have ever known. In what direction he would eventually have developed I have never been sure; his sudden death at the age of thirty-six cut short such conjectures. He believed himself to be meant for poetry and letters. . . . I felt as did most of his friends . . . that if poetry was to be his ultimate form he must pass beyond the imitative stage into fuller self-expression. But he had a naturally scholarly mind, and might have turned in the end to history and archaeology. . . .

Her comments on "Bay" Lodge remind us of the early Robinson Jeffers, the son of Dr. William Hamilton Jeffers. His father had been the last of a line of Scotch-Irish Calvinists, who had been a professor of Greek and of Latin and at the time of his son's birth, January 10, 1887, was a distinguished theologian at the Western Theological Seminary in Pittsburgh. Robinson Jeffers' early education, through the influence of his father, had been at boarding schools in Europe—in schools at Geneva, Lausanne, Zurich, and Leipzig, and in those years, the closing years of the nineteenth century, Robinson Jeffers came into impressionable contact with the very scenes that "Bay" Lodge knew. Jeffers had read his Greek (taught to him by his father), and at fifteen his imagination had been stirred by a reading of Friedrich Nietzsche's *Thus Spake Zarathustra* and Dante Gabriel Rossetti's poems; and it was said by Jeffers' biographer, Lawrence Clark

[1] By permission of D. Appleton-Century Company, Inc.

Powell, that the boy at fifteen "was able to think in Italian,
French and German." And if there was less of Schopenhauer in
the boy's mind than had been retained by "Bay" Lodge on his
return to the United States in 1897, there was a measurable influence of Schopenhauer's great disciple, Nietzsche, upon his
imagination.

Jeffers' early books, his *Flagons and Apples* (1912) and his
Californians (1916), were of that "imitative stage" of writing
that Mrs. Wharton remarked upon as she recalled the verses that
"Bay" Lodge had written. *Flagons and Apples,* with its title
taken from the fifth verse of the second chapter of The Song of
Solomon, betrayed what Mrs. Wharton had called "a naturally
scholarly mind," and the young poet had a taste for reading
poetry which had been formed by its discoveries of Rossetti
and Swinburne. Jeffers was to succeed where Lodge had failed,
but it is only because we have read *Roan Stallion* and the volumes which followed it, that we can recognize Jeffers' second
volume, *Californians,* as "transitional" poetry. The book contained what Jeffers in his foreword to his *Selected Poetry* (1938)
described as "preparatory exercises" in the writing of traditional
verse forms, which included the sonnet, blank verse, the *terza
rima,* and the Spenserian stanza. From his biographer we know
that Jeffers' university career was of a mixed and "scientific"
order, and that after he received his A.B. at Occidental College
in 1905, his studies at various universities, including the University of Zurich, and a course in medicine at the University of
Southern California, took on the character of being as experimental as his early verses. His *Californians* was neither better
nor worse than what might be expected from the writing of a
diversely educated man who had probably read the poetry of
Wordsworth and of E. A. Robinson with studious enthusiasm.
The poems were "Californian" in detail, and one might conclude from a number of them that the countryside in that Far
Western climate was better and larger than any other place on
earth. In the latter half of the volume the cheerful temper of
its lines and stanzas underwent a change to a doubting, stormy,
and rhetorical sense of loss. It was clear that the author had

begun to learn the rules of writing poetry, but he had yet to find a language that he could call his own.

Between 1912 and 1923, a transformation had taken place in Jeffers' life as well as in his poetry; he had married Una Call Kuster, a fellow student at the University of Southern California, in 1913, he had received a legacy which made him independent of immediate financial worries, and he had made his home at Carmel, California. The legend of Jeffers at Carmel has for one of its anecdotes the story of his building a stone tower with his own hands, and perhaps the incident has a private and internal relationship to the character of his poetry. But many people have built stone towers without being poets at all, and many less fortunate men than Jeffers have broken rocks and mended roads during a term in prison—and so far as literature is concerned, the results were negligible. A better index to the character of Jeffers' poetry lies in that aspect of Jeffers' legend which reveals him as a cultivated and modest man who cares little or nothing for dinner-table conversation and is inept in the arts of "literary gossip" and "small talk," and this aspect of his legend seems consistent with his determination "not to tell lies in verse." On the few occasions when Jeffers found it necessary to publish prose, his statements have been well poised and clear.

As for the moment which led to the fortunate reception of *Roan Stallion* in 1925, Lawrence Clark Powell's *An Introduction to Robinson Jeffers* [2] (Dijon, 1932) has a paragraph or two of unusual candor and of timely interest:

In 1923 the Book Club of California was preparing an anthology of verse by California writers. The poets George Sterling, James Rorty and Genevieve Taggard were the editors. Someone, perhaps having heard of *Californians,* told them of Jeffers, and the Carmel poet was asked to contribute to the venture. His "Continent's End" gave the anthology its name, but it made no stir.

The following year Jeffers again decided to undertake the printing of some of his verse at his own expense. Accordingly, *Tamar,* a long narrative poem which he had written in 1920 or 1921 but had never submitted to any publisher because of its length, was sent to a New York printer, Peter G. Boyle. Boyle was both enthusiastic and generous.

---

[2] By permission of the Author.

Tamar and Other Poems was issued in an edition of five hundred copies, and its printer sent review copies over the land. They had no effect. The remainder of 450 copies was shipped across the continent to Jeffers. . . .

Then he mailed a copy of Tamar to James Rorty because of their correspondence, and one to George Sterling because he had lived in Carmel and knew the scene of the verses. On his return to New York, Rorty showed the book to Mark Van Doren and Babette Deutsch; and led by Rorty, all three wrote enthusiastic reviews hailing "a new poet of genius," "a major poet," etc.

Jeffers "wrote," so Powell tells us, "later of some of his friends and their poetry, thus showing his gratitude to those poets who discovered him, by reviewing books of theirs. These reviews of volumes of verse by James Rorty, Mark Van Doren, and Babette Deutsch, and the memories of George Sterling are examples of beautiful prose."

The tone of Jeffers' prose was forthright and mature and he employed his occasions for writing it to advance his general views concerning poetry. In his review of James Rorty's *The Children of the Sun* [3] (1927) Jeffers wrote:

"The poets lie too much." Nietzsche wrote with brief contempt; he knew, for himself was one. Their profession is to tell the exciting truth; but a lie is an easier way to excitement—a reality is always so much more stubborn, so much harder to digest. Sometimes the lying becomes epidemic with them; then it is called a poetic tradition or a new movement; sometimes it becomes matter for cynical confession and a man writes on his title-page "mundus vult decipi"—"people want to be fooled"—Barnum's motto.

2

Whatever critical commentary might be made of Jeffers' major poems (and these include "Roan Stallion" itself and "The Tower Beyond Tragedy") Nietzsche's essay, *The Birth of Tragedy*, should not be forgotten. It was a Nietzschean "reality" that Jeffers perceived: the external appearances of Jeffers' unrhymed lines were deliberately "antipoetic" in the same sense that Nietzsche had spoken of the poetic "lie"; and what has now become a familiar aspect of Jeffers' "despair" is no less profound

[3] In *Advance*, April 1, 1927, by permission of the Author.

and as far removed from a literal instruction to the human race to commit suicide as Nietzsche's version of the story of King Midas. It was in *The Birth of Tragedy* that Nietzsche presented in his most eloquent vein his famous definitions of Apollonian and Dionysian opposites in art; and in the light with which Nietzsche illuminated the pages of his essay, it is significant that Aeschylus claimed as his source for divine inspiration the ecstasy, the voice of prophecy, the insight, and the violence of Dionysus. It was from this very source that Jeffers derived his authority to write his poem, "The Tower Beyond Tragedy," and the reality of what he had to say springs from and frequently returns to the story of King Midas that Nietzsche wrote in *The Birth of Tragedy:* [4]

There is an ancient story that King Midas hunted in the forest a long time for the wise *Silenus,* the companion of Dionysus, without capturing him. When Silenus at last fell into his hands, the king asked what was the best and most desirable of all things for man. Fixed and immovable, the demigod said not a word; till at last, urged by the king, he gave a shrill laugh and broke out into these words: "Oh, wretched ephemeral race, children of chance and misery, why do ye compel me to tell you what it were most expedient for you not to hear? What is best of all is beyond your reach forever: not to be born, not to *be,* to be *nothing.* But the second best for you—is quickly to die."

It is from these lines that Jeffers took his essential themes, the "subject matter" of both his classical and Wagnerian narratives; and the same subject matter finds its expression in all his narrative poems. Lawrence Clark Powell has spoken of the "disillusionment" that came upon Jeffers after the First World War, but since it is well established that Jeffers had long held Nietzsche's writings in high regard, this latter observation is one of secondary and perhaps negligible importance. Many writers of the period in which Jeffers found himself famous were also "disillusioned" and in 1926 F. Scott Fitzgerald published a book of short stories under the title *All the Sad Young Men.* If Jeffers was "disillusioned," his disillusionment was not of the same order as that which afflicted his younger contemporaries, and

[4] From *Ecce Homo and the Birth of Tragedy,* Modern Library ed. By permission of Random House, Inc.

they did not revive, as Jeffers did, an early reading of Nietzsche to overcome their grief.

Since the imagery and speech of Jeffers' poetry remain well within the philosophic terms that are circumscribed by the writings of Schopenhauer, Nietzsche, and Oswald Spengler, it is not surprising that Jeffers' heroines resemble Wagnerian Valkyries. In "At the Fall of an Age," Jeffers' image of the Greek Helen is more than life-size; and in a red twilight on a half-darkened stage she is obviously less Greek than post-Wagnerian. And Jeffers' Orestes "who had climbed the tower beyond time, consciously, and cast humanity" and "entered the earlier fountain" is a Greek figure only in the sense that Dionysus and Silenus are of an ancient Greek heritage and in "The Tower Beyond Tragedy" Orestes' progress is toward a heaven that lies "beyond" Nietzsche's "good and evil."

Because of Jeffers' affinity with the teachings of Nietzsche, it is dangerous to insist too warmly that his view of the world with the Pacific coast line at his back is "anti-intellectual." Jeffers' quarrel with the "intellectuals" has within it the nay-and-yea-saying paradox which Nietzsche so consistently placed before the readers of his *Thus Spake Zarathustra*. And Jeffers' conclusions (whether one accepts them entirely or not) are those of a learned and, in his own person, gently spoken man. The God whom he defines is more abstract than the majority of gods who inhabit the plural universe of other poets; and we should also remember that Jeffers speaks of his deity with an almost "intellectual" air of civilized detachment:

> Yourself, if you had not encountered and loved
> Our unkindly all but inhuman God,
> Who is very beautiful and too secure to want worshippers,
> And includes indeed the sheep with the wolves,
> You too might have been looking for a church.[5]

The argument is continued and concluded in another poem, "Triad": [6]

[5] "Intellectuals" from *Selected Poetry of Robinson Jeffers*. By permission of Random House, Inc.

[6] From *Selected Poetry of Robinson Jeffers*. By permission of Random House, Inc.

The poet, who wishes not to play games with words,
His affair being to awake dangerous images
And call the hawks;—they all feed the future, they serve God,
Who is very beautiful, but hardly a friend of humanity.

A distant ancestor of Jeffers' God was, of course, the sun, and a more recent figure of that ancient line was the Hebrew Jehovah, whose presence in the beginning was the "word," whose power was held in no visible image to his people, and whose tests of Job's virtues were certainly not those that had been inspired by friendliness or the desire to be kind. In this instance, Jeffers' reference seems to take its channel backward to a source by the way of Scotch-Irish Calvinism, and if the way seems dark to cheerful readers of poetry, it is no more unfamiliar than the darkness through which Hawthorne revealed the souls of the New England Puritans.

The non-Greco-Germanic references in Jeffers' verse are either Californian or Celtic; and for the interested reader of Jeffers' Californian narratives, his biographer has provided a map of Monterey as well as a sketch of "Continent's End," Alaska. One feels that his biographer would also have gladly provided a map of Ireland that showed the route of Jeffers' poems in the *Descent to the Dead* (1931). Maps have their charms, and many a·lecturer on British poetry in American universities has entertained his students by tracing with a pointer in his right hand the joys of a bicycle trip through Wordsworth's lake country and a stop at a tavern not too far from Stratford-on-Avon. But the use of maps (lively in themselves as they may be) is scarcely a substitute for the reading of the poetry which happens to contain the same place names that have been written on a flat, two-dimensional surface. Nor is it possible to quote fragments of "Roan Stallion" so as to illustrate its descriptive felicity, for its physical details are (as they should be) of a kind that unify and speed the progress of the story. No narrative poem written by an American during the twentieth century is a better example of the classical rules of unity than Jeffers' "Roan Stallion": place, time, action, its characters, and its emotional temper are of one piece; and even its violent scenes of action fall with propriety within the design of the poem. If they are removed from their context, individual episodes within the poem become ridiculous, but the poem itself, like a canvas filled by the seemingly harsh and "impossible" colors of Delacroix, has its own life and its own veracity, and these are as rare in poetry as they are in painting. One need go no further than Jeffers' shorter poems in his *Descent to the Dead*, to show that the imagination which gave color and motion to "Roan Stallion" has a Celtic aspect and a reference to an ancient past in Ireland. It was in the sight of Irish round towers, of memorial shrines, of dateless rocks and stones (which was to W. B. Yeats a "secret discipline") that Jeffers discovered a transatlantic affinity to nature. The affinity was by no means a complacent one; and it was of cold, gray Antrim and of Iona, the sacred island of the Hebrides, that Jeffers wrote:

> I wish not to lie here.
> There's hardly a plot of earth not blessed for burial, but here
> One might dream badly.
>
> .   .   .   .
>
> Kings buried in the lee of the saint,
> Kings of fierce Norway, blood-boltered Scotland, bitterly dreaming
> Treacherous Ireland.[7]

Jeffers' lines at Ossian's grave may be read as the "romantic" tribute which they are, yet the temperament and the eloquence in which the poem has its speech are so obviously Celtic in their origin that to call them "romantic" almost seems an understatement. In the "Ghosts in England" there is the traditional and Celtic distrust of the wealthy southern island, England,

> No pity for the great pillar of empire settling to a fall,
>   the pride
> and the power slowly dissolving.[8]

The ghosts that Jeffers raised in his *Descent to the Dead* were of the same quality that gave life to his resurrection of Achilles' Myrmidons in the dramatic poem "At the Fall of an Age." It is the dead who live and exert their powers in Jeffers' Irish poems, and of these the story of Mary Byrnes, in "In the Hill at

[7] "Iona: The Grove of Kings" from *Selected Poetry of Robinson Jeffers*. By permission of Random House, Inc.

[8] "Ghosts in England" from *Selected Poetry of Robinson Jeffers*. By permission of Random House, Inc.

New Grange" near the River Boyne, has an insight that is comparable to W. B. Yeats's "Crazy Jane" lyrics in *Words for Music Perhaps*. There is no mistaking of Mary Byrnes's origins in Jeffers' version of her speech to her lover:

> Drink, Shane; drink, dear: who cares if a hure is hanged? We kill each other in Ireland to pleasure the dead.[9]

If Nietzsche had provided a "subject matter" and a "philosophic" window through which Jeffers viewed a self-destroying humanity, the imagination and the very eloquence of the speech which expresses it owe their greatest debt to a Celtic inspiration.

3

In the years between the publication of *Cawdor* (1928) and *Be Angry at the Sun* (1941) Jeffers' position as a poet among his contemporaries became one that can almost be compared with Victor Hugo's eminence in France of the mid-nineteenth century. Jeffers' prophecies of disaster in the affairs of Europe and America had come true; that is, it was true enough that a Second World War had increased the tendency toward violence that Jeffers had foreseen—and in this connection, Amiel's remarks (severe as they may seem) on Victor Hugo are not inappropriate:

> Victor Hugo superbly ignores everything which he has not foreseen. He does not know that pride limits the mind, and that a limitless pride is a littleness of soul. . . . He is vowed to the Titanic; his gold is always mixed with lead, his insight with childishness, his reason with madness . . . like the blaze of a house on fire his light is blinding. In short, he astonishes, but provokes, he stirs, but annoys. His note is always half or two-thirds false, and that is why he perpetually makes us feel uncomfortable. The great poet in him cannot get clear of the charlatan.[10]

In Jeffers' case, it would be better to change the last sentence of the quotation to read, "The great poet in him cannot get

---

[9] "In the Hill at New Grange" from *Selected Poetry of Robinson Jeffers*. By permission of Random House, Inc.

[10] From *Essays in Criticism* by Matthew Arnold, Second Series. By permission of The Macmillan Company.

clear of Nietzsche's philosophy." There are no signs of the charlatan in Jeffers; yet Jeffers at his worst has attempted to write poetry less with words than with ideas; in the less successful of his narratives, he shows greater concern for the consistency of his general beliefs than he does for the actual sight of human conduct or the structure of his poems. His advantage is a lack of seeming preoccupied with mere talk of "writing poetry"; and in this respect his work is comparable to the so-called "artless" art of D. H. Lawrence's prose: we can assume that Jeffers' early knowledge of Greek had trained his ear in the limitations and adaptations of the classical hexameter in English verse, and his skill in writing the long line of verse in English is no mere accident. He has tuned whatever instruments he has heard or used in the past to the sound of a speaking voice, but it is the general effect, the overtone, and the central dominant rhythm or the dominant image at the center of the poem that seem to be his concern. In Jeffers' poetry, as in Lawrence's prose, the eloquence, the urgency of the speaking voice, are of primary consideration; and if, at any moment, the oracular statement shows signs of losing force, a colorful image is brought forward to fill the eye. In "At the Fall of an Age," the sight of Helen and of Achilles' Myrmidons, risen from their graves in Asia, carry the weight, and not without success, of a repetitious philosophic argument. We have already spoken of how well "Roan Stallion" fills the eye and holds the attention of the reader; its art is self-contained and the narrative is likely to survive the present age as a Californian parable, a story that has for its heritage an ancient reference to a deity in the form of a beast, and in Jeffers' poem it assumes a "local habitation and a name."

It is almost impossible to quote Jeffers' poetry successfully. For the most part, his verse must be taken whole, the good with the bad, the penetrating flashes of insight along with inflated rhetoric and heavily worded pronouncements and prophecies. In this respect, much of his poetry resembles the verse of Herman Melville and that of the later Whitman who wrote "Passage to India"— and to this one must add the personal legend of Jeffers' fame. In later years, that legend has sustained the many shorter poems he has written, poems in which Jeffers, a lonely figure, against a backdrop of the Pacific Coast, or the rocks of Antrim, or Europe in flames, takes the reader into his confidence. As he remarks upon it, the world may be doomed to self-destruction, but not Jeffers. The voice in which he has chosen to speak is the voice of one who made up his mind long ago as to what he had to say; and the sight of the eagle, the hawk, the falcon, or the wild swan may be relied upon to stir his imagination. Perhaps the most characteristic of his shorter poems is his sonnet, "Love the Wild Swan": [11]

> "I hate my verses, every line, every word.
> Oh pale and brittle pencils ever to try
> One grass-blade's curve, or the throat of one bird
> That clings to twig, ruffled against white sky.
> Oh cracked and twilight mirrors ever to catch
> One color, one glinting flash, of the splendor of things.
> Unlucky hunter, Oh bullets of wax,
> The lion beauty, the wild-swan wings, the storm of the wings."
> —This wild swan of a world is no hunter's game.
> Better bullets than yours would miss the white breast,
> Better mirrors than yours would crack in the flame.
> Does it matter whether you hate your . . . self? At least
> Love your eyes that can see, your mind that can
> Hear the music, the thunder of the wings. Love the wild swan.

The art of the poem is beautifully concealed, and it was expressed with a humility that stands in contrast to the melodrama of blood and fire which so often enters and seems to take command of Jeffers' poetry. Certainly W. B. Yeats's "The Wild Swans at Coole" is not far distant in its imagery and feeling from the last three lines of Jeffers' sonnet, and in Jeffers' recent *Be Angry at the Sun* (1941) there is a perceptible relationship between the shorter pieces in the volume and the poetry that Yeats wrote after 1919. In the same volume there is a semidramatic sketch of Hitler, quite as Wagner would have composed a ballet with incidental music for a nineteenth-century production of *Macbeth*. The appropriate insights into the phenomenon of the doomed Leader are there, and in a Wagnerian sense they are closer than

[11] From *Selected Poetry of Robinson Jeffers*. By permission of Random House, Inc.

any other attempt made by an American to define what seems essential in Hitler's personality. But it is impossible for the reader to know how consciously Jeffers echoed the bombast and the verbal nonsense of Hitler's speeches, or whether or not the lines of the poem were written in parody of an ineptly translated Wagnerian ballet into English verse. Yet the fact remains that the figures of the poem, its images of Frederick the Great, and of the Leader himself, its female soothsayer, its masked creatures, leave their impression upon the imagination of the reader. One is reminded of Amiel's commentary on Victor Hugo, and one might well say that Jeffers' "gold is always mixed with lead," and "like the blaze of a house on fire his light is blinding," and "his note is always half or two-thirds false."

4

Although the critics of the American Far West and its Pacific Coast justly regard Robinson Jeffers of Tor House in Carmel as their major poet, the sensational character of the literature which the region produced has scarcely diminished since the day when Joaquin Miller was known as the "Bard of the Sierras." The Bohemia of George Sterling and Jack London has long since declined, but in the 1930's the tendency of California to produce vehement extremes in its literature was also represented in the person of Yvor Winters, who taught English at Stanford University and was Jeffers' severest critic. Like Jeffers', Winters' birthplace was far removed from California itself; he was born in Chicago, Illinois, in 1900, and he entered the University of Chicago in 1917. Ill health interrupted his college career and he went to the Far West to improve it, and there he continued his studies in English literature. In 1927 he published a second book of poems, *The Bare Hills,* which owed some of its distinction to the clarity and visual force of its imagery, and since talk of "Imagism" was in the air, and literary circles still discussed the merits and flaws of the quarrel between Amy Lowell and Ezra Pound, Winters' book was promptly described as an example of the "new" poetry and of "Imagism." A few years later, Winters made his arrival as a moral critic, and though his moral object in criticism remained obscure, it was clear that he advanced a neoscholastic attitude in his reviews of poetry. Jeffers could well afford (in the light of his fame) to be modest, but Winters could not, and in his attack on Jeffers' volume, *Dear Judas,* in *Poetry,* February, 1930, Winters wrote: "Now the mysticism of, say, San Juan de la Cruz offers at least the semblance of a spiritual, a human, discipline as a preliminary to union with Divinity; but for Mr. Jeffers a simple and mechanical device lies always ready; namely, suicide, a device to which he has not resorted."

The violence of Winters' critical pronouncements betrayed earnest intentions and a naïve desire to assume authority. He had picked up the teachings of Irving Babbitt and of Paul Elmer More and attempted to further them by fixing rules of a neoscholastic order, but he could not free himself of a tendency to exaggerate whatever he felt was "wrong" or evil in contemporary verse. And his criticism in respect to Jeffers' poetry was like a small and one-sided war (since Jeffers could and did ignore it) between two preachers of Calvinist persuasion. Winters' temper was no less extreme than Jeffers'; and the titles of his books of criticism, *Primitivism and Decadence* (1937) and *Maule's Curse* (1938), indicate the zeal with which he pursued his course. His manner was uniformly serious, and if his verse was less forceful than his prose, his selected poems, *The Giant Weapon* (1943), showed honest intentions in the strains of minor verse and the degree of serious effort that Winters, the critic, had so often preached; but as Coleridge had once remarked of Donne, who seemed, so he said, to twist iron pokers into true-love knots, one feels that Winters has tried by a great exercise of will and well-worn platitudes to transform lovers' knots into iron pokers.

Jeffers' poetry, whatever its flaws may be, needs no defense, and he has phrased his own answer to those who have taken the trouble to dispute his general views; in "Self-Criticism in February," [12] Jeffers wrote:

12 From *Selected Poetry of Robinson Jeffers.* By permission of Random House, Inc.

But the present time is not pastoral, but founded
On violence, pointed for more massive violence: perhaps it is not
Perversity but need that perceives the storm-beauty.
Well, bite on this: your poems are too full of ghosts and demons,
And people like phantoms—how often life's are—
And passion so strained that the clay mouths go praying for destruc-
        tion—
Alas, it is not unusual in life;
To every soul at some time. *But why insist on it. And now*
For the worst fault: you have never mistaken
Demon nor passion nor idealism for the real God.
Then what is most disliked in those verses
Remains most true. *Unfortunately. If only you could sing*
That God is love, or perhaps that social
Justice will soon prevail. I can tell lies in prose.

His last answer is always a return to Nietzsche. But it is probable that his "philosophy" will have less endurance than those
gifts which enabled him to create parables of human blindness
and suffering, to see, as if for the first and last time, the austerities of a Pacific or Irish coast line, and to make his reader aware
of the physical beauty that inhabits the Californian landscape
and the sky above it.

T. S. ELIOT, THE TWENTIETH-CENTURY
"MAN OF FEELING" IN AMERICAN POETRY

There is a story told about Delacroix that could be applied to the literary figure that T. S. Eliot has created in his own name, and the story also illustrates what has been said of Eliot for the past twenty years. Delacroix had been invited to the house of a lady who was fashionable in her love of all that was then fashionable in the arts. He arrived late, and found many of his fellow artists arrayed in the velvet jackets, the scarlet waistcoats, the flowing locks of hair, in all the elaborate detail of that artful negligence which had been so dear to the advanced taste of the romantic artist of the day. Delacroix, a somber, pensive figure, formally, smartly dressed in a frock coat, polished boots, top hat, and lemon-colored gloves, made a sensational impression upon the gathering. As he gave his stick to the footman at the open door of the drawing room, several of his fellow artists hissed, and one guest in a loud whisper muttered, "Poseur! Poseur!"

In 1922, Eliot's arrival on the literary scene (with the publication of *The Waste Land* in the pages of *The Dial*), and in fact almost every subsequent phase of his career, had the same elements of surprise, of formal correctness in external manners, of being fitly dressed for the occasion that had graced the genius of Delacroix. In the past quarter-century no poet of Eliot's generation has been so fortunately reviled, denounced, defamed, buried so often, revived so often, been so enthusiastically defended, and so passionately denied (by his adverse critics) the merits of human contact and of sincerity. Ever since 1922, his antagonists have almost hourly announced the fact of his literary suicide. They implied (and some have used strong language in doing so) that if *The Waste Land* were not a hoax (which it soon proved itself not to be), admiration of the poem was a sign of sterility, if not something worse. Elder critics of poetry had just been taught, and not without difficulty, that the poetry of Edna St. Vincent Millay, Amy Lowell, Carl Sandburg, and Edgar Lee Masters was the highest expression of the "poetic renaissance," and naturally enough, many of these good men felt that though they may have been pushed too far, they were reluctant to be untaught again. The very reading of Eliot seemed to demand an entire process of "unlearning" the merits of his immediate predecessors: here was a writer whose poetry in *Prufrock and Other Observations* (1917), *Poems* (1920), and *The Waste Land* had an unfamiliar character and flavor. Was the poetry light verse? was it clever? was it slightly obscene? was it revolutionary?—or did it have that something which related it to academic discussions of "classicism"? And "classicism" was the very thing that the more outspoken participants in the "poetic renaissance" thought they had buried forever.

In the early 1920's, the more advanced young men in American colleges and universities had become champions of an anti-academic order; they learned H. L. Mencken's *Prejudices* by heart, they rejected everything that had acquired the name of "Victorianism," including the poetry of Browning, Tennyson, and Longfellow, and to these were added the "escapist" novels of Henry James, as well as anything that could be called with equal vehemence "classicism." Van Wyck Brooks's *The Pilgrimage of Henry James* (1925) and Vernon Louis Parrington's monumental *Main Currents in American Thought* (1927-30) expressed the critical spirit of young men who had left instructorships and professorships behind them to become neo-Freudian, neosocial critics of a "New Literature" in New York weeklies. And among these were young men whose enthusiasm for literature had been fostered by writing critical reviews of books for Chicago and New York newspapers.

Of the latter company Burton Rascoe was the liveliest and most conspicuous figure, a Kentucky-born, Oklahoma-bred, Chicago newspaperman, who came to New York in 1921, who wrote a weekly column of literary gossip for the *New York Tribune*, and who became a protagonist of Eliot's early reputation in the United States. Eliot's poetry, from its earliest appearance in

Poetry in 1915, held a phenomenal attraction for widely dissimilar readers; in the praise and blame that it received it had been called names of great variety, but it could never be dismissed as seeming dull. It held the same attraction that the writings of Jean Cocteau and the music of Stravinsky never fail to reawaken; even the unwilling reader of it is prompted to speak aloud in protest—and the protest against *The Dial's* award to *The Waste Land* was so general among liberal and conservative critics alike that the enthusiastic Burton Rascoe enjoyed the role of being the devil's advocate. It was not a question of being interested in or knowing precisely what Eliot's poetry said, but of being certain that it aroused partisan feeling. Rascoe admired Eliot's gifts with the same instinctive fervor with which he admired the poetry of Maxwell Bodenheim, E. E. Cummings, and Marianne Moore, as well as the prose of Ben Hecht, Thyra Samter Winslow, Ernest Boyd, Frank Moore Colby, John Dos Passos, Edmund Wilson, and Willard Huntington Wright. His admirations seemed at times to be inspired by a passionate love of reading everything, yet the reader of his *A Bookman's Daybook* (1929) will discover that he retained a few vehement dislikes, which might well have cut him off from any appreciation of T. S. Eliot, and these were Dante, Irving Babbitt, Paul Elmer More, and Henry James. Rascoe did not suffer the tensions and fears of being "untaught" anything, and he held an advantage over his New York contemporaries because he had so recently arrived from Chicago: Harriet Monroe's *Poetry*, Margaret Anderson's *The Little Review,* and the stately innovations of Scofield Thayer's *The Dial* held no terrors for him. To Chicagoans of the late teens and twenties of the present century, stray copies of Wyndham Lewis' *Blast, The Egoist* (of which Eliot in London was an associate editor), *The Little Review,* and Gertrude Stein's *Three Lives* (1909) and her *Tender Buttons* (1914) were bread and wine at dinner tables. But more important than an education in, or at least an introduction to, the mysteries of a "New Literature," which to its Chicago initiates had the freshness of the wind blowing the length of Michigan Boulevard, was Rascoe's temperamental affinity with the early Eliot.

The affinity was not a matter of literary taste and discrimination, it was not a matter of intense, nor of careful reading, but it was a matter of being far to the left or right of a liberal center; it was the same affinity that had attracted Ezra Pound to Eliot in London, and it was of a nature that baffled Amy Lowell.

Since that day Eliot has had many admirers of a more sober disposition and of greater critical distinction than Burton Rascoe, but none has been more fervent than Rascoe, or one whose word would have been (at that particular moment) heard with greater excitement in hostile circles. Rascoe's discovery of *The Waste Land* is one of the curious, yet seemingly inevitable facts in a career that was filled with curious turns and disquieting surprises. Like Eliot's poetry, Eliot's career betrayed an almost instinctive distaste of boredom, and it touched the sources of otherwise hidden emotions of the day. It was a gift that may be compared to the early Wordsworth's, and to the elder W. B. Yeats's, and its greatest victories were scored in the face of critical abuse.

Rascoe's tribute was among the first of many that had come to one of the most engaging and most powerful literary personalities in twentieth-century poetry. But long after the poetry of T. S. Eliot had become a "classic" in American colleges, long after thousands of undergraduates had gone forth into literary battles with his name upon their lips, long after his poetry had ceased to be merely a youthful source of promise and had become a generally recognized "influence," traces of the dissensions Eliot had aroused were voiced by Carl Sandburg at a *Herald Tribune* Forum, on October 23, 1940, in New York. It was true that Sandburg spoke at a moment of wartime hysteria; and it was also true that Eliot was no longer a citizen of the United States, but since 1927 had been a British subject:

If you wish to pray, or if you wish to sit in silent meditation in a corner . . . you will get it from this poet [T. S. Eliot]. But if you want clarity on human issues, he's out—he's zero. *A year ago I would have kept silent about him.* . . . Now I have to say that T. S. Eliot is anti-democratic and that he is a mediaevalist, and that he is a royalist and that he's so close to fascists that I'm off him, to use a truck driver's phrase; and we've got to consider truck-drivers in the present hour rather than the intellectuals.

The very language of Sandburg, and one might almost say
the very nature of his grief-stricken manifesto, revealed with
unmistakable clarity two divergent tendencies in American
poetry. One is inclined to agree with Allen Tate, who in a reply
to Sandburg's statement in *The Sewanee Review*, Autumn, 1944,
asked somewhat plaintively, "Why could Mr. Sandburg not have
made his particular brand of violent choice a year earlier? Why
can't we have both the truck-driver and the intellectual?"

The split between Sandburg and Eliot has long been characteristic of American divergences in its cultural life; through
Henry James, Eliot's American heritage is of a line that stems
from Hawthorne to the present day, and Sandburg's acknowledg-
ments to the past are those that carry a memory of Whitman.
Whenever our literature tends to produce too many Whitmans,
an Eliot arrives to counterbalance that cheerful and extraverted
tendency.[1]

But Eliot's value to his time and to his generation in London
has still another curiously spectacular turn that should not be
ignored. This aspect of Eliot's career has been presented by
Richard Aldington, the British novelist, translator, biographer,
and poet, who always writes of Eliot with the half-malicious intensity of a pupil who had escaped (almost too late) from the
influence of a powerful and all-absorbing schoolmaster. In his
autobiography, *Life for Life's Sake*,[2] Aldington wrote of the first
impact that Eliot's writing had made upon him:

I believe personally that Eliot's greatest service to English literature
at that time was his insistence that writers could not afford to throw
over the European tradition. Just after the war in the confusion and
reaction against everything prewar and war there was an almost unani-
mous belief among artists and writers of the vanguard that all art of
the past was so much dead stuff to be scrapped. . . . I was delighted

1 F. O. Matthiessen has shown in his commentaries on Whitman in his
American Renaissance (1941) and in his *Achievement of T. S. Eliot* that an
observant critic need not ignore the significant merits of either poet. Only
the narrowest and least perceptive of critical minds would fail to recognize
the importance of both Whitman and Eliot in discussing the character of
twentieth-century American poetry.

2 Copyright, 1940, 1941, by Richard Aldington. By permission of The Viking Press, Inc.

. . . when I came across a sensitive and well-written article on Marivaux in one of the small, arty periodicals which sprang up in 1919. Evidently here was someone who could write and who did not believe that illiteracy was a symbol of originality.

The observation that Aldington had made in London also came as a delight to Americans who had read Eliot's London letters in *The Dial*. To Americans (and in this respect, the more European Eliot became, the more American he seemed to some few of his readers) the cultural division has always been toward Europe, and away from it, toward a delicacy and a finesse beyond anything in European literature, to a classicism more classical (and certainly of a far more transcendental character) than had ever existed in Hellas or in Rome. Eliot's critical choices among the literatures of Europe had less enthusiasm than an almost Puritan concern for the ethical-esthetic value of his discoveries. His discriminations were such that they could be readily interpreted as the last words of one who had nothing further to say. No man seemed to have written so little and accomplished so much, but in actuality Eliot's production has never been as slender as it has appeared to an innocent observer; and the sometimes painful air with which he has presented both his modesties and pretensions to the readers of his prose was almost certain to exasperate his hostile critics. If the last words of an essay seemed final, the arrival of a newly written poem or a further essay always created the illusion of a fresh start—a disquieting surprise was registered, and perhaps another controversy—all of which was far from welcome among those who liked to pigeonhole and classify their literary figures. It was remembered by those who read poetry with less attention than haste, that Eliot was a member of what was then called a "lost generation," and it was hoped that he would obligingly stay "lost." That feeling was best expressed by Ernest Hemingway, himself, who might well have been described as the Chief of the Missing Persons Bureau, and if we are to believe Malcolm Cowley's lively preface to an anthology of Hemingway's prose (1944) Hemingway is reputed to have said in 1924, and in tribute to Joseph Conrad:

If I knew that by grinding Mr. Eliot into a fine dry powder and
sprinkling that powder over Mr. Conrad's grave Mr. Conrad would
shortly appear, looking very annoyed at the forced return, and com-
mence writing, I would leave for London early tomorrow with a sausage
grinder.[3]

The violence of Hemingway's remarks was not unlike that of
Sandburg's grief in 1940; and it proved that the anger which
Eliot had aroused had less reason in it than submerged emotion.
It was as though both Hemingway and Sandburg had taken the
mere existence of Eliot's literary being as a personal insult—and
by speaking in no uncertain terms, both Hemingway and Sandburg have contributed to the phenomena of Eliot's fame.

2

Almost from the very beginning of his career, Eliot has possessed the touch of genius which transformed whatever he wrote
into matters of greater importance and of more enduring interest than the facts of his biography. He was born of New England parentage in St. Louis, Missouri, in 1888, and was the seventh and youngest child of Henry Ware Eliot, a businessman,
whose ancestors were of Devonshire origin, and whose identity
with New England began when Andrew Eliot in the seventeenth
century emigrated from East Coker (the title of the second of
T. S. Eliot's *Four Quartets* [1943]) to the American colonies. The
poet's grandfather was the Reverend William Greenleaf Eliot,
and as F. O. Matthiessen observed (in the best book-length study
of Eliot, *The Achievement of T. S. Eliot* [1935], that has yet
appeared), Dr. Eliot wrote a sermon entitled "Suffering Considered as Discipline." In speaking of the poet's mother, Matthiessen makes another observation of great interest in stating that
she was the author of a dramatic poem, based on the life of
Savonarola, on which Eliot himself remarked, "This Savonarola
is a disciple of Schleiermacher, Emerson, Channing, and Herbert Spencer," and one agrees with both Matthiessen and Eliot
that the mention of the poem properly illuminates the intellectual life, as well as the very time and place, into which the poet

[3] *The Portable Hemingway.* Copyright, 1944, by The Viking Press, Inc.

was born. It is evident that Eliot's family was one of those New England families that entered the smaller cities of the Middle West, carrying with them the teachings of Emerson and the files of *The Atlantic Monthly;* and it was not at all unusual to find—and even as recently as 1912—the literary-review section of the *Boston Evening Transcript* neatly displayed upon Middle Western library tables. Those who came from New England to the Middle West spread a love of learning with a missionary zeal that their ancestors had shown in preaching the Gospel to the Indians, and their influence was felt in many a public school, in Browning Clubs, in Unitarian Church circles, and in local "poetry" societies and reading clubs.

In 1906 and after preparation for college at Smith and Milton academies, T. S. Eliot entered Harvard. His earliest verses appeared in *The Harvard Advocate,* but more important than these early signs of talent was that there he came under the combined influences of Irving Babbitt and George Santayana, and Eliot is in fact the single figure of great poetic talent who can be said to have discovered true values in the dogma of what was popularly called "the inner check." What has been interpreted as sterility in his writing was no more or less than the action of a highly developed and self-critical restraint, a quality of self-knowledge in the Greco-neoclassic-American sense of which Paul Elmer More was well aware in his *Shelburne Essays.* And Eliot himself has written:

The poet who thinks is merely the poet who can express the emotional equivalent of thought. We talk as if thought were precise and emotion were vague. In reality there is precise emotion and vague emotion. To express precise emotion requires as great intellectual power as to express precise thought.[4]

Eliot's studies included a year (1910-11) in Paris at the Sorbonne, reading French literature, and on his return to Harvard he extended his studies in metaphysics, logic, and psychology to embrace Indic philology and Sanskrit. He was awarded a traveling fellowship and was in Germany the early summer of 1914, and in the following winter was reading Greek philosophy at

[4] From *Selected Essays.* By permission of Harcourt, Brace and Company.

Merton College, Oxford. This was the beginning of his long repatriation, which as time goes on, tends to resemble more closely than any other literary parallel, the career and attachments, identities and individual growth of Henry James's long stay in England.

3

Valuable as Eliot's literary personality has been, and salutary as much of his prose (*The Sacred Wood* in 1920, *Selected Essays* in 1932) has been in offering its correctives to mere impressionism, literary gossip, and neo-Freudian extremes in twentieth-century criticism, valuable as his editorship of a quarterly review, *The Criterion* (1923-39) had been, these activities, though they supplemented and at times seemed to support it, have at no moment in his career equaled the quality of his verse. Eliot's true authority stems from his gifts in writing poetry, and in America, Edmund Wilson's essay on Eliot in *Axel's Castle* (1931) firmly established Eliot's poetic reputation. Wilson brought to the attention of his readers Eliot's debt to the literature of the French Symbolists, as well as to the poetry of the British seventeenth century. Edmund Wilson was at his persuasive and rare best, and unlike the more academic and neoscholastic critics who followed him in the discovery of Eliot's poetry, Wilson's prose took fire from its subject; to this day, it is among the superlative essays that Wilson has written.

What soon became clear was that judicious reading had been among the sources of Eliot's poetry, that Eliot's reading embraced passages of prose from the sermons of Lancelot Andrewes as well as other obscure sources including a fragment of a letter of Edward Fitzgerald as it had been quoted in an excellent biography of Fitzgerald written by A. C. Benson. But these findings, however sedulously sought for they may be (and the task, if it could ever be completed, would employ a lifetime), cannot be taken as the full explanation of Eliot's poetic genius. Eliot's habit of borrowing lines and phrases and making them his own is not a new nor a shocking one; every undergraduate in college knows how skillfully Tennyson turned elder poets to account, and how surely, how wittily, Robert Herrick, the self-confessed "son" of Ben Jonson, reset and burnished lines from Horace and Ovid—and in respect to Eliot, one may quote Sir John Denham's poem on Abraham Cowley: [5]

> To him no author was unknown,
> Yet what he wrote was all his own.
>
> .   .   .   .
>
> Horace—his wit, and Virgil's state,
> He did not steal, but emulate!
> And when he would like them appear,
> Their garb, but not their clothes, did wear.

More important than the great number of Eliot's literary sources was the synthesis of a poetic reality and its emotion that he conveyed to his readers; he gave to those who read *The Waste Land* a profound sense of the restlessness of the time, and he had found for them a rhythm and a speech that seemed to voice a hitherto unexpressed state of the soul and its disturbances. He brought certain stray insights, intentions, wandering philosophies, and dormant moods to light, and gave them a personality and a name—the direction that he led was toward the devotional resolutions of *Ash-Wednesday* (1930) and he had contributed an individual rhythm that had been heard as early as the publication of "The Love Song of J. Alfred Prufrock" [6] in 1915:

> I have heard the mermaids singing, each to each.
> I do not think that they will sing to me.

The "individual talent," rhythm and melody were heard, and they presented variations of Eliot's gifts in "Sweeney Among the Nightingales," in the Jamesian "Portrait of a Lady," and in the delicately modulated "La Figlia che Piange." With "Gerontion," these poems passed into the very language of the twentieth century, and in emotional range they foreshadowed the character of Eliot's poetry. It can be said today that this small group of Eliot's early poems also defined (as though a line in chalk were being drawn around them) his limitations. What remained

---

[5] From *Poetry of the English Renaissance* edited by Hebel and Hudson. By permission of F. S. Crofts & Company.
[6] From *Collected Poems*. By permission of Harcourt, Brace and Company.

to be explored was a greater depth of feeling, and the first step in that direction, which is neither of space nor of time, was *The Waste Land*. Its first readings were of its day, but as *The Waste Land* gave place to *Ash-Wednesday*, and *Ash-Wednesday* was followed by *Burnt Norton* in 1935, and at last by *Four Quartets* (of which *Burnt Norton* was republished as the first poem) one witnesses the progress of Eliot's religious being to a full and rich maturity. The turning points of his later development may be found within his "Minor Poems": in "Eyes that last I Saw in Tears," in the last two lines of "Usk": [7]

> Where the grey light meets the green air
> The hermit's chapel, the pilgrim's prayer.

And in "Lines for an Old Man": [8]

> The tiger in the tiger-pit
> Is not more irritable than I.
> The whipping tail is not more still
> Than when I smell the enemy
> Writhing in the essential blood
> Or dangling from the friendly tree.

And the fine modulations of "La Figlia che Piange" are endowed with a renewed intensity and strength in "Marina," whose theme is the recognition scene between father and daughter, and if the earlier poem was of the glancing sight of a vanished lady, the second is one of rediscovery, and the poet accomplishes for his reader the restoration of a lost image, and the resolution of a scene which has enduring significance—the sight of a completed vision in later life, which is

> This form, this face, this life
> Living to live in a world of time beyond me; let me
> Resign my life for this life, my speech for that unspoken,
> The awakened, lips parted, the hope, the new ships.

> What seas what shores what granite islands toward my timbers
> And woodthrush calling through the fog
> My daughter.[9]

[7] From *Collected Poems*. By permission of Harcourt, Brace and Company.
[8] *Ibid.*
[9] "Marina" from *Collected Poems*. By permission of Harcourt, Brace and Company.

It is best of all to remember that Eliot's poetry has a true affinity with Joyce's three great works in prose, *A Portrait of the Artist as a Young Man, Ulysses,* and *Finnegans Wake,* in that the majority of Eliot's poems tend to make a single book; almost everything that Joyce wrote was in reality toward a single "Work in Progress," and a "Work in Progress" might well be the all-embracing, if abstract, title of Eliot's poetry, beginning with *Prufrock,* including the choruses of *The Rock* (1934), and his two plays in verse, *Murder in the Cathedral* (1935) and *The Family Reunion* (1939), and finally, his *Four Quartets.* This is not to say that the "Work" is yet complete, but since his *Four Quartets* are a successful recapitulation of many of his earlier poems, including the choruses of his plays, it is reasonable to assume that a large arc of Eliot's circle has come into view.

"Prufrock," *The Waste Land,* "The Hollow Men," *Ash-Wednesday,* "Triumphal Arch," "Difficulties of a Statesman," and *Four Quartets* may be read (and have been read) as poems which revealed the hidden sensibilities of a quarter-century in America and in England, and from *The Waste Land* onward, each poem has its relevance in emotional temper, rather than in the literal statement of events, to a world that has suffered the presence of two world wars. In other words, the poems are written in the language of their day, yet the references to the time in which they are written merely form the top layer of their meanings. The true concern of Eliot's later poetry is the sight of the central vision of religious being, which, if it is translated into different terms, is the "Epiphany," "the showing forth," of a timeless moment, of which Joyce was so distinctly aware from the time he wrote his *Stephen Hero* (1904-1906) to the end of his life. It was that "showing forth" which was the concern of the seventeenth-century "metaphysical" poets as well as the devotional poets who followed them, and whatever else their poetry conveyed, the centers of religious being and of the timeless moment were sought and held within a single vision. The attraction of that moment is held in the best of Eliot's poetry, and if, as he himself remarked, the number of excellent devotional poems in English is small, he has added to that small but memorable selection, *Journey of the Magi, A Song for Simeon, Animula,* and *Ash-Wednesday.*

The terrors of *The Waste Land* [10] were uplifted to glory in:

> "This music crept by me upon the waters"
> And along the Strand, up Queen Victoria Street.
> O City city, I can sometimes hear
> Beside a public bar in Lower Thames Street,
> The pleasant whining of a mandoline
> And a clatter and a chatter from within
> Where fishmen lounge at noon: where the walls
> Of Magnus Martyr hold
> Inexplicable splendour of Ionian white and gold.

And in *Ash-Wednesday,* [11] as Eliot, like Dante, reiterates "Our peace is in his will," a great energy relieves the dryness of the spirit:

> And the lost heart stiffens and rejoices
> In the lost lilac and the lost sea voices
> And the weak spirit quickens to rebel
> For the bent golden-rod and the lost sea smell
> Quickens to recover
> The cry of quail and the whirling plover
> And the blind eye creates
> The empty forms between the ivory gates
> And smell renews the salt savour of the sandy earth

In "Little Gidding," the last of the *Four Quartets,* the release of energy has assumed the form of paying tribute to those gifts which are the last fruits of mature experience. (Several of Eliot's critics, including Edmund Wilson, have noted his choice of the "aged eagle," of elder men, of which Becket in *Murder in the Cathedral* is one of a large company, in whose words the central commentary of a poem or a play is spoken. In its best sense, this observation has several implications, and the most important of these is Eliot's dual respect for mature authority and poetic wit, which in *The Waste Land* was signified by the presence of the ancient, blinded seer, Tiresias, who "perceived the scene, and foretold the rest." And it should also be remembered that respect

---

[10] From *Collected Poems.* By permission of Harcourt, Brace and Company.
[11] *Ibid.*

for the wisdom of age has been voiced by many an excellent poet before Eliot's day; and these include—if one would name a few—Homer, Sophocles, Ovid, Wordsworth, Tennyson—and Eliot's near contemporary, E. A. Robinson). Little Gidding itself was Nicholas Ferrar's "Protestant nunnery" which figured so appropriately in J. H. Shorthouse's remarkable historical novel, *John Inglesant,* and the novel deserves to be reread today as a minor classic written in the nineteenth century. The following lines from the poem show the firmness of expression that Eliot has mastered:

> 'Let me disclose the gifts reserved for age
>   To set a crown upon your lifetime's effort.
>   First, the cold friction of expiring sense
> Without enchantment, offering no promise
>   But bitter tastelessness of shadow fruit
>   As body and soul begin to fall asunder.
> Second, the conscious impotence of rage
>   At human folly, and the laceration
>   Of laughter at what ceases to amuse.
> And last, the rending pain of re-enactment
>   Of all that you have done, and been; the shame
>   Of motives late revealed, and the awareness
> Of things ill done and done to others' harm
>   Which once you took for exercise of virtue.
>   Then fools' approval stings, and honor stains.
> From wrong to wrong the exasperated spirit
>   Proceeds, unless restored by that refining fire
>   Where you must move in measure like a dancer.'
> The day was breaking. In the disfigured street
>   He left me, with a kind of valediction,
>   And faded on the blowing of the horn.[12]

As, in *Ash-Wednesday,* the dryness of the soul is released into the fire of the word of God, so in the last of the *Four Quartets,* suffering and doubt are consumed in the fire that streams from humane and heavenly love:

> The dove descending breaks the air
>   With flame of incandescent terror

[12] "Little Gidding" from *Four Quartets.* By permission of Harcourt, Brace and Company.

Of which the tongues declare
The one discharge from sin and error.
The only hope, or else despair
  Lies in the choice of pyre or pyre—
  To be redeemed from fire by fire.

Who then devised the torment? Love.
Love is the unfamiliar Name
Behind the hands that wove
The intolerable shirt of flame
Which human power cannot remove.
  We only live, only suspire
  Consumed by either fire or fire.[13]

Another aspect of the *Four Quartets* is, of course, the expression of one who has lived through "the years of *l'entre deux guerres*," and in that sense *Four Quartets* is of the same importance to Eliot's generation as Wordsworth's "The Prelude, Or Growth of a Poet's Mind" was to those who read it in 1850.

Of Eliot's ventures as a playwright, one can only suppose that his activity has just begun. Although Eliot's ability to write dramatic verse within his major poems has long been recognized for its excellence, his play, *The Family Reunion,* is of an "art theater" variety, and embarrassing moments of "artiness" marred its more serious religious and esthetic values. *Murder in the Cathedral,* a play so written that it bears an analogy in its structure to the morality plays of the pre-Renaissance English stage, was far more successful. Those who saw its performance in New York in 1936 under the direction of the Federal Theater, and acted by those who spoke their parts with greater feeling than is usual upon the overly professional Broadway stage, realized the impressiveness of the event. And not the least element of interest in that production (which for a short time was well attended) was that the great majority of the audience scarcely knew Eliot's name. Many of those who came—and among them were the very poor, for whom the Federal Theater offered good productions and good plays at low prices—came because they wished to see a religious play, and they were not disappointed.

[13] "Little Gidding" from *Four Quartets*. By permission of Harcourt, Brace and Company.

In his position of one who does not fear to exercise his intelligence as well as learning, in his formality, in his ability to surprise, to shock, and at times to bewilder his critics, Eliot truly resembles in more ways than one that highly gifted—and "intellectual"—painter, Delacroix: how well, how appropriately Eliot's tigers and leopards would appear in company with Delacroix's lions and Arabs! And if this parallel seems too "romantic" in its associations for the completed intention of Eliot's poetry, it is also pertinent to quote Joyce's discussion of the classical temper in *Stephen Hero* (1944): [14]

The classical temper . . . ever mindful of its limitations, chooses . . . to bend upon . . . present things and so work upon them and fashion them that the quick intelligence may go beyond them to their meaning which is still unuttered. In this method the sane and joyful spirit issues forth and achieves imperishable perfection, nature assisting with her goodwill and thanks. For so long as this place in nature is given us it is right that art should do no violence to the gift.

This latter statement lies close to Eliot's avowed "classicism" and the major aspects of his poetry; meanwhile he has introduced his readers to a new sensibility in the poetic genius of our time; and if his quickened intelligence seems to move behind and beyond his generation, to meanings which are still unuttered, he is also to be read as "the man of feeling," the poet whose lines have caught and held the essential rhythms of twentieth-century poetry.

[14] By permission of New Directions.

PART IV

THE 1930'S

THE NATIONAL SPIRIT OF STEPHEN VINCENT
AND WILLIAM ROSE BENÉT, WITH
NOTES ON LOLA RIDGE AND
MURIEL RUKEYSER

During the middle years of a "political decade," the 1930's, the "low dishonest decade," of which W. H. Auden spoke, no poet in America saw the implications of that hour with greater clarity than Stephen Vincent Benét. He was a writer who had "found himself" as completely as John Dos Passos had in the writing of his American trilogy, *U.S.A.*, and while other writers discussed the means of reaching a public in the American Writers' Congress of 1935, Benét's major poem, *John Brown's Body* (1928), was widely read and admired in high schools and colleges throughout the country. Benét's verse was irrelevant to the usual definitions of politics and esthetics: it reflected the taste and the popular feeling of the moment; it never failed to "tell a story" that could be understood with the ease and the vividness of a Currier and Ives print or of a mural painted by Thomas Hart Benton, and it possessed those qualities of an historical imagination that were felt by readers of *The Saturday Evening Post* as well as those who shaped their opinions by the weekly digest of news in *Time* magazine. It was to that contradictory and amorphous public that Benét spoke, and his gifts were those that caught the public ear. His disciplines were those of the professional writer for widely circulated magazines: his rules for writing either prose or verse were verbal clarity, pictorial vividness, a display of humor in the manner of Mark Twain, and a discernible rhythmic beat in a stanza or a paragraph. His five novels, his seven books of verse, his numerous short stories, his miscellaneous pieces of prose and dramatic sketches seem to have been written by a hand that never blotted or scratched out a line, and in all the various kinds of writing that Benét employed, there is never an inactive page. In a foreword written to a high-school text edition of his *John Brown's Body* in 1941 Benét wrote, "Poetry . . . is not a highly complicated puzzle box which you can open only with a special set of keys. It tells its story in a different way from prose—it uses rhyme and meter and the words go to a beat"—and he was frankly describing the nature of his own verse. It must be admitted that the definition betrayed a note of impatience for any further or a more profound consideration of poetry itself, but it was clear that to Benét poetry was an evocative and impressionable means of making a story heard. And *John Brown's Body,* a narrative poem of the American Civil War, had justified the expression of Benét's opinion.

When *John Brown's Body* appeared in 1928 it enjoyed a highly attentive press; Stephen Benét's ballad, *King David,* had received *The Nation's* poetry prize in 1923, and it was generally known that the author of *John Brown's Body* had spent two years in Paris on a Guggenheim Fellowship in writing it. Most of the critics and reviewers welcomed it with enthusiasm; it held much of the same appeal that Longfellow's *Hiawatha* had for an earlier generation: its theme was American and the poem ran to some 350 book-size pages; its love stories could be enjoyed in the same spirit in which an historical novel is read and its verse forms had all the variety of the verse written in the preceding decade by Vachel Lindsay, Edgar Lee Masters, Carl Sandburg, G. K. Chesterton, and others. Nothing in the poem was unfamiliar to the eye or ear; the poem was, as Louis Untermeyer remarked, "a work of assimilation," it reassembled facts and legends concerning the Civil War, and threw into high relief its scenes of action. If Benét took everything in verse that came readily to hand, from ballads that had been sung in the Kentucky mountains to the free-verse rhythms of Masters and Sandburg, his battle scenes had the excitement, the "realism," the skill of David Wark Griffith's *The Birth of a Nation,* and if Griffith's sympathies leaned a trifle to the South, Benét tipped the balance slightly in favor of the North. Allen Tate reviewed the poem briskly in *The Nation:*

John Brown's Body has merit enough; it has hair-raising defects; and yet it deserves to be widely read and within reason praised. The poem is not in any sense an epic; neither is it a philosophical vision of the Civil War; it is a loose episodic narrative which unfolds related themes in motion-picture flashes.

Nothing could be plainer than the poem's merits: its view was that of a young American who had rediscovered the importance of the Civil War, and, in that view, historical documents, old portraits, songs, newspaper commentaries, yellowed photographs, and boyhood visits to the battlefields had come to life; its thumbnail sketches of the generals on both sides of the conflict had an air of veracity and of restless, quick-witted, authoritative notation. These were done with an historian's eye for effective detail—and among the many brief scenes of action that the poem presented to the reader few were better than the memorable and terse description of Lincoln's visit to Pickett's house after the fall of Richmond. The poem creates the impression of being expertly planned and directed, and once a scene moves into view before the reader's eye, it seems to take on the inevitable character of any sequence of events in history.

The "hair-raising defects" of the poem are those of a writer who concentrates his energies upon the immediate effect that his writing may have upon the eye and ear. The fictional characters in *John Brown's Body* are of the same stature, color, and life that are often witnessed within the pages of popular magazine fiction; their youth has charm and vivacity, they wear appropriate clothes; they fall in love or out of it; they know the emotions that accompany physical fear and courage; they enjoy the embraces of friendship or of love, but they lack the passions of grief and of more than transitory delight, and when they disappear from the page that gave them an excuse for being, the reader is not likely to feel their loss. When the poem tells its stories of its Northern and Southern soldiers and its Southern heroine, one is certain that the poem is "talking down" to its readers; the figures of Jack Ellyat, Melora Vilas, Clay Wingate, Luke Breckinridge are out of the same clothes closet that once housed the heroes and heroines of Winston Churchill's novels, those romances which began with *Richard Carvel* (1899) and reached the height of their popularity with *The Crossing* (1904). It is only in their proximity to the historical figures of *John Brown's Body* and in their participation in the events of the Civil War that the fictional characters of the poem are endowed with life.

The poem is sustained by the author's lively interest in its scenes and recollections of an historic past; when he wrote of the raid at Harper's Ferry or of boyhood memories of "the courthouse in the square" where John Brown stood his trial, or the concluding stanzas of the poem itself, the entire work seems to justify Stephen Benét's intentions. The intention (so it seems) was to awaken the American schoolboy as well as the thoughtless American who read illustrated fiction in magazines from an indifference to the events of the Civil War. And when *John Brown's Body* was selected by a book club for distribution, and when it received the Pulitzer Prize for poetry in 1929, it was assured of reaching the public for whom it had been written.

2

In the writing and the subsequent success of *John Brown's Body,* Stephen Benét had undergone a transformation. He had followed the example set by his elder brother, William Rose Benét, in choosing Yale for his college education. The very year that Stephen Benét entered Yale (which was 1915) he published a series of dramatic sketches in verse, *Five Men and Pompey,* and two years later at the age of nineteen, he received the Albert Stanburrough Cook prize at Yale for verses on Keats, "The Drug-Shop, or Endymion in Edmonstoun." As a boy he had won prizes in the columns of the *St. Nicholas,* and if one wishes to find a true "influence" upon the lighter verses written by the members of the Benét family, including Stephen's sister, Laura, the *St. Nicholas,* that best of all children's magazines ever published in English, should not be forgotten. From 1873 to 1919 the *St. Nicholas* inspired and encouraged precocious and gifted children who possessed literary ambitions; during its long and influential lifetime *St. Nicholas* published contributions from

Louisa May Alcott, William Cullen Bryant, Lucretia P. Hale, Mark Twain, Rudyard Kipling, and Frances Hodgson Burnett; it created a standard for the writing of light verse, of which Oliver Herford and Carolyn Wells were the most able practitioners. At least three generations of children sent their writings in to *St. Nicholas* with the hope of seeing their contributions published in its back columns under the heading of "St. Nicholas League"; and one is certain that two of Stephen Benét's well-known shorter poems, "American Names" and "The Ballad of William Sycamore" (as well as *A Book of Americans* [1933], which had been written in collaboration with his wife, Rosemary Benét), would have been welcomed by the editors of the *St. Nicholas* when the magazine was in its prime. How clearly the last stanza of "The Ballad of William Sycamore" [1] belongs to those readers whose memories embraced recollections of a *St. Nicholas* childhood!

> Go play with the towns you have built of blocks,
> The towns where you would have bound me!
> I sleep in my earth like a tired fox,
> And my buffalo have found me.

In a letter to the authors of the present history of recent American poetry, William Rose Benét wrote of his brother in 1944:

He read poetry from an early age . . . as my father had before him. My father also had an amazing taste in literature. He used to say that he could not always explain why he knew instinctively the good things, but that he knew he knew. If that sounds conceited, the fact remains that he was usually right. *Why* was because from a precocious childhood my father had read enormously. I used to think he had read everything. . . . He used to call Steve the "child of his old age," as Steve came twelve and fourteen years after myself and Laura. In reality Father was about forty when Steve was born, which now seems to me, at the advanced age of fifty-eight, like a mere youth! Still, Father gave him special attention, and used to love to talk to him, to read to him, and so on. Steve was the one of us nearest to my father mentally. Mother had a natural love of poetry, and good taste in it. But she inclined to devotional poets like George Herbert. Father inclined to

---

[1] From *Selected Works of Stephen Vincent Benét*, published by Farrar & Rinehart. Copyright, 1922, by Stephen Vincent Benét.

the romantic and dramatic and martial. Also to the wits, to parody, to Gilbert, Lear, Calverley, etc. That was the background at home. Steve was a rather delicate small boy and not very happy at school.

His schools were in California and in Georgia, where his father was stationed at government arsenals . . . at Yale he took his place as one of the outstanding—albeit regarded as eccentric—men of his class. He did this almost by an effort of will as he was very shy when he entered. He was an omnivorous reader like his father, reading the good, bad, and indifferent, but at one time quite strongly influenced by Browning, William Morris, and Chesterton. This was in youth. . . . He liked songs you could sing and ballads.

His friends at Yale included Phelps Putnam, author of two highly promising books of verse, *Trinc* (1927) and *The Five Seasons* (1931), Philip Barry, the playwright, Archibald Mac-Leish, and the gifted, sensitive novelist and playwright, Thornton Wilder. His publisher, John Farrar, who was also a friend at Yale, was memorably quoted by Mabel A. Bessy in her note on "The Author" in the textbook edition of *John Brown's Body:* [2]

While in Yale . . . [Stephen Benét] wrote plays and acted in them, was elected to the Editorial Board of the *Yale Record* and later, to the chairmanship of the *Yale Literary Magazine.* It was of his connection with this magazine that John Farrar remarked that Benét was the despair of all the other fellows who wanted to make the "Lit," for the editorial board could hardly reject its chairman's stuff and "the young-ster wrote so much and so well that there was often mighty little room left for any other ambitious verse-maker."

In Stephen Benét's early novels, *The Beginning of Wisdom* (1921) and *Young People's Pride* (1922), the fashion of the day, or rather the sort of light novel that was being written by young men just out of college, had left its mark. If *This Side of Paradise* (1920) expressed the ardors and desires of a young man from Princeton, *The Beginning of Wisdom* and *Young People's Pride* were the voices of urban, undergraduate Yale. All three novels represented a self-consciously restless generation whose stay at college was an introduction to the more exciting adventures of seeing New York, Chicago, Paris, and the Riviera soon after the First World War. The books were written with almost tele-

---

[2] Published by Farrar & Rinehart. Copyright, 1927, 1928, by Stephen Vincent Benét.

graphic speed, and they were models of what the "younger generation" breathed, felt, and wore, and at last communicated their observations to readers of books in the lending libraries.

But being fashionable for fashion's sake was not Benét's intention; in 1920 he took his master's degree at Yale, and continued his academic career through a fellowship at the Sorbonne; nor did a position in an advertising office nor the commercial success of his short stories exhaust or satisfy the resources of his energy; he was "at home" only in the writing of *John Brown's Body*.

The shorter poems of Stephen Benét fall within the definitions that T. S. Eliot so happily conceived for Rudyard Kipling's verse; and it should be said that both William Rose and Stephen Benét had written of Kipling in the highest terms of admiration. The nationalism of Stephen Benét was of essentially the same temper as Kipling's devotion to the British Empire, and quite as Stephen Benét had grasped the importance of the Civil War in its relevance to American life, he also recognized, in the sense that few writers of his generation had, the obvious fact that the society through which he moved was Christian, and the most successful of his satires in verse was "Carol: New Style"[3] which began with the following stanza:

> If Jesus Christ should come again,
> On Christmas day, on Christmas day,
> To bother the minds of gentlemen
> On Christmas day in the morning?

And in his "1935"[4] something of the worldly and critical gift that Kipling possessed enters the closing lines of a poem in which the ghosts of marching men were raised:

> Must you march forever from France and the last, blind war?
> "Fool! From the next!" they said.

[3] From *Ballads and Poems*, published by Farrar & Rinehart. Copyright, 1925, by Stephen Vincent Benét.
[4] From *Selected Works of Stephen Vincent Benét*, published by Farrar & Rinehart. Copyright, 1935, by Stephen Vincent Benét.

3

In 1933 Stephen Benét was awarded the Roosevelt Medal for his contribution to American literature, and five years later, he was elected to membership in the American Academy of Arts and Letters; he also became a vice-president of the National Institute of Arts and Letters, and few writers ever stepped into a position of authority and influence with a greater sense of responsibility than he. Among his loyalties was the editorship of the "Yale Series of Younger Poets"; and the series, which published a book each year by an unknown poet, was one of the means he used of doing good unobtrusively, which was graced by the rare gift of common sense. It was through his efforts that Paul Engle, an earnest, sometimes bewildered, but essentially truthful poet, found publication; his second book, *American Song* (1934), carried on its dedication page its tribute to Stephen Benét, and his four books of poems following it are a record of his uneven and yet hopeful progress. Among the more promising of the younger poets who were introduced by Stephen Benét in the "Yale Series" was Muriel Rukeyser, who in 1935 was highly praised for her *Theory of Flight,* and in a foreword to her book Benét wrote:

> . . . the mind behind these poems is an urban and a modern one. It has fed on the quick jerk of the news-reel, the hard lights in the sky, the long deserted night-street, the take-off of the plane from the ground. It knows nature as well—the look of landscape, the quietness of hills. But its experience has been largely an urban experience, and it is interesting to see the poetry of youth so based. When Miss Rukeyser thinks of energy, she thinks of a dynamo rather than a river, an electric spark rather than a trampling hoof—and that is interesting too.[5]

Muriel Rukeyser's first book, published when she was twenty-two, sharply defined her talents. It was true, as Benét so happily suggested, that her poems seemed to feel and to think in terms of energy; it was the force of the dynamo that gave them life, and the same implied force, with varying success, entered her three other volumes of verse, *U. S. 1* (1938), *A Turning Wind* (1939), and *Beast in View* (1944). Her poems seem to show the

[5] By permission of Yale University Press.

effort of trying to move forward on too many fronts, as though the poems were conceived in terms of slogans and commands. Although visual brilliance is in evidence throughout the many poems she has written, her first book is still her nearest approach to accomplishment. *Theory of Flight* contained such brilliant and unaffected poems as "Sand-Quarry with Moving Figures," and the quickening tour de force, "Ritual of Blessing." Her verse reflected the temper of a prewar generation of young women, who, like Miss Rukeyser, had left Vassar College in search of larger worlds to conquer, all of whom were well aware of the Wall Street crash of 1929, the diverse influences of Freud and of Marx upon contemporary literature, and who read with sympathetic appreciation the early verse of W. H. Auden and Stephen Spender as well as the novels of Thomas Wolfe. Miss Rukeyser's books of verse were supplemented by a commentary on the life of Willard Gibbs (1942), the distinguished American scientist. Not unlike Lewis Mumford's *Herman Melville* (1929) and *The Brown Decades* (1931) Miss Rukeyser's *Willard Gibbs* was an interpretation of nineteenth-century America reviewed in the light of social criticism. Quite as her book of poems, *A Turning Wind,* contained an indebtedness to the writings of Waldo Frank, in like measure, her *Willard Gibbs* shared the Messianic insights and diversions of the elder writer's prose; in general, the book had the same flaws and merits that characterized Waldo Frank's *Virgin Spain* (1926) and *Dawn in Russia* (1932).

Through his encouragement of younger poets, as well as his own writings, Stephen Benét participated actively in a literature that slowly prepared the United States for entrance into a Second World War; in these services, his writing supplemented the prose and verse of Archibald MacLeish; the two poets seemed to exchange "influences" upon one another's verse, and it was obvious that the same spirit that produced MacLeish's conviction that

> Men have forgotten how full clear and deep
> The Yellowstone moved on the gravel and grass grew
> When the land lay waiting for her westward people! [6]

[6] "Frescoes for Mr. Rockefeller's City" from *Poems 1920-1934*, by permission of Houghton Mifflin Company.

also entered Stephen Benét's incompleted and posthumously published narrative in verse, *Western Star* (1943), which, like *John Brown's Body*, was distributed by a book club and received the Pulitzer Prize for poetry the following year. The narrative, which paid its tribute to the memory of the *Mayflower* and Plymouth Rock, held to the belief (as Benét phrased it) that "Americans are always moving on," and in this conviction he seemed to share the view that had been advanced in Carl Sandburg's *The People, Yes* as well as in MacLeish's *Frescoes for Mr. Rockefeller's City* (1933). Stephen Benét's unexpected and early death on March 13, 1943, gave rise to an occasion for many younger poets whose work he had encouraged to express their gratitude in the pages of *The Saturday Review of Literature*, and his publisher observed that a sheet of paper placed on top of the manuscript of his uncompleted *Western Star* [7] had the following four lines written across it:

> Now for my country that it may still live,
> All that I have, all that I am I'll give.
> It is not much beside the gift of the brave
> And yet accept it since tis all I have.

It was in that devoted and patriotic spirit that Benét fulfilled the heritage of his grandfather, Brigadier General Stephen Vincent Benét.

4

Of those who wrote in tribute to Stephen Benét's memory, none spoke with deeper understanding than his brother, William Rose Benét, who was twelve years his senior. In his elegy, "S. V. B.—1898-1943," [8] William Rose Benét included the following lines:

> The fleece that was filled with dew;
> The god in the oak.

[7] From *Western Star*, published by Farrar & Rinehart. Copyright, 1943, by Stephen Vincent Benét.

[8] From *The Day of Deliverance*. Reprinted by permission of Alfred A. Knopf, Inc. Copyright, 1944, by William Rose Benét.

And legend for his own folk,
Of their toil and their mirth;
Tang of the tongue they spoke,
The savour of their earth;
Till when foul darkness stirred
To blast all singing,
Men heard his quiet word
Steady and ringing.

William Rose Benét's verse was of an elder school than that of his brother; it was written in the vein of the "Romantic Traditionists" and its happiest moments were lyrical rather than in the dramatic scenes of action that Stephen Benét found so effective in his *John Brown's Body.* As Stephen Benét wrote with thoroughly deliberated concentration upon single themes, his elder brother diffused his talents widely; William Rose Benét's verses touched upon and sometimes passed over many subjects lightly, and the very conditions of his life, his many activities in editing magazines and anthologies of verse seemed to contribute toward a neglect of his own gifts in favor of his ability to encourage and to appreciate the works of others. Like his younger brother, Stephen, he abhorred dullness as nature does a vacuum, and at Yale a decade earlier than Stephen, his training for a professional career included editorship of *The Yale Record* and *The Yale Courant*—and he was markedly of the same restless college "generation" at Yale that produced the novelist, Sinclair Lewis. The same spirit of revolt against an academic reading of literature which led Henry Seidel Canby from the English department at Yale to an assistant editorship of *The Yale Review,* and finally to the chairmanship of the Book of the Month Club in New York, seems to have entered the generation of which Canby, William Rose Benét, and Sinclair Lewis were the forerunners, and of which Archibald MacLeish, Thornton Wilder, and Stephen Benét, and latterly Selden Rodman, poet and editor, were the fortunate heirs. Behind all these, perhaps the example set by William Lyon Phelps exerted a charm that has been underrated by critics of contemporary American letters. Phelps's enthusiasm for current literature in the broadest terms has its analogy only in the adventurous spirit that possessed such Victorians as Sir Richard Burton, the translator of *The Arabian Nights*—and the title of William Rose Benét's first book of poems, *Merchants from Cathay* (1913) has something of the same adventurous character.

William Rose Benét's early verse delighted in fancy for its own sake; it glittered rather than shone, and translated quickly and lightly into its own speech the attractions that Swinburne, Rossetti, Browning, G. K. Chesterton, and Rudyard Kipling held for the young Americans in a generation that saw a "poetic renaissance" in the United States. Like his younger brother and his sister Laura, the true touchstone for the verse that seemed to move with so much ease and skill was of a family heritage— and it seems natural that his first editorial job should have been on the staff of the *Century* magazine which was closely associated (since it was then published by the same firm) with the *St. Nicholas*.

William Rose Benét's abilities turned in the direction of light verse, and his ballad on "Jesse James: American Myth" showed the skill with which his facility in writing verse was at its best advantage. The poem's qualities of lightness, brilliance, and metrical speed place it among the best of its kind in American verse and one must turn to Vachel Lindsay's verses to find something of like temper.

Of William Rose Benét's some fifteen books of verse, *Man Possessed* (1927) and *Golden Fleece* (1935) are the most representative volumes, and within them one clearly sees the reflections of a volatile, gracefully mannered, and erratic talent. His "The Falconer of God" has been reprinted in many anthologies, and it has never failed to awaken admiration for its metrical variety and skill. But Benét's verse found its best expression in an elegy, his "Inscription for a Mirror in a Deserted Dwelling," [9] which was written (it is believed) in memory of his second wife, Elinor Wylie, and which justly deserves to be remembered long after his more facile and glittering pieces are forgotten:

[9] From *Golden Fleece*. Reprinted by permission of Dodd, Mead & Company, Inc.

Set silver cone to tulip flame!
The mantel mirror floats with night
Reflecting still green watery light.
The sconces glimmer. If she came
Like silence through the shadowy wall
Where walls are wading in the moon
The dark would tremble back to June.
So faintly now the moonbeams fall,
So soft this silence, that the verge
Of speech is reached. Remote and pale
As though some faint viridian veil
The lovely lineaments emerge,
The clearly amber eyes, the tint
Of pearl and faintest rose, the hair
To lacquered light a silken snare
Of devious bronze, the tiny dint
With which her maker mocked the years
Beneath her lip imprinting praise.
Dim flower of desecrating days,
The old reflection, strange with tears,
Is gazing out upon the gloom,
Is widening eyes to find the light
In reminiscence, in the night
Of this forgone, forgotten room.
And you, the watcher, with your eyes
As wide as hers in dark distress,
Who never knew her loveliness
But guess through glass her shadowy guise,
For you around the glass I trace
This secret writing, that will burn
Like witch-fire should her shade return
To haunt you with that wistful face
At least no gesturing figures pass;
Here is no tragic immanence
Of all the scenes of small events
That pantomimed before the glass.
No bliss, no passion, no despair,
No other actor lingers now;
The moonlight on a lifted brow
Is all,—the eyes so wide aware
Of clouds that pass with stars, and suns,
Of mystery that pales the cheek,
Of all the heart could never speak,
Of joy and pain so vivid once,

That ceased with music and the lights,
Dimming to darkness and repose . . .
Lean then and kiss that ghostly rose
That was her face, this night of nights,—
And know the vision fled indeed,
The mirror's surface smooth and cold,
The words unbreathed, the tale untold,
The past unpiteous to your need!

In this poem, Benét's sensibility assumed its own character, and the poem properly distinguishes his talents from those of his younger brother, and indeed from those possessed by all other poets of his generation. His autobiography in verse, *The Dust Which Is God* (1941), showed a man who had participated actively in the years that spanned two world wars, and the reader sees reflected in its pages a busy life that enabled him to work with so much felicity in collaboration with Henry Seidel Canby and Christopher Morley in the founding and editing of *The Saturday Review of Literature*. The book received the Pulitzer Prize for poetry in 1942. In 1944, he published another book of poems, *Day of Deliverance*, whose lines expressed with great sincerity the national feeling of the day in the third year of the Second World War.

A NOTE ON LOLA RIDGE

Among William Rose Benét's many contributions to the literature of the day (which included the editing in collaboration with Norman Holmes Pearson of *The Oxford Anthology of American Literature* [1938] which was both the most authoritative and discriminating work of its kind ever published in the United States) his loyal friendship to Lola Ridge should not be forgotten. Lola Ridge was born in Dublin, Ireland, in 1871; her childhood was spent in Australia and New Zealand and after studying painting at the Académie Julienne in Sidney, in 1907 she came to the United States and settled in the neighborhood of New York's Greenwich Village. Unlike many stories of the privations suffered by poets during the years of the "poetic renaissance" in Chicago and in New York, the legend of Lola Ridge's austere devotion to her talents had more than the usual background of literal truth to support it. Her choice of living in poverty was a deliberated one, for she had proved her ability to support herself reasonably well by contributing fiction to popular magazines. Perhaps inspired by the example set before her in Edgar Lee Masters' *Spoon River Anthology,* she turned her attention to the misery of the poor who lived in Manhattan's tenements on the lower East Side, and, in 1918, *The New Republic* published her observations in her famous poem, "The Ghetto," which appeared in book form during the same year. Lola Ridge was possessed of a Celtic imagination whose insights gave life and color to her convictions; and though much of her early verse now seems hastily fashioned in the rhythms of Amy Lowell's vers libre, the honesty of her devotion to a cause remains unquestioned.

Her devotion was one that can be described only in terms of a saintliness that Paul Vincent Carroll in his one felicitous play, *Shadow and Substance,* gave to his memorable and vision-haunted Irish heroine. Those who remember Lola Ridge also remember the large, barely furnished, wind-swept, cold-water loft where she lived in downtown Manhattan. The loft was very like some neatly, frugally kept cold-water flat in Dublin, and the unworldly presence of Lola Ridge, a slender, tall, softly-speaking, thin-featured woman in a dark dress, heightened the illusion of being in a place that was not New York, but was well in sight of Dublin's purple hills. Even as one rereads her books one gains the impression that she regarded her social convictions and the writing of poetry in the same spirit in which an Irish girl invokes the will of God by entering a convent—but Lola Ridge's devotion had turned to self-taught and protestant demands, and the task, the almost impossible task, of making social and religious emotion a unified being was an effort that remained unfinished at her death.

If her five books of verse, of which the last, *Dance of Fire* (1935), was the best, had been collected between the covers of a single volume, "fire" and "shadow" are the two words that would have accurately described them. Her self-taught art was at times unknowingly "arty" and her unrhymed verses were shadowy and thin. Her devotion to the memory of Shelley's poetry was in fact a complement of Elinor Wylie's devotion to the legend of Shelley's personality. Lola Ridge wrote as thinly as Shelley did when neither his poetry nor hers was at its best, and like Shelley, Lola Ridge endeavored to give fluid words and images, such as "fire" and "light," purposeful meaning in poetry. The political martyrdom of Sacco and Vanzetti gave occasion for her long poem on Christ's crucifixion, *Firehead* (1929), and the reiterated images of light within the poem, effective as they were upon first reading, dazzled rather than enlightened the understanding of her sympathetic critics.

In *Dance of Fire* Lola Ridge's poetic maturity began, and it was evident that in the sonnet sequence, "Via Ignis," which opened her last volume, Hart Crane's revival of Christopher Marlowe's diction left its impression upon her imagination. The poems were written at a time when many of those who had read Hart Crane's *The Bridge* felt the implied force of Crane's improvisations in archaic diction; and indeed several of Lola Ridge's sonnets recalled the memory of Crane's suicide at sea:

> Balanced on high arc precariously
> He saw the fire on all lands; the flame-
> Encircled waters drew him sweetly down . . .[10]

Yet despite their dignity and perhaps because of the high, disinterested motives of their composition, the sonnets remained disembodied and curiously abstract. It was as though the poet had become aware of her lyrical gifts too late to find the words with which to express them clearly; felicitous lines and phrases flowed through the sequence of twenty-eight sonnets, and it is impossible to reread them without respect for the saintly, unworldly motives that seem to have inspired the interwoven themes of "Via Ignis." Yet no single sonnet withstands the test of being read for itself alone, and a newly acquired, slightly misplaced archaic diction still quarrels with contemporaneous themes in the very poems that should have established Lola Ridge's fame. With the same lack of completed artistry, Lola Ridge paid her tributes to Robinson Jeffers, and to Sacco and Vanzetti; and she was

---

[10] "Via Ignis" from *Dance of Fire*, by permission of Random House, Inc.

among the first of many to write of Van der Lubbe and the Reichstag Fire. Her moral courage and her imaginative insights seem to have reached beyond her strength, and if her devotion to poetry and the frustrations of the poor fell short of accomplishment in the writing of a wholly memorable poem, her failure was an honorable one. For the literary historian her verse provides a means of showing that the younger writers of the 1930's were not the first to rediscover the ghettos of New York in a city that was all too obviously ill at ease between two wars. And few of those who followed the direction she had taken wrote with the selfless idealism of Lola Ridge. On May 19, 1941, William Rose Benét wrote the notices of her death for New York newspapers; the worldly rewards she had won were few; but it was not without a measure of poetic if not ironic justice that she received the Shelley Memorial Prize for poetry in 1933 and in 1934.

ARCHIBALD MACLEISH AND THE
"INVOCATION TO THE SOCIAL MUSE"

Scarcely less brilliant in his career than Stephen Benét, Archibald MacLeish in 1930 had the advantage of seeming more controversial than his contemporary, and more closely allied with the "new" techniques in writing poetry. He had been born in the well-to-do suburb of Chicago, Glencoe, Illinois, in 1892, and was of Scotch Presbyterian–New England ancestry. Although his career at Yale and later at the Harvard Law School was one that brought with it literary honors and distinction in leadership, particularly in his studies in law at Harvard, his poetic talents were less easily recognized than those of the precocious Stephen Benét. When the biography of Archibald MacLeish is written, it will not be forgotten that his academic life had been interrupted by his commission as a captain in the First World War, that he had served in the Field Artillery in France, that he returned to Cambridge to teach in the Harvard Law School, that he practiced law in the firm of Choate, Hall, and Stuart, of Boston, and that he gave up the successful practice of law for the writing of poetry. MacLeish's academic, legal, and poetic talents were widely diffused, and one might almost say that his gifts were so brilliant, so attractive, and of such great variety that the problem of making a choice between them demanded firmness and a conscious act of will.

The highly conscious manner with which MacLeish has presented his literary career to a growing public has often deceived both his admiring and adverse critics; they have taken him at his word, which throughout the 1930's has been subject to many revisions and contradictions; to a few younger writers he has been the political poet, par excellence, neatly tacking his sails (and he has written well of a "Yacht for Sale") to each fresh

448

wind, whether it came from the right northwest or from the left southeast. Heat or cold has made little difference to the central hardness—and hardiness—of MacLeish's gifts in writing verse. For like men (and Clarence Darrow, the famous lawyer, was among them) who present a loose and friendly exterior to the world, MacLeish's verse has a hard core. "I speak to my own time/To no time after" wrote MacLeish, and, in this respect, he has successfully kept a promise which has seemed to shift with each change of popular feeling in the United States.

An illustration of how the hardiness of MacLeish's talents were underrated, even as late as 1929, has been preserved in *A Bookman's Daybook* [1] by Burton Rascoe. The scene was in Paris:

MacLeish is a clear-eyed, deferential young man, with an extremely Nordic head, quiet manners, and an ungovernable passion for discussing aesthetics—aesthetics in the round, in the general, in the specific, in the concrete—any way so long as it is aesthetics. He has not yet made up his mind whether to go free verse whole hog or none; and his pansy-like book of verse suffers from this indecision. But he is a fine lad—one can call him a lad even if he has got a boy of seven who is a handsome youngster and bright as a whip; and a wife who is charming American "quality"; and lives in a mansion fitted out in luxurious bad taste with padded damask covered walls, by a Russian prince, now down on his luck, for a mistress who enjoyed the imported American plumbing of the bathroom for three months before the crash came. Yes, he is a fine lad and a brave one. When he was yet under thirty he had achieved as much success in law as that by which the most tolerable of the "How I Became a Success" yarns tempt the gullible wage-slave; and with enough money in the bank to keep him going for some years, he threw over the law, went to Paris, reduced his expenditures (he gets the ex-prince's mansion furnished and two servants for less than $150 a month), and started out being a poet. This accounts for his extraordinary preoccupation with aesthetics.

The Hamlet of A. MacLeish (1928), which may have been one of the books to which Rascoe referred, had a clearer outline than critics of that moment had discerned; it had an obvious indebtedness to the poetry of T. S. Eliot and Ezra Pound, but it presented—and not without dramatic effectiveness—the figure of MacLeish as Hamlet. The part was extraordinarily well played—

[1] By permission of Liveright Publishing Corporation.

and if the figure was indecisive in its action, Hamlet has never been known for his ability to make up his mind. The same quality of careful planning and expert composition distinguishes *The Pot of Earth* (1925) in which MacLeish presented, with a quotation from Sir James G. Frazer's *The Golden Bough*, a version of the Adonis myth. No fault can be found with the external appearance of the poem; its flaws are those of a failure to present a definite literary personality, but they were compensated by the three books which followed it: *Streets in the Moon* (1926), *The Hamlet of A. MacLeish*, and *New Found Land* (1930), and with these three volumes the success of MacLeish's decision to turn from law to literature was well assured, and from 1930 onward, almost every activity that MacLeish entered carried with it the atmosphere of successful accomplishment.

Although a number of critics had praised *Streets in the Moon*, *New Found Land*, a book of fourteen poems, provided a true measure of MacLeish's gifts; the gifts were those of an almost Irish turn of eloquence; it was the eloquence of the John Synge of whom Yeats had been speaking when he said that poetry should be "as simple as the simplest prose, like a cry of the heart." And it was as though MacLeish had refined and revived in Paris Synge's belief that "it is the timber of poetry that wears most surely, and there is no timber that has not strong roots among the clay and worms." It was true that *New Found Land* reflected from its brilliant surfaces the teachings of Ezra Pound, but the elegiac atmosphere which pervaded the entire volume, its memories of an American heritage, with the title taken from John Donne's line in an elegy to his mistress, "O my America, my new found land," were of MacLeish's own creation. The book conveyed a unified impression of the American in Paris who had been possessed by thoughts of home, and at least three poems in the slender volume are now familiars of those who read modern poetry at all; they are "Immortal Autumn," "You, Andrew Marvell," and " 'Not Marble nor the Gilded Monuments.' " Those who had found the poetry of T. S. Eliot, Ezra Pound, and Hart Crane difficult to read soon discovered that MacLeish's variation of a "new" technique was as easy to accept as a short story by Ernest Hemingway, and indeed parallels between Hemingway's prose and MacLeish's verse will probably concern the attention of future historians of American literature.

When MacLeish returned to America in 1928, and followed his return by retracing Cortez's route in Mexico from the coast to the valley, he prepared himself for the writing of *Conquistador,* a narrative in *terza rima* based on Bernal Diaz's *True History of the Conquest of New Spain.* The book was published in 1932 and the following year it received the Pulitzer Prize. The generation of Americans who had traveled to postwar Paris and London and Madrid were beginning to rediscover Mexico, and MacLeish's poem anticipated the romantic search for violent color, action, and the vicarious sense of leisure that so many Americans have pursued in the countries southwest and south of Florida. And the general public had been prepared for *Conquistador* by an interest that had been aroused in Mexican mural painting, the murals of Rivera and of Orozco, and in New York the associations of Mexico were linked with revolutionary political activity. *Conquistador* arrived at the right moment, and the impressionistic color and movement of the poem delighted its critics and dazzled all those who read it.

The poem was a justly praised phenomenon, for the self-training and discipline that MacLeish had received in writing *The Pot of Earth* and *The Hamlet of A. MacLeish* made *Conquistador* an example of craftsmanship that was beyond the skill of any poet of his generation. Compared to *Conquistador* other narrative poems of the period were less well sustained, were less expertly planned, and it was true, as Louis Untermeyer remarked, that *Conquistador* "displays the poet's maturity." Much has been written of *Conquistador's* indebtedness to the techniques of Ezra Pound's *Cantos* and to T. S. Eliot's "Gerontion," but the actual precedent for the flaws and merits of the poem exists in Longfellow's *Evangeline.* The general reader who is unconcerned with matters of poetic technique does not care greatly whether or not *Evangeline* was written in an English version of the hexameter and *Conquistador* in an equally successful adaptation of the *terza rima.* The point is that both poems were justified in their appeal to the eye and ear; both poems—and at some length—satisfied the expectations they aroused; both poems (as the American public read them) held the exotic attraction of places near at home, and yet were far distant in their cultural tradition from the familiar, Protestant, Anglo-Saxon civilization of the cities and countrysides of the United States. And both poets had traveled extensively, Longfellow to Spain and Italy, MacLeish across Europe to the Middle East as far as Persia, and both were essentially elegiac poets, who could, on occasion, extend their gifts to the writing of brilliantly conceived narratives in verse. It could be said of MacLeish that the more he seemed to echo Ezra Pound, the more he actually resembled Longfellow; and like Longfellow, he had the same facility in adjusting the poetic innovations of his contemporaries to his own needs.

2

With the publication of *Conquistador* the recognition of Mac-Leish's gifts had traveled far beyond the circle of those who edited "little" magazines in Paris and in New York, and in the meantime MacLeish had become a member of the staff of Henry Luce's organization of *Time* and *Fortune*—and in this position he gained the admiration of younger men employed by Henry Luce. Quite as Arthur Brisbane, the gifted and liberally inclined editorial writer on Hearst's chain of newspapers, trained and inspired younger men and won their devotion in the days when Hearst was not considered "reactionary," so MacLeish set a standard for journalistic excellence by writing articles for *Fortune*. Young men from Yale, Harvard, and Princeton were among the first to realize MacLeish's qualities for leadership in highly polished and luxuriously phrased "documentary" literature; and nothing quite like it, whether the subject was housing or Yale or Rivera's murals or skyscrapers or labor-saving machines, had ever been seen in previous ventures of American journalism. Under MacLeish's direction the arts of publicity and advertising took on an air of enriched simplicity, the kind of simplicity in dress and manner which can be acquired only by the very rich. With

the same skill that distinguished his articles in *Fortune,* Mac-
Leish wrote experimental plays in verse for radio production,
The Fall of the City (1937) and *Air Raid* (1938); they were the
best of their kind among many similar experiments, and they
have not been equaled by any writer since.

MacLeish's position as a publicist was enhanced by a poem,
"Invocation to the Social Muse," which appeared in *The New
Republic,* October 26, 1932. The poem was topical, and it was a
satire so phrased as to awaken controversy in liberal publications.
MacLeish seemed to speak for the kind of poets who were eager
to confess

> We are
> Whores Fräulein: poets Fräulein are persons of
>
> Known vocation following troops: they must sleep with
> Stragglers from either prince and of both views: . . .[2]

The art of persuasion which MacLeish had served so admirably
in his elegiac poems, particularly in his "You, Andrew Marvell,"
"L'An Trentiesme de Mon Eage," and "Immortal Autumn," had
undergone a subtle change; the language in his verse shifted from
the speech of the literary manifesto (which had become so popular among American "expatriates" in Paris during the 1920's) to
the language which attempted "public speech," the kind of writing in which almost every statement, no matter how casual it
might have been, was transformed into a command.

The history of that earlier moment has been eloquently written
by Malcolm Cowley in his *Exile's Return* (1934); and today the
book holds something of the same fascination that George
Moore's *Confessions of a Young Man* once held for its readers.
Cowley himself was a poet of considerable charm, whose verse
was most successful when it re-created pastoral scenes in his native
Pennsylvania, where he was born in 1898. His first book was a
book of poems, *Blue Juniata* (1929), which in its notes (written
in prose) described the wanderings of a young man who felt
himself to be a member of a "landless, uprooted generation." He
had gone to Harvard, he had edited the undergraduate *The Har-*

[2] "Invocation to the Social Muse" from *Poems 1920-1934,* by permission of
Houghton Mifflin Company.

vard Advocate; in 1917 he had served in an American ambulance unit in France, and he had found both Greenwich Village in New York and the Left Bank in Paris to be places of his discontent. Cowley had helped in editing "little" magazines, had joined the Dadaists, had made friends easily, and his book, *Exile's Return,* glowed with the warmth of his enjoyment in recollecting Montparnasse and the evening of his "significant gesture," the time that he was "arrested and tried for punching a café proprietor in the jaw." The café proprietor was probably no better and no worse than others of his kind, but he was disliked by Malcolm Cowley's friends—and most of Cowley's friends mentioned with awe and reverence in *Exile's Return* were better known to Cowley than by the general public. He was amused to find that the incident brought him newspaper publicity:

> I reflected that French writers rarely came to blows and that they had placed a high value on my unusual action . . . I had committed an *indiscretion,* acted with *violence* and *disdain* for the law, performed an *arbitrary* and *significant gesture,* uttered a *manifesto.*[3]

The gayest and most high-spirited criticism of the period that had been described by Cowley is in Morton Dauwen Zabel's essay on MacLeish, "Cinema of Hamlet," [4] which was published in *Literary Opinion in America:*

> One of the oddest aberrations in our cultural history was the great exodus to France of 1918-1929, when literature, to be written, had to be written in Paris. Those were the days when American art moved from the Middle West to the Left Bank; when farm-hands hurried from Ohio and Wisconsin to get in on the Dada movement; when Gertrude Stein brandished the torch that lately sputtered in the grasp of Amy Lowell; when Kiki was the toast of Rotonde and Coupole; when "Ernest" proudly wheeled his well-filled go-cart among the occult biologic growths of the Dome of an evening to partake of a whiskey and parental pride; when *transition* the best of the "little" magazines in Paris edited by Eugene Jolas and Elliot Paul was young, nothing was sacred, and money was cheap; when whole generations got lost . . .

And in the same surroundings, another "Ernest" than Hemingway, an Ernest Walsh, a young poet of an extremely "poetic"

---

[3] From *Exile's Return,* published by W. W. Norton & Company, Inc.
[4] From *Literary Opinion in America,* by permission of Harper & Brothers.

temperament who died too soon to fulfill his promise, also edited
a magazine, *This Quarter;* E. E. Cummings was there, so was
Hart Crane, and so were many others—who were as exhilarated
by their experiences as Malcolm Cowley. Cowley returned to
New York to become literary editor of *The New Republic,* a
position in which he conducted not unfriendly controversies with
MacLeish and it was under Cowley's editorship that MacLeish's
"Invocation to the Social Muse" appeared in *The New Republic.*

The first of MacLeish's manifestoes, his "Ars Poetica," [5] appeared in *Poetry* in 1926; the poem was not noted for its common
sense or its wit, and the statement that

> A poem should be wordless
> As the flight of birds

was a fancy which recalled Keats's fine paradox:

> Heard melodies are sweet, but those unheard
> Are sweeter . . .

And

> A poem should not mean
> But be [6]

was another instruction whose attraction was in its rhetoric
rather than to a critical intelligence, and the difficulty was that
it had the pretension of being both serious and critical. Of course,
a manifesto of this kind would have to be unsaid the moment
another occasion for a manifesto presented itself; and in Mac-
Leish's case, a curious cycle of issuing instructions in verse had
begun; their political overtones veered from right to left, and
more than all else, they revealed a poet who seemed intent upon
having his cake and eating it too. Actually the change from
writing "Ars Poetica" and "Invocation to the Social Muse" to
"America Was Promises" in 1939 was not as great as some few
of MacLeish's critics have believed; it meant merely that Mac-
Leish had turned his attention from literary "politics" to politi-

---

[5] From *Poems, 1920-1934,* by permission of Houghton Mifflin Company.
[6] From "Ars Poetica," from *Poems 1920-1934,* by permission of Houghton
Mifflin Company.

cal "politics"; the quality of the rhetoric was the same; it was timed to suit the moment, and it was sufficient to meet the immediate occasion that had prompted it. As MacLeish spoke less of Paris and of a point of view that had once been held by Ezra Pound, the character of his verse was more in keeping with Carl Sandburg's *The People, Yes* and Stephen Benét's *Western Star*. In the writing of verse that has its source in nationalistic feeling and historical phenomena Sandburg's *The People, Yes* was a far more convincing document than MacLeish's *Public Speech* (1936) and *Land of the Free* (1938). The elder poet wrote with a confidence that he had gained from his researches into the life of Abraham Lincoln, and if he had advice to offer his readers, it was phrased in the speech of one who knew how to humor those who read him. It was not unnatural that the public response to *The People, Yes* was more widely spread and sustained for a longer period of time than the attention which had been devoted to *Public Speech* and *Land of the Free*.

The coming of the Second World War created a new series of emergencies for Archibald MacLeish: in 1939 he received an honorary degree at Yale and was appointed Librarian of Congress, and the honors brought with them those responsibilities which are attendant upon any man who steps from private life into public office. Soon his activities placed him in the Office of Facts and Figures as well as in the Office of War Information, and though the first office was soon dissolved, and the second had undergone changes which temporarily cast a shadow across MacLeish's career of political advancement, MacLeish's genius for diplomacy was rewarded—and not without the attractive stirring of controversy which had marked his earlier career in writing verse—by the appointment in 1944 as public relations counsel in the office of the Secretary of State. In accepting these responsibilities and honors, MacLeish followed the footsteps of James Russell Lowell who served as minister to Spain in 1877 and as Ambassador to the Court of St. James's from 1880 to 1885, and still another precedent for MacLeish's activities may be found in the career of John Hay (1838-1905), the author of *Pike County Ballads* (1871). Not unlike MacLeish's, John Hay's early training was in law; he was an assistant private secretary to Abraham Lincoln in Washington, and he closed a long and distinguished career in diplomatic services as Secretary of State in Theodore Roosevelt's administration. A future historian may discover that John Hay's anonymously published novel, *The Breadwinners*, which appeared serially in the *Century* magazine from August, 1883, to January, 1884, was the true ancestor of MacLeish's political verses; Vernon Louis Parrington treated the novel harshly, yet MacLeish, in his satires, seems to stand for an "educated leadership." No one doubts the sincerity of his "social" conscience, nor is there any doubt that MacLeish's devotion to public life was less self-sacrificing, less graceful, less brilliant than John Hay's.

Upon the death of Stephen Benét, MacLeish also assumed the responsibility of editing the "Yale Series of Younger Poets." Today, MacLeish's poetic reputation rests upon his *Poems, 1924-1933* (1933); and these include the poems of *New Found Land* as well as *Conquistador*. After their contradictions have been weighed, after their indebtedness to Pound and Eliot and Sandburg have been discussed and set aside, their values rest upon a lyrical gift and a phrasing of rhetoric that belong to MacLeish and to MacLeish alone. The persuasive note within them is that of a melancholy music which entered English verse with the bagpipe sounding its strains to a border ballad. Quite as E. E. Cummings disguised (and legitimately disguised) his affinity with sixteenth-century lyric forms by the use of typographical devices, so MacLeish has concealed his affinities (and rightfully so) with an elder music. We read him because of his sensibility rather than for his instructions; and it may well be that the future will find "You, Andrew Marvell" and "Immortal Autumn" of a greater hardiness in their survival than the prose of Hemingway's *The Sun Also Rises* and *A Farewell to Arms*.

THE LOST GENERATION
OF JOHN PEALE BISHOP

John Peale Bishop's death in the spring of 1944 (he was born in Charles Town, West Virginia, in 1891), which came at a moment when his verse was beginning to attract more notice than at any other stage of his career, left his friends lamenting that his work had been very much underestimated. Indeed, no poet was ever more fortunate in his friends, for they were many, influential, and loyal, and their esteem for him often led to exaggerated claims for the talents he possessed. Good fortune had also graced him with a distinguished and influential family, and after an early education at excellent private schools, he entered Princeton, where he began his long friendships with Edmund Wilson and F. Scott Fitzgerald in whose *This Side of Paradise* Bishop was said to have been portrayed in the character of Tom D'Invilliers.

During the First World War he served as a first lieutenant of infantry, and after the armistice he was placed in charge of a company guarding German prisoners. He too became, like Archibald MacLeish, one of the more fortunate and less Bohemian of the American "exiles" in Paris "when nothing was sacred and money was cheap" and he divided his time between Paris and an old country house dating from the day of Louis XIII. Three of his children were born in France, and in 1933 (as the Great Depression began to fade) he returned to the United States and settled on Cape Cod. His tastes were modest, elegant and, perhaps, expensive; as he is quoted in Fred B. Millett's *Contemporary American Authors,* he said, "I like to eat and drink, and above all to talk. . . . I am fond of looking at paintings, sculptures, architecture and formal gardens. . . . I prefer the ballet— at its best—to the theatre."

With these tastes [1] one can understand why it was that his career between the First World War and his return to France was so successfully conducted in the editorial offices of *Vanity Fair,* a magazine which at one time or another had as its staff-writers such figures as Elinor Wylie, Edna St. Vincent Millay, and Clare Boothe Luce—and one of its editors was Bishop's friend, Edmund Wilson (who, aside from his later contributions to American criticism, published a memorable elegy to his father in a book of verses, *Poets, Farewell!* in 1929). *Vanity Fair* was then (from 1919 to 1924) what *The New Yorker* or *Harper's Bazaar* became to the following decade and the present: it was reputed to contain and to encourage everything that was "smart" and fashionable. Unworldly and awkward young literary aspirants who visited *Vanity Fair's* office were struck by the gilt, the dazzle of the atmosphere. Even the office girls were more elegant (it was rumored that they wore real pearls!), smartly dressed, and formidably polite than the heroines of Bulwer-Lytton's "silver-fork" novels, those ladies who charmed the readers of *Pelham* in a Napoleonic postwar period. Frank Crowninshield, the editor-in-chief, the inspiration, the creator, the master of ceremonies of the once famous *Vanity Fair,* quoted the first of Miss Millay's "Distressing Dialogues" (1924) which appeared in *Vanity Fair* and the quotation recalled the atmosphere of that earlier day to those who read Crowninshield's memoirs in *Vogue,* November 1, 1944. It was one aspect of *Vanity Fair* to the life, and Crowninshield who was easily refreshed spoke of its "refreshing savour," and it had been written rejecting an imaginary proposal of marriage:

Sir, do you take me for an idiot? For four seasons I have parried the advances of the talented, the titled, the handsome-as-Apollo, and the verminous with wealth. It was for me that Paderewski took up politics; for me D'Annunzio became a soldier. The Grand Duke Michael has begged for my photograph in three languages—and Russian; Freud has dreamed of me; Muratore has asked me to sing Celeste Aïda by the hour; a Communist once gave me a seat in a street-car, a Count has run

---

[1] Mr. Bishop was also something of a classical scholar and did some few fine translations from the Greek. Of some of his Latin translations Dudley Fitts has said: "He was the best Roman of us all."

off with my pocket-book, and a King has made a pun about me. For what do you think I am waiting?—for you? Be reasonable! [2]

Of this slight touch of vulgarity Bishop's writing was free, and visitors to *Vanity Fair's* office described him as the most courteous and elegant of the courteous and elegant young men who held positions on its staff. At its best his verse had a professional manner, and some few of his lyrics had a delicately sensuous charm, but unfortunately the greater part of his verse suffered the strain of adapting itself to too many of the most fashionable styles of writing poetry, and his volume of *Selected Poems* (1941) could be used as a textbook illustrating changes in poetic taste from 1916 to 1940—and no single poem, no matter how polished it may have seemed upon first reading, has the distinction of an individually formed taste and imagination. With mirrorlike docility he reflected the mannerisms of Elinor Wylie, Ezra Pound, T. S. Eliot, Allen Tate—and for a brief time, even the speech of MacLeish's "Social Muse" (of which phase the less said the better), and the latter-day, Californian, neoscholasticism of Yvor Winters. Lack of space prevents us from quoting the obvious parallels of Bishop's verse to the work of other poets, but as a well-known critic remarked in a private letter to the authors of this book, "John Peale Bishop wears the finest suit of secondhand clothes in American poetry."

The phenomenon of John Peale Bishop's verse has its precedent in the line of editor-poets from Thomas Bailey Aldrich to Ridgely Torrence; Bishop had been a successful editor, quite as those who came before him were—and the best of his poetry extended the general influence that had been exerted by Ezra Pound and T. S. Eliot upon a between-the-wars generation of lesser poets. His novel, *Act of Darkness* (1935), was among the best of a school that advanced the cause of southern regionalism, and in his latter years, his name was more frequently associated with Allen Tate and Robert Penn Warren than with Edna St. Vincent Millay, Edmund Wilson, and Elinor Wylie. On the occasion of F. Scott Fitzgerald's death in 1940, Bishop wrote an elegy in

[2] From *Distressing Dialogues* by Nancy Boyd, published by Harper & Brothers. Copyright, 1924, by Edna St. Vincent Millay.

memory of Fitzgerald which appeared in the pages of *The New Republic;* the elegy recalled the memory of Fitzgerald almost not at all, but it did succeed in echoing the last "dying fall" of Malcolm Cowley's "lost generation" that had charmed the readers of *Exile's Return.* In 1942 and in collaboration with Allen Tate, Bishop published a popular anthology of American prose and verse, *American Harvest,* of which Howard Mumford Jones observed that it had on the whole selected contributions of a delicate but minor strain of verse in recent American literature.

THE CRITICAL REALISM
OF KENNETH FEARING

If Stephen Vincent Benét and Archibald MacLeish were considered the "leaders" of their poetic generation in America, their successes did not wholly obscure the merits of other poets who were less skillful than they in gaining public recognition. Not all the poets of the "political decade" arrived at a sense of "social consciousness" by way of the Left Bank in Paris; some were less enterprising in securing fellowships abroad than their contemporaries, and some were both in frail health and too poor to risk the chances of finding out that it was actually cheaper to live in Paris rather than in Chicago and in New York. Some had an American and half-cynical and almost Puritanical distaste for the Bohemia that flourished so gayly at the Rotonde and the Dôme; they actually preferred the sights of Times and Union Squares in the early days of the Great Depression; and they were in semi-revolt against the rapidly commercialized Bohemia of New York's Greenwich Village. Some had read Marx and Lenin, or, at least, spoke their names aloud with conscious pride, and some in the offices of *The New Masses* joined the John Reed Club, which was later to change its name to The League of American Writers and to welcome such writers as Waldo Frank, Malcolm Cowley, MacLeish, Hemingway, Newton Arvin, Donald Ogden Stewart and Granville Hicks to its public meetings.

The phenomenon created great local excitement, which reached its height in 1935 with the publication of *Proletarian Literature in the United States,* an anthology of verse and prose. In its criticism of poetry the movement made no discernible advance beyond Upton Sinclair's *Mammonart* (1925) and *Money Writes!* (1927); and Upton Sinclair, no matter how naïve some few of his judgments on literature may seem today, had the virtue of convincing his readers that his mind was untainted by personal ambition, that his "heart was pure," that his chivalry was irreproachable, and that not unlike Tennyson's Sir Galahad, his sincerity had armed him with "the strength of ten." His journalistic abilities were far more skillful than those employed by the younger critics who had followed the direction he had taken; and his mind remained cheerfully undisturbed by esthetic problems that bewildered the latter-day Marxians.

In 1933, *We Gather Strength,* a small paper-bound anthology, which contained an introduction by Michael Gold and poems by Herman Spector, Joseph Kalar, Edwin Rolfe, and S. Funaroff, held the promise of a left movement in poetry. Funaroff edited a little magazine of verse called *Dynamo,* and later, in 1938, published his own book of poems, *The Spider and the Clock.* Political activity, ill health, and the continued effort to earn a living seriously retarded his poetic development; his early death in 1942 was followed by a posthumous book of verses, published in 1944. Because of his promise, and the record of a troubled life he left behind him, there was a touch of pathos in his brief career, yet Funaroff was more fortunate than most young writers who shared his promise, his political convictions, and his poverty. Loyal friends saw to it that his posthumous book of verse was published and the book received praise from Louis Untermeyer in the pages of *The Saturday Review of Literature.*

It is with a sense of great relief that one turns to an elder and more prominent figure in the group, whose verse had an early publication in the *New Masses* and whose second book of poems was published in 1935 by Funaroff under the imprint of the Dynamo Press—Kenneth Fearing.

Fearing was born in 1902 in Oak Park, Illinois, which is a prosperous, middle-class suburb of Chicago, and is known to many readers of contemporary fiction as the birthplace of Ernest Hemingway. Fearing's father was a well-to-do lawyer, and Fearing was educated in Oak Park's public schools and at the University of Wisconsin. Like many another Middle Western boy of his generation, he held unattractive, manual, summer-time jobs, and because of his frail health, they probably fixed (at an early age) his determination to become a writer. By the time he arrived at the University of Wisconsin in the early 1920's, his gifts and his interests in writing poetry were clearly marked, and because of his experience in journalism (he had held for a short time a job in Oak Park as a suburban reporter for a Chicago newspaper) his attitude toward writing had a touch of worldliness that distinguished him from his contemporaries in the classroom and on the staffs of undergraduate publications. In Chicago he had made a friend of Vincent Starrett, and Starrett was a Chicago journalist of the "old school," a man who wrote engaging light verse and "mystery stories," who had a lively appreciation for the literature of the 1890's, and who loved to wander through old bookstores in the city, rediscovering "buried Caesars" among forgotten poets and prose writers. It could be said that Starrett was Fearing's first teacher, and that it was not extraordinary that Fearing won the Vilas Prize at the University of Wisconsin for an essay in appreciation of James Gibbons Huneker.

At college Fearing read the poetry of Sidney Lanier with distaste, the poetry of E. A. Robinson with sustained admiration, and the monthly numbers of H. L. Mencken's *The Smart Set* with undisguised enjoyment. The influence of H. L. Mencken's critical attitudes on Fearing's mature poetry should not be underrated; it is there, quite as E. A. Robinson's shorter poems with their portraits of urban failures created a precedent for Fearing's half realistic, half humorous presentations of New York gangsters and broken down newspaper men that filled the pages of his first book of poems, *Angel Arms* (1929). At the University of Wisconsin, undergraduate literary circles were divided between those who read *The Dial* (under Scofield Thayer's editorship) and those who read *The Smart Set*; Fearing read *The Smart Set*, but his best friends (including Margery Latimer,* a writer of vivid short stories who died too soon to fulfill her promise) read *The Dial*. And Fearing during his stay at Wisconsin was by no means unaware of E. E. Cummings, Wallace Stevens, and T. S. Eliot's *The Waste Land*.

---

* Margery Latimer was the author of four books of prose of which *Nellie Bloom* (1929) and *Guardian Angel* (1932) are memorable contributions to the American short story.

Perhaps no poet of Fearing's generation has devoted himself so exclusively to the demands of "free lance" writing in New York as he. When he arrived in New York from Wisconsin in 1924, he had the youthful charm and something of the appearance of a latter-day Ernest Dowson; his early efforts at writing novels and short stories for a living were never attended by great success, but he never relaxed his determination to earn his living by writing alone. He lacked the facility to adapt his prose to the demands of editors, and he valued his independence too greatly to play more than a passive part in left political activities. But the half-cynical humor and critical overtones of his verse were not unappreciated by critics of left persuasion—Fearing's irony in verse was irresistible; and it had personal charm and character:

> Hey? What saith the noble poet now,
> Drawing his hand across his brow?
> Claude, is the divine afflatus upon you?
> Hey? Hey Claude?
> Here are a million taxi drivers, social prophets,
> The costume for an attitude,
> A back-stage shriek,
> The heat and speed of the earth.[1]

Angel Arms, the book from which the above quotation is made, was generally ignored by book reviewers and critics. Its realistic observation and commentary, its portraits of the servant girl, "Minnie and Mrs. Hoyne," its "Cultural Notes" (a poem which should be compared with and contrasted to E. E. Cummings' "Poem, or Beauty Hurts Mr. Vinal"), its scenes of Broadway in "Saturday Night" and in "They Liked It," created an "anti-poetic" atmosphere that bewildered Fearing's early readers. Fearing had taken for his characters the heroes of the New York tabloid newspapers, and in a language that was in itself a parody of tabloid journalism, presented to his readers a kind of satire in light verse that has seldom if ever been equaled in America.

Six years later, in 1935, when his second book, *Poems,* appeared, the public that had ignored Fearing suddenly discovered his value; when the Great Depression was at its height, it was by

---

1 "Lithographing" from *Angel Arms,* copyright, 1929, by Coward-McCann, Inc.

no means difficult to perceive the hint of terror, the critical intention, the implied brutality, the wit of Fearing's "Obituary": [2]

Take him away, he's as dead as they die.
    Hear that ambulance bell, his eyes are staring straight at death.

    .   .   .   .   .   .

    Go through his clothes,
    take out the cigars, the money, the papers, the keys, take everything
        there is,

And give the dollar and a half to the Standard Oil. It was his true
    blue friend.
    Give the key of his flat to the D.A.R. They were friends of his, the
        best a man ever had.
    Take out the pawnticket, wrap it, seal it, send it along to the
        People's Gas. They were life-long pals. It was more than his
        brother. They were just like twins.

In his parody of New York journalism, Fearing created his
own language; his rhythms were prose rhythms that were arranged in the same typographical order in which Carl Sandburg
had presented many of his shorter poems—but Fearing's speech
was more direct than Sandburg's. It was clear that he had accepted Sandburg as his master, but his temperament held its true
affinity with a younger generation than Sandburg knew when he
wrote his *Chicago Poems,* a generation that was more distinctly
urban, that was self-consciously "hard-boiled," that had shared
the hopes and disillusionments of 14th Street in New York and
Union Square. At its best Fearing's verse is sharp and clear; its
wit never descends to the level of whimsy, and there is never the
least doubt that Fearing's "artless" manner is his own. But Fearing's "artlessness" has flaws of its own making: when his poems
are not at their best, they repeat the minor themes of the more
successful poems at unguarded length, and the parody of "O,
executive type, would you like to drive a floating power,/knee-
action, silk-upholstered six?" if read several times too often between the covers of a book, discourages the reader in the enjoyment of an otherwise brilliant urban scene or a fortunate turn
of social irony.

After the widely acknowledged success of his *Poems* (1935), his

[2] From *Poems,* by permission of Random House, Inc.

Dead Reckoning (1938), and the *Collected Poems of Kenneth Fearing* (1940) it was clear that Fearing, like his contemporary, the novelist, James T. Farrell (who also came from Chicago to New York, and was the author of the famous "Studs Lonigan" trilogy), had found a medium in which to write and was content to repeat the earlier successes of his writings with slight variations on a central theme. If it could be said that the poetry of Archibald MacLeish had a strong kinship with and a parallel to the prose of Ernest Hemingway, the same analogy could be made between the poetry of Fearing and the prose of Farrell; and in political terms, if Fearing veered in the direction of Stalinist Marxism, Farrell complemented Fearing by being an acknowledged Marxist of Trotskyite persuasion. Quite as Farrell justly claimed an indebtedness to Dreiser, so Fearing acknowledged a debt (by the appearance of his unrhymed verse) to Sandburg—and both the poet and the novelist were descendants of a school of social realism in American writing.

In 1939, Fearing received a Guggenheim Fellowship for creative writing, and in that year he published a novel, *The Hospital*, and this was followed by the publication of two other novels, *Dagger of the Mind*, a mystery story (1941), and *Clark Gifford's Body* (1942). Fearing's prose lacked the distinction of his verse, but not unlike Ernest Dowson, he placed a higher value on the writing of it than on his poetry. In 1943, he published his fifth book of poems, *Afternoon of a Pawnbroker*, which contained three examples of his best work, "King Juke," "Beware," and the title poem. In the pages of *The New Yorker*, where most of Fearing's verse makes its first appearance, one finds that it continues to maintain the higher standards for light verse published in that magazine. Like Farrell's prose,* it suffers from a repetitious manner of presenting its criticism; but it is unmistakably honest in its intention, and is a corrective to the merely "slick" and "professional" verse that so readily finds an audience among readers of popular magazines.

---

* But here the resemblance of Fearing's verse to Farrell's prose comes to an end. Farrell's critical writings in *A Note on Literary Criticism* (1936) and in *The League of Frightened Philistines* (1945) show a seriousness of intellectual conviction that is not to be found in the poetry of Kenneth Fearing.

HAROLD HART CRANE: DEATH AND THE SEA

No voice divine the storm allay'd,
  No light propitious shone;
When, snatch'd from all effectual aid,
  We perish'd, each alone:
But I beneath a rougher sea,
And whelm'd in deeper gulfs than he.

William Cowper, "The Castaway"

Of the poets who came into prominence during the 1930's in America, none is more likely to achieve an immortality than Harold Hart Crane. As George Saintsbury wrote of Shelley, Crane was a great poet of the second class, a list that would include the names of Hopkins, Beddoes, Coleridge, Poe, Crabbe, Ezra Pound, and William Blake. And Saintsbury continued his remarks on Shelley with an observation that also applies to the best of Crane's poetry; Saintsbury spoke of "intoxication," the intoxication that Crane deliberately (and at times too literally) sought and cherished in his own writing, "the ineffable, the divine intoxication which only the *di majores* of poetry can communicate to their worshippers." It so happens that Saintsbury in a review of Whitman's *Leaves of Grass* had more to say which is pertinent to the character of Crane's poetry; and if what he said was true of Whitman, readers of *The Collected Poems of Hart Crane* (1933) will find his statement singularly appropriate in its application to the poet and the book held open in their hands:

> But affluent as his descriptions are, there are two subjects on which he is especially eloquent, which seem indeed to intoxicate and inspire him the moment he approaches them. These are Death and the sea . . . in his connection of the two ideas (for the one always seems to suggest the other to him), and in his special devotion to Death, he is more singular.[1]

[1] From *Academy* (England), October 15, 1874.

But in spite of the fortunate commentary that Saintsbury gives us in describing the nature of Crane's poetry, our quotations do not imply that Crane was a "second Shelley" and "another Whitman." He was neither of these, and though the figure of Whitman was consciously invoked, spoken to, and praised in the "Cape Hatteras" section of Crane's poem, *The Bridge* (1930), Crane's poetry had a closer affinity to the cadences of Melville's prose than to any claim of Whitman's influence upon it. Nor was the imagination that Crane possessed (or rather, Crane sought its demon to possess *him*) of the same brilliant, half-intellectual raptures that the boyish Shelley knew. It is only in Saintsbury's happy stress upon the word "intoxication" and in Crane's willingness to confess his heritage in the romantic tradition, that a likeness between Crane and Shelley may be discerned. If Crane may be said to have any temperamental kinship with a British poet of the early nineteenth century, that poet is Thomas Lovell Beddoes—and it is extremely doubtful if Crane had ever heard of him.

A dozen years have elapsed since the news of Crane's suicide at sea, three hundred miles north of Havana, and in that time, the story of his life told in a shrewd and tactfully written biography by Philip Horton (1937) has become identified with the very mention of his poetry. Although the book firmly established Crane's reputation as a figure in contemporary American literature, and though future commentators on Crane's life and work will continue to look upon Horton's book as a source of information, it was published too soon after Crane's death (Crane leapt into the sea from the deck of a small passenger steamer on April 26, 1932) for his biographer to gain a perspective on the gossip, the clique warfare, the literary controversies of Crane's brief career. Good as Horton's book was, the general public came away from it with a slight feeling of revulsion for its central figure and for the crowd of eager, ambitious, and well-intentioned young men who surrounded him. All this was, of course, quite the contrary of the impression that Horton had wished to convey. The sensational facts of Crane's personal maladjustment, his homosexuality, his violent fits of depression, his presence at drinking parties, the occasions on which he would "weep and shout," as Katherine Anne Porter wrote, "shaking his fist, 'I am Baudelaire, I am Whitman, I am Christopher Marlowe, I am Christ,' " overwhelmed the serious aspects of Crane's poetry in Horton's "life of an American poet." Yet Horton was faced with another difficulty, that of presenting Crane's friends to the reader, and since most of them were alive and well, the task called for more adroitness than moral candor.

Today, only the discriminating reader, and preferably one who is familiar with the best of Crane's poetry, will find Horton's book a useful supplement to the critical studies that have been written on the subject of Hart Crane. The present biographical commentary on Crane will of necessity be of the briefest order: Crane was born in Garrettsville, Ohio, on July 21, 1899, and was the son of Clarence A. and Grace Hart Crane; both branches of his family were of New England heritage, and Crane's father was a well-to-do businessman who held controlling stock in a chain of retail candy stores in Cleveland, Ohio. Crane was the only son, and the "spoiled child" of parents who were divorced when the poet was seventeen, and a reference to the now familiar Freudian term of "Oedipus Complex" probably tells us all we need to know of Crane's homosexuality. To the psychiatrist, there is little doubt that his frequent use of sea imagery in his poetry has an obvious meaning in sexual pathology—but the more important fact is that Crane translated these associations into poetry. Crane's schooling was both meager and erratic; in the company of his mother he traveled to the Isle of Pines, south of Cuba, and with her he shared an apartment in Gramercy Park and in East 11th Street, New York, during the years of 1916 and 1917. His true education was of a sporadic order: at the age of fourteen he had begun writing poetry, and through a correspondence with William Vaughn Moody's widow (who lived in Chicago) Crane received his first criticism and encouragement. He read the "little" magazines of the period with great enthusiasm; his first published poem appeared in Bruno's *Bohemia,* and from that time onward he read *The Pagan, Others, The Seven Arts, The Little Review,* and *The Dial,* and it was through some few of these magazines

that Crane gained a "literary intelligence." Through correspondence, he became acquainted with their editors; he submitted
poems to them, and asked for criticism. In effect, the editors were
Crane's instructors, and their magazines, his university.

All this may well seem to have been an unsound education for
a serious poet, and, in purely academic terms, it was. Crane
formed a habit of drawing his learning from secondary sources;
his knowledge and awareness of French Symbolism came from
what he had read of it in translation, and with the aid of a
dictionary he painfully translated (in verse) three poems of
Laforgue. But through conversation with people whom he met
on his earlier visit to New York—the Padraic Colums, husband
and wife, Maxwell Bodenheim, the author of *Minna and Myself*
(1918), Margaret Anderson of *The Little Review,* and Alfred
Kreymborg of *Others,* he acquired a felicity in speaking of literary movements and names of writers. If one may accept his
later poetry as evidence, the more profound of his readings concentrated upon what he had learned in the pages of *The Seven
Arts,* edited by Van Wyck Brooks, James Oppenheim, and Waldo
Frank, for it is more than likely that his intensive reading of
Melville's *Moby Dick* had its natural beginnings in a magazine
that stressed the importance of "America's coming of age"—and
in this connection, Crane's later friendship with Waldo Frank
has particular significance. Other formative friendships were
those sustained (largely through correspondence and through a
mutual interest in the techniques of writing poetry) with Allen
Tate and Yvor Winters. Crane was the most gifted and most
unlearned figure in the group, and on his second (and prolonged)
stay in New York in 1924, it seems that he represented to those
who knew him their ideal of the "intoxicated," unschooled, literally drunken, noisy poet—but one who was in need of education through their help and advice. In respect to his poetry, Allen
Tate (of all his friends) had the deepest insight into its character
and its intentions. When Tate spoke of Crane's desire to achieve
a "single vision" he revealed a true and central value in Crane's
writing. The single and "intoxicated" vision was what Crane
sought and, in his best work, found, and when he himself wrote

in a letter to Gorham Munson (an admiring friend and critic), "The imagination is the only thing that is worth a damn," Crane meant it with deeper seriousness than the youthful, pretentious, and at times guilt-ridden statements of his published "aims and theories."

2

Although *White Buildings* (1926), Crane's first book, did not receive the praise from its reviewers that had been lavished by Tate in his introduction to the volume, it established him among those who were willing to read poetry with balanced respect and enthusiasm. The volume contained eight poems out of twenty-nine which may be read today with the same delight of perceiving actual poetry and rediscovering individual expression that they conveyed nearly twenty years ago. Of these, "Black Tambourine," "Praise for an Urn," "At Melville's Tomb," and poems II and VI of "Voyages" have an air of authority that we define as "timeless"; in these Crane caught and held his single vision, and his tribute to the memory of Melville, and Melville's *Moby Dick,* was one of obvious significance. Throughout these poems there is sustained evidence that Crane read Marlowe, Webster, Shakespeare, and the sixteenth-century translation of Rabelais as though he had held a screen that had been fashioned out of Melville's prose before his eyes—but beyond this, one refers less to literary influences, or to the devices of literary art, than to those inadequate words that describe a poet as being a "mystic" or a "metaphysical."

And what of "For the Marriage of Faustus and Helen" which appeared in the same volume and which Crane regarded as the true expression of his "aims and theories"? The poem rests too much upon his explanation in prose to be convincing. He had talked about the poem too avidly with his friends, and in rereading the poem there is the renewed impression that his intentions and pretensions were too large and too hazy to translate his vision of the Greek " 'Helen' sitting in a street car," and "the Dionysian revels of her court," and "her seduction" on "a Metropolitan roof garden with a jazz orchestra" into poetry. One suspects that he had "talked out" half his poem to his friends, and that neither his imagination nor his art could recall the completed sight of a "vision" he had once held in mind. He entered the same pitfall and torture which on a larger and far more terrifying scale Beddoes had unwittingly prepared for himself in writing his endless dramatic poem, *Death's Jest Book*. Crane's letter of his "aims and theories" to Laura Riding betrays the warmth of too much midnight talk, particularly when he spoke a shade too grandly of "our seething, confused cosmos of today."

Even as *White Buildings* found its place among the few distinguished first books of poems in its decade, Crane had begun the preparation of his never quite completed major book, *The Bridge*. In the letter to Laura Riding, he wrote, "I found that I was really building a bridge between so-called classic experience and many divergent realities of our seething, confused cosmos of today." There can be no doubt that the very image of "the bridge" had taken possession of his imagination, and that he reached toward it with something of the same emotion, an emotion which was both evangelical and despairing, that William Cowper, the eighteenth-century British poet, expressed in the writing of "The Castaway." The reader of *The Bridge* finds in it sufficient evidence to show that Crane conceived the poem on multiple levels of meaning and experience; the poem would be a test of how well his single vision held a multiple scene, and as Crane wrote of it in 1927 to Otto Kahn, the Wall Street banker of Kuhn, Loeb and Company (and Crane's patron), the poem was to be "an epic of the modern consciousness."

If there were more than one way to read Crane's conception of *The Bridge,* there is also more than one way to read his correspondence with Otto Kahn. From time to time, Crane held copywriting jobs in large advertising offices; and during the 1920's the profession of writing advertising copy was considered a desirable one for inventive young novelists and poets. Perhaps Sherwood Anderson, by his successful example, showed the way. (And Anderson himself, a native of Ohio, had been the object of one of Crane's early literary enthusiasms.) Crane's maladjustment to whatever environment he entered, whether at home in

Cleveland, Ohio, or in New York, or during his brief stay in Paris, was deep enough to cause recurrent cycles of being out of money and dependent on the hospitality of his friends. Kahn, a man of liberal interests in the arts, advanced Crane money, and Crane rewarded Kahn by sending him letters telling of the progress *The Bridge* had made. Was Crane's mention of the poem as "an epic of modern consciousness" a means of holding the banker's attention by using language that closely resembled the jargon of publicity and advertising? It may well have been. Yet throughout Crane's correspondence with Kahn one is never quite certain where the poet's pretensions came to an end and the truly felt work of his imagination had begun. Crane's intentions were less obscure than many-threaded, and he was undoubtedly sincere when he said to Kahn, "Thousands of strands have had to be searched for," and that he wished to make his bridge "the Myth of America." In theory (in prose), the poem created the illusion of being a "project," something that was to be talked about, steered, and manipulated into shape: it had a beautiful Proem to Brooklyn Bridge (in sight of which Crane had lived in Brooklyn), then a soliloquy (I) by Columbus, then (II) Powhatan's Daughter, and so on, through eight sections of the poem. *The Bridge* was to span the river, then the ocean, then time and space. Crane was, if anything, too heavily deliberate in his plans, and too dependent upon the "intoxication" of the moment for their fruition. Not unlike his "Faustus and Helen," *The Bridge* was too frequently talked about and "analyzed" in the very process of its composition.

In "The River" section of *The Bridge* the last eight stanzas of Crane's tribute to the Mississippi might well—and better— have stood alone. Few poets of twentieth-century America have approached the memorable quality of "The River's" [2] last stanza:

> The River lifts itself from its long bed,
>
> Poised wholly on its dream, a mustard glow
> Tortured with history, its one will—flow!

[2] From *Collected Poems of Hart Crane,* by permission of Liveright Publishing Corporation.

—The Passion spreads in wide tongues, choked and slow,
Meeting the Gulf, hosannas silently below.

The last line has the same authority as the last two lines of the poem which follows it, "The Dance": [3]

Now is the strong prayer folded in thine arms,
The serpent with the eagle in the boughs.

In these lines we have an accent in American poetry that may be traced back to Philip Freneau's stanzas in his "The House of Night," as well as in his better-known "The Indian Burying Ground." This is not to say that Crane had read Freneau, but that in writing the memorable passages of "The River" and "The Dance," his lines had the same felicity, the same presence of poetic imagination. The lines also remind us that for over an hundred years, Freneau's elegiac note with individual variation has been sounded in the verse of Longfellow as well as Bryant's, in the verse of E. A. Robinson as well as Santayana's, in the verse of John Crowe Ransom, the verse of Allen Tate, as well as in Hart Crane's.

The Bridge made it clear that its author had not realized his full imaginative powers. Those powers were revealed in brief passages throughout the progress of the book, in "Cutty Sark," in the first half-dozen lines of "Cape Hatteras," the paean to Walt Whitman, in the passage that recalls Poe's "City in the Sea," in "The Tunnel," and in flickering lines throughout the closing stanzas of "Atlantis." Certain obvious reasons may be advanced as to why Crane could not sustain the quality he valued most, the "intoxication" of his finest lines of verse. In years and in emotional experience, Crane was too young to realize his intentions, and although he had "found" his own style, and could speak in a language that was recognized as his own, he still echoed with inexpert skill the poetic devices of E. E. Cummings in the opening passages of "The River," and in "The Tunnel" he experimented unsuccessfully with some few of the techniques that Eliot had employed in *The Waste Land*. To these devices

[3] From *Collected Poems of Hart Crane*, by permission of Liveright Publishing Corporation.

and techniques Crane added the high-flown rhetoric of Waldo Frank—and the results, whenever their lack of success became evident, were an almost intolerable "artiness." It was all too clear that he had not assimilated his readings in contemporary verse and prose. In this connection, Philip Horton unearthed the facts relating to another source of Crane's unassimilated readings which had visibly affected his writing of "Voyages" in *White Buildings*—and that source was the unpublished manuscripts of Samuel Greenberg, a poet who died in 1916 at the age of twenty-three, "uneducated . . . unknown . . . in an institute for the destitute tubercular on Ward's Island." Readings in the Greenberg manuscript reveal a gift less disciplined than Crane's, and Crane's use of it does not involve him in the ugly and patently dishonest aspects of plagiarism. What it does show, rather, is that Crane, whenever he felt his own powers of invention flagging, whipped them to life again from external sources, and this means of restoring his "inspiration," more often than not, disjointed and dismembered Crane's effort to sustain the more ambitious sections of *The Bridge*. It could be said that Crane abused his gifts rather than fostered them; he was impatient at the workings of his own genius, and not unlike Beddoes, his nineteenth-century predecessor, he had been driven toward a large effort at a synthesis that he could not achieve.

It could almost be said that in the writing of *The Bridge* Crane unwisely sublimated the religious emotion that has a far more complete expression in "The Broken Tower," which was reputed to have been the last of his poems, written in Mexico a short time before his death. In the late 1920's and in the 1930's to confess religious emotion in New York literary circles was far more damaging to whatever went by the name of "poetic prestige" than the confession of any number of sexual or moral irregularities. In a letter to Kahn, Crane did admit that *The Bridge* had "a rather religious motivation"—but he carefully modified "religious" with the word "rather" and spoke of *The Bridge* in a mixed jargon of anthropological and historical terms. It was then highly fashionable to be "metaphysical" rather than anything else, just as today, in the fifth decade of the twentieth century, the fashion to be both "political" and "religious" has gained considerable ground. In Crane's poetry an impulse toward the full expression of religious emotion ran its course. The unsuccessful "Lachrymae Christi" of *White Buildings* contained sentimental references to the Nazarene and to Dionysus, but in the Proem to *The Bridge*,

> And of the curveship lend a myth to God,

the religious impulse had begun to find its proper language and a theme. In the progress of *The Bridge* from the physical sight of Brooklyn Bridge itself to the last section, "Atlantis," "Swift peal of secular light," the sight of wings carry the poem toward an evangelical "salvation," the desire for an immortality that Crane devoutly wished. If the divisions of *The Bridge* could be recognized for what they are, separate poems of unequal quality, Crane's last poem, "The Broken Tower," would be the last, the best, the completely realized expression of his poetic gifts. If a highly discriminating selection of Crane's poetry were made, it would include the five titles we have mentioned that were published in *White Buildings*, the Proem to *The Bridge*, and "The Broken Tower." The least well known of these is "The Broken Tower" and for that reason, as well as its own merits, we feel that it deserves quotation here:

THE BROKEN TOWER [4]

> The bell-rope that gathers God at dawn
> Dispatches me as though I dropped down the knell
> Of a spent day—to wander the cathedral lawn
> From pit to crucifix, feet chill on steps from hell.
>
> Have you not heard, have you not seen that corps
> Of shadows in the tower, whose shoulders sway
> Antiphonal carillons launched before
> The stars are caught and hived in the sun's ray?
>
> The bells, I say, the bells break down their tower;
> And swing I know not where. Their tongues engrave
> Membrane through marrow, my long-scattered score
> Of broken intervals . . . And I, their sexton slave!

[4] From *Collected Poems of Hart Crane*, by permission of Liveright Publishing Corporation.

Oval encyclicals in canyons heaping
The impasse high with choir. Banked voices slain!
Pagodas, campaniles with reveilles outleaping—
O terraced echoes prostrate on the plain! . . .

And so it was I entered the broken world
To trace the visionary company of love, its voice
An instant in the wind (I know not whither hurled)
But not for long to hold each desperate choice.

My word I poured. But was it cognate, scored
Of that tribunal monarch of the air
Whose thigh embronzes earth, strikes crystal Word
In wounds pledged once to hope—cleft to despair?

The steep encroachments of my blood left me
No answer (could blood hold such a lofty tower
As flings the question true?)—or is it she
Whose sweet mortality stirs latent power?—

And through whose pulse I hear, counting the strokes
My veins recall and add, revived and sure
The angelus of wars my chest evokes:
What I hold healed, original now, and pure . . .

And builds, within, a tower that is not stone
(Not stone can jacket heaven)—but slip
Of pebbles—visible wings of silence sown
In azure circles, widening as they dip

The matrix of the heart, lift down the eye
That shrines the quiet lake and swells a tower . . .
The commodious, tall decorum of that sky
Unseals her earth, and lifts love in its shower.

The poem was self-contained to a degree that few of Crane's poems are, and unlike so many of the longer poems in *The Bridge,* the movement of the entire poem seems inevitably attracted in the direction of its closing stanzas. Was this because Crane, on a Guggenheim Fellowship in Mexico, had fewer of his literary friends to humor his pretensions, to let him talk half the poem out of existence before it was set down on paper? This question cannot, of course, be answered, but to the reader of Philip Horton's life of Crane, the question is a reasonable one to ask. Or the poem may have been the true beginning of Crane's poetic maturity. Ten years earlier he had written to· Gorham Munson, "You know I live for work,—for poetry. I shall do my best work later on when I am about 35 or 40." At the time he committed suicide, he was thirty-three.

3

Philip Horton's book contains many amusing anecdotes of the criticism that Crane's work received during the poet's lifetime, critical reviews, which, of course, angered Crane and gave him a sense of spiritual isolation (the price that a truly gifted poet usually pays in contemporary America)—but the reviews distorted, rather than fatally injured, Crane's reputation. Edmund Wilson attacked contemporary poets (with Crane among them) for their unintelligibility (in which he echoed a foolish and ill-informed article written by Max Eastman in *Harper's Magazine*). And Yvor Winters who had long been Crane's friend (through correspondence) urged Crane to be "the complete man"; Winters was, then as now, well known for the pettiness of his views, his lack of poetic imagination—and to Winters, Crane wrote:

You need a good drubbing. . . . Wilson's article was just half-baked enough to make one warm around the collar. It is so damned easy for such as he, born into easy means, graduated from a fashionable university into a critical chair overlooking Washington Square, etc. to sit tight and hatch little squibs of advice to poets . . . as though all the names he had just mentioned had been as suavely nourished as he— as though 4 out of 5 of them hadn't been damned well forced the major part of their lives to grub at *any* kind of work they could manage by hook or crook and the fear of hell to secure! [5]

Unlike Winters, Wilson had a residue of poetic imagination that had been drained off into the channels of his colorful, energetic, lightly textured prose. In respect to poetry and his criticism of it, his tastes were not unlike those of Conrad Aiken, but his warmest appreciation of contemporary verse had been limited to the period that produced Edna St. Vincent Millay, and the poetry

[5] From *Hart Crane, The Life of an American Poet*, by Philip Horton, used by permission of W. W. Norton & Company, Inc.

of Miss Millay has been one of the touchstones by which he has judged most of the poetry he has praised.

In America Crane's poetic reputation was at its height in 1933, the year that *The Collected Poems of Hart Crane* appeared, edited by Waldo Frank, who also contributed an introductory essay to the volume. In this country the influence of his poetry was first acknowledged by Allen Tate, and Tate, in turn, and through mutual admiration, exerted an influence upon the poems that appeared in *White Buildings*. Of all Crane's critics who knew him personally Frank was the most officious and successful in attracting public recognition, and through the difficulties of personal contact with Crane, Munson had the most courage, the kindliest understanding and he was certainly—as in his early recognition of Franz Kafka's genius, of Pound's *Cantos,* and of Wallace Stevens' first edition of *Harmonium*—the most disinterested of men. Crane's influence quickly spread among younger American poets, and among these the most promising was James Agee, whose first book, *Permit Me Voyage* (the title was a quotation from the last line of the third of Crane's "Voyages"), appeared in 1934 with an introduction by Archibald MacLeish. Since that date his poetic talents have been overshadowed by his skills in journalism on the staff of *Time* and as motion-picture critic for *The Nation*.

In Britain, Crane's poetry has been belatedly discovered by younger writers, and today its influence has taken root in the poetry of those who represent a neoromantic school. It would seem that the early verse of Dylan Thomas and of Nicholas Moore show traces of reading Crane's *The Bridge,* and as a sustained and balanced appreciation of Crane's best poetry comes into being, it is probable that the immediate, and not always fortunate, effects of his influence will drop away. Among his contemporaries in American literature, his closest affinity in imaginative writing is with William Faulkner, the novelist. Some few of the same flaws that Crane's poetry had are to be found in Faulkner's *As I Lay Dying* (1930) and *The Sound and the Fury* (1929), the same feeling of "intoxication" is also conveyed through the medium of Faulkner's prose, and in the best of

Faulkner's novels and short stories there is the presence of a "single vision." Compared with Crane, Faulkner has been the more self-conscious artist, and he has had the good fortune to live and to write into a maturity that Crane never knew. Crane's single advantage over Faulkner was in the highly charged concentration of his gifts, an advantage which is always held by the poet whenever he is compared to a novelist of similar insights, depth, and imaginative quality. And Crane well knew

> The imaged Word, it is, that holds
> Hushed willows anchored in its glow.
> It is the unbetrayable reply
> Whose accent no farewell can know.[6]

[6] "Voyage VI," from *Collected Poems of Hart Crane*, by permission of Liveright Corporation.

EPILOGUE

It is time to realize that the revolutionary trend of the thirties did not profoundly transform the literary consciousness of America.

William Phillips and Philip Rahv, in *New Letters in America* (1937)

So wrote the two young editors of *Partisan Review*. Their reference was to the so-called "proletarian novel" which did not materialize in America. By 1944 the only "literary Marxian" who held to his original principles was the novelist, James T. Farrell, —and Farrell, like Kenneth Fearing, had never been a member of the "proletariat." His family was of lower-middle-class Chicago Irish, and his novels more properly represent a candid, forceful, urban regionalism than any other claim which they may have to the documentary literature of the period. The same observation holds for the poetic literature of the same decade. The naïve young critics of the period tried to instruct writers to "write down" to the "workers," and the effort failed because on the one hand gifted writers refused to compromise their moral and esthetic integrity (only lesser poets fell into the trap), and on the other hand the American public (of all classes) had a higher standard for what it cared to read than what had been praised as the "proletarian novel."

If the general movement to the left proved anything, it gave evidence of a long-recognized youthful American "vitality," which in this case responded acutely to the Great Depression and the threat of a Second World War. Its more spectacular efforts moved in the direction of journalism and away from the slow and more profound rewards of writing and reading imaginative literature. And it has been the curse of the phenomenon called "American vitality" to be praised and encouraged in terms of adolescent values. Aided by well-meaning but thoughtless critics, the "vitality" of the Saroyans, the Steinbecks, and the Hemingways of American prose projected a mindless, half sadistic, half sentimental vision of an indefinitely prolonged boyhood across the many pages of their novels and short stories and, literally, upon the Hollywood screen. And the curse was compounded by the ever present hope (and sometimes the actual fact) that "easy" writing brought with it the rewards of easy money. With this readily commercialized value placed on American "vitality," it was little wonder that the writers of fiction during a "political decade" became confused, and that they did not make a notable advance beyond the writers of a previous decade.

If the values of poetry (and criticism of it) fared better than fiction, it is because the temptations of commercial success were further removed; and though a poet may become self-deceived as to the nature of his "vitality" and his prestige, there is small danger that his work will be corrupted by large offers of money from Hollywood. On the North American continent we possess, so it has been often said, a vital language—and in saying this, we drop the quotation marks with which "vitality" passes from its all too familiar meanings to those which have a closer association with poetry. In the writings of many poets of whom we have spoken in the preceding pages, a vital language has been the medium through which their poetry has delighted and persuaded us, and today it should be our concern to give that speech a life beyond the glib rise and fall of voices heard on the radio or in the lecture hall. The gay and bright rhetoric of the advertising agency, which twenty years ago seemed so refreshing, has grown shrill and thin; the speech of the political manifesto (which, so some have said, had been imported from Paris soon after the First World War) has grown heavy and pontifical; and as if to counteract the first two extremes of rhetorical exercise, a neoscholastic rhetoric of poetry as well as criticism, based, as someone said, upon a Henry James version of the Bible, came into being—and all of it contained the elements of what some of us had too fondly called American vitality, and then had been forced to confess that it had small chance of surviving the pains of "growing up" into something that would endure. But a true and adult vitality cannot be patronized in the fashion we have just described, and instead of applying the word without reservation to the poetry of younger writers, let us say, rather, that first and second books of poetry written in this country are seldom dull.

2

Since 1940, younger American poets, superficially at least (although among the weaker of them, the influence became subcutaneous), keenly felt the presence of three British poets, W. H. Auden, Stephen Spender, and Louis MacNeice, across the waters of the Atlantic. Perhaps the most immediate influence that was widely and quickly spread by the younger British poets was a renewed respect for traditional forms in English verse. For a brief moment it was forgotten that traditional forms in verse had been employed by every American poet of more than passing distinction from 1900 to the arrival of Archibald MacLeish. But the point is that, with the exception of Stephen Spender, the British poets moved with great freedom and facility within the traditional forms of lyric verse, and the immediate results were spectacular.

In practice the verse of Louis MacNeice was the most readily adaptable; he seemed to write his verse in the way that he defined, "as one enjoys swimming or swearing." In other words, his gift was easily assumed, often journalistic, extraverted and at its worst, flat, dull, and wordy. In its lighter moments, the verse was brisk, acrid, amusing, and at its best it emulated (in a fine adaptation of one of Horace's odes) the clarity and strength of a Latin heritage in English verse, but in itself and in its influence upon younger American writers, it very nearly founded a school of poetic insensibility. Its metrics were tone deaf, and only the most obvious half-and-full rhymes and cadences were heard within it. And as one makes the effort to reread *Poems 1925-1940* there is indeed something that more resembles "swimming" and "swearing" in it than poetry. MacNeice's technique, his verse forms, his manner of seeming to know the world, were quickly adopted by two promising poets, Randall Jarrell, author of

Blood for a Stranger (1942), and Karl Jay Shapiro, whose editor published two volumes of verse, *Person, Place and Thing* (1942) and *V-Letter* (1944). The three books received universal praise, but the clearest tendency that was expressed in them was a half sentimental, half hard-boiled effort to rewrite the "MacNeice manner" into acceptable magazine verse. We shall have to wait another five years for their maturity.*

Stephen Spender's second volume, *Poems* (1933), moved in an opposite direction from that of Louis MacNeice's verse; and since the publication of Rupert Brooke's *Collected Poems* in 1915, no single book of poems by a young and unknown British poet has received so much praise. Its promise still holds the attention of its readers, nor does the promise diminish when one becomes aware that the majority of the poems betray a sometimes naïve and always sensitive reading of Rainer Maria Rilke. It is enough to know that the sources of Spender's early poems were freshly inspired, unspoiled, unhackneyed. His *Ruins and Visions* (1942) was less reassuring. Something of Spender's fine sensibility remained between (one almost says) its lines, but one feels that the sensibility had become blunted and battered by a series of unfortunate encounters with psychology, history, and politics. One must look for felicitous single lines in the book, and not for completed poems; the book is filled with portents, speculations, slogans, ruminations, which in their immature phrasing have all

---

* On his return from the Pacific, Shapiro published an *Essay on Rime*, 2,000 lines of verse on the "confusions" of poetry (1945), which promises to be a historical phenomenon and which reflected those attitudes and opinions that had become familiar to all readers of the *Partisan Review* (1935-1945). Meanwhile, his *V-Letter* had received the Pulitzer Prize for poetry in 1944. *Essay on Rime* confirms the character of his first two books of poems; with remarkable showmanship and a vigorous facility, Shapiro's heavily weighted periods, his use of such words as "signification" and "resultantly," showed a greater debt to MacNeice's verse than to the "influence" of Auden's poetry which Shapiro claims and acknowledges. In his *Essay* Shapiro's remark on John Donne's prosody ("A prosody of thunder-clap and bullets") is more vigorous than brilliant or perceptive and, as Charles Poore observed, "more novel than convincing." Although *Essay on Rime* increased rather than diminished current "confusions" in criticism of modern American poetry, Shapiro's adverse critics should not underrate his gifts for showmanship and poetic journalism—which, in their energy if not in their lack of wit and gaiety, curiously resemble the similar gifts of William Saroyan in prose.

too rapidly become clichés. The truism that poetry is written with words and not ideas leaves a negative impression upon a volume whose title described its contents with an imaginative and fatal accuracy.

Of the three British poets, and though it now seems gratuitous to say so, W. H. Auden alone has sustained the brilliance of his early promise. Auden's early verse revealed, among other things, a literary personality, the created figure of a young British poet, who moved with great and brilliant ease in a fashionable intellectual and social milieu of the day. And the figure that Auden had created spoke the language of that day, its particular brand of Oxford communism, its "Americanisms," its private jokes, its literary quarrels, its ambitions for "leadership," with an admirable show of poetic wit. The figure was and still remains the kind of "genius" that is the very spirit of its time and place, and it inhabited a pre-Second World War milieu that was presented on the screen by Alfred Hitchcock, and made its presence known to the readers of fiction in the novels of Grahame Greene, Evelyn Waugh, Eric Ambler, and Christopher Isherwood. The figure drew from that active scene a speech and a manner whose resources seemed inexhaustible; the gifts that he possessed relieved him of those responsibilities that fall to the lot of the island Englishman; and as readers of *Letters from Iceland* (1937) can testify, he assumed the role of a latter-day Lord Byron, the rare phenomenon of a British poet who carried at heart the events and ideas of Mid-Europe, as well as its north and northwestern islands.

Since Auden's arrival in America during the late 1930's, his literary personality has been deprived of that rich source of immediate reference in language and events which had existed in an Oxford-London-Orient Express milieu; his "Americanisms" were less effective because they lacked the appropriate setting of a European context; and he had been put to the difficulty (and not without natural failures) of inventing another language in which to convey the expression of poetic wit and personal authority. For this reason the speech of *The Double Man* (1941) was less refreshing than the language of *On This Island* (1937) and *Another Time* (1940) and it soon became almost as "dated" as that eldest document of vital literature, which is always yesterday morning's edition of the *New York Times*. In five years from now it is highly probable that the "ideas" and the "private jokes" which so genuinely delighted the readers of Auden's *Poems* (New York, 1934, London, 1930) will be as desperately out of fashion as D. H. Lawrence's manifestoes on sex and obscenity are today.

Auden's poetry bears the same relationship to American poetry today as D. H. Lawrence's prose did to the "American scene" of twenty-five years ago. The presence of D. H. Lawrence in this country could not be otherwise than salutary; and both Auden and Lawrence created a literary character who happened to have the same name as the author of their books. As we become aware of that relationship, the likeness becomes all the more convincing: both characters, though under the separate names of Lawrence and Auden, treated "ideas" and interest in intellectual affairs with the passion and intensity of one who becomes the leader or the devotee of a cult.

What then seems to have the quality of endurance in the best of Auden's poetry? The very best which came to light in *On This Island* (1937), and that flickered with less sustained but equal brilliance in *Another Time* (1940), and in his latest book, *For the Time Being* (1944)? What true example does it offer us behind the ephemeral speech and gestures of the personality which seems to utter its shifting convictions, or the lack of them, with such facility? What is the nature of the art or spirit which has endowed his poetry with a measurable size, and weight, and depth? One answer is that his poetry exists—and with appropriate freedom and wit—within the tradition of English lyric verse. From that tradition it derives its true authority; and even in its deliberate parodies and satires, it pays its respects to a range of lyrical conceit in poetry that extends from Sir Philip Sidney to Alfred, Lord Tennyson—and embraces at the close of the nineteenth century the verse of Kipling and of A. E. Housman. This describes the nature of its "size"; and if some of the spaces within it are imperfectly filled, it is because the creation of a literary personality and its legend tends to dissipate those energies which should have been concentrated upon and within certain individual poems. As to the "depth" and "weight" of Auden's gift, an analogy may be found among his literary ancestors, in the verse of the gifted, and today all too little known, seventeenth-century poet, Richard Lovelace—and this is not an analogy of kind, but rather of true weight in which something like a balance can be struck between the lyrical brilliance of Auden's poetry at its best and the songs, odes, pastorals, elegies, and reflective verses of Lovelace. The strain in Auden's verse which has always held a relationship to what has been called "metaphysical" poetry may be rediscovered in reading the poetry of Lovelace. How "Freudian," how Audenesque these few lines from one of Lovelace's songs now appear!

> Hark! O hark! you guilty trees,
> In whose gloomy galleries
> Was the cruel'st murder done
> That e'er yet eclips'd the sun.
>
> .   .   .   .
>
> Feel no season of the year
> But what shaves off all your hair;
> Nor carve any from your wombs
> Aught but coffins and their tombs.[1]

It is perhaps unnecessary to add that such lines are very nearly certain to stir and to delight the reader's imagination; and it is superfluous to remark that as long as Auden's poetry is at its best it achieves the same result. It is rather more than likely that William Empson, that fine and able disciple of the teachings of I. A. Richards and the author of a distinguished volume of verse, *The Gathering Storm* (1940), would insist that the pleasure derived from the reading of Lovelace's lines came from their author's perception of a poetic, and thoroughly legitimate, ambiguity. Such an accomplishment in poetry—and it may also be found in the poetry of T. S. Eliot and Hart Crane—is always a source of delight, and those distinctions which refer to nationality, to sex, to race, to whether or not the verse is major or minor, or "romantic" or "classical," become matters of secondary

[1] "The Song" from *Minor Poets of the Seventeenth Century*, Everyman's Library, E. P. Dutton & Company.

importance and tend to melt away. It is therefore natural to relate Auden's title, "The Double Man," to Lovelace's lines in his second poem to "The Snail"—even the metrics of the poem resemble those of "The Double Man"—and Lovelace had the advantage of writing his poem in considerably less than Auden's seventeen hundred lines:

> Yet the authentic do believe,
> Who keep their judgment in their sleeve,
> That he is his own double man,
> And, sick, still carries his sedan:
> Or that like dames i' th' land of Luyck,
> He wears his everlasting huke.
> But, banish'd, I admire his fate,
> Since neither ostracism of state,
> Nor a perpetual exile
> Can force this virtue change his soil:
> For wheresoever he doth go,
> He wanders with his country too.

It is in the concealed fashion of Lovelace's snail, and not in the fashionable milieu through which Auden has traveled with so much success and such great ease, that the true virtues of his poetry are to be found; and Lovelace's remarks upon the snail are precisely those that one welcomes in the presence of Auden's literary legend and his poetry.

Of those who felt the presence of Spender and of Auden with particular keenness, and yet with discrimination, the most gifted American was Frederic Prokosch, who is now better known for his novels than for his verse. His distinction rests, however, upon the rare and delicate qualities in his verse which denote the possession of a lyrical "ear." His verse has charm and it creates the illusion of being written with the ease of one who is in the habit (a habit from which Auden himself is not quite free) of playing, for the sake of whiling away the time, several bars of one of Chopin's melodies with the left hand. And the ease rewards us with its moments of true pleasure. The best of Prokosch's several books of poems is *The Carnival* (1938), and readers of contemporary verse are likely to find in it passages of relief from the tone-deaf, small-minded, ugly-tempered, sarcastic rather than satiric improvisations of those Americans who followed MacNeice with scant wisdom and thoroughly docile admiration.

3

A near contemporary of Prokosch, and both poets were born in the American Middle West, and both had traveled extensively in Europe, is Richard Eberhart. During the past fifteen years, Eberhart has published four books of verse, of which *Song and Idea* (1940) is the most characteristic. His verse is notoriously uneven in its quality; it is both artful and artless, and whenever a good poem appears on a page of one of his books, it seems to arrive with the spontaneity and freshness of a fortunate accident. One concludes that Eberhart is a bad self-critic, that he has yet to find a poetic style that is completely his own, and that his progress has been one of leaping forward rather than of steady growth. At his best his poems show the presence of a true imagination; he has written four or five fine poems of which "The Groundhog" is the most complete, and "In Prisons of Established Craze" the most indicative of his promise. His choice of language is less American than British, and it seems to stem from the period that produced the anthologies of Georgian Poetry from 1911 to 1922. Another poet, who happens to be some ten years younger than Eberhart (who was born in 1904), but who is of the same mixed European-American heritage in his verse, and has the same evidence of promise, is Thomas Merton, the author of *Thirty Poems* (1944). Merton is a Trappist Monk in Our Lady of Gethsemani, Kentucky; little is known of him or his poetry, but the promise of his first book indicates, as Eberhart's best verse implies, a revived devotional spirit in contemporary poetry.

The sensitive quality of Robert Fitzgerald's verse has gained more recognition than Richard Eberhart's. And the recognition has been justly given to his two volumes, *Poems* (1935) and *A Wreath for the Sea* (1943). Fitzgerald has depended not at all upon the hopes of easily won success, but like the best of those who wrote in the generation that preceded his, he has allowed time for the natural growth of his abilities. In *A Wreath for the*

Sea, his verse shows a fine appreciation of those classical values that have existed and continue to exist in British and American poetry, and the following lines inspire admiration:

> The epithalamion, the hush were due,
> For I had fasted and gone blind to see
> What night might be beyond our passages;
> Those stars so chevalier in fearful heaven
> Could not but lay their steel aside and come
> With a grave glitter into my low room.[2]

The portrait-elegy for and of John Wheelwright, which we have quoted in the preceding pages of this book, is an elegy that has been written well within the best tradition of English verse, and it is not, as so many contemporary elegies have been, a strained and fortuitous use of an elegiac title to record anything that may have floated through the poet's mind. Among Fitzgerald's "Mementoes," [3] there is an excellent tribute to Henry James's heroines:

> Milly and Daisy and Henrietta
> And Isabel, beauties, pray for us
> In your fresh heaven, on those lawns
> By Thames under the copper beeches,
> Behind the iron gates in ducal
> Shadow: ambassadors! At Venice
> Where the old and weary and splendid
> Spiders of the world devoured you,
> Who were not ever in anything
> Quite so correct as they. Sisters,
> Mothers later corrupted, maidens
> Living like men into bewilderment
> With a stiff upper lip: you masks
> At operas and marriages,
> Matriarchs with knobby canes,
> Goodbye, goodbye gentlewomen.

At first reading, the associations of these lines may seem too "literary," and so they are, until it is remembered that James's heroines belong to an American past that is our common

[2] "Souls Lake" from *A Wreath for the Sea,* Arrow Editions, by permission of New Directions.

[3] From *A Wreath for the Sea,* Arrow Editions, by permission of New Directions.

heritage, and that their lives exist today as in a mirror whose rays reflect a light that illuminates a twentieth-century sensibility.

In collaboration with Dudley Fitts, Fitzgerald has translated *The Alcestis of Euripides* (1936) and *The Antigone of Sophocles* (1939) which have been praised for their sensibility in reviving the essential qualities of Greek dramatic verse for presentation on the modern stage. Fitzgerald has also written an English version of Sophocles' *Oedipus at Colonus* (1941),[4] and the following chorus from it shows the tact and flexibility of Fitzgerald's lyrical gift:

> The land beloved of horsemen, fair
> Colonus takes a guest;
> He shall not seek another home,
> For this, in all the earth and air,
> Is most secure and loveliest.
>
> In the god's untrodden vale
> Where leaves and berries throng,
> And wine-dark ivy climbs the bough,
> The sweet, sojourning nightingale
> Murmurs all day long.
>
> No sun nor wind may enter there
> Nor the winter's rain;
> But through the haunted shadow goes
> Dionysus reveler,
> Immortal maenads in his train.
>
> Here with drops of heaven's dews
> At daybreak all the year,
> The clusters of narcissus bloom,
> Time-hallowed garlands for the brows
> Of those great goddesses we fear.
>
> The crocus like a little sun
> Blooms with its yellow ray;
> The river's fountains are awake,
> And his nomadic streams that run
> Unthinned forever, and never stay;
>
> But like perpetual lovers move
> On the maternal land.

4 By permission of Harcourt, Brace and Company.

And here the choiring Muses come,
And the divinity of love
With the gold reins in her hand.

Other lesser known poets of the period that followed in the wake of a "political decade" were John Malcolm Brinnin, Winfield Townley Scott, Kenneth Rexroth, and Weldon Kees. Of these Brinnin was the most deeply influenced by the fashions of the day. His book, *The Garden Is Political* (1942), ran the chances in its very title of being a parody of what seemed to have happened to the "new poetry" of the ,1930's, and like Muriel Rukeyser's gift, Brinnin's brilliant promise seems half concealed in poetic activity rather than in the actual writing of poetry. Scott's promise is of an entirely different order; it is one of slow maturity. He has lived almost all his life in Providence, Rhode Island; and he has held serenely to a New England environment. *The Sword on the Table* (1942), a long narrative poem of Thomas Dorr's Rebellion, proved the seriousness and the cross-grained honesty of Scott's speech and its intentions. The poem itself was pedestrian in its movement, but Scott's unvarnished, intractable, blunt Rhode Island manner has its virtues. Scott's merits are those of the regional American poet, who is a New Englander, and who has found in the poetry of E. A. Robinson an example of moral and national integrity. Kenneth Rexroth in *In What Hour* (1940) published regional verse that reflected the charm of the Pacific Coast, and the meditative if somewhat belated contact of a poet with the political and esthetic "conversations" of his day. He had the advantage of his isolation, with the result that his writing retained its personal character. Of the same forthright and direct intention that both Scott and Rexroth showed, Weldon Kees in *The Last Man* (1943) pursued a course that had a keener edge and a true respect for formal distinction in writing poetry. His greatest debt was to the poetry of Allen Tate, and Kees's promise seems to be in achieving a balance between direct prose cadences and those of verse. All of these poets have contributed either to James Laughlin's "poets of the month" series or to his annual, *New Direc-*

tions; and they represent divergent tendencies in American poetry.

Of the same general group (and the list of contributors to eight successive issues of *New Directions* is a long one) Delmore Schwartz and Kenneth Patchen attracted wide attention. Both poets were of an esthetic heritage that had been marked by the publication of an earlier annual, *The American Caravan,* edited by Van Wyck Brooks, Lewis Mumford, Paul Rosenfeld, and Alfred Kreymborg. Although both Schwartz and Patchen have published several books of verse, of which *In Dreams Begin Responsibilities* in 1938 was the best of Schwartz and *First Will and Testament* in 1939 was the best of Patchen, their promise was more in evidence than their achievement, and both carry with them some few of the flaws and merits of the generation which preceded them. In his later prose and verse Patchen has emulated the example set before him by Henry Miller, and in his criticism and verse Schwartz has followed a style that has been acceptable to the editors of *The Southern Review.*

4

It is scarcely necessary to say that if we think of poetic vitality in terms of great variety, of expectations awakened each year by the introduction of several unknown poets, the prospect becomes too broad, too varicolored in its depths and shallows, to endow the sight of life and its activity with anything more than vague shadows of protean movement. What American poetry needs most is the courage (since there are many diversions and easily won rewards not to do so) to mature. But it is also an impertinence on the part of any critic for him to insist too strenuously that individual poets suddenly "grow up." The "growth" of an individual poet is a private matter, and as Keats wrote in one of his memorable letters,

I have written independently *without judgment*. I may write independently, and *with judgment,* hereafter. The Genius of Poetry must work out its own salvation in a man. It cannot be matured by law and precept, but by sensation and watchfulness in itself. That which is creative must create itself. In Endymion I leaped headlong into the sea, and thereby have become better acquainted with the soundings, the quicksands, and the rocks, than if I had stayed upon the green shore, and piped a silly pipe, and took tea and comfortable advice.[5]

And as for the twentieth century in American poetry, examples may be found of a mature vitality in the poetry of E. A. Robinson, of Robert Frost, of T. S. Eliot—and across the Atlantic, where Eliot has become a British subject, the example is furthered in the later poetry of Thomas Hardy, of W. B. Yeats, and of Edith Sitwell. American vitality as a youthful attribute, with its admitted strength and charms, cannot be substituted, year after year, for the more enduring values of individual maturity and distinction, and as we view the human process of "growing up," questions of morality, religious and social being, and esthetic responsibility continue to play an increasingly larger part in the evaluation of twentieth-century American poetry.

[5] *The Life and Letters of John Keats* by Lord Houghton, by permission of E. P. Dutton & Company, Inc., publishers in the United States.

A DESCRIPTIVE BIBLIOGRAPHY

A literary history, however inclusive its scope may be, must respect the limitations of its narrative. Certain titles of books of poems have been omitted; but for the sake of furthering information, we have supplemented our narrative with the following list of titles:

Ideal Passion (1917) by George Edward Woodberry (1855-1930) who was a characteristic minor poet of Stedman's "twilight interval." He believed in "not turning aside to the eccentric, the sensational, the abnormal, the brutal, the base," and that "life-experience spiritualized is the formula of all great literature." His sonnets in *Ideal Passion* were of the same "classicism" that guided the hand of William Wetmore Story (1819-95) in his sculpture; Woodberry wrote:

> in a flying marble fold
> Of Hellas once I saw eternity
> Flutter about her forms; all nature she
> Inspirits, but round her being there is rolled
> The inextinguishable beauty old
> Of the far shining mountains and the sea.

Rose of the Wind (1910) by Anna Hempstead Branch (1875-1937), a lyric poet who was greatly admired by Conrad Aiken and whose best-known poem was "The Monk in the Kitchen"; the sentiments of her verse were divided between the exalted and the trivial, and at her best, her lyricism resembled the quality of Ridgely Torrence's verse. Miss Branch was a descendant of a highly respected New England family; in Boston and New York literary circles she had many friends; the latter part of her life was almost exclusively devoted to settlement-work on New York's East Side at the Christadora House.

Bluestone (1920) by Marguerite Wilkinson (1883-1928), a lyricist whose devotional poems were less well known but touched deeper springs of emotion than were revealed in Miss Branch's "The Monk in the Kitchen." Mrs. Wilkinson was better known as the editor of an anthology, *New Voices* (1919), than as the author of her own books of verse.

Collected Poems of John G. Neihardt (1926); Neihardt, who was born in Illinois in 1881, was a well-known and widely respected regional poet. His life has been devoted to the writing of "frontier epics" in verse which showed commendable industry and honesty of intention. He has received many tokens of respect from the Indians with whom he has lived, honorary degrees from the Universities of Nebraska and Creighton, and prizes from various poetry societies. More industriously pursued than Mary Austin's (1868-1934) *The American Rhythm* (1923), Neihardt's work represents an attempt to join the diverse cultures of the Anglo-Europeans and the Indians who inhabit the North American continent. So far the attempts of Anglo-Europeans to interpret Indian culture and its literature have been more "primitive" and of lesser esthetic value than the "originals" from which the interpretations have been drawn. Such attempts, however, show a well-meant desire to promote good will between two highly developed cultures.

The Sea (1923) by James Oppenheim (1882-1932) who was an editor of *The Seven Arts* (1916-17) and also a poet whose tastes and insights were reflected in the writings of Waldo Frank, Lewis Mumford, Randolph Bourne, Alfred Kreymborg, Paul Rosenfeld, and Dorothy Norman, the editor and publisher of *Twice-a-Year*. An historical interpretation of the poetry written by Muriel Rukeyser, Delmore Schwartz, Paul Goodman, and Kenneth Patchen would disclose the fact that Oppenheim's "free verse" foreshadowed the verse of a younger generation; Oppenheim's language was more "idealistic," less worldly, looser in phrasing than the speech of a *Twice-a-Year, New Directions* generation, whose first books of poems were published in a period that gave lip service to the heritage of Whitman, "rediscovered" Melville, and feared the moral and "idealistic" teachings of Emerson.

Selected Poems (1945) by Alfred Kreymborg who was a genial and "familiar" historian of American poetry in *Our Singing Strength* (1929), and who will probably be remembered as the author of a cheerful, informal autobiography, *Troubadour* (1925) which was a near contemporary of Harry Kemp's *Tramping on Life* (1922) and preceded other books of a similar nature, including Malcolm Cowley's *Exile's Return* (1934), Mabel Dodge Luhan's *Intimate Memories* (1933-37), and Joseph Freeman's *An American Testament* (1936). All these books reflected (from various points of view) the same esthetic, the same literary milieu, the same interest in being, as Mrs. Luhan phrased it, "movers and shakers," and "rebels." Kreymborg's anthologies of the "new" verse, *Others* (1916, 1917, 1919), showed an early awareness (that was not without critical discrimination) of the verse of T. S. Eliot, Marianne Moore, Wallace Stevens, and Mina Loy. *Others* created a precedent for the less well-poised, less well-informed, and yet curiously similar series of "new" poetry anthologies, edited by Oscar Williams under the titles of *New Poems 1940, New Poems 1942, New Poems 1943, New Poems 1944*. These latter-day (twenty years after Kreymborg!) compilations of contemporary verse included British as well as American examples of the "new" poetry, and the selections were enlivened by the inclusion of the latest camera portraits of the poets whose writings appeared in the volume. Reviewers of the *New Poems* anthologies agreed that Williams' editing rivaled his British contemporary's, Thomas Moult's, *Best Poems* series of annual anthologies, but it is more likely that Williams' *New Poems* series will be remembered as the true heir of *Others;* the standard of taste employed by Williams was of the same character that endows *Others* with a historical interest. Kreymborg's own verse is of wide variety, and the charms of its "free forms," its puppetlike humors in *Plays for Poet-Mimes* (1918) received the admiration of Conrad Aiken and other critics of Aiken's generation.

Poems 1911-1936 (1936), by John Hall Wheelock, represented the work of a "Romantic Traditionist," who was born in 1886, and who, while at Harvard in 1905, published in collaboration with Van Wyck Brooks *Verses by Two Undergraduates.* Wheelock's sensibility in the writing of his verse (which he has defined as "lyrical metaphysics") is not unlike the so-called "poetic" sensibility of Van Wyck Brooks's prose; but for the obvious reason that Wheelock was not the author of *The Flowering of New England,* his name is less well known than Brooks's, but his temperamental affinities are of the same order. As Brooks's prose made its appeal to the eye, so Wheelock's poetry was "addressed to the ear"; and like Brooks's prose, its effect upon the reader was less profound than spirited, more professional in its graces than highly polished, and unquestionably more sincere than rational in arriving at its conclusions. *The Black Panther* (1922) was the best of Wheelock's single volumes, and "The Lion-House" was one of the best lyrics in that volume.

Four Saints in Three Acts (1934) and *Portraits and Prayers* (1934) by Gertrude Stein (1874-1946) have exerted the salutary influences of verbal wit and a high regard for accuracy in verbal expression upon twentieth-century American poetry. Miss Stein's excellent teachings include a lack of pretension in writing poetry; her comedy in verse, *Four Saints in Three Acts,* is a superlative example (among many that have been far less successful) of presenting verse upon the twentieth-century stage. It is more than likely that Miss Stein's *Four Saints* will have greater endurance than the highly commercialized versions of "Elizabethan blank verse" that Maxwell Anderson has given the Broadway stage in *Elizabeth the Queen* (1930), and with which he offended the ears and befuddled the brains of his audiences in *Winterset* (1935). In *Four Saints* Miss Stein's talent for writing "operatic" verse shines like a beacon through the inflated rhetoric of "radio dramas" and plays in verse that have been written by Miss Stein's younger contemporaries in America, and are heard on "coast-to-coast" radio programs.

The Collected Poems of Lew Sarett (1941) are further examples of a regional tendency that had been expressed by the *Collected Poems of John G. Neihardt* in 1926. Sarett was born in 1888, but like Neihardt was a native of Illinois, and like Neihardt and Mary Austin he professed an identity in his verse with the speech of the North American Indian. In his own definition of poetry, "triumphant shouting" is a significant phrase, and such phonetic phrases as "Ha-a-a-ah-eeeeeeee-oooooooooo . . . Hi-yee! Hi-yee!" and "Ugh!" and "Ho!" seem to offer him particular delight in transcribing their noises to the printed page. Like Neihardt's verse, Sarett's *Collected Poems* is the record left by a seriously minded, patient, industrious, and well-intentioned man.

Collected Poems of Robert P. Tristram Coffin (1939) is the uncompleted lifework of one who is a phenomenon of Maine (where he was born in 1892) rather than a writer. Few of his poems are poems in themselves, nor are his novels novels—they are the projections of a commercially successful, rotund, energetic, adolescent—and often wistful—literary personality. The value of his work rests upon the number of people who are willing to enjoy the rhymed presence of a man who is determined not to "grow up" and whose greatest pleasure is to be a boy among boys on a farm in Maine. Coffin has done for Maine what Jesse Stuart, the author of *Man with a Bull-tongue Plow* (1934), has done for Kentucky; both men have taught school, Stuart in Kentucky and Coffin holds the Pierce Professorship of English at Bowdoin College; both affect a "homespun" manner in their verses; both are shrewd, prolific, and successful in advancing their literary careers. They have given Hollywood versions of farm life in America to readers who are the sons and daughters and grandchildren of those who listened to the dramatic recitals of James Whitcomb Riley and who read (not without tears and laughter) Alice Hegan Rice's *Mrs. Wiggs of the Cabbage Patch* (1901). As a phenomenon, Coffin threatens to rival the British-born poet, Edgar Guest; in 1936, his sixth book of verses, *Strange Holiness,* received the Pulitzer Prize.

The Devious Way by Theodore Morrison (1944). One of the best novels in verse in recent years. Morrison is a too little-known poet whose lyric verse always carries a quiet distinction. His other books of poetry are *The Serpent in the Clouds* (1931) and *Notes on Death and Life* (1935).

In Tract of Time (1936) by Helen Cornelius (1892-1933). Helen Cornelius is a poet who died too soon to have made a solid contribution to the poetry of her time. Yet this little volume, neglected when it appeared and almost forgotten now, deserves a better fate, for it has some fine lyrics, many of which when they appeared in *The New Republic* aroused interest in the author. The style was that of the "metaphysical" ladies of the 1920's, chief among whom were Louise Bogan and Genevieve Taggard, but Miss Cornelius had more distinction and maturity. Anthologists who are looking for a few fine neglected lyrics would do well to examine this small book.

O City, Cities! (1929) by Raymond Larsson. A curious and sensitive document by a genuine poet and valuable as a contribution to the period so well described by Malcolm Cowley in *Exile's Return*. The chief influence in this and in Larsson's most recent book is T. S. Eliot, but the music and sensibility especially in the liturgical rhythms of *Weep and Prepare* (1940) is Larsson's own. At his best Larsson is one of the few fine devotional poets of our time.

The Hesitant Heart (1919) by Winifred Welles (1893-1939). The first book by a slight and charming poet whose work was really an extension of the better women poets of the "twilight interval." There is a closer resemblance to Lizette Reese and Sara Teasdale than to her later feminine contemporaries. The titles of her books also include *This Delicate Love* (1929), *Blossoming Antlers* (1933), *A Spectacle for Scholars* (1935), and a posthumous volume which did nothing to increase or decrease her reputation for a certain kind of fanciful and delicate verse. Her chief fault was an occasional excruciating whimsy which was, however, considered a great charm by her not inconsiderable number of admirers.

Epistle to Prometheus (1931) by Babette Deutsch. Probably her best book and the book in which she has been able to exercise her not inconsiderable gifts to the full measure of her particular talents which, unlike most women who have made verse their medium, is not lyrical. Miss Deutsch is that rare thing, a genuine woman of letters, and has written verse, novels, translations, and with her husband, the distinguished Slavonic scholar Avrahm Yarmolinsky, has edited anthologies of Russian and German verse. She has been particularly successful in the field of writing children's books. In fact the range of her literary activities and her industry make her a close rival of Mark Van Doren. Her last book of verse, *Take them, Stranger* (1944), has the customary values of her best work, a dignity of thought and a depth of feeling. But she has an insensitive ear and her diction is always flat and occasionally clumsy. She is also the author of *This Modern Poetry* (1935), a serious study of recent British and American poetry, written under the influence of Parrington and which is the work of one who has accepted thoughtfully the critical attitudes of the liberal weeklies.

Poems by Dunstan Thompson (1943) is a brilliant first book of poems by one who has felt the presence of a Harvard milieu as well as the rapidly accelerated influences of Grahame Greene, W. H. Auden, George Barker, Evelyn Waugh, and the Second World War in which he has participated overseas. The promise that his first book holds is of a line that links it to the work of the "Romantic Traditionists" of an earlier generation. Thompson's *Poems* also show a well-trained "ear" and an appreciation of the lighter modes of composing verse.

From Jordan's Delight (1937) by R. P. Blackmur, born in 1904, is a first book of poems, honestly if ruggedly accomplished by a writer who is better known for the criticism he has published in *Hound & Horn*, *The Southern Review*, the *Kenyon Review*, and in *Accent*. The verses written in tribute to Jordan's Delight (an island off the coast of Maine) offer the reader a fortunate and opposite extreme from the kind of regionalism that has been expressed in the *Collected Poems* of Robert P. Tristram Coffin. Blackmur's speech is tortured, harsh, and unrhythmical—but the honesty of his intentions is plain and it strikes a proper counterbalance to the far less serious professional ease of Coffin's rhymes and fancies.

Of the anthologies which were not mentioned in the preceding narrative, the most compact and rewarding compilations are Conrad Aiken's *Modern American Poets* (1927), his *American Poetry, 1671-1928* (1929), and Selden Rodman's *A New Anthology of Modern Poetry* (1938). All three are good examples of the anthology that has been edited so as to reach a large public, and all three have been successful in attracting public attention. Rodman was born in the city of New York in 1909, and graduated from Yale in 1931; his own verse (*Mortal Triumph* [1932] and *Lawrence: The Last Crusade* [1937]) stems from the Yale heritage of Stephen Benét and Archibald MacLeish; Rodman's gifts are those of a poetic energy that has yet to mature.

Of the books in prose which may be of interest to those who have read the present volume and desire supplementary readings in the same subject as well as in the critical sources of twentieth-century poetry, the following short list is offered:

T. S. Eliot's *The Use of Poetry and the Use of Criticism* (1933) is one of the most valuable of Eliot's critical commentaries concerning poetry, which might well be supplemented by Kenneth Burke's *Counter Statement* (1931), a series of essays which deal with problems of communication between the writer and his reader, the playwright and his audience. In this connection, William Empson's *Seven Types of Ambiguity* (1933) and I. A. Richards' *Practical Criticism* (1929) are excellent sources to read for those who find themselves baffled by what seem to be intractable prose and obscure reference in the criticisms of poetry which have been published in current quarterly reviews. If the prose is frankly recognized as "Cambridge English" greater ease is enjoyed in reading it, and some of its more forbidding mannerisms tend to lose their frightening aspects. Both Richards and his disciple, Empson, are critics of high integrity and of stimulating purpose; one application of their principles may be found in Cleanth Brooks's *Modern Poetry and the Tradition* (1939). Another example of the salutary effects of Richards' influence may be found in Elizabeth Drew's and John L. Sweeney's *Directions in Modern Poetry* (1940), which is a brilliant, unorthodox study of those techniques in poetry which had attracted and at times bewildered the readers of "modern verse." The Drew-Sweeney book is for the sophisticated reader who is innocent only in respect to the technical innovations in twentieth-century poetry. For readers who have an interest in the theoretical aspects of twentieth-century American verse from a singular and able point of view, Allen Tate's *Reactionary Essays on Poetry and Ideas* (1936) has its rewards, and it is particularly valuable in bringing to rest and correcting any popular misconceptions which may have arisen concerning the poetry of Hart Crane.

A serious, thorough, and pioneer work of great value to the study of Canadian verse is A. J. M. Smith's *The Book of Canadian Poetry: A Critical and Historical Anthology* (1943). This book has the potential values in its own field that were once held by Stedman's *An American Anthology* in 1900. Smith's anthology represents, of course, a literary heritage that lacked the physical presence of a nineteenth-century "American renaissance" in New England; one is inclined to say that Smith's book offers a renewed hope for the future of Canadian verse, and Smith himself is one of the best contemporary Canadian poets, along with Patrick Anderson, Abraham Klein, Ralph Gustafson and E. J. Pratt.

INDEX

Æ., 236
Abercrombie, Lascelles, 156, 157
Accent, 501
Adams, Franklin P., 306
  So Much Velvet, 306
Adams, Henry, 25, 30-31, 41, 70, 74,
  116, 170, 399
Adams, Leonie, 291-99
  "Death and the Lady," 296-98
  "Ghostly Tree," 296
  High Falcon, 291, 296, 298
  "Kennst Du Das Land," 298
  "Moon and Spectator, The," 296
  "Mount, The," 295
  This Measure, 299
  Those Not Elect, 291
Aeschylus, 53
Agee, James, 480
  Permit Me Voyage, 480
Aiken, Conrad, 70, 146, 217-25, 259,
  310, 319, 479, 497, 502
  American Poetry (ed.), 502
  And in the Human Heart, 225
  Bread and Music, 219
  Jig of Forslin, The, 219
  Modern American Poets (ed.), 502
  "Morning Song of Senlin," 222
  "Prelude LVI," 222-23
  "Preludes for Memnon," 222
  Priapus and the Pool, 219
  Punch: The Immortal Liar, 218,
  219
  Selected Poems, 225
  "Senlin: A Biography," 222
  Time in the Rock, 222, 223-24
à Kempis, Thomas, 82
Alcott, Louisa May, 435
Aldington, Richard, 169, 170, 183-84,
  189, 193, 417-18
Aldrich, Mary A. S., 383
Aldrich, Thomas Bailey, 16, 39, 460
  "Heredity," 16

Altgeld, John P., 239, 242
Ambler, Eric, 487
Amiel, Henri Frédéric, 407, 410
American Anthology, An, 8-11, 16,
  19, 20, 83, 503
American Bookman, The, 369
American Caravan, 495
American Harvest, 461
American Mercury, The, 220, 231
American Poetry, 502
Anderson, Margaret, 142, 166, 317,
  375, 415, 471
Anderson, Maxwell, 499
Anderson, Patrick, 503
Anderson, Sherwood, 64, 203, 243,
  301-2, 398, 473
Andreyev, Leonid, 256
Appleseed, Johnny, 239
Arensberg, Walter Conrad, 255
Arlen, Michael, 219
Arnold, Matthew, 4, 5, 8, 66, 186, 293
  "Dover Beach," 293
Arvin, Newton, 462
Atherton, Gertrude, 398
Atlantic Monthly, The, 16, 60, 109,
  186, 317, 420
Auden, W. H., 7, 32, 188, 299, 382,
  432, 439, 485, 487-89, 501
  Another Time, 488
  Double Man, The, 487, 490
  For the Time Being, 488
  Letters from Iceland, 487
  On This Island, 487, 488
  Poems, 488
Austen, Jane, 82, 110
Austin, Mary, 182, 498, 499
Ayscough, Florence, 182

Babbitt, Irving, 302, 411, 415, 420
Baker, George Pierce, 43
Barham, Richard Harris, 241
Barker, George, 501

Barnes, Djuna, 216
Barry, Iris, 165-66
Barry, Philip, 436
Baudelaire, 47, 259, 330, 331
  Fleurs du Mal, 259
Beardsley, Aubrey, 166, 218, 330
Beddoes, Thomas Lovell, 468, 469, 473
  Death's Jest Book, 473
Beer, Thomas, 134
Bellamy, Edward, 51
Benét, Laura, 434, 442
Benét, Rosemary, 435
  Book of Americans, A, 435
Benét, Stephen Vincent, 251, 300, 397, 431-37, 438, 439, 441, 448, 456, 457, 462, 502
  "American Names," 435
  "Ballad of William Sycamore, The," 435
  Beginning of Wisdom, The, 436
  Book of Americans, A, 435
  "Carol: New Style," 437
  "Drug-Shop, The," 434
  Five Men and Pompey, 434
  John Brown's Body, 251, 431-34
  King David, 434
  Western Star, 439, 440, 456
  "1935," 437
Benét, William Rose, 268, 285, 287, 300, 434, 435, 440-44, 447
  Dust Which Is God, The, 444
  Falconer of God, The, 442
  Golden Fleece, 442
  "Inscription for a Mirror in a Deserted Dwelling," 442-44
  "Jesse James: American Myth," 442
  Man Possessed, 442
  Merchants from Cathay, 442
  Oxford Anthology of American Literature, The (ed.), 196, 207, 444
  "S. V. B.—1898-1943," 440-41
Benson, A. C., 421
Benton, Thomas Hart, 432
Bessy, Mabel A., 436
Bethune, George, 283-84
Bierce, Ambrose, 51, 55, 56, 57, 58, 62 136
Birth of a Nation, 432

Bishop, John Peale, 458-61
  American Harvest (ed.), 461
  Selected Poems, 460
Blackmur, R. P., 177, 346, 501, 502
  From Jordan's Delight, 501, 502
Blake, William, 47, 311, 468
Blast, 166, 167, 317, 415
Blunden, Edmund, 309
Bodenheim, Maxwell, 219, 415, 471
  Minna and Myself, 471
Bogan, Louise, 277-80, 294, 500
  Body of This Death, 277
  "Hypocrite Swift," 278
  "M., Singing," 278
  "Man Alone," 278
  "Single Sonnet," 278
  Sleeping Fury, The, 277
  "Spirit's Song," 278
Bohemia, 470
Bond, Carrie Jacobs, 18
Boni, Albert, 258
Book of American Negro Poetry, The, 387, 389, 390, 391, 392-93
Book of the Dead, 242
Bookman, The, 165
Boston Evening Transcript, 391, 420
Bourne, Randolph, 498
Boyd, Ernest, 415
Boyd, Nancy, 460. (See also Millay, Edna St. Vincent)
Bragdon, Claude, 97
Braithwaite, William Stanley, 391-92, 396, 397
Branch, Anna Hempstead, 497
  "Monk in the Kitchen, The," 497
  Rose of the Wind, 497
Bridges, Robert, 7, 309
Briggs, Professor, 293
Brinnin, John Malcolm, 494
  Garden Is Political, The, 494
Brisbane, Arthur, 54, 452
Brontë, Charlotte, 82
Brontë, Emily, 82
Brooke, Rupert, 167, 269, 294, 394, 486
  Collected Poems, 486
  "Great Lover, The," 394
Brooks, Cleanth, 155, 157, 294, 360, 383, 502

Brooks, Van Wyck, 16, 32, 40, 87, 190, 301, 359, 414, 471, 495, 499
Brown, George Douglas, 134
Brown, Nicholas, 255
Brown, Sterling A., 396-97
   Southern Road, 396
Browne, Sir Thomas, 84
Browning, Elizabeth Barrett, 190, 268, 283
Browning, Robert, 10, 40, 41, 47, 144, 172, 414, 442
   Pied Piper of Hamelin, The, 40
   Ring and the Book, The, 172
   Sordello, 172
Bruno, Guido, 470
Bryan, William Jennings, 228, 239
Bryant, William Cullen, 176, 227, 435, 475
   Library of Poetry and Song (ed.), 110
   "Thanatopsis," 176
"Bryher" (*see* Macpherson, Mrs. Winifred D.)
Bullen, Frank Thomas, 185
Bulwer-Lytton, Edward, 372, 459
Bunyan, John, 82, 250
Burgess, Gelett, 55
Burke, Kenneth, 502
Burnett, Frances Hodgson, 435
Burns, Robert, 388
Burr, Amelia Josephine, 141
Burton, Sir Richard, 442
Bynner, Witter, 15, 255
   "Greenstone," 15
   Young Harvard, 15
Byron, Lord, 47, 163, 227
   "Churchill's Grave," 163
   Tales, Chiefly Oriental, 47

Cabell, James Branch, 218, 360, 363, 364, 365, 367, 368, 372, 386, 398
Cabot, Mabel, 186
Caldwell, Erskine, 384, 395
Campbell, James Edward, 390
   "De Cunjah Man," 391
Campbell, Mrs. Patrick, 8
Campion, Edmund, 85
Campion, Thomas, 295
Canby, Henry Seidel, 441, 444

Carman, Bliss, 11-15, 20, 37, 152, 167, 268
   Along the Trail, 12, 15
   Songs from Vagabondia, 12, 13, 15, 38
   "Vagabonds, The," 13
   Wild Garden, 14
Caroling Dusk, 396
Caroline poets, The, 84
Carroll, Lewis, 160
Cavalcanti, Guido, 177
Cawein, Madison, 16-17, 19, 373, 386
   "Rain-Crow, The," 17
Century, The, 97, 141, 442, 457
Chaplin, Charles, 345
Chapman, John Jay, 183
Chatterton, Thomas, 86
Chesterton, G. K., 432, 442
Chicago Tribune, The, 144
Chief Modern Poets of England and America, 220-21
Churchill, Charles, 163-4, 345
   Poems, 345
Churchill, Winston, 433
"Claire Marie," 256. (*See also* Evans, Donald)
Claredon, Lord, 83, 84, 86
Clark, Robert Edward, 345
Claudius, Matthias, 296
   Der Tod und das Mädchen, 296
Clemens, Samuel, 66. (*See also* Twain, Mark)
Cocteau, Jean, 167, 240, 415
Coffin, Robert P. Tristram, 500, 501
   Collected Poems, 500, 501
   Strange Holiness, 500
Colby, Frank Moore, 415
Coleridge, Samuel Taylor, 157, 174, 242, 411, 468
Collins, William, 377
   "Ode to Fear," 377
Colum, Padraic, 14, 471
Conrad, Joseph, 143, 418
Coolidge, Calvin, 160
Cooper, Fenimore, 185
Corbière, Tristan, 167, 330
Cornelius, Helen, 500
   In Tract of Time, 500
Cournos, John, 169

Cowley, Malcolm, 361, 418, 453-54, 455, 461, 462, 498, 501
  Blue Juniata, 453
Cowper, William, 468, 473
  "Castaway, The," 468, 473
Crabbe, George, 110, 468
Crane, Hart, 27, 57, 294, 374, 375, 450, 455, 468-81, 489, 503
  "Atlantis," 475, 477
  "At Melville's Tomb," 472
  "Black Tambourine," 374, 472
  Bridge, The, 446, 473, 474, 475, 476, 477, 478, 480
  "Broken Tower, The," 476, 477-78
  "Cape Hatteras," 475
  Collected Poems, 468, 480
  "Dance, The," 475
  "For the Marriage of Faustus and Helen," 472
  "Lachrymae Christi," 477
  "Praise for an Urn," 472
  "River, The," 474-75
  "Tunnel, The," 475
  "Voyages," 472, 476, 480, 481
  White Buildings, 472, 473, 476, 477, 480
Crane, Stephen, 133-37
  Black Riders, The, 133, 134, 136
  Collected Poems, 133
  "Heart, The," 134-35
  War Is Kind, 133, 134
Crapsey, Adelaide, 91-97
  "Angelique," 95-96
  "Arbutus," 95
  "Cinquains," 91-92, 94
  "Guarded Wound, The," 94
  "Mourner, The," 97
  "Poem to John Keats," 95
  "To the Dead in the Graveyard Underneath My Window," 96-97
  "Vendor's Song," 95
  Verse, 91
Criterion, The, 375, 421
Crowninshield, Frank, 459
Cullen, Countee, 387, 396
  Color, 396
  Caroling Dusk (ed.), 396
Cummings, E. E., 129, 135, 216, 264, 294, 299, 306, 318, 319, 336-47,

349, 355, 356, 359, 415, 455, 457, 464, 465, 475
  Collected Poems, 347
  Eimi, 336, 338
  Him, 346
  "Poem, or Beauty Hurts Mr. Vinal," 465
  Tom, 346
  Tulips and Chimneys, 336
  1 X 1, 344
Curran, Sarah, 85

Damon, S. Foster, 184, 186-87
Dana, Katherine, 185
Dana, Richard Henry, 185
Dance Index, 325
Dane, Clemence, 267
Daniel, Arnaut, 171, 172
Dante, 53, 213, 231, 415, 425
  Divine Comedy, The, 213, 231
Darrow, Clarence, 449
Davidson, Donald, 275, 380
Davies, W. H., 392
De Casseres, Benjamin, 257
Decision, 224
Delacroix, Ferdinand Victor Eugène, 413
De la Mare, Walter, 56, 102, 196, 295
  "The Listener," 196
Dell, Floyd, 15, 255, 267, 393
Denham, Sir John, 325, 422
  Poem on Abraham Cowley, 422
Detzer, Karl, 247, 249
Deutsch, Babette, 402, 501
  Epistle to Prometheus, 501
  Take them, Stranger, 501
Dial, The, 6, 147, 263, 317-19, 415, 418, 464, 470
Diaz, Bernal, 451
Dickens, Charles, 82, 110
Dickinson, Emily, 11, 17, 133, 134, 137, 182, 190, 277, 295, 321
Dobson, Austin, 388
Dodge, Mabel, 256, 394. (*See also* Luhan, Mabel Dodge)
Dodge, Professor R. E. N., 293
Donne, John, 282, 292, 293, 294, 295, 311, 345, 366, 411, 458
  "Canonization, The," 345

Donne, John (Cont.)
"Holy Sonnet XIV," 292
Doolittle, Hilda, 169. (*See also* H. D.)
Dos Passos, John, 250, 339, 415, 432
Douglas, Major, 170
Dowson, Ernest, 26, 55, 166, 467
Draper, Muriel, 255
Dreiser, Theodore, 57, 227, 232, 467
Drew, Elizabeth, 272, 502
Dryden, John, 292, 371-72
   All for Love, 371
Dunbar, Paul Laurence, 387-90, 396, 397
   "After Many Days," 389
   "Circumstances Alter Cases," 390
   Complete Poems, 390
   "Despair," 389
   Lyrics of a Lowly Life, 388
Dunbar, William, 383-84
   "Lament for the Makaris," 383
Duncan, Isadora, 144, 220
Duse, Eleanora, 186
Dynamo, 463

Earle, Ferdinand, 268
Eastman, Max, 15, 393, 394, 497
Eberhart, Richard, 491
   "Groundhog, The," 491
   "In Prisons of Established Craze," 491
   Song and Idea, 491
Eggleston, Edward, 8
Egoist, The, 415
Eliot, Charles William, 67, 69, 70, 72
Eliot, T. S., 6, 7, 70, 98, 146, 147, 157, 160, 174, 180, 188, 196, 197, 202, 216, 222, 257, 264, 292, 293, 294, 295, 299, 318, 320, 321-22, 330, 341, 369, 374, 375, 384, 413-28, 437, 449, 450, 451, 457, 460, 464, 475, 489, 496, 498, 501, 502
   "Animula," 425
   Ash-Wednesday, 422, 423, 424, 425, 426
   "Burnt Norton," 384, 423
   "Difficulties of a Statesman," 424
   "Eyes that last I Saw in Tears," 423
   Family Reunion, The, 424, 427
   "For Lancelot Andrewes," 292

Eliot, T. S. (Cont.)
   Four Quartets, 384, 419, 423, 424, 425, 426
   "Gerontion," 422, 451
   Hollow Men, The, 424
   Journey of Magi, 425
   "La Figlia che Piange," 422, 423
   "Lines for an Old Man," 423
   "Little Gidding," 425-26
   "Love Song of J. Alfred Prufrock," 146, 422, 424
   "Marina," 423
   "Minor Poems," 423
   Murder in the Cathedral, 424, 425, 426
   Old Possum's Book of Practical Cats, 160
   Poems, 414
   "Portrait of a Lady," 422
   Prufrock and Other Observations, 414
   Song for Simeon, A, 425
   "Sweeney Among the Nightingales," 422
   "Triumphal Arch," 424
   "Usk," 423
   Waste Land, The, 6, 147, 222, 263, 318, 413, 414, 415, 416, 422, 423, 424, 425, 464, 475
Elliot, William Yandell, 380
Emerson, Ralph Waldo, 10, 11, 110, 124, 239, 498
   "Fate," 124
   Poems, 124
Emmet, Robert, 85
Empson, William, 489, 502
   Gathering Storm, The, 489
Engle, Paul, 438
   American Song, 438
English Review, The, 166
Evans, Donald, 255-63, 291
   "Dinner at the Hotel de la Tigresse Verte," 257
   Discords, 257
   "En Monocle," 258
   "Failure at Forty," 261
   "For the Haunting of Mauna," 257
   "Frail Phrases," 257
   "In the Vices," 259-60
   Ironica, 257, 261

Evans, Donald (Cont.)
"Mary Douglas Bruiting the Beauty of the Hands of Monsieur Y.," 257
"Portrait of Carl Van Vechten," 260
"Rouge for Virgins," 257
Sonnets from the Patagonian, 257, 259
"Two Deaths in the Bronx," 257
"Two Portraits of Mabel Dodge," 260

Farrar, John, 81, 82, 436
Farrell, James T., 467, 483
Father Tabb (*see* Tabb, John Bannister)
Faulkner, William, 480-81
Fauset, Jessie Redmon, 394-95
Fearing, Kenneth, 462-67
Afternoon of a Pawnbroker, 467
Angel Arms, 464, 465
"Beware," 467
Collected Poems, 467
"Cultural Notes," 465
Dagger of the Mind, 467
Dead Reckoning, 467
"King Juke," 467
"Lithographing," 465
"Minnie and Mrs. Hoyne," 465
"Obituary," 466
Poems, 465-66
"Saturday Night," 465
"They Liked It," 465
Ferrar, Nicholas, 426
Ficke, Arthur Davidson, 261
Field, Eugene, 59, 64
Filsinger, Ernst, 102
Fitts, Dudley, 354-59, 493
Alcestis of Euripides, The, 358, 493
Anthology of Latin American Poetry (ed.), 357
Antigone of Sophocles, The, 358, 493
"Epitaph for a Sailor," 356
"Fifth Anniversary," 357
Homage to Rafael Alberti," 357
More Poems from the Palatine Anthology, 355

Fitts, Dudley (Cont.)
One Hundred Poems from the Palatine Anthology, 354, 355, 358
Poems 1929-1936, 355, 358
"Priam," 358
"Retreat," 357
"Valentine for a Lady, A," 355, 356
Fitzgerald, Edward, 421
Fitzgerald, F. Scott, 263, 267, 339, 403, 458, 460-61
Fitzgerald, Robert, 353, 358, 491-92
Alcestis of Euripides, The, 358, 493
Antigone of Sophocles, The, 358, 493
"Mementoes," 492
Oedipus at Colonus, 493-94
Poems, 491
"Portrait," 353-54, 492
"Souls Lake," 492
Wreath for the Sea, A, 353, 491-92
Flanner, Hildegarde, 279-80
If There Is Time, 280
Time's Profile, 279
"Sonnets in Quaker Language," 279-80
Flaubert, Gustav, 258, 330
Fletcher, John Gould, 166, 199, 201-206, 217
Black Rock, The, 205
"Color Symphonies," 204, 205
"Cycle of Liguria," 205
"Ghosts of an Old House, The," 204, 206
Goblins and Pagodas, 204
Preludes and Symphonies, 204, 205
Selected Poems, 201
Flint, F. S., 168, 169
Ford, Ford Madox, 135, 164, 166, 169, 192-93
Fortune, 452, 453
Forum, The, 152
France, Anatole, 364
Frank, James Marshall, 380
Frank, Waldo, 439, 462, 471, 476, 480, 498
Frankfurter, Felix, 70
Frazer, Sir James G., 450
Freeman, Joseph, 498
French, Joseph Lewis, 108, 113

Freneau, Philip, 11, 154, 475
  "House of the Night, The," 475
  "Indian Burying Ground, The,"
    475
  "To a Wild Honeysuckle," 154
Frost, Robert, 21, 129, 150-62, 167-68,
    169, 224, 245, 250, 294, 299, 312,
    361, 371, 496
  "Acquainted with the Night," 159
  Boy's Will, A, 154, 155, 157, 158,
    161
  "Come In," 155-56
  "Death of the Hired Man," 157,
    159
  "Further Range, A," 160
  "Gift Outright, The," 161-62
  "Home Burial," 159
  "I Could Give All to Time," 161-
    62
  "Lesson for Today, The," 151, 160,
    371
  "Love and a Question," 161
  "Master Speed, The," 159
  Mountain Interval, 154
  "My Butterfly," 154-55
  "New England Eclogues," 168
  New Hampshire, 157, 159, 160
  "Never Again Would Birds' Song
    Be the Same," 161
  North of Boston, 154, 157
  "Serious Step Lightly Taken, A,"
    159
  "Soldier, A," 159
  "To E. T.," 157
  "Twilight," 152
  "Vantage Point, The," 159
  Witness Tree, A, 155
Fugitive, The, 360
Fugitives: An Anthology of Verse,
    379-80, 382, 384, 386
Funaroff, S., 463

Gainsborough, Thomas, 153
Garland, Hamlin, 46, 61
Gaudier-Brzeska, Henri, 169
Gautier, Théophile, 258, 277
Georgian poets, The, 156-57, 167
Georgian Poetry, 157, 382, 491
Gibbon, Edward, 20-21
Gibbs, Willard, 439

Gibson, Wilfred, 156, 167
  "Golden Room, The," 156
Gide, André, 70, 167
Gilbert, W. S., 356
Gilder, Richard Watson, 9, 14
Gold, Michael, 463
Goodman, Paul, 498
Gosse, Sir Edmund, 17, 74, 87, 167
Gould, Joseph Ferdinand, 319
Graves, Robert, 380, 382
Gray, Thomas, 11
  "Elegy Written in a Country
    Church-Yard," 11
Greenberg, Samuel, 476
Greene, Grahame, 487, 501
Greenslet, Ferris, 186
Grierson, Herbert J. C., 293, 294
Griswold, Rufus W., 10
  Poets and Poetry of America, The,
    10
Guest, Edgar A., 307, 501
Guiney, Louise Imogen, 83-91
  "Beside Hazlitt's Grave," 85
  "Five Cards for Christmastide," 87
  "Friend's Song for Simoisius, A,"
    90-91
  Happy Ending, 84, 85, 86, 87, 88,
    89, 90
  "On Leaving Winchester," 85
  "Planting the Poplar," 89
  Recusant Poets (ed.), 86
  "Sanctuary," 89
  "Siege of London, The," 88
  Songs at the Start, 83
  "Talisman, A," 84
  "Tears," 83
  "Wild Ride, The," 88
Guiney, General Patrick, 87-88
Gustafson, Ralph, 503

H.D., 91, 169, 184, 188, 192-200, 208,
    216, 325
  Collected Poems, 195
  "Gift, The," 194
  "Hermes," 193
  "Let Zeus Record," 196
  Red Roses for Bronze, 196
  Sea Garden, 194
  "Sea Gods," 194-95
  "She Watches Over the Sea," 194

H.D. (Cont.)
"Spare Us from Loveliness," 193
"Toward the Piraeus," 195
Tribute to the Angels, 199-200
"Triplex," 196
Walls Do Not Fall, The, 197
Hagedorn, Hermann, 42, 43, 108
Hale, Lucretia P., 435
Halleck, Fitz-Greene, 47
Hardy, Thomas, 7, 58, 82, 129-30, 189-90, 496
Harland, Henry, 144, 166, 218
Harper's Bazaar, 260, 459
Harper's Magazine, 60, 141, 479
Harte, Bret, 46, 238
Harvard Advocate, The, 112, 335, 420, 454
Hatcher, Harlan, 301
Hawthorne, Nathaniel, 82, 111, 125, 269, 352, 405, 417
Hay, John, 8, 456-57
Pike County Ballads, 456
Hayne, Paul Hamilton, 373
Hazlitt, William, 84, 85, 110
Hearst, William Randolph, 452
Hecht, Ben, 415
Heine, Heinrich, 307-8
Hemingway, Ernest, 135, 201, 293, 339, 418-19, 451, 457, 462, 463, 467
Henley, W. E., 10, 15, 18, 166, 317
Hospital Sketches, 10
"Invictus," 15
Henry, O., 60
Herbert, George, 82
Herford, Oliver, 435
Hergesheimer, Joseph, 190, 398
Herrick, Robert, 17, 79, 330, 422
Poetical Works, 79
"To Dianeme," 79-80
Herring, Robert, 82, 196-97
Herron, Ima Honaker, 117-18
Hicks, Granville, 462
Hillyer, Robert, 76, 300, 305, 309-11
Collected Verse, 309
Letter to Robert Frost, A, 76, 305, 309, 310
"Pastoral II," 310
"Pastoral VII," 310
Riverhead, 311

Hillyer, Robert (Cont.)
Seventh Hill, The, 309
Sonnets and Other Lyrics, 311
Hitchcock, Alfred, 487
Hoffenstein, Samuel, 271
Poems in Praise of Practically Nothing, 271
Hollis, Cornwall, 261
Holmes, Oliver Wendell, 10
Homer, 53, 180, 426
Odyssey, The, 180
Hood, Thomas, 110
Hopkins, Gerard Manley, 27, 84, 133, 295, 468
Hoppé, E. O., 164
Horace, 160, 162
Horton, Philip, 374, 380, 469-70, 476, 478, 479
Hound & Horn, 501
Housman, A. E., 10, 39, 307, 488
A Shropshire Lad, 11
Hovey, Richard, 11-15, 19, 37, 152, 167
Along the Trail, 12, 15
"Isabel," 13
Songs from Vagabondia, 12, 13, 15, 38
Stein Song, A, 13
"Unmanifest Destiny," 15
Howells, William Dean, 8, 16, 134, 237, 368
Howgate, George W., 71, 72, 73
Hoyt, Nancy, 286
Portrait of an Unknown Lady, The, 286
Hueffer, Ford Madox, 177. (See also Ford, Ford Madox)
Hughes, Glenn, 167
Hughes, Langston, 395-96
Fine Clothes to the Jew, 396
Shakespeare in Harlem, 396
Weary Blues, The, 395
Hugo, Victor, 47, 53, 407, 410
Hulme, T. E., 168, 169, 174-75, 176, 361
Huneker, James Gibbons, 257, 464
Hunt, Leigh, 110
Hunt, Violet, 166
Huxley, Aldous, 225
Huysmans, J. K., 167

Illustrated London News, The, 320
Imagism & the Imagists, 167
Imagistes, Les, 58, 135, 167, 169, 176, 188, 193, 204, 205, 207, 212, 294
Independent, The, 152
Ingersoll, Robert, 228
Irving, Sir Henry, 66
Isherwood, Christopher, 487

Jackson, Andrew, 239
James, Henry, 8, 29, 70, 74, 111, 119, 129, 134, 143, 166, 173, 175, 202, 265-66, 271, 272, 286, 322, 414, 415, 417, 421
Jarrell, Randall, 485
   Blood for a Stranger, 486
Jeffers, Robinson, 58, 398-410, 411
   "At the Fall of an Age," 404, 406, 408
   Be Angry at the Sun, 407, 409
   Californians, 400
   Cawdor, 398, 407
   Dear Judas, 398, 411
   Descent to the Dead, 405, 406
   Flagons and Apples, 400
   "Ghosts in England," 406
   "In the Hill at New Grange," 406
   "Intellectuals," 404
   "Iona: The Grove of Kings," 406
   "Love the Wild Swan," 409
   Roan Stallion, Tamar and Other Poems, 398, 401, 402, 405-406, 408
   Selected Poetry, 400
   "Self-Criticism in February," 411-12
   Tower Beyond Tragedy, The, 402, 403, 404
   "Triad," 404-405
   Women at Point Sur, The, 398
Johns, Orrick, 268
Johnson, Lionel, 26, 84, 152, 166, 282
Johnson, James Weldon, 392
   Book of American Negro Poetry, The (ed.), 387, 389, 390, 391, 392-93
   "Creation, The," 393
   Fifty Years and Other Poems, 393
   God's Trombones, 393, 396

Johnson, Samuel, 4, 22, 101, 128, 132, 235-36, 291-92, 294, 297, 321, 325
   Irene, 128
Johnson, Stanley, 380
Jones, Howard Mumford, 461
Jonson, Ben, 21, 422
Josephson, Matthew, 70
Joyce, James, 310, 424, 428
   Chamber Music, 310
   Pomes Pennyeach, 310

Kafka, Franz, 480
Kahn, Otto, 473-74, 476
Kalar, Joseph, 463
Keats, John, 17, 18, 35, 152, 160, 182, 227, 283, 434, 455, 495
Kees, Weldon, 494
   Last Man, The, 494
Kemp, Harry, 498
Kenyon Review, The, 370, 378, 383, 501
Keys, Florence V., 93
Kilmer, Joyce, 268
Kipling, Rudyard, 7, 10, 47, 435, 437, 442, 488
   Barrack Room Ballads, 10
Klein, Abraham, 503
Kreymborg, Alfred, 134, 141, 219, 471, 495, 498, 499
   Plays for Poet-Mimes, 499
   Selected Poems, 498
Kuster, Una Call, 401

Laforgue, Jules, 167, 330, 331
Lamb, Charles, 82, 83, 84, 110, 242
Landor, Walter Savage, 47, 180, 282, 283, 312
Lang, Andrew, 388
Lanier, Sidney, 92, 360, 367, 372, 373, 375, 386, 464
Lark, The, 55
Larsson, Raymond, 500-501
   O City, Cities!, 500-501
   Weep and Prepare, 501
Latimer, Margery, 464
Laughlin, James, 494
Laver, James, 345
Lawrence, D. H., 184, 188-89, 398, 408, 488
Lawrence, Sir Thomas, 153

Lear, Edward, 160, 233
Leavis, F. R., 179, 180, 294
Lee, Robert E., 239
Le Gallienne, Richard, 268
Leonard, William Ellery, 300-305
  "Ægyptian Papyrus, An," 301, 303
  Aesop and Hyssop, 304
  Beowulf, 301
  "Latin Scholar, The," 305
  "Lynching Bee, The," 304
  On the Nature of Things, 301, 303
  Socrates, 303
  Son of Earth, A, 301, 302
  Two Lives, 301, 302
  "War Movie, A," 304
Letter to Robert Frost, A, 76, 305, 309, 310
Lewis, Sinclair, 267, 441
  Main Street, 267
Lewis, Wyndham, 166, 168, 169, 317, 415
Liberator, The, 394
Liebknecht, Wilhelm, 352
Life and Letters Today, 196, 317
Lincoln, Abraham, 229, 239, 456, 457
Lindsay, Vachel, 66, 141, 145, 146, 226, 231, 233-42, 247, 249, 268, 304, 352, 395, 432
  "Bryan, Bryan, Bryan, Bryan," 238, 240
  "Chinese Nightingale, The," 238
  Collected Poems, 233, 237
  "Congo, The," 238
  "Factory Windows Are Always Broken," 240
  "Flower-Fed Buffaloes," 239
  "General William Booth Enters into Heaven," 66, 237
  "Golden Book of Springfield, The," 237
  "I Heard Immanuel Singing," 233-35
  "Sea Serpent Chantey, The," 238-39
  "Simon Legree—A Negro Sermon," 241-42
Lippmann, Walter, 70, 319
Literary Opinion in America, 454
Little Review, The, 142, 166, 317, 318, 375, 415, 470, 471

Liveright, Horace, 258
Lodge, George Cabot, 19, 25, 26, 29-32, 33, 34, 41, 70, 76, 111, 116, 170, 301, 348, 399
  Poems and Dramas, 30, 31
  Song of the Wave, 29
  "Soul's Inheritance, The," 29
  "To Giacomo Leopardi," 31
Lodge, John Ellerton, 33
Lomax, John, 387
London, Jack, 55, 57, 410
Longfellow, Henry Wadsworth, 10, 12, 60, 63, 158, 164, 176, 264, 321, 414, 432, 451-52, 475
  Evangeline, 12, 451
  Hiawatha, 432
  "My Lost Youth," 158, 264
Lope de Vega, 171
Lorca, Garcia, 369
Louis XV, 153
Lovett, Robert Morss, 27
Lovelace, Richard, 489
  "Snail, The," 490
  "Song, The," 490
Lowell, Amy, 109, 133, 169, 182-91, 203, 204, 205, 207, 219, 227, 244, 256, 261-62, 283, 286, 336, 347, 350, 410, 414, 416
  Dome of Many-coloured Glass, A, 182, 187
  Can Grande's Castle, 182, 189
  Men, Women and Ghosts, 182, 187
  On Looking at a Copy of Alice Meynell's Poems, 191
  "Patterns," 190
  Pictures of the Floating World, 182
  "Sisters, The," 190-91
  Sword Blades and Poppy Seeds, 182
Lowell, James Russell, 9, 10, 16, 59, 184, 311, 388, 456
  "How Old Brown Took Harper's Ferry," 9
Loy, Mina, 498
Luce, Clare Booth, 459
Luce, Henry, 452
Ludecke, H., 285
Luhan, Mabel Dodge, 498. (*See also* Dodge, Mabel)
Lyric Year, The, 268

MacDonald, Ramsay, 54
MacDowell Colony, The, 155
MacGowan, Kenneth, 255
McKay, Claude, 393-4
MacLeish, Archibald, 72, 188, 213, 250, 307, 334, 397, 436, 439, 441, 448-57, 458, 460, 462, 467, 480, 485, 502
  Air Raid, 453
  "America Was Promises," 455
  "Ars Poetica," 455
  Conquistador, 213, 307, 451, 452, 457
  Fall of the City, The, 453
  Frescoes for Mr. Rockefeller's City, 250, 439, 440
  Hamlet of A. MacLeish, The, 449, 451
  "Immortal Autumn," 450, 453, 457
  "Invocation to the Social Muse," 453
  "L'An Trentiesme de Mon Eage," 453
  Land of the Free, 456
  New Found Land, 450, 457
  "Not Marble nor the Gilded Mountains," 450
  Poems, 1924-1933, 457
  Pot of Earth, The, 450, 451
  Public Speech, 397, 456
  Streets in the Moon, 450
  "You, Andrew Marvell," 450, 453, 457
MacNeice, Louis, 384, 485-86, 491
Macpherson, Mrs. Winifred D., 325
Madariaga, Salvador de, 71
Maeterlinck, Maurice, 13
Maillol, Aristide, 145
Mallarmé, Stéphane, 167, 332
Mangan, James Clarence, 85
Mann, Thomas, 198, 224, 318
Mansfield, Katherine, 285
Markham, Edwin, 15, 31, 44, 49, 50-54, 55, 58
  Gates of Paradise, The, 51
  Lincoln and Other Poems, 51
  "Man with the Hoe, The," 15, 51, 52, 54
  New Poems: Eighty Songs at 80, 51, 53

Markham, Edwin (Cont.)
  Shoes of Happiness, The, 51
  "Slaves of the Drug," 54
  "Song of the Followers of Pan," 53
Marks, Lionel, 40
Marlowe, Christopher, 42
Marryat, Captain, 185
Marsh, Edward, 156, 167
Marvell, Andrew, 363
  "Horatian Ode," 362
  "To His Coy Mistress," 362
Masefield, John, 38, 196, 268
  Everlasting Mercy, The, 268
Masses, The, 275
Masters, Edgar Lee, 19, 64, 117-18, 134, 145, 226-32, 233, 236, 356, 414, 432, 445
  "Ann Rutledge," 230
  Domesday Book, The, 231
  Fate of the Jury, The, 232
  Hill, The, 229
  New Spoon River, The, 231
  "Petit the Poet," 230
  Spoon River Anthology, 19, 64, 66, 226-30, 232, 356, 414, 432, 445
  "Thomas Trevelyan," 230
  "Village Atheist, The," 230-31
Matisse, Henri, 145
Mattiessen, F. O., 419
Melville, Herman, 11, 408, 469, 471, 472, 498
  Battle Pieces, 11
  Clarel, 11
Mencken, H. L., 6, 220, 231, 301, 414, 464
Meredith, George, 128, 289, 301
  Modern Love, 289, 301
Merton, Thomas, 491
  Thirty Poems, 491
Meteyard, Tom Buford, 12
  Songs from Vagabondia, 12, 13, 15, 38
Meynell, Alice, 18, 87, 191
Mill, John Stuart, 174
  On Liberty, 174
Millay, Edna St. Vincent, 15, 94, 101, 105, 135, 255, 264, 265-75, 276, 277, 278, 279, 280, 281, 282, 283, 284, 294, 306, 394, 414, 459, 460, 479

Millay, Edna St. Vincent (Cont.)
"Apostrophe to Man," 270
"Aubade," 270
Buck in the Snow, The, 281
"Cameo, The," 273
"Childhood Is the Kingdom Where Nobody Dies," 271
Conversation at Midnight, 271, 272, 276
"Euclid Alone Has Looked on Beauty Bare," 267, 272
Few Figs from Thistles, A, 267, 271, 272, 306
"First Fig," 267
"Fledgling, The," 271
"God's World," 267
"Hardy Garden, The," 281
Harp Weaver and Other Poems, The, 267, 272
King's Henchman, The, 272
"Memorial to D. C.," 272-73
Poet and His Book, The, 274
Renascence, 267, 268, 270
"Return, The," 274
"Two Sonnets in Memory of Sacco and Vanzetti," 270
"What Lips My Lips Have Kissed," 266
Miller, Henry, 495
Miller, Joaquin, 44-50, 51, 52, 55, 58, 173, 238, 410
"Columbus," 45, 46
"Comanche," 48
"Gold that Grew by Shasta Town, The," 48
"Kit Carson's Ride," 48
Poetical Works, 45, 48, 50
"Walker in Nicaragua," 50
Miller, Muriel, 13-14
Millet, Fred B., 164, 246, 299, 308, 458
Milton, John, 92, 204, 362
Lycidas, 92, 362
Samson Agonistes, 362
Mitchell, S. Weir, 8
Modern American Poetry, 305, 308, 321, 367
Modern American Poets, 502
Monro, Harold, 157, 167, 169

Monroe, Harriet, 12, 31, 55, 57, 58, 134, 141-49, 157, 166, 183, 184, 187-88, 190, 192, 195, 203, 229, 233, 237, 249, 305, 327
"Chosen Poems," 148
"Columbian Ode, The," 144-45
"Hotel, The," 146
"Love Song I," 148
New Poetry, The, 145, 158
"Plaint," 148
Montcorbier, François, 171
Moody, William Vaughn, 19, 20, 25-28, 31, 32, 33, 34, 40, 42, 43, 111, 113
"Daguerreotype, The," 27
"Gloucester Moors," 28
Great Divide, The, 42
"Ode in Time of Hesitation," 28
"On a Soldier Fallen in the Philippines," 28
Poems and Plays, 28
Selected Poems, 27
Moore, George, 258, 318, 453
Moore, Marianne, 98, 146, 147-48, 193, 216, 294, 317-25, 330, 335, 348, 415, 498
"Marriage," 322
"No Swan So Fine," 323
Observations, 318
"Octopus, An," 322
"Pangolin, The," 322
"Plumet Basilisk, The," 322
"Poetry," 319-20
Selected Poems, 320
"Silence," 325
"Sun," 325
Moore, Merrill, 380
Moore, Nicholas, 480
Moore, Thomas, 267, 373
Irish Melodies, 267
More, Paul Elmer, 115, 411, 415, 420
Morley, Christopher, 306, 365, 444
Translations from the Chinese, 306
Morrison, Theodore, 500
Devious Way, The, 500
Notes on Death and Life, 500
Serpent in the Clouds, The, 500
Mumford, Lewis, 439, 495, 498
American Caravan (ed.), 495

Munson, Gorham B., 151, 472, 479, 480
Munsterberg, Hugo, 70
Murry, John Middleton, 183

Nash, Ogden, 306
  Free Wheeling, 306
Nation, The, 122, 311, 335, 383, 432, 480
Nation, The (London), 259
Nation and Athenaeum, The, 225
National Observer, 18, 166
Neihardt, John G., 497-98, 499
  Collected Poems, 497, 499
Nelson, John Herbert, 220
  Chief Modern Poets of England and America, 220-21
Nerval, Gérard de, 167
New Age, The, 203
New Anthology of Modern Poetry, 502
New Directions, 167, 494-95
New English Weekly, The, 369
New Masses, The, 462
New Republic, The, 32, 38, 131, 272, 299, 453, 455, 461, 500
New York Evening Post, The, 365
New York Globe, The, 356
New York Times, The, 320, 353, 488
New York Tribune, The, 414
New York World, The, 108, 114, 145
New Yorker, The, 260, 277, 459
Newcastle, Duchess of, 283
Newman, Cardinal, 84
Nietzsche, Friedrich, 399, 400, 402, 403, 404, 407, 408, 412
Nijinsky, 144
Norman, Dorothy, 498
Norton, Charles Eliot, 112
Noyes, Alfred, 118

O'Neill, Eugene, 232, 398
  Desire Under the Elms, 398
Oppenheim, James, 471, 498
  Sea, The, 498
Orage, A. R., 203
Osborn, Mary Elizabeth, 91, 92
Others, 134, 142, 470, 471, 498, 499
Ovid, 6, 426
  Metamorphoses, 6

Oxford Anthology of American Literature, The, 196, 207, 444
Oxford Book of American Verse, The, 14

Pagan, The, 470
Pall Mall Gazette, 18
Parker, Dorothy, 271, 306
  Enough Rope, 306
Parrington, Vernon Louis, 414, 457, 501
Parrish, Maxfield, 17
Partisan Review, 484
Patchen, Kenneth, 495, 498
  First Will and Testament, 495
Patmore, Coventry, 27
  Angel in the House, The, 27
Pavlova, Anna, 144, 325
Peabody, Josephine Preston, 40-43, 107, 114, 186
  "Cradle Song," 41
  Marlowe, 43
  Piper, The, 41
Peacock, Thomas Love, 282, 283
Peale, Charles Wilson, 348
Pearson, Norman Holmes, 444
  Oxford Anthology of American Literature, The (ed.), 444
Perry, Bliss, 301
Peterson, Houston, 218, 219, 221
Phelps, William Lyon, 60, 62, 441
Philadelphia Public Ledger, The, 365
Phillips, Stephen, 41
Picabia, Francis, 145
Picasso, Pablo, 145
Pickford, Mary, 239
Piers Plowman, 303
Pipkin, Charles, 360
Poe, Edgar Allan, 11, 41, 53, 176-77, 233, 259, 298, 372, 383, 468, 475
  "City of the Sea," 475
Poetry, A Magazine of Verse, 12, 31, 44, 58, 141-49, 158, 176, 188, 203, 229, 237, 249, 299, 305, 319, 327, 333, 375, 411, 415
Poets and Poetry of America, The, 10
Pompadour, Marquise de, 153

Pope, Alexander, 292, 311, 320, 376
  "Epistle to Dr. Arbuthnot," 311
  Essay on Man, An, 328
  "Windsor Forest," 320
Porter, Katherine Anne, 470
Pound, Ezra, 7, 58, 84, 136, 145, 149,
  156, 163-81, 188, 192, 193, 197,
  201, 203-204, 207, 208, 209, 216,
  224, 259, 294, 317, 319, 335, 341,
  355, 361, 374, 410, 416, 449, 450,
  451, 452, 456, 457, 460, 468, 480
  A B C of Reading, 171
  "Altaforte," 168
  Canzoni, 166
  Cathay, 180
  Culture, 171
  Draft of XXX Cantos, A, 163, 172,
    180, 181, 451, 480
  "Envoi," 181
  Exultations, 166, 201
  Homage to Sextus Propertius, 180,
    355
  Hugh Selwyn Mauberly, 179, 355
  Personae, 163, 166, 179, 201
  Polite Essays, 171, 209
  Provença, 166
  Ripostes, 169
  "River Merchant's Wife, The," 180
  *Sonnets and Ballads of Guido
    Cavalcanti,* 177-78
  Spirit of Romance, The, 170-71,
    172, 173-74, 176, 180, 181
Powell, Lawrence Clark, 400, 401,
  403
Pratt, E. J., 503
Prokosch, Frederic, 490-91
*Proletarian Literature in the United
  States,* 462
Pushkin, Alexander, 397
Putnam, Phelps, 436
  Five Seasons, The, 436
  Trinc, 436

Rambler, The, 101
Ransom, John Crowe, 294, 295, 360-
  72, 378, 379, 380, 473
  "Address to the Scholars of New
    England," 370
  "Amphibious Crocodile," 368

Ransom, John Crowe (Cont.)
  "Antique Harvesters," 295-96, 367-
    68, 386
  "Armageddon," 365-66
  "Blackberry Winter," 365
  "Blue Girls," 367
  Chills and Fever, 361, 362, 367, 379
  "Dog," 368
  "Fresco," 368
  God Without Thunder, 369
  "Here Lies a Lady," 367
  New Criterion, The, 364, 369
  "Philomela," 362-63
  "Piazza Piece," 367
  "Plea in Mitigation, A," 367
  "Spectral Lovers," 371
  "Survey of Literature," 368
  "Tall Girl, The," 363
  Two Gentlemen in Bonds, 295, 361,
    367, 368
  "Winter Remembered," 365
Rascoe, Burton, 414-16, 449
  Bookman's Daybook, A, 415, 449
Read, Herbert, 174
Recusant Poets, 86
Redon, Odilon, 145
Reed, John, 15, 319, 394
Reedy, William Marion, 228
Reedy's Mirror, 229
Reese, Lizette Woodworth, 79-83, 98,
  501
  Branch of May, A, 80-81, 82
  "Girl's Mood, A," 81
  Handful of Lavender, A, 82
  "In Time of Grief," 80
  Pastures, 82
  Quiet Road, A, 82
  Spicewood, 82
  Selected Poems, 81
  "Street Scene, A," 80
  Wild Cherry, 81, 82
  Worleys, 81
Remington, Frederic, 46
Review of Reviews, 237
Rexroth, Kenneth, 494
Reynolds, Sir Joshua, 153
Rice, Alice Hegan, 500
Richards, I. A., 489, 502
Richards, Mrs. Laura, 131

Ridge, Lola, 444-47
  Dance of Fire, 445, 446
  Firehead, 446
  "Ghetto, The," 445
  "Via Ignis," 446
Riding, Laura, 379-83, 473
  Collected Poems, 381, 382
  "Vain Life of Voltaire, The, 381
Riley, James Whitcomb, 8, 59-66,
  160, 227, 387, 388, 500
  "August," 65
  "Backward Look, A," 65
  "Courtin', The," 61
  "Happy Little Cripple, A," 62
  Home Folks, 62
  "Old Friend, An," 64
Rimbaud, Arthur, 167, 222, 331
Robinson, Edwin Arlington, 11, 12,
  13, 19-20, 34, 37, 41, 42, 43,
  107-32, 137, 152, 224, 260, 400,
  424, 464, 475, 494, 496
  "Aegeus," 112
  Amaranth, 114, 131
  "Archibald's Example," 130
  Avon's Harvest, 125
  "Ballad of Old London, A," 118
  "Ben Jonson Entertains a Man
    from Stratford," 125-26
  "Bewick Finzer," 113, 131
  Captain Craig, 41, 110, 111, 116-21,
    127, 130, 132
  Children of the Night, 34, 109, 112
  Collected Poems, 131
  "Dear Friends," 109
  "Flammonde," 122
  "For a Dead Lady," 123
  "Garden, The," 34
  "Haunted House, The," 129
  King Jasper, 131
  Lancelot, 130
  "Luke Havergal," 37, 113
  Man Who Died Twice, The, 124,
    130-31
  "Master, The," 126
  "Miniver Cheevy," 116
  "New England," 129
  *Torrent and the Night Before,
    The*, 111
  Town Down by the River, The,
    42, 116, 123, 126

Robinson, Edwin Arlington (Cont.)
  Tristram, 128, 132
  "White Lights, The," 42-43
Rodman, Selden, 441, 502
  Lawrence: The Last Crusade, 502
  Mortal Triumph, 502
  New Anthology of Modern Poetry
    (ed.), 502
Rolfe, Edwin, 463
Romney, George, 153
Roosevelt, Theodore, 20, 108, 114-15,
  457
Roosevelt, Col. Theodore, 393
Root, John Wellborn, 144
Rorty, James, 402
Rosenfeld, Paul, 495, 498
  American Caravan, The (ed.), 495
Rossetti, Christina, 98-99, 100
Rossetti, Dante Gabriel, 49, 98, 118,
  177-78, 399, 400, 442
Rukeyser, Muriel, 438-39, 494, 498
  Beast in View, 438, 439
  "Ritual of Blessing," 439
  "Sand-Quarry with Moving Fig-
    ures," 439
  Theory of Flight, 438
  Turning Wind, A, 438, 439
  U. S. 1, 438
Ruskin, John, 110, 326

Saintsbury, George, 468
Saltus, Edgar, 256
St. Nicholas, 434, 435, 442
San Francisco Examiner, 51
Sanborn, Pitts, 255
Sand, George, 265, 272
Sandburg, Carl, 133, 141, 145, 146,
  226, 242-251, 294, 387, 395, 397,
  414, 416, 432, 440, 456, 457, 466,
  467
  American Songbag, The, 247, 387
  Chicago Poems, 242, 244, 397, 466
  "Cool Tombs," 248
  "Early Moon," 246
  Good Morning, America, 245
  "Grass," 248, 249
  Home Front Memo, 251
  "Old Timers," 248
  People, Yes, The, 247, 440, 446
  Selected Poems, 246

Sandburg, Carl (Cont.)
  "Shenandoah," 248
  "Shirt," 248
  Slabs of the Sunburnt West, 245
  Smoke and Steel, 245
  "Spring Grass," 245
Sanders, Gerald DeWitt, 220
  Chief Modern Poets of England and America (ed.), 220-21
Sanine, 256
Santayana, George, 11, 67-78, 105, 420, 475
  "Avile," 72
  Hermit of Carmel, A, 68
  Lucifer, 68
  "Minuet on Reaching the Age of Fifty, A," 76-78
  "Odes, III," 71
  "On an unfinished statue—", 76
  Poems, 68, 71, 72, 73, 75
  "Sapphic Odes," 70-72
  Sonnets and Poems, 68
Sargent, John Singer, 326
Sarrett, Lew, 499-500
  Collected Poems, 499, 500
Sassoon, Siegfried, 309
Saturday Evening Post, The, 431
Saturday Review of Literature, The, 440, 444, 463
Savoy, The, 55
Schopenhauer, Arthur, 348, 399, 400, 404
Schwartz, Delmore, 495, 498
  In Dreams Begin Responsibilities, 495
Scott, Sir Walter, 185, 373
Scott, Winfield Townley, 183, 494
  Sword on the Table, The, 183
Scribner's Magazine, 60
Second Mrs. Tanqueray, The, 8
Sedgwick, Ellery, 186
Seldes, Gilbert, 255
Seven Arts, The, 470, 471, 498
Sewanee Review, The, 417
Shakespeare, William, 53, 268, 316
Shapiro, Karl Jay, 486
  Person, Place and Thing, 486
  V-Letter, 486
Shaw, Bernard, 6, 41, 172

Shelley, Percy Bysshe, 144, 152, 184, 227, 283, 446, 468
Sherman, Stuart P., 44, 49
Shorthouse, J. H., 426
Sidney, Sir Philip, 288
Sill, Edward Rowland, 152, 161
  "Truth at Last," 153
Sinclair, Upton, 57, 462-63
Sitwell, Edith, 196, 197, 285, 299, 496
Sitwell, Osbert, 196
Smart, Christopher, 233, 235-36
  "Song to David," 233
Smart Set, The, 464
Smith, A. J. M., 503
  Book of Canadian Poetry, The, 503
Smith, Effie, 141
Sorel, Georges, 174
Soupault, Philippe, 216
Southern Review, The, 360, 383, 495, 501
Southey, Robert, 157, 312, 313
  Curse of Kahama, The, 312
  Roderick, 312
Spector, Herman, 463
Spencer, Herbert, 227
Spencer, Theodore, 293
Spender, Stephen, 439, 485, 486, 490
  Ruins and Visions, 486
Spengler, Oswald, 404
Spenser, Edmund, 293
Spingarn, J. E., 301
Starrett, Vincent, 464
Stedman, Edmund Clarence, 8-12, 14, 16, 19, 20, 83, 98, 105, 107, 143, 144, 305, 497, 503
  American Anthology, An (ed.), 8-11, 16, 19, 20, 83
Stein, Gertrude, 204, 216, 256, 260, 415, 499
  Four Saints in Three Acts, 499
  Tender Buttons, 256
Stendhal, de, 174
Sterling, George, 15, 44, 49, 55-58, 410
  "Ode on the Centenary of Robert Browning," 56
  Omnia Exeunt Mysterium, 58
  Testimony of the Suns, The, 56
Stevens, Wallace, 146, 160, 208, 211, 212, 213, 216, 255, 261, 262, 294, 322, 326-35, 346, 464, 480, 498

Stevens, Wallace (Cont.)
"Anglais Mort à Florence," 327
"Comedian as the Letter C, The," 327
"Fish-Scale Sunrise, A," 335
Harmonium, 326, 329, 333, 480
Ideas of Order, 327, 329
"It Must Be Abstract," 334-35
"Laocoön," 212-13
"Last Looks at the Lilacs," 331
"Le Monocle de Mon Oncle," 261
"Lions in Sweden," 327
Man with the Blue Guitar, The, 329, 330, 332, 334
"Mystic Garden & Middling Beast," 332
Notes Toward a Supreme Fiction, 329, 334
"Paltry Nude Starts on a Spring Voyage, The," 327
Parts of a World, 329, 334
"Peter Quince at the Clavier," 327, 330-31
"Pleasures of Merely Circulating, The," 329
"Romanesque Affabulation," 333
"Sad Strains of a Gay Waltz," 328
"Sunday Morning," 333
"Thought Revolved, A," 332
"To the One of Fictive Music," 333, 334
"Woman that Had More Babies than That, The," 327
"Worms at Heaven's Gate, The," 331
Stevenson, Alec Brook, 380
Stevenson, Robert Louis, 10, 17, 82, 143
Child's Garden of Verses, A, 10
Stewart, Donald Ogden, 462
Stickney, Trumbull, 19, 20, 25, 26, 32-37, 41, 70, 76, 111, 113, 116, 170, 173, 301, 303, 348
"Age in Young," 34
IV, 34
"Fragment V," 35
"In Ampezzo," 35
"It's Autumn in the Country I Remember," 37
"Lucretius," 33

Stickney, Trumbull (Cont.)
"Mnemosyne," 33
Poems, 34
"Song," 35-36
Stoddard, R. H., 9
Story, William Wetmore, 99, 497
Stuart, Jesse, 384, 500
Sullivan, Louis, 144
Sullivan, Sir Arthur, 356
Sweeney, John L., 272, 502
Swinburne, Algernon, 118, 167, 364, 400, 442
Symons, Arthur, 5, 167, 256
Synge, J. M., 26, 145, 226, 244, 450
Playboy of the Western World, The, 244
Poems and Translations, 145

Tabb, John Bannister, 17-19
"Going Blind," 18-19
Taggard, Genevieve, 272, 275-76, 500
Calling Western Union, 275
"Enamel Girl, The," 275
For Eager Lovers, 275
"To an American Worker Dying of Starvation," 276
Traveling Standing Still, 275
Words for the Chisel, 275
Tagore, Rabindranath, 236
Tarkington, Booth, 65
Tate, Allen, 206, 294, 300, 305, 360, 361, 372-79, 382, 383, 417, 432, 460, 461, 471, 475, 494, 501
"Aeneas at Washington," 377, 386
American Harvest (ed.), 461
"Idiot," 374, 376
"Ignis Fatuus," 377
"Mediterranean, The," 377, 386
Mr. Pope and Other Poems, 373, 376
"Ode to the Confederate Dead," 373, 375
"Ode to Fear," 377-78
Pervigilium Veneris (tr.), 377
"Seasons of the Soul," 378-79, 386
Selected Poems, 361, 383
"Sonnets of the Blood," 376
"Subway, The," 373
Taylor, Bayard, 11, 12, 372
Taylor, Deems, 272, 393

Taylor, Jeremy, 84
Teasdale, Sara, 98-106, 186, 219, 394,
　　501
　"All That Was Mortal," 105
　"Arcturus in Autumn," 103-104
　"Autumn (Parc Monceau)," 104
　Collected Poems, 105-106
　Dark of the Moon, 102
　Flame and Shadow, 103
　"Fontainebleau," 104
　"In a Darkening Garden," 105
　"Leaves," 101
　"Let It Be Forgotten," 103
　"Long Hill, The," 103
　"Look, The," 100, 101
　"Love Me," 100, 102
　Love Songs, 99, 100, 105
　Rivers to the Sea, 100, 101
　"Song for Colin," 102
　Sonnets to Duse and Other Poems,
　　99
　"Spring Night," 219
　Strange Victory, 105
Tennyson, Alfred, Lord, 10, 13, 31,
　　40, 47, 63, 110, 118, 127, 145, 186,
　　414, 421, 463, 488
　Becket, 40
　Idylls of the King, 13
　"In Memoriam," 31
Terry, Ellen, 40
Thackeray, William Makepeace, 82
Thayer, Scofield, 415, 464
This Quarter, 455
Thomas, Dylan, 299, 480
Thomas, Edward, 156-57, 169
Thompson, Dunstan, 501
　Poems, 501
Time, 431, 452, 480
Times Literary Supplement, The, 74,
　176
Timrod, Henry, 373
Tolstoy, Leo, 320
Torrence, Ridgely, 38-40, 65, 108,
　　131, 460, 497
　"Bird and the Tree, The," 39
　"Eye-Witness," 38
　Hesperides, 38
　House of a Hundred Lights, The,
　　38, 65
　"Light," 40

Torrence, Ridgely (Cont.)
　"Prothalamion (To a bride in
　　wartime)," 39
　*Selected Letters of Edward Arling-
　　ton Robinson* (ed.), 108
　"Winter Crystal," 39
Towne, Charles Hanson, 44, 141
Transatlantic Review, The, 166
Treece, Henry, 299
Trollope, Anthony, 82
Trotsky, Leon, 348
Twain, Mark, 46, 93, 238, 431, 435
Twice-a-Year, 498

Unamuno, Miguel de, 75
Untermeyer, Louis, 52, 101, 141, 189,
　　221, 268, 272, 300, 305-309, 432,
　　451, 463
　—and Other Poets, 307
　"Archibald MacLeish," 307
　From Another World, 101, 308
　Including Horace, 307
　Modern American Poetry (ed.),
　　305, 308, 321, 367
　Selected Poems and Parodies, 308
　"So Rein Und Shön," 306
　"To Chloe," 307

Van Doren, Carl, 285, 287
Van Doren, Mark, 294, 300, 311-16,
　　365, 383, 385, 402, 501
　American Poets (ed.) 316
　Anthology of World Poetry (ed.),
　　316
　Collected Poems, 316
　"End, The," 315
　Jonathan Gentry, 312, 313, 385
　Mayfield Deer, The, 312
　Now the Sky, 311
　"Spectral Boy," 314
　Spring Thunder, 311
　"Strike the Rusted Springs," 314
　Winter Diary, A, 313
Van Dyke, Henry, 8
Van Gelder, Robert, 232
Van Vechten, Carl, 190, 218, 255,
　　263, 383, 395
Vanity Fair, 260, 275, 459, 460
Vaughan, Henry, 82
Veblen, Thorstein, 361

Verlaine, Paul, 13, 47, 210, 222
Verne, Jules, 185
Very, Jones, 11
Victorian Anthology, A, 10
Viereck, George Sylvester, 257
Villon, François, 240
Vivas, Eliseo, 369-70
Vogue, 260, 459
Voltaire, 21-22, 179

Waley, Arthur, 196
Walker, Margaret, 397
Waller, Edmund, 179
Walsh, Ernest, 454-55
Ward, Artemus, 238
Warren, Robert Penn, 360, 361, 375,
    380, 383-86, 460
    "Ballad of Billy Potts," 384, 385-86
    "Bearded Oaks," 384-85
    Eleven Poems on the Same Theme,
    383
    "Ode to Fear," 383
    Selected Poems 1923-1943, 383, 384
    Thirty-Six Poems, 383
Washington, George, 239
Waugh, Evelyn, 487, 501
We Gather Strength, 463
Webster, Jean, 93, 97
Webster, John, 35
Weirick, Bruce, 74
Welby, Mrs., 383
Welles, Winifred, 501
    Blossoming Antlers, 501
    Hesitant Heart, The, 501
    Spectacle for Scholars, A, 501
    This Delicate Love, 501
Wells, Carolyn, 435
Wells, H. G., 86
Wendell, Barrett, 302
West, Rebecca, 246, 247
Westminster Review, The, 47
Wharton, Edith, 286, 287, 288, 399,
    400
Wheelock, John Hall, 268, 499
    Black Panther, The, 299
    "Lion-House, The," 499
    Poems 1911-1936, 499
    Verses by Two Undergraduates,
    499

Wheelwright, John Brooks, 347-54,
    355, 359, 381-82
    "Ave Eva," 350-52
    "Dinner Call," 350
    Masque with Clowns, 353
    Mirrors of Venus, 349
    "Mossy Marbles," 349
    Political Self-Portrait, 348
    Rock and Shell, 348
    Selected Poems, 352
    "Small Prig in a Big Square, A,"
    350
    "Train Ride," 350, 352
Whicher, George F., 276
Whistler, James McNeill, 143, 164,
    166, 171-72, 326, 335
Whitehead, Professor, 329
Whitman, Walt, 10, 11, 12, 13, 19,
    31, 45, 46, 47, 62, 134, 137, 203,
    239, 408, 417, 468, 498
    Leaves of Grass, 468
    "O Captain! My Captain!", 45, 46
    "Passage to India," 46, 408
    "When Lilacs Last in the Door-
    yard Bloom'd," 46
Whittier, John Greenleaf, 16
    Snow-bound, 16
Wilcox, Ella Wheeler, 59, 176
Wilde, Oscar, 55, 218, 335, 381
Wilder, Thornton, 441
Wilkinson, Marguerite, 497
    Bluestone, 497
    New Voices (ed.), 497
Williams, Oscar, 498
    New Poems (ed.), 498-99
Williams, William Carlos, 188, 193,
    207-16, 319, 334
    Al Que Quiere, 208
    "Botticellian Trees, The," 209
    "Burning the Christmas Greens,"
    213-15
    Collected Poems, 211
    Complete Collected Poems, 209
    "Cure, The," 215-16
    "Elegy in Memory of D. H. Law-
    rence," 213
    "Jungle, The," 209, 210
    "Nantucket," 209
    "Rain," 210
    "Sea Elephant, The," 209

Williams, William Carlos (Cont.)
  Wedge, The, 213, 215
  "Yachts, The," 212
  "Young Housewife, The," 208
  "Young Sycamore," 209
Wills, Jesse, 380
Wilmot, John, 344
Wilson, Edmund, 32, 269, 272, 286,
    415, 421, 424, 458, 459, 460, 479
  Poets, Farewell!, 459
Wilson, Woodrow, 60
Winslow, Thyra Samter, 415
Winter, William, 8, 9
Winters, Yvor, 410-11, 460, 471, 479
  Bare Hills, The, 410
  Giant Weapon, The, 411
Wolfe, Thomas, 439
Woodberry, George Edward, 16, 268,
    497
Woolf, Virginia, 98
Wordsworth, William, 37, 157, 174,
    312, 400, 405, 416, 427
  "Prelude, The," 427
World Almanac, The, 248
Wright, Frank Lloyd, 144
Wright, Willard Huntington, 415
Wylie, Elinor, 129, 190, 263, 282-91,
    294, 442, 446, 459, 460

Wylie, Elinor (Cont.)
  "Address to My Soul," 285
  Angels and Earthly Creatures, 285,
    289
  "Beauty," 287
  "Castilian," 284
  "Chimaera Sleeping," 290
  Collected Poems, 285
  Incidental Numbers, 282
  Nets to Catch the Wind, 282

Yale Courant, The, 441
Yale Record, The, 441
Yale Review, The, 189, 441
Yarmolinsky, Avrahm, 401
Yeats, William Butler, 5, 7, 26, 141,
    145, 152, 160, 164, 226, 229, 236,
    244, 282, 295, 318, 382, 406, 407,
    409, 416, 450, 496
  "Wild Swans at Coole, The," 409
  Words for Music Perhaps, 407
Yellow Book, The, 55, 144, 166, 218,
    262
Young, Art, 54
Youth's Companion, The, 152

Zabel, Morton Dauwen, 99, 122, 123,
    454